Corruption in British Politics

Corruption in British Politics

1895–1930

G. R. SEARLE

CLARENDON PRESS · OXFORD

1987

Oxford University Press, Walton Street, Oxford OX2 6DP
Oxford New York Toronto
Delhi Bombay Calcutta Madras Karachi
Petaling Jaya Singapore Hong Kong Tokyo
Nairobi Dar es Salaam Cape Town
Melbourne Auckland
and associated companies in
Beirut Berlin Ibadan Nicosia

Oxford is a trade mark of Oxford University Press

Published in the United States
by Oxford University Press, New York

© G. R. Searle 1987

British Library Cataloguing in Publication Data
Searle, G.R.
Corruption in British politics 1895–1930.
1. Great Britain—Politics and government—1901–1936
2. Great Britain—Politics and government—1837–1901
3. Corruption (in politics)—Great Britain—History
I. Title
320.941   JN231
ISBN 0–19–822915–1

Library of Congress Cataloging in Publication Data
Searle, G. R. (Geoffrey Russell)
Corruption in British politics, 1895–1930.
Bibliography: p.
Includes index.
1. Great Britain—Politics and government—1901–1936.
2. Corruption (in politics)—Great Britain. I. Title.
JN231.S46 1987   354.41009'94'09   87–11018
ISBN 0–19–822915–1

Set by Hope Services, Abingdon, Oxon.
Printed in Great Britain by
The Alden Press, Oxford

ACKNOWLEDGEMENTS

IN the eight years or more spent preparing and writing this book I have accumulated a mass of debts. I must first acknowledge the support I have received from the University of East Anglia, which allowed me several sessions of study leave to pursue my researches without losing confidence that eventually something publishable would result from my labours. Then there are my immediate colleagues who have done a great deal to help me with their criticism and advice. I am especially grateful to Professor Paul Kennedy, who carefully read the early drafts and encouraged me to enlarge the chronological scope of the book, and who, since leaving these shores for Yale University, has continued to keep an eye on its progress. Other colleagues, happily still in Norwich, have been generous with their support and encouragement, in particular Dr John Charmley and Professor J. R. Jones. Dr Stephen Wilson kindly gave me some guidance in the matter of the French bibliography of scandal. Dr Franz Coetzee, Dr R. T. Davenport-Hines, Dr Dilwyn Porter, and Dr Christopher Smith have all made helpful suggestions and drawn my attention to material I might otherwise have missed, as have my research students, past and present, Maureen Montgomery and Barry Doyle. All have saved me from making foolish errors; but the responsibility for the shortcomings that remain is of course entirely mine.

Secondly, I am particularly grateful to Mr R. H. Harcourt Williams, the Archivist at Hatfield House, who proved especially helpful. My thanks are also due to all the librarians and archivists who made their collections accessible and patiently dealt with my many requests, namely the staff at the following institutions: the Manuscripts Department and the Newspaper Library of the British Library; the House of Lords Record Office; the India Office Library; Cambridge University Library; the Bodleian Library, Oxford; the National Library of Scotland; the Scottish Public Records Office; Birmingham University Library; the West Sussex Records Office, Chichester; the Norfolk Records Office; Trinity College, Cambridge; Churchill College, Cambridge; Nuffield College, Oxford; the National Maritime Museum; the Imperial War Museum.

This study relies heavily upon the use of material in collections of unpublished political papers. I am therefore greatly indebted to owners and custodians who have given me permission to cite material from these papers. I give their names, with the title of the manuscript collection in brackets: the Marquess of Salisbury (3rd Marquess of Salisbury, 4th Marquess of Salisbury, Chelwood, Quickswood), Lord Gainford (Gainford), Mrs R. M. Stafford (Steel-Maitland), Mrs Gascoigne

(Viscount Harcourt), Mrs Maxse and Mrs P. Gill (Leo Maxse), Mr Mark Bonham Carter (Asquith), Vice-Admiral Sir Ian Hogg (H. A. Gwynne), the Keeper of Manuscripts, British Library (Balfour, Campbell-Bannerman, Cecil of Chelwood, Viscount Gladstone, Northcliffe, C. P. Scott, Spender), Trustees of the Bedford Estates and the National Maritime Museum (Arnold White), the University of Birmingham (Austen, Joseph, and Neville Chamberlain), the Syndics of Cambridge University Library (Baldwin, Crewe, Templewood), Trinity College, Cambridge, and Mr Milton Gendel (Montagu), Norfolk Records Office (Oliver Locker-Lampson), Trustees of National Library of Scotland (Elibank, Haldane, Rosebery), the Clerk of the Records, House of Lords Records Office (Beaverbrook, Blumenfeld, Bonar Law, Davidson, Lloyd George, Samuel, Strachey, Wargrave, Willoughby de Broke), A. J. P. Taylor, on behalf of the Beaverbrook Foundation (Beaverbrook, Blumenfeld, Bonar Law, Lloyd George, Wargrave), the India Office Library and Records (Reading), the editor of the *Spectator* (Strachey), the Bodleian Library (Bryce, Ponsonby, Sandars, Selborne), Trustees of the Imperial War Museum (Henry Wilson).

In addition, I wish to express my warm thanks to the owners of copyright in manuscript material who have given me their permission to quote from this material. It must be slightly disconcerting to be asked, out of the blue, whether the words of a member of one's family may be included in a forthcoming book on 'Corruption'! But nearly everyone responded in a helpful fashion, several being so kind as to volunteer pieces of information relevant to my work and to spur me on with words of encouragement. One elderly peer, I am told, was cheered up on his sick bed on being confronted with his grandfather's abusive words about Lloyd George, so perhaps I have unwittingly been of help to some of *them*! Mr Julian Amery wishes me to point out that in the period covered in my book letters were often used to express speculative views which today would be expressed over the telephone or in personal discussion.

Here is a list of copyright owners of manuscript material whose written permission I have secured, with the name of the actual author in brackets: the Rt. Hon. Julian Amery (L. S. Amery), Viscount Bledisloe (First Baron Bledisloe), Mr Mark Bonham Carter (Asquith, Margot Asquith), Lord Croft (First Baron Croft), Viscount Esher (Second Viscount Esher), Lord Gainford (First Baron Gainford), Sir John Edwards-Moss (Sir Thomas Edwards-Moss), Sir William Gladstone (First Viscount Gladstone), Earl Grey (Fourth Earl Grey), Lord Harlech (Third Baron Harlech), Trustees of the Imperial War Museum (Henry Wilson), Professor H. K. S. Lambton (Lord Cecil of Chelwood), Mr A. D. Maclean (Sir Donald Maclean), Trustees of the National Library of Scotland (Viscount Haldane, Lord Murray of Elibank), the National Trust (Rudyard Kipling), Viscount Northcliffe Will Trust (Northcliffe),

Lord Ponsonby of Shulbrede (First Baron Ponsonby), Earl of Rosebery (Fifth Earl of Rosebery), the Marquess of Salisbury (Third and Fourth Marquesses of Salisbury, Lord Quickswood), the Earl of Selborne (Second Earl of Selborne), the Duke of Somerset (Fifteenth Duke of Somerset), the University of Birmingham (Austen Chamberlain, Joseph Chamberlain, Neville Chamberlain), Lord Willoughby de Broke (Nineteenth Baron Willoughby de Broke), the Librarian, Windsor Castle (King Edward VII, Lord Stamfordham, First Baron Wigram). Every effort has been made to trace and secure permission from holders of copyright. I apologize to anyone whose right I might inadvertently have infringed.

Finally, I must also acknowledge my indebtedness to Edward Arnold (Publishers) Ltd. in respect of quotations from *Anti-Semitism in British Society 1876–1939* (1979) by Colin Holmes; A. & C. Black (Publishers) Ltd. in respect of a quotation from *The History of the English People in the Nineteenth Century*, vol. vi (1934) by Élie Halévy; to Blackstaff Press Ltd. and the author in respect of a quotation from *C. P. Trevelyan 1870–1939: Portrait of a Radical* (1977) by A. J. A. Morris; to Cambridge University Press in respect of quotations from *Wars, Plots and Scandals in Post-War France* (1970) by Philip M. Williams, *The Story and Significance of Imperialism* (1965) by R. Koebener and H. D. Schmidt, *Liberals and Social Democrats* by Peter Clarke, *Property and Politics 1870–1914* (1981) by Avner Offer, *The Impact of Labour 1920–1924* (1971) by Maurice Cowling, and *The Liberal Mind 1914–1929* (1977) by Michael Bentley; to Century Hutchinson Ltd. in respect of quotations from *Diaries 1915–1918 (1968)* by Cynthia Asquith, and *My Life of Strife* (n.d.) by Lord Croft; to William Collins Sons & Co., Ltd. in respect of quotations from *Hankey: Man of Secrets*, vols. i and ii (1970 and 1972) by Stephen Roskill, *Downfall of the Liberal Party 1914–1935* (1966) by Trevor Wilson, *The Scene Changes* (1939) by Basil Thomson, *The Decline and Fall of Lloyd George* (1963) by Lord Beaverbrook, and *The Political Diaries of C. P. Scott, 1911–1928* (1970) edited by Trevor Wilson; to Constable & Co. Ltd. in respect of quotations from *The Rise of the Plutocrats* (1978) by Jamie Camplin, *C-B: A Life of Sir Henry Campbell-Bannerman* (1973) by John Wilson, and *King George V* (1952) by Harold Nicolson; to Croom Helm Ltd. in respect of a quotation from *The Best Circles* (1973) by Leonore Davidoff; to David & Charles Ltd. in respect of a quotation from *Unionists Divided* (1972) by R. A. Rempel; to Eyre & Spottiswoode Ltd. in respect of a quotation from *The Unknown Prime Minister* (1955) by Robert Blake; to Hamish Hamilton Ltd. in respect of a quotation from *Rise and Fall of the Political Press in Britain*, vol. ii (1984) by Stephen Koss; to Liverpool University Press in respect of a quotation from *Democracy and Sectarianism* (1981) by P. J. Waller; to Longman Group Ltd. in respect of quotations from *The Age of Balfour and Baldwin* (1978) by John Ramsden; to Macmillan Publishers Ltd. in respect of a quotation from the essay by Gillian Peele in *By-Elections in British Politics* (1973) edited by C. Cook and J. Ramsden, and a quotation from *Life with Lloyd George: The Diary of A. J. Sylvester* (1975) edited by Colin Cross; to Manchester University Press in respect of quotations from *The Crawford Papers* (1984) edited by John Vincent; to John Murray (Publishers) Ltd. in respect of quotations from *Inside Asquith's Cabinet* (1977) edited by E. David; to Oxford University Press in respect of quotations from *Thomas Jones: Whitehall Diary*, vols. i and ii (1969) edited by K. Middlemas, *The Liberal Party and the Jameson Raid* (1968) by J. Butler, *Lloyd George Family Letters 1885–1936* (1973) edited by K. O. Morgan, *Consensus and Disunity* (1979) by K. O. Morgan, *H. H. Asquith: Letters to Venetia Stanley* (1982) edited by Michael and Eleanor Brock, and *The Holmes–Laski Letters* (1953) edited by M. Howe; to Routledge & Kegan Paul, Ltd. in respect of a quotation from C. Trebilcock's essay in *Edwardian Radicalism 1900–1914* (1974) edited by A. J. A. Morris; to Sidgwick & Jackson, Ltd. in respet of a quotation from *The History of the Liberal Party 1895–1970* (1971) by Roy Douglas; to Virago Ltd. in respect of a quotation from *The Diary of Beatrice Webb*, vol. ii (1983) edited by Norman and Jeanne MacKenzie, in association with the London School of Economics and Political Science (Editorial Matter and Arrangement: © Norman and Jeanne MacKenzie, 1983; the Diary of Beatrice Webb, The Passfield Papers: © The London School of Economics and Political Science, 1983). Dr John Ramsden has kindly given me permission to include extracts from his edition of the Bayford letters, *Real Old Tory Politics* (1984).

Material from *The Leo Amery Diaries, vol. i* (1980) edited by John Barnes and David Nicholson is reprinted by kind permission of Curtis Brown Ltd. (p. 93, 11 words; p. 94, 6 words; p. 141, 14 words; pp. 355–6, 24 words; p. 334, 3¾ words).

Material from the biography of *Winston S. Churchill* by Randolph Churchill and Martin Gilbert (1967–77) is reprinted by kind permission of Curtis Brown Ltd. on behalf of C. & T. Publications; vol. ii (R. Churchill), p. 58, 18 words: © 1967 C. & T. Publications; vol. ii (R. Churchill), cviii, p. 1747, 17 words: © 1969 C. & T. Publications; vol. iii (Gilbert), cvii, p. 1474, 14 words: © 1969 C. & T. Publications; vol. iv (Gilbert), p. 787, 17 words: © 1975 C. & T. Publications; vol. iv (Gilbert), cviii, pp. 1932–3, 28 words: © 1975 C. & T. Publications).

Finally I would like to thank Ivon Asquith of Oxford University Press for his kindness and encouragement.

CONTENTS

ILLUSTRATIONS

TABLES

ABBREVIATIONS

ASE	Amalgamated Society of Engineers
BL	British Library
BSA Co.	British South Africa Company
DBB	*Dictionary of Business Biography*
DPP	Director of Public Prosecutions
EPD	Excess Profits Duty
HLRO	House of Lords Records Office
ILP	Independent Labour Party
PLP	Parliamentary Labour Party
PP	Parliamentary Papers
Parl. Deb.	Parliamentary Debates
RPE	Radical Plutocrats Enquiry

Introduction

A book about political corruption in modern Britain may occasion some surprise; precisely what, many may wonder, will such a book be about? Britain may have experienced the occasional sexual scandal in which the career of a leading politican has been destroyed; one thinks of Charles Dilke and Parnell, to go no further. But in late Victorian and Edwardian Britain pride in the purity of public life was a sentiment shared by Britons of all classes, creeds, and party affiliations. 'We in this country have happily been free for two or three generations from any imputation of mercenary or corrupt motives on the part of our public men, a thing which can be said of few other countries.'[1] The words were those of the Liberal Leader, Campbell-Bannerman, speaking in a Commons debate in May 1900, but almost identical phrases were ritually intoned by Conservative and later by Labour MPs.[2]

Certainly nothing happened in Britain which resembled the Panama Canal Scandal of 1892–3, which gave France an unenviable reputation as a state where representative government was threatened by the venality and rapacity of its public men.[3] Late Victorian and Edwardian commentators, basking complacently in the praise of their own political system, could also compare their country favourably with the United States—home of Tammany Hall and of a Congress whose decisions were often distorted by log-rolling and cynical pressure groups on the look-out for legislative favours. 'Isn't everybody corrupt there?' was the question which visitors returning from the United States were invariably asked, according to James Bryce.[4]

Even when due allowance has been made for the possibility that some potentially serious political scandals failed to break simply because their perpetrators succeeded in hushing them up'[5] there does

---

[1] *Parl. Deb.*, 4th ser., lxxxii. 1335–6 (8 May 1900).

[2] e.g. as late as the Lynskey Affair of 1948–9, the Labour Prime Minister, Attlee, appealed to all parties to draw together in defence of the principle that 'public administration in this country and public life in this country stand unrivaled in their high standards of service and incorruptibility' (cited by Madeline R. Robinton, 'The British Method of Dealing with Political Corruption', in Heidenheimer, Arnold J. (ed.) *Political Corruption: Readings in Comparative Analysis* (N. Brunswick, 1970; 2nd edn., 1978), p. 249).

[3] e.g. J. E. C. Bodley's influential book, *France* (London, 1898; revised edn., 1899), the sixth chapter of which is entitled 'Corruption Under the Republic' and gives the writer's reflections not just on Panama but also on the 'Wilson Scandals'.

[4] Bryce, J., *The American Commonwealth* (London, 2nd rev. edn., 1889), p. 149. But perhaps in this book Bryce himself helped to fix that stereotype by depicting America very much in the terms that educated American 'reformers' of the 1880s had employed. (See Ions, E., *James Bryce and American Democracy 1870–1922* (London, 1968), pp. 136–7.)

[5] Recent anxieties about local government have been well handled in Doig, A., *Corruption and Misconduct in Contemporary British Politics* (London, 1984). See also

seem broad justification for the general belief in the honesty and incorruptibility of Britain's ruling élite in late Victorian Britain. This, after all, was the period in which the implementation of the Northcote–Trevelyan Reforms was bringing about a sharp curtailment of the patronage at the disposal of ministries, while the passing of the Corrupt and Illegal Practices Act in 1883 had put an end to the grosser kinds of electoral malpractice. In retrospect, it is tempting to view the late nineteenth and early twentieth centuries as an interlude of near-total political purity separating the 'Old Corruption' of earlier decades from the post-1960 period, in which anxieties about local government and police corruption and improper parliamentary lobbying have frequently been expressed.[6]

Why, then, did I ignore this conventional view of the British political system and embark on a study of corruption? My interest in the subject developed slowly. It first began when I was working in the late 1970s on aspects of the Radical Right in Britain.[7] Here I was confronted with politicians and journalists on the fringes of the political system who bitterly assailed the pre-war Liberal Administrations of Campbell-Bannerman and Asquith, alleging that they owed their existence to unspeakable corruption, the like of which had not been seen since the days of Walpole. Though episodes like the Marconi Incident gave a certain substance to these outbursts, it was initially tempting to treat them as expressions of frustration on the part of the patriotic Right, as they contemplated their opponents' seemingly unshakeable grip on national power. Given the unbalanced personalities of some of their spokesmen, it even seemed possible to interpret their utterances as evidence of political paranoia, calling for psycho-historical analysis.

However, I soon realized the inadequacy of such an approach to politicians and pamphleteers, many of whom were in no way psychologically disturbed. Similarly, I dismissed as an evasion those accounts of scandalmongering in the Edwardian period which reduced it to a mere sub-chapter in the history of anti-Semitism. True, anti-Semitism forms a thread in the story told by this book. But by no means all the critics of the Liberal Government who shouted 'corruption' were anti-Semites (Loe Strachey, for example, cannot be so

Fennell, P., 'Local Government Corruption in England and Wales', in Clarke, M. (ed.), *Corruption: Causes, Consequences and Control* (London, 1983), and Chibnall, S. and Saunders, P., 'Worlds Apart: Notes on the Social Reality of Corruption', *British Journal of Sociology*, xxviii (1977), 138–54.

[6] e.g. see the recent revelations about Lord Randolph Churchill's relationship with Baron Nathan Rothschild, in Foster, R. F., *Lord Randolph Churchill: A Political Life* (Oxford, 1981).

[7] Searle, G. R., 'Critics of Edwardian Society: The Case of the Radical Right', in O'Day, A. (ed.), *The Edwardian Age: Conflict and Stability 1900–1914* (London, 1979), pp. 79–96; and Searle, G. R., 'The "Revolt from the Right" in Edwardian Britain', in Kennedy, P. and Nicholls, A. (eds.), *Nationalist and Racialist Movements in Britain and Germany Before 1914* (London, 1981), pp. 21–39.

categorized), and though some of the targets of their attacks were Jewish, like Rufus Isaacs, quite as many were not. As the anti-Semitic Hilaire Belloc once conceded, nobody less Jewish than Lloyd George could possibly be imagined.[8] The scandalmongering of the Edwardian period would surely have occurred, even had there been no 'Jewish problem'. Moreover, one can go further and suggest, as some contemporaries did, that the overt anti-Semitism of journals like the *New Witness* was positively helpful to the reputation of Liberal statesmen, who were able to defend themselves by deploring the anti-Semitic nature of the charges, while ignoring the substance of the accusations being made against them. This in turn has coloured the historiography of Edwardian politics, where, at least until recently, blatantly Whiggish interpretations have dominated the field.

Without accepting the charges of corruption at face value, there seemed, then, to be a case for taking them more seriously than historians had previously done. But how to set about examining the issue of corruption, which, it soon became apparent, was a highly ambiguous one? The allegations could not be simply proved or disproved, if only because the behaviour complained of was seldom of the kind that would have led to its perpetrators being prosecuted. After all, a 'corrupt' act need not necessarily be an illegal one. Thus, while most Britons thought honours trafficking dishonourable, it was not a criminal offence until 1925. The Government's critics were in nearly all cases doing no more than accuse Ministers of a singular want of 'delicacy' which threatened public confidence in the political system by violating some of its unwritten laws. But what was this hypothetical code of conduct and what did it enjoin?

A few semi-formal rules of conduct did exist. For example, in 1892 Gladstone's Cabinet bound its members to divest themselves of all their directorships in public companies on entering office, and this self-denying ordinance—though not without considerable argument and acrimony—eventually became accepted by all the political parties as one of the ground-rules of British politics. Successive rulings by the Speaker also imposed restrictions on what Members of Parliament could do. So did the Contractors Act of 1782, a rare attempt to prevent by law the possibility of conflict between a Member's pecuniary interests and his public duty. These issues have been ably delineated by D. C. M. Platt, in an important article to which political historians have given insufficient attention.[9] But the indifference of modern historians was matched by the ignorance of most contemporary politicians. Caught in the snares of Marconi, Rufus Isaacs was discovered by a colleague ruminating out loud about the duties of a

---

[8] See Ch. 9, p. 211.
[9] Platt, D. C. M., 'The Commercial and Industrial Interests of Ministers of the Crown', *Political Studies*, ix (1961), 267–90.

Minister—a subject to which the Attorney-General seems previously to have given little thought and about which he was clearly not that well informed.[10]

In any case, rules and statutory prohibitions only touch the fringes of the problem of corruption. It was something of a commonplace, subscribed to by both major parties, that gross misconduct could never be eradicated by the application of formal rules. As Bonar Law put it during the Marconi debate in June 1913, the problem 'could only be dealt with by a general sense of propriety in these matters'.[11] Britain's most effective barrier against corruption, it was said, lay in the 'character' of her public men. (Exactly the same sort of thing was being said in the 1970s.)[12]

Now, the cardinal virtue invoked by those who waxed eloquent about character was 'disinterestedness', the high-minded subordination of personal advantage and selfish interests to a rational pursuit of the common good. Voters and, still more, politicians were expected to display scrupulous personal integrity and a disinterested approach to public life. Admittedly, scrupulosity could be carried too far. An exaggerated concern for purity, it was said, would do nothing to discourage rogues and adventurers from seeking a political career, but might frighten away honest men with highly sensitive consciences, in which case the standard of political morality might actually decline.[13] Nor should the emphasis on disinterestedness be interpreted in such a way as to bar men with business interests from political involvement, since the Commons was not a university debating society, but a national forum in which experienced men from a variety of practical backgrounds discussed practical issues.[14] So when politicians of different traditions came together to praise the character of British statesmen, they seem to have had in mind practical experience, combined with fastidious moral standards, acquired through being brought up from birth in a particular tradition of public service.

But disinterestedness had other meanings than this. For not only was

[10] Lucy Masterman's diary, in Masterman, L., *C. F. G. Masterman* (London, 1939), p. 255.

[11] *Parl. Deb.*, 5th ser., liv. 646 (19 June 1913).

[12] e.g. Redcliffe-Maud, J. and Wood, B., *English Local Government Reformed* (Oxford, 1974), p. 169.

[13] Thus, when Strachey argued that politicians should avoid all business involvement that might even possibly conflict with their public duties, the Liberal journalist, Harold Spender, retorted: 'There is an old saying, containing some shrewd truth: "The best is the enemy of the good". So I am afraid if you attempted to apply your standard to all political life you would really make things far worse. For as it is really an impossible standard to live up to, it would inevitably produce a reaction, with all its accompaniments of hypocrisy and cynicism' (Spender to Strachey, Apr. 1912, HLRO, Strachey papers, S/13/13/2).

[14] As one Unionist MP put in in 1903, 'Was the Government to be composed of mere doctrinaires and pedants who had no practical knowledge of anything going on?' (*Parl. Deb.*, 4th ser., cxviii. 417–18 (20 Feb. 1903).

personal integrity in a politician highly valued but there was also an insistence that political groups and parties should pursue a common good or a national interest which overrode sectional or class interests. Central to this view of politics were the writings of John Stuart Mill, which contain eloquent warnings of the dangers of 'class legislation', that is to say, 'of government intended for (whether really affecting it or not) the immediate benefit of the dominant class, to the lasting detriment of the whole'. Interestingly, Mill defined a class as 'any number of persons who have the same sinister interest'.[15]

It was not only Liberals who subscribed to this creed. The Conservatives, too, professed belief in a national good transcending class interests and presented themselves as the natural custodians of that 'good'. Indeed, so dominant in British political culture was this distaste for class that even Socialists, or at least the majority of them, played down this aspect of their creed. In a famous pasage from *Socialism and Society* (1905), James Ramsay MacDonald wrote: 'Socialism marks the growth of Society, not the uprising of a class. The consciousness which it seeks to quicken is not one of economic class solidarity, but one of social unity and growth towards organic wholeness.'[16]

In short, there was widespread agreement that the survival of Britain's system of representative government called for fastidious honesty in all her citizens, most noticeably in her politicians. Moreover, however illogical this may seem, such beliefs became inextricably entangled with an abhorrence of 'sectionalism' and 'class selfishness'. These views united people across almost the entire political spectrum.

However, in the interpretation and application of these beliefs there was plentiful scope for disagreement and conflict. Indeed, party political life throughout the late Victorian and Edwardian period in some ways centred around such conflicts, in which the objective was to identify one's own party with the 'common good' while branding one's opponents as selfish promoters of mere interests. Thus, professions of belief in the high standards supposedly prevailing in British politics were usually the prelude, as in the Campbell-Bannerman quotation of the first paragraph, to a party political attack.

Allegations of *personal* misconduct, too, were usually shaped by personal predilections, family traditions, and class prejudice. The political ethics of a Welsh Radical like Lloyd George necessarily diverged from those of someone brought up, as Lord Robert Cecil had been, in the aristocratic ambience of Hatfield House. Thus, the motives and 'interests' of the scandalmongers and the political

---

[15] Mill, J. S., *Considerations on Representative Government* (London, 1861; Everyman edn., 1910), p. 254.
[16] MacDonald, J. R., *Socialism and Society* (London, 1905), p. 127.

moralists stand in as much need of critical scrutiny as does the
misconduct of those whom they were attacking. (To look at it in
another way, most of the political corruption which figures in this
book would be categorized by political scientists as 'gray', not 'black'
or 'white'.)[17]

All these reflections have taken me a long way form my original
concern with 'Liberal corruption' in Edwardian Britain. But it soon
became apparent that my new broader approach to political corruption
was one that could not be confined to the years of Liberal rule from
1905 to 1914. So I started to push my investigations back into the
1890s and forward to about 1930. The rationale for these chronological
parameters will be justified at greater length in the book's Conclusion.
    Once I had decided to enlarge the scope of my study so that it took
in, not a decade, but over thirty years of political life, certain
consequences naturally followed. First, it was necessary for me to
synthesize my own original work with other historians' findings, since
no one could cover all the relevant episodes and issues single-
handedly. I hope that I have fully acknowledged my many debts to
those historians upon whose research I have drawn. Secondly, the
length of the period covered meant the curtailment of certain topics
and themes that perhaps deserve fuller treatment. For example,
admirable though Frances Donaldson's study of the Marconi Scandal
is, there should now be a new full-length book on the subject
incorporating the mass of primary source material that has become
available in the last twenty years or so. Indeed, many of my chapters
could profitably have been extended. But rather than see an interesting
subject broken down into a series of 'safe', conventional monographs, I
wanted to show the essential unity of a thirty-five year period, in
which certain themes, dilemmas, and personalities made repeated
appearances, and to trace the connections between episodes, often
separated by many years, which combined to form what I see as an
intricate pattern of paranoia and suspicion.
    To keep the book down to a reasonable length I have also had to
excise certain aspects of political corruption in the years under study.
In particular, I soon decided to leave *electoral* corruption out of
consideration, in part because it has already attracted several competent

----

[17] Arnold Heidenheimer means by 'gray corruption' activities that some groups in
society would like to see punished, though some would not, while many would feel
ambiguous. 'Black corruption' denotes activities which an overwhelming majority of
people would want to see suppressed as a matter of principle. 'White corruption' would
cover activities which most people tolerated or felt would not be worth the cost of
suppression. (Heidenheimer (ed.), *Political Corruption*, pp. 26–7). Heidenheimer, with
American experience in mind, is, however, mainly interested in conflicts of value and
interest between 'élites' and 'mass opinion', not those between political parties and
social classes of the sort that feature in this book. Note, took that his classificatory
scheme cuts across the distinction, drawn above, between 'legal' and 'illegal' corruption.

studies,[18] but also because I accept the general view that after the passing of the 1883 Corrupt and Illegal Practices Act, electoral bribery and intimidation were issues of diminishing significance. There were, it is true, 'scandalous' episodes, like that which led to the disfranchisement of the borough of Worcester for systematic corruption following the 1906 General Election.[19] But significantly, this was the last time such drastic action needed to be taken. The combined effect of secret ballots, enlarged constituencies, and the emergence of mass parties, as well as better legislative controls, meant that the cost of party politics was being steadily transferred in these years from the constituencies to the party headquarters—a development which arguably gave rise to *new* kinds of corruption, but which greatly reduced the level of traditional electoral malpractice. Also excluded from this study is any examination of corruption in local politics and the police force.[20]

This, then, is a study of national politics. It deals incidentally with the foibles of individual politicians and with the malicious rumours which grew up around them; but its main purpose is to explore the assumptions and values which underlay competing theories about what needed to be done to purify British public life. For a preoccupation with this subject was never far from the surface of politics during the first three decades of the twentieth century, as even a cursory examination of parliamentary debates, the press, and political correspondence will quickly confirm. True, nothing took place in Britain which remotely resembled the 'Tweed Days in St Louis', revealed by Lincoln Steffens; but the absence of such blatant corruption in no way reassured British public opinion. Indeed, it is arguable that in countries where gross corruption is endemic its occurrence is often viewed with cynical forbearance, while in countries like Britain the discovery of even minor irregularities may excite much greater concern. One might go further and argue that 'corruption', both as a phenomenon and as a subject arousing anxiety, tends to assume the greatest prominence in those societies which have developed strong 'community-regarding

[18] Gwyn, W. B., *Democracy and the Cost of Politics in Britain* (London, 1962); O'Leary, C., *The Elimination of Corrupt Practices in British Elections 1868–1911* (Oxford, 1962); Howe, J. R., 'Corruption in British Elections in the Early Twentieth Century: Some Examples From Gloucestershire', *Midland History*, v (1979–80), 63–77.
[19] Pelling, H., *Social Geography of British Elections 1885–1910* (London, 1967), pp. 192–3, 429–30.
[20] This is the subject of Alan Doig's interesting book, *Corruption and Misconduct in Contemporary British Politics*; although it mainly concerns the period after the Second World War, I have found the early chapters stimulating and helpful in many ways.
Political scientists are generally agreed that the incidence (though not, of course, the scale) of corruption tends to increase as one descends the political hierarchy. See the invaluable anthology: Heidenheimer (ed.) *Political Corruption*.

norms' and in which the concepts of public duty and responsibility have been raised to a high level.[21]

This book, however, is not really an attempt to write a history of political corruption in Britain. Indeed, such a history would be quite impossible to put together, given the fact that, as Joel Hurstfield has argued, corruption is 'the easiest charge to make and the most difficult charge to refute'.[22] Significantly, where corruption laws do exist, the problems of enforcement remain peculiarly difficult because such laws deal with motives as much as with actions and with intentions as much as with consequences.[23] The historian faces similar difficulties. All he can really do, as Walter Lippmann observes, is to write 'the history of the exposure of political corruption',[24] in other words to describe and analyse *political scandal*. In some ways this is unfortunate. The fact that political corruption often comes to light only because it has been discovered by chance in bankruptcy proceedings or through investigatory journalism necessarily encourages highly-coloured, sensational treatment of conduct which may be regarded as quite 'normal' by its practitioners and their work colleagues.[25] But there is also substance in the claim of the French historian, Jeannine Verdès-Leroux, who has written:

Chaque régime a les scandales qui'il mérite, chaque scandale donne une image fidèle du régime . . . On connaît un régime en déchiffrant ses scandales, non en lisant les discours de ses maîtres.[26]

---

[21] Ibid. 9, 22, 60. As one political scientist puts it, 'Corruption . . . is a product of the distinction between public welfare and private interest which comes with modernization' (Huntington, S. P., *Political Order in Changing Societies* (New Haven, 1968), p. 61).

[22] Hurstfield, J., *Freedom, Corruption and Government in Elizabethan England* (London, 1973), p. 139. The extremely rigorous criteria which Professor Hurstfield lays down for distinguishing corruption proper from mere rumour would make it difficult for a historian ever to assert that real corruption had taken place. See the stimulating discussion in Ch. 5 of his book.

[23] Chibnall and Saunders, 'Worlds Apart', p. 149.

[24] Walter Lippmann, 'A Theory About Corruption', Heidenheimer (ed.), *Political Corruption*, p. 294.

[25] See the stimulating article by Phil Fennell, 'Local Government' in Clarke (ed.), *Corruption*, p. 22.

[26] Verdès-Leroux, J., *Scandale financier et antisémitisme catholique: Le Krach de l'Union Générale* (Paris, 1969), p. 206.

Prelude: The Hooley Affair

'THE Hooley revelations have caused a far wider and deeper interest than any domestic political event this year': so wrote the *National Review* in December 1898.[1] It took nothing less than the Fashoda Crisis to distract public attention away from the bankruptcy court where the extraordinary life and times of Ernest Terah Hooley were being opened up to scrutiny. Hooley was a company promoter. By the time he finally filed his bankruptcy petition, he had been responsible for at least fourteen flotations, including Dunlop, Schweppes, and a number of cycle companies, with an aggregate capital of nearly £12,500,000. For his part in these transactions Hooley had scooped about £3,000,000. In the summer of 1898 his rickety business empire collapsed.[2]

The rise of this one-time Nottingham lace manufacturer from obscurity to a dazzling role in London Society, followed by his subsequent downfall, proved to be irresistibly fascinating to contemporaries. For a start, Hooley's character was a puzzle. On one level, he was an unscrupulous swindler; but at another level, he was able to project himself quite plausibly as a 'Holy Fool', an innocent provincial who had wandered into a sphere of life which escaped his comprehension. As he later put it when writing his memoirs in a prison cell, he was 'the biggest "mug" that ever was born'.[3]

Of financial and business organization Hooley clearly knew very little,[4] the methods by which he had amassed his fortune being in essence childishly simple. As the financial journalist, W. R. Lawson (better known for his part in a later scandal) shrewdly observed, Hooley's 'genius' was to perceive that 'the average Englishman takes less pains over a five thousand pound investment than over the choice of a coat' and that the speculating public cared only for surface appearances.[5] So Hooley brought to his various company promotions all the arts of the professional advertising man. Hooley candidly confided to the court that the most important part of his prospectuses was the front page, on which he was prepared to spend almost £100,000 in the case of the Dunlop Company.[6] Some of this money went on gifts to solicitors and brokers, additional to their professional fees. There

[1] *National Review*, xxxii (1898), 477.
[2] On Hooley, see *The Hooley Book* (London, 1904); Camplin, J. *The Rise of the Plutocrats: Wealth and Power in Edwardian England* (London, 1978), pp. 64–7, 120–1, 191–3; Richardson, K. and M., 'Ernest Terah Hooley', *DBB* (London, 1985), iii. 329–32.
[3] Hooley, E. T., *Hooley's Confessions* (London, n.d.), p. 108.
[4] O'Hagan, H. O., *Leaves From My Life* (London, 1929), i. 411.
[5] Lawson, W. R., 'Company Promoting "À La Mode" ', *National Review*, xxxii (1898), 113.
[6] *Daily Mail*, 28 July 1898.

were also the 'press calls'[7] and, most important of all, the acquisition of the names of titled notables to add lustre and solidity to his precarious enterprises. For example, the Earl de la Warr, Hooley's prize capture, was paid £25,000 to join the Dunlop Board. De la Warr in turn brought in other peers. Lord Albermarle, the Duke of Somerset, and Lord Winchelsea were only three of the illustrious 'guinea pig' directors whom Hooley used to fool an investing public which was as snobbish as it was credulous.[8]

In his financial methods Hooley was not really an innovator. But few company promoters in the 1890s operated quite so blatantly on the principle that 'every man has his price'. Hooley's gold was used to ensnare friends, to buy off rivals, and to neutralize enemies. Gifts were showered on journalists, lawyers, businessmen, and aristocrats—on anyone, in fact, who might aid his purposes. Lawson understood this side of Hooley's nature to perfection:

Himself an out-and-out believer in money and nothing else, he assumed that every human being he came in contact with was the same. He gave no one, man or woman, rich or poor, credit for being able to resist the touch of his illgotten gold. He carried the coarsest form of bribery into the bank parlour and up to the very steps of the altar. Bribery seems to have become so engrained in his own nature, that in his own mind it tainted every monetary transaction he did. Whoever got money from him, even in the ordinary course of business, he set down as a blackmailer or a man he had bought and paid for. The simplest service that could be rendered to him was liable to be afterwards twisted by him into something corrupt and dishonourable.[9]

Not content with the simple possession of a fortune, Hooley set about buying his way into 'High Society'. Lured by Hooley's wealth, the fashionable world of London thronged to the Midland Grand Hotel, where the great financier held court, rumour having it that some prospective clients were prepared to pay £500 for an audience.[10] Meanwhile Hooley was spending money like water. He acquired a string of racehorses. He took up yachting, annoying the Queen by the purchase of the Prince of Wales's yacht, the *Britannia*, for £10,000. Driven on by an intense social ambition, Hooley also set himself up as a country gentleman by acquiring Papworth Hall in Cambridgeshire, where he dispensed lavish hospitality. Later he was nominated as High Sheriff and Deputy-Lieutenant for Cambridgeshire and Huntingdonshire.[11] The *Daily News* expressed grim amusement over the spectacle of Mr Hooley sitting in judgement on petty criminals.[12] But, prior to his

[7] See Ch. 2, pp. 36–7.
[8] *Daily Mail*, 28 July 1898; *The Hooley Book*, p. 34. Most of Hooley's companies were oversubscribed and the stock heavily watered.
[9] *National Review*, xxxii (1898), 110.
[10] *DBB*, iii. 330.
[11] *The Hooley Book*, *passim*; Hooley, *Hooley's Confessions*, p. 107.
[12] *Daily News*, 15 Nov. 1898.

bankruptcy, there were no barriers to Hooley's social advancement. He even received an invitation to Sandringham.[13]

The political world, too, seemed ready to embrace him. The Conservatives of the Ilkeston Division of Derbyshire adopted him as their parliamentary candidate. Moreover, and this was the most sensational of the revelations to come out of the bankruptcy court, Hooley purchased admission to the Carlton Club and also tried to acquire a baronetcy by donations to Conservative Party Funds.[14] In his eagerness for a title, Hooley made princely contributions to charities, though it is unlikely that he disbursed £250,000 in this way as he boasted of doing. St Paul's Cathedral was presented with a gift of gold plate, which it later had to return to help meet the claims of Hooley's creditors![15]

In the course of his adventurous life Hooley twice served a prison sentence—on one of these occasions meeting up with his fellow-swindler, Horatio Bottomley.[16] But his bankruptcy in 1898 entailed nothing worse than the ruining of his social career. He managed, for example, to keep possession of Papworth Hall, and publicly boasted of living still at the rate of £15,000 a year. Moreover, by the simple expedient of trading in his wife's name, he was even able after a short interval to resume his company-promoting activities. Yet the Official Receiver in Bankruptcy in his 1899 Report enumerated several offences which Hooley had committed, involving breaches of the Bankruptcy Act and of the Debtors Act. Why, then, did the Director of Public Prosecutions do nothing, to the disappointment of thousands of creditors and shareholders, ruined in the crash? Contemporary rumour had it that there were good reasons for not putting Hooley on trial. Indeed, Hooley himself had told the press, while awaiting the DPP's decision, 'Look here! I have not yet said one-fifteenth part of what I can say about the British peerage. I have still got a lot of cards up my sleeve.'[17]

Even as things stood, the proceedings of the bankruptcy court had revealed how many notable public figures had compromised themselves through association with the fraudulent company promoter. A striking feature of the case was the queue of barristers appearing in court anxious to refute the suggestion that their clients, 'noble and otherwise', had sullied their hands with Hooley's money.[18] Indeed, several of the aristocratic 'guinea pig' directors, including de la Warr

---

[13] *The Hooley Book*, p. 88. Camplin says that one of the royal courtiers, Sir Jacob Wilson, an investor in one of Hooley's companies, was instrumental in introducing him to the Prince of Wales. Hooley claims that in 1896 he purchased 2,000 acres adjoining Sandringham, which he later sold to the Prince (Camplin, *Rise of the Plutocrats*, p. 109).

[14] *Daily Chronicle*, 3 Nov. 1898. For the details, see Ch. 4, pp. 88–9.

[15] *The Hooley Book*, p. 76.

[16] Symons, J., *Horatio Bottomley* (London, 1955), p. 260.

[17] *The Hooley Book*, p. 151.   [18] *Daily Mail*, 2 Aug. 1898.

and Albermarle, may actually have offered inducements to Hooley to withdraw his allegations.[19]

Thus, for aristocratic Society the whole affair constituted a humiliating experience. A number of famous peers were made to look foolish and grasping, if not corrupt. Hooley himself blatantly played to the gallery and deliberately set out to present himself as an innocent who had been fleeced by people of high standing.

But then nobody who figured in the Hooley Case emerged with much credit. The evidence brought before the bankruptcy court, argued the *Spectator*, indicated the prevalence of 'a low and vulgar standard of morals which it is painful to contemplate. . . . Turn which way we will, the case reeks with moral garbage.'[20] Though some Liberal newspapers could not repress their glee at the discomfiture of the Carlton Club and the Conservative Party managers, the *Spectator's* note of moralistic concern was echoed by most sections of the press. Nor did this concern die away once Hooley himself had disappeared from the headlines. For the revelations of the autumn and winter of 1898 had dramatized issues that for several years had been causing anxiety. For example, the ease with which Hooley had exploited the investing public suggested the need for improvements in the company laws.

But legal reforms, however necessary, hardly seemed adequate to contain the evil. For the fact that an amoral adventurer like Hooley could acquire, albeit briefly, so remarkable a social ascendancy seemed to indicate a decay of morals and manners and a lowering of the whole tone of public life. As for the other 'scandals' exposed by the Hooley 'Trial', like honours trafficking and the manipulation of a venal press, the existence of such abuses had long been suspected, though never had they been so clearly demonstrated.

The British had been wont to boast that they were free of the corruption which was endemic in the public life of less favoured nations like France and the United States. But by the late 1890s observers of the contemporary scene were no longer sure that this was so. It was the beginning of an anxiety about 'corruption'—an ambiguous term with a multiplicity of meanings—that was to influence the course of British politics for the next thirty years.

[19] Ibid. Hooley told the court he had offered to punch the head of the 'little man' who had approached him on Albermarle's behalf.
[20] *Spectator*, 5 Nov. 1898.

1
The Problem of Plutocracy

In the opinion of the *Spectator* the moral of the Hooley Case was that a way needed to be found to moralize the great wealth which had recently been created by the economic exploitation of the globe. 'The race for wealth is the great factor of our time', it observed; but unfortunately 'the growth of social morality has not kept pace with the growth of wealth.'[1] Like other commentators on the social scene coming from his sort of background, Loe Strachey, the editor, was distressed over what he saw as the deterioration of manners and morals that had followed in the wake of the emergence of a 'new plutocracy' and he feared that this development was bringing serious corruption, both commercial and political, in its train.

But who were the so-called 'plutocrats'? One would look in vain for any common economic characteristics linking the galaxy of eccentric Edwardian millionaires described in Jamie Camplin's stimulating book, *The Rise of the Plutocrats*. Some were retailers and manufacturers who had successfully exploited the new consumer market opened up by rising real wages in the 1880s and 1890s, like Thomas Lipton, the grocer, William Lever, the soap manufacturer, and Alfred Harmsworth, the newspaper proprietor. Secondly, there were the 'Park Lane millionaires', wealthy South African financiers and mine owners, of varied national origins, who had made a fortune out of Kimberley diamonds or Witwatersrand gold and then settled in London to pursue their social ambitions; this group, many of whose members were Jewish, included Sir Julius Wernher, Alfred Beit, and J. B. Robinson. Thirdly, there was a new class of banker cum company promoter, of whom Hooley stands as a disreputable example, while, at the respectable end, can be found a figure like Sir Ernest Cassel, King Edward VII's close friend. Finally, there were American expatriates, like Waldorf Astor, who were attracted to London because of the fame it enjoyed as the social capital of the world.

Economically diverse though these men were, they had certain things in common which enabled contemporaries to identify them as a group. They were all immensely wealthy, several being multi-millionaires, and they all exercised *personal* control over their stupendous fortunes. As Camplin observes, the Edwardian plutocracy was a transitional phenomenon which looked back to the era of individual achievement, but also 'looked forward to the impersonal future—to remote rule at

---

[1] 'Bribery and Public Duty', *Spectator*, 5 Nov. 1898, p. 645.

the head of the modern business corporation'.[2] Indeed, Camplin goes on to show that nearly all his plutocrats had difficulty, even within their own lifetime, in maintaining control over the vast economic enterprises they had brought into being. But these difficulties were exacerbated, in many cases, by a tendency to neglect the running of the business as they tried to buy their way into the exclusive circles of London Society. This burning social ambition, as Camplin notes, testifies to the plutocrat's confidence, but also to his need for constant reassurance— reassurance that his wealth was real and that he was a person who really commanded respect.[3]

For, with a few exceptions, the plutocrats did not despise the conventions that regulated Society and felt neither jealousy nor resentment of the position held by the landed aristocracy; rather, they were seeking to legitimate their wealth by acquiring the various status symbols and privileges traditional within Britain's ruling élite. Indeed, they were prepared to pay a very high entrance charge in their anxiety to break into Society. And this need dovetailed with the financial requirements of a section of landed society.

Few historians today would contend that landowners as a class were ruined by the agricultural depression that settled over the countryside in the closing decades of the nineteenth century; even the inroads made into landed wealth by Harcourt's death duties budget of 1894 and Lloyd George's land taxes fifteen years later were not as severe as their victims liked to pretend. In any case, the economic fortunes of landowners were too diverse to permit such generalizations. Where the landlord possessed mineral resources or owned urban land, for example, he might see his income rise rather than fall.

On the whole, however, it is true to say that *agricultural* land by itself could no longer sustain landed society in the social role which had become traditional. So, to secure an adequate income, other strategies needed to be adopted—including the making of advantageous marriages with social outsiders, including Americans, and becoming involved, in unprecedented ways, in the world of business and finance, whether as shareholders or as company directors. But F. M. L. Thompson is right to warn against the mistake of seeing such strategies simply as a rational response to economic difficulties. For, slowly but significantly, the value system of the aristocracy was changing. In Thompson's words, landed society now 'had a new respect for money, especially money not furnished by agricultural estates, and growing affinities with those who made money in large-scale enterprises, particularly overseas'.[4] Thus there occurred a process of fusion

---

[2] Camplin, J., *The Rise of the Plutocrats. Wealth and Power in Edwardian England* (London, 1978), p. 37.
[3] Ibid. 237.
[4] Thompson, F. M. L., *English Landed Society in the Nineteenth Century* (London,

between traditional aristocrats and first-generation businessmen and financiers anxious to secure acceptance into high society. As the contemporary journalist, T. H. Escott neatly put it: 'Our territorial nobles, our squires, our rural landlords great and small have become commercial potentates; our merchant-princes have become country gentlemen.'[5]

What differentiated the late Victorian and Edwardian plutocrats from their predecessors was that they had, in nearly all cases, been raised by their vast wealth from obscurity and relative poverty to social prominence within the space of their own lifetimes. This meant that they had not been prepared by education or prior experience for the kind of role which they now aspired to play. However, fortunately for them, there existed impoverished ladies and gentlemen of genteel and even of aristocratic background, who were prepared to guide the *nouveaux riches* through the intricate rituals of the London Season. 'A lady in the smartest society in London wishes to chaperone a young lady. Terms £1,000 for one year. Highest references given and required': so ran one advertisement carried by a Society newspaper.[6] Sums of £500 or even £1,000 are rumoured to have been paid for the introduction of royal or ultra-fashionable guests to a garden party.[7] The Jesuit priest, Father Bernard Vaughan, believed that such behaviour was not uncommon. Time was when young people used to hire the chairs for the guests; now they hired the guests for the chairs, he quipped.[8] But it could be unwise for a social climber to attempt to pursue a relationship with his newly acquired fashionable friends once the formal occasion had ended. 'I went to your d——d dinner and got your d——d money for it', Labouchere reports an English gentleman as saying to a foreign nobleman. 'That was a matter of business, and the business is now at an end. How dare you presume to pester me, you cad!'[9]

But to make a real mark in Society, one needed to have a country house and an estate, with facilities for field sports, from which to dispense hospitality. In fact, for several generations businessmen translated to the House of Lords had registered their changed social position by the purchase of land.[10] Good railway connections even made it possible to live in the country while continuing to run one's

1963), p. 302. See also Spring, D., 'Land and Politics in Edwardian England', *Agricultural History* (1984), pp. 17–42, esp. pp. 22–44, where aristocratic ventures into the Stock Exchange are described.

[5] Escott, T. H., *England: Its People, Polity, and Pursuits* (2nd edn., London, 1880), ii. 23.

[6] Quoted in Davidoff, L., *The Best Circles: Society, Etiquette and the Season* (London, 1973), p. 63.

[7] Stutfield, H. E. M., *The Sovranty of Society* (London, 1909), p. 232.

[8] Vaughan, B., *The Sins of Society* (London, 1906), p. 177.

[9] MacNeill, J. G. S., *What I Have Seen and Heard* (London, 1925), p. 304.

[10] Thompson, *English Landed Society*, p. 297.

family business, as Harold Perkin shows.[11] On the other hand, there is evidence that by the end of the nineteenth century not all middle-class men of wealth were bothering to acquire a landed estate, once they had been ennobled; Professor Thompson has calculated that between 1886 and 1914 only about half of those capable of buying an estate chose to do so, and the proportion was declining during these years.

Such statistics take no account of the growing habit of renting a country mansion for part of the year. Here was another way in which the social needs of the plutocrat met the financial needs of the aristocrat. Ernest Cassel, for instance, took out a rent on Lord Willoughby de Broke's ancestral home of Compton Verney in Warwickshire for a short period. Did this humiliating experience contribute to that proud peer's public attack on the evils of plutocracy and the resulting decay of manners?[12] However, most of the plutocrats described in Camplin's book preferred outright purchase to rental. Cassel himself eventually acquired a country house of his own, Moulton Paddocks, conveniently close to the Newmarket racecourse. And, most spectacular of all such purchases, Waldorf Astor proceeded to buy the Cliveden Estate and Hever Castle.[13]

For the plutocrat the countryside was a place where money was spent, not made. A few, like the banker, Stuart Samuel, took an interest in their 'model farms'. But, as their critics complained, such men usually had little understanding of agriculture and valued their properties almost entirely because of the social prestige which they conferred and the recreational facilities which they offered. The plutocrats were particularly keen in their pursuit of the aristocratic field sports. Cassel's unfortunate habit of falling off his horse may have amused the landed society of Warwickshire, but the single-minded determination of the banker to master these unfamiliar rural pastimes well illustrates the sacrifices which the plutocrat was prepared to make in his attempt to 'join' fashionable Society.[14]

It was also characteristic of the plutocracy that it brought to traditional sports a new technological sophistication and a new concern for the creature comforts, both of which its vast wealth made possible. 'Shooting requires, no doubt, in its modern developments, great skill of hands and eye', complained the journalist Hugh Stutfield, 'but it was a much more fascinating recreation in former years, before Plutocracy had laid its rapacious paws on it and made it a toilless

[11] Perkin, H., *The Origins of Modern English Society 1780–1880* (London, 1969), p. 432.

[12] On Cassel and the later fate of Compton Verney, see Camplin, *Plutocrats*, pp. 203, 272.

[13] Ibid. 203, 182–5.

[14] Ibid. 203. This social failing was cruelly mocked, after Cassel's death, during Lord Alfred Douglas's trial of 1923. 'Do you remember what he looked like when sitting on a horse?', asked Douglas's counsel (Croft-Cooke, R., *Bosie* (London, 1963), p. 307).

pastime for the lazy and the luxurious.' Now the sportsman 'has but to drive or motor up the glen, so soon as the stalkers have "located" the stags (as the Americans say), and the unsuspecting quarry can be pursued and slain with "convenience and despatch".'[15] The record 'bags' of the Edwardian period can be explained in a number of ways. Strict rules for game preservation played a part, and so did the increased acreage under root crops and a succession of warm and dry springs and early summers. But the sporting records achieved during these years also owed much to the grandiose and expensive way in which shooting was being organized.[16]

Where plutocracy led the way, the aristocracy was quick to follow. The individual plutocrat might be a smaller man on a more crowded stage, suggested the *Saturday Review*, but plutocracy itself largely gave 'the tone to society and influence[d] the manners of a vast circle outside society'.[17] This influence was most obviously exercised in the direction of raising the cost of social life. When she wrote her memoirs in 1906, the society hostess, Lady Dorothy Nevill, was particularly struck by the magnitude of the changes that had occurred since she was a young girl.

When Samuel Warren wrote his famous novel 'Ten Thousand a Year', such an income was considered princely, and its fortunate possessor rich beyond the dreams of avarice. What is it to-day? Why, your modern millionaire gives as much for a single picture, whilst up-to-date entertaining on such a sum is hardly possible. . . . What was luxury fifty years ago is now the merest comfort, whilst what was then considered comfort is now called squalor.[18]

Lady Dorothy goes on to enumerate the luxuries which Society people had recently come to think of as necessities: 'houses, hotels, horses, motors, pictures, and other works or art, and very likely, in addition to all of these, most costly of all—a yacht'.[19]

Nor did the social round of the fashionable man and woman stop there. It might also include big-game hunting in Africa, trips to the casino tables of the Riviera, skiing holidays in the Alps, visits to a German spa town to recuperate from indulgence in over-rich food and heavy drinking. As William Clarke, the Fabian essayist, noted in January 1899, a vast army of servants now existed to serve the requirements of wealthy seekers after pleasure. 'Who shall measure the growth of hotels, restaurants, cafés, clubs which has changed the face of London in less than a generation?' he asked. Whatever its industrial

---

[15] Stutfield, *Sovranty of Society*, pp. 270–1.
[16] Middlemas, K., *Pursuit of Pleasure: High Society in the 1900s* (London, 1977), p. 127
[17] *Saturday Review*, 16 May 1914.
[18] Nevill, R. (ed.), *The Reminiscences of Lady Dorothy Nevill* (London, n.d.; Thomas Nelson edn.), p. 123.
[19] Ibid. 125.

future might be, Clarke predicted that England seemed set fair to become the pleasure-ground for wealthy people from all over the world: 'a land of equable climate, pleasant if not grand scenery, a large and ample life organised for sport, amusement, and the kind of enjoyments pleasing to the leisured classes—how can England help being attractive to the wealthy people who speak her own language?'[20]

The ever-growing love of luxury was also noted with disapproval by Stutfield. He took as an example the cost of a lady's dress allowance, which had enormously increased during the previous thirty years, as had the number of social occasions for which she must be properly equipped: namely, 'balls, dinner and garden-parties, race-meetings, travel, country-house visits, riding, yachting, golf, motoring . . . '.[21] Had there ever been a society in which so much importance was attached to the display of wealth, and so little to historic tradition and the claims of birth and social station, the critics wondered. Moralists recoiled in horror before such spectacles as the 'improvements' carried out by the company promoter, Whitaker Wright, to his country house at Lea Park, near Godalming, where a billard room with a glass ceiling had been constructed under a lake, so that between strokes the players could oberve the carp swimming above them.[22] The palatial home of the South African millionaire, Sir Julius Wernher, was free of such vulgarities as these, but Beatrice Webb, after observing the company assembled there, noted caustically in her diary: 'There might just as well have been a Goddess of Gold erected for overt worship—the impression of worship in thought, feeling and action could hardly have been stronger.'[23]

A dislike of the way in which hedonistic values were spreading played an important part in eugenical thought. In the growing eugenics movement it was argued that the love of luxury was physically and morally debilitating; from the racial standpoint, it was also extremely dangerous, since it encouraged men and women to seek out marriage partners who possessed wealth rather than those who came from 'sound stock'. Quoting Francis Galton, eugenists warned that peers who attempted to rehabilitate their economic fortunes by marrying a rich heiress ran a statistically significant risk of acquiring a barren wife. Moreover, along with other moralists, they deplored the popularity of the small family and the practice of family limitation, which they

[20] Burrows, H. and Hobson, J. A. (eds.), *William Clarke: A Collection of His Writings* (London, 1908), pp. 51, 53–4.
[21] Stutfield, *Sovranty of Society*, p. 98.
[22] Hyde, H. M., *Lord Reading* (London, 1967), p. 49.
[23] Beatrice Webb's diary, 2 July 1906, in MacKenzie, Norman and Jeanne (eds.), *The Diary of Beatrice Webb*, iii (London, 1984), 42. But Beatrice Webb exempted Wernher himself from this condemnation.

blamed on the wife's ignoble fear of pain and on the husband's selfish addiction to materialistic pleasures.[24]

The behaviour of the plutocrats seemed to threaten traditional landed society in other ways also, not least by forcing those who wished to lead a fashionable life to devote more thought to making the money necessary for its realization. An experienced Society columnist, writing in the *Daily Mail* in 1913, argued that the London Season no longer acted primarily as a marriage market. The 'Americans, the merely rich, and even the very successful financier, manufacturer, or merchant' whom the King had helped into Society had more basic preoccupations on their minds:

In these days of greatly increased luxury and the greatly increased cost of luxuries they who merely know how to spend money cannot for long compete with those who mainly know how to make it. Many drawing-rooms in the West End are little else now than auxiliary stock-exchanges, men meeting in them less for purposes of civility and conversation than to promote somewhat irregular business. It is the millionaire who is the chief attraction at them, not woman nor the wit. Everything is for sale; family portraits, treasures accumulated through the ages, the estate, wines, cigars, motor-cars, titles, friends, sons and daughters.[25]

Exaggerated, partial, and unfair such criticisms may be, but the frequency with which they were made in the late Victorian and Edwardian periods gives them significance. Thus, Stutfield notes how the fashionable world burned its fingers during the 'Kaffir Boom' of 1895. This was the time, he recalls, when smart young men, acting as 'runners' for Stock Exchange firms, began appearing in West End drawing rooms and spreading market tips to all who wanted to hear. By the end of the decade, he adds, company promoting 'had become as much a recognised industry for all social classes, including the highest, as stockbroking. Money had to be made somehow to meet increased expenditure, and the pressure of need relaxed scruples as to the means employed.'[26]

The question of company promotion will be considered in greater detail in the next chapter. But, as contemporaries were aware, the Stock Exchange scandals which occurred around the turn of the century had a moral as well as an economic origin. The financial journalist, Van Oss noted in 1895: 'In clubs and trains, in drawing-rooms and boudoirs, people are discussing "Rands" and "Modders"; even tradesmen and old ladies have taken to studying the *Mining Manual*, the rules of the Stock Exchange, and the highways and byways of stockbroking. . . . In short, we are in the midst of one of

[24] See Searle, G. R., *Eugenics and Politics in Britain, 1900–1914* (Leyden, 1976), pp. 57–8.
[25] *Daily Mail*, 3 June 1913.
[26] Stutfield, *Sovranty of Society*, pp. 156–7.

those eras of feverish speculative activity . . .'.[27] It was hard to avoid comparisons with the South Sea Bubble of the previous century.[28] Similarly, in the aftermath of the Whitaker Wright collapse, another journalist identified 'a restless unsettling spirit of speculation all through society', which was destroying the traditional Victorian virtues of thrift and providence.[29]

Why was this occurring? In some of his articles Stutfield laid the blame on 'ingenious money-spiders' who enmeshed other classes in their financial games.[30] But so gullible was the investing public that it rushed eagerly into the arms of the most bare-faced swindler.[31] Thus there was a sense in which the crooked financier was less the cause than a symptom of the prevailing 'moral leprosy'.[32] A. J. Wilson, the Radical who edited the *Investors' Review*, railed in despair at his readers; preaching caution to investors at a time of market activity, he observed, was as futile as preaching 'self-restraint to a troop of wild Zulus'.[33]

For this state of affairs there had to be some underlying cause. In Stutfield's view it was 'the desire to grow rich quickly and easily in order that people might indulge the passion for amusement and social display'.[34] A. J. Wilson agreed; the 'habit of gambling in the present day' he attributed to 'a spirit of emulation in extravagance . . . Fight that wasteful spirit, by ceasing to emulate its extravagance, by cultivating contentment of mind, and it may in time be conjured away.'[35] The abuses associated with 'guinea pig directors' were also rooted in a false set of social values, or so Wilson believed. 'Poor fellows', he wrote in an anlysis of the 'professional director', 'they are the victims of an over-luxurious age, which compels the mass of educated society-pretending men to live always beyond their means. . . . It is hard, but what can he do? He must have his carriages and horses, his retainers in livery, his house in town, his yacht or his shooting box; he must bet a little to be in the fashion, and gracefully lose now and then at baccarat.'[36] Perhaps the road to national decadence could therefore be halted by the passing of sumptuary laws? Not entirely seriously, perhaps, Arnold White called for 'the reasonable taxation of

---

[27] Van Oss, S. F., 'The Gold-Mining Madness in the City', *Nineteenth Century*, xxxviii (1895), 538.

[28] Ingall, G. D. and Withers, G., *The Stock Exchange* (London, 1904), pp. 101–2.

[29] Anon., 'Whitaker Wright Finance', *Blackwood's Magazine*, clxxv (1904), 409.

[30] Stutfield, H. E. M., 'The Higher Rascality', *National Review*, xxxi (1898), 84.

[31] 'Whitaker Wright Finance', p. 397.

[32] Anon., 'The Game of Speculation', *Quarterly Review*, cxcvii (1903), 88.

[33] Wilson, A. J., *Practical Hints to Investors. And Some Words to Speculators* (London, 1897), p. 53.

[34] Stutfield, *Sovranty of Society*, p. 157.

[35] Wilson, A. J., 'The Ethics of Gambling', *Investors' Review*, June 1897, republished in his volume *An Empire in Pawn* (London, 1909), pp. 302, 306.

[36] Wilson, A. J., 'Professional Directors', *Investors Review*, Nov. 1893; *An Empire in Pawn*, pp. 317–18.

silks and satins, of diamonds and laces, of patés de foie gras, caviare and ortolans, of motor-cars, saphires and ostrich feathers, and the products of Parisian artists in ladies' dresses and of German low-class, sweated, and unnecessary toys'.[37]

In this 'modern Mammon-worship'[38] the Prince of Wales, later King Edward VII, can be treated as both victim and instigator. The Kaiser pitied him for his indebtedness to Lipton and the Jewish bankers, and rumours circulated about the King's obligations to the rich men who had taken responsibility for his debts and who managed his finances. Lady Paget thought that he had 'a great deal of ability but is always surrounded by a bevy of Jews and a ring of racing people. He has the same luxurious taste as the Semites, the same love of pleasure and comfort.'[39] A guest at Sandringham in 1890 was shocked to find that baccarat was being played on a real table, with rules modelled on the tables at Monte Carlo—though this was technically illegal.[40] The craze for gambling drew the plutocrats in hordes to the French Riviera, and horse-racing continued to enjoy the enthusiastic support of the fashionable rich, and in both these fields the King symbolically led the way.

How far Edward can be considered as an agent of social change is a moot point. The journalist, T. H. S. Escott wrote a somewhat sycophantic article in 1901, arguing that in social matters the King had 'accepted a situation created by forces before his time and beyond his control. Plutocracy, Semitic or American, with the modish smartness that is its product—the former Prince of Wales has dealt with these much in the same way as they were manipulated by Disraeli, in the interests of the new conservatism', making them, in fact, 'the guarantees and defences of Crown and even of altar'.[41] Escott's interpretation was eccentric, but most commentators were agreed that the King, as the unchallenged arbiter of social manners, had secured a quick entrée into select society for people who would otherwise have been severely handicapped by their birth and background. Margot Asquith spoke of his loyalty to his 'female admirers, Jewish financiers and Newmarket bloods',[42] while others noted his liking for the company of smart, rich, American women.

'Smartness' was in fact the word commonly used to describe the 'Marlborough House Set' and the influence exerted by the King and his friends on London Society around the turn of the century. As Escott put it, 'the husband and the Court of Queen Victoria began by making

[37] *Sunday Sun*, 24 Jan. 1904.
[38] Stutfield, 'Higher Rascality', p. 76.
[39] Camplin, *Plutocrats*, p. 101; Middlemas, *Pursuit of Pleasure*, p. 15.
[40] Ibid. 141.
[41] Escott, T. H. S., 'The New Reign and the New Society', *Fortnightly Review*, lxx (1901), 684.
[42] Asquith, M., *The Autobiography of Margot Asquith* (London, 1922), ii. 115.

English society respectable. Edward VII went on to make it smart.'[43] The same idea was in the mind of Stutfield when he observed that, whereas 'the Victorian era was the era of respectability, . . . the Edwardian will probably be known as the epoch of that frisky futility which is known as smartness.' Gentility, thought Stutfield, had gone out of fashion. 'Smart Society would rather be stigmatised as wicked than genteel; it prides itself on a certain modish superiority to those conventional proprieties which are still respected by people belonging to the older school of manners.' Respectability had taken flight from aristocratic society and found refuge amongst the middle and lower-middle classes.[44]

It would be more accurate perhaps to say that 'smartness' was the distinctive mark of *fashionable* Society, for it still met resistance from aristocrats who remained wedded to traditional values. The resulting clash between the new and the old codes of conduct within 'High Society' provides one of the themes in Howard Sturgis's novel, *Belchamber* (1904), which savagely satirizes the corruption within Edwardian Society.[45]

When Edward was still Prince of Wales a group of aristocratic ladies, called the 'Lambeth Penitentes', appealed to Princess Alexandria to join them in promoting 'the moral improvement of society'.[46] The appeal clearly went unanswered. And once he had ascended the throne, Edward could no longer be criticized in public. But there was an undertow of criticism of the King in publications like Arnold White's pamphlet, *Society, Smart Society and Bad Smart Society* (1901), which set out to shame the traditional aristocracy into reasserting its influence against plutocratic intruders who were bringing Society as a whole into disrepute.[47] Arnold White's notion of 'bad' smart Society is interesting because it also carries with it the notion of 'decadence',[48] which suggests that the anxieties stimulated by the Oscar Wilde Trial had not yet abated. Indeed, White himself clearly felt that financial and sexual corruption were manifestations of the same disease and that both were associated with disloyalty to one's country. 'Sodomism in London is an allied and friendly Power with all foreigners that hate us', he wrote in November 1902.[49] This was a theme which was later to be developed by Pemberton Billing in his famous trial of 1918—in which

[43] Escott, T. H. S., *King Edward and His Court* (London, 1903), p. 30.
[44] Stutfield, *Sovranty of Society*, pp. 93, 180–1.
[45] See Sturgis, H., *Belchamber* (London, 1904; 1965 edn.), p. 70.
[46] See also Benson, E. F., *As We Were: A Victorian Peep-Show* (London, 1930; 1934 edn.), pp. 98–103.
[47] White, A., *Society, Smart Society and Bad Smart Society* (London, 1901).
[48] This theme was emphasized in a somewhat hostile review in the *Spectator* (10 Feb. 1900) of White's *Daily Chronicle* article of 5 Feb. 1900.
[49] *Daily Dispatch*, 13 Nov. 1902.

Arnold White, significantly enough, was scheduled to appear as a witness.[50]

Another personality who figured in the Pemberton Billing Trial was the Jesuit priest, Father Bernard Vaughan, who first came to prominence in 1906 when he delivered a series of sermons indicting the fast Smart Set—appropriately enough, during the London Season from the Church of the Immaculate Conception in Mayfair. Father Vaughan created a sensation by his method of drawing parellels between some of the more licentious events recorded in the Bible and behaviour which, he alleged, passed as 'normal' in London's fashionable society. Herodias, he claimed, would today be treated as 'a really Smart Woman of the Smart Set'; 'provided she and Herod gave good dinners and rare entertainments there would be no difficulty in finding excuses for their actual life of incest.' He also hinted that vice of every kind was commonplace in modern society; gambling, drug addiction, dishonesty, and sexual misconduct had now become acceptable, so long as their perpetrators were careful to avoid the sin of being poor.[51]

Ironically—and Father Vaughan was aware of the irony—these sermons became a fashionable success with the very people whose morality and way of life were being condemned. Attracted by considerable press publicity, the fashionable world flocked to the Church of the Immaculate Conception. Towards the end of the series of sermons the church was crammed to the doors with well-dressed ladies and gentlemen; extra chairs were placed in every conceivable place, 'to the no small discomfort of the congregation on such a sultry afternoon'. One journalist estimated that one of the sermons attracted an audience of 2,300, with an equal number turned away for want of room. The area around the church was congested with smart carriages. How far had Father Vaughan exaggerated in his portrayal of contemporary mores? The newspapers, and the readers who contributed to their correspondence columns, debated this issue inconclusively for several weeks. But that the Jesuit preacher had drawn attention to an important social phenomenon seems evident from the interest which he aroused. Later in 1906 his sermons were published under the title, *The Sins of Society*, and the book quickly went through fourteen editions.[52]

Meanwhile, notwithstanding his punctiliousness about certain of the social proprieties and a pernickety concern over correct etiquette in matters of ceremonial, decorations, uniforms, and such like, the King continued to surround himself with a coterie whose sexual licentious-ness, love of gambling, and taste for luxurious entertainments made for

[50] See Ch. 11, pp. 261–2.   [51] Vaughan, *Sins of Society*, esp. pp. 131, 99.
[52] Ibid. The postscript to the book contains a generous anthology of newspaper comment on the sermons. See also Martindale, C. C., *Bernard Vaughan, S. J.* (London, 1923), pp. 82–9.

24   *The Problem of Plutocracy*

a prevailing tone of hedonism, which spread far beyond the narrow confines of the Court.

The King, as one of his biographers has noted, also 'enjoyed a flutter on the Stock Exchange as much as he enjoyed a stroll along the Paris boulevards'. Indeed, prominent members of the Court themselves became involved in a minor City scandal. The affair was described in shocked tones in December 1907 by Lord Carrington, upholder of a more traditional aristocratic code of manners. A Siberian gold-mining company, he noted, had been formed by some 'Jew speculators'. Among the directors were Francis Knollys, the King's Secretary, and Horace Farquhar, Master of the Royal Household, who was supposed to have roped in the other celebrities and to have 'netted' £70,000 through trading in the company's shares. How deplorable it was, thought Carrington, that members of the Court should have been involved in such an affair.[53]

Farquhar, it is worth noting, was in large part responsible for so administering the King's finances that he lived within his income, though HRH was also helped by his many millionaire friends, like Sir Blundell Maple, the furniture retailer, and, of course, by Cassel.[54]

Another way in which Edward VII typified 'smart' Edwardian Society was in possessing a restless disposition which would not let him settle in one place for any length of time. This craving for constant changes of environment also marked the behaviour of the 'homeless, nomadic' rich. 'Aping their betters', grumbled Father Vaughan, the Smart Set 'beat round about after happiness, whirling, gyrating through the summer months from Mayfair to Cowes, and then on to Carlsbad, and back again to Scotland, till winter send them first hunting and shooting at home, and then golfing and gambling abroad.'[55] It is hardly surprising that the restless monarch should have developed a passion for motoring. He served as a patron of the Automobile Club, and limousines were in constant attendance at Marienbad and Biarritz. The King liked his chauffeur to overtake all cars in front of him, and once in 1906 his car reached a maximum speed of 60 m.p.h. on the Brighton road.[56]

The motor-car was, in fact, the consumer good which was most often used to symbolize the new plutocracy. Showering humbler folk with dust as they raced noisily through the countryside, the motorists, a small and privileged albeit expanding class, flaunted their wealth in a highly irresponsible way. Selfish motorists, said the Edwardian wags, were converting more people to socialism than Karl Marx had ever done.[57] But motoring not only created dust and noise on the

[53] Magnus, P., *King Edward The Seventh* (London, 1964), p. 389.
[54] Aubyn, G. St., *Edward VII Prince and King* (London, 1979), pp. 366–7.
[55] Vaughan, *Sins of Society*, p. 106.   [56] Middlemas, *Pursuit of Pleasure*, p. 124.
[57] *Saturday Review*, 2 Nov. 1912, p. 538; Camplin, *Plutocrats*, pp. 252–4.

untarmacadamed Edwardian roads; it also, or so the critics alleged, destroyed the sense of space and feeling for historical association and continuities upon which a true love of the country depended. Lowes Dickinson, the Cambridge don, poured out article after article for the Liberal monthlies, calling on the government to put down the 'motor tyranny' and protesting at the despoiling of nature which resulted from the 'vulgar' modern mania for travel. Motorists, he said, were using, or rather abusing, their privileges 'with an inconsiderate insolence which illustrates forcibly the extent to which the wealth of England, during the past half century, has passed away from the hands of gentlemen'.[58] Readers of *Howard's End* (1910) will recall the symbolic significance which Dickinson's friend, E. M. Forster, assigns to the motor-car in that most socially sensitive of novels.

The restless behaviour of the plutocrat denoted a certain rootlessness, and this, in turn, was linked to a 'cosmopolitanism' of outlook and lifestyle. Critics of Edwardian plutocracy were especially concerned to attack the 'financier', who was necessarily a cosmopolitan, since the wealth in which he dealt was fluid and could readily be shifted across national frontiers—unlike land, the ownership of which bound a man to one locality and was supposed to create a sense of responsibility towards neighbours and dependants. Lowes Dickinson portrayed the financier as the typical figure of the age, because the people whom he manipulated themselves worshipped money. Equally censorious was the aristocratic Liberal, Arthur Ponsonby, for a time Campbell-Bannerman's private secretary, who wrote a pamphlet, *The Camel and the Needle's Eye* (1909), in which he set out 'to expose a state of social corruption which can only be corrected in the long run by being brought fully into the light'. The pamphlet attacked 'stock-brokers, company-promoters, and other financiers, who (were) the high priests of money'; the influence of these men, it alleged, had debauched the press and threatened to make democracy a meaningless charade.[59] Like many other Radicals, Ponsonby subscribed to the theory that the Second Boer War had been engineered, and support for it sustained, by the South African mineowners and other sinister financial interests.

This kind of suspicion of the influence of the 'Randlords' often gave rise to anti-Semitic prejudices. Many 'Little England' Radicals, even

---

[58] Dickinson, G. L., 'The Motor Tyranny', *Independent Review*, xi (1906), 17. See also Masterman, C. F. G., *The Condition of England* (London, 1909), p. 65: 'The action of a section of the motoring classes, . . . in their annexation of the highways and their indifference to the common traditions, stands almost alone as an example of wealth's intolerable arrogances . . .'.

In 1904 there were only 8,465 licensed cars, but by 1914 the total had reached 132,015 (Middlemas, *Pursuit of Pleasure*, p. 124). See also Green, P., *Kenneth Grahame 1859–1932* (London, 1959), pp. 167–8. The Edwardian 'road hog' forms, of course, the starting-point for the character of Toad.

[59] Ponsonby, A., *The Camel and the Needle's Eye* (London, 1909; 1910 edn.), esp. pp. 99, 108–9.

such high-minded men as J. A. Hobson, were prepared to use the word
'Jew' in a pejorative sense to denote 'cosmopolitan finance' or 'finance
capitalism'; while in his novels and verses Hilaire Belloc gave open
expression to his anti-Semitic convictions. So, in a different way, did
ultra-patriots like Arnold White, who passionately supported the
British Government's cause during the Boer War, but hated the
manipulative role which they believed the Jewish financiers were
playing in politics and international life. 'I like dis news; it vill gif a
goot shake-out to shtocks—dat iss healthy', White makes a 'well-
known German Jew hanger-on of smart society' say during the Boer
War.[60]

In addition, a simple snobbish disdain for rich Jews can be found
amongst Englishmen of all social classes and all political persuasions.
·Lord Northcliffe, who was certainly no anti-Semite, ordered the editor
of the *Daily Mail* to see that his 'Society' correspondent kept 'his Jews'
out of the social column: 'What with the Ecksteins, Sassoons and
Mosenthals, we shall soon have to set the column in Yiddish'.[61] The
strong Jewish presence within the royal entourage also excited much
hostile or caustic comment, as we have seen.[62] Arnold White lamented
that so many Jewish financiers should be surrounding the throne,
while rabid anti-Semites, like Joseph Banister, speculated publicly
about whether the King himself might not be Jewish.[63] Even Escott
admitted that 'the incorporation of the Hebrews into the most august
parts of the social fabric has been paid for at a certain moral price.' It
had meant the social and political eclipse 'of the country gentleman
after the Henley pattern, so well known in the Disraelian House of
Commons', because the expense of London had been raised by their
influence to a prohibitive level. And in a passage which would have
confirmed the anti-Semites' worst fears, he added:

. . . if the latter-day cosmopolitanism has been largely promoted by the 'golden
international', of which the Rothschilds are ornaments, it is because the
highest sections of the polite world have voluntarily placed themselves under
the Hebrew hegemony. . . . One leader after another in society and politics has
practically admitted the impracticability of a social or political organisation in
conformity with the taste of the time, except with the help, and under the
auspices, of the great Semitic capitalists.[64]

Interestingly, Escott followed up these remarks about Jewish
financiers with an analysis of the influence exercised by rich

[60] White, A., *Efficiency and Empire* (London, 1901; 1973 edn., Brighton, edited by
Searle, G. R.), p. 79.
    [61] Northcliffe to Marlowe (copy), 6 Oct. 1912 (BL, Northcliffe papers, Dep. 4890/46).
But for a different view of Northcliffe, see Morris, A. J. A., *The Scaremongers: The
Advocacy of War and Rearmament 1896–1914* (London, 1984), p. 454 n. 6.
    [62] See also Holmes, C., *Anti-Semitism in British Society 1876–1939* (London, 1979),
Ch. 5.
    [63] Ibid. 87.   [64] Escott, *King Edward and His Court*, pp. 203–4, 211.

Americans who had chosen to settle in London; both groups, he suggested, were 'of a nervous temperament, highly strung, most at ease in movement, only breathing freely in an atmosphere of excitement'.[65] Those holding such prejudices viewed transatlantic marriages with considerable disquiet. Not untypical of contemporary comment was an article appearing in the *Contemporary Review* in June 1905, where titled colonials were compared with titled Americans—naturally, to the latter's disadvantage. Anglo-American marrriages, the article concluded, had no sound basis whatever, as could be seen from the fact that they were significantly less fertile than aristocratic marriages with colonial women; Americans may have helped to make society brighter, 'but they have also helped to make it shallower, more extravagant, and more vulgar than it ever was before'.[66]

Stutfield, too, gives over many pages to a savage dissection of the rich American woman. 'Principally, it seems to me, she stands for a very frank Mammonism, for a view of life that is essentially trivial and material, and, I fear it must be added, slightly sordid.' The new American woman was 'the fine flower of a perfect egoism, goddess and empress of the new aristocracy of wealth'. What worried Stutfield was less the propriety of transatlantic marriages, but rather the various intangible ways in which Americans had 'succeeded in infecting us with their spirit, in forcing us to regard their country as the controller of our destinies—the model, the exemplar to which we must conform if we would escape individual and national discomfiture'.[67] A love of sensationalism, unscrupulous self-advertisement, 'pushy' behaviour, and a manic restlessness: these were the qualities which critics of social manners thought that rich Americans possessed.

But if 'the inner informing spirit of most modern Society (was) the spirit of America', as Stutfield alleged,[68] this was surely because the values of modern Society were rooted in nothing save wealth. Lady Colin Campbell, in her book, *The Etiquette of Good Society*, noted the existence of a trade in crests and titles, commenting that in this brazen age anything could be bought.[69] It is true that the *Saturday Review* thought that talk of this sort exaggerated the social power of money, and argued that 'even the possession of a great fortune is not sufficient by itself to secure social position for its possessor'.[70] But the weight of opinion backed the verdict of the Society paper, *The Queen*, that nowadays it was often enough to acquire certain status symbols—'yacht, house, grouse moor, race horses, cars'—to be admitted to hitherto

[65] Ibid. 224.
[66] 'Colonial', 'Titled Colonials v Titled Americans', *Contemporary Review*, lxxxvii (1905), 861–9.
[67] Stutfield, *Sovranty of Society*, pp. 243, 262.
[68] Ibid., Ch. 13.
[69] Camplin, *Plutocrats*, p. 120.
[70] *Saturday Review*, 5 May 1900, p. 553.

exclusive social circles.[71] The 'rise of the plutocrats' testifies to the broad truth of this claim.

Horrified by this 'service of Mammon', Ponsonby predicted in 1912 that 'a reaction—even a fashionable reaction' against extravagance and vulgar ostentation might soon take place.[72] And, indeed, such a reaction can be said to have occurred with the accession of George V, who gave a quite different tone to the royal court. 'The atmosphere at Balmoral has undergone a great change', as Ponsonby himself observed in a private letter of January 1911, 'harlots and Jews have been exchanged for tutors and governesses. Not so amusing for the courtiers.'[73]

Yet though the new King, in contrast to his father, was a model family man, content, so far as his position allowed, to lead a quiet life, the social tendencies of the age were opposed to the simple domestic virtues. The spread of fashionable hotels and restaurants from the late nineteenth century onwards encouraged the practice of eating out, especially in connection with trips to theatres or other public places of pleasure and amusement. In fact, the trend during these years was for social events to take place in public. The very fashionable yachting regatta at Cowes would be an example of this. Admittedly, these occasions for public display were often preceded by social gatherings of a very private and exclusive kind. But in general, the activities of the very rich were becoming more 'visible', and this dramatized and publicized the 'problem of plutocracy'. Photography gave a further impetus to this trend; so did descriptions of 'The Upper Ten Thousand' purveyed by Society journals and by the gossip columnists employed by nearly all the major newspapers, including those aimed at a mass readership.[74]

Much of this press coverage of 'High Society' was designed to convey a glamorous and flattering picture of the rich and famous. But towards the *nouveaux riches* there was also considerable animosity. The critics who attacked plutocracy did so from a number of different vantage-points. Father Vaughan, for example, elected to play the role of Savanarola, and the purpose of his celebrated series of sermons was to call the idle rich to prayer and repentance. But there was also criticism of a more obviously political nature, and this can be discussed under four broad headings: the socialist, the liberal moralistic, the traditionally aristocratic, and the technocratic.

Socialists who indicted the behaviour of the irresponsible rich adopted the obvious ploy of contrasting the material circumstances

[71] Davidoff, *Best Circles*, p. 73.
[72] Ponsonby, A., *The Decline of Aristocracy* (London, 1912), p. 313.
[73] Ponsonby to Herbert Gladstone, 10 Jan. 1911 (BL, Herbert Gladstone papers, Add. MS 46,063, fo. 212).
[74] Davidoff, *Best Circles*, p. 62; Camplin, *Plutocrats*, pp. 91–2.

and social expectations of rich and poor. As W. C. Anderson, the Chairman of the Independent Labour Party put it, when addressing the party conference in March 1913:

On the one side there is the labourer or railwayman toiling laboriously for a pound a week, and finding that his pound somehow buys less and less as the months go by; on the other side are those whose life, an endless whirl of social gaiety, excitement, and costly pleasures, is made up of receptions, dinner parties, dances, bridge parties, hunting parties, shooting parties. These conditions are unjust, and, being unjust, they afford no safe or lasting foundation for a State.[75]

The second group comprised democratic Radicals, like Ponsonby, who feared that 'Mammon worship' was undermining the theory and practice of liberalism. It is noticeable, however, that Ponsonby, unlike the Socialists, devotes little attention to how the plutocracy has acquired its wealth, but focuses on the ways in which this wealth is being *spent*. His polemic, *The Camel and the Needle's Eye* therefore ends, appropriately enough, not with an attack on economic conditions, but with an appeal for a change of heart among *all* citizens, rich and poor; only 'the cleansing spirit of enlightened thought' could destroy those baneful social habits and conventions which led men to worship the false god of worldly riches. Ponsonby's writings seem to belong to the genre of the lay sermon, and his attacks on plutocracy can be viewed as a secular equivalent to Father Vaughan's calls to repentance.[76] However, it is important to note that Ponsonby does not simply direct his attack against wealthy parvenus, but also aims his fire at the landed aristocracy proper; for, as an authentic Radical, he hated the 'sham feudalism' which surrounded the 'Big House', and the 'toadyism' and 'cringing' which aristocracy encouraged.[77]

Quite separate from Ponsonby, therefore, were traditional aristocrats and their defenders. This third group viewed plutocracy with snobbish disdain and insisted that nobility of *birth* was the sole basis for legitimate social and political leadership. Such a viewpoint enabled the Diehard peer, Lord Willoughby de Broke, to explain the 'Great Labour Unrest' as a protest from the common people directed against self-made men—'the plutocracy'—who lacked the manners and traditions of good government inherent in a hereditary ruling class.[78]

Finally, there were technocrats, like Stutfield, who objected to plutocracy on the ground that it was frivolous. Stutfield feared that

[75] ILP Conference Report, 1913, p. 41. For the Webbs' view, see the *New Statesman*, 19 July 1913, pp. 461–3.
[76] Ponsonby, *Camel*, pp. 185–7. Ponsonby actually quotes from the Epistle of St James in support of his views: 'Go to now, ye rich men, weep and howl for your miseries that shall come upon you!' (p. 176).
[77] Ibid. 78–9. A similar stance was adopted by C. F. G. Masterman in Chapter 2 of *The Condition of England* (London, 1909).
[78] *Parl. Deb.*, 5th ser. (Lords), xv. 272–3 (23 Feb. 1914).

women, who merely consumed wealth, were acquiring a social dominance over men, the actual creators of that wealth, and that this trend engendered false values, militated against seriousness, and diverted attention from the vitally necessary task of promoting greater 'National Efficiency'.[79]

These are, of course, 'ideal types'. In practice it was possible for an individual—Beatrice Webb, for example—to combine elements from all four lines of criticism, socialist, democratic, aristocratic, and technocratic, in the denunciation of the new plutocracy. For this reason one would not expect to find the hostile reaction to plutocracy identified with any one party or any one ideology. But in the years around the turn of the century the 'problem of plutocracy' seemed to be intimately connected with the fortunes of the Unionist Party and the behaviour of certain Unionist Ministers. Why this was so will become clearer after an examination of the attempts that were made to eradicate the various malpractices, commercial and political, which Hooley's bankruptcy had exposed.

[79] Stutfield, *Sovranty of Society, passim.*

UNIONIST PRELUDE
1895–1905

2
'Company Promoting "À La Mode"'

The Company Promotion Boom

THE historians of the Stock Exchange have argued that although there were fraudulent issues in the 1890s, they were less numerous than might have been expected: 'it is hard to find parallels to the de Beranger, Poyais or Honduras railways frauds of earlier years'.[1] Contemporaries, however, were not able' to affect this kind of detachment. 'Let us cease talking about the Panama scandals of France until we have cleansed our own Augean stable', wrote one financial journalist.[2] Even allowing for some exaggeration, wrote another, in the aftermath of the Hooley case, 'the fact remains that the world of company-promotion and trust-mongering finance is a disgusting centre of corruption, which constitutes a standing menace to commercial stability as well as morality'.[3]

Some of the abuses which unscrupulous company promoters inflicted upon shareholders and creditors were itemized by the Lord Chief Justice, Lord Russell of Killowen in November 1898. The main one—which lay at the heart of Hooley's initial success and eventual failure—was the buying up of companies, which were then resold with their capital grotesquely inflated. There was also the practice of going to allotment, when shares were not freely taken up, on insufficient capital, with directors protecting themselves by issuing debentures which enabled them to sweep away all the assets when the inevitable crash took place.[4] Then, too, the issue of a false prospectus in order to sell worthless properties had by this time become a well-developed art. So had the practice of rigging the market, along with other kinds of stock manipulation, and the use of sub-trusts and 'baby companies' for the purpose of unloading shares on to an unsuspecting public. Bribery, whether subtle or brazen, could then be employed to square the press and 'puff' a newly launched company.[5] No one seriously contested that all these abuses were rife in the 1890s.

---

[1] Morgan, E. V. and Thomas, W. A., *The Stock Exchange: Its History and Functions* (London 1962), p. 138.
[2] *Critic*, 19 Nov. 1898.
[3] Stutfield, H. E. M., 'The Company Scandal: A City View', *National Review*, xxxii (1898), 575.
[4] *The Times*, 10 Nov. 1898.
[5] e.g. Stutfield, H. E. M., 'The Company Monger's Elysium', *National Review*, xxvi (1895) 836–48; Van Oss, S. F., 'The Gold Mining Madness in the City', *Nineteenth Century*, xxviii (1895), 537–47; Stutfield, H. E. M., 'The Higher Rascality', *National*

In any case, comparisons with the railway scandals of earlier years are difficult to make, because the situation which gave rise to such careers as Hooley's was of comparatively recent origin. Limited liability legislation went back to 1856; but over the next twenty years this legislation was modestly used. In 1880 limited liability companies only accounted for between 5 and 10 per cent of all important businesses and were largely concentrated in the fields of cotton, shipping, and iron and steel.[6] As the financial journalist, W. R. Lawson noted in his article, 'Company Promoting "A La Mode" ' of December 1898, the industrial group was still a very small and unimportant part of the Stock Exchange.[7] In 1882 'there was only £64 million of stock exchange investment in British industry, out of a total of nearly £5,800 million of quoted securities'.[8] Most manufacturing firms were still private concerns.

There followed, however, a very rapid phase of company promotion between 1894 and 1898, stimulated perhaps by low interest rates, which drove investors away from Consols, which yielded only about 2½ per cent, to other more risky ventures which offered a better return. Hence in the middle of the decade there occurred the frenetic speculation in South African shares ('Kaffirs'). When the Kaffir Boom burst in the autumn of 1895, the speculators turned their attention to other commodities, and this happened to be precisely the moment when Hooley started launching his companies, many of them connected with cycles. All this while an amalgamation movement was taking place in British industry, with smaller firms merging and forming themselves into limited liability companies. About sixty-seven firms a year were disappearing in the course of the 1890s. On the other hand, the annual registration of limited liability companies more than doubled between 1893 and 1897 alone. This particularly affected such industries as textiles, iron and steel, cement, and tobacco. By the start of the twentieth century the amount of capital invested in manufacturing and commercial companies had risen to £654 million, a tenfold increase since 1882 and a fourfold increase since 1892.[9]

But there were dangers in this process. Lawson, for example, believed that the structure of the limited liability company, which had

---

Review, xxxi (1898), 75–86; Lawson, W. R., 'Company Promoting "À La Mode" ', National Review, xxxii (1898), 103–15; Van Oss, S. F., 'The Limited Company Craze', Nineteenth Century, xliii (1898), 731–44; Lawson, W. R., 'Stock Jobbing Companies', National Review, xxv (1901), 869–81; Anon., 'The Game of Speculation', Quarterly Review, cxcvii (1903), 88–114.

[6] Payne, P. L., 'The Emergence of the Large Scale Company in Great Britain, 1870–1914', Economic History Review, xx (1967), 520.

[7] National Review, xxxii (1898), 104.

[8] Morgan and Thomas, Stock Exchange, p. 133.

[9] Ibid. 133–6; Payne, 'Large Scale Company', p. 527; Hannah, L., The Rise of the Corporate Economy (London, 1976), Ch. 1; Cottrell, P. L., Industrial Finance, 1830–1914 (London, 1980), pp. 173–9.

proved suitable in the past for railways and financial houses, was less appropriate in its existing form to the myriad of manufacturing concerns that had recently 'gone public'.[10] There was another difficulty. In Britain the merchant banks and joint stock banks very seldom took responsibility for company issues, and this forced many companies to engage the services of a company promoter, who could take charge of the conversion, arrange the underwriting, and bring the venture to the notice of the investing public. H. O'Hagan is the best-known example of the efficient promoter; on his retirement he could congratulate himself on the soundness of all his flotations.[11] But, as Cottrell has pointed out, most 'professional' promoters in the 1890s lacked a day-to-day business career which would provide them with a secure and reliable income, and so were tempted to make a major 'killing' from each new promotion.[12] It was a temptation to which Hooley readily succumbed, as did such contemporaries as J. H. Lawson and Horatio Bottomley.

Long before the Hooley crash the morality of company promoting and the speculative mania which accompanied it had come in for caustic criticism. For example, the whole development was satirized by Gilbert and Sullivan in their operetta, *Utopia Limited* of 1891, which featured that very modern social type, Mr Goldbury, with his penchant for bringing the most unlikely commercial activities to Stock Exchange quotation. Public anxieties about this trend were widespread and were sustained by a steady stream of bankruptcies, of which Hooley's was only the most sensational.[13] The Report of the Inspector-General for Company Liquidation of 1899 showed that over the preceding eight years over 9,000 companies had been wound up. Even if allowance was made for those concerns whose liquidation could be accounted for by reconstruction, amalgamations, and other acquisitions, which involved no loss to the shareholders, that still left 1,345 companies which had collapsed in the course of 1899 alone.[14]

The General Purposes Committee of the Stock Exchange had power to expel or suspend any of its members who had broken its rules or who were adjudged 'guilty of dishonourable or disgraceful conduct'.[15] But, as even a friendly observer noted in 1904, it was impossible 'to deny that the Committee of the Stock Exchange appears lately to have to some extent relaxed the Draconian severity of its code, and that the complicity of members, in thinly disguised partnership with non-

[10] *National Review*, xxxii (1898), 104.

[11] Cottrell, *Industrial Finance*, pp. 186–7; Morgan and Thomas, *Stock Exchange*, pp. 137–8; O'Hagan, H. O., *Leaves From My Life*, 2 vols. (London, 1929).

[12] Cottrell, *Industrial Finance*, p. 187.

[13] The theme of speculation and financial collapse was a favourite one with contemporary novelists, e.g. Gissing, G., *The Whirlpool* (London, 1897).

[14] Cited in Hess, H. (ed.), *The Critic Black Book* (London, 1902), p. XII.

[15] Withers, H., *Stocks and Shares* (London, 1910), pp. 31, 279.

members, in various acts of market-rigging and other flagrant crimes against the Rules, has been allowed to pass unchallenged by the very body of men who are annually elected to keep the atmosphere of the Exchange pure'.[16] As things stood, certain jobbers were 'only too willing to allow themselves to be made the cat's-paw of the promoter in working the various discreditable market "rigs" which [had] lately become notoriously frequent'.[17]

Any complacency about the operation of the Stock Exchange which may have survived the Hooley revelations disappeared with the collapse of Whitaker Wright's London & Globe Corporation in 1902, which left thousands of shareholders ruined.[18] As in the case of Hooley's companies four years earlier, men of high public standing, including the Duke of Dufferin and the Duke of Connaught, were shown to be associated with a failed commercial venture. What is more, the public could not understand why the Attorney-General, R. Finlay, had taken so long to initiate proceedings against Wright, in view of the fact that the latter had almost certainly issued a fraudulent balance-sheet. The matter was debated in the Commons, while ugly rumours spread throughout the City that Wright was being protected by 'friends in high places'.[19] It was only when a High Court Judge had granted the application of one of the creditors that a warrant was sent out for Wright's arrest. The disgraced company promoter was apprehended in New York in March 1903 and brought back to London for trial, and on being sentenced for fraud, he committed suicide by swallowing a capsule of cyanide.[20]

The campaign to clean up these City scandals was waged intermittently in certain quarters of the press. But though the financial journalists, a new professional group, claimed to supply disinterested advice and information to the investing public, many of them partook in the very corruption they purported to deplore.[21] Charles Duguid, one of the few respectable City editors, painted a sombre picture of the temptations to which financial journalists were exposed in his classic book, *How To Read the Money Article* (1901). A standard ploy was for the promoter to give a newspaperman £100 or £200 for inserting a 'puff' of his company into his financial column, or, more common still, to offer him a call upon the shares of the new company, which he then

[16] Ingall, G. D. and Withers, G., *The Stock Exchange* (London, 1904), p. 2.
[17] Ibid. 39.
[18] Anon., 'Whitaker Wright Finance', *Blackwood's Magazine*, clxxv (1904), 397–409.
[19] Thus the Liberal MP, George Lambert, spoke of rumours 'that certain exalted personages have been mixed up in these matters' (*Parl. Deb.*, 4th ser., cxviii. 349 (19 Feb. 1903)).
[20] For a useful summary of Wright's rise and fall, see Hyde, H. Montgomery, *Lord Reading* (London, 1967), pp. 47–54.
[21] Porter, Dilwyn, 'The Expansion of the Financial Press in the Nineteenth and Early Twentieth Centuries'. Paper delivered at Institute of Commonwealth Studies Seminar, 6 Dec. 1984.

had a vested interest in praising. Duguid claimed that so much a matter of course had such bribery become that there had been 'wagers in the City as to how long a certain editor would stand on his pedastal of honesty'. Bribery from the promoter was naturally complemented by blackmail from the journalist. Indeed, as Duguid put it, it was all a question of supply and demand. 'If the supply of bribes exceeds the demand, bribery is the characteristic of the market; if the demand for bribes exceeds the supply, business becomes blackmailish.'[22]

An expert practioner in this area was the journalist, Harry Marks, founder of the *Financial News*. This paper, the first daily newspaper of its kind in Britain, posed as 'an outspoken and fearless critic' of impropriety and as 'the bugbear of dishonest promoters'. Its unearthing of a scandal at the Metropolitan Board of Works pushed Parliament into passing the Public Bodies Corrupt Practices Act in 1889. But a subsequent series of libel and slander cases badly dented Marks's reputation. In 1903 Mr Justice Bigham dubbed him 'a dishonest rogue' and 'a scoundrel', and allegations of financial irregularity followed him throughout his controversial political career.[23]

The same was true of the Liberal MP, Henry Labouchere, also famous as a theatre critic and a Society wit, who in 1877 had founded the weekly, *Truth*, which, in accordance with its motto, *Cultores Veritatis Fraudio Inimici*, set itself up as the scourge of wickedness in high places and, in particular, as the protector of the innocent shareholder. But 'Labby', well versed in the ways of the City, frequently used his paper for personal self-enrichment—for example, by praising shares which he happened to own. 'What greater proof can I give of my belief in the shares I write up than buying them?', was his delightful rejoinder to someone who had reproached him for this practice.[24] But it brought him the implacable hostility of Henry Hess of the *Critic*, which boasted that it had fought more libel actions 'brought by company-promoters, directors, and bucket-shop keepers than all the daily, weekly and monthly financial newspapers combined'.[25] The *Critic* regularly listed firms and individuals who had incurred the editor's suspicions (Bottomley, for example, was one of its targets),[26] and eventually got the better of Labouchere in a protracted slanging-match when Hess published a pamphlet in 1905 which was distributed

[22] Duguid, *How To Read the Money Article* (London, 1901), p. 105. See also Wilson, A. J., *Practical Hints to Investors. And Some Words to Speculators* (London, 1897 edn.), esp. pp. 50–2.
[23] For this paragraph I am indebted to Dilwyn Porter's stimulating article, 'Journalist, Financier, "Dishonest Rogue", "Scoundrel": The Life and Times of Harry Hananel Marks, M.P.', *Moirae*, viii (1984), 65–83.
[24] Emden, P. H., *Randlords* (London, 1935), p. 166.
[25] Hess (ed.), *Critic Black Book*, from inside cover.
[26] Bottomley successfully sued Hess for libel (Symons, J., *Horatio Bottomley* (London, 1955), pp. 60–1).

to all MPs, in which one of Labby's cynical share-rigging deals was exposed. Labouchere did not stand for Parliament again.[27]

Of course, there were papers, like A. J. Wilson's *Investors' Review*, and the *Economist*, that held aloof from the venality and corruption into which so much of the financial press had plunged. But clearly, if a moral campaign was to be launched with any conviction against fraudulent company promoters, it would have to come from a respected public figure, knowledgeable about City affairs, yet detached from them in a way that financial journalists were not. Rather improbably, given his passion for cards and the turf, the role of 'conscience-keeper of the country' was accordingly assumed by the Lord Chief Justice, Lord Russell of Killowen.[28] On 9 November 1898, as the Hooley Case was drawing to an end, the Lord Chief Justice made a very well-publicized speech on the occasion of his annual visit to the Courts of the Lord Mayor of London.

For several years past Russell had felt disquiet at the spread of commercial dishonesty, flagrant examples of which regularly came to his professional notice, and he had already spoken publicly about the dangers which this represented. Russell rehearsed much of this material in November 1898 when he claimed that the limited liability system was being 'prostituted by the greed of unscrupulous persons in the hurry to obtain great wealth without being willing to put forth for its acquirement honest toil and honest endeavour'. If allowed to go on with impunity, he added, such transactions must have a serious effect 'upon the public mind and conscience'. Russell also believed that commercial fraud was on the increase and that this, too, was 'working insidiously to undermine and corrupt that high sense of public morality which it ought to be the common object of all interested in the good of the community to maintain'.[29]

That the Lord Chief Justice had skilfully touched a troubled spot in the nation's conscience was evident from the way in which the press reacted to his 9 November speech. The *Daily Mail* thought that the warning 'against reckless and dishonest company promoting was badly needed'.[30] The *Daily Chronicle* 'rejoiced' at the speech and said it was fitting that it should have been made in the City, since City men, or a minority of them, were deeply implicated in recent scandals; all the more regrettable, then, that 'the just men of the City' had not bestirred

---

[27] Hind, R. J., *Henry Labouchere and the Empire, 1880-1905* (London, 1972), p. 35 The feud between Hess and Labouchere goes back at least as far as Nov. 1897, when Hess was described in *Truth* as 'a swindling attorney' (4 Nov.).

[28] *National Review*, xxxii (1898), 477. Russell's passion for cards and horse-racing is dealt with in O'Brien, R. B., *The Life of Lord Russell of Killowen* (n.d., Nelson edn.), pp. 330-2, 343-50. O'Hagan, *Leaves From My Life*, i. 467-8.

[29] O'Brien, *Russell of Killowen*, pp. 289-301. The speech was later quoted at some length by the Webbs in their book, *The Decay of Capitalist Civilisation* (London, 1923), pp. 105-7.

[30] *Daily Mail*, 10 Nov. 1898.

themselves so as to check 'the tide of demoralisation which has threatened at times to turn the British Empire into a more or less shady company concern'.[31] In the view of the The Times there had to be 'a higher sense of duty on the part of the directors', but this in turn would require the formation of a vigilant and alert public opinion, as well as certain improvements in the law.[32]

In his moral crusade the Lord Chief Justice was especially concerned with the eradication of two kinds of abuse. The first covered the payment of bribes or 'secret commissions'. Since the Public Bodies Corrupt Practices Act of 1889, it was already a criminal offence to corruptly give, promise, offer, or receive any gift, loan, fee, or reward in a dealing with a member or servant of any local government public body.[33] Russell wanted, in effect, to widen the scope of this Act so that it covered every kind of commercial dealing, both public and private. He first spoke out on the necessity of such legislation when he gave judgement in the Oetzman v. Long case in July 1896. His words were picked up and elaborated by the judge, Sir Edward Fry, who wrote two letters on the subject to The Times. The London Chamber of Commerce then took up the issue by establishing a committee of enquiry, which reported in July 1898 in favour of statutory curbs on the giving and taking of secret commissions. Obviously the Hooley disclosures gave a further boost to the reform campaign. Russell and Fry entered into correspondence with one another, and between them drew up a bill which was introduced into the Lords in 1899.[34]

In August 1900 Russell died. But his Bill, with some modifications, was taken over by his successor as Lord Chief Justice, Lord Alverstone. It then suffered a complex fate, being repeatedly brought before Parliament, only to lapse for want of time. The Lord Chancellor, Lord Halsbury, was not entirely sympathetic to the measure, because he feared it might inadvertently encourage the practice of blackmail.[35] Thus it was left to Campbell-Bannerman's Liberal Administration to achieve the reform on which Russell had set his heart.

Russell's second objective was the eradication of abuses associated with the founding and running of incorporated companies. The Hooley Affair had convinced most remaining doubters that Britain's company laws were, to use the Spectator's words, among 'the least safe for the investor of any in the civilised world', and that creditors, as well as

[31] Daily Chronicle, 10 Nov. 1898. [32] The Times, 10 Nov. 1898.
[33] This issue is well handled in Doig, Alan, Corruption and Misconduct in Contemporary British Politics (London, 1984), pp. 69–73.
[34] O'Brien, Russell of Killowen, pp. 290–9; Leonard, R. M., The War Against Bribery (London, 1913), pp. 4–10.
[35] Doig, Corruption and Misconduct, pp. 74–5. R. M. Leonard blamed Halsbury for his insistence that, to reduce the risk of blackmail, the Attorney-General must first give his consent to a prosecution (War Against Bribery, p. 10). See also Parl. Deb., 4th ser., lxx. 25 (20 Apr. 1899).

shareholders, were in urgent need of protection.[36] In fact, limited liability and company law had been under intense scrutiny since the mid-1880s. Several specialized and technical measures, like the Directors' Liability Act of 1889, had already been placed on the statute book, and in 1894 the Liberal Government introduced a comprehensive measure of reform. This Bill was first considered by a Board of Trade committee under Lord Davey and was then sent up to the Lords, where a Select Committee examined it in such a dilatory way that many suspected that obstructive tactics were being deliberately employed.

This was the point which had been reached when Hooley came up for trial and Russell made his great speech. The Unionist Government, initially reluctant to act, now felt obliged to bring in a bill of its own. Though but a pale imitation of the measure which Davey had recommended four years earlier, the Companies Act of 1900 did go some way to protecting shareholders against fraudulent company promoters. For example, it provided against the evil of bogus or fictitious subscriptions with the aim of ensuring that new companies started life with sufficient capital. Moreover, limited companies were now obliged to make more information available to the public, while, in an effort to curb the worst abuses of 'guinea pig directorships', it was stipulated that directors should not be appointed if they were unqualified for the work.[37]

The Guinea Pig Director and Politics

The main purpose of the 1900 Companies Act was to offer protection to shareholders and creditors. But the growing use of guinea pig directors carried with it other dangers, which were political rather than commercial. We have already seen how Hooley and Whittaker Wright persuaded the bearers of ancient and noble names to lend their social authority to business ventures that were highly dubious. In the House of Lords about one quarter of the assembly were holding company directorships in 1896; some thought the proportion was even higher.[38] Moreover, in contrast to an earlier period, peers now often had associations with companies quite unconnected with their localities or estates. In an interesting article published in the *Critic* in September 1898, Hess was actually able to prove that no fewer than sixty-nine members of the Lords had sat on the boards of companies which had failed during the preceding three years; none of these peers had an

[36] *Spectator*, 5 Nov. 1898, p. 645.
[37] Cottrell, *Industrial Finance*, pp. 64–75.
[38] Thompson, F. M. L., *English Landed Society in the Nineteenth Century* (London, 1963), pp. 306–7. John Burns claimed that 435 peers were company directors (*Parl. Deb.*, 4th ser., lxxxii. 1141 (9 May 1900)).

obvious connection with the 'failed' company, and several of them were persistent offenders.[39]

In the House of Commons a similar state of affairs existed. The Irish Nationalist MP, Swift MacNeill, who made a speciality of this subject, announced in 1900 that 30 per cent of all MPs were directors of public companies.[40] According to John Burns, the proportion was highest among Liberal Unionists (4¾ companies per MP), followed by Conservatives (2¼) and Liberals (1¾).[41]

Who were these company directors? They can be roughly grouped, for convenience, into three sets. Firstly, there were the financiers and company promoters who perceived that there were advantages in membership of a legislative assembly that was increasingly concerned with the regulation of commercial life. In 1900 Burns was expressing anxiety at the prospect of 'the dregs and scum of the Stock Exchange' breaking into Parliament.[42] The kind of MP Burns obviously disliked was Harry Marks, who sat as a Conservative from 1895 to 1900 and was later re-elected in a scandalous by-election in Thanet in 1904.[43] Arnold White, angry at the friendship between Marks and Whitaker Wright, complained furiously about the entry into Parliament of men with very shady reputations, and referred to 'the art of corruption in 1904'.[44] Bottomley stood unsuccessfully for Parliament in 1900, before being returned as Radical Member for South Hackney in 1906, while even Hooley perhaps entertained parliamentary ambitions.[45]

A second group of company director MPs consisted of impecunious backbenchers trying to place their political careers on a more secure footing by acquiring the sort of financial independence which business connections might give them. Such an MP was the young Lloyd George, ever on the look out for any company directorships which would not be prejudicial to his career; thus, he reluctantly declined a place on the board of a company whose products included saucy penny-in-the-slot machines, sensing that this was not a suitable enterprise for a Welsh Member representing a Nonconformist constituency.[46] But all the while he was assiduously cultivating his newly acquired business friends on the Liberal backbenches, among them a young Scotsman,

[39] 'Guinea Pig Peers', *Critic*, 17 Sept. 1898.
[40] *Parl. Deb.*, 4th ser., lxxxii. 1131 (8 May 1900).
[41] Platt, D. C. M., 'The Commercial and Industrial Interests of Ministers of the Crown', *Political Studies*, ix (1961), 274. This article gives a very clear account of the issue of 'conflicting intersts' in the years around the turn of the century.
[42] *Parl. Deb.*, 4th ser., lxxxii. 1138 (8 May 1900). See also Burns's speech about the commercialization of public life (ibid. cii. 942–4 (10 Feb. 1902)).
[43] Porter, 'Harry Hananel Marks', *Moirae*, viii. 76–83.
[44] *Sunday Sun*, 9 Oct. 1904.
[45] Before his disgrace, Hooley had been adopted as the Conservative candidate for Ilkeston. But this was a safe Liberal seat, so, by agreeing to contest it, Hooley was perhaps more concerned to do a financial service to the Party—in the hope of being given an honour at some later date.
[46] George, W. P. R., *Lloyd George Backbencher* (Llandysul, 1983), pp. 280–1.

Henry Dalziel. This forms the background to Lloyd George's often dubious business ventures in the 1890s, which included his disastrous quest for Patagonian gold.[47]

But most of the MPs who joined the boards of public companies were neither financiers and businessmen by origin, nor poor men on the make. This third group came from landed society and from the respectable professions. In some cases they were members of families who had suffered from the Agricultural Depression; in other cases they simply sought to supplement their already large incomes in order to keep up with the hectic pace which now prevailed in High Society. Whatever their motives, they were prepared to sell their family name and their political reputation in return for the easily earned money of directors' fees. 'No matter how high honourable Members' mansions in Mayfair may be', observed MacNeill, 'if I were a betting person I would bet that every room in them could be papered with the prospectuses sent out in a period of six months on which the magic letters 'M.P.' appeared on the front page.'[48] This was the 'guinea pig nuisance' of which many Members complained. Harcourt, for example, called it 'an infinite social evil which (was) working immense mischief in all classes of Society'; he added that, unfortunately, he observed 'its evil influences in this House'.[49]

The danger that certain Members of Parliament might put their business interests before the interests of their constituents and the common good was all the greater because the rules of the House, as interpreted by the Speaker, gave insufficient guidance about what was and what was not permissible conduct. Leaving aside Private Bills, for which special provision had been made since the 1840s and 1850s,[50] the main ruling was still that of Speaker Abbott, who had declared in 1811 that 'no Member who has a direct or pecuniary interest in a question should be allowed to vote upon it.' But successive Speakers had interpreted this ruling very liberally, in order to ensure that the interest was 'immediate and personal, and not merely of a general or remote character', to quote Erskine May.[51]

Indeed, there was only one clear case of an MP's vote being

---

[47] Grigg, J., *The Young Lloyd George* (London, 1973), esp. Ch. 7.

[48] *Parl. Deb.*, 4th ser., lxvi. 972 (14 Feb. 1899).

[49] Ibid. cii. 939 (10 Feb. 1902).

[50] In 1844, faced by a mass of railway legislation, the Commons set up a number of small committees, attendance on which was compulsory; but before being selected for membership, an MP had to sign a declaration to the effect that his constituents had no interest in the matters under discussion and that he himself had no pecuniary interests either. This procedure was extended in 1855 to all Private Bills. Paradoxically, this safeguard seems to have lowered standards once Private Bills came before the whole House; Members presumably felt that the Bill was now a matter of general concern on which they were entitled to vote, whatever their personal interests (Cocks, Sir Barnett (ed.), *Thomas Erskine May, A Treatise upon the Law, Privileges, and Usages of Parliament* (18th edn., 1971), pp. 913, 922, 402).

[51] Ibid. 398. Platt, 'Commercial and Industrial Interests', p. 271.

disallowed on a question of public policy during the entire Victorian period. Thus happened in 1892 when the indefatigable MacNeill successfully called attention to an infraction of the privileges of the House by three Conservative Members who had voted for a Motion in favour of a grant-in-aid to finance a preliminary survey for a railway to link the East African coast to Lake Victoria-Nyanza. The survey was being undertaken on behalf of the Government by the British East Africa Company, of which all three Members were shareholders and of which two were also directors. The three accused MPs protested that the Company had no interest whatever in whether the railway was built, since the aim was the elimination of slavery, not commercial profit, and the Company was simply being reimbursed for the costs it had incurred by performing a public service for the Government. However, the Speaker ruled against the three MPs on the ground that their votes had been given on a Motion which involved a grant of *money* to a company.[52]

Moreover, as Parliament became more and more involved in the regulation of commercial life and interest groups began lobbying in a highly professional way, public anxiety increased. In April 1896 Lloyd George objected that the Conservative MP, Sir W. Houldsworth, had voted on the London and North-Western Railway Bill, although he was a director of the railway company involved and therefore had 'a direct personal and pecuniary interest'.[53] The protest was not upheld, but the episode probably contributed to the setting up of a Commons Select Committee to examine the whole question of Members' Private Interests. The Report turned out to be a very cautious document. Existing procedures could not be formalized in a standing order, it said, since no conceivable formula could cover all the likely contingencies; therefore, the attempt to frame one might even *encourage* impropriety.[54] The 1896 Committee also stuck narrowly to its brief and dealt solely with the circumstances in which Members' *votes* were valid, ignoring the question of whether they should also declare an interest before they *spoke* in debate. Of course, even in the nineteenth century there was a convention that MPs should treat the House frankly, and deliberate attempts to deceive were definitely frowned upon. But the general practice of declaring an interest only became commonplace in the inter-war years.[55] In the absence of such a convention, suspicion and rumour could easily spread.

[52] *Parl. Deb.*, 4th ser., ii. 323–32 (8 Mar. 1892); Erskine May, *Treatise on the Law*, p. 399; MacNeill, J. G. S., *What I Have Seen and Heard* (London, 1925), pp. 238–40; Platt, 'Commercial and Industrial Interests', p. 272.
[53] Grigg, *Young Lloyd George*, p. 206.
[54] Report of Select Committee on Members of Parliament (Personal Interest), 1896, xi. The Commons Select Committee of 1969–70 took broadly the same line.
[55] Report of Select Committee on Members' Interests (Declaration), 1969–70, xiv. 159. Erskine May, *Treatise on the Law*, p. 403.

There was, indeed, one Act of Parliament which defined a Member's duties and obligations. Under the terms of the Contractors Act of 1782 an MP had to resign his seat, if a company of which he was a partner had a contractual relationship with the Government of the day. This measure was invoked against two Conservative MPs, the Gibbs brothers, whose family firm had acted as brokers on behalf of the Chilean Government in executing a contract for the sale of two warships to the British Admiralty. In February 1904 a by-election was held in which Vicary Gibbs was defeated, though his brother, Alban, was returned unopposed.[56]

But the Contractors Act was limited in its scope; in particular, it applied neither to corporate trading companies nor to companies consisting of more than ten persons when the contract was entered into for the public benefit.[57] By the late Victorian period this made neither political nor commercial sense. All it did was to encourage such evasive activities as that of the well-known contractor and Liberal MP, Weetman Pearson, who in 1897 converted his family firm, S. Pearson & Co., into a limited liability company solely in order that he could continue to undertake government contracts without running foul of the law.[58] More controversially, the Chamberlains were also alleged to have deliberately circumvented the Act when they bought out and reconstructed the ship appliances firm of Hoskins.[59]

But it was not just backbench MPs who still had a considerable freedom in combining their political careers and their business interests. So too did Ministers of the Crown. Not until 1906 was the principle clearly established that ministers must divest themselves of their directorships in public companies as soon as they entered office. It is true that in 1892 Gladstone's Cabinet bound itself to just such a self-denying ordinance.[60] But when Salisbury and the Unionists returned to office in 1895, this rule was allowed to lapse. By 1900, 52 per cent of Salisbury's Ministers held directorships in public companies, a higher proportion than obtained for the House as a whole (30 per cent).[61] Balfour, the Leader of the House, was forced to admit that on coming into office the Unionist Ministry held no fewer than sixty directorships in all, though by 1899 the number had dropped to forty-one.[62] Nor were all these directorships held in 'traditional' and

[56] *Parl. Deb.*, 4th ser., cxxix. 75–6 (2 Feb. 1904); ibid. 194–9 (3 Feb. 1904). See also letter from Rufus Isaacs to Asquith, 11 Nov. 1912 (Bodleian, Asquith papers, vol. xxiv, fos. 220–2).
[57] Platt, 'Commercial and Industrial Interests', pp. 272–3.
[58] Spender, J. A., *Weetman Pearson First Viscount Cowdray* (London, 1930), pp. 22–5. Lloyd George drew attention to this anomaly in his Commons speech of 10 Dec. 1900 (*Parl. Deb.*, 4th ser., lxxxviii. 398). [59] See Ch. 3 pp. 54–6.
[60] Gladstone to Queen Victoria, 27 Oct. 1892, in Buckle, G. E. (ed.), *The Letters of Queen Victoria: Third Series*, ii (London, 1931), 171.
[61] *Parl. Deb.*, 4th ser., lxxxii. 1131 (8 May 1900).
[62] Ibid. lxvi. 1006–7 (15 Feb. 1899).

relatively harmless concerns like railway companies.[63] Yet Salisbury and his successor, Balfour, seemed perfectly happy to leave it to the conscience and good sense of individual Ministers to protect the Government's reputation. Only when a Minister was connected with a company which had failed was it thought necessary that he should resign, as happened, for example, to the Financial Secretary to the Treasury, Hayes Fisher, in 1903.[64]

But such scandals as the Hooley Affair dramatized the problem of the guinea pig director and gave an impetus to the campaign to drive him out of government and even, though this was obviously utopian, out of Parliament itself. Indeed, many journalists—not all of them Radicals—complained that company law reform was being obstructed in the Upper House precisely because so many peers held directorships and so had a stake in the very evil they were supposed to be tackling. For example, Hugh Stutfield, a Tory journalist, referred to 'the depressing atmosphere of the House of Lords Select Committee' that was examining the Davey Bill, and thought it significant that seven of its eleven members happened to be company directors.[65]

But the main attack was launched within the House of Commons by the Irish Member of South Donegal, John Swift MacNeill, described in the *Dictionary of National Biography* as 'an eccentric warm-hearted Irish Protestant gentleman'. MacNeill had already drawn attention to himself by his personal success in challenging the votes of the three Conservative MPs in the Mobassa Railway survey affair. He had also published in 1894 a pamphlet, *Titled Corruption*, which exposed the sordid transactions by which most Irish Peers had received their titles one hundred years earlier. The Member for South Donegal was trying in this way to discredit those Irish Unionists who had recently helped block the Second Home Rule Bill.[66] He had clearly been annoyed, too, by the accusations of corruption which Unionist politicians persistently directed against the Irish Nationalist Leaders. He had been particularly offended when in early 1893 the Liberal Unionist Whip, Lord Wolmer (who later became Lord Selborne), spoke disparagingly about the way in which the Nationalist Party was financed; Wolmer was obliged to

[63] Not that all railway directorships were 'harmless'. 'How ill-advised of Arthur Balfour to allow Ailwyn Fellowes to become director of the Great Eastern Railway, at a time when there is conflict between railways and agriculture in respect of railway rates; Fellowes representing the Board of Agriculture in his parliamentary capacity, and at the same time defending a railway company attacked by his own department' (Balcarres's diary, 10 July 1904, in Vincent, J. (ed.), *The Crawford Papers. The Journals of David Lindsay, twenty-seventh Earl of Crawford and tenth Earl of Balcarres 1871–1940 during the years 1892 to 1940* (Manchester, 1984), p. 75).

[64] *Parl. Deb.*, 4th ser., cxx, 1254–8 (7 Apr. 1903). But in 1913 Hayes Fisher was still 'the source of gossip about his financial ventures' (Balcarres's diary, 2 Feb. 1913, in Vincent (ed.), *Crawford Papers*, p. 307).

[65] *National Review*, xxxii (1898), 578.

[66] MacNeill, J. G. S., *Titled Corruption: The Sordid Origins of Some Irish Peerages* (London, 1894).

make a partial retraction and the House formally ruled that the reporting of the offending words in *The Times* amounted to a breach of privilege.[67]

No wonder that Irish MPs like MacNeill and William Field were so keen to launch a counter-attack on aristocratic corruption. But why concentrate on the events surrounding the passage of the Act of Union where there were so many more recent manifestations of corruption to expose? Salisbury's seeming indifference to ministerial involvement in business life gave MacNeill just the opening he needed, and, with his growing command of parliamentary procedure, he soon became a skilful and relentless foe of the guinea pigs occupying the Government Front Bench.

In this campaign MacNeill soon acquired allies in all parts of the House. The most vociferous of these were well-known troublemakers like Labouchere and Captain 'Tommy' Bowles, a persistent Tory rebel. Then there was the Lib-Lab MP, John Burns, who brought to the attacks on titled corruption his own colourful brand of proletarian class-consciousness. Moreover, these critics soon started to pick up support even in journals normally sympathetic to the Government. For example, in February 1899 the *Spectator* published an article, 'Directors in Parliament', which dealt more in sorrow than in anger with the lax standards prevailing in Salisbury's Government.[68] A Radical like F. W. Hirst of the *Economist* felt less need to mince his words:

If salaries of £5,000 a year are not enough to enable Ministers to compete with the ambitious poverty of West-End life, let them be increased. . . . We all know how insidious are the ways of corruption, how unconsciously motives of private gain may work upon virtuous resolves. Stringent, then, is the duty imposed upon men in office to live and move in a cleaner air far above the atmosphere of suspicion.[69]

The occasion for the *Spectator* article was MacNeill's action in moving an amendment to the Address on 14 February 1899 in which the holding of a company directorship was said to be 'incompatible with the position of a Minister of the Crown' and likely to 'lower the dignity of public life'. This led to an interesting two-day debate, at the end of which the amendment was lost by 143 votes to 247.[70] But the most significant feature of this debate was that it supplied clear evidence that the Liberal Party itself was now swinging into line behind MacNeill in his indictment of a corrupt Unionist Ministry. There had already been signs of this happening in the Select Committee's deliberations two and a half years earlier, when it had

---

[67] *Parl. Deb.*, 4th ser., viii. 1587–1608 (16 Feb. 1893).
[68] *Spectator*, 18 Feb. 1899.
[69] Hirst, F. W., Murray, G., and Hammond, J. L., *Liberalism and the Empire* (London, 1900), p. 115.
[70] *Parl. Deb.*, 4th ser., lxvi. 971–92, 996–1056 (14, 15 Feb. 1899).

been the Liberal Members, Campbell-Bannerman, Haldane, and Lloyd George, plus MacNeill and Courteney, who pressed for tighter restrictions on MPs' behaviour, with the Unionists favouring leniency and the status quo.[71]

In February 1899 it also became clear that the critics were by no means confined to the Radical backbenches. In words that were to ring strangely in the aftermath of the Marconi Affair, Asquith called for firmer rules, binding on ministers as well as civil servants, to preclude all possibility of corruption: 'no man who enters (the service of the State)', declared Asquith, 'should place himself in a position in which by any conceivable or reasonable possibility his public duty and private interest (should) come into collision the one with the other'.[72] It was left to Balfour to riddle MacNeill's proposal with every objection he could think of.[73]

In these various debates the House was not solely concerned with discussing the problem of company directorships in abstract terms. Inevitably, there were personal attacks on particular Ministers. For example, the Duke of Devonshire, President of the Defence Committee of the Cabinet, had recently been Chairman of the Hematite Iron Company, whose products were used in the construction of battleships. Apologists for the Government seemed uncertain whether or not the Duke had resigned this position when he re-entered the Cabinet in 1895.[74] But opponents frequently raised the issue. Incidentally, the concern being expressed here foreshadowed the later outcry against the influence allegedly wielded by the so-called 'merchants of death'.[75]

Another Minister often under criticism, especially from the Irish MPs, was Lord Selborne, who for a time had combined the office of Under-Secretary at the Colonial Office with a directorship in the P&O Company, which did business with his own Department. It was also pointed out that the P&O Company had been allowed for some years to evade the law relating to adequate provision for Lascar seamen—an irregularity for which Selborne, it was implied, bore some

[71] Report of Select Committee on Members of Parliament (Personal Interest), 1896, xi. The defeated amendment read: 'Your Committee thinks it desirable that the position and votes of Members who are directors or shareholders in companies affected by Private Bills should be regarded more strictly than has been the case of late years. Such instances as those of directors and shareholders who have undertaken to represent their companies in conducting Bills through the House appear to come within the spirit if not the letter of the rule.'

[72] Parl. Deb., 4th ser., lxvi. 1050 (15 Feb. 1899).

[73] Ibid., 1032–46. The arguments were rehearsed in later debates on this subject, held in May 1900 and February 1903 (ibid. lxxxii 1131–44 (8 May 1900) and cxviii. 381–92, 407–32 (19, 20 Feb. 1903)).

[74] Marder, A. J., The Anatomy of British Sea Power (Hamden, Connecticut, 1940), p. 27. Among the many references, see Parl. Deb., 4th ser., lxvi. 1008–9 (15 Feb. 1899) and lxxxii. 1140 (8 May 1900).

[75] See Appendix I.

responsibility.[76] This ill-chosen company directorship was an acute embarrassment to Selborne, who was never allowed by his political opponents to forget it.[77] More quickly forgotten was the situation of Gerald Balfour, who had to face a parliamentary grilling in 1900 about how he reconciled his tenure of the Presidency of the Board of Trade with his retention of his company directorships.[78]

MacNeill and his friends stopped short of suggesting that there should be a ban on ministers holding *shares* in public companies. Yet Arthur Balfour was not alone in finding this distinction illogical. Why, he asked, should Lord Tweedmouth have felt obliged to resign his directorship in Meux's Breweries when he sat in Gladstone's recent Cabinet, while continuing to hold shares in that company? After all, a politician's directorships could easily be ascertained from a reading of the *Directory of Directors*, whereas his shareholdings were much easier to conceal and so afforded greater temptations to an unscrupulous minister.[79] But of course, no one thought it feasible for ministers to sell off all their stocks and shares on entering office, still less for them to impose similar conditions on their close relatives. All that could reasonably be expected was a display of prudence and discretion.

Yet these qualities seemed to be lacking in many Ministers. Balfour himself, for example, took a keen interest in the Stock Exchange, which led him into a number of foolish speculations, including the investment of £1,000 in Whitaker Wright's ill-fated London & Globe—word of which somehow got about and gave rise to malicious rumour.[80]

Joseph Chamberlain also showed poor judgement in these matters. Leaving aside for the moment his family's involvement in local armaments firms,[81] was it sensible of him to have retained Royal Niger Company shares, bought many years earlier for £3,000, after he

---

[76] *Parl. Deb.*, 4th ser., lxxxii. 1419 (11 May 1900). The attack was launched, predictably, by an Irish Member, John Dillon. Selborne, warned by this experience, took much greater care subsequently. In 1910 he wrote to Balfour, asking whether he should take the chairmanshp of a very big armour-plate and shipbuilding business; he said he instinctively felt that to accept it 'might hereafter impair my opportunities for political usefulness' (Selborne to Balfour, 6 July 1910, BL, Balfour papers, Add. MS 49,708, fo. 211).

[77] e.g. Swift MacNeill's letter ('Purity in Politics') to the *Manchester Guardian*, 23 Feb. 1914.

[78] Gerald Balfour assured his interrogators that he had in fact resigned his one directorship on becoming President of the Board of Trade in 1900—though not during the previous five years when he held Cabinet office (*Parl. Deb.*, 4th ser., lxxxviii. 47, 209, 461, 471, 808 (6 Dec., 7 Dec., 14 Dec. 1900)).

[79] Ibid. lxvi. 1038–9 (15 Feb. 1899). But the Liberals later inverted the argument. In 1912 Harold Spender offered a partial defence of Liberal Ministers' share-dealing by bringing up the large number of directorships held by the late Government. He commented: 'if shares are perilous, what about Directorships? For there you have not merely a shadowy conflict of interest but a real and actual conflict of control' (Spender to Strachey, Apr. 1913. HLRO, Strachey papers, S/13/13/2).

[80] See above, p. 36 and Ch. 8, pp. 192–3.   [81] See Ch. 3.

had become Colonial Secretary? This became a public talking-point in the summer of 1899 when the Government was assuming power to revoke the Royal Niger's Charter and to administer the territory which it had hitherto controlled. Several Irish MPs and backbench Radicals, Lloyd George included, had already attempted to reduce the compensation due to shareholders, believing that the Government's terms were too favourable, when the press started to carry stories about the Colonial Secretary's involvement in the Company. An angry Chamberlain made a personal explanation to the Commons. As soon as the question of revoking the Royal Niger Company's Charter was mooted, he said, he had informed the Prime Minister of his interest and begged 'to be excused from offering any opinion on the transaction'. Its handling was then entrusted to the Chancellor of the Exchequer, Hicks Beach. Thus, claimed Chamberlain, his conduct had been entirely honourable from first to last; and in any case, the deal eventually worked out by the Government was positively disadvantageous to the Company's shareholders.[82]

Most Unionist newspapers declared themselves to be entirely satisfied with this explanation and deplored the insinuations which had been directed against the Colonial Secretary.[83] But, not for the first time, the *Spectator* broke ranks by calling the Government's bargain with the chartered company 'very improvident'.[84] The Liberal press went further. The *Westminster Gazette* thought it highly inconvenient that the Colonial Secretary should have been 'out of court' when the Nigerian matter came under discussion: 'What should we say if the Secretary of State for War declared himself unable to give an opinion on the question of a new weapon, because he held a few shares in a small-arms factory?', it asked.[85] And the *Speaker*'s verdict was even harsher. Chamberlain's statement, it said, had 'astonished even some of those who thought they knew (him) best', and it deplored his remarks about the Company having got a poor bargain as 'bad taste'; on the contrary, the Company had 'undoubtedly made a good (bargain), and the tax-payer cannot be blamed for thinking he would have paid less to a company which contained no member of the Cabinet . . .'.[86]

No one suggested that in this instance the Colonial Secretary had behaved corruptly, but the episode could plausibly be presented as yet more evidence of the Government's 'carelessness' about its own reputation. A similar deduction was drawn from the Prime Minister's controversial decision in the autumn of 1900 to allow the newly appointed Indian Under-Secretary, Lord Hardwicke, to retain his

---

[82] *Parl. Deb.*, 4th ser., lxxiv 40–1 (6 July 1899); *Annual Register*, 1899, pp. 146–7.
[83] 'There is really no arguing with such austerity as this', commented the *Pall Mall Gazette* contemptuously (7 July 1899).
[84] *Spectator*, 8 July 1899, pp. 38–9.
[85] *Westminster Gazette*, 7 July 1899.   [86] *Speaker*, 29 July 1899. p. 92.

connection with his stockbroking firm and hence his membershp of
the Stock Exchange. In the Upper House Rosebery declared that
nothing of the kind had happened since the time of Lord North, and
spoke of a precedent having been set which was 'of the very greatest
danger to the political life of our country'. Hardwicke was driven into
making a personal statement about his financial embarrassments,
supported by the Prime Minister, who mocked at Rosebery's 'clap-trap
cry', claimed that the field of selection of ministers was smaller in
Britain than in other countries, and said that the real danger came from
most Ministries and Parliaments knowing too little about business,
not too much.[87] But Rosebery was not convinced;[88] nor was Arnold
White, who kept up his attacks on Hardwicke, whose stockbroking
firm, he was later able to show, enjoyed close ties with Whitaker
Wright![89]

To make things worse, most Ministers publicly gave the impression
that they simply could not understand what it was about their conduct
which others found reprehensible. On the question of company
directorships, for example, Hicks Beach apparently felt that he had
successfully vindicated his position when he had demonstrated to his
own satisfaction that the time he devoted to his business interests did
not impair the quality of his political or administrative work.[90] The
point about a possible conflict of interest was often ignored. Despite
the ingenuity of his speeches Balfour showed a similar obtuseness, to
the private unease of some of his followers who wished that the
Government's approach to ministerial directorships was not so
tolerant.

Without making accusations of actual corruption, the critics also
alleged that some Cabinet Ministers were too familiar with dubious
businessmen and financiers. 'Mr Balfour is in the habit of spending his
weekends with hosts whose power in the world of cosmopolitan
finance enables them to exercise great influence on the questions of
the day', complained Arnold White in 1904.[91] And five years earlier,
in the course of fulminating over the Government's surrender of
the public interest to the National Telephone Company in what it
called 'the most scandalous lobbying which the oldest members of
Parliament can recollect', the *Speaker* commented that though Balfour
was 'not himself a director of any company', yet 'in the Cabinet he

---

[87] *Parl. Deb.*, 4th ser., lxxxviii. 48–9, 801–11 (6 Dec., 14 Dec. 1900).
[88] Ibid. 806–7 (14 Dec. 1899).   [89] *Daily Dispatch*, 13 Nov. 1902.
[90] *Parl. Deb.*, 4th ser., lxvi. 986 (14 Feb. 1899). When W. H. Smith became First Lord of
the Admiralty in 1877 his mind had moved along similar tracks. After retiring from
active partnershp in the family firm, he explained his action to Salisbury as follows: 'I do
not understand the difference between public and private time. If a man does not think of
his work except when he is in his office, he does not rise to my conception of what a good
Public Servant should do' (Viscount Chilston, *W. H. Smith* (London, 1965), p. 140).
[91] *Sunday Sun*, 3 July 1904.

breathes an atmosphere of directorships, and he has been unable to stand up against a gang of corrupt intriguers.'[92]

It was this jaundiced view of the Unionist Ministry which underlay the Opposition's hunt for 'contracting scandals' during the Second Boer War. And these 'scandals' in their turn intensified the suspicions felt by many Radicals, Irish Nationalists, and Socialists about the motives behind British policy in South Africa, and indeed their suspicions about Imperialism as a whole.

[92] *Speaker*, 29 July 1899, p. 92.

3

Contracting Scandals and Stock-Jobbing Imperialism

Boer War Scandals: Kynoch's and Hoskins

THE issues which Swift MacNeill and his friends had broached might not have aroused so much interest had it not been for the outbreak of the Boer War in October 1899. Scarcely had hostilities broken out than the air was alive with rumours that contractors were making exorbitant profits at the taxpayer's expense. On 26 March 1900 a Conservative backbencher, Sir Carne Rasch, was provoked by these rumours into asking 'whether the Government would consider the advisability of appointing a small Parliamentary Committee to examine and report upon the alleged cases of fraud in connection with Army and Navy contracts'. Balfour agreed that this was necessary in order to dispel any notion that scandals were being concealed.[1] In May a Select Committee was set up.

But friends and foes of the Ministry concurred in the view that the Report which this Committee produced three months later raised more questions than it answered. For example, it declared that 'the discovery of frauds and secret commissions by the methods of examination' open to the Select Committee had been 'extremely difficult'. 'It is rather by accident that such irregularities can be detected by such methods', it said. The Report also spoke of the 'widespread belief' in the existence of bribery, and argued that there was 'ground for suspicion' that the payment of secret commissions was as prevalent in the public service as in private commerce, though definite proof of this was lacking.[2] *The Times* was not the only paper which regretted that the charges of corruption that had been made against the Service Departments had not been probed to the bottom, and it wished that the enquiry had been 'handed over to a tribunal furnished with larger powers'.[3]

However, one specific rumour was dealt with in some detail by the Select Committee, and that concerned the allotment of cordite contracts to the firm of Kynoch & Co of Birmingham, whose Chairman, Arthur Chamberlain, was the brother of Joseph Chamberlain, the

---

[1] *Parl. Deb.*, 4th ser., lxxxi. 316–17 (26 Mar. 1900).
[2] Report from Select Committee on War Office Contracts, 1 Aug. 1900, vol. ix, paras. 37–8.
[3] *The Times*, 9 Aug. 1900; Doig, *Corruption and Misconduct*, pp. 75–6. The Lord Chancellor's response was to introduce a bill to outlaw gifts or considerations given corruptly or secretly, but this was withdrawn for lack of time.

Colonial Secretary. It had been alleged that favouritism was being shown to this firm. The Select Committee demonstrated that this allegation was not without foundation. For Kynoch's had been allowed to revise their original tender, a privilege not accorded to any of their rivals; and they had then been given a large share of the cordite order, even though their revised price was still higher than that of most of the other armaments firms.[4] On whose advice had this seemingly irregular arrangement been made?

The Select Committee's investigations suggested that one strong influence had been that of Patrick O'Brien, the MP for Kilkenny, anxious that employment should be provided for his constituents working in Kynoch's Arklow Works.[5] Moreover, the Admiralty representatives had urged that concessions should be given to Kynoch's on account of its specialized experience.[6] This was odd advice, since the available evidence indicated that Kynoch's had a record of bad workmanship and poor deliveries.[7] But what of the family relationship with the Colonial Secretary? Naturally Arthur Chamberlain, when summoned to give evidence, claimed that his brother's position gave his firm no advantage whatever, and he indignantly denied that he had influence to secure orders.[8] This disclaimer was accepted by the Select Committee, which criticized the Kynoch's deal but declared that the Services Departments had had the best interests of the country at heart and had not succumbed to illegitimate pressure from outside.[9]

But in the highly charged political atmosphere surrounding the Boer War it was unlikely that this verdict would be universally accepted. Even before the publication of the Select Committee Report, Liberal newspapers were expressing amusement at the notion that the Unionist Government was apparently so ready to defer to the wishes of an Irish Member.[10] And other critics noted that the Financial Secretary to the War Office, the minister responsible for the allocation of contracts, was Powell Williams, a close associate of Chamberlain's and a fellow Birmingham MP. Was it really likely that Williams was not aware of the Chamberlain family interest in Kynoch's or that he had in no way been influenced in his decision by such knowledge? Moreover, no one could be in doubt that the Chamberlain involvement in Kynoch's was an important one after the *Morning Leader*, a metropolitan Liberal daily, had published the latest list of shareholders filed at Somerset House, which showed that the family held shares in the

[4] Report on War Office Contracts, paras. 25–33.

[5] Ibid., qs. 6550, 10035–42, 6487. It was not uncommon at this time for MPs to promote the industrial interests of their constituents by securing contracts for local firms. See Davenport-Hines, R. P. T., *Dudley Docker. The Life and Times of a Trade Warrior* (Cambridge, 1984), pp. 61–3.

[6] Report on War Office Contracts, para. 33.

[7] Ibid., qs. 7182–220.

[8] Ibid., qs. 9990–4.

[9] Ibid., para. 33.

[10] *Morning Leader*, 2 Aug. 1900.

company which would be worth about £140,000 if they currently came onto the market.[11]

On 8 August the Select Committee Report formally appeared, and this was an occasion for the attack on Chamberlain to be taken up in the Commons, where the running was made by Lloyd George, who was clearly out to 'get' the Colonial Secretary. Like other Radicals, he drew attention to the contrast between the Government's professed concern to 'redress grievances in and purify the administration of the Transvaal' and its indifference to rather similar abuses at home.[12] In particular, Lloyd George attacked the favoured treatment received by Kynoch's, a firm which, he said, had been 'made' by the War Office. And he added, 'Whatever party in the country suffered by the war, one party in the country was doing well out of it.'[13] Stung by this gibe, Joseph Chamberlain furiously denied that he had any interest, direct or indirect, in Kynoch's, or that he had ever discussed the matter of the contracts with its Chairman: 'it is a gross abuse', he complained, 'to attack a public man through his relatives, for whom he is not responsible.'[14] This outburst shows that Lloyd George had succeeded in his original objective—deflecting public criticism from his own opposition to the War by a savage counter-attack on the motives and good faith of the dominant figure in the Unionist Ministry.[15]

It is just possible that the controversy might then have died down but for the resourceful and determined campaign against the Chamberlain family which the *Morning Leader* continued to conduct throughout the late summer and autumn of 1900. The paper's most notable coup was the publication of an article on 18 September which revealed the connection of the Chamberlains with the firm of Hoskins & Sons Ltd., of which Neville Chamberlain, Joseph's second son, was managing director. For the *Leader* was able to document that this small concern, which supplied fittings for the Navy, was virtually owned by Chamberlain's immediate family, and that among the major shareholders (with £3,000 worth of shares) was Austen Chamberlain, the Civil Lord of the Admiralty. Moreover, the Chamberlain family had acquired control of Hoskins in December 1897, that is to say, over two years *after* Austen Chamberlain had taken up his Admiralty post. This made it a much more difficult arrangement to defend that the one at Kynoch's, where Arthur Chamberlain had been company chairman long before his brother became Colonial Secretary.[16]

---

[11] Ibid., 3 Aug. 1900.
[12] *Parl. Deb.*, 4th ser., lxxxvii. 1011–13 (8 Aug. 1900). For this line of attack, see also: *Speaker*, 13 Oct. 1900; *Star*, 20 Sept. 1900.
[13] *Parl. Deb.*, 4th ser., lxxxvii. 1012 (8 Aug. 1900).   [14] Ibid. 1014.
[15] Grigg, *Young Lloyd George* pp. 268–9. Lloyd George had first raised the question of Chamberlain's connection with Kynoch's in 1895 and had returned to the theme in April 1900 (ibid. 269).
[16] *Morning Leader*, 18 Sept. 1900.

It also seemed suspicious that the Chamberlains had been trading under the 'alias' of Hoskins, and that among the original shareholders in 1897 were five clerks, each with £10 in shares, inherited from the former firm. The *Morning Leader* suspected that the latter arrangement was designed to bring the total number of partners to ten, so enabling Austen to evade the provisions of the 1782 Contractors Act.[17] In fact, these suspicions were probably misplaced. In a private letter to Austen, Neville explained that the clerks had been taken on as partners simply for administrative convenience and that 'there certainly was no question of evading the clause about MPs, of which he and his business associates had been entirely ignorant.'[18]

But few Radicals believed such assurances, and the *Morning Leader*'s 'exposure' of the Hoskins connection created a minor sensation. For although the Government press initially tried to boycott the story, the Liberals played it up for all it was worth. Thus, the *Manchester Guardian* mischievously affected to believe that there must be some mistake; surely the Chamberlains would shortly be able to supply a satisfactory explanation?[19] Meanwhile, the *Westminster Gazette* seized the opportunity to contrast the prudent behaviour of recent Liberal Ministries with the 'slackness' which had crept into public life during the years of Unionist rule.[20] A more savage note was struck by the anti-imperialist Radical weekly, the *Speaker*, which declared the Hoskins Affair to be 'of a class that, in France, America or Germany, would have produced a political trial'.[21]

Much to the frustration of the Chamberlain family, which was looking for an opportunity of taking its critics to court, the *Morning Leader* and the other Radical journals were careful not to make allegations of actual corruption against Austen Chamberlain. 'There is no reason to suppose that he would use his public office to further his private interests', wrote the *Morning Leader*, 'but how difficult has he rendered the position of his subordinates in Whitehall!'[22]

In an attempt to clear his name, Austen Chamberlain released a letter to the *Birmingham Daily Post*, in which he admitted that Hoskins had indeed done 'a small trade in certain ship's fittings with the Admiralty', but claimed that this was 'only an infinitesimal proportion of the company's business', and that in any case it was no part of the duty of a Civil Lord of the Admiralty to deal with

---

[17] Ibid., 6 Oct. 1900. The *Star* said: 'If Mr Chamberlain were a shady company promoter, we could understand his attitude . . .' (29 Sept. 1900). See also *Speaker*, 15 Dec. 1900.

[18] Neville Chamberlain to Austen Chamberlain, 7 Dec. 1900 (Birmingham University, Austen Chamberlain papers, AC 11/2/3). Austen Chamberlain tried to deal with the issue in the 10 Dec. parliamentary debate: (*Parl. Deb.*, 4th ser., lxxxviii. 448–9).

[19] *Manchester Guardian*, 19 Sept. 1900.

[20] *Westminster Gazette*, 18 Sept. 1900.

[21] *Speaker*, 22 Sept. 1900.

[22] *Morning Leader*, 18 Sept. 1900.

contracts.[23] This assurance was repeated by the Financial Secretary to the Admiralty, William Macartney, who informed the world that Chamberlain had never spoken to him on the topic of contracts. But this statement brought down on its author the ridicule of the *Speaker*, which along with other Radical papers speculated out loud about why the fortunes of Hoskins & Sons should have improved so markedly after 1897.[24]

Yet the attacks on Austen Chamberlain lacked venom. One suspects that the Civil Lord of the Admiralty was far too amiable a man to have made many personal enemies. It was his father, the Colonial Secretary, whom the critics wanted to smash. And here Joseph Chamberlain had played into his enemies' hands by his reckless denial in the Commons in August that he had had any interest direct or indirect in any company supplying warlike stores to the Government. Since his wife, two sons, and two daughters all held shares in Hoskins, this claim was clearly untrue. What is more, the *Morning Leader* continued throughout September and October to unearth other companies in which the Chamberlain family had a large stake, all of them enjoying some kind of contractual relationship, albeit often indirect, with the War Office or Admiralty.

For example, Austen and Joseph Chamberlain both held shares in an investment trust which had put part of its assets in 'Tubes' (another company chaired by Arthur Chamberlain), and 'Tubes' in turn had supplied boilers to the Admiralty.[25] The Chamberlains greeted this disclosure by protesting that only a very small part of the work of 'Tubes' was in fact given over to public contracts, but the Liberal MP, McKenna, was later to throw doubt on the truth of this claim.[26] Moreover, there were other family links with companies supplying the Service Departments: for example, Elliotts' Metal Company, in which 9,260 of the 20,280 ordinary shares and 3,841 out of the 7,099 preference shares were held by immediate members of Chamberlain's family, including Neville and Austen.[27] Although it was only in the case of Kynoch's that any suggestion of 'favouritism' could be found, the Chamberlains clearly had not succeeded in severing their ties with the armaments firms of the West Midlands—which prompted the *Morning Leader* to make the sly observation that it seemed 'only fitting that as one brother makes our wars, the other should make our ammunition'.[28]

In late September and October 1900 the country went to the polls.

[23] *Birmingham Daily Post*, 21 Sept. 1900. The goods made by Hoskins under Admiralty contract cost only £374 in 1897, £528 in 1898, £669 in 1899, and £910 in 1900 (Dilks, D., *Neville Chamberlain*, i. *1869–1929* (Cambridge, 1984), pp. 83–4).

[24] *Speaker*, 13 Oct. 1900.

[25] *Morning Leader*, 22 Sept., 5 Oct. 1900.

[26] *Parl. Deb.*, 4th ser., lxxxviii. 445–6, 454 (10 Dec. 1900).

[27] *Morning Leader*, 28 Sept. 1900.   [28] Ibid., 17 Sept. 1900.

Labouchere alleged, rather implausibly, that the Government had dissolved Parliament prematurely in an attempt to distract attention from the 'contracting scandals'.[29] If that were the intention, it did not succeed, since the issue of Kynoch's, Hoskins, and the other Chamberlain companies was frequently raised during the election campaign. The *Speaker* urged that the motto of every good Liberal should be: 'Fight corruption in high quarters; fight Minister contractors; fight Minister speculators; fight those who turn public misfortunes into private lucre.'[30] In addition, the *Morning Leader* boiled its contracting articles down into a concise leaflet. Available at 6*d*. for 50 or at 5*s*. per thousand, the leaflet was widely circulated by Radical candidates—among them Lloyd George, who made personal attacks on Chamberlain a central feature of his campaign.[31]

In London, in particular, many Liberals brought the 'contracting scandals' to the fore. The evening paper, the *Star*, which backed them in this tactic, relayed a story of a man who had been heard in a restaurant charging another with being 'on the Kynoch', meaning 'on the make', and wondered whether this expression was 'to be added to the language as was the name of Captain Boycott'.[32] And in Bethnal Green an election meeting resounded 'with cries from working men who had read their *Morning Leader* and *Star* of "What about Hoskins?" and "That's all Kynoch." '[33] Not that this ploy necessarily did the Liberals much electoral good. B. S. Straus in St George's got nowhere near winning the usually Liberal seat, which the Unionists had held by only four votes in 1895; and in Hoxton, where the Government contracts also featured prominently in the election, the Unionist majority *increased* from 128 to 271.[34]

Despite their Party's triumph in the Khaki Election, Joseph and Austen Chamberlain nevertheless smouldered with resentment over what they saw as the monstrously unfair attacks to which they had been subjected. The Colonial Secretary had to suffer the additional ignominy of being taunted with having made a generous profit out of his Department's acquisition of the Royal Niger Company, in which he was a shareholder.[35] Never a man to endure personal abuse philosophically, Chamberlain soon convinced himself that his opponents were trying to drive businessmen out of public life altogether. 'Every man in every Government who has saved money must invest it somewhere', he wrote in a Memorandum of 15 December, 'and it is difficult to see what form the investment, English or Foreign, he could choose which would not lay him open to such

[29] Ibid., 29 Sept. 1900. [30] *Speaker*, 29 Sept. 1900.
[31] *Morning Leader*, 29 Sept. 1900; Grigg, *Young Lloyd George*, pp. 269–72.
[32] *Star*, 20 Sept. 1900. [33] Ibid., 25 Sept. 1900.
[34] See *Star*, 20 Sept., 2 Oct. 1900.
[35] e.g. *Speaker*, 22 Sept. 1900. On the Royal Niger Company Affair, See Ch. 2, pp. 48–9.

scandalous imputations' as those he had recently had to endure. Chamberlain claimed that he had nobly given up all chances of further money-making when he embraced a political career, but there was no reason, he said, why his brother should follow suit, and he thought it insupportable that Arthur's business successes should now be brought up against them both. Chamberlain declared that his 'middle class commercial honour' had been touched and that his feelings had been deeply hurt.[36]

The Colonial Secretary would have liked to sue the papers, including the *Morning Leader*, which had so tormented him, but he was advised by three different lawyers not to initiate proceedings on the ground that specific accusations of personal corruption had been carefully avoided.[37] And so Arthur was left to 'vindicate the family honour' when he brought a suit against the *Star* for defamation of character. He won the case, though the jury awarded only £300 damages, which perhaps detracted somewhat from the 'moral victory'.[38]

Austen Chamberlain, meanwhile, was doing the very thing which he found so reprehensible in his opponents, namely, sending investigators to Somerset House to enquire into the shareholdings of former Liberal Ministers. These searches revealed that Gladstone's First Lord of the Admiralty, Lord Spencer, had retained 2,300 shares in a trust company with holdings in the Fairfield Shipbuilding Company, and that Sir Thomas Brassey, a junior Admiralty Minister between 1880 and 1885, had actually increased his investments in a shipping company while holding office.[39] Austen Chamberlain's 'detective' also amassed some potentially embarrassing information about the business interests of Hartington (now the Duke of Devonshire), though this could hardly be used against a fellow minister. In addition, there was obviously a desire to demonstrate that Asquith had an interest in the Nobel Dynamite Company through his father-in-law, Sir Charles Tennant; however, evidence for this was lacking, and the information he had gathered about the shareholdings of various members of the Gladstone family was similarly inconclusive.[40]

It seems probable that the point of these investigations was to procure material which could later be used, if need be, in parliamentary debate. Such a debate quickly followed the assembly of

[36] Chamberlain's Memorandum of 15 Dec. 1900 (Birmingham University, Joseph Chamberlain papers, JC 12/2/2/2); Parker Smith's Memorandum of conversation with Chamberlain, Dec. 1900 (?) (ibid.).

[37] Memorandum of 30 Nov. 1900 in Chamberlain papers (JC 12/2/2/1).

[38] *The Times*, 21 Mar. 1901. See also Walker-Smith, D., and Clarke, E., *The Life of Sir Edward Clarke* (London, 1939), pp. 276–7.
Neville Chamberlain, too, won a case against the *Star*, but that concerned his management of a sisal plantation (Dilks, *Neville Chamberlain*, pp. 84–5).

[39] Memorandum, n.d. (Austen Chamberlain papers, AC 11/2/6).

[40] Unsigned typed Memorandum of 5 pages in Austen Chamberlain papers, AC 11/2/5.

the new Parliament, when Lloyd George moved an amendment to the Address calling on Ministers of the Crown to give up their interests, direct or indirect, in firms and companies competing for government contracts, or at the very least to take precautions which would 'prevent any suspicion of influence or favouritism in the allocation of such contracts'.[41] Swift MacNeill's campaign against ministerial directorships was being given a new twist.

The December 1900 debate produced few dramatic revelations. Chamberlain insisted that he had sold out his interest in Kynoch's at a loss as soon as he entered office to avoid compromising himself.[42] Lloyd George, on the other hand, was able to show that when the Unionists formed their Administration in 1895, Kynoch's shares had risen by 33 per cent.[43] And another up-and-coming Liberal backbencher, Reginal McKenna, who had sat on the recent Select Committee, made a very telling speech, in which he pointed out that Arthur Chamberlain's connection with the Colonial Secretary was actually mentioned in the letter of introduction used by the travellers acting for his company.[44] 'The fact is that when officials have to deal with companies which have the guarantee of great names behind them their judgement and independence are paralysed', he commented.[45] It also emerged during the debate that Chamberlain had, at an earlier date, publicly spoken out on Kynoch's behalf, using his position as an MP, but not declaring a personal or family interest.[46] The cases of Hoskins, Elliotts, 'Tubes' and other companies were also debated, without anything new of substance being produced.

After the December debate the facts about the Chamberlains' business interests were no longer in dispute. But politicians and journalists continued to argue over the question of whether anything corrupt or reprehensible had been done. The Government's critics made three general points. First, they pointed out how unfair it would be if civil servants were to receive heavy punishment for combining private business interests with public office, while ministers were left free to do the same thing with impunity.[47] Secondly, they argued that, though the Chamberlains had not acted corruptly, yet, in Lloyd George's words, 'things [had] been done which would set up a precedent which could legitimately be used later on to justify corruption itself'. Here Joseph Chamberlain had played into his detractors' hands when he had earlier criticized the appointment as British High Commissioner in

---

[41] *Parl. Deb.*, 4th ser., lxxxviii. 421 (10 Dec. 1900).
[42] Ibid. 442. [43] Ibid. 413–14.
[44] 'You will be interested to know that the chairman of the company is Mr Arthur Chamberlain, brother of the present Colonial Secretary.'
[45] *Parl. Deb.*, 4th ser., lxxxviii. 456. [46] Ibid. 430–1 (Robson).
[47] Ibid. 400, 469. The *Speaker*, too, observed that under Section 193 of the Public Health Act of 1875 shareholders in a joint stock company could not be salaried officers of a municipal corporation, though they could be members of one (13 Oct. 1900).

South Africa of Hercules Robinson, a man known to have a deep involvement in various Rhodesian enterprises: 'It is not only necessary that [the Queen's representative] should be pure, but, like Caesar's wife, he must not be suspected.'[48] These words were now thrown back in Chamberlain's face. 'A person appointed to represent the Queen', said Lloyd George, 'should be not only pure, but, like Caesar's wife, above suspicion.'[49] Of course, as John Grigg observes, the Radical MP, with the Welsh Patagonian disaster recently behind him, was not the best man to make this point, and after the Marconi Affair broke, he must often have rued his display of unctuous righteousness in December 1900.[50]

The third general argument deployed against the Chamberlains was that their behaviour was doing something to jeapardize confidence in the British political system, which still had a high reputation—in contrast, say, to that of the United States, where the air was full of accusations of corruption. 'What differentiates the British Parliament from any other parliaments?', asked John Burns in the course of a much-interrupted speech:

It is because it does not 'Panama' as the French Parliament has occasionally done. It does not do what 'Tammany' has done in America, and it has not yet been under the influence of 'the chosen people', of capitalist rings and other monopolists that are accustomed to reign in the representative institutions in other parts of the world.[51]

The *Economist*, a fierce critic of the Government's entire South African policy, put it slightly differently: 'We cannot afford to permit, as a nation, the faintest beginnings of a lax system which might in time yield such evil results as marked our public records in the last century'.[52]

In replying to these charges, Ministers and their supporters put on a fiery display of indignation, deploring the fact that so much mud had been thrown at them and murmuring about 'a conspiracy of insinuation', as Joseph Chamberlain put it.[53] *The Times*, which scornfully dismissed the Opposition allegations, also expressed dismay: 'It will be an evil day for this country when charges of corruption which cannot be substantiated are allowed to be put forward by way of innuendo.'[54] If such practices once became widespread, said Austen

[48] *Parl. Deb.*, 4th ser., lxxxviii. 415–16.

[49] Ibid. 399. This was a close paraphrase of what Chamberlain himself had earlier said about Robinson. The invocation of 'Caesar's wife' was also made by Rosebery (ibid. 49 (6 Dec. 1900)).

[50] Grigg, *Young Lloyd George*, p. 276. In Apr. 1913 one of Bonar Law's correspondents wrote: Lloyd George should be '*made* to recant his petty Pecksnifferies about Kynochs etc and his cheap and easy virtue at the public expense' (Sichel to Bonar Law, 4 Apr. 1913, HLRO, Bonar Law papers, 29/3/3).

[51] *Parl. Deb.*, 4th ser., lxxxviii. 468.

[52] *The Economist*, 8 Dec. 1900.

[53] *Parl. Deb.*, 4th ser., lxxxviii. 433.

[54] *The Times*, 9 Aug. 1900.

Chamberlain, 'good men' would be less inclined to accept public office, which in any case 'was at no time a bed of roses'.[55] And Balfour, perhaps ignorant of what the Chamberlains were up to, waxed indignant at the activities of 'paid gentlemen searching the records of Somerset House, searching out all the private investments of [the two Ministers] and of all their relations, their uncles, sisters, cousins, and aunts'.[56] Never, it was claimed, had partisan spite been carried to these degrading lengths.

It was also possible to argue, as Joseph Chamberlain himself did, that he was being victimized simply because he came from a successful business family. 'I come of a family', he said, 'which boasts nothing of distinguished birth, or of inherited wealth; but who have a record—an unbroken record of nearly two centuries—of unstained commercial integrity and honour.'[57] To enlist men from such a practical business background strengthened the British political system, he implied.

The third line of defence adopted by the Unionists was to claim that they were behaving no differently from their political opponents. Austen Chamberlain did not quote from the material that his 'detective' had compiled for him, but Government spokesmen hinted that they might be forced to 'retaliate'. *The Times* also made threatening noises in its editorial of 11 December:

If Mr Chamberlain and his family are to be the subject of such imputations as were thrown out in last night's debate, why should the process of investigation stop at that point? Why should not the country have a full disclosure of all the holdings in limited liability companies and other concerns of all members of all recent Administrations, from Mr Gladstone downwards, during the last thirty years?[58]

The Kynoch's debate of December 1900 turned out to be a straightforward party contest. Admittedly, as *The Times* observed, there was something a little strange about the spectacle of a 'freelance' (i.e. Lloyd George) instigating the attack on Chamberlain, while the official Opposition leaders gave guarded support to the Amendment without having to commit themselves to all the arguments which Lloyd George was using.[59] Yet with 127 MPs voting for the Amendment and 269 against, the division followed fairly strict party lines. Even the Liberal Imperialist, Haldane, spoke in the debate, though he privately confessed that only his sense of public duty drove him into so disagreeable an act.[60] In addition, most of Haldane's fellow Liberal

[55] Cited in Petrie, Sir C., *Life and Letters of Sir Austen Chamberlain*, i (London, 1939), 93.
[56] *Parl. Deb.*, 4th ser., lxxxviii. 464.　　　　　　　　[57] Ibid. 440.
[58] *The Times*, 11 Dec. 1900. Joseph Chamberlain, in the 10 Dec. debate, also issued some veiled threats against former Liberal Ministers (*Parl. Deb.*, 4th ser., lxxxviii. 453).
[59] *The Times*, 11 Dec. 1900.
[60] Haldane to Elizabeth Haldane, 18 Dec. 1900 (National Library of Scotland, Haldane papers, vol. 6010, fo. 178).

Imperialists, including Asquith, cast their votes against the Chamberlain family.[61] Divided about the justice of the British cause in South Africa, Liberals of all shades of opinion could briefly unite in deploring the lack of 'delicacy' shown by the Colonial Secretary and his relatives. This, indeed, may have been the chief significance of the Kynoch's Affair, so far as the Opposition were concerned.

Joseph Chamberlain took the matter very personally. He swore that he would never speak to Harcourt again and he waxed indignant at the behaviour of Asquith, telling Margot Asquith that her husband 'had set a precedent of inquiry into the action of relatives for whom you were not responsible which he himself would suffer from'. 'Fancy the son-in-law of that old speculator [i.e. Charles Tennant] taking that line', was his private comment.[62]

A partial balm to Chamberlain's hurt feelings must have been the receipt of shoals of sympathetic letters (over seventy of them are preserved in his papers), a few of them coming from Liberals ashamed at the line their party had taken. Among the latter was Lord Esher, formerly a Liberal MP, who made the interesting admission that he occupied the same position as the Chamberlains 'inasmuch as among the many investments which I find my Trustees hold in "industrial concerns" is a considerable holding in a firm with which I also find we do business in this Department!' (i.e. HM Office of Works).[63] More typical is this message from the Tory Duke of Somerset:

The disgraceful way you have been maligned has disgusted all decent people. I could not belong to a party which allowed even the scum of its followers to descend to such brutal meanness—but with the Radicals men who think they are gentlemen did not scruple to join in the cry. It is too disgusting and disgraceful.[64]

This was also the tone adopted by nearly all the pro-Government press, where only the *Spectator* dared to question the propriety of the Chamberlains' behaviour.[65] The editor of this highly respected weekly, Loe Strachey, occupied, in fact, a somewhat unusual position, in the sense that he was vehemently 'Anti-Rhodes', yet supported the South African War, being quite convinced that, contrary to what most Radicals were saying, it was in no way 'a capitalist war'.[66] This somewhat detached stance had already brought Strachey into conflict

---

[61] Rosebery, too, made some harsh observations about Chamberlain, though he admitted that he knew nothing about the current 'contracts scandal' (*Parl. Deb.*, 4th ser., lxxxviii. 47–9 (6 Dec. 1900)).

[62] Parker Smith's Memorandum (Joseph Chamberlain papers, JC 12/2/2/2).

[63] Esher to Chamberlain, 11 Dec. 1900 (ibid., JC 12/2/2/15).

[64] Somerset to Chamberlain, 12 Dec. 1900 (ibid., 12/2/2/56).

[65] For a loyalist defence of Chamberlain's conduct and expressions of indignation directed at his critics, see *Pall Mall Gazette*, 11 Dec. 1900. The freelance journalist, Arnold White, however, offered some mild criticism (*Weekly Sun*, 22 Dec. 1900).

[66] Strachey to Chamberlain, 4 Mar. 1900 (Joseph Chamberlain papers, JC 12/2/2/80).

with Chamberlain in March,[67] and relations between the two men deteriorated still further when the *Spectator* declared that episodes like the Kynoch's Affair produced 'a sense of unrest and uneasiness in the public mind'.[68] There was no direct criticism of Joseph or Austen Chamberlain, though Strachey caused some amusement in Opposition circles by suggesting that the Colonial Secretary was not 'a man of the world' and therefore did not sufficiently 'trouble about appearances'.[69] The *Spectator*, incidentally, had comparatively little to say about the Hoskins connection, but concentrated almost exclusively on the Kynoch's Affair, where (or so the paper argued) the Colonial Secretary had been put into a false position as a result of *Arthur* Chamberlain's tendering for government contracts while his relatives held high office.[70]

Arthur Chamberlain was furious over this criticism, and so was his brother. In a private letter to Strachey Joseph Chamberlain said that he could not 'understand how an educated gentleman [could] encourage' an attack on the honour of public men instigated by 'the baser sort of radicals'. The task of a responsible newspaper, he suggested, was to allay ill-founded suspicions, not to encourage them. He continued:

If it is to be laid down as an axiom that character, position, responsibility go for nothing and that no one must accept office unless he can show that neither he nor any of his relatives have any pecuniary interest in any matter with which the Government of the Country have to deal, where are you going to find your Ministers? There is certainly not a member of the present Government who could pass such a test and yet I venture to say there is not a single member of this Government who would not cut off his right hand rather than that the country should suffer in order that he might make some petty gains . . .[71]

Strachey replied that Chamberlain seemed to have missed the point of the *Spectator* article:

I never dreamt of saying that a man must refuse or leave office because his brothers were in a business closely connected with Government contracts. Of course, he ought not to do any such thing. What I did say was very different, namely that one had a right to expect that the brother of a man with high

[67] Ibid. See *Spectator*, 24 Feb. 1900, pp. 261–2. The comments in these 'notes' were friendly enough towards Chamberlain but very hostile to Rhodes.

[68] *Spectator*, 11 Aug., 18 Aug. 1900, pp. 163, 198–200. But the *Spectator* expressed little sympathy with Lloyd George, whose 10 Dec. speech was criticized for its 'silly suspiciousness' (15 Dec. 1900, p. 875).

[69] Ibid., 6 Oct. 1900, p. 451. Strachey still professed a great admiration of Chamberlain, and actually proposed that he be sent in to 'purify' the War Office—a suggestion which provoked predictable mirth in the Radical press (e.g. *Star*, 26 Sept. 1900, *Speaker*, 20 Oct. 1900).

[70] Even the *Speaker* thought that that was going too far; all would have been well, it argued, if Joseph and Austen Chamberlain and those who lived under their roofs had disposed of all their holdings (15 Dec. 1900, p. 287).

[71] Chamberlain to Strachey, 18 Aug. 1900 (HLRO, Strachey papers, S/4/6/13).

Cabinet rank should not take while he was in power an active part in obtaining Government contracts.

Arthur Chamberlain, Strachey complained, had responded to this observation by violent attacks on his own honour, which he deeply resented. But Strachey insisted that he could not abandon his editorial right 'to comment with the utmost liberty on public affairs because "radicals of the baser sort" have made those affairs the ground for an unjust attack on you'. He said that he agreed with Chamberlain that it would be disastrous if the government of the country passed into the hands of 'professional politicians', but he denied that that would be the consequence of ensuring that public life was regulated by a strict code of conduct:

To begin with, it would not act upon Cabinet Ministers, but only on their near relatives and only on them in very rare cases, and need not do them any great pecuniary damage. I cannot myself see anything wrong in expecting men to make certain sacrifices for the good of their country. In our various ways we all have to do it.[72]

But the Colonial Secretary was neither convinced nor mollified. The *Spectator* article, he reiterated, would be interpreted by the wider public as an indication that members of the Chamberlain family had done something shameful. On the question of what relationship should obtain between business and politics, Chamberlain expressed his position as follows:

I am aware of the precedent of Caesar's wife; but you are extending this, and I imagine that in the case Caesar was anxious for other reasons to get rid of the lady. The demand that all the relatives of a public man should make what in many cases might be an enormous sacrifice, not for any public interest, but as a concession to the suspicions, and pretended suspicions, of his political opponents, is both unfair and futile . . .

Chamberlain concluded his letter by curtly indicating that he regarded both the correspondence and his relationship with Strachey finally closed.[73]

The disagreement between Strachey and Chamberlain was not susceptible to an easy solution. And herein lay the significance of the Kynoch's Contracts Affair: that it provided a dramatic illustration of how a minister with a variety of business interests and contacts might unwittingly find himself involved in a potentially serious conflict of interests. But many Radicals worried about the growth of political corruption thought that this episode was also significant in quite

[72] Strachey to Chamberlain, 21 Aug. 1900 (Joseph Chamberlain papers, JC 12/2/2/83).
[73] Chamberlain to Strachey, 22 or 23 Aug. 1900 (Strachey papers, S/4/6/13). Strachey was later able to claim that he had consistently followed his principles, without reference to party loyalties or personal friendship. See Strachey to Margot Asquith (copy), 7 Jan. 1919 (Strachey papers, S/11/7/68).

another way. 'The more the Empire expands, the more the Chamberlains contract', one wit had quipped in December 1900. Certain opponents of the Government had always believed that corruption was inherent in the process of Imperialism, and the events of the South African War had strongly reinforced these beliefs.

The Attack on Imperialism

Such a hostile view of Imperialism can be traced back at least as far as the founding of the various chartered companies, like the Royal Niger Company and the British South Africa Company (BSA Co.). Initially, it is true, these organisations had found favour with politicians of all parties because they promised to effect a promotion of Britain's world interests 'on the cheap'. But, as the events of the 1890s were to show, there were dangers in vesting in a business company two very different functions: 'the right to government and the desire to make money'.[74] The BSA Co.'s suppression of the Matabele Rising in 1893 brought this issue out into the open; Campbell-Bannerman, for example, told the Commons how undesirable it was to entrust 'the administration of a great territory to a trading company—or rather not to a trading company, but to a speculative financial company—with administrative powers'.[75] As this remark indicates, some of the chartered companies were thought to have an unsound financial base. And was it wise to put such terrifyingly wide powers into the hands of men of often doubtful character?

The most persistent of all the critics of the chartered companies was Henry Labouchere. In November 1893 he lectured the Commons on the 'financial jobbery' which underlay the granting of a charter to the BSA Co., gave information about its major shareholders, and described how the company had enlisted public sympathy and money by means of Rhodes's clever manipulation of the press, where his enterprises were regularly 'puffed'.[76] Another mordant critic of Rhodes was the independent Radical, A. J. Wilson, editor of the *Investors' Review*, which in 1894 carried a long two-part article entitled 'Rhodesian Finance; or a New Story of a Golden Fleece'; the Government had no right, it said, to hand over the people of that country—'savages' though they might be—'to a small troop of stock-jobbing adventurers'. The article went on to warn prudent investors to steer clear of 'this kind of company-begetting and share-multiplying', the sole purpose of which

---

[74] The remark was made by the Unionist backbencher, Arnold-Forster. Cited in Porter, B., *Critics of Empire* (London, 1968), p. 61.

[75] Ibid.

[76] Hind, R. J., *Henry Labouchere and the Empire 1880–1905* (London, 1972), pp. 20–2. The prelude to this campaign was the attack made earlier by Labouchere and other Radicals against the political influence of the Egyptian bondholders.

was the raising of money 'in order to fill promoters' pockets'.[77]

Then in December 1895 the Jameson Raid took place. The critics of Rhodes and his business friends now had a far more serious accusation to make against the BSA Co. For it seemed to many that Britain and the Boer Republics were being driven into an avoidable international conflict by men concerned only with the hope of financial gain. Radical 'Little Englanders', allied to many Irish Nationalists and Labour men, were accordingly loud in their denunciations of 'stock-jobbing Imperialism' and of the shady financiers they thought were pursuing their nefarious activities under cover of the Union Jack.

In the aftermath of the Jameson Raid, the Commons set up the South Africa Committee in an attempt to allocate responsibility for what had happened. One of its members was Labouchere himself, who, unsupported by his fellow Liberals, attempted to use the Committee as a forum for the exposure of the chartered company. In articles in *Truth* and in another published by the Belgian journal, *Gaulois*, the Radical scandalmonger boldly claimed that there was a syndicate of financiers who had hoped to make money out of the raid. Unfortunately, 'Labby's' victims did not, as expected, bring in a libel suit which might have furnished him with the evidence he needed to substantiate his case. In consequence, Labouchere was forced to tender an apology, while the Select Committee almost entirely ignored the question of how the BSA Co. had raised its money and manipulated its shares.[78] In fact, the other Liberals were intensely irritated by Labouchere's behaviour. Campbell-Bannerman later held him partly responsible for the Committee's failure: 'He was continually running about declaring that he had got wonderful evidence in his pocket which when it was examined always came to nothing.'[79]

Nevertheless, Labouchere's indictment of the 'capitalist interests' at work in South Africa played an important part in the developing Radical-Socialist critique of British Imperialism. His case was concisely stated in a letter of 28 May 1897:

Rightly or wrongly, I have contended in the House and out of it, that the Rhodes group has subordinated everything (?) to the Stock Exchange. It started with a huge paper Capital, as the Chartered Cy, having then alone Mashonaland. Finding no gold there, it seized on Manicaland from the Portuguese. When no gold was forthcoming, and as there was no gold there it found itself in this position . . . a smash was certain. Therefore they had only one chance—to get hold of some new territory, and they raided and revolutionized in the Transvaal, to be able to annex the rich Rand District. . . . Never since the South Sea Bubble has there been such an impudent financial

---

[77] *Investors' Review*, Mar., Apr. 1894, later republished in Wilson, A. J., *An Empire in Pawn* (London, 1909), Chs. 17–18.

[78] *Truth*, 9 Jan., 16 Jan. 1896; Butler, J., *The Liberal Party and the Jameson Raid* (Oxford, 1968), p. 174.

[79] Hind, *Labouchere*, pp. 24–6. Butler, *Jameson Raid*, p. 177.

speculation against the public as that of these people, trading under the guarantees involved in a Royal Charter, and a lot of grandees being put on the Board by the Government.[80]

Some of these points were restated in Labouchere's 'minority report' on the South African Committee. 'The plan was devised', he claimed, 'and sought to be carried out, in order that certain wealthy men might become more wealthy.' Labouchere was particularly scathing about Alfred Beit, whom he described in language strikingly similar to that which the Radical Right would later use about the so-called 'Radical Plutocrats'; 'He is a German subject, living under the protection of our laws, and profiting by our hospitality to pursue his remunerative calling.' Because the Committee had not been given access to the BSA Co.'s books, Labouchere admitted that it was impossible to *prove* that the organizers of the Jameson Raid had been strongly influenced by financial considerations of a personal character, but he believed that the available evidence pointed in that direction.[81] This was also the opinion of other Radical MPs, like Philip Stanhope, who, in a Commons attack on the chartered company in July 1897, spoke of a *'fin-de-siècle* patriotism, which had its nursery on the Stock Exchange'.[82]

The view that Imperialism was fuelled by sinister capitalist interests, aided and abetted by a 'bought' syndicated press, received a futher boost when Britain found itself at war with the Transvaal and the Orange Free State in October 1899. Both socialists and Lib.-Lab. working men instinctively distrusted anything that suggested 'the capitalist exploitation of labour'.[83] Their viewpoint was, to some extent, shared by Irish Nationalists like MacNeill, who spoke of 'a Stock Exchange Government promoting a Stock Exchange war for Stock Exchange purposes'.[84]

True, once the War had broken out, most senior Liberal MPs who criticized it did so by attacking the provocative diplomacy of Milner and Chamberlain which had made hostilities inevitable, steering clear of theories of 'capitalist conspiracy', for which in any case firm evidence was lacking. This was also a course of political prudence. The hot-headed Liberal backbencher, Arthur Markham, was unwise enough to make a speech outside Parliament in which he charged Messrs. Beit and Eckstein with being thieves and swindlers in the part they had played in operations in South Africa; for his pains, he was sued for libel and forced to make a humiliating retraction.[85]

[80] Labouchere to Harcourt, 28 May 1897, cited in Butler, *Jameson Raid*, pp. 175–6.
[81] Second Report from the Select Committee on British South Africa Company, 1897, vol. ix, esp. p. lix.   [82] *Parl. Deb.*, 4th ser., li. 1098 (26 July 1897).
[83] Porter, *Critics of Empire*, p. 128; Koebner, R. and Schmidt, H. D., *The Story and Significance of Imperialism: A Political Word 1840–1960* (Cambridge, 1965), p. 231.
[84] *Parl. Deb.*, 4th ser., lxxxii. 1131 (8 May 1900).
[85] Walker-Smith and Clarke, *Edward Clarke*, pp. 279–80.

J. A. Hobson shared this anxiety to uncover the economic interests which underlay the conflict in South Africa. But, following in the footsteps perhaps of men like Labouchere, he also made an important modification of the Cobdenite view of politics which had coloured the 'anti-Imperialism' of most late Victorian Radicals. As Koebner and Schmidt put it, in Hobson's theory of Imperialism 'a Cobdenite ground-plan is unmistakable. But the original motive has been transferred, so to speak, to another historical level. The pernicious parasites are no longer identified with the privileged remnants of feudal society; they are the outgrowth of capitalist society.'[86]

In fact, there are two somewhat distinct elements in Hobson's economic theory of Imperialism, as Bernard Porter has shown. On the one hand, there is the argument that maldistribution of wealth at home produces under-consumption and over-saving, and hence speculative investment in underdeveloped overseas territories, which in turn is the prelude to subsequent conquest and annexation. On the other hand, in his account of the Boer War Hobson emphasizes the sinister role of 'Randlords' and financiers seeking to involve the British State in the furtherance of their selfish interests.[87] 'We are fighting in order to place a small international oligarchy of mine-owners and speculators in power at Pretoria', claimed Hobson in 1900.[88] Chamberlain was merely an 'instrument' in the carrying out of their designs.

In such 'conspiracy theories' Cecil Rhodes was, understandably, frequently singled out for denunciation. But equally common was the portrayal of the 'international Jew' of Johannesburg as the hidden manipulator of British Government policy. Labour men and Irish Nationalists were particularly prone to voice these sentiments.[89] But Hirst of the *Economist* took a similar line. As far as he was concerned, the South African War was a Stock Exchange ramp, pure and simple. 'How is democracy to know or even to suspect', he wrote in 1900, 'that its Ministers are a row of puppets, and that a board of international financiers sitting in Paris or Berlin or London pulls the wires, expecially if that same board controls a great part of the press?' Hirst was caustic about 'certain organ-voices which always sing private interests to the accompaniment of patriotic airs: "God save the Queen and enrich Baron Glückchild", "Rule Britannia and ennoble Herr Oppenbeit" '.[90] This takes us into Hilaire Belloc's fictional world,

---

[86] Koebner and Schmidt, *Imperialism*, p. 254.

[87] Porter, *Critics of Empire*, pp. 190–206.

[88] Hobson, J. A., *The War in South Africa: Its Causes and Effects* (London, 1900), p. 197.

[89] Koebner and Schmidt, *Imperialism*, p. 228.

[90] Hirst, F. W., Murray, G., and Hammond, J. L., *Liberalism and the Empire* (London, 1900), pp. 59, 30.

which is peopled by such great patriots and Builders of the Empire as Mr I. Z. Barnett.[91]

There was also an anti-Semitic tinge to the utterances of men like John Burns, and to the writings of Hobson himself. For as Peter Clarke notes, Hobson had a particular reason for emphasizing the manipulative role of the big Jewish financiers: he 'wanted to confute twice over the patriotic claim that the interests at stake [in South Africa] were "national"; once by showing that they were sectional, and again by showing that they were cosmopolitan'.[92] Anti-war Radicals could find no more telling way of indicating their own patriotism than by seeking to show that Imperialism was a conspiracy to draw the British Government into a fight for 'international Jewish interests'.

From this crude starting-point Hobson went on to fashion the sophisticated critique of British overseas expansion which he communicated to the world in his famous book, *Imperialism* (1902). And in this book Hobson made a shrewd prediction: the subjugation of the Boer Republics, he wrote, would shortly be followed by an attack on the principles and practice of Free Trade.[93]

When this did, indeed, occur with Chamberlain's launching of the Tariff Reform crusade in May 1903, the issue of corruption was once again brought into the very forefront of political discussion. Chamberlain's opponents, those within the Unionist Party as well as those outside it, had a large array of arguments to use against fiscal reform, but fundamental to the Free Trade case was the proposition that Chamberlain's programme amounted in practice to Protection, which in turn threatened the basis of British public life.

Protectionism, said the Liberal MP and shipowner, Russell Rea, meant 'the deterioration of the moral standard both of commerce and politics'.

The inner history of every modern protective tariff is a history of commercial and political corruption. When once it has been established in a democratic State, the minute minority of protected capitalists, in alliance in some cases with an agrarian party, always manage to rule the community in their own interests. Whatever may be the momentary subject of political controversy, whatever may be the issue of which the voters are conscious at a general election, at the back stand the financial potentates and monopolists to guard the tariff by which they live and were brought into being. If public opinion is becoming rebellious, public opinion is found to be an article which can be manufactured at a cost—newspapers are started or captured and subsidised, universities are endowed, the springs of truth and knowledge are poisoned, the fountain of justice itself is contaminated. Above all, the organisations of

---

[91] Belloc, Hilaire, *Emmanuel Burden* (London, 1904). Note also the *Speaker's* mocking invocation of a fictitious Rhodesian candidate for West Barford—Albert Stäubenschwängl (6 Oct. 1900).

[92] Clarke, P., *Liberals and Social Democrats* (Cambridge, 1978), p. 92.

[93] Hobson, J. A., *Imperialism: A Study* (London, 1902), esp. p. 67.

political parties are made secure, party funds are always insufficient, the 'sinews of war' decide the event, and pensioners inevitably become tools.

Russell Rea cited the United States to prove his point that 'the forces of greed, of corruption, and of wealth' would inexorably strangle freedom in a democracy where Protectionism held sway.[94]

Faced by what he saw as a 'pitiful Birmingham swindle', the idiosyncratic A. J. Wilson was confirmed in his earlier economic views. He blamed it on the landowning classes for plunging into expenditure far beyond their means. Finding that there were no longer such rich pickings to be had from directorships and having lost vast amounts of money themselves in recent speculations, the landlords, said Wilson, were now turning 'with feverish eagerness towards a protective tariff, a duty on corn, as the one last hope of salvation'. Moreover, the greedy company promoter, whose sins were now finding him out, was clamouring for some way of escape, 'some device whereby the consequences of his misdeed [might] be kept concealed for a little time longer, and he himself secured in the enjoyment of dividends wrung out of defrauded labour by dishonestly excessive capitalisations'. Wilson concluded: 'Thus national extravagance is in harmony with private extravagance, and dishonesty in the public services with dishonesty in business at large—particularly joint-stock business—in producing a combination of interests determined to drive the country back into Protectionism.'[95]

More orthodox were the 'moral' objections to Chamberlain's Tariff Reform initiative mobilized by Sydney Buxton in a much-used political handbook:

(a) That it would be impossible to decide which particular industry should be selected for protection; and pressure, wire-pulling, and corruption would be rampant; (b) That, under Protection, the general interest is left out of account. In the United States, the capitalists and protected manufacturers spend millions at the elections, dictate to a considerable extent the nomination of members of Congress, control its actions, own the great newspapers, purchase favourable legislation, and debauch the people.—(c) That free trade has done much to maintain a high standard and absolute purity in the British Government, House of Commons, and Civil Service.[96]

These arguments carried conviction to those who remembered the dispute in Parliament over the railway rates question in the 1890s, when industry was pitted against industry, and locality against locality, as each affected interest group sought to achieve a preferential

---

[94] Rea, R., *Free Trade in Being* (London, 1908), pp. 211–12.

[95] Wilson, A. J., 'The Forces Behind Protection', *Investors' Review*, 10 June 1905, republished in *An Empire in Pawn*, pp. 189–90.

[96] Buxton, S., *A Handbook to Political Questions of the Day* (London, 1903 edn.) p. 372.

treatment for itself.[97] How much worse would be the manœuvring that accompanied the introduction of a general tariff.

Chamberlain did his best, of course, to quieten these fears; for example, he avoided the term 'Protection', with all its sinister connotations, adopting instead the more progressive-sounding 'Tariff Reform'. Moreover, in Chamberlain's great speeches the safeguarding of vital home industries against 'unfair foreign competition' was invariably subordinated to the larger design of Imperial Preference, aimed at preserving Britain's relative power in an international environment where the scales were tilting against her. Chamberlain also tempered the 'materialism' of his appeal by calls for patriotic sacrifice.

But critics looked behind Chamberlain's rhetoric to the business groups that were financing the rapidly expanding Tariff Reform League and noted that the impressive Tariff Commission, which had been set up to work out how in practice a tariff schedule might operate, was staffed, not just by academics, like its secretary, Professor Hewins, but also by representatives of industries hard hit by foreign competition, notably, iron and steel, tin, glass, and chemicals.[98] Could men drawn from such a background allow themselves the luxury of treating the fiscal issue in an impartial and scientific manner? Winston Churchill, a backbench Conservative who was soon to cross the floor of the House, largely because of his abhorrence of Tariff Reform, articulated the fears of traditionalists in all parties when he wrote to Balfour, predicting that Chamberlain's policy, once begun, 'must lead to the establishment of a complete Protective system, involving commercial disaster, and the Americanisation of English politics'.[99] And Lord Hugh Cecil, a Unionist Free Fooder who stayed loyal to his Party, later wrote bitterly: 'We are passionately afraid of Protection. We think that it will lead to corruption and class divisions, to a general Americanizing of our politics. . . .'[100] This brand of political moralism was important to all the Free Traders, and presumably made a contribution to the Liberals' sweeping victory of 1906, in a general election dominated by the fiscal argument.

In time the Tariff Reformers ceased to be so defensive about the 'interests' supporting their cause and counter-attacked by asking questions about who precisely it was that was financing the Free Trade organizations and the Liberal Party. They concluded that a high

---

[97] Williams, P. M., 'Public Opinion and the Railway Rates Question in 1886', *English Historical Review*, lxvii (1952), 37–73.

[98] Semmel, B., *Imperialism and Social Reform* (London, 1960), pp. 102–4; Mock, W., *Imperiale Herrschaft und nationales Interesse* (Stuttgart, 1982), pp. 121–55.

[99] Churchill to Balfour, 25 May 1903, cited in Churchill, Randolph, S., *Winston S. Churchill, ii. Young Statesman 1901–1914* (London, 1967), p. 58.

[100] Hugh Cecil to Balfour, 4–6 May 1907 (BL, Balfour papers, Add. MS 49, 759, fos. 185–6).

proportion of the Free Traders' money came from 'cosmopolitan financiers', some of them 'aliens' with little interest in those issues of national security which underlay the Tariff Reform campaign. By March 1914 the pro-Tariff Reform *National Review* could proclaim: 'Cobdenism stands for corruption, that is the long and the short of it.'[101] But all that lay in the future. Prior to the 1906 election it was the Liberal Opposition and the Unionist Free Fooders who had taken possession of the high ground of morality, while the fiscal reformers seemed to be putting at risk Britain's nobler political traditions in their pursuit of material gain.

Contracting Scandals: The Butler Committee Report

The closing years of the Unionist Administration were also marked by a fresh batch of contracting scandals arising out of the South African War. These scandals, unlike the Kynoch's Affair, did not touch the *honour* of ministers, but they did bring their capacity into question, while, more important still, they gave ammunition to those Radicals and Socialists eager to associate Imperialism with corruption. 'Whoever may have suffered', quipped Campbell-Bannerman, 'it is clear that the contractor has done well out of the war.'[102] And *Punch* later published a Bernard Partridge cartoon, depicting 'the Boa-War-Contractor' crushing the taxpaying rabbit to death.[103]

Discontent with the waste and venality surrounding the allocation of contracts re-surfaced in March 1902, when the Opposition brought forward the following Motion: 'That a select committee be appointed to inquire into all contracts and purchases made by or on behalf of the Government for His Majesty's forces in South Africa in respect of remounts, meat, forage, freights, and transport.'[104] This time Lloyd George did not join in the attack. 'I have no interest' in the matter, he confided to his wife on 14 March. 'There is not much of a case and personally I do not care a scrap how much they are swindled over their contracts. The one great crime is the war itself. All the rest follows.'[105]

Campbell-Bannerman's Motion was negatived by 346 votes to 191. It may not have been sensible to press for a division at all. For the Government took the line that holding an enquiry while the War was in progress would simply clog the wheels of the administrative machine. Moreover, argued Ministers, such an action might even prejudice Britain's conduct of future campaigns, since officials would be afraid to assume responsibility for sanctioning extraordinary

---

[101] *National Review*, lxiii (1914), 14.
[102] *Parl. Deb.*, 4th ser., cv. 187 (17 Mar. 1902).
[103] *Punch*, 21 June 1905. See Figure 1.
[104] *Parl. Deb.*, 4th ser., cv. 185 (17 Mar. 1902).
[105] Lloyd George to Wife, 14 Mar. 1902, cited in Morgan, K.O. (ed.), *Lloyd George Family Letter 1885–1936* (Cardiff, 1973), pp. 129–30.

THE BOA-WAR-CONTRACTOR.

Tax-payer Rabbit. "TAKE NOTICE! THIS IS POSITIVELY THE *LAST* TIME I SUBMIT TO THIS TREATMENT!"

["Are the tax-payers of this country to continue to be the sport of questionable contractors?"
Report of the Committee on the Army Stores Scandals.]

1. The Boa-War-Contractor
(*Punch*, 21 June 1905)

expenditure at a time of crisis. Consequently, the Government chose to treat the motion as one of no confidence in itself. And since there was no majority in the House for turning the Government out, the Opposition attack was bound to be beaten off easily. But there was disquiet over the malpractices which had undoubtedly taken place. The best that could be said of the War Office's bungling performance was that, in contrast to the Crimean campaign, the British troops were not suffering any great privation and the only way in which the war effort had been hindered was through the poor quality of the remounts—a matter into which the Government soon afterwards authorized a specific investigation.[106]

On the other hand, Campbell-Bannerman had good cause to protest at the way in which the taxpayer's money had been squandered. The Cold Storage Company, for example, had secured so favourable a contract that it had been able to pay out dividends and bonuses equal to a return of 30s. on every £1 share, as well as placing another £1 million in the reserves.[107] The critics also made great play with the fact that the War Office seemed to have been taken advantage of by syndicates of contractors whose motives scarcely stood up to examination. 'Large vested interests', complained Campbell-Bannerman, 'have apparently quartered themselves upon the war', and he spoke bitterly of

the syndicates and combinations, which reach from the River Plate to the meat factories of Queensland, embracing the great mining corporation of De Beers, great firms of shipowners, who also turn out to be horse-dealers and meat producers, embracing, also, English—for the most part naturalised English—meat contractors and Johannesburg financiers whose names for good or for evil ring throughout the world.[108]

In one of his last effective parliamentary speeches Labouchere went on to throw some light on the complicated world of these men, who bore names like Bergl, Joel, Meyer, and Weil. Ministers may have been 'perfectly honest, well-meaning and painstaking', 'Labby' conceded, but they were no match for these unscrupulous operators.[109]

But though Ministers themselves may have been gullible rather than corrupt, the same could not be said of all the army officers and War Office officials concerned with the provisioning of the troops in South Africa.[110] So much became apparent when in June 1905 an Army

---

[106] *Parl. Deb.*, 4 ser., cv. 185–287, 334–438 (17 Mar., 18 Mar. 1902).
[107] Ibid. 194 (17 Mar. 1902).   [108] Ibid. 187.   [109] Ibid. 201–16.
[110] Corruption was rife in other departments of the British Army, especially in the army canteens, which were investigated by a War Office Committee in 1902. It concluded that 'bribery and corruption [had] flourished under the regimental system, tenancy system and district contract system alike' (Cd. 1424). The Report persuaded the Lord Chancellor to reintroduce his Bill dealing with bribes and commissions, but it again failed for want of parliamentary time, after successfully passing through the Lords (Doig, *Corruption and Misconduct*, pp. 76–7).

Council Committee, appointed to consider the question of Sales and Refunds to Contractors in South Africa, produced what *The Times* called 'one of the most startling documents presented to Parliament for a great number of years'—a report which had caused 'a profound impression not merely amongst the lovers of scandalous "sensations", but amongst all who have at heart the honour and the welfare of the Army and of the Empire'.[111]

The impact made by this report was partly reduced by the extravagant and, some thought, tasteless rhetoric in which it was couched. There are not many Blue Books which contain phrases like 'some clumsy pantaloon in putties—even some agile harlequin in a helmet'.[112] In fact, both the language and the censorious tone of the report clearly owed much to the Committee's Chairman, General Sir William Butler, an irascible Irishman, with remarkably progressive opinions for a senior army officer. Campbell-Bannerman privately called Butler 'perhaps our foremost military authority: advanced Radical: Home Ruler: Catholic—no means to spare', and wondered whether he could be persuaded to run for the next Parliament as a Liberal candidate. This did not prove possible,[113] but Butler was clearly not averse to helping the Liberals by causing the Unionist Government maximum embarrassment.

But even if allowance is made for Butler's personal spleen and political prejudice, it is still the case that the 'story told by the report was most startling and disagreeable'.[114] For the Butler Committee revealed that, long after the War had ended, huge quantities of stores had continued to pile up in the South African depots. The Sales Department established by the Army Service Corps at Pretoria had then proceeded to sell off goods to contractors at very low prices, only, in some cases, for these same goods to be subsequently sold back to the Army at a huge profit. The most quoted example was one which involved the machinations of a contractor called Meyer.[115] It was also disturbing to learn that the original Director of Supplies, responsible for the disposal of stores, Colonel Morgan, was the brother of a certain Frank Morgan, described in the Report as 'the agent of "mushroom

[111] *The Times*, 15 June 1905.
[112] Report of Committee Appointed by the Army Council to Consider the Question of Sales and Refunds to Contractors in South Africa, 1905, Cd. 2435, para. 60. *Punch* (21 June 1905) expressed delight with this novel literary style and hoped it might become standard for official documents.
[113] Campbell-Bannerman to Herbert Gladstone, 23 Dec. 1904 (BL, Herbert Gladstone papers, Add. MS 45,988, fo. 134). Butler came close to being adopted as the Liberal candidate for East Leeds, but he finally withdrew because his views on the education question, though acceptable to the local Irish community, were irreconcilable with those of most Liberal voters (Bernstein, G. L., 'Liberalism and the Progressive Alliance in the Constituencies, 1900–1914: Three Case Studies', *Historical Journal*, xxvi (1983), 626).
[114] *Annual Register*, 1905, p. 174.   [115] Cd. 2435. paras. 64–71.

companies" [and] the salaried servant of favoured firms', including that of Meyer.[116] As for Meyer himself, 'various nationalities are ascribed to him', said the Report. One of the few hard facts was that he had formerly been connected with the Cold Storage Company![117]

The Butler Report censured a number of army officers, including Colonel Morgan and his successor, Colonel Hipwell, who was adjudged to be 'entirely unfit' for his postion.[118] It also criticized the War Office's administrative system. A high-ranking officer aided by trained staff, it argued, should have been sent out to South Africa as soon as the War had ended. Instead, officers who were 'tired and stale from their labours on active service' found themselves pitted against men 'versed in every detail of the Colonial contractor's art, who would be certain to redouble their various financial activities in the face of the cessation of the source of profit from which they had already drawn so large a harvest'.[119] Butler's anti-Imperialist sympathies came over most clearly in his rhetorical denunciation of such men: 'Are the taxpayers of this country', he asked, 'to continue to be the sport of the many questionable contractors who are as ready to follow their several avocations in the wake of a war *as they are also willing to be its pioneers?*'[120] Thus did a distinguished General heading an official enquiry give further encouragement to the idea that colonial wars had their origin in the corrupt machinations of a handful of interested speculators and entrepreneurs.

But the Butler Report also produced evidence which suggested that some officials and soldiers were probably guilty of corruption. The Committee said that it had been forced to abandon its original view that the 'scandals' it had unearthed were due to individual error or culpable negligence, and had fallen back on 'the impression of cleverly-arranged contrivance'.[121] Such obscurely phrased sentences caused understandable irritation; specific accusations should have been made, it was said, or, failing that, the innuendoes should have been entirely dropped.[122] In any case, as the embarrassed War Secretary, Arnold-Forster, pointed out in his preface to the Report, the evidence was 'clearly and admittedly incomplete' and the document could not therefore be 'regarded as a judicial finding'.[123]

But this, of course, did not propitiate the Opposition, which lost no time in publicly raising the whole question of the South African War Stores. The Liberals' main concern was to pin responsibility for what had gone wrong on the Cabinet. Not that there was any suggestion that Ministers had 'intended to connive at corruption, or anything of that

---

[116] Cd. 2435. paras. 41, 23.   [117] Ibid., para. 25.
[118] Ibid., para. 101.   [119] Ibid., para. 46.   [120] Ibid., para. 59.
[121] Ibid., para 33. There were other similar phrases: for example, a reference to 'substantial financial persons moving in a background which we cannot pierce' (para. 39).
[122] *The Times*, 15 June 1905.   [123] Cd. 2435, preface.

kind', as Robert Reid put it, but the Butler Report strongly implied that some of them had been incompetent, inattentive, and dilatory in taking remedial action, once it had become obvious that something was seriously amiss.[124]

In the face of this attack, the Unionist Administration was obliged to promise that a further investigation of the charges would shortly take place; in the meantime, officers who had been censured or who were under suspicion were suspended from duty.[125] And so a Royal Commission of Enquiry was set up, which reported twelve months later, when the Liberals were back in office.

Though the tone of this second Report could hardly have differed more sharply from Sir William Butler's document, it reached broadly similar conclusions. It estimated that the total preventable loss to the taxpayer during the twenty-two months following the end of the War had been between £750,000 and £1,125,000. Such figures, however, could only be a rough estimate, since, as the Royal Commission explained, the Army's accounting procedures were so rudimentary. And this absence of an adequate system of accounts, it suggested, may well have contributed to both 'improvidence and peculation in South Africa'. Moreover, the business of the Director of Supplies was found to have been conducted 'with inexcusable carelessness and extraordinary ineptitude', and, more worrying still, the Auditor-General, to whose vigilance and pertinacity the revelations made were largely due, had actually been obstructed in his enquiries by certain War Office officials. The Royal Commission concluded that large surpluses had been 'fraudulently disposed of', and though the highest officials were all exonerated, it spoke of the prevalence of petty corruption among the NCOs involved.[126]

The incoming Liberal Government quickly acted upon this Report. Twelve officers were punished, some being dismissed from the Army, and action was also taken against a number of NCOs and private soldiers. In addition, to prevent a recurrence of such administrative bungling, the new War Secretary, Haldane, decided to send certain members of the War Office's administrative staff to be trained on a special course organized by the London School of Economics.[127] Once these actions had been announced, public interest in the South African war contractors simply melted away.

Yet the issue was important in three quite different ways. In the first place, it had alerted the country to what would later be called 'profiteering'. As Robert Reid put it in 1902, there were certain kinds of

[124] *Parl. Deb.*, 4th ser. cxlviii. 107 (26 June 1905).
[125] Ibid. cxlvii. 1103–6 (20 June 1905).
[126] Report of Royal Commission on War Stores in South Africa, 1906, Cd. 3127, esp. paras. 218–24.
[127] Beatrice Webb's diary, 21 Nov. 1906, in MacKenzie (eds.), *Diary of Beatrice Webb*, iii. 59.

contractor 'prowling about the Army and the departments of State anxious to make an unclean profit out of the sacrifices of the country'.[128] These evil men, a reader of *Hansard* would have learned, were often of indeterminate nationality, bore Germanic-sounding names, and in many cases were Jewish. Those that had British citizenship tended to be naturalized. They moved in a murky world which it was difficult for outsiders to penetrate, but they often turned out to be connected, in some way or other, with a prominently placed official. Moreover, they lacked any spark of patriotic feeling, were sometimes members of a syndicate with international ramifications, and were animated purely by material greed. Thus a stereotype of the 'war profiteer' came into being. The word had not yet been coined, but the attributes of this sinister figure had already been clearly described, ready for use once the First World War broke out.

Secondly, the war contracts scandals helped draw attention to the growing importance of international syndicates and combines. This had not been true of the Kynoch's Affair. As Clive Trebilcock has noted, there was no suggestion that Kynoch's was part of a Trust; indeed, 'the exact point of the allegations was that, owing to a special family connection, a *single* armament firm had been preferred to others.'[129] Belief in the existence of a vast armaments 'ring' straddling national frontiers was not widespread until British pacifists and anti-war socialists began echoing the charges which Liebknecht made in the Reichstag in 1913.[130]

On the other hand, it is significant that in the Commons debate of 1902 many MPs discussed the worrying possibility that groups of contractors ostensibly in competition with one another were actually in collusion, and there were hints that the British Government had fallen dependent for some of its supplies upon supra-national organizations enjoying a quasi-monopolistic position. Was it a mere coincidence that this debate occurred at almost the same time as Pierpont Morgan was successfully amalgamating Atlantic shipping in a single Trust, which threatened to bring nearly all the major British shipping firms, bar Cunard, under partial American control?[131] Coincidence or not, the two events made many British people, on both the Left and Right, fearful of the sinister power of 'Trusts' and of the 'cosmopolitan

---

[128] *Parl. Deb.*, 4th ser., cxlviii. 108–9 (26 June 1905).

[129] Trebilcock, C., 'Radicalism and the Armament Trust', in Morris, A. J. A. (ed.), *Edwardian Radicalism, 1900–1914* (London, 1974), p. 191.

[130] See below, Ch. 8, p. 197 and Appendix I.

[131] Heindel, R. H., *The American Impact on Great Britain, 1898–1914* (New York, 1968; 1st edn., 1940), pp. 150–1; *Parl. Deb.*, 4th ser., cvii 458–94 (1 May 1902) and cviii. 846–69 (28 May 1902). It is interesting that one of the most outspoken of the critics of 'Trusts' was Lord Charles Beresford. See also Macrosty, H. W., 'State Control of Trusts', Fabian Tract no. 124, 1905.

financiers' who directed them. Much more was to be heard about this development during the decade that followed.

Thirdly, and on a quite different plane, the mishandling by the Government of the allocation of war contracts adversely affected the public standing of the Unionist Administration. The reputation not only of the War Secretary but also of the Prime Minister suffered damage. For when the Butler Report first came before Parliament in June 1905, Balfour was very slow to respond to the mood of the House, and, to quote the *Annual Register*, had 'had to be practically coerced by pressure' in the Commons to take the matter seriously.[132] He had then procrastinated when faced by demands for a Royal Commission with powers to take evidence on oath (i.e. a statutory Commission).[133] On 22 June the Prime Minister finally accepted this as the only possible *modus operandi*, but, to again quote the *Annual Register*, 'an appreciable amount of time, and still more of Mr Balfour's reputation for the conduct of Parliamentary business, was lost through these passages'.[134] Thus the affair of the South African war contracts contributed, albeit in a minor way, to the disintegration of the Unionist Government later in the year.

[132] *Annual Register*, 1905, p. 175.
[133] *Parl. Deb.*, 4th ser., cxlvii. 1217–24 (21 June 1905) and 1341–8 (22 June 1905).
[134] *Annual Register*, 1905, p. 175.

4

Honours Trafficking and the Problem
of the Press, 1895–1905

Radical Views of the Unionist Administration

THE Radical-Liberal assault on the laxity allegedly shown by the Salisbury and Balfour Governments should not be seen merely as the effort of an opposition party to discredit its opponents. For when Liberals censured Unionist Ministers for their lack of 'disinterestedness', they were invoking an ideal which was central to their political thought, in which sectional and class interests were held in abhorrence.[1] Indeed, Liberals were inclined to preen themselves as historical agents of political purification. They recalled with pride their assaults earlier in the nineteenth century on 'Old Corruption' and their campaigns to abolish favouritism and nepotism in the civil service.

Yet Liberals believed that, despite these achievements, the vestiges of a corrupt pre-industrial order—or 'feudalism', as they often called it—had survived the movement for reform, thanks to the efforts of their opponents. It was this belief which underlay their attacks on the Conservative Party, which they portrayed as engaged in an aristocratic conspiracy against 'the People'. Landlords, in particular, were accused of treating politics as a means of perpetuating the 'unearned' privileges which enabled them to prey upon the wider community.

In 1896 the Liberal Party was confirmed in this view of the world by the Unionist Government's introduction of the Agricultural Land Rating Bill, a measure intended to relieve farmers of part of their financial burdens at a time of acute agricultural depression by using £1 million of Exchequer money to relieve the rates on agricultural land. But the Opposition argued that the main beneficiaries of the legislation would be not the farmers, but the Tory Party's friends, the squires and the parsons. The *Speaker* complained that the already vast rentals of the Duke of Devonshire and the Duke of Bedford had been increased, and that what had really happened was that a landlord-dominated Cabinet had paid out 'huge doles' to the landlords.[2] William Harcourt led the Liberal onslaught on the Rating Bill—which his admiring biographer dubbed a 'daring raid on the public purse in the interests of

---

[1] The tradition can be traced from John Stuart Mill's attacks on 'class legislation' through T. H. Green's concept of the 'common good' to L. T. Hobhouse's belief in the possibility of 'social harmony'.

[2] *Speaker*, 1 Dec. 1900.

a class'.[3] And Lloyd George virtually accused prominent Ministers of corruption by estimating the financial benefits they were likely to secure from their legislation; the Prime Minister would be better off by £2,000, he claimed, the Duke of Devonshire by £10,000, Balfour by £1,450, and Chaplin, who as President of the Local Government Board was responsible for the measure, by £700.[4] In the 1900 Election some Radical candidates repeated these allegations, linking the rating issue to the Boer War contracting scandals, both being presented as evidence of the Unionist Government's propensity to 'look after its own'.[5]

The narrow social composition of the Unionist Cabinet was also attacked, particularly after the 1900 reshuffle which gave rise to the joke about Britain being governed from the 'Hotel Cecil'. 'We must resolutely protest against an oligarchic attempt to govern the country through one or two great families', wrote *The Economist*.[6]

Halsbury's behaviour as Lord Chancellor fitted easily into this picture of governmental impropriety. *Truth* fulminated at his 'shameless abuse of his powers',[7] and many others were convinced that Halsbury was perpetrating 'jobs' by making appointments to the judicial bench on narrowly political grounds. Within the legal world ritual stories are still told about Halsbury's jovial cynicism in this area of his work.[8] One of his most unpopular judicial appointments was that of Charles Darling, a young barrister whose main claim to fame was his composition of light verses, but who had ingratiated himself with the Conservative managers by winning and holding for nine years the marginal seat of Deptford. So strongly did some barristers feel about Darling's elevation in 1897 that they presented a petition of protest to the Bar Council.[9] Halsbury may, in fact, have been unfairly treated in this respect. Historical research has shown that he was perhaps responsible for six 'bad' appointments out of a total of thirty,[10] but, surprisingly, it has also been shown that he selected proportionately fewer 'politicians' for the judicial bench than were selected in the 1850–1901 period, taken as a whole.[11]

Less easy to defend is Halsbury's policy with regard to filling

---

[3] Gardiner, A. G., *Life of Sir William Harcourt*, ii (London, n.d.), 406.

[4] See Offer, A., *Property and Politics 1870–1914* (Cambridge, 1981), pp. 208–10; Grigg, *Young Lloyd George*, pp. 203–5. Lloyd George and four other MPs were suspended for refusing to go into the division lobby as a protest against the closure of this Bill (ibid. 205).

[5] *Star*, 20 Sept. 1900. The candidate was B. S. Straus in St George's.

[6] *The Economist*, 15 Dec. 1900.

[7] *Truth*, 21 Dec. 1905. Why had the son of Finlay, the Attorney-General, been appointed to the post of Junior Counsel to the Board of Inland Revenue, it also asked (ibid., 14 Dec. 1905).

[8] Heuston, R. F. V., *Lives of the Lord Chancellors 1885–1940* (Oxford, 1964), pp. 36–7.

[9] Ibid., 55.

[10] Griffith, J. A. G., *The Politics of the Judiciary* (London, 1978), pp. 21–2.

[11] Duman, D., *The English and Colonial Bars in the Nineteenth Century* (London, 1983), pp. 181–2.

vacancies in the magistracy. Even before the Unionists' return to office in 1895 the Liberal Party had been complaining that their opponents had an unfair advantage due to the fact that the overwhelming majority of magistrates in rural areas were Unionists. This situation had largely come about through the wholesale desertion of the Liberal Party by the landed interest following Gladstone's espousal of Irish Home Rule. In consequence the Lords-Lieutenant who forwarded nominations to the Lord Chancellor's Office were nearly all Unionists and they tended to favour men with similar opinions—and social backgrounds—to their own.[12] In May 1893 the Liberals carried a resolution in the Commons declaring that county magistrates should not in future be appointed exclusively on the recommendation of the Lord-Lieutenant. Indeed, the Liberal Lord Chancellor, Lord Herschell, found his patience sorely tried when Liberal MPs, individually and in groups, tried to pressurize him into filling vacancies with 'good sound party men'.[13] It was a foretaste of the difficulties which would be experienced by the Liberal politician who next held that office thirteen years later.

But Halsbury during his tenure of office from 1895 to 1905 then proceeded to aggravate the imbalance by reversing Herschell's policy and relying solely on the Lords-Lieutenant, which meant that almost no one got on to the Commission of the Peace who was not a Conservative. The Liberals were determined that they would correct this anomaly as soon as they returned to power. Meanwhile they were bitter at what they saw as the blatantly partisan spirit being shown by the Unionist Lord Chancellor.

The Netheravon Affair

A controversy of an entirely different kind was that which involved the Chancellor of the Exchequer, Sir Michael Hicks Beach, the central figure in the so-called Netheravon Affair. This was perhaps a trivial enough episode in itself, but since it regularly cropped up in political debate right until the outbreak of the Great War, it merits brief discussion.

The trouble began when Hicks Beach was informed by Lansdowne, the War Secretary, that the War Office wanted to purchase part of his estate at Netheravon in Wiltshire for a new training ground—the origins of the present-day Salisbury Plain site. Hicks Beach agreed, but turned over responsibility for choosing the area and setting its price to Balfour and Lord Goschen, a former Chancellor. On counsel's advice the Government decided to proceed by compulsory purchase. The

[12] Heuston, *Lord Chancellors*, p. 114.
[13] Ibid. 114–17; Lee, J. L., 'Parliament and the Appointment of Magistrates. The Origins of Advisory Committees', *Parliamentary Affairs*, xiii (1959), 88–9.

valuation of the site was then entrusted to two arbitrators, who speedily reached a settlement which obviated any need for Goschen and Balfour to intervene.[14]

But the episode was a political embarrassment to Hicks Beach, since the sale of the estate brought in £93,700, freeing him from the financial difficulties into which he had been plunged by the agricultural depression, and as such it was bound to be seized upon by hostile critics. Perhaps it was embarrassment which made Sir Michael lose his temper when the issue was brought before the Commons in 1899. On this occasion the interrogator promptly apologized for having inadvertently wounded the Chancellor's feelings: 'we all know that the right hon. Gentleman is the very soul of honour', he said.[15]

But the Netheravon Affair was to haunt Hicks Beach for the rest of his life. His main tormentor was the gad-fly journalist, Arnold White, who kept nagging away at the subject for over a decade, perhaps hoping that he might goad his victim into filing a libel suit. White insisted that the Netheravon site had been grossly overvalued and that a reasonable price would have been between £33,000 and £38,000, if the basis of calculation had been its net rental. As custodian of the national finances, complained White, Sir Michael had failed in his responsibilities and this failure had cost the taxpayer a large sum of money, while he himself had benefited to the tune of £55,700.[16] White darkly hinted that 'the full facts have not come out' and that damaging evidence on the subject was in the hands of an unspecified Member of Parliament.[17]

This attack had enough substance to attract journalists with a greater reputation for accuracy and sound judgement than White ever commanded. In particular, Loe Strachey's *Spectator* came in time to the view that the Netheravon Affair had not been satisfactorily handled, though initially it went out of its way to defend Hicks Beach's role.[18] Later the whole episode was to be revived in a big way by Liberal politicians and journalists during the Marconi Scandal who used it as proof of the hypocrisy of Unionist claims that they had the purity of British public life close to their hearts. This in turn persuaded the junior partner of the solicitor who had acted for the War Office in the purchase to put on paper his understanding of what had occurred, an account which was then passed on to Bonar Law in case he needed to allude to it during the Marconi debate. The solicitor believed that

[14] Hicks Beach, Lady Victoria, *Life of Sir Michael Hicks Beach*, ii (London, 1932), 70–2.

[15] *Parl. Deb.*, 4th ser., lv. 880–1 (31 July 1899).

[16] White, A., *Efficiency and Empire* (London, 1901), p. 9.

[17] *Daily Dispatch*, 6 Nov. 1902.

[18] *Spectator*, 26 Aug. 1899, where it says (p. 27) that the sale has 'the appearance of a job', but that the Chancellor had 'behaved quite properly'. On 2 Sept. it hoped for an end to the controversy, in fairness to Hicks Beach (p. 303).

the Government had desperately wanted to buy this piece of land, which, in fact, it acquired quite cheaply at £11 18s. 11d. an acre; for when the Liberals later returned to power, the War Office had to pay out £26 an acre for an adjoining estate. This, he argued, proved that, had Hicks Beach 'declined to sell on account of his position, his estate would now be worth to him fully £200,000 on the War Office's own basis of value'.[19] But the solicitor's explanation of the Netheravon Affair was given in a confidential private letter, written a dozen years after the events it described. At the time the Chancellor's refusal to answer or to sue his critics allowed the suspicion to spread that perhaps something dishonourable really had occurred.

Unionist Honours Lists

More significant, however, than the Netheravon Affair was the howl of outrage which greeted Balfour's Resignation Honours List, divulged to the press in December 1905. Indeed, those who viewed with suspicion the behaviour of the Unionist Ministries between 1895 and 1905 had from the start assumed that the award of honours was far too closely tied to the party's fund-raising activities. All that Balfour's Resignation List had done was to underline these suspicions.

It has been argued that it was the unstable political situation in the mid 1880s, with three ministries between 1885 and 1886, followed by the Golden Jubilee of 1887, which was marked by its own honours list, which gave the initial impetus to the inflation in honours.[20] This was the period, too, when Prime Ministers and their Patronage Secretaries started to relax the conditions which qualified a man for a title. Before 1885 few businessmen received a peerage, since mere wealth, allied to business success, was not thought to provide a proper preparation for subsequent ennoblement.[21] Strangely enough, the Prime Minister who first took decisive steps to broaden the social composition of the peerage was the highly aristocratic Lord Salisbury, during his 'Caretaker Ministry' of 1885–6, when the brewer, Allsopp, and the banker, Mills, were made barons;[22] in all 23 per cent of Salisbury's creations went to businessmen.[23] Just as the barriers maintaining the exclusivity of 'Society' began to crumble, so the admission of 'social

---

[19] The solicitor's letter was forwarded to Bonar Law by Lord Bathurst on 18 June 1913 (HLRO, Bonar Law papers, 29/5/32).

[20] Lant, J. L., *Insubstantial Pageant: Ceremony and Confusion at Queen Victoria's Court* (London, 1979), p. 187.

[21] Hanham, H. J., 'The Sale of Honours in Late Victorian England', *Victorian Studies*, iii (1960), 278.

[22] Lant, *Insubstantial Pageant*, p. 188.

[23] Pumphrey, R. E., 'The Introduction of Industrialists into the British Peerage: A Study in Adaptation of a Social Institution', *American Historical Review*, lxv (1959), 8–9.

outsiders' into the ranks of the knighthood, baronetcy, and peerage proceeded apace.

'When is the "honour" correspondence to end?', Goschen asked Salisbury in 1887; 'it is frightful.'[24] But the embarrassment felt by some Ministers as they contemplated the growing mania for honours and decorations of all kinds was tempered by more earthy considerations. For as Michael Pinto-Duschinsky has explained, the fund-raisers of both parties were now ready to adopt increasingly unorthodox measures to fill their central war chests. The Corrupt and Illegal Practices Act of 1883 may have stamped out the cruder forms of electoral corruption by imposing upper limits on what candidates could spend in their constituencies, and one consequence of this, judging by the returns made by the candidates' agents, was a fairly steady decline in the sums of money devoted locally to election campaigns. Moreover, three years later Salisbury himself finally abolished the Secret Service Fund out of which governing parties had traditionally financed their electoral campaigns.[25]

But these two steps created considerable problems for both major parties. The sources of income for the central headquarters had been reduced just when they were being asked to increase their assistance to impecunious candidates and to undertake new propaganda activities. In contrast to what was happening at constituency level, the cost of national politics appreciably rose. Whereas in 1880 the Liberals' general election fund had been a modest £50,000, by 1910 the party was spending around £100,000 in each of the two elections fought in that year. Professor Hanham has calculated that the regular annual expenditure of the Liberal Party increased approximately tenfold between the 1860s and 1912.[26] A similar situation prevailed with their opponents. How did the financial managers of the parties succeed in raising these huge sums, deprived as they now were of the old Secret Service Fund and often competing with a host of semi-independent political pressure groups for their revenue?

One obvious expedient was for the Chief Whips to trade upon their power of bestowing honours and titles by promising to reward rich supporters who contributed generously to the party funds. The Liberals were exposed to this temptation as much as the Conservatives, and the first real 'honours scandal' broke in the mid 1890s as a consequence of a decision made by the Liberal Chief Whip and the Chief Party Organizer, Arnold Morley and Schnadhorst. In 1891 these two men seem to have struck a bargain with Sydney Stern, a Jewish banker, and James Williamson, a wealthy linoleum manufacturer, both of whom

[24] Cited in Lant, *Insubstantial Pageant*, p. 190.
[25] Pinto-Duschinsky, M., *British Political Finance 1830–1980* (Washington, 1981), pp. 26–8, 33.
[26] Hanham, 'Sale of Honours', p. 282.

had only recently joined the Liberal Party and carried no political authority; as a reward for large gifts of money to the party funds, Stern and Williamson were each promised a peerage when the Liberals returned to power. Gladstone himself must have approved of this transaction. Rosebery, Gladstone's successor as Liberal Leader and Prime Minister, felt obliged to honour the bargain, but the outcome led to criticism from all sides of the House.[27] Rosebery publicly denied that he had received 'one-farthing of corrupt consideration for these peerages' and called the suggestion that this had happened a 'scandalous lie'; 'we in the Liberal Party do not traffic in titles in that way'.[28] Such disclaimers did not save Williamson (or Lord Ashton, as he was now known) from social ostracism and worse.[29]

No one seriously doubted, even in the 1890s, that contributions to party funds led to the offer of an honour or title. It was quite another matter, of course, to prove the existence of a causal relationship between the two transactions. Moreover, the ethics of the honours trade were by no means easy to define. Everyone could agree that honours should only be given to men who had performed some distinguished public service; but what precisely was meant by 'public service'? Presumably, no one otherwise qualified for an honour should forfeit his claims simply because he had supported one of the main parties. Indeed, as Whiteley was later to argue, this might be taken as an additional recommendation in so far as it indicated a disinterested commitment to some political cause.[30] The second stage, however, was more controversial. Was it proper to give an honour to a man whose *principal* claim to fame was his generosity to the party? And what about rich nonentities whose 'public service' had taken the form of conspicuous support for a reputable charity, with one eye obviously fixed on the forthcoming honours list?

The third stage was reached when a perfectly honourable man, who had done nothing spectacular to put the country in his debt, was allowed to buy his title by means of a simple cash transaction, arranged perhaps by an intermediary or 'tout'. Fourthly—and all could agree on the impropriety of this—honours might be blatantly sold to rich men

[27] Ibid. 283–6. But for a different view of the episode, see Masterman, N., *The Forerunner: The Dilemmas of Tom Ellis 1859–1899* (Swansea, 1972), p. 255. An old acquaintance of the Stern family wrote to Gwynne in 1927 saying that he believed that Stern had given £50,000 to Liberal Party funds (Unknown to Gwynne, 7 Sept. 1927, Bodleian Library, Oxford, Gwynne papers, vol. 21).

[28] Speech at Wolverhampton, 18 Mar. 1896, cited in *Daily Express*, 8 Sept. 1927.

[29] He was still a hated figure during the Great War, Lord Balcarres believing that Ashton had virtually threatened to close his linoleum factory unless the recruiting officers stopped approaching his employees, a stand followed by other manufacturers in his home town of Lancaster who were under business obligations to him (Balcarres to Gwynne, 20 Jan. 1915, Gwynne papers, vol. 20).

[30] Whiteley's evidence to the 1922 Royal Commission on Honours (Cambridge University Library, Templewood papers, I.ii).

with shady reputations, even to men with criminal records, as happened in one or two cases during Lloyd George's later premiership. It was somewhere between stage one and stage three that a point was reached where the permissible shaded off into the downright corrupt, and it was in this murky, controversial area that the Unionist Ministry, like the Liberal Ministries which followed it, was obliged to operate during what Pinto-Duschinsky has aptly called 'The Plutocratic Era'.[31]

Many years later in 1922 Selborne told the Royal Commission on Honours that during the period when he had been the Liberal Unionist Whip (1887–92) and in the period prior to his appointment as South African High Commissioner in 1905 when he was still in touch with Conservative Central Office, 'he could not remember a single case . . . in which a man who had obviously no claim to special recognition had been able to purchase an Honour.'[32] This was an equivocal statement since it did not rule out the possibility that the chances of an otherwise title-worthy man might have been enhanced by generous contributions to the party funds. A few years earlier Selborne, in a confidential Memorandum which he showed to his brother-in-law, was somewhat franker; when he was Liberal Unionist Whip, he said, he had raised large sums of money 'with no difficulty and with clean hands', though he did recall one instance of honours trafficking which had been 'carried out by J(oseph) C(hamberlain)'s organisation in Birmingham'. But he added that Conservative Central Office had already set up the 'system' which Lloyd George was later to carry to much greater lengths.[33]

Despite the brief furore over the Williamson and Stern peerages, public opinion still viewed the idiosyncracies of the honours system more with amusement than alarm. When the Liberal MP, Wilfrid Lawson, brought a motion before the Commons in May 1894 urging Her Majesty to issue a statement of the services which recipients of honours had rendered, the ensuing debate was conducted in a frivolous spirit, with good-humoured badinage very much the order of the day. The House roared with laughter over the story of one mythical MP who had allegedly seceded to the other party in order to be made a baronet, before later returning to his original party to be made a peer. Harcourt joined in the spirit of the occasion and begged the House not to destroy the romance of titles and end a good deal of amusing debate as to why on earth certain people had been singled out for the Queen's recognition. The Motion was carried by 52 votes to 34.[34]

---

[31] Pinto-Duschinsky, *British Political Finance*, Ch. 2.

[32] Selborne's evidence to 1922 Honours Commission (Templewood papers).

[33] Selborne Memorandum, 17 Sept. 1918 (Hatfield, Fourth Marquess of Salisbury papers, 83/143–4).

[34] *Parl. Deb.*, 4th ser., xxiv. 410–17 (4 May 1894).

However, there was very little laughter when Hooley revealed in the bankruptcy court that not only had he paid over £30,000 to gain admission to the Carlton Club but that he had also handed over £50,000 to the Conservative Party managers in the hope of getting a baronetcy in the Jubilee Honours List. The Radical press wept crocodile tears over the humiliation which had been visited on the Carlton Club. 'What It Costs To Enter the Carlton', ran the *Daily News* headline, and in an accompanying editorial Hooley was somewhat implausibly described as 'a pillar of the party which loves to call itself Constitutional'.[35] Conservative journals were correspondingly dismayed. Wrote the *National Review*: 'The great majority of the members of the Carlton are honourable English gentlemen, who are thoroughly disgusted with this unpleasant transaction, whereby the reputation of their club has been compromised.' The *Review*'s editor, Maxse, went on to express the hope 'that a searching investigation will be held within the club to discover who are responsible for selling memberships to Hooleys and other vulgar bounders, whose room is more agreeable than their company'.[36]

What made the affair so embarrassing to loyal Conservative supporters was the role played by Sir William Marriott, a former Conservative MP and Solicitor-General and a Privy Councillor; Hooley first made his acquaintance as the man who 'did all the dirty work for the Conservative Party'.[37] Marriott, it was clear, encouraged Hooley in the belief that a baronetcy was purchasable. The two men had had a sordid haggle over its price, which had ended with the company promoter paying out £50,000 and Marriott stipulating that he would want £10,000 for himself when the deal was done. Marriott, without any doubt, was one of the early honours touts. Of course, Hooley's statements in the bankruptcy court should not be accepted at face value. On the other hand, it is significant that Marriott did not deny the charge on oath. Instead he contented himself with observing that both political parties were alike in their fund-raising methods.[38]

At Conservative Central Office all was consternation. Captain Middleton, the Party's Principal Agent, was 'bothered to death by the Press men trying to find out all about the Hooley donation to the funds—some apparently think old ? and myself have jumped it between us.'[39] At the Attorney-General's suggestion, Middleton then wrote the Prime Minister a formal explanation of his part in the transaction. According to this, he had told Marriott that Hooley's hope of purchasing an honour was 'ridiculous' and he had only, with reluctance, accepted the cheque after Marriott had asked him to keep it

---

[35] *Daily News*, 3 Nov. 1898.   [36] *National Review*, xxxii (1898), 475.
[37] *Daily Chronicle*, 15 Nov. 1898.   [38] Ibid.
[39] Middleton to 'Pom' McDonnell, 3 Nov. 1898 (Hatfield, Third Marquess of Salisbury papers, E).

securely in his safe for the period that Hooley was out of town; on the company promoter's reappearance in London, Marriot took the cheque away.[40] In addition, the Party Trustees paid back to Hooley's creditors another cheque—for £10,000—which had earlier been accepted. Middleton and Akers-Douglas felt that by doing this they would 'obtain in the end larger subscriptions from the virtuous shocked portion of the Party'. 'I agree', Salisbury minuted sardonically; 'they can hardly help themselves.'[41]

The general public was obviously not privy to these confidential communications, and the wildest rumours flourished. The *Spectator* made the easily forgotten point that Hooley had *not*, in the event, secured his baronetcy, and praised Salisbury for his 'vigilance', suggesting that 'a careless Premier' might have let his name slip through.[42] The *National Review*, by contrast, gave credence to the (false) story that Hooley's name had initially appeared on the Jubilee Honours List before the Queen intervened and 'saved the country from this further humiliation' by striking it off.[43] The *Daily Mail* perhaps best caught the prevailing mood of anxiety when it lamented that 'the system of granting titles should be so managed as to induce our Hooleys for a moment to imagine that a cheque can possibly pass them into the ranks'.[44] Hooley's methods, as the *Spectator* noted, were 'very crude . . . he did not understand forms, or despised them, and so made a blunder which when revealed in Court covered him with ridicule and his helpers in the affair with a sort of social disgrace'.[45] But the implication here was that, had he shown more subtlety, Hooley could have used his wealth to procure the title he so much craved. The fact of the matter, grumbled the *National Review*, was that there was 'far too much buying and selling in politics just now', and for some time the distribution of political honours had excited 'misgivings'.[46]

'Labby' mischievously came forward at this point and reminded his own Liberal friends that they

had no right to find fault with their opponents for selling Titles for they themselves do a very lively trade in those articles. How about the newest Liberal Peerages? What did Baron Stern pay to his Party before blooming into Lord Wandsworth? The pot must not call the kettle black.[47]

[40] Middleton to Salisbury, 25 Nov. 1898 (ibid.). McDonnell commented: 'I think Marriott has played rather a dirty trick on him' (McDonnell to Salisbury, 26 Nov. 1898, ibid.).

[41] McDonnell to Salisbury, 21 Nov. 1898, with Salisbury's annotation (Hatfield, Third Marquess of Salisbury Papers, E).   [42] *Spectator*, 19 Nov. 1898, p. 734.

[43] *National Review*, xxxii (1898), 476.   [44] *Daily Mail*, 15 Nov. 1898.

[45] *Spectator*, 19 Nov. 1898, p. 734.   [46] *National Review*, xxxii (1898), 475.

[47] *Truth*, 17 Nov. 1898. His first attack was in *Truth* on 10 Nov.: 'any rich man, ready to pay the price, can buy [an honour], provided that his name is not too odious'. The paper also claims, *re* the Hooley affair, 'either the Queen or Lord Salisbury put a veto on this little game' (ibid., 17 Nov. 1898).

The *National Review* was only too pleased to give publicity to Labouchere's remarks. And, foreshadowing its campaign against the Radical Plutocracy fourteen years later, its editor, Maxse, suggested that the Liberals were 'much more at the mercy of money than the Conservatives', because the financial weakness of the Liberal organization gave Stern, Sir John Brunner, and other 'semi-educated plutocrats' the opportunity of 'calling the tune'.[48]

But the Conservative Party had wealthy, unscrupulous, and ambitious backers of its own, to whom it was accumulating political debts. For example, in the year of the Hooley Affair, the banker, Horace Farquhar was made a baron after only three years' service on the Conservative backbenches—a rapid promotion which he confidentially explained as resulting from the fact that he had subscribed more than the 'accepted tariff'.[49] We have already observed the faintly disreputable part which Farquhar played when he involved prominent members of King Edward VII's Court in a risky speculation; his equally controversial role as a Treasurer of the Conservative Party will be touched upon later.

Farquhar at this time was a protégé of the Duke of Devonshire, who had been insistently pressing his claims since 1892, but Salisbury's Secretary warned his 'Chief' in 1895 not to give the Duke any promise until he had had the chance of a private word—'a great deal depends on it'.[50] The following year the Jameson Raid put further obstacles in the path of Farquhar's ambition since he was a Director of the British South Africa Company, and Chamberlain argued that 'Farquhar's peerage had better be deferred until the inquiry has at least been opened and it is seen what allegations if any are made against the Directors.'[51] When in 1898 the award was eventually made, there were rumblings of discontent. 'It surely cannot be that having entertained His Royal Highness the Prince of Wales and other distinguished persons that such a marked honour should be accorded to him', wrote a Mr W. B. Horsfall. 'If so, I should like to request a member to bring the matter before the House when it meets next month.'[52]

In fact, Salisbury, who regarded the whole honours business with world-weary cynicism, was certainly not prepared, as this correspondent implied, to give in to royal pressure. This became evident in 1902 when King Edward VII urged that two of his close personal friends, Thomas Lipton, the grocer, and Cassel should receive peerages. Cassel, it will be recalled, had done much to bring order into the King's chaotic

[48] *National Review*, xxxii (1898), 476–7.

[49] Lant, *Insubstantial Pageant*, pp. 230–1. But the author is mistaken when he says that Farquhar only got his peerage in the new reign.

[50] McDonnell's note of 30 Oct. 1895, *re* Farquhar-Devonshire correspondence (Third Marquess of Salisbury papers, E).

[51] Devonshire to Salisbury, 28 Nov., 6 Dec. 1896 (ibid.).

[52] W. B. Horsfall to Salisbury, 10 Jan. 1898 (ibid., H).

finances and was continuing to give him much-needed financial assistance. But Salisbury adamantly refused to fall in with the royal command, and there was some ill-will between King and Prime Minister, though the conflict abated when Lipton was awarded a baronetcy and Cassel a privy councillorship and knighthood.[53]

On the other hand, the steady inflation of the peerage continued during the years of Unionist rule. Between 1895 and 1905 sixty-two peerages and about 150 baronetcies were created.[54] As for knighthoods, these were distributed so lavishly that, as a contemporary put it in 1902, one could not 'throw a stone at a dog without hitting a knight in London'.[55]

One manifestation of the growing discontent with the honours system was the violent attack which Arnold White launched in the *Weekly Sun* on 7 July 1900 and later republished in his swashbuckling book, *Efficiency and Empire* (1901). White recalled that Hooley's £50,000 cheque had 'remained in the safe custody of one of Her Majesty's Ministers for weeks' and argued that this proved that 'the purchase of baronetcies is by no means an unthinkable proposition by the Front Bench'. The bestowal of honours in recent years, wrote White, had become a 'sordid farce', for which both parties deserved condemnation. Salisbury himself was criticized for conferring hereditary titles on 'financiers and men of pleasure' and for using the honours system to silence press criticism of his government. 'Men with the manners of an organ-grinder and the morals of his monkey' were being singled out for official recognition, while self-sacrificing servants of the State went unrewarded. The remedy, White thought, was simple: 'Let the services of every man who received a national honour be recorded and published at the time the honour is bestowed.'[56] This was precisely what Lawson had proposed in the Commons seven years earlier. The difference was that the subject no longer seemed suitable for playful witticisms.

To the disgust of the moralists, Balfour, who succeeded his uncle as Prime Minister in 1902, continued to take a decidedly easy-going view of the compilation of the honours lists. Although adequately informed about what was being done in his name and why, he entrusted the detailed work to his Chief Whip, Acland-Hood, who in turn sought assistance from one of his predecessors in that office, Akers-Douglas, and from Balfour's confidential private secretary, Jack Sandars. Acland-Hood, familiarly known as the 'Pink Un', had inherited a party fund of

[53] Marsh, P., *The Discipline of Popular Government: Lord Salisbury's Domestic Statecraft, 1881–1902* (Hassocks, 1978), pp. 313–14. Salisbury had also been deaf to the Prince of Wales's suggestions about honours at the time of the 1887 Jubilee (Lant, *Insubstantial Pageant*, p. 195).

[54] These figures cover all new creations, but exclude 'steps' in the peerage.

[55] Marsh, *Discipline of Popular Government*, p. 192.

[56] White, *Efficiency and Empire*, Ch. 6.

£150,000, but he was anxious to add to that sum, hoping to reach the position where he could securely invest £200,000, and then after financing the next election still have £100,000 left.[57]

How did the Unionist Chief Whip set about this task? His methods are clearly enough expressed in his letter to Sandars of 28 September 1905: 'Haig [the Chief Agent] is rather keen to have Stewart Mackenzie of Seaforth made a Peer . . . and if it means (as Haig thinks) Fifty it is worth doing.'[58] Haig was also launching a big fund-raising scheme in the City.[59] This eagerness on the Whips' part to make contact with wealthy supporters was paralleled by a readiness on the part of many rich men to press their claims for honours on the Whips' Office.[60] Often such claimants shied away from making direct approaches but made their wishes known through third parties. One rich merchant, for example, took advantage of a visit to Hatfield House to complain that his political exertions for the party had not been recognized; the request was duly passed on to Sandars, who in turn reminded his 'Chief' that the claimant was 'rich and very friendly to you', and that although the peerage he wanted was out of the question, perhaps a baronetcy might be considered.[61] In the event this man received nothing. More successful was the overture from Lord Zetland, who wrote to Acland-Hood that his neighbour, Mr S. W. Duncan had voted for the Party for twenty-five years and had three times contested an election at his own expense and was now prepared to give at least £20,000 to Central Office by depositing a signed cheque that could only be drawn when 'the condition' was fulfilled;[62] Duncan duly entered the ranks of the baronetcy in December 1905.

Acland-Hood was clearly not an over-scrupulous man.[63] But he wanted certain 'decencies' to be observed. He was therefore embarrassed when in 1905 the Conservative Whips' Office came under pressure from the King—as had earlier happened to Salisbury. On 4 December 1905 the King wrote in his execrable handwriting, accepting the Prime Minister's honours list, but asking that four additional names be included: 'As Sovereign I claim to have a right to bring them

---

[57] Acland-Hood to J. Sandars, 9 Sept. 1905 (BL, Balfour papers, Add. MS 49,771, fos. 63–4).

[58] Acland-Hood to Sandars, 28 Sept. 1905 (ibid., fo. 81).

[59] Ibid., fos. 83–4.

[60] For earlier brazen examples of honours begging, see Chilston, 3rd Viscount, *The Political Life and Times of Aretas Akers-Douglas First Viscount Chilston* (London, 1961), pp. 197–200.

[61] Sandars to Balfour, 6 Jan. 1905 (Balfour papers, Add. MS 49, 763, fo. 21).

[62] Zetland to Acland-Hood, 19 Oct. 1905 (ibid., Add. MS 49,771, fo. 96).

[63] In February 1908 Blumenfeld called at Acland-Hood's office and found him even redder in the face than usual. He was riled by the disfranchisement of Worcester for corruption. ' "We are becoming a nation of priggish noodles", said the irate colonel. "If a candidate or his agent just smile on a baby nowadays he is looked upon as a criminal. Give me the good old days of a hundred years ago".' (Blumenfeld's diary, 1 Feb. 1908, in Blumenfeld, R. D., *R. D. B.'s Diary 1887–1914* (London, 1930), pp. 203–4).

prominently before the ? outgoing Prime Minister', he said. The King wanted a baronetcy to be conferred on Buckle, the editor of *The Times*, who subsequently declined the honour,[64] and a privy councillorship for Colonel Lockwood.[65] More controversially, he also pressed for peerages for Alfred Harmsworth, the newspaper proprietor, and for H. Stern, a younger brother of the man whom the Liberals had made Baron Wandsworth.[66] Balfour acquiesced in this arrangement:

All these gentlemen are persons of high character and position, influential supporters of the party to which Mr Balfour belongs and worthy of recognition. . . . Sir A. Harmsworth and Sir H. Stern have very recently been made Baronets on Mr Balfour's recommendation; and for this reason he did not add them to the list of those who were to be made Peers on the change of Government. But Mr Balfour quite recognises that they are (in different ways) gentlemen to whom the Party owes much, and who occupy great positions in the country; they would, without doubt, have, at no distant date, received the further honour which it is now proposed to confer upon them.[67]

But Acland-Hood was displeased. In an intriguing letter to Sandars he observed:

I hardly know how to answer your wire—obviously the King means Harmsworth to have a Peerage. If he doesn't get it now he will get it when CB makes his Peers on taking office—we should then lose all his money and influence—I very much dislike the business, but as we *can't* stop it in the future why make so handsome a present to the other side!

Of course some of our men will be furious and I can't blame them. We have to weigh that and the difficulty with Buckle against the giving an enormous card to the other side—I think in this case we might allow our virtue to be raped.[68]

The King's wishes were duly met. But Hood remained apprehensive about the changes made to the List: 'I am sick about the Honours Business', he wrote to Sandars three days later. 'I think the original List was respectable and moderate, and would have caused no comment, tho' a certain amount of jealousy. The Party additions to this List are all right, but the additions from a Higher Quarter are bound to cause us trouble.' Did Acland-Hood, in writing this, know of the rumour that the King was seeking to reward Harmsworth and others for the

---

[64] On Buckle, see Koss, S., *The Rise and Fall of the Political Press in Britain*, ii. *The Twentieth Century* (London, 1984), pp. 52–3.

[65] Lockwood had been a Conservative MP since 1892. The *Morning Post* (9 Dec. 1905) said that he 'recently had the honour of entertaining the King at his seat, Bishop's Hall, near Romford'.

[66] Edward VII to Balfour, 4 Dec. 1905 (Balfour papers, Add. MS 49,685, fos. 75–6).

[67] Balfour to Edward VII (copy), 5 Dec. 1905 (ibid., fos. 77–83).

[68] Acland-Hood to Sandars, 5 Dec. 1905 (Bodleian, Sandars papers, vol. 750, fos. 147–8). But Hood later claimed that Northcliffe offered him 'a very large cheque' after being made a peer, which he refused (Peter Sanders's diary, 8 May 1919, in Ramsden, John (ed.), *Real Old Tory Politics: The Political Diaries of Robert Sanders Lord Bayford 1910–1935* (London, 1984), p. 125).

financial assistance they had allegedly given his mistress, Mrs Keppel?[69]

As the Chief Whip predicted, Balfour's Resignation Honours List received a bad press, with the ennoblement of Harmsworth and the elevation to the peerage of another Stern receiving most of the caustic comment. *Truth* carried a mocking article about 'The "Title Boom" ',[70] and the *Saturday Review* included a piece on 'The Adulteration of the Peerage', in which it was said that Balfour's creations 'cannot but lower one of the greatest of our institutions in the eyes of educated men', and warning was given that 'a House of Lords composed of plutocrats will not survive the test of modernity'.[71]

The 'Problem of the Press'

When the *Saturday Review* complained that Harmsworth had done 'more than any man of his generation to pervert and enfeeble the mind of the multitude',[72] it was voicing a common complaint. It seemed that, while the rich were being corrupted by the plutocratic ethos, the populace at large was being corrupted by the triviality and mendacity of the 'Yellow Press'. G. M. Trevelyan railed against the new 'White Peril', which he likened to the music hall, and argued that these two social forces were destroying civilized standards and eroding the very basis of the national character.[73] Unfairly in many ways, the Harmsworth brothers became the target of all those who held such views.

Recent historical writing has tended to play down the important of the so-called 'New Journalism' of Harmsworth, Newnes, and Pearson, by showing that there was no sharp breach between their journalistic practices and those of their predecessors. The 'Americanization' of the press, for example, had been in progress for several decades, and the newspaper reading public of the 1890s was becoming familiar with such devices as banner headlines, short paragraphs, interviews with 'celebrities', and copious illustrations. The *Daily Mail*, which Alfred Harmsworth launched in 1896, was in many ways a fairly traditional paper; its front page, for example, was covered in advertisements. On the other hand, the editorial staff of the *Mail* was clearly making a determined bid to attract members of the public who had not in the

[69] Acland-Hood to Sandars, 8 Dec. 1905 (Sandars papers, vol. 750, fo. 204). For the rumour about Northcliffe and Mrs Keppel, see Cecil King's diary, 16 Feb. 1974, in King, C., *Diaries, 1970–1974* (London, 1975), p. 345.

[70] *Truth*, 14 Dec. 1905; 'Baronetcies, in particular, are rising rapidly. Such distinctions as knighthoods and K.C.M.G.'s are also very attractive at the present comparatively modest prices.'

[71] *Saturday Review*, 16 Dec. 1905, pp. 769–70. But *The Times*, in its leader of 9 Dec. 1905, made no mention whatever of Stern and Harmsworth and merely observed that the List contained 'some interesting items'.

[72] *Saturday Review*, 16 Dec. 1905.

[73] Trevelyan, G. M., 'The White Peril', *Nineteenth Century*, l (1901), 1043–55.

past bought a daily newspaper at all. Not only was its price lowered to
½*d*., but the material was simplified and lightened.[74]

But Harmsworth's originality lay less in devising new journalistic
techniques than in the thoroughgoing way he applied the latest
methods of business organization to newspaper production—in particular,
his use of up-to-date technology and distribution techniques to build
up a mass readership, and his determined quest for advertising
revenue. Such business methods added to the initial cost of starting
new journals and encouraged the development whereby existing
newspapers became grouped into 'chains'. The *Daily Mail*, it is true, is
said to have begun life with a capital of only £15,000.[75] But, as A. J. Lee
has shown, in his excellent study of the rise of the popular press,
whereas most nineteenth century newspapers had been built up as
family businesses, by the 1880s syndicates and corporations had come
into existence, foreshadowing the amalgamated press of the twentieth
century.[76] By 1910 66.9 per cent of the circulation of metropolitan
morning newspapers was accounted for by three business organisations,
of which that of Northcliffe (formerly Alfred Harmsworth), with a 39
per cent share of the market, was easily the largest.[77] For some
proprietors the acquisition of more and more titles became almost an
end in itself, but it was also a rational way of achieving economies of
scale by employing expensive printing machinery and elaborate
distribution networks at something approaching full capacity.

We have already seen the fears that were being expressed around the
turn of the century over the emergence of trusts and combines, which
were thought to signal an undesirable Americanization of British life
and to constitute a threat to the consumer's freedom of choice.[78] The
application of such a form of business organization to the activities of
Fleet Street was accordingly resented. But in this case there were
additional grounds for unease. For one of the consequences of the
amalgamation movement was a shifting of power from editors and
journalists to proprietors; the men and women who wrote for
newspapers were coming increasingly under the control of those who
financed and organized them. Indeed, whereas in the early and mid-
nineteenth century the same word, 'journalist', was used to cover both
groups, by the end of the century it was clearly recognized that there
was an important difference of function and interest between them.[79]
True, Northcliffe himself had started off as a journalist and retained
throughout his life an instinctive sympathy for the working journalist's
point of view; but his brother, Harold, later to be Lord Rothermere, saw
newspapers largely from a business perspective.

---

[74] See Pound, R. and Harmsworth, G., *Northcliffe* (London, 1959), p. 199.
[75] Ibid. 206–7. It is by no means certain that this story is true.
[76] Lee, A. J., *The Origins of the Popular Press, 1855–1914* (London, 1976), p. 79.
[77] Ibid. 293.   [78] Ch. 3, pp. 78–9.   [79] Lee, *Popular Press*, pp. 94, 114.

Ramsay MacDonald was well aware of the significance of this change, alleging that the 'cheap press' had become 'the organ of the advertisers and the convenience of the capitalist'.[80] But this line of criticism was by no means confined to socialists. A dislike of the commercialization of the press was felt by many journalists and writers, of all persuasions, who naturally resented the threat to their job security. Thus in an article on 'The Ethics of Editing', the distinguished Radical journalist, Massingham, complained that the individuality of his craft was being destroyed by the new breed of press proprietors, who virtually dispensed with the editors altogether in their anxiety to secure the largest and swiftest return on their capital investment.[81]

Indeed, in the opening years of the twentieth century it was Radical-Liberals who were generally the most vocal in their denunciations. This can be explained in a number of ways. As we have seen, Radical anti-Imperialists like Hobson and Hirst believed that the South African financiers and mineowners had succeeded in controlling and manipulating not only the English-speaking press of South Africa, but large parts of the London press as well—a development to which they assigned considerable responsibility for the outbreak of the Second Boer War.[82] More generally, there was a belief in Liberal circles that an insistence upon Radical principles tended to antagonize proprietors and advertisers and that this explained both the loss of newspaper support which Liberalism had sustained since 1886 and also the consequential electoral set-backs of their party. During the 1906 General Election Campbell-Bannerman, aware of the fact that the Unionist press in London had a circulation three times greater than that of the newspapers friendly to his own party, publicly lamented that the 'newspaper press has largely . . . got into the hands of combinations of capitalists'.[83]

In retrospect such fears seem exaggerated. The Liberal Party still enjoyed considerable support among that sector of the business community involved in the financing and organization of newspapers; Newnes himself, for example, was actually a Liberal MP. And, especially after their return to power, Liberals became very adept at using the amalgamated press in their own interests. But, quite apart from that, dislike of what the Harmsworth brothers represented was never confined to Liberals and Socialists alone. Even in the 1890s many traditional Conservatives viewed the changes taking place in Fleet Street with a jaundiced eye. Most, though by no means all, of the new press barons may have inclined to the Conservative side, but they

[80] Ibid., 217.
[81] Massingham, H. W., 'The Ethics of Editing', *National Review*, xxxv (1900), 256–61.
[82] Ch. 3, pp. 67–9.
[83] Russell, A. K., *Liberal Landslide* (Newton Abbot, 1973), p. 139.

were often self-made men with a reputation for 'unreliability', in the sense that they had no real party loyalties at all. This was even true of Alfred Harmsworth after his disastrous experience as a Conservative parliamentary candidate.[84] It was not so much that Conservatives feared that Alfred Harmsworth would follow his brothers into the Liberal camp. Rather they perceived that the commercial success of the *Daily Mail* had made its owner financially independent of *all* parties. Indeed, along with his rivals, Pearson and Newnes, Harmsworth knew that his interests would be best served by building up a mass circulation which crossed barriers of class and party. And as Stephen Koss has shown, this in turn had the important consequence of bringing about the 'de-politicization' of the popular press from the late Victorian period onwards.[85] Many newspapers no longer covered politics as extensively as had once been customary, and they certainly did not assume in their readers an all-consuming interest in party affairs.

But that is not to say that these new newspaper proprietors 'were speculators, in the strict sense'.[86] They were certainly more complex figures than that. Though not a sound party man, Alfred Harmsworth was intensely hungry for political power and had a strong sense of his own mission to guide the fortunes of the British people. This explains his acquisition of *The Times* in 1908, a very poor use of capital judged by purely commercial criteria, but a rational step to take, given Northcliffe's wish to influence policy-making at the highest level.[87]

Naturally enough, practising politicians tended both to resent and to fear the intrusion of these new rivals into what they regarded as their own domain. Yet how could they control or restrain the press barons' political ambitions? The only effective instrument to hand was their power to bestow, or promise, honours and titles to newspapermen prepared to be friendly. In fact, this practice can be traced back to the early 1880s; Algernon Borthwick, the owner of the *Morning Post*, received a knighthood from Disraeli in 1880 and a baronetcy from Salisbury in 1887, before being admitted into the ranks of the peerage in 1895. But many of these early recipients of honours, Borthwick included, had also had political careers in their own right, in addition to holding a social position which seemed to justify the titles eventually conferred upon them.[88] Harmsworth's elevation in 1905 could not be defended on these grounds.

---

[84] Rather surprisingly, Koss argues that Alfred Harmsworth was very traditional in his allegiance to party (Koss, *Rise and Fall*, i. 369). But he goes on to show that even in the 1890s Harmsworth had links with the Liberal as well as with the Conservative Party.

[85] Koss, *Rise and Fall*, ii. *passim.*

[87] See *The History of the Times: The Twentieth Century Test 1884–1912* (London, 1947), Ch. 18.

[88] Lee, *Popular Press*, p. 205. Borthwick was a Unionist MP from 1885 to 1905 and served as Chairman of the Metropolitan Unionist MPs in the late 1880s.

In any case, was it healthy that Governments should attempt to employ so blatant a system of press management? Arnold White thought not, and in 1901 he was voicing sentiments that were to be repeaded *ad nauseam* during the succeeding decades:

It is interesting to watch the criticism of a newspaper knight on the politics of his patron. It is thus that political opinion is medicated, the springs of truth poisoned, jobs hushed up, and incapacity condoned—in the interests of a Government.[89]

But equally worrying was the possibility that the bestowal of honours would *fail* to 'tame' the press barons or deflect their wish to convert their commercial strength into political influence. Once again Alfred Harmsworth provides an interesting case. In some respects he was a typical plutocrat as described in Chapter 1, not least in his craving for honours and titles—though he also knew how commercially useful they could be.[90] On the other hand, whereas most plutocrats longed to be 'accepted' by those who possessed high social status and political authority, the attitude of the press barons such as Harmsworth was decidedly ambiguous. For although they wanted to be the advisers and confidants of prime ministers, they did not wish to forfeit their position as clamorous outsiders with a self-proclaimed mandate to speak up on behalf of the common man.

This ambiguity in turn affected the way in which the mass circulation press handled scandals and allegations of corruption. The *Daily Mail* liked to see itself as a fearless crusader for justice, ready to stand up to Westminster and Whitehall. And the press barons gave one or two of the sensation-mongering freelance writers a newpaper column—Arnold White, for example, was employed in this capacity by the *Daily Express* just before and during the Great War. On the other hand, since such papers were intended to cater for the whole family and depended for bare survival on achieving huge circulations, they could not carry material that would cause offence or lose readers. G. K. Chesterton thus had good cause to lament the 'mildness' of the 'Yellow Press', which shied away from stories that really were sensational.[91] Certainly, none of Harmsworth's editors cared to emulate the methods of a man like W. T. Stead, who had genuine courage and a clear sense of social purpose. Nor did they play a *major* role in exposing any of the financial scandals which involved prominent politicians in the late nineteenth and early twentieth centuries.

Here the initiative was more often taken by well-established family-

---

[89] White, *Efficiency and Empire*, p. 59.   [90] See Koss, *Rise and Fall*, i. 370.
[91] Chesterton, G. K., *Heretics* (London, 1905), Ch. 8. As Chesterton notes: 'With the whole world full of big and dubious institutions, with the whole wickedness of civilisation staring them in the face, their idea of being bold and bright is to attack the War Office' (ibid., p. 117).

owned newspapers, like the right-wing *Morning Post*, by the socialist press, and, most important of all, by the often influential, but small circulation, weeklies and monthlies that were still widely read in political society. Very often journals of the latter type were owned by their editors—for example, Loe Strachey's *Spectator* and Leo Maxse's *National Review*—and this gave them an independence which enabled them to comment freely and to attack political abuses of all kinds, restrained only by their concern not to infringe the libel laws or to offend their readers' sense of decorum. From 1911 onwards the *Eye-Witness* (later renamed the *New Witness*), run by Cecil Chesterton and Hilaire Belloc, played a similar role.

Now, 'muck-raking' journals like the *Eye-Witness* and the *National Review* (the *Spectator* was perhaps too old-fashioned and stately in its language to warrant this description) usually looked in vain for support from the mass circulation newspapers. Indeed they soon came to see the syndicated press as an integral part of the very 'corruption' they wished to expose. It is true that Maxse had a soft spot personally for Northcliffe (he even publicly welcomed his peerage in 1905),[92] perhaps because the two men shared a number of political convictions, not least an intense fear of German expansionism. But the *National Review*, like other journals of its type, inveighed bitterly against the tendency for newspapers and periodicals to come under the irresponsible authority of a single great capitalist or board of directors; 'One man one newspaper' was the mock Radical slogan which Maxse later became fond of using.[93]

Both sets of party managers, too, resented the power which had accrued to wealthy newspaper proprietors, with their vast political ambitions unrestrained by party ties or obligations. Hence, in the discussions about the alleged spread of corruption which took place during the first decades of the twentieth century, considerable emphasis was given to 'the problem of the Press', and the press barons and those who trafficked with them became objects of deep suspicion. As we have seen, the Unionist Administration of 1895–1905 was the first to attract criticism on these grounds. But, perhaps surprisingly, even more was to be said about 'the problem of the Press' after the Liberals' electoral victory in 1906.

[92] *National Review*, xlvi (1906), 776. Strachey, too, congratulated Northcliffe on his elevation (Strachey to Northcliffe, 12 Dec. 1905, BL, Northcliffe papers, Res. Mss 131/23).
[93] e.g. *National Review*, lxii (1914), 919.

LIBERAL RULE
1905–1914

5
The Liberals in Office, 1905–1914

Introduction

WE have seen that at the start of the twentieth century the protest against plutocracy, in so far as it assumed a political form at all, came mainly from the Radical wing of the Liberal Party. It may readily be imagined with what abhorrence the Nonconformists viewed the new social developments, especially the increase in gambling and luxurious expenditure. The emerging group of 'Social Radicals', like Hobson, L. T. Hobhouse, and H. W. Massingham, joined them in deploring the self-indulgence of the rich, who ignored the plight of the 'people of the abyss' and excited class animosity by their vulgarity and pretentiousness. In the case of Hobson, this feeling was combined with anger against 'cosmopolitan financiers', whom he thought were the guilty men responsible for the South African War. Joined on occasions by independent-minded journalists like Arnold White, it was Radical-Liberals who set themselves up as moral judges and called upon the fashionable and the wealthy to repent the error of their ways.

It was also the Radicals, more than any other group, who were on the look-out for political corruption. After their repeated attacks on the lax standards of the Balfour Administration, the new Liberal Ministers were therefore most anxious that their own period in office should be free from any hint of scandal. It was appropriate, then, that one of Campbell-Bannerman's first acts on becoming Prime Minister was to ask his colleagues for details of the directorships they held, making it clear that he did not want the Front Bench to become a 'sty for guinea pigs'.[1] All directorships had to be relinquished, except those connected with philanthropic undertakings and directorships in private companies. Campbell-Bannerman did not set his ministers a deadline, because he thought it was 'not desirable that these things should be done in an inconvenient way'; nor would he agree with MacNeill, who wanted the Government's 'excellent rule' to be embodied in legislation. 'I hope that legislation will not be necessary. A good example has been set', he replied.[2] There was some good-humoured persiflage about what constituted a philanthropic company, and MPs also differed over whether the distinction being made between public and private companies was a valid one.[3] But it seemed that MacNeill's determined attempts to root out 'ministerial

---

[1] Wilson, A. J., *A Life of Sir Henry Campbell-Bannerman* (London, 1973), p. 496.
[2] *Parl. Deb.*, 4th ser., cliv. 234–5 (20 Mar. 1906).
[3] Ibid. 639–40 (22 Mar. 1906) and 1084–5 (27 Mar. 1906), and clv. 186 (2 Apr. 1906).

guinea pigs' had been brought to a successful and decisive conclusion.[4]

Symbolically, the first measure to reach the statute book after the Liberals' accession to power was the Prevention of Corruption Act. The King's Speech of 1906 had promised that such a measure would be quickly introduced, but the new Lord Chancellor, Loreburn, allowed Halsbury, his predecessor, who had already done much work on this reform, to have the honour of formally sponsoring it. Both men then received a blessing from the Archbishop of Canterbury, who said that he had received many communications on the subject, which showed the strength of feeling 'in these large questions of principle and morality which underlie the proposals of the measure'.[5]

To monitor the new Act, a body called the Secret Commissions and Bribery Prevention League came into existence; Fry served as its President, and among its Vice-Presidents were a number of public figures prominently concerned with the more general quest for 'purity' in public life, for example, the Fourth Marquess of Salisbury.[6] Public meetings were held in an attempt to draw attention to the issue, and the League also circulated millions of copies of the Act and other propaganda material. It also on occasions instituted prosecutions under the Act when circumstances made it difficult for individuals to do so, and in 1912 the Liberal businessman MP, Albert Spicer, one of the League's Vice-Presidents, brought in a Private Member's Bill which would have deprived the Attorney-General of his right of veto; however, pressure of parliamentary business prevented this bill from making any further progress.[7]

As well as sponsoring the Prevention of Corruption Act, the Liberals also moved promptly to provide further protection to shareholders and creditors by bringing in the 1907 Companies Bill, which forced every public company either to issue a proper prospectus or else to deposit with the Registrar of Joint Stock Companies a full statement containing the information which would otherwise have appeared in the prospectus.[8] The passing of this Act was attended by many ironies.

---

[4] On the problems subsequently thrown up by this distinction between public and private companies, see Conclusion, p. 413.

[5] *Parl. Deb.*, 4th ser., clii. 1253–6 (1 Mar. 1906). The background to the Act is well handled in Doig, *Corruption and Misconduct*, pp. 75–7, and its provisions are described on pp. 79–80.

[6] Leonard, R. M. (the League's secretary) to Lord Robert Cecil, who had once been a member of it, 19 Feb. 1914 (BL, Cecil of Chelwood papers, Add. MS 51, 161, fos. 108–9).

[7] Leonard, R. M., *The War Against Bribery* (London, 1913), pp. 31–4.

[8] *Parl. Deb.*, 4th ser., clxxi. 164–76 (14 Mar. 1907) and clxxx. 465–84 (8 Aug. 1907). The introduction of the Bill was preceded by the submission of a report from a departmental committee set up by Gerald Balfour, the President of the Board of Trade in 1905, whose members comprised the Chairman of the Stock Exchange, the Chairman of the Associated Chambers of Commerce, Lord Faber, Sir Felix Schuster, and Sir Edgar Speyer—under the chairmanship of Loreburn.

For example, the Minister responsible for its parliamentary progress was the President of the Board of Trade, Lloyd George, whose irresponsible quest for Patagonian gold ten years earlier had only been possible because such legislative protection for gullible shareholders had then been lacking.[9] It is also surprising to find that stern upholder of lofty standards of rectitude in public life, Lord Robert Cecil, attacking the 1907 Companies Act, partly because he feared that it would hit the 'honest fool', while missing the 'clever rogue', but also because he preferred to leave individuals to look after their own commercial interests and take whatever remedies the existing law offered them.[10]

As always, appearances were deceptive. But, to the superficial observer at least, the Liberals' return to power promised to bring about a higher level of political morality. For although Campbell-Bannerman was not without his critics, no one ever cast doubt upon his financial probity or questioned his fastidiousness where matters of money were concerned. Moreover, marriage to a valetudinarian wife prevented the Liberal Leader from taking any part in the activities of 'Society', and this too helped endear him to his backbenchers and to his Labour and Irish Nationalist allies.

There is a case for saying that, leaving aside the personal inclinations of its leaders, the Liberals were not likely to be welcomed in 'Society' anyhow, in view of the hostility which their policies were soon exciting. Certainly, within the higher reaches of the Court, the Civil Service, and the Armed Services, support for the Liberal Party perceptibly declined between 1906 and 1914. Moreover, during the intensely bitter conflicts over the Constitutional Crisis and over Irish Home Rule, the once-close ties between the two Front Benches became loosened. On becoming Opposition Leader in 1912, Bonar Law declared that personal friendship between political opponents had been carried too far and that it might prove necessary to disband the *Other Club*, that social focus for cross-party familiarities.[11]

Nevertheless, between 1908 and 1914 there was a sustained attack on the 'Radical Plutocracy', in which the Liberals found themselves constantly held up to censure and ridicule for their alleged hedonism, luxuriousness, and fondness for the trappings of great wealth. Even more damaging to their reputations, it was said that the Liberals, despite their criticism of their Unionist predecessors, were guilty of corruption, the like of which the country had not seen since the days of Walpole. Not all Conservatives would have gone as far as Maxse who

---

[9] Grigg, John, *Lloyd George: The People's Champion 1902–1911* (London, 1978), pp. 111–12.

[10] *Parl. Deb.*, 4th ser., clxxx. 472–4 (8 Aug. 1907).

[11] Riddell's diary, Nov. 1911, in Lord Riddell, *More Pages From My Diary 1908–1914* (London, 1934), pp. 27–8.

once wrote, 'Such men are little better than pirates—they are out for loot',[12] but the underlying sentiment was one that many level-headed and responsible Opposition leaders broadly shared. For example, in October 1912 the Unionist Chief Whip, Balcarres, wrote in his diary:

The common talk of the lobby and the City is government corruption—personal corruption. The radicals seem to vie with one another in payment for honours and in recoupment via public contracts. Never before have such rumours been so prevalent, nor has there been so much ground for their foundation . . .[13]

Nor did the criticisms take the form of mere generalized abuse. There were also some very detailed and specific accusations. In 1912–13 the Asquith Ministry was caught up in the famous Marconi Scandal, but this was only one of a number of incidents which suggested that the relationship between Liberal Ministers and the business world was irregular, to say the least. Running parallel to these accusations was an outcry against honours trafficking and against abuses in the Liberals' dispensation of government patronage. By the eve of the War the increasingly accident-prone Liberal Party had become associated in the minds of its opponents and even in the minds of some of its erstwhile supporters with shady transactions and chicanery. The Balfour Ministry had never attracted quite this volume of abuse.

The very extravagance of this abuse has led many historians to minimize the significance of the Liberal 'scandals' or to attempt to explain them away. For example, one can plausibly argue that the Opposition was simply seeking revenge. So spiritedly had the Liberals protested against the 'corrupt' proclivities of the Unionists earlier in the decade that they had unwittingly set up a standard of purity in public life by which they found it impossible to guide their behaviour when they came to power. The angry and embittered Opposition would be quick to pounce on any lapses which substantiated their belief in Liberal 'hypocrisy'. This did indeed happen to some extent. Moreover, when the Unionists suffered further defeats during the general elections of 1910, their bitterness assumed an even greater intensity. It was natural for Opposition politicians to convince themselves that a Radical Ministry which was prepared to harry the King into an early grave was capable of any enormity. Besides, the passing of the Parliament Act in 1911 released the Unionists from many of the restraints which customarily inhibit the behaviour of Opposition parties. Attacking the individual and collective integrity of Liberal Ministers could be seen in these circumstances as a perfectly legitimate tactic.

[12] *National Review*, lvii (1911), 383. The 'plunderbund' was one of Maxse's names for the Asquith Ministry.
[13] Balcarres's diary, 14 Oct. 1912, in Vincent (ed.), *The Crawford Papers*, p. 280.

Thus the Constitutional Crisis raised the temperature of party political warfare and created the atmosphere in which accusations of corruption were likely to be made. But it is arguable that, in addition, the Liberals' emphasis on social reform as a device for improving the condition of the people, and their success in consolidating their hold on the working class electorate also played a part. As Bentley Gilbert has perceptively noted, the Opposition may not have dared to block the social reform legislation of the Liberal Government, knowing that it would be electoral suicide for them to do so, but may instead have opted to assail the reputations of leading Ministers, notably Lloyd George.[14]

This, however, is not entirely satisfactory, if only because many leading Conservatives *did* articulate their disapproval of Liberal policy. For example, Lord Selborne was not concerned to attack Liberal Ministers for corruption simply as an indirect way of discrediting social reform; he also believed that social reform was corrupt *in itself*, and was quite prepared to say so publicly. Thus in his pamphlet, 'Mr Lloyd George and the Land', issued by the National Union of Conservative Associations, Selborne expressed horror at the election address recently put out by a Liberal candidate (R. L. Outhwaite), with its many promises of social reform to come:

If Mr Outhwaite had given an elector five shillings from his own pocket, he would have been unseated and declared guilty of corrupt practice. But to *offer all* the *electors* a *share in millions of pounds* belonging to other people is *lawful and respectable*! Truly we are a people who strain at gnats and swallow camels.[15]

Admittedly, the Unionists who accused the Liberals of corruption had ulterior motives. But their allegations would not have been taken seriously, had people outside their ranks not found them partly credible. And in fact changes *were* occurring in British politics which made the Liberals vulnerable to attacks on their integrity. Two of these must now be briefly examined: Payment of Members, and the emergence of the 'New Liberalism'.

Payment of MPs

During the first decade of the twentieth century politics was becoming less the preserve of gentlemen of independent means who performed public service out of a sense of obligation, and more a career which

[14] Gilbert, B. B., *The Evolution of National Insurance in Great Britain: The Origins of the Welfare State* (London, 1966), p. 451.
[15] Selborne, 'Mr Lloyd George and the Land', pamphlet in Steel-Maitland papers, GD 193/103/2 (Scottish Record Office). See Balcarres's description of old age pensions as 'the most corrupting bit of legislation passed in my time' (Balcarres's diary, 12 July 1908, in Vincent (ed.), *The Crawford Papers*, p. 112).

attracted the ambitious. True, the social backgrounds of Liberal Cabinet Ministers did not differ that widely from the backgrounds of their predecessors, since John Burns, the working man, was an anomaly, and as many as twenty-two of the thirty-three men who held Cabinet office between 1906 to 1914 can be described as landed gentlemen or lawyers.

On the other hand, some of the Liberal Ministers lacked financial independence, among them Lloyd George, who actually alluded to his straitened circumstances when testifying before the Marconi Select Committee.[16] This performance annoyed the Unionist lawyer, A. V. Dicey. Lloyd George, he wrote, should be told 'that though poverty was no disgrace, poverty ought to be combined with dignity, and that an official who is poor should be even more careful than a Duke or a millionaire to avoid even the remotest indelicacy in matters of money'.[17] Dicey's insinuation was that a poor politician could easily be put under an 'obligation' by those with whom he came into contact.

Moreover, politics was becoming more of a career than it had once been, and this change was symbolized by the establishment of Payment of MPs in 1911. As such the measure was bound to excite controversy. Introducing it, Lloyd George argued that a 'modest allowance' like £400 a year would have the effect of broadening the composition of the Commons and enabling men without private means, including working men and trade unionists, to play a fuller part in public life. But, while pretending to share this goal, prominent Unionists, notably Arthur Lee, also expressed horror at 'the violation of the principle of gratuitous public service', and predicted that Payment would lower the tone of the House by encouraging an assortment of political adventurers to stand for parliamentary elections.

Indeed, much of Lee's case rested upon the belief that a paid legislature would be a corrupt legislature: 'I challenge anyone to name a single paid legislature in the world which has such a well-deserved reputation for purity and independence as the British House of Commons', he said. 'There has not been even a suspicion of corruption in the British House of Commons.'[18] If the proposed change was adopted, argued Lee, Members would have the odious task of voting salaries to themselves out of public funds. Moreover, Payment would also encourage corrupt bargains at constituency level, with well-off candidates being expected to hand their £400 over to their constituents in one form or another. Finally, the critics invoked American experience in support of their view that Payment did not of itself guarantee an increase in the number of manual workers being elected,

[16] Grigg, *Lloyd George: The People's Champion*, p. 141.
[17] Dicey to Strachey, 2 Apr. 1913 (HLRO, Strachey papers, S/5/6/9). On background to this, see Ch. 6, pp. 124–5.
[18] *Parl. Deb.*, 5th ser., xxix. 1392 (10 Aug. 1911).

but that public-spirited citizens might in future be deterred from standing for Parliament.[19] So widespread were these sentiments—or prejudices—that the Annual Conference of the National Union regularly passed motions calling for an end to Payment, and nine Unionist MPs, including Lee, returned their cheques to the Paymaster-General and asked him not to send any more, while others announced that they were passing on the money to local charities and hospitals.[20]

In paying lip-service to the ideal of more working-class men in Parliament, the Unionists could be accused of the very hypocrisy with which they frequently charged their opponents. But Lord Robert Cecil, for one, also had the courage to speak frankly about his apprehensions over current developments. 'Poorer men are likely to be in Parliament in the future than in the past', he said during the Marconi debate in June 1913. 'I rejoice at that. But, of course, it adds to the danger of personal corruption. (An Hon. Member: "Why?") It is not an accusation against anybody. You cannot corrupt millionaires. (Hon. Members: "Oh! Oh! Oh!").[21] If pressed to justify these provocative remarks, Cecil would probably have argued that the poor MP without private means who depended on his salary would be extremely loath to precipitate a dissolution, because he would fear to lose his livelihood as well as his seat in the ensuing election. Indeed, it quickly became a commonplace of Conservative rhetoric that one reason why the 'Ministerialists' did not throw out the 'treasonable' Cabinet that was tampering with the Union and the Church Establishment and neglecting the country's defences was that MPs were not prepared to forfeit their salaries, just as Ministers were clinging to office out of pecuniary considerations.

Yet it would be a mistake to suppose that the parliamentary Liberal Party, at any time before 1914, consisted predominantly of poor men. Nor did the critics of the Asquith Government always present it in such terms. 'The danger is not that there are too many poor men in the House', wrote Arnold White in 1913, 'but that there are not enough. Unscrupulous adventurers in the House of Commons are more often rich than poor.'[22] White clearly meant these remarks to apply to a section of the Radical Party. Now, on the face of it, it seems puzzling that Edwardian Liberalism could be simultaneously attacked for encouraging the political aspirations of poor men and also for being

[19] Ibid. 1383–98.
[20] Gwyn, W. B., *Democracy and the Cost of Politics in Britain* (London, 1962), p. 223. Frank Meyer, the prospective Unionist candidate for Norwich, declared in June 1914 that payment 'attracts the very worst class that a country can be governed by—the caucus-fed professional politicians. Log-rolling and corruption are the inevitable corrollary.' He added: 'one of the great tasks which is before the Unionist Party is the purification of the present system of Government; in that purification the abolition of payment of members will take a leading place . . .' (*Norwich Unionist*, June 1914).
[21] *Parl. Deb.*, 5th ser., liv. 463 (18 June 1913).
[22] *Daily Express*, 2 June 1913.

dominated by millionaires. Even more paradoxical was the position of Lloyd George, sometimes denounced by his opponents as a 'socialist' and sometimes as the crony of 'plutocrats'. To understand how such seemingly contradictory criticisms could be made we must first identify the sociological characteristics of the Liberal Party between 1906 and 1914.

The New Liberals and Social Policy

In 1906 the Liberals won one of the most outstanding election victories in modern times, picking up 400 seats. They did so because the Unionists after ten years in office had managed to alienate almost every interest group in the land. Such was the scale of the population's disenchantment with the Unionists that the Liberals notched up wins in almost every region and in almost every conceivable type of constituency, so that briefly they could claim that they were a 'national' party, not beholden to any particular class or sectional interest.

This happy situation could not survive long, and it finally disappeared in the winter of 1908–9 when economic recession sharpened class antagonisms. The socialists used the mounting unemployment as evidence of the failure of capitalism, the Tariff Reform wing of the Unionist Party as proof of the breakdown of Free Trade. The Liberals did badly in a series of by-elections, losing eight seats between January 1908 and March 1909. A more aggressive and positive stance was clearly needed if the Liberals were to avoid disaster, and this was provided by the 'New Liberals', Lloyd George and Churchill, whose power and influence were greatly enhanced by the Cabinet reshuffle which followed Campbell-Bannerman's resignation in April 1908. Lloyd George was obviously not a 'socialist', as his critics inside and outside the Party sometimes claimed. Like Joseph Chamberlain in the mid-1880s, his prime objective, shared with his ministerial colleagues, was to fend off the threat from Labour by involving working men with the bourgeois Radicals in a crusade for social justice.

This crusade entailed, firstly, a return to the traditional Radical policy of attacking the landed interest and its parasitical hangers-on in Court, the Armed Services, the Anglican Church, and so on. It also meant an attempt to modify the meaning of Radicalism, so that the emphasis no longer fell so heavily on political rights, and so that social improvement received greater recognition. Through the assault on 'feudalism', on the one hand, and the pursuit of welfare politics, on the other, the Liberals hoped to re-establish their credentials as the 'People's Party' and as the natural party of government.

But the two general elections of 1910, held in the middle of the Constitutional Crisis caused by the Lords' rejection of the 1909

Budget, showed that the Liberals had only half succeeded in their objectives. True, they managed to stave off electoral defeat, and, with the support of the Labour and Irish Nationalist Parties, were able to continue in office. But an analysis of the election results shows that the Liberals, in their rhetorical denunciations of 'privilege', had not only totally alienated the landed interest, which was no doubt unavoidable, but had also lost ground in suburban constituencies among middle-class voters upon whose support they had previously been able to count. Professor Blewett has shown that whereas in working-class and mining constituencies the swing to the Unionists was only 3.8 and 0.5 per cent respectively, in urban constituencies where the middle classes predominated the swing was much higher (6.2 per cent).[23] The British electoral system, it could be argued, was becoming more overtly 'class-based' than it had ever been in the past.

Indeed, there are historians who assert, with some plausibility, that in the years before 1914 the Unionists had successfully staked out their claim to be the defender of all property rights, both industrial and landed, while the Liberals, with their insistence on expensive welfare reforms to be financed by a more progressive tax system, were emerging as a kind of 'social democratic party', capable of identifying with the class needs of the working man—the Labour Party proper having been trapped into a so-called Progressive Alliance with the much larger Liberal Party, from which only the First World War enabled it to escape.[24] In support of this interpretation it can legitimately be argued that by 1914 the Liberals had abandoned much of the ideological lumber they had inherited from the Gladstonian era, and in its place the theoreticians of the 'New Liberalism', like J. A. Hobson and L. T. Hobhouse, were providing the Party with a new programme and a new creed.[25] Even the arguments about Free Trade and Tariff Reform, it has been contended, had become transmuted into what was in effect a dispute about how best to finance social reform, with the Liberals proposing a modest, but significant, redistribution of income, while the Unionists wooed the middle-class income-tax payers by presenting the tariff as an effective way of raising revenue so that the burden would fall, ostensibly, on the 'foreigner', but in practice on the broad mass of consumers.

That these trends were occurring between 1908 and 1914 is not in doubt, but the social composition of the Liberal Party, at parliamentary level anyhow, was not undergoing corresponding changes. The Party which campaigned for the 'People's Budget' and promulgated Old Age Pensions and National Insurance was not only overwhelmingly

[23] Blewett, N., *The Peers, the Parties and the People: the General Elections of 1910* (London, 1972), p. 400.
[24] Clarke, P. F., *Lancashire and the New Liberalism* (Cambridge, 1971), *passim.*
[25] Clarke, P., *Liberals and Social Democrats* (Cambridge, 1978), *passim.*

middle class, but also a party of which businessmen, many of them very wealthy, formed a necessary component. Whatever system of classification is adopted, the same result is achieved: at least one-third of all Liberal MPs in the Edwardian period came into politics from a business career, and, despite what is sometimes claimed, this proportion did not decline as a result of disillusionment with Lloyd George's advanced radicalism. Indeed, the Liberal leadership remained dependent on business support at a number of different levels. The Party had no machinery for collecting money for its Central Fund from the subscriptions paid by a mass membership, and therefore relied upon a small number of wealthy supporters. Herbert Gladstone, the Liberal Chief Whip from 1899 to 1906, drew most of the cash he needed for the 1900 and 1906 general elections from a mere twenty-seven wealthy men, eighteen of them businessmen from the North of England and Scotland. His successors found themselves in the same situation.[26] Paradoxically, the greater the effort which Liberals made to run talented young professional men and intellectuals for Parliament, the more dependent they became on their financial backers. The institution of Payment of Members in 1911 made no substantial difference in this respect.

Moreover, as we shall see in Chapter 6, many Liberal leaders had 'social needs' which drew them into the company of the Party's wealthy businessmen. Lloyd George, in particular, was often mocked for moving in these circles. But in fairness to him, it should be said that, like many of his colleagues, Lloyd George had a genuine admiration for the self-made businessman. After the deadlocked general election of January 1910 there is a record of the Chancellor playing with the idea of a 'government of businessmen', in which public office would go to great Liberal capitalists like Alfred Mond and Christopher Furness. During his period as President of the Board of Trade between 1905 and 1908 Lloyd George got on well with the businessmen who came into contact with his Department, though he also found that they were 'very simple people' and that he could do what he liked with them. The point is that the Liberals, as well as seeing themselves as the 'People's Party', also tried on occasion to present themselves as the friends of capitalist enterprise. Even Lloyd George, in his demagogic speeches in support of the 1909 Budget, drew attention to the way in which businessmen were disadvantaged by the existing land system—the 'landlords' tariff on industry', as he called it—and he tried hard to enlist these businessmen in the Liberal ranks. Both for practical, financial reasons and to sustain their self-image as a party representative of all the 'productive classes' in the nation, the Liberals could not afford to see their traditional business support drain

[26] Searle, G. R., 'The Edwardian Liberal Party and Business', *English Historical Review*, xcviii (1983), 41.

away. Some defectors there undoubtedly were, but right up until 1914 and beyond Liberalism continued to appeal to certain members of the business community, in particular to those working in industries that benefited from Free Trade, and to those who through education or social background found difficulty in securing acceptance in the Unionist Party, which was less 'open' to outsiders than its antagonist.[27]

The Edwardian Liberal Party, therefore, was in a paradoxical situation. It had adopted a 'democratic' reform programme with which, until 1910 at least, it was successfully appealing to the working-class electorate; but after the miners had affiliated to the Labour Party in 1908 it boasted a mere handful of working-class MPs. Liberal Ministers were largely drawn from the respectable professions and landed society, and the Party's funds from businessmen, many of whom were on intimate terms with the Liberal leadership. Given this situation, it is hardly surprising that the Opposition should have drawn attention to this mismatch between Liberal ideals and the Party's 'material base'. The way in which they did this was to mount an attack on what they described as the 'Radical Plutocracy', arraigning prominent Liberal businessmen and politicians for hypocrisy and sometimes for corruption. But before tracing that campaign, it is necessary to identify the individuals and groups which took the leading part in it and to ascertain their motives.

The Scandalmongers

Most Unionists on occasions attacked the lifestyle of particular Liberals. In this they received little encouragement from Balfour. But his successor, Andrew Bonar Law, showed fewer inhibitions. Moreover, during the Bonar Law regime, the National Union's monthly organ, *Our Flag*, made a regular feature of ridiculing plutocratic Liberals, or £iberals as it facetiously called them, notably the hated Lloyd George—alias £loyd George.[28] Nevertheless, it is a fair generalization that 'official' Conservative politicians and Central Office tended to doubt both the expediency and the good taste of personal vendettas. This left the field open to a strangely variegated assortment of moralists and scandalmongers.

Prominent among the former were members of the aristocratic Cecil family.[29] The Cecils, it is true, shrank from the coarser kind of invective and deprecated a vulgar descent into 'personalities'. At the same time they made something of a speciality of exposing what they regarded as the scandalous behaviour of Liberal Ministers, whom they believed to be indifferent to the finer traditions of British public life,

[27] Ibid., *passim*.   [28] e.g. *Our Flag*, Aug. 1913, p. 123.
[29] For portraits of all the children of the Third Marquess of Salisbury, see Rose, Kenneth, *The Later Cecils* (London, 1975).

even though they were not actually corrupt. Arthur Balfour, a nephew of the Third Marquess of Salisbury, was too involved in the compromises of high politics to strike these self-righteous attitudes, but the Fourth Marquess of Salisbury and the latter's younger brothers, Lord Robert and Lord Hugh Cecil, seldom lost an opportunity of reminding the general public of how standards were liable to slip once high offices of state were allowed to pass into the hands of men from outside the traditional ruling class. Loosely associated with these three men was their brother-in-law, Lord Selborne, who had served as First Lord of the Admiralty between 1900 and 1905, had then succeeded Lord Milner as High Commissioner in South Africa, and had then returned to England, where he played a leading part in the Diehard revolt against Balfour's leadership during the Constitutional Crisis. Selborne was a Liberal Unionist, whereas the three Cecil brothers were stern, unbending Church-and-State Tories of the old school, but all four men were alike in combining a general loyalty to the Unionist cause with a certain detachment from party ties, which enabled them to speak out in an independent way whenever an issue arose which stirred their highly sensitive consciences.

This detachment from party owed something to a certain haughtiness of spirit, but it became much accentuated after the eruption of the fiscal controversy, in which the three Cecil brothers (Selborne's position was more complex) fiercely opposed Chamberlain's Imperial Preference scheme—so fiercely, in fact, as to come into collision, not just with the Tariff Reform League and the 'Confederates', but later with the official party leadership. What angered the Cecils was the 'gross materialism' of Chamberlain's appeal, Chamberlain being in any case a politician whom they despised because of his manufacturing background and distrusted because of his Radical past. To such devout Churchmen as the Cecils, Chamberlain's connections with Dissent and his continuing, though now muted, support for Disestablishment was an offence which no display of imperialistic ardour could expunge. Hence their anger knew no bounds as they contemplated the prospect of Church, Monarchy, and Constitution being jeopardized by Chamberlain's demagogic gamble. Characteristically, they worried lest the 'new departure' meant the vulgarization of politics and the introduction of American-style corruption. As Lord Robert Cecil wrote revealingly to Balfour in January 1906 on the subject of the 'Chamberlainites': 'It is not by any means only the Fiscal Question upon which I differ from them. It is their whole way of looking at politics. It appears to me to be utterly sordid and materialistic, not yet corrupt but on the high road to corruption.'[30]

[30] Cecil to Balfour, 25 Jan. 1906, cited in Rempel, R. A., *Unionists Divided: Arthur Balfour, Joseph Chamberlain and the Unionist Free Traders* (Newton Abbott, 1972), p. 109.

The Cecils never abandoned this view of Tariff Reform nor minced their language on the subject. But, once the Liberals were in office, they seem to have been under an overwhelming psychological compulsion to demonstrate that they were concerned with their party opponents' 'lapses' as well as with those of their colleagues. Through their attacks on the laxness and corruption that they saw creeping into politics under Liberal rule, the Cecils were perhaps expressing in an indirect way their disquiet at developments taking place within their own Party: the 'materialistic' appeals to the electorate, the domination of the 'caucus', a crude exploitation of the powers of patronage, the growing influence of businessmen, and so on. Underlying all these anxieties was a desire to return to an earlier period of aristocratic politics, when a handful of great families easily dominated public life. Already bitter at the partial take-over of the Unionist Party by Chamberlain and his friends, the 'Cecil connection' later came to see Lloyd George and other 'Radical Plutocrats' as possessing all of Chamberlain's faults without any of his few redeeming features.[31] Lloyd George understood this well enough, and, whenever possible, got his own back on them.[32]

No one journal reflected the convictions of the Cecil brothers. But, though strictly a Liberal Unionist rather than a Conservative organ, the weekly *Spectator*, edited by Loe Strachey, often found itself echoing their high-minded, but backward-looking, views of how politics should be conducted.

A similar dislike of the character and ambitions of Liberal Ministers motivated the Diehards—to whose protest movement, in fact, the Cecil brothers made a significant contribution. But most of the Diehards (that is to say, the Unionists grouped around the 'Reveille' in 1910–11 and later around the Halsbury Club) differed in their attitudes from the Cecils in several important respects. For a start, most of them managed to reconcile their belief in the 'natural leadership' of the country gentleman with support for Chamberlain's fiscal programme; indeed, men like Willoughby de Broke were fanatical Tariff Reformers, 'whole hoggers' to use contemporary jargon. Moreover, whereas the Cecilian approach to politics was frankly backward-looking and nostalgic, most of the Diehards took the view that aristocratic values

---

[31] In April 1922 Walter Long told Austen Chamberlain that he had been reading the first two volumes of Lady Gwendolyn's life of Lord Salisbury and could not help being struck by the close parallel between the feelings of Salisbury for Disraeli and of Salisbury's sons for Lloyd George (Long to Chamberlain, 27 Apr. 1922, Birmingham University, Austen Chamberlain papers, AC 33/1/62). Yet the Third Marquess did in time learn to co-operate with Disraeli, his sons never succeeded in doing so effectively with Lloyd George.

[32] For example, during the debate on Welsh Disestablishment, Lloyd George taunted the Cecils by accusing their ancestors of dishonesty in the way they had acquired Church property. See Grigg, John, *Lloyd George: From Peace to War 1912–1916* (London, 1985), pp. 28–31.

could only be preserved in the face of Radical attacks if the gentlemen of England were prepared to play the Radicals at their own game. Whereas the Cecils feared democracy, or, at best, viewed it with aristocratic reserve, Willoughby de Broke and his friends enjoyed the cut-and-thrust of platform speaking, and even supported the adoption of the plebiscite, believing that the masses were sound at heart and would respond if an appeal was made to their patriotic instincts; for they considered the existing alliance between Labour and Radical-Liberalism to be artificial and temporary. Selborne, whose importance perhaps lay in the fact that he acted as an intermediary between men like Willoughby and the Cecil brothers, expressed the robust confidence of the Diehards when, in a letter to the *Morning Post* in July 1912, he wrote, 'Take off the coat, and the Englishman will be found to be exactly the same man underneath, whether he be a peer or a dock labourer.'[33]

In the view of the Diehards conservatism was a limited creed because it offered resistance to all change; whereas *their* view of the world was modern—indeed, much more modern than that espoused by their radical and socialist opponents who were still imprisoned within a Victorian thought-world. Such political innovations as the referendum, drastic reform of the composition of the House of Lords, Tariff Reform, and compulsory military service, held no fears for these men, because they believed that whatever was conducive to the strengthening of the Empire would contribute to greater class harmony and national unity, and hence to a continuation of their own social and political influence.[34]

How, then, did the Diehards account for the Radicals' success in three successive general elections and for their own decisive defeat over the 1911 Parliament Act? First, they bitterly criticized the feebleness and effeteness of official Unionism, suspecting its leaders of 'collusion' with the Liberal Ministry. Secondly, they spoke of a variety of 'corrupt practices' which had entered British politics and which were 'distorting' the electorate's wishes. And thirdly there was a xenophobic strand in their thinking which led them to believe that the Empire was being undermined from within by treachery and by the malign influence of various 'alien' groups: Celts, German immigrants, and 'cosmopolitan financiers', all of whom were playing Berlin's game. (Incidentally, it is striking how large an overlap there was between the

---

[33] Draft letter to *Morning Post*, July 1912 (Bodleian, Selborne papers, vol. 79, fo. 94).

[34] Searle, G. R., 'The "Revolt From the Right" in Edwardian Britain', in Kennedy, P. and Nicholls, A. (eds.) *Nationalist and Racialist Movements in Britain and Germany Before 1914* (London, 1981), pp. 29–30; Phillips, G. D., 'Lord Willoughby de Broke and the Politics of Radical Toryism, 1909–1914', *Journal of British Studies*, xx (1980), 205–24. For a different view of Willoughby de Broke, see Sykes, A., 'The Radical Right and the Crisis of Conservatism Before the First World War', *Historical Journal*, xxvi (1983), 661–76.

Edwardian 'Scaremongers' and the scandalmongers.)[35] Belief in all these things, if intense enough, was sufficient to detach people from 'mainstream' conservatism altogether. That is why, to describe such people and their attitudes, historians have had recourse to the concept of the 'Radical Right'.[36]

'Radicalized' patriots, of the sort described above, had an inbuilt distrust of organizations and the bureaucrats who ran them. Consequently they tended to express their collective identity not through formal organizations, but through the medium of journals and newspapers. Two such journals were especially important as transmitters of 'Radical Right' attitudes: the daily *Morning Post*, edited by H. A. ('Taffy') Gwynne, and the monthly *National Review*, edited and owned by Leopold Maxse. Both were tireless in their efforts to track down scandals and corruption, reckless in the language with which they conveyed their suspicions, and by no means averse to criticizing the Unionist leadership for being implicated in the misdemeanours they had unearthed. Maxse, in particular, eschewed all accepted ideas of decorum and good taste in his violent and often extremely funny philippics against those he disliked. In fact, there is a sense in which he positively owed his livelihood to his reputation for 'irresponsibility', since many readers presumably bought his journal in the expectation of being shocked and amused. Quite literally, if scandals had not existed, the *National Review* would have had to invent them.

However extravagant their language, Gwynne and Maxse were at least treated seriously by many leading politicians and credited with sincere, if extreme, convictions. But the Radical Right also comprised rootless patriots whose reputation was more shaky. One of these we have already met: Arnold White, the freelance journalist. White had stood as a Liberal candidate in the 1885 General Election, before breaking with Gladstone over Home Rule. Thereafter, he combined a strident, xenophobic nationalism with flamboyant scandalmongering. Posing as the instrument of popular indignation against wealthy and powerful men who were unworthy of their position, White had rendered some useful public service by his part in exposing the swindling company promoter, Whitaker Wright—indeed, so energetic had been White's campaign that it briefly landed him in gaol for contempt of court.[37] But more typical of a later phase in Radical Right propaganda was his libellous vendetta against Hicks Beach over the Netheravon Affair.[38] Why Hicks Beach did not take legal action

[35] See Morris, A. J. A., *The Scaremongers: The Advocacy of War and Rearmament 1896–1914* (London, 1984).

[36] Searle, G. R., 'Critics of Edwardian Society; The Case of the Radical Right', in O'Day, A. (ed.), *The Edwardian Age: Conflict and Stability 1900–1914* (London, 1979), pp. 79–96.

[37] White, A., *Efficiency and Empire* (1901; ed. by Searle, G. R., Brighton, 1973), p. x.

[38] See Ch. 4, pp. 82–4.

remains something of a mystery. Perhaps he hesitated to give White, a notorious publicity-hunter, any further opportunity for self-advertisement, and like other victims of such personal attacks, he must have known how slim were his chances of recovering damages.

In 1906 White finally over-reached himself when he alleged that the late Financial Secretary to the Admiralty, Ernest Pretyman, had received favourable treatment from Admiralty officials over acquisition of land in Essex—an incident which led to the severance of his connection with the *Sunday Sun*.[39] But he soon secured another assignment as the hard-hitting columnist, 'Vanoc', on the *Referee*, where he was allowed a free hand in celebrity-baiting. It should be noted that White, unlike Maxse, was never a member of the Unionist Party: indeed, in the early years of the century he was an 'independent' commentator on politics who, if anything, tended to favour the Liberals.

But with the Liberals in office White had soon adopted an oppositional role.[40] This was the characteristic posture of all Radical Right journalists. As Austen Chamberlain later philosophically remarked to Maxse: 'I think that the real difference between us is that . . . my bias is governmental, whilst yours is anti-governmental.' If everyone was like Maxse, thought Chamberlain, 'no Government would escape whipping—indeed no Government would endure'.[41] White shared this predilection for holding up the powerful to censure, and it was not long before he was abusing the Asquith Ministry in the most intemperate way. In an article published in the *Daily Express* in November 1913, entitled 'Government of Political Gehazis: "Unclean" ', he likened Cabinet Ministers to lepers: 'Unpublished depths of corruption have been created within the last seven years by squeezable and unclean Ministers, uncontrolled by Parliament and drunk with power', he fulminated.[42] This was a characteristic utterance.

In assessing the role of Radical Right journalists in stirring up scandal, it must never be forgotten that there were thousands of readers who enjoyed these attacks for the excitement they provided, and that White and Maxse were public entertainers of a specialized kind, and rather skilful ones at that. Such journalism could therefore be quite lucrative, and this was shown by the phenomenal success of Horatio Bottomley's *John Bull*, which was founded in 1906 and had built up a circulation of half a million only four years later. Unlike Maxse and White, Bottomley was a mere cynical adventurer, and until

[39] *Sunday Sun*, 19 Aug. 1906, and material in Arnold White papers, vol. 158 (National Maritime Museum).
[40] Compare his contributions to the *Sunday Sun* in 1905 with the 'Vanoc' column.
[41] Austen Chamberlain to Maxse, 10 Nov. 1917 (West Sussex Record Office, Maxse papers, vol. 474, N 268).
[42] *Daily Express*, 17 Nov. 1913.

he threw himself into the recruitment campaign during the First World War, there is little evidence that his paper had more than a slight nuisance value.[43] *John Bull* can be seen as a parody of the newly emergent Radical Right school of journalism, which claimed to stand for the 'Little Man' and the 'Average Englishman' in the face of corruption and inefficiency in high places.

A weightier journal, because of the literary reputations of those who ran it, was the *Eye-Witness*, founded in June 1911 and reissued as the *New Witness* seventeen months later. This was the medium through which the Chesterton brothers and Hilaire Belloc purveyed their highly idiosyncratic blend of anti-Semitism, distributivism, medieval Christianity, anti-statism, and jovial hedonism. It may be questioned whether this little group should be bracketed with the Radical Right at all. Cecil Chesterton had once been a Fabian, and Hilaire Belloc had sat as Liberal Member for Salford South between 1906 and 1910. The *New Witness* also differed from the other independent patriotic journals in taking a favourable view of Irish Home Rule, in promulgating an egalitarian philosophy, and in denouncing the total rottenness of industrial society. On the other hand, it shared with the rest of the Radical Right an aversion to the secret party funds and to the contemporary party system, which it regularly denounced as a corrupt conspiracy.[44] The *New Witness* was savagely hostile to the Asquith Ministry, but neither did it spare the Opposition. 'The real political division', it declared in April 1914, 'is becoming more and more not a division between "Liberals" and "Conservatives" or between "Socialists" and "Individualists", but simply between honest and dishonest men.'[45]

In one respect the *New Witness* rather weakened the causes which it espoused. For it was an outspokenly anti-Semitic journal. For example, it carried the lunatic denunciations of 'the Rodent Race' penned by Hugh O'Donnell, who often 'went too far' even for Belloc;[46] and few opportunities were lost of drawing attention to the sinister part played by Jews in the scandals which were featured in its pages.

How integral a part, in general, did anti-Semitism play in Radical Right propaganda before 1914? Certainly, White himself had first come to public notice in the 1890s as a demagogic 'restrictionist' and had been partly instrumental in forcing the Balfour Government to set up a Royal Commission to study 'alien' (i.e. Jewish) Immigration, which led to the Aliens Act of 1905. In common with Maxse, White also took

---

[43] But note Bottomley's own extravagant claims about the paper's influence made in his letter to Goulding, 13 June 1910 (HLRO, Wargrave papers).

[44] See Ch. 7, pp. 160–1.   [45] *New Witness*, 2 Apr. 1914, p. 681.

[46] *New Witness*, 8 Jan. 1914, p. 309. For Belloc's reservations, see Speaight, R., *The Life of Hilaire Belloc* (London, 1957), p. 311. However, in a series of articles on 'The Jewish Question' published in the *Eye-Witness* between 7 Sept. 1911 and 26 Oct. 1911, Belloc had revealed the extent of his own considerable anti-Semitism.

pleasure in baiting rich Jewish financiers and businessmen whose 'loyalty' to Britain he questioned and whose way of life he portrayed as a threat to the sturdy traditional British virtues. Maxse and White were wont to claim that they were only warning Jews for their own good of what would befall them if they obstinately clung to an 'anti-national' line.[47] The final step of denouncing Jews because they were Jews was not taken, and popular outbursts of crude anti-Semitism deplored. Instead, the Jew figured in most Radical Right writing as a symbol of 'bad smart society', of rootless cosmopolitanism, and of acquisitive finance capitalism. Whether this makes Maxse and White anti-Semites is obviously a matter of how that vague concept is defined. Certainly, there was an anti-Semitic tinge to much Edwardian scandalmongering. But equally the allegations of corruption in high places in no way *depended* on the exposure of Jews. Even the *New Witness*, when it came to practical action, kept the anti-Semitic theme in the background, as we shall see when we come to examine the activities of the National League for Clean Government, an organization hosted by that paper.[48] The *Spectator*, of course, would have nothing to do with anti-Semitism,[49] neither would the Cecil brothers—Lord Robert, incidentally, being very suspicious of the *New Witness*.[50]

But even the more 'respectable' attacks made by patriotic independents on the corruption of Liberal politics were bound to be viewed by the leaders of the Unionist Party with mixed feelings. Anything which weakened the Asquith Ministry would obviously help the Unionists back to power. On the other hand, as we shall see, most of them feared to associate themselves with the more outspoken allegations for fear of goading their opponents into retaliation. Moreover, the motivation of the scandalmongers filled orthodox Conservatives with some unease. The power brokers inside the Party knew that, in the last analysis, the Cecil brothers could be depended upon, tiresome though their obsessive concern to uphold a particular concept of public morality might be. But the Radical Right, even as allies, posed a threat. For there were revolutionary implications in the quest for corruption in high places, and orthodox Conservatives were wise to keep their distance from it.

[47] For example, White in *Daily Express*, 8 Feb. 1913.

[48] Lunn, K., 'Political Anti-Semitism Before 1914: Fascism's Heritage?', in Lunn, K. and Thurlow, R. C. (eds.), *British Fascism: Essays on the Radical Right in Inter-War Britain* (London, 1980), p. 28. See also Ch. 7, pp. 160–1.

[49] Dicey, superfluously, urged Strachey in March 1913: 'Do not on any consideration give the least encouragement to Anti-Semitism. It is one of the glories of England to have escaped this prejudice.' (Dicey to Strachey, 26 Mar. 1913, Strachey papers, S/5/6/9).

[50] 'Have you seen the New Witness meat scandal?', wrote Cecil to Gwynne in January 1914. 'On the face of it it looks rather bad—but coming from such a source one is naturally cautious about accepting it' (Bodleian, Gwynne papers, vol. 17, Cecil to Gwynne, 6 Jan. 1914). In Parliament the 'meat scandal' was being pursued by the Conservative MP, Rowland Hunt.

Labour and the Socialists

Interestingly enough, these fissures on the Right were paralleled by fissures on the Left, where the Labour and socialist movements were uncertain what line to take over the scandals. It must be remembered that the Labour Party had been involved since 1903 in an informal electoral alliance with the Liberals—an alliance which operated in the three subsequent general elections. Moreover, when after January 1910 the Asquith Ministry lost its overall majority and fell dependent on Irish Nationalist and Labour support, Ramsay MacDonald, the Chairman of the Parliamentary Party, deemed it prudent to keep the Liberals in office rather than risk a return to Unionist rule. But this meant that Labour had to perform a delicate balancing act, since the Party was supposed to be independent and many of its supporters resented the way in which its identity was being lost as it became integrated into the 'Progressive Movement', which the much larger Liberal Party inevitably dominated.

What is more, the Labour Party from its foundation had been a loose federation of socialist societies and affiliated trade unions; in other words, it contained many Socialists but was not, as an organization, committed to Socialism as a goal. In general, the non-Socialists were ready to co-operate with the Radical wing of the Liberal Party, the political opinions of which did not greatly differ from their own. By contrast, most of the 'born again' socialists within the ILP wanted Labour to dissociate itself from *both* capitalist parties, and saw no particular reason why working men should show a preference for the Liberal capitalists.

The doctrinaire Socialists, therefore, were quite prepared to join the Radical Right in attacks on Liberal corruption, firstly, because they were predisposed to believe that corruption was endemic to the capitalist system and that it was the duty of socialists to expose it, and, secondly, because they saw these issues as a way of embarrassing MacDonald and the 'reformist' leadership and of prising Labour away from the entanglement of the 'Progressive Alliance'. MacDonald and his friends, on the other hand, believed that Labour neither could nor should go it alone, and so felt obliged to play down the so-called scandals and to defend Liberal Ministers from their detractors.

Thus the allegations of corruption made against the Liberal Party had the effect of dividing both the Unionist and the Labour Party, and, of course, they elicited a variety of responses from Liberals themselves. But none of the major parties could afford to ignore these scandals, each of which might by itself have been dismissed as of little significance, but which, in combination, seemed to add up to something much more important.

This is apparent from the letter which Lord Robert Cecil wrote to Gwynne in early Janary 1914:

Don't you thnk we ought to have an amendment to the Address deploring that no step is announced to check the increasing corruption of Public Life with examples from Marconi, Wick Harbour, Purchase of Railway Stock during the Coal Strike, Isaacs as Lord Chief Justice and peer, Meat scandal (?), sale of honours, with side lights from Payments of Members, and this new scheme of building cottages by Central Government—a well known form of bribery in the form of Public Works in other countries?[51]

Gwynne was sceptical about the existence of a 'meat scandal', but he said in reply that he would be 'delighted to see an amendment such as you suggest moved to the address'.[52] On 19 February Cecil and another Unionist MP, James Hope, tried to do precisely this by tabling an amendment regretting the failure of the Government 'to take any steps for preventing the growing debasement of the accustomed standard of purity in public life'.[53] As they later explained through the pages of the *Morning Post*, Cecil and Hope were anxious 'to track the evil results to the public life of the country which arise, separately and cumulatively, from such practices as the Sale of Honours, Payment of Members, the Marconi Scandal, the Appointment of the Lord Chief Justice, Lord Murray's Party Investments, and the conduct of the Wick Election'.[54] Unfortunately for them, the Speaker thought the amendment one 'of a rather indefinite and vague character' and he did not allow time for its discussion.[55]

But R. M. Leonard, the Secretary of the Secret Commissions and Bribery League, was stimulated by Cecil's move into considering the formation of a new pressure group, which could concern itself in a general way with 'purity in public life', something which his own League was powerless to do. Though Leonard claimed to have the support of *The Times* and the *Spectator*, nothing came of this venture.[56]

What these desultory discussions of early 1914 do reveal, however, is the belief of many opponents of the Asquith Government that the various mishaps in which it had become involved formed part of an interconnected system of corruption. And manipulating this 'system', so claimed the critics, was a gang of cynical and hypocritical 'Radical Plutocrats'— a popular target of Opposition abuse.

---

[51] Cecil to Gwynne, 6 Jan. 1914 (Bodleian, Gwynne papers, vol. 17).
[52] Gwynne to Cecil, 7 Jan. 1914 (BL, Cecil of Chelwood papers, Add. MS 51, 161, fo. 69).
[53] *Parl. Deb.*, 5 ser., lviii. 1268–70 (19 Feb. 1914).
[54] *Morning Post*, 19 Feb. 1914.
[55] *Parl. Deb.*, 5th ser., lviii 972–3 (18 Feb. 1914).
[56] Leonard to Cecil, 19 Feb. 1914 (Cecil of Chelwood papers, Add. MS 51, 161, fos. 108–9).

6
The Attack on 'Radical Plutocracy'

Social Life of the Liberals

IN December 1923 Winston Churchill won a famous libel case against Lord Alfred Douglas. In the course of the trial he easily exposed as absurd Douglas's far-fetched stories of how he had abused his official position during the War to help a syndicate of wealthy Jews. But Churchill did admit that late in 1905 the Jewish banker, Ernest Cassel, who had previously been a good friend of his father's, had furnished the sitting room in his new house—a gift which Churchill said that he had accepted 'as an act of spontaneous friendship'.[1]

The relationship with Cassel did not have the sinister significance which the paranoid Douglas supposed. But neither was it an isolated case. For example, in 1906 Churchill became friendly with the Baron de Forest, the rich adopted son and heir of Baron Hirsch, and he was often entertained by the Baron at his estate in Austria and went on cruising holidays with him.[2] This friendship had certain political consequences. After de Forest had unsuccessfully contested Southport as a Liberal candidate in the January 1910 Election, Churchill vigorously lobbied the Chief Whip in the hope of securing for him a winnable seat.[3] In the following year de Forest eventually got elected to the Commons as Member for West Ham North. Controversies followed him throughout his career. But Churchill loyally stuck by his eccentric friend, and the Liberal Party benefited from the friendship, at least in the financial sense. De Forest, for example, contributed heavily to Lloyd George's Land Enquiry.

The case of de Forest can be cited to illustrate the dependence of the Liberal Party on its rich financial backers. It also shows how Churchill—and he was not alone—was driven by social ambition into the sort of plutocratic environment which a 'good democrat' might prudently have avoided. Indeed, the very possession of office permitted those ministers who were attracted by 'Society' to gain an easy entry into it. Moreover, aristocrats and landed gentlemen who already belonged to this world discovered that their offices gave them

---

[1] Gilbert, Martin, *Winston S. Churchill*, vol. v, Companion vol. i (London, 1979), p. 81. In his will Cassel left money to the Asquiths, Churchills, Lord and Lady Reading, and Birkenhead, among others. See Pat Thane's entry in *DBB* i. 612.

[2] Churchill, *Winston S. Churchill*, ii. *Young Statesman*, pp. 156–8. On de Forest, see also Churchill, R. S., *Lord Derby: 'King of Lancashire'* (London, 1959), pp. 110–13; Grigg, John, *Lloyd George: From Peace to War 1912–1916* (London, 1985), p. 42.

[3] Churchill to Elibank, 26 May 1910 (National Library of Scotland, Elibank papers, vol. 8802, fo. 63).

additional opportunities for lavish social entertaining. When he was First Lord of the Admiralty, for example, Churchill took full advantage of the Admiralty yacht, the *Enchantress*, using it not only to carry out official inspections, but also as a kind of floating hotel which could be placed at the disposal of family and friends.[4]

Asquith, too, under the influence of his Society-loving wife, Margot, found that being Prime Minister guaranteed him a luxurious and stimulating social life and an assured place in the activities of the 'smart set'. That Asquith had a drink problem was soon fairly well known to those whose business it was to be informed about the personal lives of the famous and the great.[5] Balcarres wrote primly to a friend: 'Asquith is all the time touting for invitations to country house parties—many of his colleagues do the same—for they thoroughly enjoy the good things of life. I never saw a lot of men who so thoroughly appreciate a good dinner party and a good vintage . . .'.[6] Six years earlier Beatrice Webb had noticed the contrast between the ménage of Lord George Hamilton, the Tory country gentleman, and the luxuriousness of an Asquith dinner party, with its 'Second Empire' setting and ladies who were very 'décolletées'.[7] It would be silly to make too much of censorious comments like these. But Asquith's reputation as an *habitué* of decadent High Society was sufficiently widespread to compel his Private Secretary, Edwin Montagu, to remind him in 1908 that the Liberal Party was essentially a nonconformist party which frowned on luxury and frivolity; the occasion for this remark was the presence at an Asquith garden party of the dancer, Maud Allan, who was to figure in Asquith's life, in grisly circumstances, nearly ten years later.[8] Perhaps from 1912 onwards the Prime Minister was also harmed by the activities of his son, Raymond, the centre of a young fashionable set called 'the Corrupt Coterie', who, in Lady Diana Cooper's words, were 'unafraid of words, unshocked by drink, and unashamed of "decadence" and gambling'.[9] It was the Unionist Leader, Bonar Law, a gloomy, stern, and abstemious man, who seemed cut out by temperament to lead the Liberal Party.[10]

The case of Lloyd George is more difficult to describe, but because

[4] See Lady Violet Bonham Carter's account of the Mediterranean cruise which Churchill organized for his family and friends in May 1914 (Bonham Carter, V., *Winston Churchill As I Knew Him* (London, 1965), Ch. 19: 'Interludes of Delight').

[5] e.g. Balcarres's diary, 30 Oct. 1912, in Vincent (ed.), *The Crawford Papers*, p. 282.

[6] Balcarres to Lady Wantage, 25 Mar. 1910 (ibid. 149). See also Wilfrid Blunt's diary, 3 Oct. 1909, Blunt, W. S., *My Diaries: Being a Personal Narrative of Events 1888–1914* (London, 1932), p. 692.

[7] Beatrice Webb's diary, 20 Mar. 1906, in MacKenzie (eds.), *The Diary of Beatrice Webb*, iii, 34–5; see also entry for 13 Mar. 1910 (ibid. 136).

[8] Waley, S. D., *Edwin Montagu* (London, 1964), p. 30. See Ch. 11, pp. 261–2.

[9] Brock, M. and E. (eds.), *H. H. Asquith: Letters to Venetia Stanley* (Oxford, 1982), p. 117.

[10] Riddell's diary, Nov. 1911 (Riddell, *More Pages From My Diary*, p. 27).

his personality and way of life were the subject of much comment in the 1909–14 period, they must be examined. Lloyd George, it seems fair to say, lived his social life, just as he lived his political life, on more than one level and had the ability to move from one to another with bewildering rapidity. Frugality and abstemiousness were the qualities with which some of his contemporaries associated him. His friend George Riddell, after visiting him at his home on Wandsworth Common in late 1908, was struck by the unpretentiousness of the house and the simplicity of his way of life. We need not doubt Lloyd George's word when he told Riddell in December 1912 that he had few wants: 'a cut of mutton, and good, bright company' were what he enjoyed.[11] Certainly the Chancellor disliked aristocratic society; he was indifferent to the lure of stately homes and only rarely set foot in one.[12] Moreover, as he wrote to his wife after a visit to Balmoral, 'I am not cut out for Court life. I can see some of them revel in it. I detest it.'[13] Nor did Lloyd George fit into the world of Margot Asquith's smart dinner parties. In a letter to Elibank of November 1910 he referred contemptuously to the 'weekend snobs' who exercised a baleful political influence over her.[14] In fact, the Prime Minister and his Chancellor led social lives which scarcely intersected at any point.

Whether Lloyd George could have afforded to emulate the Asquiths, even had he shared the latter's social ambitions, is a moot point. On becoming Chancellor of the Exchequer, his official salary had risen from £2,000 to £5,000 a year. Prior to that his comparative poverty caused friends and party admirers to suggest that an allowance should be made to him from party funds or from private contributions; after some initial hesitation Lloyd George refused, fearing to jeopardize his political independence. But in 1908 he still claimed that he could not afford more than £1,000 for his house at Criccieth, and in the spring of 1913, when he appeared before the Marconi Select Committee, he claimed to be a relatively poor man.[15]

On the one hand, then, Lloyd George genuinely admired the self-abnegation and modest lifestyle of the Welsh tenant farmers, small shopkeepers, and struggling professional men among whom he had been brought up, and it was to his political advantage to stress his allegiance to their values. But there was another side to the Chancellor's character—the side which induced him to sit on the Wine and Cigars

[11] Riddell's diary, 5 Dec. 1912 (ibid. 107).
[12] Grigg, *Lloyd George: The People's Champion*, pp. 141–5.
[13] Lloyd George to wife, 16 Sept. 1911, in Morgan, K. O. (ed.), *Lloyd George Family Letters 1885–1936* (Cardiff, 1973), pp. 158–9. The letter continues: 'The whole atmosphere reeks with Toryism.'
[14] Lloyd George in Elibank, 29 Nov. 1910 (Elibank papers, vol. 8802, fo. 149).
[15] Amery, a member of the Committee, commented caustically in his diary (28 Mar. 1913): 'It really requires an Aristophanes to do justice to these situations' (Barnes, J. and Nicholson, D. (eds.), *The Leo Amery Diaries, i. 1896–1929* (London, 1980), p. 93).

Committee of *The Other Club*, of which he was a founder member.[16] His Welsh friend, D. R. Daniel, said of him: 'always the best hotels, the best food, the most comfortable seats—whatever the cost this was his motto always, and his weakness was that he never had a sense of delicacy when receiving gifts or favours'.[17] John Grigg, Lloyd George's biographer, denies the insinuation that obligations were incurred in this way. But he admits that the Chancellor liked Brighton and the company of the 'Metropole' type.[18] Examples of this type presumably include Charles Solomon Henry, a millionaire metal broker of Australian descent, and his wife Julia, an American Jewess; Julia for a time was one of Lloyd George's mistresses, and the Henrys entertained him lavishly in their various houses and on Continental motoring trips.[19] Some political opponents suspected, wrongly, that Henry must somehow have been involved in the Marconi Affair.[20]

Lloyd George also became very fond of Nice and the French Riviera, though he prudently refused to set foot in Monte Carlo casino lest he be recognized.[21] But the Mastermans, who accompanied Lloyd George to the Riviera in early 1910, found themselves in some embarrassment because he set a scale of expenditure that was too high for them.[22] There is piquancy in the spectacle of Masterman, who had mordantly dissected the plutocratic 'conquerors' in *The Condition of England* (1909), being rushed around the pleasure haunts of France in Lloyd George's motor-car.

'These penniless ministers are not living at their extravagant rate upon their official salaries', grumbled Balcarres. 'Lloyd George is not building his new house out of his salary. Somebody must be financing him. Who, and above all, why?'[23] In fact, it was the press proprietor, Riddell, who supplied the Chancellor with his country house at Walton Heath, where he could indulge his passion for golf on the nearby links.[24] Later in 1912 and 1913 Lloyd George, along with his friends Rufus Isaacs and the Master of Elibank, took advantage of the hospitality of another newspaper proprietor, the much-despised Harold Harmsworth,[25] who put 'La Dragonnière', his villa at Cap Martin, at his disposal. The villa was situated in a fashionable area—the Radical politicians had the Empress Eugénie as their close neighbour. According to a newspaper report,

[16] Coote, C.R., *The Other Club* (London, 1971), p. 23.
[17] Grigg, *Lloyd George: The People's Champion*, p. 128.   [18] Ibid. 144.
[19] Ibid. 128–9. Rufus Isaacs was another Liberal politician who often enjoyed Henry's hospitality (Reading, Marquess of, *Rufus Isaacs: First Marquess of Reading, 1860–1914* (London, 1943), p. 171).
[20] H. de Costa Andrade to Bonar Law, 20 Mar. 1913 (HLRO, Bonar Law papers, 29/2/29).
[21] Masterman, Lucy, *C. F. G. Masterman* (London, 1939), p. 155.   [22] Ibid. 180.
[23] Balcarres's diary, 14 Oct. 1912, in Vincent (ed.), *The Crawford Papers*, p. 280.
[24] Rowland, P., *Lloyd George* (London, 1975), pp. 227–8.
[25] See e.g. the contemptuous remarks about him cited in Koss, *Rise and Fall*, ii. 75.

La Dragonnière is situated in the forest, is surrounded by olive trees, and overlooks a valley now golden with the rich harvest of countless orange trees. Although small, the villa boasts a white marble staircase, winding from the sunny library to the red tiled roof. A loggia, screened from the sunshine by great jalousies, opens from Mr Lloyd George's bedroom, and gives a wide view of the Mediterranean, of Monte Carlo and of Mentano.[26]

It was in this exotic setting that some of the key episodes in the 'Marconi Scandal' were later to be played out.

Not, of course, that Lloyd George and his friends were alone in pursuing these luxurious pleasures. Captain Arthur Murray, a Liberal MP and brother of the Master of Elibank, records in his diary in February 1913 an occasion when Lloyd George, Isaacs, Jack Pease, and himself were dining at the Casino in Cannes, when they noticed that Balfour was a few tables away. 'After dinner Balfour came up to us with the remark: "Well, how is this criminal assembly getting on!"'[27] And the chairman of the Ramsgate Conservative Association could hardly believe his eyes when, on a visit to Nice, he saw Bonar Law playing golf with Isaacs and Lloyd George.[28]

As well as availing himself of the hospitality of his newly acquired plutocratic friends, Lloyd George tried to supplement his official salary by shrewd investments. Though he might shun the gaming tables of the Riviera, he had from his early days been fascinated by the prospect of Stock Exchange 'killings'.[29] The responsibilities of office did not curb these speculative propensities. The *Family Letters* show him in 1912 informing his wife of 'quite a good thing I have got' and coaching his relatives on how to play the Stock Exchange.[30] One of the commonest rumours of the Edwardian period was that Lloyd George, when President of the Board of Trade, had speculated in various dock shares at the time of the Port of London Bill.[31] In late 1909 Northcliffe gave Lloyd George's secretary a friendly warning of the kind of thing that malicious critics were saying on this topic.[32]

It will already be apparent how different from the circle of the Asquiths was that in which Lloyd George moved. Almost without exception, the Chancellor's political friends and business contacts were very wealthy men who for one reason or another made no serious

[26] *Daily Chronicle*, 10 Jan. 1912. See also Pound, R. and Harmsworth, G., *Northcliffe* (London, 1959), p. 440; Grigg, *Lloyd George: From Peace to War*, pp. 15–16.
[27] Arthur Murray's Diary, 28 Feb. 1913 (Elibank papers, vol. 8814, fo. 107).
[28] Edward Moyle to Bonar Law, 5 Apr. 1913 (Bonar Law papers, 29/3/6).
[29] See Ch. 2, pp. 41–2.
[30] Morgan (ed.), *Lloyd George Family Letters*, pp. 161–2.
[31] Grigg, *Lloyd George: From Peace to War*, p. 47, for rumour that Lloyd George had speculated in Surrey Commercial Dock Shares. Amery diary, 8 Dec. 1912, in Barnes and Nicholson, *Leo Amery Diaries*, p. 87.
[32] Enclosure in Northcliffe's letter to Lloyd George, 25 Dec. 1909 (not sent) (BL, Northcliffe papers, Add. MS 62,157).

attempt to join fashionable Society. The comfort and luxury which they sought could be attained in other ways. Riddell, Charles Henry, Isaacs (who had made a fortune at the Bar but had earlier in his career been 'hammered' for debts on the Stock Exchange): none of these men was quite 'respectable'. They were 'Metropole types' and they can be said to have constituted a kind of 'counter-Society', which aped the raffishness of King Edward's Court, while ignoring its dignified and ceremonial aspects.

Critics of the new plutocracy, and as we have seen they were many, understandably took exception to the social environment which Lloyd George found so congenial. But Conservatives were additionally contemptuous of it, because it was at almost total variance with the Chancellor's platform rhetoric. It is hardly surprising, therefore, that a section of the Conservative press should have attempted to discredit the Liberal Government by making personalized attacks on its wealthy members and supporters. It was in this context that the label 'Radical Plutocrat' was invented.

Attacks on Liberal Businessmen

First to be singled out for this hostile treatment were prominent Radical businessmen. For example, attacks were launched on W. H. Lever, the soap manufacturer, who also served as Liberal MP for the Wirral between 1906 and 1909. Although by the turn of the century Lever was a millionaire, his firm, like that of other soap manufacturers, was hard hit in these years by a combination of rising material costs, diminishing returns, and a frenzied advertising war. Lever responded by reducing the weight of his 'Sunlight' soap bars from 16 to 15 ounces, and in 1906 he brought together the major firms in a combine which hoped to effect economies by means of bulk purchases and common marketing arrangements. In September 1906 the manufacturers disclosed their scheme, and Lever started to take steps to lay off redundant agents and to cancel an expensive press advertising campaign which had been planned.

This last move angered the newspaper proprietor, Northcliffe, whose papers proceeded to launch a series of vituperative attacks against Lever, accusing him of conspiring to defraud the public through the machinations of an American-style 'Trust'. So successful was this campaign that Lever Bros.' sales dropped by 60 per cent and their share prices by approximately 25 per cent. But the jubilation of the *Daily Mail* and its stable-mates was short-lived. For Lever promptly sued Northcliffe for libel, and when the case was heard at Liverpool in July 1907 Lever won the then record sum for damages of £50,000. By the time all the litigation had been completed the Northcliffe Empire had lost £150,000.[33]

This episode cannot perhaps be categorized as part of the campaign against the 'Radical Plutocrats', since Northcliffe was himself a 'plutocrat' of a slightly similar type to Lever, and he had purely commercial reasons for behaving as he did. But the methods employed in the campaign—incessant newspaper denigration, the employment of agents who spied on Lever's works and interviewed disgruntled ex-employees—were to become commonplace in the taunting of other wealthy Radical businessmen during the next five or six years.[34]

Northcliffe was sufficiently chastened by the Lever Affair never again to indulge in vendettas against rich individuals in the business community. Indeed, he subsequently discouraged his newspapers from engaging in scurrilous activity of this sort. But other journalists were less fastidious. Not long after the Lever Trial came another libel case, this time involving George Cadbury, the chocolate-manufacturer. Cadbury was well known as a model employer and philanthropist, and also for being an enthusiastic supporter of a variety of Radical causes. But in 1907 he was arraigned in the *Standard* for financing his good works out of profits made possible by slave labour practised on the island of San Thomé, off the Angolan coast, which, between 1900 and 1908, was supplying the Cadbury firm with a significant proportion of its raw cocoa. Cadbury sued the *Standard*, and when the case was held in 1909 he was able to show that he had spared no efforts to stamp out the abuses of the indentured labour system, as soon as these had been brought to his attention, and, moreover, that he would have stopped the purchases altogether, had he not been dissuaded from doing so by Edward Grey and the Foreign Office officials, who argued that the Government could exert greater diplomatic pressure on the Portuguese if commercial contact was not broken. Cadbury won his case, but, impressed by Carson's powerful speech for the defence, the jury awarded him only a farthing in damages. At the time the trial aroused tremendous interest because of its strong political overtones. Cadbury's newspaper, the *Daily News*, had been unforgiving in its moral condemnation of the outgoing Balfour Government for employing 'Chinese slavery' in the South African mines, and the temptation to hit back at Cadbury by exposing his hypocrisy was irresistibly tempting to

[33] Pound and Harmsworth, *Northcliffe*, pp. 302–5; Jolly, W. P. *Lord Lever. A Biography* (London, 1976), pp. 46–57.

[34] Ibid. (both references). One interesting aspect of the trials was the unscrupulous behaviour of Lever's counsel, F. E. Smith, then an up-and-coming Conservative MP. Unbeknown to Lever, Smith was soon having private conversations with Northcliffe. 'He can help me greatly. L[ever] of no use to me', Smith is reported as saying. Northcliffe rewarded Smith for his 'treachery' by giving him some useful investment tips (Pound and Harmsworth, *Northcliffe*, p. 304; Jolly, *Lever*, p. 56; Campbell, John, *F. E. Smith: First Earl of Birkenhead* (London, 1983), p. 175; Smith to Northcliffe, 20 Apr. 1909, Northcliffe papers, Add. MS 62,156, fo. 155).

Conservative politicians, especially on the eve of a general election. In the end, the inconclusive nature of Cadbury's victory left him vulnerable to snide innuendos for the rest of his life.[35]

Attacks on the 'Cocoa Trust' also continued, thanks to an anomaly whereby the Liberal Government retained the import duty differentiating between raw and manufactured cocoa. This duty was repealed in 1911, to the considerable relief of the manufacturers themselves. The measure of protection afforded by this tax had played an insignificant part in the commercial success of Cadbury, Rowntree, and Fry, but the fact that such staunch Free Traders should benefit at all from the protection they so frequently denounced gave their many political opponents plentiful ammunition.[36] 'Cadbury, Cocoa, and Cant' became indelibly associated in the minds of Radical Right journalists.[37] The *World* gave currency to an even more popular epithet, 'the Cocoa Press', to describe the newspapers which the Cadbury and Rowntree families owned or part-owned. The *Spectator* and the *National Review* kept up the vendetta, while Strachey and Maxse congratulated one another on the good work they were doing. But Strachey was disgusted at the refusal of the 'incriminated journals' to publish material vilifying themselves.[38]

In fact, there was no way in which Cadbury and Rowntree could satisfy their detractors. If, for example, they cut betting news out of their papers, as an act of moral principle, they were denounced for interfering with the pleasures of the poor. After all, as the *New Witness* put it, no Liberal newspaper believed that 'the plutocrat should be saved from himself when he "makes a book"'; nor had Cadbury's papers had much to say about Liberal Ministers' little 'flutter' in Marconi shares.[39] On the other hand, when, after acquiring the *Star* and the *Morning Leader*, Cadbury reluctantly retained their racing columns in order not to lose too many readers, he was bitterly attacked by the *Spectator* 'as an odious example of the sleek hypocrite who profited by the degradation and vice of others'.[40] A refusal to credit the proprietors of the 'Cocoa Press' with any genuinely held beliefs inspired critics to argue that Cadbury and Rowntree only gave publicity to temperance propaganda because they wanted to boost the sales of their own particular beverages! The main charge against Cadbury, however, was that his Quaker pacifism made him a danger to the country in its hour of peril; he was, thought Maxse, one of those cosmopolitan cranks, the curse of modern British politics, who seemed to be oblivious of the security of their country, so long as they were

---

[35] Gardiner, A. G., *Life of George Cadbury* (London, 1923), pp. 242–51.
[36] Ibid. 240–2.   [37] *Outlook*, 8 Feb. 1913.
[38] Strachey to Maxse (copy), 20 Sept. 1911 (HLRO, Strachey papers, S/10/9/18).
[39] *New Witness*, 5 June 1913, p. 133.
[40] Paraphrased in Gardiner, *Cadbury*, p. 231.

free to make money out of its gullible inhabitants. Rowntree, who was less prominently identified with extreme Radical views, came in for less abuse; but his position as the leading social investigator on Lloyd George's Land Committee led even *The Times* to suggest mockingly that, if the functions of landowners were to be closely scrutinized, it might be a good moment to inquire into the composition of the chocolate industry, and the profits made from it—'in the interests of public health'.[41]

In one respect, however, none of the Cadburys or Rowntrees fitted the stereotypical image of a 'Radical Plutocrat'. Cadbury, for example, openly denounced the extravagant behaviour of 'speculators, tout-mongers, and owners of enormous wealth', lived a relatively simple and abstemious life for one of his financial means, and refused to accept either a peerage or a privy councillorship, saying that he did not see how this could be 'in the interests of the poor suffering people'.[42]

More central to the Opposition's idea of a 'Radical Plutocrat' were Sir John Brunner and Sir Alfred Mond, who both served as Liberal MPs while continuing to oversee the fortunes of the great chemical firm, Brunner, Mond & Co. Not only were they immensely rich, but they also wielded considerable influence within the Liberal Party. Brunner retired from Parliament in 1910 to hold the post of President of the National Liberal Federation for a few eventful years, while Mond, as well as being an MP, was part-proprietor of the *Westminster Gazette*.[43]

Like the 'Cocoa Magnates', Brunner and Mond laid themselves open to attack because they were eloquent advocates of Free Trade, while building up their family firm until it enjoyed a near monopoly of the alkali and nickel ore trades:

By the acquisition of patents and by agreements with foreign firms they have created practically a world-wide monopoly, by means of which they exploit the necessities of the poor, not only in Great Britain, but in other parts of the world. Out of this monopoly they make enormous profits, from which, no doubt, they are prepared to subscribe handsomely for propaganda against the two millions of landowners in Great Britain whom they allege to hold a monopoly. Sir John Brunner takes his 27 per cent out of his monopoly, but grudges a scanty 3 per cent to the owners of land.[44]

Brunner and Mond also had their records as employers critically scrutinized. These criticisms occurred despite Mond's painstaking attempts to improve labour relations at the Winnington plant, and his provision of a wide range of welfare facilities for the employees. The

---

[41] *The Times*, 23 Sept. 1912.
[42] Cited in Camplin, *Rise of the Plutocrats*, p. 231. See also Basil G. Murray's entry in *DBB* i. 553.
[43] His fellow directors included such prominent 'Radical Plutocrats' as Weetman Pearson, Charles Solomon Henry, Brunner, Newnes, and, later, the Master of Elibank.
[44] *Gleanings and Memoranda*, xl (1913), 1.

fact remained that some of the workforce were only drawing the low wage of 22s. a week. As in the case of Lever, disgruntled ex-employees were given ample opportunity to air their grievances in public. When contesting the Chester constituency, Mond could only reassure working-class electors after he had sent five working men to inspect his Babberton mines to refute Tory charges of bad labour conditions there. Mond ran into similar difficulties in the Swansea constituency in January 1910, when it took a libel action to force his Socialist opponent, Ben Tillett, to drop his allegations about the maltreatment of the workforce employed by Brunner, Mond & Co.[45]

Critics from the Radical Right were less easily silenced. An open letter in the *Outlook* in 1913 taunted Mond in what had by then become the conventional language of abuse:

Had your shareholders been content with, say, two-thirds of their huge dividends, and assigned less than one half of the remainder to a fund for the comfort of the poor workers whose arduous toil has provided for them their gluttonous wealth, they would still have had enough for the necessaries of their own pampered lives—for their thousand-guinea motor-cars, their palaces in Mayfair, their preserves, their deer-forests, their luxurious yachts—for these things are among the necessaries of the alien multi-millionaires whom we welcome in free-trade England.[46]

The final gibe was a reference to the fact that Mond was a Jew whose father had been born in Germany. Brunner's family was of Swiss extraction, but his critics seem to have supposed that he, too, was of German background. No doubt Brunner's attempts to reduce 'bloated armaments' and to secure an Anglo-German reconciliation fuelled these suspicions. Maxse was encouraged by these circumstances to launch a savage onslaught against Brunner in 1909, when in the pages of the *National Review* he wrote sarcastically about Messrs. Brunner and Mond as 'gentlemen of alien extraction who do us the honour of living among us, and of making great fortunes out of us, but who remain superbly indifferent as to the fate of our over-hospitable community'. Stung to the quick, Brunner sent Maxse a letter denouncing his 'vile' methods of controversy: 'I, whose fortune has been made in Cheshire, and is rooted in Cheshire, cannot be indifferent to the fate of the English community. . . . You speak of men as being "of alien extraction". Your origin is probably Dutch, but I know little and care less about that.'[47] In no way abashed, Maxse started a

[45] Bayliss, G. M., 'The Outsider: Aspects of the Career of Sir Alfred Mond First Lord Melchett' (University of Wales Ph.D., 1969, pp. 35, 62–5).

[46] *Outlook*, 18 Jan. 1913, pp. 73–4. The attack was picked up in the *Norwich Unionist* (June 1914), p. 8.

[47] Koss, S. E., *Sir John Brunner: Radical Plutocrat 1842–1919* (Cambridge, 1970), p. 238; Brunner to Maxse, 9 Mar. 1909 (West Sussex Record Office, Maxse papers, vol. 459, R51).

campaign in the *Daily Mail* to prevent aliens owning land in Britain.[48] Meanwhile his post-bag was full of letters from sympathizers in all ranks of life, most of them expressing delight at 'your spirited attack on Sir John Brunner and on the legion of scouts of all kinds sent here by the German Government'.[49] Maxse also voiced his anger when the Liberal Ministry conferred a baronetcy on Mond in 1910, and a privy councillorship on him three years later. (Brunner was already in receipt of both honours.)

A combination of Jewish origins, vast personal wealth, involvement in the City of London, and a commitment to the Liberal Party was the hallmark of yet another group of 'Radical Plutocrats', the 'Cosmopolitan Financiers'. Arnold White hit out at this group with unconcealed relish:

When Mr Lloyd George complains of the wealth of the Party to which he is opposed he suppresses the fact that the Party of the rich have been in power since 1906. Sir Sigismund Neumann, Sir George Albu, Sir A. D. Kleinwort, Sir E. Speyer, Mr H. H. Kleinwort, Sir Alfred Mond, Sir John Brunner, Sir Ernest Cassel, the late Lord Swaythling, and Mr E. A. Strauss, M.P., are examples of foreign-born millionaires who have successfully combined Liberal or non-Party politics with personal gain. How far the country is strengthened or enriched by the increasing sway of cosmopolitan financiers is an open question.[50]

Our Flag flaunted its prejudices even more crudely in its cartoon satirizing 'Sir Ludwig Saurkraut' of 'Sweatem Towers'.[51]

Attacks on Liberal Politicians

Not content with attacking businessmen and financiers, the critics of 'Radical Plutocracy' also devoted increasing attention to the personal lives of ministers. Those who conducted themselves with modesty and self-restraint, like John Burns, escaped censure of this kind. Others, however, were held up to ridicule because of the gap between their public posture of being friends of the poor working man and their private predilection for luxury and comfort. Not surprisingly, Churchill's pleasure jaunts in the *Enchantress* came in for much amused and ironic comment, some of it mildly affectionate, as in *Punch*.[52] But Maxse and the *National Review* affected to believe that the hard-pressed taxpayer was being intolerably burdened by the cost of entertaining the First Lord's friends: 'How much coal has been consumed by the *Enchantress* this year, and at what price?', it asked. 'How many lobsters have been eaten? How many magnums of

[48] *Daily Mail*, 13 Mar. 1909.
[49] F. Ware to Maxse, 18 Mar. 1909 (Maxse papers, vol. 459, R54).
[50] *Throne*, 19 June 1912.   [51] *Our Flag*, Aug. 1912. See Figure 2.
[52] *Punch*, 19 June 1912, p. 473. But this applies specifically to Asquith.

TYPES OF THE ENEMY—No. 1.

Sir Ludwig Saurkraut, Bt., of Little Britain, E.C.,
and Sweatem Towers, Kent, one of our Free
Trade Stalwarts. Author of "England for the
English," "Foreign Competition for Famishing
Families," etc., etc.

2. The Radical Plutocrat
(*Our Flag*, August 1912)

champagne have been drunk? To say nothing of the other delicacies composing a democratic diet.'[53] Again, some journalists wondered quite what *public* value attached to Edwin Montagu's leisurely tour around India between October 1912 and March 1913.

Churchill was a member of the landed aristocracy and behaved as to the manner born. It was even more annoying to Opposition critics to see ministers from humbler backgrounds enjoying the expensive pastimes of the upper classes, while retaining the right on other occasions to denounce these pastimes as anti-social. Lloyd George caused considerable anger when he delivered a well-publicized lay sermon to the City Temple in 1910 in which the ordinary man's healthy preference for cultivating flowers and vegetables was contrasted with the aristocracy's passion for blood sports. This homily was reported in the Liberal *Daily News* under the banner headline, 'BLOOM v. BLOOD'. Maxse, infuriated by what he called 'a ghastly piece of clap-trap', commented that he could not 'imagine the Prime Minister sitting at home on a vegetable patch, watching his flowers and his fruit; rather do we think of him like his Chancellor of the Exchequer "scorching" through the country in a motor-car to the total destruction of all bloom within several miles of his wild career or roaming over spacious golf links, where flowers and fruit and vegetables have been ruthlessly extirpated in order that "statesmen" may ineffectually endeavour to deposit gutta-percha balls in tin holes.'[54]

Lloyd George's love of golf also prompted the *Spectator* to some sardonic reflections. Why had the Chancellor, it wondered, exempted golf links from the undeveloped land tax of the People's Budget?[55] Unwisely, Lloyd George allowed himself to be nettled by his criticism into devoting a section of his next speech at Crediton to indignant self-justification and retaliatory abuse against the *Spectators*'s editor, whom he dismissed as 'an exceedingly pretentious, pompous and futile person'.[56] This, of course, simply encouraged Conservative MPs to make further snide remarks about Lloyd George's golfing activities. During the controversy over the Land Campaign, Henry Page Croft said to his Bournemouth constituents: 'When they came to think about it, there had been more land turned out of cultivation for the royal sport of Mr Lloyd George than was the case for game preservation, because no one would try to preserve partridges in any country where there was not cultivated soil.'[57]

[53] *National Review*, lx (1912), 38. [54] Ibid. lvi (1910), 373–5.
[55] See File in Strachey papers.
[56] Ibid. These remarks, Strachey later claimed, had 'always been a great source of enjoyment and amusement to me. It was so human an outbreak that it always gave me a pleasant feeling about Lloyd George and made me think better of him. . . .' (Strachey to Harold Spender (copy), 8 Apr. 1913, ibid. S/13/13/2).
[57] *Bournemouth Echo*, 19 Nov. 1913 (Churchill College, Croft papers, 3/3). See also Prothero's letter to *Morning Post*, cited in *National Review*, lxii (1913), 392.

The Government's enemies were well aware of Lloyd George's weakness for the good things of life, and drew attention to this in an attempt to expose him as an insufferable hypocrite. Thus in February 1912 *Our Flag* carried an article entitled: 'The Gospel of Self-Denial. WHAT DO *YOU* THINK?' Appended was a photograph—doctored—of the Chancellor in bowler hat and fur-lined coat, leaning out of a railway carriage, winking, en route to the Cap Martin villa. The paper reminded its readers that in a recent address to the churches in Cardiff Lloyd George had spoken about the need to make sacrifices for the cure of poverty, and wondered how these words could be reconciled with such behaviour.[58] The *Standard* embroidered on this theme at greater length:

It is not a crime to wear fur coats, or to travel in trains de luxe, and hire expensive villas on the Riviera. Anybody is entitled to do these things, if he pleases, and can afford the expense; but it is a little inconsistent for a person whose heartstrings are supposed to be wrung by the inequality of social conditions. . . . Mr Lloyd George cannot have the best of both worlds. He has, like other people, reconciled himself quite comfortably with the Mammon of politics, got all he could get out of it, taken nearly a hundred pounds a week out of the public funds as his remuneration, and expended part of the proceeds on giving himself those frequent and delightful holidays which only fall to the lot of 'dukes', plutocrats and well-paid politicians.[59]

The *Saturday Review* had similar observations to make about the Chancellor's double standards when news of ministerial speculation in American Marconi shares burst upon an astonished world.[60] And when Riddell made available to Lloyd George the weekend cottage at Walton Heath, Maxse made the by now familiar deduction. Lloyd George, he said, was 'entitled to buy, build, or hire as many houses as he pleases . . . as also to tour abroad in the magnificent motors of his millionaire friends and to luxuriate at palatial hotels; but he is not entitled to hold up to execration other people who lead infinitely more laborious and less luxurious lives, who have the misfortune to own land instead of "pleasure-houses", merely because they are of different politics, nor is he entitled to pose as a poor man.'[61]

It will be seen that the size of ministerial salaries as well as their consumption patterns came in for occasional criticism from those intent on discrediting the 'Radical Plutocrats'. Maxse was wont to list methodically the salaries of all members of Asquith's Cabinet. The point of the exercise was once more to poke fun at Lloyd George, who had been reckless enough to say publicly that if wealth were properly distributed, every family in the country would have £200 a year. What a pity, Maxse said, that the Government had not introduced, as the first bill of the new session, 'a Bill to bring the salaries of Cabinet

[58] *Our Flag*, Feb. 1912, p. 26.   [59] Cited in *Our Flag*, Feb. 1912, p. 26.
[60] *Saturday Review*, 26 Apr. 1913, p. 509.   [61] *National Review*, lxi (1913), 37*.

Ministers more in conformity with the Chancellor of the Exchequer's creed and the people's need, thus reducing the huge sums the country pays its politicians for the tragic mismanagement of national business'.[62]

Linked to these complaints was indignation, real or simulated, about the huge fees that government lawyers were able to earn, as during the *Titanic* Enquiry, when Isaacs, the Attorney-General, and Sir John Simon, the Solicitor-General, were paid fees of over £2,400 each for appearing as 'Counsel for the Board of Trade'.[63] It was not only from journalists like Arnold White and Hilaire Belloc that cries of outrage rent the air when the news was announced in the Commons. The *Saturday Review* commented that it was the payment of enormous fees like these which converted men to socialism.[64]

Indeed, a hatred of rich lawyers and a suspicion of lawyers in politics was an emotion which brought together political extremists of Left and Right. White complained that 'lawyers [had] got society into their grip, as the Churchmen of the Middle Ages obtained ascendancy over kings and carls alike'.[65] Like other members of the Radical Right, he objected to lawyers because their training led them to treat politics as a ritualized game in which forensic eloquence counted for more than wisdom or administrative capacity.[66] Also, the existence of so many lucrative openings for successful lawyers, he feared, was attracting into Parliament a particular social type: the job-hunting opportunist whose sole interest in politics was what he could get out of it.

But that, in brief, was how many critics saw the Liberal Cabinet itself—and its lawyer Prime Minister.[67] In the bitter atmosphere created by the passage of the Parliament Act in 1911 and the re-emergence of Irish Home Rule as an issue, extremist opponents of the Government tended to succumb to the view that the Liberals were only pursuing their criminal and insane policies because they feared for the loss of their ministerial salaries. It was perhaps predictable that the Marxist weekly, *Justice*, should sneer at Churchill, whom it represented as 'a member of that by no means unknown variety of "statesmen" to whom politics means a strenuous endeavour to obtain and keep £5,000 a year maintained for him at public cost'.[68] But from the opposite end of the political spectrum the same point was made by White when he wrote: 'To some Ministers, Irish politics is [sic] the raw material of champagne, of motor cars, of pate de foie gras, of trips to the Riviera, of tips on the Stock Exchange, and, generally, of a good time

---

[62] Ibid. lx (1913), 728–9.   [63] Ibid. 729.

[64] *Saturday Review*, 2 Nov. 1912, p. 538.   [65] *Daily Express*, 2 June 1913.

[66] *Referee*, 1 Mar. 1908, 2 Feb. 1913.

[67] F. S. Oliver wrote to Maxse on 31 Dec. 1913: 'Of course the Aged Squiff is about as low a character as ever came into British politics—with his mean, narrow lawyer's view of things' (Maxse papers, vol. 468).

[68] *Justice*, 18 Oct. 1913.

all round.'[69] The implication was clear: the Liberals were vulgar *arrivistes*, who lacked the finer manners of Britain's 'natural' ruling élite, men of broad acres and large inherited wealth.

The contrast thus drawn between landed and non-landed wealth was to play an important part in the political polemics of the late Edwardian period. In general, of course, the Liberals, especially those from its Radical wing, disliked landowners, whom they presented as an 'idle' class which exploited its monopolistic position to the detriment of all 'productive' workers. 'Profiteering' was how some Radicals described this relationship.[70] In fact, the distinction between real and personal wealth was very much in Lloyd George's mind when he launched his famous Land Campaign. But this Campaign quickly ran into furious resistance from the Conservative Party. In so far as they were prepared to distinguish at all between different types of wealth, Conservatives tended to take the view that landowners were far more useful and public-spirited than the big capitalists. For in acquiring a landed estate, a man assumed onerous responsibilities towards his dependents and was an important source of employment in his locality, whereas the capitalist, especially the financier, was free to shift his capital around the world in the search for maximum profits. We have already seen this line of argument being employed against the chemical tycoons, Sir John Brunner and Sir Alfred Mond.

The Radical Plutocrats Enquiry

But the Land Campaign offended most Conservatives for another reason. It was spearheaded by a semi-official committee, which called upon sympathizers to help in the compilation of detailed information about landlords as a class. Nor surprisingly, this was widely construed as an underhand, inquisitorial investigation into the lives of individuals. So offended was the Duke of Montrose that on 5 August 1912 he had a letter published in *The Times* attacking the Radicals and what he characterized as their sinister and secretive proceedings. But the Duke ended on a positive note. Why not retaliate, he suggested:

. . . a general feeling prevails that there is a wide field of taxation unexplored from which revenue could be obtained from those who are in the enjoyment of

---

[69] *Daily Express*, 8 Dec. 1913. One of White's 'informants' wrote to him complaining that while Parliament was sitting, the Cabinet met every Monday night in a private room in the Hotel Cecil, where they made a great deal of noise. 'I am thoroughly disgusted that the affairs of the State should be discussed at dessert after copious libations, the amount of which the hotel books would no doubt disclose.' He blamed the situation on 'the Jewish section of the Cabinet', who were perhaps defraying the expense (Arthur Kay to White, 16 May 1914, National Maritime Museum, Arnold White papers, vol. 83).

[70] Hyder, J., *Profiteering in Land, An Armoury of Facts* (London, n.d.). Hyder was Secretary of the Land Nationalization Society.

personal estates as distinct from real estates. Could not a small committee of enquiry be brought together for the purpose of obtaining authentic information as regards the wealth of all members of His Majesty's Government, its supporters, and all those pressing this unwarranted land taxation scheme? The committee might inquiry how these fortunes were obtained, how and where they are invested, what use is made of the proceeds, and whether the capital, or interest, pays it due share of Imperial or local taxation. For the purpose of obtaining this information, investigators would have to be appointed to take charge of this work. It is a labour which would obviously be greatly facilitated if your readers would suggest the names of some private detectives, bank clerks, Government employees, and other confidential servants, who would be likely to be of service in this connexion.

The *National Review* quickly spotted the mischievous possibilities suggested by the Duke of Montrose's letter; and its enthusiastic endorsement of the idea of a 'Radical Plutocrats Enquiry' elicited considerable support.[71] On 31 October 1912 some twenty-eight Opposition MPs met in a room in the Commons to set up a rudimentary organization.[72] There was a further meeting on 12 December, presided over in the first instance by Sir Frederick Banbury (then hot on the trail of those notorious Radical Plutocrats who ran the financial house of Samuel Montagu) and subsequently by George Wyndham. At the end of the meeting a representative committee of twelve backbench Conservative MPs came into existence, with G. Lane-Fox as Chairman and Major Archer-Shee as Secretary. By the end of the year the RPE had acquired premises at Westminster and had already sent all MPs two circulars, the first dealing with honours, the second with the behaviour of Radical landlords.[73] The *Spectator* was one of a number of journals which supported the venture: 'The movement began in a joke, but we see no reason why this attempt to unveil the disgusting hypocrisy of those posing plutocrats, who try to pass themselves off as earnest and simple-living working men and wear the red cap studded with diamonds, should not lead to sound practical results.'[74] The *Outlook*, the *Saturday Review*, and the *Daily Express* also joined in the fun.

The RPE, then, was more than simply an ingenious device for protecting the landed interest against its political assailants. It was also, as one of its officers declared, an attempt to 'destroy the dangerous legend which has been most assiduously fostered to our detriment that Unionism is the Party of the Rich, and Radicalism the Party of the Poor', and the aim was to 'make it impossible for wealthy Radicals to finance class attacks, as they do at present'.[75] An article in

[71] *National Review*, lx (1912), 19–20.
[72] Ibid. 716–17; Maxse papers, vol. 467.
[73] *National Review*, lx (1912), 716–17; Maxse papers, vol. 467.
[74] *Spectator*, 14 Dec. 1912, p. 998.
[75] Report of acting honorary secretary of RPE, 29 Nov. 1912 (Maxse papers, vol. 467).

Our Flag listed the names of some of the Liberal Party's richest supporters and members, under the banner headline: 'Which Is The "Party of Wealth"?'[76] But the RPE was also set up because men like Maxse thought that Radical demagogues could only be silenced if they were given 'homeopathic doses of their own medicine'.[77] The movement was frankly intended to intimidate. When the New Years Honours List of 1913 was published, the *National Review* attributed its modest and unoffending character to the fear which its own campaign had inspired; and Lloyd George's delays in developing his Land Campaign were also explained—quite erroneously, as it happened—to the fact that the 'Radical Plutocrats' had now 'been made to "sit up"' and 'realise the grotesqueness of their position'.[78]

The Enquiry quickly assumed the form of an attack on the rich businessmen who financed the Liberal Party. These 'cosmopolitan millionaires', thundered Maxse, were rich beyond the dreams of avarice in possessions which, to a large extent, escape the tax-gatherer's net, yet they sought 'to cast on to land the burden that should rightfully be placed on their own broad shoulders'.[79] The *Daily Express* reduced the issue to even cruder terms in a pugnacious article, headlined: 'TAX 'EM: Liberal Plutocrats Who Could Bear Georging. NO LAND—BUT TONS OF MONEY'. There existed, according to this article, 'landless Liberal millionaires far better able to pay taxes than the landlords whom Lloyd George proposed to drive out of existence', millionaires who, if taxed at a realistic level, would supply the country with the funds for building three Dreadnoughts to Germany's one, doubling old age pensions, and putting health insurance on a sound and honest footing. The author of this article obligingly provided his own personal list of fifty prominent Radical Plutocrats (most of them recently entitled) whose financial circumstances could usefully be investigated.[80] The *National Review* carried out a similar exercise.[81]

But the RPE also directed its fire at 'Radical Plutocrats' who did own landed estates. The Government's critics were, of course, aware that the Asquith Cabinet contained a number of wealthy traditional landowners—perhaps four Ministers answer to this description.[82] But although informers provided the organizers of the RPE with scurrilous allegations against Earl Beauchamps, for example,[83] great Whig landlords of this kind were spared the most savage of their attacks. Thus, despite his wealth, Lord Rosebery's name appeared on only one

[76] *Our Flag*, Oct. 1912, p. 155.   [77] *National Review*, lx (1912), 911*.
[78] Ibid. 911–14, 911*.   [79] Maxse papers, vol. 467.
[80] *Daily Express*, 6 Sept. 1912.   [81] *National Review*, lix (1912), 604.
[82] Beauchamps, Crewe, Edward Grey, Harcourt. Of the thirty-three Ministers who served in the Liberal Cabinets of 1905–14, perhaps nine can be classified as landowners.
[83] Maxse papers, vol. 467. The complaint came from the Unionist candidate in the constituency where Beauchamps's estates were situated.

of the lists of 'Radical Plutocrats'. Apart from anything else, such 'grand seigneurs' occupied a position so elevated that they could very easily brush aside any personal criticism that came their way. Thus, on 12 October 1912 a certain Philipp Carr wrote to Lord Crewe asking him how he reconciled his policy of letting part of his Madeley Manor estate for shooting with Lloyd George's recent speech at Bradford attacking the landlords' obsession with field sports. Crewe returned a polite and reasoned reply, commenting to one of his secretaries that the missive he had received was 'quite a nice candid letter of a rather stupid man'.[84]

'Loulou' Harcourt, an enthusiastic sportsman and a sizable landowner in his own right, was more vulnerable. The secretary of the RPE wrote to Lloyd George, suggesting that as he was 'now taking such a very great interest in the management of landed properties', he might like to consider the case of his colleague, the Colonial Secretary. For example, was it true that Harcourt had created only one smallholding on his Nuneham Courteney estate? There followed solicitous questions about the wages and working conditions of Harcourt's farm labourers, and a query as to whether 'the number of partridges shot on this estate in one season constitutes a record for that part of the world'. 'What shall I say in answer to enclosed?', wrote Lloyd George to Harcourt. 'It is a sheer piece of impertinence. We have conducted no such enquiry into the management of individual estates on the Tory side. Give me the material for a "snorting" reply.'[85] The Colonial Secretary duly supplied some relevant facts and figures. But his case, like Crewe's, illustrates the truth of Avner Offer's observation that 'Liberals were compromised by their complicity in the culture of the rural ascendancy.'[86]

However, it was upwardly mobile middle-class Radicals who had recently purchased estates whom the organizers of the RPE were mainly concerned to pillory, since they assumed that these were the men who, by their vulgarity and selfishness, were giving the landowning class as a whole a bad name. Having devoted part of his enormous wealth to buying out some impoverished Tory Peer, wrote Maxse, what does the Radical Plutocrat set out to do? 'He not infrequently proceeds to stop the pensions of the poor old people, to evict farmers in order to make room for keepers' lodges, and generally to sacrifice the peasant to the pheasant, which is the reverse of what Sir Henry Campbell-Bannerman promised to do when his party came into power

[84] Carr to Crewe, 12 Oct. 1912; Crewe to Carr, 17 Oct. 1912 (Cambridge University Library, Crewe papers, C/5).

[85] Peter Wright to Lloyd George (copy), 28 Oct. 1913, enclosed with letter from Lloyd George to Harcourt, 30 Oct. 1913 (Bodleian, Lewis Harcourt papers, vol. 443, fos. 187–91). Peter E. Wright was to make a number of appearances in the history of early twentieth-century scandalmongering. See Ch. 13, p. 303 and Ch. 14, p. 329.

[86] Offer, A., *Property and Politics 1870–1914* (Cambridge, 1981), p. 371.

seven years ago.'[87] 'Then again', claimed Maxse, 'look at the manner in which your purse-proud Radical plutocrat encroaches on common land, closes footpaths, denies access to his park to his humbler neighbours, and generally devotes himself to "swank" in the shape of huge battues of unoffending pheasants imported for the day in £1000 motor-cars.' The Enquiry under way would, he suggested, show that 'in nine cases out of ten the mushroom Radical squire is an infinitely harsher employer, a more inconsiderate, indifferent and ignorant landlord than his wicked Tory neighbours.'[88]

It was with these suspicions in their mind that the RPE released to the press on 18 December 1912 a questionnaire based in many ways on the Land Committee's controversial 'Rural B' form. The questionnaire asked its informers whether Radical landlords in their locality had helped the country people to purchase smallholdings on their estates, as Radical land reformers had urged; whether they brought pressure on their dependents to vote for the Government, while preventing their opponents from using schools under their control for political meetings at election times; and there were also questions about footpaths, access to parks, game preservation, and so on.[89]

Judging by the contents of Maxse's post-bag, this request for information brought in enough scandalous tit-bits to keep the campaign against the 'Radical Plutocrats' going for several years,[90] and it is therefore perhaps a surprise that the RPE simply dropped out of existence after a few months. In practice, the campaign went on, but in different forms; Maxse became obsessed, almost to the point of monomania, with the Marconi Affair, and other critics of the Government preferred to make specific charges of corruption, for example, over honours trafficking and 'jobbery'. One must also assume that the prospect of libel actions must have discouraged the leaders of the RPE from publicizing the confidential information which was in their possession.

But there were more general political dangers involved in conducting vendettas against particular individuals, and these led potential supporters to hold aloof from Maxse's activities. For example, after some perfunctory references to the RPE, Northcliffe's *Daily Mail* denied it any further publicity. Maxse wrote the press lord a letter on 19 December 1912, trying to persuade him that his campaign was not a device for 'booming the *National Review*', and explaining that the questionnaire had been drafted by ten or eleven Opposition MPs, 'many of them expert on the Land question'.[91] But Northcliffe

[87] *National Review*, lx (1913), 911*.
[88] Ibid. 912*. See also Derby's counter-attack against de Forest, taken up by the *Daily Express* (Churchill, *Derby*, pp. 110–12).
[89] Maxse papers, vol. 467. Published in *National Review*, lx (1913), 913–14.
[90] Maxse papers, vol. 467.
[91] Maxse to Northcliffe, 19 Dec. 1912 (Northcliffe papers, Res. MSS 131/23).

impatiently replied: 'I think that the "Daily Mail" was quite right not to print your Radical Plutocracy inquiry. Your little joke has already been given publicity in "The Times". Surely that is enough.'[92] Such rebuffs, of course, confirmed Maxse in his dark suspicions that sections of the Unionist press were holding back because they feared the withdrawal of Radical advertisements.

But Maxse's correspondence with various Conservative MPs shows that he faced more serious difficulties. Pretyman, the Opposition's spokesman on agriculture, for example, declared that he found the project 'distasteful': 'I may be wrong, but my own feeling is that the country is getting utterly disgusted with these swine and that we can preserve both our dignity and our property by fighting in the old-fashioned way.'[93] And Wyndham wrote: 'I would not collect evidence in the sneaking way adopted by Hirsch and George.'[94] Not surprisingly, those self-constituted guardians of the proprieties of public life, the Cecils, would have nothing to do with the campaign either.

Revealing, too, is the attitude of another leading Conservative Front Bencher, Alfred Lyttelton, who wrote: 'The question of how a man spends his time and his money is one for his own conscience, and I do not think that the spectacle of rich Radicals and rich Conservatives disputing with one another as to which has made the most use of the gifts of God, could be an edifying one for the people—even if it could be proved—and it can't—that the Radicals are all black and ourselves whiter than snow!'[95] There was a very real danger, many Conservatives feared, that agitations like the RPE would stir up class feeling and endanger the position of all wealthy men. Why do the Socialists' dirty work for them? Moreover, as Lane-Fox, the RPE chairman, reminded Maxse: 'It [was] really a check on the Radical side to have a capitalist section. . . .'[96] Was it really sensible for Conservatives to try to drive these men out of the Liberal Party, so polarizing the political system on class lines—the very thing which they were in the habit of accusing ministers like Lloyd George of doing?

But there were even greater dangers than this to the official Conservative Party. Ostensibly Maxse and his friends were attacking *Radical* Plutocrats, but it is obvious that they also had a quarrel to pick with *all* 'Plutocrats', including those who had gravitated into the Conservative Party. Cassel, for example, was often portrayed as a

[92] Northcliffe to Maxse, 20 Dec. 1912 (Maxse papers, vol. 466).
[93] Pretyman to Maxse, 17 Oct. 1912 (ibid., vol. 467).
[94] Wyndham to Maxse, 18 Oct. 1912 (ibid.).
[95] Lyttelton to Maxse, 21 Oct. 1912 (ibid.).
[96] Lane-Fox to Maxse, 30 Oct. 1912 (ibid.). It is ironic that when Lloyd George in 1914 found his Budget held up by the hostility of the rich businessmen in the Party, he should, if Asquith is to be believed, have attributed the trouble to 'the "Radical millionaires", i.e. Mond, Molteno, de Forest & Co' (Asquith to Venetia Stanley, 18 June 1914, cited in Brock (eds.), *Letters to Venetia Stanley*, p. 89).

'Radical Plutocrat', whereas, in fact, though keeping scrupulously clear of public controversies and being prepared to work confidentially with any government, he was a secret financial backer of the Tariff Reform League and a Conservative in his sympathies.[97]

The propaganda of the RPE tried to convey the impression that the Liberals stood for the interests of Capital, while the Conservatives were the party of landed property. But this was only partly the case. By the time that Bonar Law, himself a businessman, became Opposition Leader, about a quarter of his parliamentary followers were pursuing, or had pursued, business careers, and many more had business interests—a smaller proportion than was to be found in the Liberal Party, it is true, but a significant proportion nevertheless. The attack on 'Radical Plutocracy', therefore, was not quite what it seemed to be on the surface. For at a deeper level, it signified a protest against the changes that were beginning to transform the Conservative Party, as power slowly drifted away from the aristocratic connection to new men of wealth.

It was logical, then, that Maxse and his colleagues should later take part in a furious vendetta against those Unionists, many of them businessmen, who moved into Lloyd George's orbit and supported his Coalition Governments. But we must first describe the other attacks that the pre-war Liberal Administrations had to endure; and of these none caused more trouble than the allegation that Asquith and his Chief Whips were engaged in blatant honours trafficking.

[97] Mock, W., *Imperiale Herrschaft und nationales Interesse* (Stuttgart, 1982), pp. 256, 291; Pat Thane's entry in *DBB* i. 612–13.

7

The Liberals and the Sale of Honours Scandal, 1905–1914

Liberal Chief Whips in Action

UNDER the pre-war Liberal Governments the inflation of honours gathered still further momentum. During their ten years of office the Liberals created 102 peerages, as against the 81 elevated during the roughly comparable period of time during which Salisbury and Balfour held power between 1895 and 1905. This generosity upset even many of the Liberal stalwarts, while their opponents viewed it with a mixture of outrage and admiration. 'The Liberals', wrote Balcarres in his diary in November 1910, 'bleed their plutocrats, they distribute their honours, and they silence their malcontents with a skill which we cannot emulate.'[1] Indeed, there were those who later traced the excesses of the Lloyd George Coalition directly back to the behaviour of Campbell-Bannerman's and Asquith's whips—a charge which Herbert Gladstone indignantly denied.[2] But, if Pinto-Duschinsky's surmise is correct, the two major parties between them had raised at least £1,250,000 more than they actually spent in the decade prior to 1914, with the Liberals, like their opponents, amassing huge sums of money from a relatively small number of wealthy supporters.[3] To what extent was this achieved by corruption and a flagrant abuse of the Government's powers of patronage?

Herbert Gladstone, Liberal Chief Whip from 1899 to 1905, sub-sequently claimed that 'only a fifth [of the money disbursed while he was Whip] came from persons whose names appeared on the Honours List with which I was connected.'[4] He admitted that he had met precursors of what would later be called honours touts, but said that these people were courteously shown the door. Not in one single case, he boasted, did he 'hint directly or indirectly at an honour' when engaged in fund-raising.[5] Gladstone did confess to feeling some unease at the ennoblement of the coalowner, James Joicey, who hinted that he would give the Party £10,000 in return for a secondary honour; but since this honour was justifiable on quite other grounds, the peerage

---

[1] Balcarres's diary, 17 Nov. 1910, in Vincent (ed.), *The Crawford Papers*, pp. 167–8.
[2] Herbert Gladstone's Memo. (BL, Herbert Gladstone papers, Add. MS 46,118, fos. 105–12). Gladstone emphasized that the fund he had controlled was a Trust Fund, administered in the interests of the Party, whereas Lloyd George's was a personal one.
[3] Pinto-Duschinsky, *British Political Finance*, p. 54.
[4] Herbert Gladstone papers, Add. MS 46,021, fos. 167–8.
[5] Gladstone's draft autobiography (ibid., Add. MS 46,118, fos. 65–7, 69).

was indeed conferred.[6] There were clearly one or two more 'border-line decisions' of this kind.[7] In contrast to the confident moralizing of his later reflections is this contemporary note, dated December 1905: 'The ice may have been thin. But transactions should be regarded as a whole. If the letter of the law has not always been observed . . . let every one ask himself if in tax-rating and other matters, he has always observed the letter of the law.'[8]

Yet standards only began seriously to slip under Gladstone's successor, George Whiteley. A prosperous cotton manufacturer, Whiteley sat as a Conservative MP from 1893 to 1900, when he was returned for another constituency as a Liberal; henceforward, he served his new party with all the zeal of a convert. Gladstone expressed satisfaction when Whiteley became Patronage Secretary, and may in fact have suggested him for the post.[9] But in later years he was inclined to the view that the improprieties which marked the Lloyd George regime may have begun under his successor.[10] Even at the time Acland-Hood privately expressed amazement at the promotion and thought that the Government Whips would not enjoy serving under Whiteley at all: 'I am told he is quite unscrupulous and very cunning, and that all arrangements with him must be in writing.'[11] Campbell-Bannerman's Private Secretary, Arthur Ponsonby, watched Whiteley's methods with fascination and disgust. In drawing up the 1906 Birthday Honours List he noted that 'Whiteley enjoyed the money squeezing part of it which I think is particularly disagreeable', while the other Secretary, Vaughan Nash, agreed that, though affable, the Patronage Secretary seemed to be 'quite devoid of any "mind or political quality"'.[12]

Ponsonby was soon recording that the Prime Minister had become 'alarmed when he found that Whiteley the Chief Whip was sometimes extracting very large sums of money from [applicants for honours]. This had to be severely restrained.'[13] In a letter to Lord Ripon, Campbell-Bannerman had earlier expressed a fear that Whiteley may have been trying to wring money out of supporters, although he had been assured, of course, that nothing of the kind had occurred.[14] But

[6] Lloyd, T. O., 'The Whip as Paymaster: Herbert Gladstone and party organization', *English Historical Review*, lxxxix (1974), 809.

[7] e.g. the case of Horniman (ibid. 810). But note also Horniman's hectoring letter to Gladstone of 22 Nov. 1905 (not quoted in Lloyd): 'Considering what I have done for you and the Party and what I am doing at the Election, I depend on your bringing about the matter named between us' (Herbert Gladstone papers, Add. MS 46,021, fo. 85).

[8] Ibid., Add. MS 46,107, fo. 73.

[9] Hudson to Herbert Gladstone, 10 Dec. 1905 (ibid., Add. MS 46,021, fo. 103).

[10] C. P. Scott's diary, 1 July 1923, in Wilson, Trevor (ed.), *The Political Diaries of C. P. Scott, 1911–1928* (London, 1970), p. 441.

[11] Acland-Hood to Sandars, 19 Dec. 1905 (Bodleian, Sandars papers, vol. 750, fo. 274).

[12] Ponsonby's Downing Street diary, 3 July 1906 (Bodleian, Ponsonby papers, vol. 653, fo. 14); Nash to Ponsonby, 28 Jan. 1907 (ibid., vol. 654, fo. 27).

[13] Wilson, J., *CB: A Life of Sir Henry Campbell-Bannerman* (London, 1973), p. 584.

[14] Ibid. 580.

such bland disclaimers are hardly convincing. Whitley's successor, Jack Pease, who served as his Junior Whip, talked over the delinquencies of his former chief with Asquith, the new Prime Minister, in April 1908. 'We . . . discussed Whiteley's characteristics and his methods, the way in which money had been collected from those given honours was obviously most distasteful'. Pease recorded that two months later, Asquith told him that 'Whiteley had been skating on too thin ice, in selling honours', and that he asked him 'to pursue [a] different course'.[15]

The Honours Lists of 1906–8 which Whiteley compiled were unusually long—a fact only partially explained by the Liberals' long sojourn in the wilderness. They also contained some dubious names, among them the South African financier, J. B. Robinson, who had donated £30,000 to the Party when in Opposition and then made a scene when it seemed that he was not being put forward for a baronetcy. He enlisted the support of the Colonial Under-Secretary, Winston Churchill, who urged his promotion on account of his 'important public service' in employing white labour in the South African gold mines; but he also seems to have used threatening language about what might ensue if the Government turned down his claims.[16] Robinson received his baronetcy in July 1908—an event which in retrospect seemed to mark a decisive turning-point.[17]

It may also be significant that Whiteley's period as Chief Whip coincides with the first spate of rumours concerning the existence of honours touts. True, Humphrey Davies, Whiteley's Secretary, later claimed that his chief had taken steps to 'suppress' the touts.[18] And when in 1922 he appeared before the Royal Commission on Honours, Whiteley himself, while admitting that touts had been at work during his tenure of the Whip's Office, denied that they had exercised any influence.[19] Such claims can neither be proved nor disproved. What, however, is incontrovertible is that when Whiteley entered office, he inherited about £20,000, and that when he retired in June 1908, pleading ill-health, the Fund stood at £514,000.[20] No wonder Gladstone

[15] Pease's diary, 7 Apr., 5 June 1908 (Nuffield College, Gainford papers, vol. 38, fos. 4, 12).
[16] Lloyd, 'The Whip as Paymaster', p. 810; Wilson, *CB*, pp. 582–3; Herbert Gladstone to Ponsonby, 16 Dec. 1907 (BL, Campbell-Bannerman papers, Add. MS 41,217, fos. 308–9).
[17] Selborne told the 1922 Royal Commission on Honours that it was this award which first led him to expect 'a change of system'. He was also struck by the fact that it had been conferred without consultation with himself, then South African High Commissioner, or with the South African Prime Minister (Cambridge University Library, Templewood papers).
[18] Douglas, R., *History of the Liberal Party, 1895–1970* (London, 1971), p. 159 n. 4.
[19] Templewood papers.
[20] Blewett, N., *The Peers, the Parties and the People: the General Elections of 1910* (London, 1972), p. 291.

believed that the Party was becoming too rich for its own good.[21]

Whiteley was replaced by the Quaker, Jack Pease, who, in response to the Prime Minister's appeal, perhaps tried to get away from the more controversial of Whiteley's methods. But a reading of Pease's personal diary suggests that no fundamental changes occurred under his stewardship. On 4 June 1908 he records a meeting with Whiteley to consider 'who I might tap of his list'.[22] The following day he approached Herbert Roberts, whose name Whiteley had given him, and congratulated him on his prospective baronetcy; Roberts immediately said that 'he recognised the necessities of party and asked me to suggest what help I should like. I said £5,000, he offered £4,000, with a further £1,000 if I needed it before year's end.'[23] This was not exactly a sale of an honour, but came perilously close to it.

One new development, however, Pease could not condone. In December 1909 he learned that Lloyd George was raising funds for the Budget League by selling honours. Pease denounced Lloyd George to his face and said such behaviour was 'scandalous'. 'He took it lying down', though Churchill, who was present, spoke out on his friend's behalf. In a later conversation, Asquith admitted that Lloyd George had indeed asked for an honour for a Welsh friend who was anxious to do something for Welsh education and seemed a possible supporter of the Budget League. Pease records in his diary: 'I told Asquith what my opinion was of my slippery friends and how I raised cash without ever directly associating distinctions with party funds, and alluded to Kleinwort who had that morning responded by a cheque for £20,000 for the Election on my bare request.'[24] Since Kleinwort was made a baronet before the end of that year, Pease's moral distinction does seem a somewhat tenuous one.

Most revealing of all, in the matter of Pease's fund-raising, is the letter which he wrote in November 1910 to his successor, the Master of Elibank:

In reply to your question whether I think you might appeal to Kearley to further help the party having regard to his services and past assistance, I would say that the first time I approached him was when he was still working with Lloyd George at the Board of Trade, and he did not relish remaining on and had no intention (and naturally so) of playing second fiddle to Winston. He said the PM had offered him a baronetcy, and that George Whiteley had suggested if he liked he thought that generosity might be further acknowledged by a peerage. I think Kearley rather resented the suggestion, but he told me that if he later on took a peerage he would like to voluntarily help the Party by £25,000 or so, but he wasn't going to buy it. I merely thanked him and there the matter was left.

[21] Lloyd, 'The Whip as Paymaster', p. 790 n. 1.
[22] Pease's diary, 4 June 1908 (Gainford papers, vol. 38, fo. 10).
[23] Ibid., 5 June 1908, fo. 12.
[24] Ibid., 3 Dec. 1909, fo. 82.

I afterwards included his name among the Privy Councillors, and I hoped that I might have at the last election received something. I believe he wanted to help me, but he was ill and went abroad, and our interview never came off. I feel sure that if you now approached him he would like to respond in the direction indicated by him, at the interview I first had with him, and I know full well how much a Whip . . . can get for a General Election![25]

One should add that Hudson Kearley not only got his privy councillorship, but did indeed receive a peerage, becoming Lord Devonport in July 1910—an event immortalized by Hilaire Belloc in a famous squib.[26]

Meanwhile Jack Pease, who had prepared the Liberal Party well for its efforts in the January 1910 Election, in which over £110,000 was spent from central funds, a pre-war record,[27] was duly appointed to the Cabinet in February 1910. His successor was the Master of Elibank. Pease trusted Elibank even less than he trusted Whiteley and did what he could to dissuade Asquith from his choice; Elibank, he said, was 'a bit too scheming and wanted a steady hand over him', and he suggested that Seely would be a more suitable man.[28] Asquith ignored this warning.

Elibank is in many ways the central figure in the story of Edwardian corruption. Contemporaries all spoke with grudging admiration of 'Alick's' energy, resourcefulness, and persuasiveness. Margot Asquith described him as a 'rare combination of grit and honey',[29] and the Liberal journalist, J. A. Spender, has written of his skill at getting large cheques out of rich Liberals 'to be used for their own despoiling'.[30] From an early stage in his career Elibank cultivated the friendship of the great and the powerful by a judicious distribution of gifts and flattery. He had great charm of manner, though some people found it embarrassingly florid—Maxse's later nickname, 'The Master of Oilybank', was appropriate in more than one sense. He loved intrigue for its own sake, and was never so happy as when closeted with his particular cronies, Lloyd George and Rufus Isaacs, in a private room at the Café Royal or when holidaying on the French Riviera. From this association there later developed the Marconi Scandal, which nearly destroyed all three men's careers. Incidentally, it was from the South of France that Isaacs, Masterman, and Lloyd George allegedly sent

---

[25] Pease to Elibank, 18 Nov. 1910 (National Library of Scotland, Elibank papers, vol. 8802, fos. 146–7).

[26] Quoted in Churchill, *Winston S. Churchill ii. Young Statesman*, p. 284.

[27] Blewett, *Peers, Parties and People*, p. 293. This probably underestimates the Liberal expenditure in the Jan. 1910 Election. See Pinto-Duschinsky, *British Political Finance*, p. 42.

[28] Asquith to Pease, 2 Feb. 1910; Pease to Asquith (draft?), 4 Feb. 1910; Asquith to Pease, 4 Feb. 1910 (Gainford papers, vol. 88).

[29] Asquith, M., *The Autobiography of Margot Asquith*, ii (London, 1922), 145.

[30] Spender, J. A., *Life, Journalism and Politics*, i (New York, n.d.), 235.

Elibank a telegram of congratulation on 'one of his most flagrant Honours Lists' bearing the ironic words, 'all for merit!'.[31]

Of Elibank's exact methods as a fund-raiser we will always remain in ignorance. His papers contain some interesting letters, but the collection is on the thin side; in any case, someone so obsessively fond of the telephone[32] would not have committed any of his more reckless dealings to paper. A few surviving letters suggest that, in association with Lloyd George, he was only too ready to trade honours for cash, which he needed for his Party Fund and also for the 'Westminster Gazette Syndicate', which Pease had set up in 1908.[33]

To knowledgeable insiders Elibank was the 'fraudulent cherub',[34] and even colleagues, who viewed him in action at close quarters, found him an object of amused distrust. From Central Office Hudson wrote to Herbert Gladstone, now South African High Commissioner, in November 1911: 'Elibank is very well—and very daring.'[35] Geake, of the Liberal Publications Department, had written a few months earlier: 'Your successor, the Chief Whip, gives great satisfaction and apparently [has] plenty of money—though these are high mysteries which happily concern us not, so long as my LPD requests are met, as they always are'.[36] Pease was less indulgent about Elibank's idiosyncracies. In August 1911 there was a row when the Master objected to what he called Pease's continued interference in the Whip's Office. Pease sent off a stiff letter: 'Whether Elibank eats humble pie, or remains nasty I care not. I can cope with a creature of his methods (which I know inside out) *if* it is to be "silent war", but I expect he will eat the leek, after I have stood up to him!'[37]

Elibank's period as Chief Whip saw a record number of peerages and baronetcies: fifteen peerages in 1910, twenty-two in 1911, and ten in 1912, though the Coronation accounts for the large number of creations in 1911. Baronetcies numbered thirteen in 1910, thirty-five in 1911, and twenty in 1912—again a startlingly large number. Criticisms of Elibank's methods mounted both within the Party and outside it. In August 1912 he resigned his office, assumed a peerage (becoming Lord Murray of Elibank), and joined the firm of the great contractor, Lord Cowdray (a Liberal creation of July 1910), who wanted his services in searching for oil contracts in South America. Pamela McKenna thought it 'utterly squalid of the Master of Elibank to leave

[31] Lloyd George to Reading, 14 Aug. 1929 (India Office Library, Reading papers, EUR 118/127). Reading read out this letter to Grey, but left out the reference to this 'jocular telegram' (Reading to Lloyd George (copy), 21 Aug. 1929, ibid.).
[32] Riddell's diary, 19 Jan. 1913, in Riddell, *More Pages From My Diary*, pp. 117–18.
[33] See Elibank papers, vol. 8802, *passim*; Koss, *Rise and Fall*, ii. 191–3.
[34] Knollys to Sandars, 12 June 1911 (Sandars papers, vol. 763, fo. 92).
[35] Hudson to Gladstone, 14 Nov. 1911 (Herbert Gladstone papers, Add. MS 46,021, fo. 132).
[36] Geake to Gladstone, 11 Jan. 1911 (ibid., Add. MS 46,042, fos. 199–200).
[37] Pease to wife, 1 Aug. 1911 (Gainford papers, vol. 520).

us, all for the sake of filthy lucre. I always thought he had a mean spirit.'[38] But there were also signs that Elibank's health had been strained by his strenuous exertions of the previous two years. Lord Riddell was informed by Sir Charles Nicholson, MP, that Elibank had retired because he 'carried his methods too far. He could not keep them up'.[39] Perhaps too he had some premonition that his name would figure in the scandal that was shortly to break over ministerial speculation in American Marconi shares. From the Opposition benches Peter Sanders, who had at first supposed that Elibank's retirement was inspired by a desire to make money to restore his family estate, later concluded that the explanation was to be found in the Marconi Affair.[40]

The Marconi Scandal, and Elibank's part in it, is discussed in the next chapter, and the only aspect which need be mentioned here is the light which it casts on the Liberal Party's way of managing its finances. As Chief Whip, the Master of Elibank, as it later transpired, had felt free to purchase 3,000 American Marconi shares for the Party without consulting anyone or making any written record of the transaction. The money for the purchase had come from a 'Special' Account separate from the main Liberal Funds. On leaving office, Elibank had given his successor, Illingworth, a long list of securities, but had made no mention of the American Marconis. Instead, after consulting his legal adviser, he had handed over these shares in confidence to his brother, Captain Arthur Murray, himself a Liberal MP, giving as his reason a desire to shield the Liberal Party from further embarrassment until the Marconi business had been 'cleaned up'.[41]

Not that there was any suggestion of Elibank feathering his own nest. In fact, as the Opposition leadership soon privately discovered, he had later to pay out over £40,000 from his own pocket to the Liberal Party to replace what had been lost by the defalcation of his stockbroker.[42] But the whole episode cast doubt on the wisdom of allowing a single man unfettered discretion of this sort. Moreover, Elibank's refusal to return from Bogota to 'face the music' and give evidence before the Marconi Select Committee, and the exaggerated touchiness of the Liberal members of that Committee, Booth and Falconer, whenever the Party Funds were brought into the discussion, together created the impression that the Liberals were sitting on

---

[38] Pamela McKenna to Pease, 9 Aug. 1912 (ibid., vol. 90).

[39] Riddell's diary, 23 Dec. 1912, Riddell, *More Pages From My Diary*, p. 111.

[40] Peter Sanders's diary, 11 Aug. 1912, 10 June 1913, in Ramsden (ed.), *Real Old Tory Politics*, pp. 49, 64. See also *Our Flag*, Sept. 1912.

[41] Donaldson, F., *The Marconi Scandal* (London, 1962), p. 196.

[42] Balfour was confidentially informed of this in Nov. 1913 by his secretary, Sandars, who wrote of how 'we' had 'had access to the books of the absconding stock broker . . .' (Sandars to Balfour, 4 Nov. 1913, BL, Balfour papers, Add. MS 49,768, fo. 71).

further financial scandals that they were desperate to conceal.[43] In retrospect, Elibank publicly admitted that, though he had done nothing corrupt, his Party had every right to be cross with him.[44] Certainly, Massingham, the Radical journalist, was articulating a widely held opinion when he described the system of secret party-funding as 'the Achilles heel of Liberalism'.[45] And H. G. Wells was not alone when he drew from the Marconi Affair the lesson that the Liberal Party needed to open 'its large black bag' and effect a 'clean up' of its financial operations.[46]

The effect of the Marconi Inquiry was to make the new Patronage Secretary, Percy Illingworth, look rather foolish. But it is to his credit that someone who was initially thought not to be 'man enough for the job' should have dealt with the crisis with such cool common sense.[47] Like Whiteley Illingworth left no papers, so it is difficult to form an opinion about his methods as a Whip, but it seems probable that, appreciating the damage which Elibank had inflicted on the Party's reputation, he decided to act with greater circumspection. The Birthday Honours List of 1913 was on a remarkably modest scale, compared with its predecessors: two baronetcies, three privy councillorships, and no peerages. The Liberal press breathed a sigh of relief, and the Opposition newspapers offered the Government their ironic congratulations.[48] Illingworth's caution was encouraged by Asquith, who in the summer of 1914 was showing unusual sensitivity to the likely press reactions to the forthcoming Honours List.[49]

How well informed, in general, were the Liberal Prime Ministers with what their Chief Whips were doing in their name? The official version was that trafficking in honours was not happening, and that, even if a few minor irregularities did occasionally occur, this was without the knowledge of the Prime Minister, since it was an axiom of British public life that party leaders left all matters involving the raising and disbursement of funds to the untrammelled discretion of their Whips. This hoary myth was repeated in a Memorandum in the Asquith Papers, composed in 1919, which describes the Leader of the Liberal Party as a person wholly unconcerned with the financial transactions of the Chief Whip.[50]

---

[43] Donaldson, *Marconi Scandal*, Ch. 14.

[44] Report from Select Committee of House of Lords on the Charges Against Lord Murray of Elibank, 1914, vol. lxvi, para. 640. See also his apologetic letter to Lloyd George of 20 Aug. 1913 (HLRO, Lloyd George papers, C/6/5/6).

[45] *Nation*, 14 June 1913.   [46] *Daily Mail*, 19 June 1913.

[47] Peter Sanders's diary, 11 Aug. 1912, in Ramsden (ed.), *Real Old Tory Politics*, p. 49. But Hudson thought that 'Illingworth makes an *excellent* Whip' (Hudson to Gladstone, 17 Sept. 1913, Herbert Gladstone papers, Add. MS 46,021, fo. 142).

[48] *Westminster Gazette*, 3 June 1913.

[49] Asquith to Venetia Stanley, 18 June 1914, in Brock (eds.), *Letters to Venetia Stanley*, pp. 89–90.

[50] Bodleian, Asquith papers, vol. 148, fos. 72–3.

But what happened in practice? Campbell-Bannerman may indeed initially have been unaware of Whiteley's fund-raising methods, though his suspicions were aroused in 1907, as we have seen. An old and sick man, Campbell-Bannerman did not concern himself with such mundane matters, and his Secretaries, Ponsonby and Vaughan Nash, had too great a repugnance for this aspect of party politics to interfere on the Prime Minister's behalf.

But with Asquith it was different. For, as Pease's diary shows, Asquith knew a great deal about what his Whips were doing in the financial field and why particular individuals were nominated for honours. Indeed, it shows him adding or subtracting names on his own initiative. Pease's later testimony to the 1922 Royal Commission actually includes a table showing that, whereas during his period as Chief Whip he had successfully sponsored thirty-nine men for privy councillorships, baronetcies, and knighthoods, the Prime Minister was responsible for sixty-six elevations in the same period. (There were also three peerages awarded between 1908 and 1910, all of them, according to Pease, on Asquith's recommendation.)[51]

In any case, the Prime Minister was obliged to keep himself reasonably well informed about the personalities and aptitudes of the men who figured on the Honours Lists, if only so that he could defend 'controversial' nominations from a royal counter-attack—for the King's approval could never be taken as a mere formality. It may be true, therefore, as Asquith wrote to Spender, that there was nothing that gave him 'so much trouble, (or I may well add such profound disgust) as the allocation of honours. In the case of the smaller fry I am obliged to act mainly on the advice of the Whips and other such experts.'[52] But, as his whole career testifies, Asquith did not have a critical or enquiring mind, and he accepted the bestowal of honours as a tiresome and distasteful, but necessary, part of the political system, although he knew of the sometimes sordid transactions with which it was associated.

The Honours System

To what extent, then, did the Liberals preside over an exchange of titles for cash? It is difficult to give a precise answer to this question. As even the straight-laced Herbert Gladstone conceded, the British political system, as it operated in his day, did not allow for a complete separation of the conferring of honours from the administration of the party finances. If one assumed, as all the Liberal Whips did, that political parties were a force for good, then those who gave financial

[51] Pease's submission to 1922 Royal Commission on Honours (Templewood papers).
[52] Asquith to J. A. Spender, 11 Nov. 1909 (BL, Spender papers, Add. MS 46,388).

support to a party were rendering a valuable public service.[53]

The 'title cadger' was well aware of such considerations. But the more persistent of them went further and took the initiative in pressing the Whips for the honour which they thought they deserved. Pease later recalled that such supplicants invariably observed that they did not covet a baronetcy or knighthood for themselves but felt that it would be a gratification to their wife! This heart-rending plea, said Pease, was sometimes accompanied by an offer of money—which move he always countered by dimissing the supplicant from his presence.[54] However, on other occasions the Whips themselves, or their agents, approached a wealthy supporter with requests for money, dropping thinly veiled hints that this would lead in due course to an appropriate 'recognition'.

Moreover, honours touts were already plying their trade in the Edwardian period. Almost all the witnesses to the 1922 Royal Commission admitted as much, though they tended to picture the touts as impostors, who lacked the power to deliver what they were promising. Indeed, Whiteley claimed that the Whips took no notice of their efforts, and said that he found it difficult to explain why touting should have continued 'without any success'.[55] A similar line was taken by Pease, who recalled that he had received about three visits from touts, whom he described as 'men of not very high standing', acting as intermediaries between Whitehall and rich self-made men; he believed that the touts were freelances, who tried to collect a commission from the recipients of honours by falsely claiming that they were responsible for the bestowal.[56] Douglas Moffat, one of Gregory's future agents, was certainly operating in the pre-war years,[57] and there were undoubtedly others, too.[58]

Unionists were convinced that the selling of honours was taking place, and there was even talk of a regular tariff.[59] In November 1913 Lord Robert Cecil told his wife that one of his constituents had alleged that his cousin had been offered a baronetcy for £2,000 and that when he refused the offer, it had been sold to one of his neighbours![60] A leading fund-raiser for the Tariff Reform League, Joseph Lawrence, had

[53] As Whiteley later put it, party work was a good ground for the bestowal of an honour, 'and a contribution to Party Funds would be regarded as an additional merit' (Templewood papers).

[54] Ibid. [55] Ibid. [56] Ibid.

[57] Moffat's letters to J. J. Bell-Irving, written in Aug. and Sept. 1913, came into the hands of Gwynne in 1922, and can be seen in the Gwynne papers, vol. 8 (Bodleian). The correspondence was published in the *Morning Post*, 12 Sept. 1922.

[58] The Duke of Northumberland informed the 1922 Royal Commission of the activities on the eve of the War of a Glasgow agent who had offered an honour to 'a certain well-known gentleman in the North of Scotland'. He said that he possessed some incriminating letters but did not have permission to quote them (Templewood papers).

[59] Oliver Locker-Lampson, the Conservative backbench MP, claimed that a peerage cost £30,000 (*Parl. Deb.*, 5th ser., lxii. 1794 (19 May 1914)).

[60] Cecil to wife, 26 Nov. 1913 (Hatfield, Chelwood papers, CHE 5/124).

circumstantial evidence that the Liberal Government was approaching rich businessmen with promises of honours if they contributed to the party war chest. Barratt, the chairman of Pears Soap, told Lawrence that he had been followed to the seaside by a man who said he understood that he was 'desirous of an honour'; and a wealthy Liverpudlian had told him a similar story of a 'very sinister attempt' to get him to pay £4,000 for a baronetcy. Lawrence concluded:

This Government is perfectly shameless in going to *anybody*, provided they are wealthy (and vulgar) enough to pay a big price. One of these instigators and intermediaries . . . openly confessed that he would intercept about 20% of the money for himself and his friends for their success. He was brutally frank. This Government must have roped in *fabulous sums* in the past seven years by the sale of honours.[61]

This testimony might be dismissed as a partisan outburst were it not for the existence of broadly similar complaints from loyal Liberal Party members. For example, in 1922 an informant wrote to Donald Maclean, reminding him that 'many years ago when Mr Asquith was Prime Minister I ventured to approach the Whips Office with the modest request that the Government should confer a knighthood upon the late Mr John Conacher for the eminent services which he had rendered in bringing about the fusion of the South African Railways.' The informant went on: 'I forget who it was I interviewed on that occasion, but, while agreeing that Mr Conacher had rendered most valuable services, I was informed that nothing could be done unless I was prepared to put up £5,000. I politely told the gentleman to go to Hell or thereabouts.'[62]

Opposition indignation at the way in which the Liberals were abusing their powers of patronage was increased by the suspicion that, especially during Elibank's period as Patronage Secretary, the Liberals had begun the practice of 'poaching', that is to say, exchanging honours for cash with wealthy men whose political sympathies lay with the Conservative Party. Riddell raised this matter directly with Elibank in June 1912, and the latter's embarrassment and evasive response convinced him that 'poaching' was indeed taking place.[63] The Conservative Chairman, Steel-Maitland, certainly believed that the Liberals were breaking the unwritten code of conduct which had traditionally regulated these transactions and preserved harmony between the two Front Benches. His papers contain lists of all recipients of honours and titles from the Liberal Ministry, with marks

[61] Lawrence to Maxse, 14 June 1912 (West Sussex Record Office, Maxse papers, vol. 466, P97–P98).
[62] ? to Maclean, 2 Nov. 1922 (Bodleian, Maclean papers, vol. 466, fo. 172).
[63] Riddell's diary, 11 May, 6 June 1912, Riddell, *More Pages From My Diary*, pp. 60, 67.

made against the names of 'suspicious' cases.[64] Such cases formed a
very small proportion of the total numbers, but they may have made a
major contribution to the Opposition's sense of outrage. Lawrence,
too, believed that many of the recently titled men were 'flabby Tories
whose "wives wanted the honour"' and 'nominal Unionists' who,
sometimes because of the fiscal issue, had voted Liberal in 1906 and
given money to the Liberal Party in anticipation of future honours—a
class of persons, in Lawrence's view, who were even more to be
despised than genuine Radicals.[65]

There was also unease about whether all the names that figured on
the Honours Lists were worthy ones. True, even so severe a critic of
the Liberal Party as Henry Page Croft was later prepared to admit that
Asquith's Lists, reprehensible though they were, did not include men
found guilty in the law courts or ostracized by society.[66] In practice,
though, the Prime Minister took an indulgent view of the frailties of
human nature. Thus, in conversation with Pease in June 1908, he
argued that trying to seduce a girl did not bar a man from the peerage;
nor did he feel it to be a disqualification that a potential recipient of a
baronetcy was rumoured to have married his wife only at pistol
point.[67]

But this was not what Joseph Lawrence had in mind when he
complained of the Liberals' lack of scruple in bestowing honours on
anyone rich enough to be able to afford the 'going rate'. Behind such
complaints lay a well-founded belief that the Liberals were conferring
peerages and baronetcies on men whose social background differed
from that of Salisbury's and Balfour's creations. In particular, the
Liberals stood accused of altering the character of the House of Lords,
for the worse, by dumping there men whose way of life was
incompatible with what was expected from a peer of the realm.
Comparisons are not easy to make, but closer investigation does reveal
some interesting and significant contrasts between the Liberals and the
Unionists in the matter of the bestowal of honours (see Table 1).[68]

Start of Attack on Honours Trafficking

Ironically, the initial protests against the Liberals' operation of the
honours system did not come from Conservatives, but from disgruntled

[64] Steel-Maitland papers (Scottish Record Office), GD, 193/108/3, GD 193/388.
[65] Lawrence to Maxse, 14 June 1912 (Maxse papers, vol. 466, P97–P98).
[66] *Parl. Deb.*, 5th ser., clvi. 1786 (17 July 1922).
[67] Pease's diary, 11 June 1908 (Gainford papers, vol. 38, fo. 13).
[68] However, the situation seems to have been different in the case of knighthoods. F.
M. L. Thompson's researches suggest 'an all-round enlargement of the opportunities for
earning knighthoods rather than any pronounced alteration in the recruiting grounds for
knights' (Thompson, F. M. L., 'Britain', in Spring, D. (ed.), *European Landed Elites in the
Nineteenth Century* (Baltimore, 1977), pp. 40–1).

TABLE 1: *Reasons for Conferral of Baronetcies and Peerages*

	Unionists (%)	Liberals (%)
Political Services	22.2	30.4
Law	14.8	12.7
Other Public Office	24.7	19.6
Businessmen	16.0	27.4
sat as MPs	7.4	19.6
not MPs	8.6	7.8
Others	21.0	9.8

Radicals, who wanted the total abolition of the House of Lords, or at least a severe curtailment of its powers, and so were puzzled at the seeming willingness of their Government to strengthen the Upper House by adding to its numbers. The cantankerous Member for East St Pancras, H. C. Lea, felt so angry about this that he wrote a letter to *The Times*, published on 12 July 1907, in which he implored the Prime Minister not to create any more baronetcies and peerages:

These honours are bought and sold, the proceeds going principally to the war chest of the party in office at the time that so-called honours are conferred. . . . At times of election, if candidates come forward and cannot pay their expenses *in toto*, grants in aid are given. And should the candidate become a Member, his vote and support of the Government are looked upon as secure, no matter what the issue or what pledges he may have given his constituents.

This threat to the 'independence' of the Commons could only be averted, he implied, if the names of donors to the party funds were made available to the public. He concluded by expressing the hope that his protest might be a means to 'abolishing one of the hypocrisies of public life'.[69]

This outburst might well have been ignored, had Robert Cecil not moved a Motion on 15 July which claimed that Lea's letter constituted a breach of privilege and asked for the allegations to be investigated by a Select Committee of the House.[70] Cecil's object, of course, was to help Lea by forcing the Commons to take his accusations seriously. But Cecil's plan was foiled when Campbell-Bannerman, supported by Balfour, intervened to say that the only possible breach of privilege contained in Lea's letter was that section which impugned the independence of MPs; the bestowal of honours, the Prime Minister claimed, was purely a matter for the Crown. On the former issue Campbell-Bannerman declared that the House would look foolish if it took notice of Lea's 'impropriety', and he called on Members to proceed to the business of the day. After an angry outburst

[69] *The Times*, 12 July 1907.
[70] *Parl. Deb.*, 4th ser., clxxviii. 346–9 (15 July 1907).

by the Liberal backbencher, Arthur Markham, the Commons rejected Cecil's Motion by 235 votes to 120, the majority consisting of the two Front Benches and their loyal followers, the minority of rebels from the major parties, plus the Labour and Irish MPs.[71] This was to set the scene for future battles.

Parliament next debated the honours question in February 1908 when Hilaire Belloc moved a Motion attacking the secrecy of the party funds and calling for an auditing of their accounts. Like other Radicals, Belloc denied the necessity for these large accumulations of wealth, saying that the cost of politics could easily be reduced by transferring election expenses from the candidates to the State. But Belloc spent most of his speech on the alleged threat to the independence of the House posed by the system of party subventions—a charge that was considerably weakened by his candid admission that he himself was the beneficiary of such help![72] Journalists were agreed that Belloc's speech was a flop.[73] The debate only came to life when Lea proclaimed it to be 'a matter of common knowledge and gossip in the House, in the clubs, and in the streets that the titles and decorations in vogue in this country were just as lacking in dignity, prestige, and moral worth as the methods by which they were obtained were loathsome, corrupt, and nauseous'.[74]

But once again the Front Benches moved in quickly to prevent the allegations from being properly investigated. In a transparently cynical move, Stanley Buckmaster, on behalf of the Government, put down an Amendment deploring 'the way in which large sums, derived from the secret funds of the Tariff Reform League and other similar societies, are spent in electoral contests without being returned in the candidates' expenses'.[75] This manœuvre successfully switched the debate on to a 'safe' and conventional track, and the debate petered out innocuously with the carrying of Buckmaster's Amendment by 134 votes to 60. Belloc's original Motion was never put.[76] Only a handful of newspapers took this February 1908 debate seriously.

But on Belloc himself it obviously had a powerful effect. For it left him more than ever convinced that the party system involved a complex of corrupt transactions carried out at the expense of the general public but sustained by tacit collusion between the two Front Benches. This conspiratorial view of politics assumed fictional form in

[71] Ibid. 346–62.   [72] Ibid. clxxxiv. 899–905 (19 Feb. 1908).
[73] e.g. *Saturday Review*, 22 Feb. 1908, p. 223.
[74] *Parl. Deb.*, 4th ser., clxxxiv. 908 (19 Feb. 1908).
[75] Ibid. 917. Liberals were obsessed with the notion that their opponents were evading the provisions of the Corrupt and Illegal Practices Act through the help they were receiving from friendly pressure groups like the Tariff Reform League which were thought to be fabulously wealthy. In a forthcoming *Historical Journal* article Dr Franze Coetzee shows this to be a myth.
[76] *Parl. Deb.*, 4th ser., clxxxiv. 899–940 (19 Feb. 1908).

Belloc's novel, *Mr Clutterbuck's Election* (1908). In collaboration with Cecil Chesterton, Belloc then set to work on another polemic, *The Party System* (1910). 'Everyone acquainted in the smallest degree with the inside of politics', claimed the authors, 'knows that there is a market for peerages in Downing Street, as he knows that there is a market for cabbages in Covent Garden'.[77] Both parties engaged in these transactions, they said, but the Liberals were the greater hypocrites.

The appearance of *The Party System* happened to coincide with an event which was to lend greater urgency to the 'Sale of Honours' Scandal. For the Constitutional Crisis brought the Liberal Government face to face with the possibility that they might have to create upwards of 400 peers in order to force the Parliament Bill through a hostile House of Lords. This would have meant an 'adulteration of the peerage' with a vengeance! In fact, Asquith and the Whip's Office went so far as to draw up a provisional list of 249 Liberal supporters who were deemed suitable candidates for ennoblement.[78] This list, which, of course, was never published, comes as something of a surprise to anyone who has studied the actual Honours Lists pushed through by the pre-war Liberal Governments. It contains the names of politicians, businessmen, and celebrities in various walks of life who looked favourably on the Liberal cause (for example, Baden-Powell, J. M. Barrie, Bertrand Russell, Joseph Rowntree), but very few 'Radical Plutocrats' are included; in fact, only eight of the 249 persons listed went on to receive peerages or baronetcies between 1910 and the formation of the First Coalition Government in May 1915—an interesting commentary on what a Liberal Honours List might have looked like if the 'financial factor' could have been eliminated. In the event, of course, the capitulation of the House of Lords in August 1911 removed the need for a mass creation of peers.

Nevertheless, the events of 1910–11 were important in two respects. First, they greatly raised the political temperature and created a situation in which an embittered Opposition was looking for any opportunity to vent its spleen on the Liberal Government; and the issue of the sale of honours provided one of several emotive issues that could be exploited to that end. Secondly, and more importantly, they convinced most Conservatives that the Liberals and their allies were cynical opportunists who, in their anxiety to maintain their ministerial salaries, were prepared to play ducks and drakes with the Constitution, even if this meant humiliating an Upper Chamber which dared to offer resistance. In that context, Elibank's blatant operations as Patronage Secretary could be seen to symbolize something far more sinister. The link between the Constitutional Crisis and honours trafficking was brought out with particular clarity in a letter sent to *The Times* in July

[77] Belloc, H. and Chesterton, C., *The Party System* (London, 1911), p. 104.
[78] The list is published in Jenkins, R., *Asquith* (London, 1964), pp. 539–42.

1911 by a correspondent bearing the pseudonym 'Anti-Corruption', who observed that 'if even 100 of the new peers paid the much reduced subscription of £5,000 apiece, there would at once be half a million for the Liberal Government to play with—to subsidize candidates, double the efficiency of the organization, buy up local Opposition newspapers, and generally fortify the party position in the country and make it almost impregnable.'[79]

National League for Clean Government

In some ways the most ambitious attempt to embarrass the Liberal Government on the honours issue was made by Belloc and his friends. Having failed to get returned to Parliament in December 1910, Belloc joined Cecil Chesterton in founding the *Eye-Witness*, which was renamed the *New Witness* in November 1912. In the summer of 1913 this journal spawned an organization. 'The National League for Clean Government', which quickly attracted the support of an interesting collection of eccentrics and extremists.[80] An open letter published in the *New Witness* in October 1913, for example, went out over the names of—among others—Thomas Burt, the Lib.-Lab. miners' MP; James Barr, a leading member of the Eugenics Education Society; Fred Jowett, the Bradford socialist; G. K. Kekewich, the former Board of Education official and one-time Liberal MP; Rowland Hunt, a Conservative MP who was shortly to unearth the 'Meat Scandal';[81] and, inevitably, Arnold White.[82] The League set out 'to demand purity of Government and to expose and punish political corruption' and 'to prevent the sale of honours', as part of its wider campaign for the reform of the party system and the strengthening of Parliamentary institutions.[83]

The League may have made slightly more of an impact than is customarily recognized through its interventions in by-elections, which helped to keep the Marconi Affair and honours trafficking before the electors' eyes. For example, it was perhaps pressure from the League which encouraged Kerr Clark, the Unionist candidate in the Poplar by-election of February 1914, to make some strong speeches about Marconi.[84] Moreover, the League also put out a questionnaire to all candidates at by-elections inviting their views on its programme for cleaning up the abuses associated with secret party funds and political honours.[85] It then published the replies of all the candidates, failure to answer being construed as hostility, and, with the help of a paid

[79] *The Times*, 22 July 1911. [80] *New Witness*, 24 July 1913, p. 357.
[81] *Parl. Deb.*, 5th ser., lxviii. 465–6 (13 Feb. 1914); ibid. 752 (17 Feb. 1914); ibid., lxix. 1505–8 (12 Mar. 1914).
[82] *New Witness*, 30 Oct. 1913, p. 811. [83] Ibid.
[84] Ibid., 19 Feb. 1914, pp. 489–90.
[85] The League's questionnaire is published in *New Witness*, 4 Dec. 1913, p. 136.

organizer, campaigned on behalf of the candidate whose answers were deemed to be most satisfactory.

The *New Witness* was particularly pleased at the result of such intervention in the South Lanark by-election of December 1913, in which the Conservative who gave broadly favourable replies to all the questions was returned for the hitherto Liberal seat.[86] The League also congratulated itself on securing the defeat of Liberal candidates in Reading in November 1913 and in Bethnal Green South-West (where the loser was Masterman) in February 1914. These claims are difficult to substantiate, especially in the case of the Reading contest, where, as the *New Witness* ruefully conceded, the triumphant Unionist candidate flatly refused to give the League the assurances it wanted.[87] There were so many different issues embarrassing the Liberal Party in these months—dislike of Home Rule, the continuing unpopularity of National Insurance, and the intervention for the first time of Labour/Socialist candidates, for example—that it is difficult to see these election results as a simple mandate for 'clean government'. On the other hand, the results in two of these contests were very close: the Unionists won in Bethnal Green by a mere 20 votes and in South Lanark by 251 votes. And where the main candidates were running neck and neck in this way, it is not unreasonable to suppose that the National League for Clean Government, through its leaflets, public meetings, and canvassing of doubtful voters, might have decisively tilted the balance against the Liberals.[88]

The Campaign of Lords Salisbury and Selborne

The League saw itself as an organization of outsiders trying to change the ground rules of politics by mobilizing an aroused public opinion. However, from groups much closer to the 'Establishment' there was also grumbling about the evils to which the administration of the honours system had given rise. The key figure here was Selborne, who felt himself to be well qualified to speak on the subject since he had briefly served as a Junior Whip himself. Selborne's initial aim was to use his many contacts with people in high places to persuade the Unionist leadership to dissociate itself from the practices currently bringing the Liberals such discredit. Accordingly he wrote a joint letter to Bonar Law and Lansdowne in May 1912. In this letter Selborne said that he had been influenced in his 'onslaught on the sale of honours by the fact that it [was] a noxious and dangerous accretion to a legitimate

---

[86] Ibid., 18 Dec. 1913, pp. 202–3. The Labour candidate also gave a favourable response.

[87] Ibid., 4 Dec. 1913, p. 136. Here only the Socialist candidate responded favourably.

[88] For a description of its election methods, see ibid., 26 Feb. 1914, p. 525. On the National League for Clean Government, see also Lunn, 'Political Anti-Semitism Before 1914', pp. 28–33.

and reasonable system of recognising acquired position and rewarding public service', and declared that the abuse was 'doing grave and increasing damage to the prestige of the Crown and debasing public morality by enhancing the value of mere wealth'. While he said that he had no desire to fetter the Prime Minister's discretion, he argued that it was evil to give an honour to a man who had 'done no public work and holds no special position which can fairly be considered to justify it . . . [simply] because . . . he has engaged to pay cash for it'. Selborne continued:

To my certain knowledge honours have been recently hawked about by agents, the bargains made by them have been sealed and crowned in the gazette, and the price of 'honour' has been paid by those agents into the radical treasury after the deduction of a handsome commission.

He called upon the Conservative Leaders publicly to abjure these evil practices, in the hope that the Radicals might be shamed into following suit. He also offered his own services as a fund-raiser, should this be thought helpful.[89]

To this impassioned plea Bonar Law and Lansdowne turned a deaf ear. Lansdowne, while agreeing with Selborne's 'principles', privately felt that little could be done save wait until the Unionst Party was once again in office, when they might be able to lead by example; but that date, he conceded, still lay at some distance in the future.[90] Indeed, six months after sending his letter, Selborne had still not received a reply to it. True, the two party treasurers, one of them Horace Farquhar, had expressed sympathy with what Selborne was trying to achieve, 'but I expect friend Horace was foxing', Selborne later observed.[91] To break the deadlock he therefore threatened to bring in a Motion on the subject, knowing that this might embarrass his Party Leaders.

Bonar Law's dilemma can easily be appreciated. For, undeterred by the outcry over Balfour's Resignation List, the Unionist Whip, Acland-Hood, had continued to promise honours to potential subscribers, in his efforts to strengthen the Party's financial position. By the time he resigned in 1911, he had built up a 'nest egg of over £300,000', although this meant that 'a year's peerages [were] hypothecated'.[92] Without getting too involved in the murky details of these transactions, Balfour and, later, Law were broadly aware of what was being done in their name.

[89] Selborne to Lansdowne and Bonar Law, 11 May 1912 (HLRO, Bonar Law papers, 26/3/21).

[90] Lansdowne to Bonar Law, 15 May 1912 (ibid. 26/3/21).

[91] Selborne to Salisbury, 2 Nov. 1912 (Hatfield, Fourth Marquess of Salisbury papers, 72/144).

[92] Blake, Robert, *The Unknown Prime Minister: The Life and Times of Andrew Bonar Law 1858–1923* (London, 1955), p. 100.

In July 1911 Arthur Steel-Maitland was appointed Conservative Chairman and given responsibility for fund-raising. Perhaps surprisingly, Steel-Maitland seems to have felt confident that the behaviour of Conservative Central Office was irreproachable in this matter. At any rate, he was quite prepared to engage in an all-out attack on the Radicals' abuses. Thus, the official organ of the National Union, *Our Flag*, in true 'Radical Right' style, carried in its February 1914 number a spoof report and balance sheet allegedly placed by the 'Titles Manufacturing Company, Unlimited'. Founded in December 1905, this company claimed to have turned out 1,771 Peers, Baronets, and Knights, some of them 'of foreign origin'; the Chairman assured his shareholders that it took only 40 hours to turn out a complete Peer, Baronet, or Knight, and, though there had recently been a set-back, he was optimistic that 'the whole question of an accelerated output' would soon be satisfactorily solved.[93] Such witticisms might bring a smile to the lips of the Conservative readership. But was it wise of the Party to adopt this attitude of lofty disdain? Bonar Law and Lansdowne clearly felt not.

Nor could they have been pleased when Selborne returned to the fray in April 1913 with the suggestion that the Gazette should specify the 'public service' for which an honour was awarded, and a vetting committee be set up to 'screen' all nominations—ideas which he had 'adopted' from his brother-in-law, Lord Hugh Cecil.[94] *Something* must be done, Selborne told Lansdowne: 'I do not want to be prudish but I do want to be more particular than Lloyd George'.[95] But the Unionist Leader was discouraging, saying that neither he nor Bonar Law could see how any Prime Minister could consent to such a reduction of his powers[96]—an objection which Selborne had anticipated would be raised by Curzon but which he was surprised to find on Lansdowne's lips.[97] Bonar Law, too, continued to stone-wall; his new excuse was that 'the present time was ill-chosen for raising the subject, on the ground that it would tend to obscure the Marconi issue'.[98]

Selborne then met Asquith for an exchange of views. Predictably, the Prime Minister poured cold water on his expression of alarm, claimed that no vetting committee would have the knowledge to do the work that was being suggested for it, and said that he had no intention of talking things over with Law, since the latter had no experience in the honours field.[99] Selborne reported the substance of this conversation

---

[93] *Our Flag*, Feb. 1914, p. 27.
[94] Selborne to Hugh Cecil, 1 Sept. 1913 (Bodleian, Selborne papers, vol. 79, fo. 143).
[95] Selborne to Lansdowne (copy), 16 Apr. 1913 (ibid., fo. 120).
[96] Lansdowne to Selborne, 23 Apr. 1913 (ibid., fos. 121–2).
[97] Selborne to Robert Cecil, 1 Sept. 1913 (BL, Cecil of Chelwood papers, Add. MS 51,157, fo. 76).
[98] Robert Cecil to Selborne, 2 July 1913 (Selborne papers, vol. 79, fo. 131).
[99] Selborne to Asquith (copy), 11 Aug. 1913 (ibid., fos. 139–40).

to Lord Hugh Cecil, who found Asquith's assurance that he was innocent of his Chief Whip's doings quite implausible:

This used to be so in my father's time, perhaps, but I suspect that both Asquith and AJB know quite well that honours are sold, though they regret it and have not bothered themselves about details. It is incredible that Lord Michelham was made a peer or that Sir A. Mond was made a Privy Councillor for any except mercenary reasons, or that the Prime Ministers who recommended those honours were not perfectly aware of the nature of the transaction they were carrying out.[100]

By the summer of 1913 the persistent Selborne thought he had at least persuaded a reluctant Lansdowne to call a Party meeting which would consider the whole issue of honours and fund-raising. The idea seems to have been that there should be a gathering at Lansdowne House, attended by Lansdowne, Bonar Law, Steel-Maitland, Devonshire, Curzon, Selborne, and perhaps Salisbury. But no firm date was fixed.[101] In an attempt to keep the subject alive, Selborne abandoned the controversial proposal for a Privy Council vetting committee,[102] and contented himself with a mild resolution which attempted to bind Ministers not to treat a subscription to party funds as a consideration in the recommendation of a peerage or other honour.[103] Lansdowne's response was that he did not object to the new formula, but doubted whether it would do any good.[104] Then in late September the proposed meeting was postponed, allegedly so that the Party could concentrate on Ulster and the Land Question.[105] His patience now exhausted, Selborne wrote to Bonar Law on 3 November 1913, saying that in the circumstances he had no alternative but to proceed on his own behalf and that he would shortly be tabling a Resolution for discussion in the House of Lords.[106]

The debate duly took place on 23 February 1914. Selborne's Resolution, amended by Lord Ampthill, ran:

That in the opinion of this House a contribution to Party funds should not be a consideration to a Minister when he recommends any name for an honour to His Majesty; that it is desirable that effective measures should be taken in order to assure the nation that Governments, from whatever political Party they are drawn, still act according to this rule; and that this House requests the concurrence of the House of Commons in the foregoing Resolution.[107]

[100] Hugh Cecil to Selborne, 6 Sept. 1913 (ibid., fo. 153).
[101] Lansdowne to Bonar Law, 5 June, 18 June 1913 (Bonar Law papers, 29/5/8, 29/5/35), and Selborne to Bonar Law, 25 Sept. 1913 (ibid., 30/2/22).
[102] Lord Robert Cecil first misunderstood the exact nature of the proposal that Selborne was putting forward (Selborne to Robert Cecil, 5 Sept. 1913, Cecil of Chelwood papers, Add. MS 51,157, fos. 79–80).
[103] Lansdowne to Bonar Law, 18 June 1913 (Bonar Law papers, 29/5/35).
[104] Lansdowne to Bonar Law, 18 June 1913 (Bonar Law papers, 29/5/35).
[105] Lansdowne to Bonar Law, 2 Oct. 1913 (ibid., 30/3/3).
[106] Selborne to Bonar Law, 4 Nov. 1913 (ibid. 30/4/6).
[107] *Parl. Deb.*, 5th ser. (Lords), xv. 295–6 (23 Feb. 1914).

Strangely enough, this Resolution was carried without a vote, with even the sceptical Lansdowne and Government spokesmen assenting. But it was a lacklustre debate. From the Liberal side, the Leader of the Lords, Crewe, was suavely dismissive; no corruption was occurring, he said, and in any case things had been much worse before the passing of the Great Reform Act![108] The occasion was saved from mediocrity by a perky speech from Willoughby de Broke and a solemn jeremiad from Lord Milner.[109] 'I wish indeed we could have had you in the debate', Milner wrote subsequently to Rosebery. 'It threatened at one time to sink to a very low level, though Selborne made quite a good speech in opening. Even at the best there was never any real "grip" in the thing.'[110] Certainly few of the peers who took part in the February debate seem to have believed that much was amiss, and even fewer wanted to create a scene.[111]

But this time, in contrast to February 1908, the press dealt seriously and at some length with the ethical issues involved. Selborne received considerable support, not just from the more outspoken Opposition newspapers, but also from *The Times*.[112] There was a sequel when the Conservative backbencher, Oliver Locker-Lampson, introduced a Bill making the Traffic in Titles illegal.[113] It passed its first reading, but the Irish Crisis supervened before a second reading debate could be held. In fact, once again the Government adopted delaying tactics; there was no time for Locker-Lampson's Bill, Asquith told the Commons on 21 May.[114] So there, inconclusively, matters rested until Lloyd George's brazen behaviour as Prime Minister revived the issue in a much more intense way.

Conclusion

Why, then, despite the public concern, was nothing done to tackle the abuses surrounding the award of honours prior to 1914? First, as Selborne had discovered, there was no easy solution to the difficulties he had raised. Even someone who sympathized with his objectives, like Lord Robert Ceil, felt privately that 'public service' would be difficult to define.[115] A vetting committee of the Privy Council, which Selborne had taken up and then abandoned, was open to the objection that it interfered with the responsibilities of the Prime Minister—and

---

[108] Ibid. 282–7.   [109] Ibid. 268–73, 276–81.

[110] Milner to Rosebery, 24 Feb. 1914 (National Library of Scotland, Rosebery papers, vol. 10,124, fos. 140–1).

[111] See the cartoon in *Punch*, 4 Mar. 1914, p. 173: Figure 3.

[112] *The Times*, 24 Feb. 1914.

[113] *Parl. Deb.*, 5th ser., lxii. 1792–1800 (19 May 1914).

[114] Ibid. 2143–4 (21 May 1914). Four days earlier Lloyd George had told Lord Robert Cecil that the Government, while agreeing with the Lords' Resolution, did not intend to bring any proposals before the Commons (ibid. lix. 1852–3 (17 Mar. 1914)).

[115] Robert Cecil to Selborne, 8 Sept. 1913 (Selborne papers, vol. 79, fo. 155).

Lord CREWE (*to Lord* SELBORNE *on his way to the Debate on the Sale of Honours*). "I trust we shall have no stone-throwing."

Lord SELBORNE. "I'm entirely with you. Too much stained-glass about, what?"

3. The Sale of Honours Debate, 1914
(*Punch*, 4 March 1914)

also with the prerogatives of the Monarch. The opening up of party funds and their subjection to public audit, as Belloc and others demanded, seemed to the party officials and Front Bench spokesmen to be incompatible with the maintenance of the party system itself. After all, contributors to party funds who hoped to receive an honour wanted the outside world to believe that they had secured their title by merit; they would not give money to political parties at all, unless secrecy was observed.[116] Nor was either of the major parties confident that it could raise revenue by alternative methods, once the 'traditional' practices had been outlawed.[117]

Moreover, powerful interests existed to defend the status quo. The Liberal Ministry would not admit that anything was amiss, and few Liberal MPs, whatever their worries on the subject, were prepared to criticize their leaders; this was especially so after 1909, when party passions were running so strongly. Meanwhile, Bonar Law and Lansdowne were doing everything they could to induce Selborne to abandon his campaign. They probably feared a Liberal counter-attack designed to show that the Opposition Front Bench itself was deeply implicated in corrupt practices. Indeed, Selborne himself was frankly admitting that the existing evil had not originated during the Liberals' period of office.

Moreover, the critics of the 'system' found it difficult to unite because they were acting from a variety of motives. The Conservatives tended to feel a deep respect for the House of Lords as the institutionalized expression of the landed aristocracy, and wanted to thwart any further attempt to 'water' the composition of the peerage by the ennoblement of wealthy parvenus. These prejudices were particularly evident in the fulminations of the Radical Right. Maxse denounced what he called the 'White Slave Traffic' in honours, by means of which power was being transferred to 'the least desirable section of the plutocracy, i.e. cadgers after titles, who naturally get a "pull" on the party which they have privily helped to finance'.[118] His New Year wish for 1913 was that the country might be spared a further 'crop of despicable Barons, dubious Privy Councillors, bounding Baronets, and Knights galore who may have served their Party not wisely but too well'.[119] Whatever their differences of method and style, the Radical Right and the Cecils could agree that the Government was

[116] See Pinto-Duschinsky, *British Political Finance*, p. 55.

[117] In his draft Autobiography Herbert Gladstone describes the failure of his attempt to raise the money he needed from a large number of small subscribers. The campaign had brought in only £5,000 (Herbert Gladstone papers, Add. MS 46,118, fo. 63). Collecting money in large once-and-for-all donations was also less time consuming for the Chief Whips.

[118] *National Review*, lxii (1914), 713–14. Maxse called on Bonar Law to make a public self-denying ordinance.

[119] Ibid. lx (1913), 727.

intent on degrading the House of Lords—an objective which they often linked to other dangerous items in the Radical programme—like patronage abuses.[120] Indeed, the sale of honours was sometimes coupled with the Payment of MPs and the spread of 'socialism', all of which were treated as common symptoms of a growing and insidious 'materialism'.[121]

Conservatives of this stamp also entertained chivalrous feelings towards the Royal Family and felt very angry at the way in which both parties, but particularly the Radical Ministries, were 'polluting the fountain of honour'. Forcing the King to bestow honours on unworthy or mediocre nominees was perhaps all that could be expected from a Government which, Conservatives believed, had harried Edward VII into an untimely grave and subjected the inexperienced George V to merciless bullying during the Constitutional Crisis. In a more general way the Conservative critics of the system repeated what others of a different persuasion were saying, namely, that allowing wealthy nonentities to buy their way into a position of titular distinction meant the dishonouring of those whose receipt of an honour was a genuine recognition of merit and community service. As the *Morning Post* put it, official honours should be 'what prizes are in a school, rewards for merit'.[122] Other Conservatives, however, simply wanted to maintain the exclusivity of the House of Lords, and had little sympathy with 'meritocratic' ideals.[123]

One other argument deployed in the Unionist press against honours trafficking must be mentioned. Such activities, it was sometimes suggested, were discrediting the ruling élite and playing into the hands of Labour agitators. The *Morning Post* rebuked Lord Ribblesdale for his facetious intervention in Selborne's honours debate of February 1914, observing that now was not 'quite the time to be funny about the abuses of the party system'.

There are men about who want to see an end made of our whole system of government. They believe in 'direct action'. They believe that our political system is in the hands of rich men and the prey of corruption. They would like to destroy it, and when they find a Peer jesting about the sale of entry to his own House and order, they find evidence of the truth of their convictions. The old parties have to deal with a new electorate.[124]

Orthodox Conservatives wanted an issue on which to attack the Liberal Government. But they did not question the party system itself.

[120] See Selborne's speech of Oct. 1911, *The Times*, 21 Oct. 1911.
[121] Marriott, J. A. R., 'The Constitution in Suspense', *Nineteenth Century*, lxxv (1914), esp. 11.
[122] *Morning Post*, 28 Jan. 1914.
[123] See *Saturday Review*, 2 May 1908, p. 556.
[124] *Morning Post*, 26 Feb. 1914. See also *Pall Mall Gazette*, 24 Feb. 1914, Editorial, 'Keep Honour Bright!'.

This was where they differed from Belloc and the Chestertons, 'Tommy' Bowles, Arnold White, and, in some respects, Maxse. Characteristically, these mavericks were not just concerned with the sale of honours but equally or more so with the way in which the party funds so accumulated were being spent. The obsessive theme in Bowles's *Candid Quarterly* is the danger represented by the growth of the 'Caucus' which, through its wealth, was manipulating ministers and electorate alike, destroying the independence of the ordinary MP, and enslaving the press. In the face of this Reign of Terror, claimed Bowles, the average citizen was helpless.[125] This, in essence, was also the conspiratorial view of politics purveyed by Belloc and Cecil Chesterton in *The Party System*. Echoes of this indictment can also be found in Maxse's *National Review*, which repeatedly warned that honours trafficking was not only disreputable on its own account, but was also allowing an unscrupulous Radical Ministry to 'muzzle' the press by a judicious distribution of titles among susceptible press lords and editors. The fact, for example, that the *Daily Mail* made little reference to the sale of honours and later took an indulgent view of Ministers' Marconi speculations simply convinced Maxse that Northcliffe was too deeply implicated in the sinister underworld to welcome a proper investigation of it.[126] Logically enough, the Radical Right wanted the formal power of the party machines to be broken down, so that the electors and their representatives could again enjoy genuine independence. As so often, setting off from Conservative premises, the Radical Right had finally worked its way round to a distinctly Radical set of conclusions.

Orthodox Liberals, by contrast, obviously had no quarrel to pick with the party system. Indeed, the *Westminster Gazette* went further and actually defended the status quo with the argument that honours trafficking *shielded* Britain from the serious corruption which prevailed in other lands: 'the mere fact that a man takes a peerage in such circumstances is proof that his claims are exhausted, and, so far as the public are concerned, in an innocent way. The really dangerous men are the secret givers, who are not paid off, and who are all the time expecting a return for their money'—for example, in the form of legislative or administrative favours. Like other Liberals, the writer of this *Westminster Gazette* editorial went on to recommend as a remedy a reduction of the expenses of politics and the transfer of as large a part of them as possible to the public purse. As it pertinently noted, Payment of Members had had the effect of freeing the MP from the

[125] e.g. 'The Caucus and the Sale of Honours', *Candid Quarterly Review of Public Affairs*, iii (1914), 649–61.

[126] But Maxse thought that it was at least 'natural' for a 'convinced Radical' like Harold Harmsworth to accept a peerage from the Government in 1914 (*National Review*, lxii (1914), 916–17).

pressure of the Whip's Office, in so far as he now received a salary from the State; hence, it was 'worse than useless to denounce party funds, and at the same time to fulminate against payment of members as the end of all things'.[127]

The one major Liberal journal to take a strongly moralistic line against the misdemeanours of successive Liberal Whips was Massingham's *Nation*, a fact not perhaps unconnected with the disillusion felt by the editorial staff with Grey's 'reactionary' foreign policy.[128] Following the revelations of Elibank's handling of the party funds during the Marconi Affair, a much-quoted article appeared in the issue of 14 June 1913. The secret party fund, proclaimed the *Nation*, 'was the Achilles' heel of Liberalism':

So far as that fund is fed by contributions from sympathisers who give to their party as they give to their Church, expecting no return save in the advance of Liberal ideas and the success of the Government promoting them, we have nothing to urge. But so far as it accrues from the sale of honors [*sic*], a taint flows from it, and saturates the entire party system of Britain.[129]

The *Nation* favoured a public audit of the party funds. But as yet few Liberals were ready to embrace so novel an idea.

The Labour Party, too, was racked with disagreements on this issue. On the one hand, the Labour Left believed that it would benefit from a publicizing of Liberal corruption. Thus, as the outcry against honours trafficking increased, so did the amount of space devoted to it in papers like Hyndman's *Justice*, Blatchford's *Clarion*, the ILP weekly, the *Labour Leader*—now controlled by the fiercely anti-MacDonaldite, Fenner Brockway—and Lansbury's *Daily Herald*. For, as well as discrediting the Liberal Party, the goings-on of Elibank could also be used to demonstrate the moral decadence of capitalism.[130] *Justice*, for example, thought that the recent revelations might help to enlighten the working man and show him just how it came about that 'John Smith, sweater of several thousands of men, women and children' should suddenly 'blossom forth into Sir John Smith', and that this would force working-class Liberals and Tories to question their traditional allegiances.[131] Moreover, even the most 'moderate' of Labour men often urged the two capitalist parties to follow Labour's excellent example and publish their financial accounts in full.

But, looked at from a socialist standpoint, did moralistic posturing against the honours system make much sense? Swift MacNeill, the Irish MP who had done so much to raise the issue in the first place, enjoyed poking fun at the stupid snobbery of those who craved for

[127] *Westminster Gazette*, 24 Feb. 1914.
[128] Havighurst, A. F., *Radical Journalist: H. W. Massingham* (Cambridge, 1974), Ch. 8.
[129] *Nation*, 14 June 1913.
[130] e.g. *Daily Herald*, 19 Feb. 1914.   [131] *Justice*, 28 June 1913.

titles. Were he Chancellor of the Exchequer, he told the Commons in February 1908, 'he would create new honours, and raise revenue by the sale of them'.[132] The socialist weekly, the *New Age*, repeated the joke.[133] In more serious vein, it conceded that large secret funds constituted 'the main means by which plutocrats exercise[d] control over their political wire-pullers', but it also observed that this was 'the price the public must pay for maintaining the profiteering system at all'; 'our only hope of abolishing the party fund', it concluded, lay 'in abolishing that which makes it necessary, namely, the system of profiteering'.[134] Moral indignation was neither here nor there. The *New Statesman* broadly agreed, calling Lord Selborne's debate 'only a storm in a teacup, and an artificial one at that'.[135] More prosaic considerations also held Labour back, since most of its MPs depended on electoral collaboration with the Liberals and certainly had no wish to bring the Asquith Ministry down.

Yet despite the failure of the campaign against it, honours trafficking undoubtedly damaged the pre-war Liberal Party. One reason was that, as Pinto-Duschinsky has suggested, the Party in these years was accumulating more money than was needed to cover current expenditure, and though this surplus cash might theoretically have been used to field many more working-class candidates, in practice the existence of a large central fund served to discourage membership drives and to weaken the Party's organization at local level.[136]

In addition, discussions about the sale of honours drew attention to the links between the Liberal Party and the 'new plutocracy'. Many sincere members of the Party viewed this development with distress, while the 'Progressive Alliance', on which Liberals had come to depend, was perceptibly strained. Moreover, the morale and prestige of Liberalism were affected by its association with shady financial transactions about which it was impossible to speak frankly. Had the 'sale of honours scandal' stood alone, less damage might have been inflicted. Unfortunately for the Liberal Party, this controversial episode ran parallel to the Marconi and the 'Indian Silver' Scandals. It is to an analysis of these events that we must now turn.

---

[132] *Parl. Deb.*, 4th ser., clxxxiv. 916 (19 Feb. 1908).
[133] *New Age*, 29 Feb. 1908, p. 343.
[134] Ibid., 26 June 1913, p. 218.
[135] *New Statesman*, 28 Feb. 1914, pp. 644–5.
[136] Pinto-Duschinsky, *British Political Finance*, pp. 57–8.

8
Marconi

Introduction

IN her skilful account of the Marconi affair, Frances Donaldson describes it as 'an isolated incident without . . . much historical significance'.[1] While recognizing that Lloyd George was lucky to emerge from it with his career still intact, most historians have followed her in this interpretation, leaving it unexplained why the Marconi Affair should have aroused so much excitement in its day. But once Marconi is related to the agitation over honours trafficking, the anti-social behaviour of the 'Radical Plutocrats', and other 'scandals', it becomes much easier to understand why in mid-June 1913 the Liberal Government trembled on the edge of resignation, with well-informed experts anticipating a dissolution which would involve the Liberal Party in massive electoral defeat.

In broad outline the facts of the case are well known, and have been ever since the appearance of the Select Committee's reports in June 1913. The affair originated in a decision by the Government to construct a chain of eighteen wireless stations to link together different parts of the British Empire. By 7 March 1912 a tender had been signed between the Post Office and the Marconi Wireless Telegraph Company covering arrangements for the erection of the first six stations, and the contract was awaiting parliamentary ratification when the Government was forced into a postponement because of widespread criticism of the agreement and also because of rumours emanating in the City, but soon current at Westminster, which linked leading Ministers to speculative transactions in Marconi shares.

On 11 October 1912, in a Commons debate covering many aspects of the Marconi agreement, Ministers implicated in the rumours took the opportunity of protesting their innocence. But the Government nevertheless agreed to set up a Commons Select Committee of Enquiry. By the time this had submitted its reports—for there was a minority as well as a majority report—it had been conclusively established that, while no Minister had trafficked in English Marconi shares, Lloyd George, Rufus Isaacs, the Attorney-General, and the Master of Elibank (the Patronage Secretary) had made speculative purchases in *American* Marconi shares, while Elibank, on his own initiative, had bought a further 3,000 shares as an investment out of Liberal Party funds. The initial purchase had been effected through Godfrey Isaacs, who had offered his brother, Rufus, a batch of newly

[1] Donaldson, *Marconi Scandal*, p. 249.

issued shares at the low price of £1. 1s. 3d. Rufus Isaacs declined this offer, but a week later agreed to purchase 10,000 of these shares at the appreciated price of £2 through the intermediation of a third brother, Harry. Rufus then offered 1,000 shares each to his close political friends, Lloyd George and Elibank. A complicated set of transactions followed in which the Ministers bought and sold American Marconi shares, ending up, in fact, with a loss. This behaviour was foolish, but was it, in any serious sense, corrupt? At the time the Ministers themselves cannot have believed that it was, because they traded in the shares in their own names, when they could easily have done so through intermediaries.

Moreover, the incriminated Ministers, with the official blessing of their party, continued to protest both in public and in private that they had done nothing worse than commit a minor indiscretion. The centre of their defence was that the American Marconi Company was quite separate from the English Company and had no interest, direct or indirect, in the negotiations being undertaken by the Post Office. The *Manchester Guardian*, which throughout the affair took a friendly view of the Ministers' actions, went so far as to claim that all talk about 'the interdependence of the two companies . . . [was] largely a matter of hypothesis and surmise'.[2] But these protestations do not carry much conviction. For a start, the English Company had a holding in the American Company, with three of the English directors sitting on the American board, and Godfrey Isaacs himself also happened to be Manager of the English Company. As well as this interlocking membership at directorship level, the two companies were linked because they employed the same patent; thus, any evidence that the British Government preferred the Marconi system of wireless broad-casting to the rival Telefunken and Poulsen systems was bound to produce a rapid appreciation in the share values of *all* Marconi companies, and this did, in fact, happen. L. S. Amery, a Unionist member of the Select Committee, believed that the American Marconi flotation was, in fact, intimately connected 'with the whole series of market operations for which the Imperial contract provided the leverage' and claimed that Rufus Isaacs was 'well in the know all through'; 'if he bought American rather than English Marconis', thought Amery, 'it was only as a measure of precaution.'[3]

Moreover, although few serious critics alleged that the Ministers had acquired a financial inducement to bring the negotiations with the English Marconi Co. to a successful conclusion, the three men did have a personal interest of some kind in securing its ratification. Indeed, as contemporaries often pointed out, all three Ministers, by virtue of their office, had placed themselves in a potentially embarrassing

[2] *Manchester Guardian*, 14 June 1913.
[3] Amery to Bonar Law, 20 Mar. 1913 (HLRO, Bonar Law papers, 29/2/28).

situation, since Isaacs might well have been asked to give an opinion on the legal aspects of the case, and Lloyd George to discuss its long-term financial implications; also Elibank, had he not resigned his office in mid-summer, would have had the task, as Chief Whip, of steering the agreement through a sceptical House of Commons. By purchasing *any* Marconi shares, the Ministers were thus putting themselves in a position where their personal interests 'might in fact have come at any moment into *direct* conflict with [their] official duty', as Amery observed.[4]

It can also be argued that Isaacs, Lloyd George, and Elibank derived a pecuniary advantage from their association with Godfrey Isaacs. This was not so much the result of their possession of inside information concerning the possibility of a forthcoming agreement between the Post Office and the English Marconi Company, since by April 1912 so much was already common knowledge. But the Ministers were undoubtedly helped by Godfrey Isaacs to acquire American Marconi shares at a time when they could not be obtained on the Stock Exchange and at prices considerably lower than their 'true' value. Indeed, the jobbing firm of Heybourn and Croft, which was responsible for introducing these new American Marconi shares, was later suspended from entering the Stock Exchange for a period of five years, following an internal investigation.[5] It seemed to many to be unfair that the jobber should be punished in this way, while senior Ministers who benefited from his activities escape scot free.[6] In any case, was it seemly for the Chancellor of the Exchequer to be seen having a Stock Exchange 'flutter'? Few would have disagreed with the Conservative pamphleteer who pointed out that it was difficult to imagine the late Mr Gladstone condoning Lloyd George's behaviour, let alone indulging in it himself.[7] Anxieties were also expressed about the bad example that the Ministers had set to their permanent civil servants, whose code of conduct was much stricter.[8]

It is often said that the Marconi Scandal would not have taken on significant proportions if the peccant Ministers had had the pluck to make a manly apology in October 1912 and if they had given Parliament a full and frank explanation of what they had done. Given the poisonous atmosphere of party politics in 1912, such a claim must be greeted with some scepticism. On the other hand, the attempts of Isaacs and Lloyd George to cover up their transactions, together with the slow but inexorable exposure of their indiscreet behaviour,

[4] Amery to Bonar Law, 22 Mar. 1913 (ibid. 29/2/34).

[5] Donaldson, *Marconi Scandal*, pp. 231–2.

[6] Unionist pamphlet, 'The Deal in Marconis and How Mr Lloyd George Took His Profits' (1914/63).

[7] Unionist pamphlet, 'The Two Chancellors. What Would Mr Gladstone Say About Marconis?' (1914/119).

[8] Lord George Hamilton to Bonar Law, 17 June 1913 (Bonar Law papers, 29/5/30).

certainly did more than anything else to convert a minor incident into a scandal which imperilled the very existence of the Government.

The moment for frankness came and went in the summer of 1912. It is now clear that Asquith knew the salient facts of the case in July.[9] Yet when the Commons debate took place on 11 October all reference to the purchase of American Marconi shares was deliberately suppressed. Asquith was feeling indisposed at the time, and so did not attend the debate; in any case, so he later explained, it never occurred to him that the action of the three Ministers had any bearing on the issues under investigation. Elibank, now a backbencher, did not attempt to speak, although he was present. But Lloyd George, in an emotional interjection, protested his innocence and spoke of 'sinister rumours, that have been passed from one foul lip to another behind the backs of the House'.[10] A more calculated effort at deception came with the carefully prepared and worded speech of Isaacs, who categorically denied that he had had any dealings in the shares of 'that company'; a similar formula was used by the Postmaster-General, Herbert Samuel, who already knew what his colleagues had done and was clearly anxious to protect them.[11] Little wonder that MPs and journalists on both sides of politics should have been so angry when the full truth finally emerged. As Lord Robert Cecil later remarked, 'Is it not amazing that in their own interests Ministers did not disclose the whole story months ago?'[12]

What in fact happened was that in February 1913 Isaacs and Samuel, prior to their appearance before the Select Committee, initiated a suit against the French paper, *Le Matin*, which had inadvertently libelled them; the case was undefended, but it provided an opportunity for the counsel of the two Ministers to make a statement on their clients' behalf, in which public mention was first made of the purchase of the American Marconi shares. The decision to sue a French paper, when violent abuse from the *Eye-Witness* had gone unanswered for months, caused amusement and outrage. In a letter to Samuel of 14 August 1912 Isaacs argued that on reflection he had thought 'it was better to treat the rag with contempt—its malevolence and prejudice were so marked that only the most blinded partisan could be led to believe the statements.'[13] Asquith, asked for his opinion, concurred. Moreover, both Samuel and Isaacs seem to have believed that *Le Matin*'s misreporting of Select Committee evidence provided them with the first opportunity that they had had of taking action because for the first time a definite and specific charge had been made. Again, Asquith

[9] Judd, D., *Lord Reading* (London, 1982), p. 99.
[10] *Parl. Deb.*, 5th ser., xlii. 714 (11 Oct. 1912).
[11] Ibid. 718, 726.
[12] Robert Cecil to Gwynne, 29 Mar. 1913 (Bodleian, Gwynne papers, vol. 17).
[13] Isaacs to Samuel, 14 Aug. 1912 (HLRO, Samuel papers, A/38, fo. 9).

concurred, though adding that it was 'a little unfortunate that the peccant journal should be a French and not an English newspaper'.[14] All of this may be convincing so far as it goes, but Frances Donaldson is not alone in her belief that what had flushed Ministers out into the open was Maxse's evidence before the Select Committee on 12 February. Hence, the sooner Ministers made a clean breast of things, the less disreputable their conduct would ultimately appear.[15]

If Isaacs and Lloyd George were evasive, Elibank simply avoided the rumpus by disappearing. In January 1913 he left the country for South America in search of oil contracts for his new employer, Lord Cowdray. Later, when as a result of the action of the absconding stockbroker the public first learned of Elibank's purchase of American Marconi shares with party money, Elibank blandly refused all invitations to return home and face interrogation at the hands of the Select Committee. As Northcliffe complained, this caused 'the wildest rumours' to circulate in London.[16]

Eventually in February 1914 Elibank (now Lord Murray of Elibank) was obliged to make a statement to the House of Lords, after which he suffered the additional indignity of a Lords' investigation into his conduct. By this time Elibank was ready to admit that his initial concern had been to protect the reputation of the Liberal Party, come what may, and that, though he would have told the Select Committee about his *personal* investment in Marconi shares, he would not have volunteered any information about his use of party funds because he had hoped that this transaction might never have become public. Thus it is often said that but for the 'accident' of his stockbroker's bankruptcy, Elibank's 'guilty secret' would never have come to light.[17] (There is, however, some evidence that Opposition MPs had got wind of it during the course of the Chesterton Trial earlier in the year.)[18]

Elibank's cheerful cynicism caused less annoyance than did Isaacs's legalistic prevarications. By the same tortuous reasoning that had led him to suppose that it was improper to buy American Marconi shares from Godfrey, but permissible to do so once they had passed through Harry's hands, so he seems to have believed that the words which he employed in October 1912 were satisfactory because, though misleading, they were strictly accurate. He displayed the same sort of pedantry and logic-chopping in his evidence to the Select Committee and in the Commons debate of June 1913. Such behaviour infuriated Northcliffe,

---

[14] Asquith to Samuel, 14 Feb. 1913 (ibid. A/38, fo. 82).

[15] Donaldson, *Marconi Scandal*, p. 99.

[16] Northcliffe to Churchill, 6 June 1913, in Churchill, Randolph S., *Winston S. Churchill, ii. Companion Vol.* (London, 1969), Part III, p. 1747.

[17] But Oliver Locker-Lampson believed that it was the Chesterton Trial which was responsible for revealing this information. See Locker-Lampson to Bonar Law, 9 June 1913 (Bonar Law papers, 29/5/12).

[18] Amery to Bonar Law, 20 Mar. 1913 (ibid. 29/2/28).

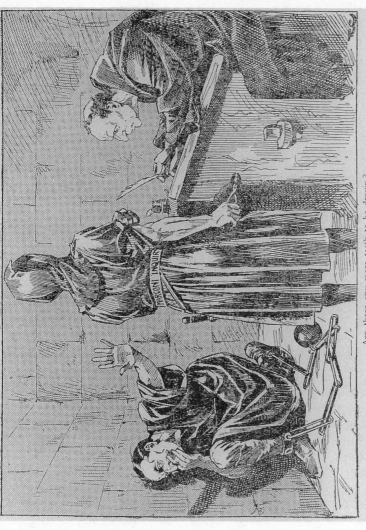

"DENTAL" RESERVATIONS.

Are there any more teeth to be drawn?

"We feel that this apparent shrinking from a full disclosure of the whole of the transactions of Ministers in
American Marconi shares is largely responsible for an uneasy impression that perhaps even now the whole
truth is not known."—(Extract from Lord Robert Cecil's Report.)

4. Consequences of Liberal Evasiveness over Marconi
   (*Pall Mall Gazette*, 18 June 1913)

who was trying to prevent his papers from taking a censorious line,[19] and it left loyal Liberals uncertain to the end whether there were not further damaging secrets awaiting disclosure. In the words of the *Manchester Guardian*, 'the most harmless facts will hurt if they are drawn out like teeth.'[20]

Liberal Self-Justifications

While Liberal Ministers brought discredit on themselves through their evasiveness, the determination of large sections of the Liberal Party to rush to the defence of their endangered colleagues constituted, in some people's eyes, a political scandal in its own right. Not, of course, that blind partisanship was the monopoly of the Liberal Party. As the independent MP, Tommy Bowles, observed: 'Almost without exception Ministerialists voted in favour of the incriminated Ministers and Unionists voted against them. When the thing was over, Ministerialists maintained that the charges were inspired by pure spite, and Unionists maintained that their adversaries were animated by mere dishonesty.'[21] It is significant that most members of the Unionist Party reacted with savage fury to the relatively neutral line adopted by the Northcliffe Press. For the Opposition's aim was to exploit the Marconi revelations in the hope that this might bring down the detested Liberal ministry. Yet, in pursuit of this goal, Unionist critics did at least have a genuine interest in searching out the truth. By contrast, Liberal partisans who rallied to the support of Lloyd George and Isaacs were quite brazenly attempting to stifle all independent enquiry.

So much quickly became apparent once the Select Committee had been set up. The Liberal MP who chaired the Committee, Albert Spicer, was well intentioned, as befitted one of the leading lights of the Secret Commissions and Bribery Prevention League. But he was somewhat deaf and ineffectual and control of affairs was soon wrested from him by two Liberal backbenchers, Falconer and Handel Booth.

Unionists quickly developed a deep suspicion of Booth, a northern industrialist with an unsavoury reputation. Amery was not alone in believing that Booth 'had been in the business' himself, because he betrayed great agitation when Lord Robert Cecil vainly asked the Liberal members of the Select Committee to go into the box and solemnly declare their disinterestedness.[22] This issue surfaced once

[19] Northcliffe to Churchill, 11 Apr. 1913, in Churchill, *Winston S. Churchill*, ii. *Companion Vol.*, p. 1740.

[20] *Manchester Guardian*, 10 June 1913. See also the cartoon in the *Pall Mall Gazette*, 18 June 1913 (Figure 4).

[21] *Candid Quarterly Review of Public Affairs*, ii (1914), 377.

[22] L. S. Amery's diary, 1 May 1913, in Barnes and Nicholson (eds.), *Leo Amery Diaries*, i. 94.

more in June 1913 when Oliver Locker-Lampson, who was emerging as one of the Conservative Party's most persistent Marconi sleuths, raised it on the motion for the adjournment. Booth's ingenious reply might have given a careless hearer the impression that he had never dealt in these shares, but it was worded in such a way as to avoid a direct disclaimer.[23]

From the start Booth and Falconer made it clear that they sáw their task as members of the Select Committee as being that of shielding the incriminated Ministers from their assailants' attacks. In fact, great indignation was later aroused when Isaacs revealed to the Committee in March 1913 that he had already told Falconer and Booth in confidence about his controversial share purchase; for not only had the two Liberal MPs made no effort to transmit this important information to the Chairman or to their colleagues, but they probably used it, in their cross-examination of the journalists, to steer debate away from dangerous ground. An even more blatant piece of partisanship was the attempt made by Liberal members of the Committee to block any probing into Elibank's investments from party funds.

In private, Falconer even tried to persuade Spicer to exclude all mention of the American Marconi transactions from his report. When this ploy was resisted, the Liberals simply used their majority on the Committee to strike twenty-six paragraphs out of Spicer's draft, which they thus converted into a document totally exonerating the Liberal Ministers, who were portrayed as victims of a malignant conspiracy.[24] The tone of the Majority Report, 'that monstrous, that childish, that exasperating majority report', as H. G. Wells dubbed it,[25] proved to be too much even for the Liberal press, and it was to all intents and purposes thrown over by the parliamentary Liberal Party when it voted on 19 June 1913 for a resolution which accepted Ministers' regrets for their behaviour, which was an admission that, although they had not acted corruptly, their actions had been indiscreet and unwise.

But the very guarded and qualified nature of the apology made by Lloyd George and Isaacs on 18 June was not likely to appease their many critics.[26] As one Unionist MP, Alfred Lyttelton, pertinently observed, what Isaacs seems to have regretted was not his 'partial disclosure to the House on 11 October, but that he had failed to perceive at that time and to appreciate how uncharitable, how censorious, and how suspicious the Opposition was'.[27] In any case, whatever good impressions might have been created by these apologies was largely undone when Lloyd George made his famous speech to the

[23] O. Locker-Lampson to Bonar Law, 18 June 1913 (Bonar Law papers, 29/5/28); *Parl. Deb.*, 5th ser., liv. 178 (16 June 1913).

[24] Donaldson, *Marconi Scandal*, Ch. 15.   [25] *Daily Mail*, 19 June 1913.

[26] *Parl. Deb.*, 5th ser., liv. 423–49 (18 June 1913).

[27] Ibid. 545 (19 June 1913).

National Liberal Club of 1 July 1913, in which he lashed out at his detractors and gave a piteous account of the wrongs he had patiently endured at their hands.[28] Leo Amery's contemptuous description of Lloyd George as 'St Sebastian of Limehouse' was quickly picked up in the Opposition press. In fact, the Chancellor had been urged by several of his friends, including Gardiner of the *Daily News*, to state his case soberly and not to work 'the tu quoque overmuch'.[29] The *Nation* subsequently admitted that Lloyd George had been 'cruelly treated' in some quarters, but gave him a little homily about the virtues of 'measure and self-control'.[30] The Unionist press, for its part, pointed out that the Radical demagogue had frequently dealt in personalities in his own platform speeches, and all that was now happening was that he was being served up with some of his own medicine.[31]

Even stronger reactions were excited, understandably enough, when in October 1913 Asquith promoted Isaacs, the central figure in the Marconi Affair, to the vacant post of Lord Chief Justice, an action which inspired Kipling's poem of hatred, *Gehazi*, and prompted the *New Witness* to observe that, if the Government were allowed to get away with this, 'a line will have been passed. It is by passing such lines that Governments often provoke revolutions; or, if there be no revolution, it is by suffering such lines to be passed that often nations die.'[32] One can recognize that Asquith was in an impossible dilemma, since it was customary for the Attorney-General to have the reversion of the Lord Chief Justiceship, and Isaacs was confidently anticipating his promotion. And although it was predictable that this appointment, coming so soon after the Marconi Incident, would create a storm, Asquith must have reasoned that if Isaacs was unfit to be Lord Chief Justice, he was also unfit to be Attorney-General, and that passing him over would therefore not have saved his Government from attack. It has also been argued that the aftermath of Marconi left Isaacs no option but to accept the offer, whereas, had he been a free agent, he might have preferred to stay in the political world.[33]

This brings us to the very centre of the Liberals' predicament. Initially, most Liberal MPs and journalists seem to have taken it for granted that the inneundoes being spread about ministerial corruption lacked all justification, and so the denials of Lloyd George, Isaacs, and Samuel during the 'Festival of Truth' on 11 October were greeted with

---

[28] See Grigg, *Lloyd George: From Peace to War*, pp. 56–60.

[29] A. G. Gardiner to Lloyd George, 25 June 1913 (HLRO, Lloyd George papers, C/9/4/65).

[30] *Nation*, 5 July 1913 ('A London Diary').

[31] *Daily Express*, 18 Feb. 1914.

[32] *New Witness*, 24 July 1913, p. 353. This comment was made about the *prospect* of Isaacs's promotion and about the decision to go ahead with the Marconi contract.

[33] Judd, *Reading*, pp. 109–10. But Maxse, characteristically, argued that this was a deliberate attempt to prevent citizens bringing actions against the Marconi Ministers.

satisfaction and relief.[34] Satisfaction gave way to positive jubilation
when W. R. Lawson of the *Outlook*, whose attacks on Marconi had
triggered off the crisis, broke down under Falconer's interrogation and
abjectly withdrew his allegations.

But this short-lived triumph only made the more bitter the series of
revelations which started in February 1913 with the statement issued
on behalf of Isaacs and Samuel covering the purchase of the American
Marconi shares. The nadir came with the disclosure of the Master of
Elibank's employment of Liberal Party funds. From the lobby correspondents of newspapers of different party colours it is possible to piece
together a picture of how Liberal MPs reacted to these disturbing
disclosures. Following the *Le Matin* statement, a cynical MP summed
up the feeling of both sides in the Commons by observing: 'The Tories
pretend to be shocked, and are not in the least shocked; while the
Liberals are shocked, but pretend not to be.'[35] Privately, many Liberal
MPs and some Ministers were highly critical of the three accused
men—Isaacs attracting more criticism than Lloyd George; and there
was even some feeling that Isaacs should have been asked by the Prime
Minister to resign. But in public a brave face was put on the situation.

It was news of Elibank's investment of party funds which caused the
real consternation. The entire Cabinet, including Lloyd George and
Isaacs, seems to have been caught by surprise by the revelation.[36]
Moreover, Illingworth's efforts at explaining the mystery to the Select
Committee in the absence of the elusive Elibank created a 'stunning'
effect on the Liberal members; according to the *Daily Mail* correspondent, they sat back with blank depression registered on their
faces.[37] As for the parliamentary party as a whole, journalists noted an
initial reluctance to believe the facts that had come to light.
Incredulity was followed by anger. According to the *Morning Post*,
supporters of the Government were furious at the lack of candour
displayed in October 1912, and there was scarcely a Liberal Member
who was 'not fearful that even now there may not be further
revelations in store with respect to Stock Exchange operations
involving the party or prominent members of it'.[38]

'Things go badly here', wrote a junior Minister to his wife on 10
June: 'Elibank investing party funds in the Marconis is shocking. He
was a beastly gambler and intriguer. We paid too dearly for his

[34] *Westminster Gazette*, 12 Oct. 1912. The author of 'Notes of the Day' thought that
ministers' statements would 'carry conviction to any decent or honest mind'.
[35] *Nation*, 5 Apr. 1913.
[36] See Churchill to Northcliffe, 5 June 1913, Churchill, *Winston S. Churchill*, ii.
Companion Vol., pp. 1746–7. There seems no reason to doubt the truth of this claim. For
a different interpretation, see Grigg, *Lloyd George: From Peace to War*, Ch. 2.
[37] *Daily Mail*, 10 June 1913. The damage to Liberal reputations was the subject of a
cartoon in the *Pall Mall Gazette*, 23 June 1913 (Figure 5).
[38] *Morning Post*, 10 June 1913.

5. Damaged Liberal Reputations
(*Pall Mall Gazette*, 23 June 1913)

cleverness. There is nothing dishonest, but it is all not above-board. He knew it was a queer thing to do, or he wouldn't have concealed it.'[39] After a few days' reflection, morale somewhat revived. On 28 June the *Nation* observed that the parliamentary party had 'recovered from the ridiculous flutter of last week; but something of its fire and spirit has gone, and time will be wanted for its recovery.'[40] It even seemed possible that the Government would break up and the Liberal Party go down to defeat in the ensuing general election.[41] Recent by-election reverses for the Government at Newmarket and Whitechapel, held in the atmosphere of suspicion created by Marconi, were cited in support of this contention.[42] As one Cabinet Minister, Charles Hobhouse, observed, Liberal Nonconformists in the provinces were also much upset by what they had recently learned, though leading dissenters like Sylvester Horne and John Hugh Edwards wrote to Lloyd George offering him their support.[43]

But the very scale of the danger forced Liberals to rally round the accused Ministers. Asquith really had no option but to stand by Lloyd George in his hour of need, something for which his critics were slow to forgive him.[44] Similarly, however much they might grumble in private, the Liberal backbenchers felt it necessary to come to the aid of their leaders. In the vote of 19 June the Government won the crucial vote by 346 votes to 268. 'Three Liberals voted with the Opposition, Messrs. D. M. Mason, J. Martin and Munro-Ferguson, the last-named cancelling his pair and travelling a long way to do it.'[45] But party solidarity was well maintained throughout the crisis, and, backed by Redmond's Irish Nationalists and by the majority of Labour MPs, the Government secured a comfortable enough parliamentary victory.

The Liberal press, similarly constrained, made out as good a case as it could for the Ministers. As with the 'sale of honours scandal', the

---

[39] Morris, A. J. A., *C. P. Trevelyan 1870–1958, Portrait of a Radical* (Belfast, 1977), pp. 91–2. As an illustration of the way one 'scandal' suggested another in politicians' minds, it is interesting to note that this letter goes on to refer to 'another party scandal' which Trevelyan thought was about to break. This involved a Liberal MP suing his wife for divorce and citing a fellow Liberal MP as a co-respondent. The latter was Lloyd George's PPS, Crawshay-Williams.

[40] *Nation*, 28 June 1913.

[41] See Peter Sanders's diary, 10 June 1913, in Ramsden, (ed.), *Real Old Tory Politics*, p. 64.

[42] Strachey told Bonar Law: 'I feel it difficult to keep my delight over Newmarket and Altringham within the bounds of decency. . . . I feel convinced that the Marconi business has a great deal to do with them and will do more to bring down the organised hypocrisy.' (Strachey to Bonar Law, 3 June 1913, HLRO, Strachey papers, S/9/8/9). On the Whitechapel by-election, see Ch. 9 pp. 206–7.

[43] Hobhouse's diary, 13 June 1913, in David, E. (ed.), *Inside Asquith's Cabinet* (London, 1977), p. 138; Sylvester Horne to Lloyd George, 23 June 1913 (Lloyd George papers, C/9/4/60). J. H. Edwards to Lloyd George, 23 June 1913 (ibid. C9/4/63). But see the distinctly hostile letter from another Nonconformist (ibid. C/9/4/52).

[44] See Strachey to Margot Asquith (copy), 7 Jan. 1919 (Strachey papers, S/11/7/68).

[45] Donaldson, *Marconi Scandal*, p. 230.

only significant rebellion came from the *Nation*. As early as 10 May the author of the paper's London Diary suggested that not only should Isaacs resign but that Lloyd George should be moved from the Treasury: 'his work at the Exchequer is done; his work for social Radicalism is still to do.' Then on 14 June came its celebrated article, 'The Party and the Affair', which called on Liberal Ministers to 'make full and frank admission of error', and discussed how to stop the evils associated with the secret party fund. The force of such comment was cushioned by the *Nation*'s outspoken attacks on the Ministers' critics. But this attempt at even-handedness was very rare among Liberal papers.[46]

For, whether out of instinctive loyalty or as a calculated response to a highly dangerous situation, most Liberal editors chose to pretend that Lloyd George and Isaacs were the victims of vile allegations which lacked all substance. The *Westminster Gazette*, for example, admitted that Ministers should behave in such a way as not to invite suspicion, but it added that this rested on 'the assumption that the suspicions in question [were] those of sane and reasonable people'. Lord Robert Cecil, author of the Minority Report, apparently did not meet that criterion.[47] In another editorial, the *Gazette* assured the public that it need have no anxiety 'about the purity of public life, so far as it is illustrated by this incident. If a real grafter were looking on at these proceedings he would wonder what it was all about, and what kind of Academy it was which got so violently excited about the mere possibility of a suspicion of corruption.'[48] So partisan was J. A. Spender's paper that it even tried for a time to pretend that Elibank's telegram to the Select Committee did not refer to his attempt to conceal from his successor as Chief Whip the fateful share purchases. Its treatment of the June 1913 debate is well summed up in its headline: 'The Marconi Debate: Personal Explanations by Ministers: Enthusiastic Scene: How the House Cleared its Accused Colleagues'.[49]

Behind the scenes, C. P. Scott gave Lloyd George some of his familiar fatherly advice. But the *Manchester Guardian* editorials would admit to nothing worse than a 'mistake'.[50] The *Daily News* was, if anything, even more dismissive of the Opposition case; on 10 June it claimed

[46] See also *Nation*, 15 Feb., 28 June 1913 (though the former article was mainly an attack on Lawson and Maxse). One other Liberal newspaper, initially sympathetic to the Marconi Ministers, which rounded censoriously on them once it learned the full facts, was the *Westminster Review*. See *Westminster Review*, clxxix (1913), 339; ibid. clxxx (1913), 86–7.

[47] *Westminster Gazette*, 14 June 1913.

[48] Ibid., 19 June 1913.

[49] Ibid. See also the *Gazette*'s cartoon of 18 June 1913 (Figure 6).

[50] C. P. Scott to Lloyd George, 7 June 1913, in Wilson, *Political Diaries of C. P. Scott*, pp. 70–1; *Manchester Guardian*, 19 June 1913.

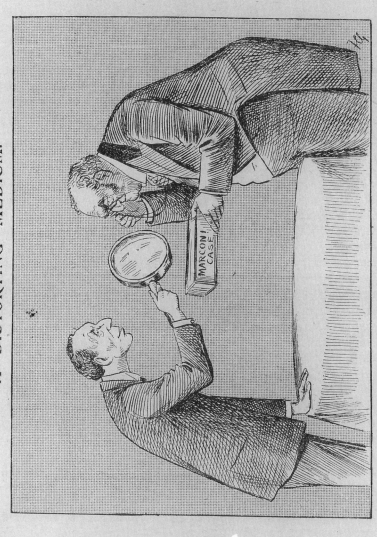

6. A Liberal View of the Marconi Minority Report
(*Westminster Gazette*, 18 June 1913)

that 'the charge of corruption has shrunk to quibbles about "discretion and delicacy"', and on 14 June it rhetorically asked, 'Did ever such a mouse emerge from such a mountain?'[51]

The report which was presented to the National Liberal Federation Conference in November 1913 echoed this complacency:

Now that a little time has elapsed since what is known as the Marconi affair was an exciting topic of the moment, it is possible to view it in more correct perspective. The original charges, either insinuated or made against Sir Rufus Isaacs, Mr Lloyd George, and Mr Herbert Samuel, were of the most serious description; if they had proved to be true, or to be anything like true, none of the Ministers could or would have been able to remain in public life. When the real facts came to be known, it was discovered that the charges were scandalously untrue. No cause could be more important than the maintenance of the purity of our public service; nothing could be meaner than to exploit this cause in a partisan attempt to injure Liberal Ministers and their effectiveness as statesmen.[52]

The above statement illustrates a tactic which the Liberals pursued from an early stage in the affair—the tactic of diverting attention away from the accused Ministers and turning it into an opportunity to expose Lawson, Maxse, Chesterton, and other outspoken journalists who had dared to impugn the Ministers' good name. It was these men, not Isaacs or Lloyd George or Elibank, whom Liberals thought should be put on trial. The fierce interrogation of Lawson and Maxse by Falconer and Booth was a central feature of this strategy. By a seeming paradox the Liberal press always chose to give emphasis to the more outrageously extreme attacks on Ministers, as a way of illustrating its thesis about the threat which the gutter press posed to democratic politics. When Cecil Chesterton lost the libel suit brought against him by Godfrey Isaacs in early June 1913, the judge's summary was given full-scale treatment in the Liberal press. The *Daily News* argued that the Opposition wanted nothing less than the destruction of the Government and its policies, and that the alleged concern for the purity of public life was a transparent lie: 'They have failed to stem the steady progress of Liberalism towards its purposes . . . And so the baser elements in it have fallen back on the expedient of poisoning the public mind about the private character of Ministers.'[53]

The Liberal press also played up the anti-Semitic nature of the campaign waged by Belloc and the Chestertons. Indeed, as the *Morning Post* shrewdly observed, Cecil Chesterton, in particular, had 'been very useful to Ministers. His charges, so preposterous, so foolish, so ignorant as to pass all credence and belief, have been placed in the

[51] *Daily News*, 10 June, 14 June 1913.
[52] National Liberal Federation Report (1913), pp. 33–4.
[53] *Daily News*, 9 June 1913.

forefront of the apologies. . . . his silly slanders are easy to kill, and make as fine a show as Falstaff's men in buckram.'[54]

From an orthodox Liberal standpoint, then, the real danger of corruption did not come from the activities of government, but rather from the 'new style', the readiness of Opposition politicians and journalists to use the weapons of personality assassination, innuendo, coarse abuse, and so on. Such disgraceful methods, said the Liberals, struck at the roots of parliamentary democracy, because if persisted in, they would make rational discussion of political differences quite impossible. This, too, was the view of the *New Statesman*, which proclaimed: 'Libel as a method of political controversy is as dangerous in practice as it is indefensible in theory.'[55]

The Unionists' Dilemma

Many of the staider members of the Opposition were very sensitive about this kind of counter-attack. 'Let us sedulously attack [ministers] for what they can't deny,' urged A. V. Dicey, 'and as far as possible keep off matters which are suspicious but not proved. Their greatest chance of escaping censure lies in their being accused of unproved offences. . . . Violence like that of Maxse and Amery however well meant can only damage a good cause.'[56]

Moreover, none of the more extreme accusations survived the investigations of the Select Committee. Lawson was obliged to retract his allegations; Maxse, by refusing to name his sources, emerged from the Committee with a lessened reputation; Cecil Chesterton was successfully sued for libel by Godfrey Isaacs; and at the end of the day even so severe a critic of the Government as Lord Robert Cecil could find no evidence that any Minister had behaved corruptly, in the full meaning of that word. The Minority Report said nothing more than that the accused Ministers had conducted themselves in a manner which was inconsistent with the better traditions of public life and that they had placed themselves in a false position by behaving in a way which, though not corrupt in itself, might set a precedent for subsequent actions that really were corrupt—offences which were compounded by ministerial evasiveness in the October 1912 debate.

The principal muck-rakers in the Marconi Affair never, of course, accepted this view. But most Unionist MPs vied with one another in protesting during the June debate that they had never made specific accusations of corruption against anyone. Indeed, one of the most dramatic episodes in this debate occurred when Lloyd George rounded on Walter Guinness, the Conservative MP who owned the *Outlook*

---

[54] *Morning Post*, 10 June, 20 June 1913.
[55] *New Statesman*, 14 June 1913, p. 293.
[56] Dicey to Strachey, 8 June 1913 (Strachey papers, S/5/6/12).

and was thus responsible for Lawson's 'libels'. Shuffling with embarrassment, Guinness lamely replied that he had performed a public service by allowing Lawson to formulate his charges, which in turn had given the accused Ministers an opportunity of clearing their names![57] But the Liberals insisted that the Opposition had given every possible encouragement to the scandalmongers and were only now beating a retreat because they had no option. The Liberal press likewise affected to see no difference between the *Outlook*, the *National Review*, and the *New Witness*, on the one hand, and a paper such as the *Spectator*, on the other. The *Manchester Guardian* commented: 'No Liberal minds being pelted with dirt by the "Outlook" or the "National Review". As Bacon says of the pricking of thorns and briars, they only do it "because they can do no other". But the "Spectator" has a character.'[58] Strachey was clearly upset by this sort of criticism, and when in June Lloyd George lumped together the *National Review*, the *Eye-Witness*, and the *Spectator* as 'confederates' in the same cause, the *Spectator* protested, and with some reason—after all, both Cecil Chesterton and Maxse had recently been attacking it for *sheltering* the Liberal Ministers.[59]

Some Opposition newspapers, on the other hand, abstained altogether from the vendetta against the Marconi Ministers. For example, Northcliffe forced the reluctant editorial staff of the *Daily Mail* and *The Times* to hold back from attacking Lloyd George and Isaacs—a service for which both men later wrote him effusive letters of thanks.[60] There has been no shortage of explanations, then and since, of why Northcliffe should have shown this indulgence, but the views he expressed in a letter to Lloyd George on 24 March 1913 may well provide the clue:

I adopted my line about this Marconi business, because five minutes' lucid explanation showed me that it was the fairest one. Moreover, I am not a rabid party man nor an anti-Semite. . . . (Moreover), a week-end glance at the French and German newspapers convinces me that this country has before it more urgent business than personal or party issues. . .[61]

The subsequent revelation of Elibank's indiscretions tried Northcliffe's patience, and a somewhat more critical tone crept into his newspapers,[62] but the *Daily Mail* affected throughout to be bored by the Marconi

[57] *Parl. Deb.*, 5th ser., liv. 476 (18 June 1913).

[58] *Manchester Guardian*, 23 June 1913.

[59] *Spectator*, 21 June 1913, p. 1041.

[60] Lloyd George to Northcliffe, 21 Mar. 1913 (BL, Northcliffe papers, Dep. 4890/5); Hyde, *Lord Reading*, p. 144; *The History of* The Times, iv. (London, 1952), 1054–60.

[61] Northcliffe to Lloyd George (copy), 24 Mar. 1913 (Northcliffe papers, Dep. 4890/5).

[62] Northcliffe wrote about Elibank as follows in a private letter to Churchill: 'I have made some bad bungles myself, but the stage-management of this business beats any record of mine' (Churchill, *Winston S. Churchill*, ii. *Companion Vol.*, p. 1747).

Affair.[63] Later it criticized both Majority and Minority Reports of the Select Committee for their unnecessary partisanship, claimed that Lloyd George and Isaacs had made 'honourable amends' in their Commons statement of June, and also found much to admire in the parliamentary performances of Asquith and Balfour—though not, significantly, in the speech of Bonar Law.[64] Northcliffe later tried to exact a *quid pro quo* from the Liberal Government by asking it to moderate its Irish policy—though to no avail.[65]

As for the Opposition Front Benchers, their relative moderation over Marconi seems to have owed much to the camaraderie of the Commons and friendships between the two major parties, which not even the Constitutional Crisis or the Home Rule struggle had completely killed. In February Lloyd George and Bonar Law were still playing golf together, and in May the Opposition Leader told Lord Riddell in confidence that he was sorry for Lloyd George and Isaacs: 'There was no corruption, but they acted imprudently.'[66] Prompted by followers like Amery, Bonar Law took a much tougher line in public—indeed, his fiercely partisan speech in June[67] contrasted with the contribution of Balfour, who, adopting the role of elder statesman, ostentatiously tried to preside over a national settlement of the disagreements that divided the House.[68] Other Front Bench politicians were simply concerned to avoid involvement in the affair. Austen Chamberlain, for example, contented himself with a few sententious observations to his stepmother,[69] but perhaps remembering the Hoskins episode, made no public criticism of the Marconi Ministers.

It is also striking what little interest the parliamentary leadership took in pursuing Elibank on his return from South America. But for Maxse's accusations against the former Patronage Secretary in the *Morning Post*,[70] it is unlikely that the Lords would have instituted their enquiry in February 1914. And even then it required a backbench peer of independent views, Lord Ampthill, to force the pace, while Lansdowne, his Leader, inclined to hold back.[71] Admittedly, the Party

---

[63] e.g. *Daily Mail*, 9 June 1913, where the editorial spoke of how the proceedings of the Select Committee had 'too frequently repelled public interest by their dreary waste of time. . .'.

[64] *Daily Mail*, 19 June, 20 June 1913. However, the 19 June issue carried H. G. Wells' attack on the improprieties of the Liberal Government, 'What Are We Liberals To Do?'

[65] Northcliffe to Churchill (copy), 1 Apr. 1914 (Northcliffe papers, Dep. 4890/4).

[66] Riddell's diary, 4 May 1913, in Riddell, *More Pages From My Diary*, p. 146.

[67] *Parl. Deb.*, 5th ser., liv. 643–53 (19 June 1913). Privately, Bonar Law wrote: 'I did not like my job about the Marconi business, because it was so personal, but it could not be helped' (Bonar Law to Aitken (copy), 23 June 1913, HLRO, Beaverbrook papers, C/201). [68] *Parl. Deb.*, 5th ser., liv. 570–2 (19 June 1913).

[69] Austen Chamberlain to Mary Chamberlain, 4 June 1913, in Chamberlain, A., *Politics From Inside* (London, 1936), pp. 564–5.

[70] *Morning Post*, 9 Feb. 1914.

[71] Ampthill to Willoughby de Broke, 15 Feb. 1914 (HLRO, Willoughby de Broke papers, WB/8/82).

Chairman, Steel-Maitland, declared in a private letter that he would be 'really delighted to see Murray hammered'[72]—a belligerent attitude which was perhaps reflected in a succession of hard-hitting pamphlets on Marconi issued by the Party organization.[73] But the parliamentary leaders continued to give the impression that they would have been quite happy to see the whole issue disappear.

This made many of the Party rank and file somewhat suspicious, as became apparent when the National Union met for its annual conference in Norwich in November 1913. Maxse moved a motion, which was carried 'with enthusiasm', roundly condemning 'the conspicuous bad faith with which Mr Asquith and his colleagues have acted throughout the Marconi controversy and kindred questions'. And in the ensuing debate on this motion Ampthill urged Conservatives to keep Marconi before the public, adding: 'He did not think that the House of Commons, or even the Unionist Party in the House of Commons, dealt with this matter at all adequately (hear, hear).'[74]

What also aroused a good deal of comment was that Carson and F. E. Smith, prominent Unionist MPs, should have served as counsel to Samuel and Isaacs in the *Le Matin* trial. Many Opposition newspapers denounced this as an act of treachery, and Bonar Law was inundated with complaints, among them a letter from Lord Charles Beresford, who declared that feeling against Carson was so 'violent' that some 'loyalists' were holding back their party subscriptions, while others feared for the fate of the Union.[75] Carson and Smith defended their action by arguing that as barristers they could not refuse a brief simply because it came from a political opponent.[76] But there was more to it than that. Carson, for one, clearly disapproved of scurrility and personal abuse as political weapons, and was on friendly terms with Isaacs, with whom he had rubbed shoulders on the Circuit for over ten years. Isaacs was duly appreciative of the help that he had received from 'dear Ned'.[77]

Nor were such attitudes confined to politicians caught up in the camaraderie of the Bar. Even Robert Cecil, a strong critic of the incriminated Ministers and of anyone who sought to shield them, would have nothing to do with the suggestion that he attempt to discredit Handel Booth by using scandalous tit-bits concerning the

[72] Steel-Maitland to Midleton (copy), 30 Jan. 1914 (Scottish Record Office, Steel-Maitland papers, GD/193/108/2).

[73] e.g. 'Mr Lloyd George and "Unearned Increment"' (1913/81); 'The Marconi Mystery: Truth Extracted Tooth by Tooth' (1913/85); 'Is This Justice?' (1913/86).

[74] Report of National Union of Conservative and Unionist Associations Conference, held in Norwich, 13–14 Nov. 1913.

[75] Beresford to Bonar Law, 25 May 1913 (Bonar Law papers, 29/4/22).

[76] For a full statement of Carson's position, see Carson to Gwynne, June 1913 (Gwynne papers, vol. 17).

[77] See Carson to Isaacs, 22 Oct. 1913, in Colvin, I., *The Life of Lord Carson*, ii (London, 1934), 183.

latter's private life.[78] There were civilized conventions which had
traditionally regulated the contest between the two main parties, and
many old-fashioned Conservative MPs were not happy at the prospect
of these conventions being discarded. Equally important would seem
to be the fact that MPs like Lyttelton and Balfour, who had known
Lloyd George and Isaacs for years, found it hard to suppose that these
familiar figures could have engaged in transactions that were really
corrupt; and when criticism could no longer be avoided, they shrank
from saying or doing anything that would create unnecessary
unpleasantness.

A final reason for proceeding cautiously was the realization on the
Opposition Front Bench that if they pressed home their attacks too
ruthlessly, they might force a desperate Liberal Ministry to attempt an
exposure of incidents in their own past which they wanted to remain
forgotten. Throughout June 1913 the Liberal press was quite blatantly
warning the Unionists of this possibility. The *Daily News*, for
example, accused its opponents of instituting 'a policy of slander
which is without parallel in our day' and warned them that this could
not 'fail to have its reaction upon a party whose record [was] black with
doubtful episodes'.[79] Interestingly enough, as early as April Lloyd
George's journalist friend, Harold Spender, was busily employed in
assembling a list of directorships held by members of the last Unionist
Cabinet—evidently for use in an emergency.[80] Meanwhile, the Liberal
press was reviving the Netheravon Affair once more. So blatant were
such threats that the *Morning Post* warned the Unionist leaders, on the
eve of the June 1913 debate, that they must on no account tone down
their criticisms, because this might give the public the impression that
the two political parties were in collusion with one another.[81]

It is possible, nevertheless, that some Unionist MPs were indeed
frightened into moderation by the prospect of counter-exposure. There
was one especially significant incident in the period immediately
following the Government's pyrrhic victory in June 1913. Exasperated
by the self-righteous tone being adopted over Marconi by Lord Wolmer,
Lloyd George wrote to *The Times* on 5 September 1913, saying that if
Wolmer wanted 'to take a high line as to Ministerial investments, let
him and his fellow Cecils begin giving their lessons at home.' 'I could

[78] When a certain Alfred W. Harris wrote a couple of letters to Cecil about Booth's
behaviour in the card room of the National Liberal Club, where stock exchange
speculation allegedly took place in the company of Godfrey and Harry Isaacs, saying that
this information should 'largely discredit Booth and his antics', Cecil promptly sent
copies of these letters to Booth. Harris was furious at the 'breach of confidentiality' (BL,
Cecil of Chelwood papers, Add. MS 51,160 fos. 230–1, 233–5, 237, 246, 250; Harris to
Cecil, 5 Apr., 9 Apr., 15 Apr. 1913; Cecil to Harris (copy), 11 Apr., 21 Apr. 1913). But this
material later found its way into print in the *Financial News*, 16 Oct. 1916.
[79] *Daily News*, 14 June 1913.
[80] Harold Spender to Lloyd George, 4 Apr. 1913 (Lloyd George papers, C/9/4/24).
[81] *Morning Post*, 12 June 1913.

furnish them with one or two or more instances of the need for such instruction in that quarter', the Chancellor added. Lord Salisbury was foolish enough to rise to the bait and publicly asked Lloyd George what on earth he meant by these aspersions on the good name of his family.[82] Lloyd George duly replied to the challenge with a long letter which was published in *The Times* on 22 September. It gave three 'instances' of members of the Cecil family behaving in ways which transgressed the lofty principles they were now laying down.

The first charge involved the former Prime Minister, the Third Marquess of Salisbury, who, according to Lloyd George, had once placed his interest as a landowner with real estate in London before his duty as a legislator when an improvement bill sponsored by the Metropolitan Board of Works came before the Lords. This charge, interestingly, had first been made against Salisbury by Joseph Chamberlain, way back in 1885.[83] The third 'instance' was that of a relative of the present marquess who, so readers of *The Times* were reminded, had once been a director as well as a shareholder in a company that was negotiating with the government department in which he held office. This, of course, was a reference to Selborne, Wolmer's own father.

The second 'instance' seemed more obscure. Lloyd George referred to 'a distinguished member of the Cecil family', who 'had held very high office himself' and who had 'had a "flutter", to use another Cecilian phrase, in Whitaker Wright's fraudulent concern, and he certainly found on that occasion that public duty and private interest came into conflict.' In fact, Lloyd George had already spoken of this case during a heated exchange of views with Salisbury and with Lord Robert Cecil. The latter had at once passed on his remarks to Balfour; for it was Balfour, no less, against whom the allegation was being directed.

What all the fuss was about was that during his premiership Balfour had lost £1,000, which he had been foolish enough to invest in the London & Globe Finance Company, which collapsed in 1903.[84] Lloyd George was simply repeating the rumours, widespread at the time, that Balfour had pressurized his Attorney-General, Sir Robert Finlay, into not immediately instituting proceedings against Wright for fear that his own involvement might become public knowledge.[85]

Cecil thought this accusation damaging: 'I know how indifferent you are to personal abuse', he wrote to Balfour. 'No doubt George relied on that in making his charge. But such methods of controversy are intolerable and an action is the only effective way of stopping them.'

[82] *The Times*, 5 Sept., 15 Sept. 1913.
[83] *Parl. Deb.*, 4th ser., lxxxviii. 399 (10 Dec. 1900).
[84] Short to Robert Cecil, 17 Oct. 1913 (Cecil of Chelwood papers, Add. MS 51,071, fos. 27–8).   [85] *Parl. Deb.*, 4th ser., cxviii. 347–80 (19 Feb. 1903).

Balfour, however, declared that he had no wish to mix himself up in 'this sordid squabble', and dismissed Lloyd George's charges against him as 'childish'. Finlay's decision was one with which he had happened to disagree, Balfour explained, but it would have been improper for either the Prime Minister or the Cabinet to instruct the Attorney-General on how to behave in a case where he exercised quasi-judicial functions. However, this explanation was reserved for a private letter.[86] For Balfour ignored his cousin's advice and made no attempt to sue the Chancellor. This somewhat absurd episode does at least show the lengths to which Lloyd George and his friends were prepared to go to save their political careers. And it may also go some way to explaining the reticence shown by some of the Conservative Front Benchers.

As the *Morning Post* feared, such reticence fuelled the suspicions of those who were predisposed to believe that both sets of party leaders shared a common involvement in corruption. On 29 March 1913 Hyndman, the leader of the Marxist British Socialist Party, wrote to Blumenfeld, the editor of the *Daily Express*: 'I am very glad to see that you do not intend to let this Marconi Scandal be hushed up, as Tories as well as Liberals are trying to hush it up. As a mere matter of good journalism I cannot understand the attitude of some of your party organs.' If the Tory leaders had had the courage of their convictions, he thought, they would long ago have destroyed Lloyd George. By the end of the year Hyndman was convinced that Bonar Law and Lloyd George were secretly in collusion.[87] This, of course, was the position which had been taken from the start by the *New Witness*, which argued that the relatively moderate resolution moved by the Conservatives in the June 1913 debate could only be explained by the fact 'that the Front Opposition Bench . . . are no more anxious to revive memories of such incidents as Hicks-Beach's sale of his own estate to himself than they are concerned to discredit further the political system out of which both parties have done so exceedingly well.'[88]

A few extreme Conservative activists seem to have drawn similar conclusions. In May 1913 an irate correspondent complained to Bonar Law that 'the Marconi revelations find you and a great part of the Unionist Press endeavouring to screen [Lloyd George] and his Hebrew associate from any unpleasant consequences. . . . My non-party friends are making the sneering comment, "Oh, the Unionists were in it, too!" . . . Why on earth, Sir, should I be a Unionist?'[89] And later Cecil Manners expressed the view that the Unionists, with Balfour the

[86] Robert Cecil to Balfour, n.d. (Cecil of Chelwood papers, Add. MS 51,071, fos. 25–6; Balfour to Cecil, 7 Oct. 1913 (ibid., fos. 22–3).
[87] Hyndman to Blumenfeld, 29 Mar. 1913 (HLRO, Blumenfeld papers, HY2); see *Justice*, 23 Mar. 1913.
[88] *New Witness*, 19 June 1913, p. 195.
[89] Claude Sisley to Bonar Law, 26 May 1913 (Bonar Law papers, 29/4/25).

chief culprit, had virtually acquiesced in the misconduct of the Marconi Ministers, with serious long-term consequences.[90]

Maxse himself adopted a somewhat less severe line, if only because he had much greater confidence in the honesty and patriotism of Bonar Law. But he too waxed eloquent on the 'treachery' of the Unionist press. The *National Review* was especially cross with Northcliffe, who by 1913 had forfeited the respect in which Maxse had once held him. Northcliffe's brother, Harold Harmsworth, also came in for censure. Like other 'Radical Right' critics, Maxse saw a sinister significance in the fact that Isaacs, Lloyd George, and Elibank had had the use of Harold Harmsworth's villa at Cap Martin. In fact, it was from this villa that Elibank had sent off a much-quoted telegram, enquiring after the fate of his American Marconi purchases.

Maxse would have felt vindicated in his suspicions, had he been in a position to observe how strenuously Harmsworth had worked throughout the crisis on the Liberal Ministers' behalf. In March 1913 he had pleaded with his brother to 'soft pedal' the Marconi Affair in the *Daily Mail*, so as not to wreck Isaacs's career.[91] Later, in January 1914, he was telling Blumenfeld that, in the event of his acquiring control of the *Daily Express*, he would insist on a complete cessation of the attacks on Murray and the Lord Chief Justice, whom he described as his two particular friends.[92] And a week later he was urging Aitken to throw the *Express* and *Globe* behind Lord Murray when he made his statement in the House of Lords.[93]

These interventions can hardly be unconnected with the Liberal Government's elevation of Harmsworth to the peerage in the 1914 New Year's Honours List, when he assumed the title of Lord Rothermere. This event gave Maxse a certain grim satisfaction: 'He is essentially the right man in the right place and has well earned this "honour" by his services to [the Radical] Party.'[94] Here, indeed, was the 'proof' for which the *National Review* had long been looking of the existence of a corrupt alliance between the syndicated press and the Asquith Ministry. But Maxse thought that this alliance was only allowed to flourish because of the timidity of the 'mandarins' who controlled the Unionist Party.

The Marconi Case thus shows how complex was the relationship between official Conservatism and the 'Radical Right'. At certain

---

[90] Cecil Manners to Lord Salisbury, 11 Dec. 1918 (Hatfield House, Fourth Marquess of Salisbury papers, 84/125).

[91] H. Harmsworth to Northcliffe, 10 Mar. 1913, in Pound and Harmsworth, *Northcliffe*, p. 441.

[92] Rothermere to Blumenfeld (copy), 20 Jan. 1914 (Beaverbrook papers, C/282A).

[93] Rothermere to Aitken, 28 Jan. 1914 (ibid. C/282A).

[94] Maxse to Steel-Maitland, 2 Jan. 1914 (Steel-Maitland papers, GD 113/108/2). But the *National Review* referred to the ennoblement in angry tones: *National Review*, lxii (1914), 916–18.

points in the story the two groups were closely identified in their onslaught on the Liberal Party, but in the end the episode rather served to emphasize the gap between conventional party politics and those activities which the 'Radical Right' thought were needed to meet a wholly unprecedented situation.

Reaction of Irish Nationalists and Labour

But a parallel of sorts can be found in the divided counsels of their opponents. The Irish, it is true, had no option but to toe the line and give the Government their unqualified support. The Nationalist members of the Select Committee behaved, in fact, just as though they were fully fledged members of the Liberal Party. Willie Redmond later tried to trade on this when he pleaded with Lloyd George in March 1917 to settle the Irish Question on a Home Rule basis: 'I stood by you in many a fight! When those who are now fawning on you tried to destroy your honour over the Marconi affair, I fought for justice for you and Rufus Isaacs. . . .'[95] At the time the Irish MPs were 'furiously angry' over Elibank's escapades, fearing that this had put the Home Rule Bill 'in real jeopardy'.[96] But the Party voted solidly for the Adkins Resolution in June 1913; even the O'Brienites contented themselves with abstaining. But to the Irish Nationalists Marconi could not have seemed other than a worrying distraction, and in reacting to it their sole concern was how best to further the Home Rule cause.

But the Parliamentary Labour Party, upon whose support the Liberal Government also depended, was forced to take Marconi more seriously, especially those of its members who believed that their socialist convictions gave them a unique insight into the origins of the crisis. Thus Fred Jowett, in his *Clarion* column of 27 June 1913, argued that Marconi showed capitalism at work. This was also the view of the *Daily Herald*, which later claimed to have been the first newspaper to take the Marconi Affair seriously.[97] Not only did the *Herald* give Cecil Chesterton a fulsome write-up, describing him, after his trial had ended, as having had the 'enviable honour' of being one of the Government's 'chief executioners', but it also gave space to G. K. Chesterton's reflections on the affair.[98] Through Will Dyson's vitriolic cartoons and slashing headlines—for example, 'Swinging the Whitewash Brush: Marcornered Ministers Handed Haloes by Committee. No Gambling, No Corruption, No Nothink! Treasury Bench Their Resting Place But Heaven is Their Home'[99]—the *Herald* used the crisis to hold the Liberals up to persistent ridicule and abuse.

[95] Willie Redmond to Lloyd George, 1 Mar. 1917 (Lloyd George papers, F94/1/64).
[96] *Morning Post*, 6 June 1913.　　　　　　　　[97] *Daily Herald*, 11 June 1913.
[98] Ibid., 9 June, 21 June 1913.
[99] Ibid., 14 June 1913. For the Will Dyson cartoon of 17 June 1913, see Figure 7.

The Daily Herald

No. 368. [REGISTERED AT THE G.P.O. AS A NEWSPAPER.]   TUESDAY, JUNE 17, 1913.   ONE HALFPENNY,

"THE MASTER TOUCH."

GENTLEMEN WHO ARE SOMETHING IN THE CITY: "Ah, Mr. Booth! You don't know how we gents appreciate this Marconi masterpiece of yours!"

MR. BOOTH (whose zeal with his little pot of Couleur de Rose is in danger of getting him another handle to his name): "Yes. Of course that chap Chesterton and others painted the picture, but the thing was nothing till I altered the title."

7. A Socialist View of Marconi
(*Daily Herald*, 17 June 1913: a Will Dyson cartoon)

Significantly, it was George Lansbury, the moving force behind the paper, who had been the one MP to mention the prevalence of rumours about ministerial corruption when Marconi was first debated in October 1912—an action which brought him a verbal lashing from Lloyd George but won him the approval of Maxse, who voiced his admiration of Lansbury's 'pluck'.[100]

More measured in its language but equally censorious in its opinions was the ILP weekly, the *Labour Leader*. With Fenner Brockway, its new editor, setting an example, it was calling in 1913 for Socialists to use Marconi as part of a renewed offensive against the Government. On the far left there was an even greater violence of tone. As early as October 1912 the Marxist paper, *Justice*, called the Marconi contract 'one of the most disgraceful jobs to which a great public department like the Post Office has ever been made a party', and thought the 'swindle' a good illustration of the true nature of Liberalism. Liberals, it said, were solely concerned with the benefit of the capitalist class generally.[101] In Hyndman's view the Tories were bad enough, but the Liberals were worse; since Asquith had become Prime Minister, 'department after department has had its very ugly scandal. . . . Caucasians and Semites, Semites and Caucasians are all "in it".'[102]

It is noticeable that once the Unionist Opposition took up Marconi in a serious way, *Justice* somewhat lost interest in the issue; perhaps more recent events were proving difficult to reconcile with Hyndman's oft-repeated belief in the existence of collusion between the two front benches. The *Herald*, for its part, in an editorial of 11 June 1913, explained that its initial concern with Marconi was to show up 'ministers and politicians in order to put the wage slave on his guard, to reveal the sort of folk they are, and how little he had to expect in such quarters'; recently, however, Marconi had become no more than a counter in the party game, serving to distract attention from the cruelties of industrial life, such as the current Black Country strike.[103] Similarly, the *Labour Leader* thought that the Marconi Affair should not be allowed to overshadow its own 'sensational' exposure of Cabinet Ministers' presence as shareholders in an armaments firm.[104] But the socialist press was almost unanimous in arguing that the PLP would cover itself in ignominy unless it came out in condemnation of the Marconi Ministers.

But that, of course, was not a course of action likely to recommend itself to the parliamentary leadership. Exposing the reactionary nature of the Liberal Party might be all very well in its way, but to withhold

---

[100] *National Review*, lx (1912), 362. [101] *Justice*, 19 Oct. 1912.
[102] Ibid., 30 Nov. 1912. [103] *Daily Herald*, 11 June 1913.
[104] 'WORSE THAN THE MARCONI SCANDAL: CABINET MINISTERS AND BISHOPS AS SHAREHOLDERS IN WAR TRUST: UNHOLY ALLIANCE OF CHURCH, STATE, PRESS, AND JINGOES' (*Labour Leader*, 12 June 1913). Also, see Appendix I.

support from the Liberal Government in June 1913 could possibly nature precipitated a general election which Labour was in no position to fight. The 'official' thinking of the Party was revealed when Arthur Henderson publicly declared that he had no wish to drive two Ministers out of public life for a 'mistake' for which they had apologized.[105]

But the key statement came from the otherwise taciturn MacDonald, who on the eve of the June debate gave out his views on Marconi to his Leicester constituents: 'The fact of the matter is that both sides are pretty much alike', he declared, but the Liberals had the better record; 'the whole thing, from beginning to end, is a humbugging fraud.'[106] This made it clear enough which way MacDonald intended to vote. An even clearer indication was provided by the one Labour MP on the Commons Select Committee, James Parker, who by his speeches and votes largely identified himself with his Liberal colleagues. Indeed, it had been Parker's vote which enabled Falconer and Booth to sabotage Spicer's draft report, so clearing a path for their own whitewashing document, which Parker duly signed. Interestingly, Parker later made a speech to his constituents in which he is reported as saying that he personally had only consented to the final version of the Majority Report on the understanding that Ministers intended to make a full apology; the implication was that Isaacs and Lloyd George had then gone back on their promise.[107] Prior to the June debate, however, the other Labour leaders kept in regular contact with Parker, and, so the lobby correspondent of the *Manchester Guardian* claimed, 'it is understood that his attitude on the Committee meets with their approval.' The *Guardian* added, however, that Parker's actions 'were not in harmony with the known views of a number of Labour members, and certainly not with those of the rank-and-file of the ILP'.[108]

That was a considerable understatement. Many left-wing activists were furious at the way in which Labour had been compromised by Parker's actions and no less furious at MacDonald's Olympian comments on the affair. The *Morning Post* believed that MacDonald's speech marked 'the last stage in the degradation of the Labour Party'; 'was ever such servility known?', it asked.[109] Labour's left wing would have agreed with this stricture.

What gave particular spice to the ensuing disagreement was that it coincided with a by-election campaign at Leicester. The Labour leaders

---

[105] Quoted in *Clarion*, 27 June 1913.   [106] *Morning Post*, 16 June 1913.
[107] *Yorkshire Observer*, 22 Aug. 1913.
[108] *Manchester Guardian*, 16 June 1913. Even as early as March Strachey had declared that Parker was 'a man who impressed me most unfavourably'. He 'did not seem to be what I call a good type of Labour member' (Strachey to A. V. Dicey (copy), 31 Mar. 1913, Strachey papers, S/5/6/9).
[109] *Morning Post*, 17 June 1913.

had only with great difficulty dissuaded local activists from running a candidate for the seat made vacant by MacDonald's Liberal partner in this two-member borough, and an 'independent' socialist candidate had entered the field to register his protest.[110] In an editorial in the *Labour Leader* Philip Snowden, one of MacDonald's ILP critics, drew the appropriate moral: 'When, as in the case of the Marconi Committee Report, we see the Labour Party completely absorbed in the Liberal element in the Committee, one is compelled to feel some sympathy with those who would throw off the Liberal "alliance", even if doing this resulted in the temporary loss of all Labour representation in Parliament.'[111] Marconi and the Leicester by-election raised the same fundamental issue: what risks should Labour be prepared to run in order to vindicate its principles and assert its claims to independence?

The events immediately preceding the Commons debate of June 1913 are not easy to reconstruct. The Parliamentary Party held two meetings, on 18 and 19 June, and clearly had great difficulty reaching agreement about what line it was going to take. They emerged from the second meeting with an amendment of their own, the terms of which were never made public and which MacDonald in the event had no opportunity of moving.[112] In its later report to the 1914 Labour Party Conference, the PLP supplied the following explanation of its attitude. Parker, it said, had signed the Majority Report because 'the transactions of Ministers in American shares were outside the purview of any Select Committee, but belonged to the House of Commons itself'; the PLP had then voted for the Adkins Motion, 'which, while not in effect either censuring or whitewashing the Ministers concerned, accepted their expressions of regret and put on record that such transactions were not proper and would not be repeated'.[113] But the plain facts of the case are these. When the Commons debate took place Parker made a brief personal statement, but no other Labour MP so much as spoke. Moreover, when the division lists were later published, it was seen that thirty Labour MPs, including MacDonald, Henderson, and Parker, had voted for the Adkins Motion, but that five MPs, Snowden, O'Grady, Jowett, Thorne, and Walsh, had deliberately abstained.

The divisions within the Labour Movement surfaced once more at the Party Conference in January 1914. MacDonald's attempts at defending the PLP's approach to Marconi did not convince angry rank-and-file delegates. A member of the Workers Union 'said that the signing of the Marconi Report had done more harm to the Movement

[110] This candidate, E. R. Hartley, secured only 2,580 votes, not enough to prevent the victory of the Liberal, on 10,863 votes; the Conservative came second with 9,279 votes.
[111] *Labour Leader*, 26 June 1913.
[112] A complicated explanation was furnished in the *Labour Leader*, 26 June 1913.
[113] Report of the 14th Annual Conference of the Labour Party, held at Glasgow, 27–30 Jan. 1914, p. 42.

than the Members of the Labour Party had any idea. He knew that members of the Workers Union had refused to continue to pay their levy because of it, and what was true of his Union was true of other unions.' An ILP delegate said that his organization believed that Parker should have brought in a separate report, instead of throwing himself 'holus-bolus on the side of Tweedledum and against Tweedledee'. Brownlie of the ASE regretted that Parker had 'lost the opportunity of showing that there was at least one honest man of the people who had the courage to say what ought to be done'.[114] Thus, although the platform defeated an attempt to refer back the Marconi section of the party report, the episode nicely reveals the strains and tensions within the Labour and socialist worlds on the eve of the Great War. It also shows how increasingly difficult it was becoming for Labour's moderate parliamentary leaders to pursue a strategy favourable to the 'Progressive Alliance' without running the risk of a serious party revolt. This was not the least of the consequences of the 'scandals' which rocked the Asquith Ministry in 1913–14.

Moreover, tactical questions apart, Marconi confirmed many Socialists in their belief that corruption was inseparable from the profit-making system. Marconi, they argued, had revealed capitalism in action. Admittedly, some Socialists viewed the affair with mixed feelings. Even the *Labour Leader* had initially welcomed Ministers' protestations of innocence in the October 1912 debate: 'Vices of public men, to whatsoever party they belong, rebound heavily on the Socialist Party. For socialists stake their all on the hope that public men will be pure, and if that hope is baseless the towers of Utopia tumble.'[115] But the general line was for Socialists to argue that purity in public life would only be achieved when all the major industries had been brought into public ownership, since this would put an end to Stock Exchange gambling and thus destroy the conditions which had brought the Marconi Scandal into existence. Socialism would also see a transformation of human nature, and the virtual disappearance of greed, selfishness, and acquisitiveness. This was, indeed, a utopian approach to politics, but it was one which Socialists applied, not just to Marconi, but to the other 'scandals' which were simultaneously attracting considerable public attention.

[114] Ibid. 77–80.
[115] 'Ministers in Dock. The Importance of Public Probity' (*Labour Leader*, 17 Oct. 1912).

9
Silver and Oil

The Silver Scandal

IT is in the nature of scandals that they never come singly but in clusters, each controversial episode reacting upon the others and giving credence to the notion of an interlocking network of corruption far more sinister in its entirety than are its component parts. So it was in late 1912 and 1913, when the Marconi Incident ran parallel to the so-called Indian Silver Scandal and overlapped with a new series of allegations involving the Mexican Eagle Oil Company. The Marconi Incident ended up by overshadowing these other issues; but there was a quiet interlude, the period separating the 'Festival of Truth' in October 1912 from the start of the disclosures which came thick and fast after February 1913, during which the Radical Right press concentrated its fire on Indian Silver, recognizing perhaps the public's growing boredom with the slow-moving Marconi saga.

The Indian Silver Affair originated in early 1912 with the decision of the Financial Committee of the India Office to purchase silver bullion in order to mint more rupees. Had past precedents been followed, the Committee would have approached one of two London financial houses which specialized in this line of work and commissioned them via the Bank of England to make the requisite purchase. But the India Office had reason to suppose that this long-drawn-out procedure simply alerted speculators to the fact that the Government was about to enter the bullion market, so pushing up the price of silver. In order to break the 'ring', they therefore approached another banking firm, which had never yet been employed in this role, and asked it to purchase silver on the Government's behalf surreptitiously and in small amounts, so as not to excite attention. In July 1912 the Governor of the Bank of England was privately informed of the India Office's plans and gave his approval, but the Bank was not formally notified, and steps were taken to disguise what was happening from its officials.[1]

Such cloak and dagger methods might have aroused controversy at any time but when they were unmasked in November 1912, in part through the vigilance of rival firms,[2] the Government's critics, still

[1] Special Report from Select Committee on Vacation of Seat (Member Holding Contract), PP ix (1912–13), 452.
[2] D'Avigdor-Goldsmid, H., 'The Little Marconi Case', History Today, xiv (1964) 284. Goldsmid writes: 'A watch by Montagu's competitors on railway stations and ports disclosed what was going on.'

influenced by the prevailing 'Marconi atmosphere', were bound to be exceedingly distrustful. For the inexperienced financial house which had received the Government's commission in these highly unusual circumstances was none other than Samuel Montagu & Co., a family firm, whose partners included two of the brothers, the brother-in-law, and the cousin of Edwin Montagu, the Under-Secretary at the India Office. The suspicious jumped to the conclusion that a Minister was 'putting a good thing' in the way of his close relatives.

In fact, Edwin Montagu had a good defence to make, but he could not do so effectively because the 'scandal' happened to break when he was in the middle of an official fact-finding tour of India—a tour, incidentally, which had already been sharply criticized on account of its expense. Montagu, a notoriously volatile man, was plunged into the depths of despair. 'I am lastingly depressed by the silence of my friends and the perverseness of Liberal newspapers', he confided to his journal, and he wrote of his fear that his political career might be irretrievably damaged by the revelations.[3] Yet though claiming that he had a burning desire to clear his name before the House of Commons, Montagu would not curtail his tour, as his critics urged. Instead, he pleaded with Lord Crewe, his departmental chief, to defer the parliamentary debate until his return to England some time in the spring of 1913.[4] But this course of action was totally impractical.

Meanwhile, from November 1912 to February 1913, the cable lines between India and London were alive with a succession of agitated messages from Montagu. He never so much as knew of the silver purchases, he said; indeed, when he entered the India Office he had agreed with Crewe not to see or initial any papers dealing with finance, such matters falling within the province of the Secretary of State and of the Financial Committee. Nor, Montagu protested, had he ever been involved in the work of the family firm. (There was a moment of panic in late November 1912 when it briefly seemed that he might have acquired a partial interest in the company through a bequest from his late father, but this proved not to be the case.)[5]

Montagu bitterly resented the insinuations of corruption being broadcast by Opposition newspapers and politicians. True, Crewe and Harold Baker, Financial Secretary to the War Office, did their best to defend their absent colleague; Crewe actually went so far as to claim in the House of Lords on 14 November that Edwin Montagu had had 'no more to do with the finance of India at the India Office than he has to do with the finance of the Panama Canal, and . . . he has no more

---

[3] Waley, *Edwin Montagu*, p. 55.

[4] Montagu to Crewe (copy), 27 Jan. 1913 (Trinity College, Cambridge, Montagu papers, AS-II-5, fo. 63).

[5] See exchange of telegrams between Montagu and Crewe in late Nov. 1912 (ibid., fos. 30–2).

connection with the firm of Samuel Montagu and Co. than he has with the firm of Marshall and Snelgrove.'[6] This statement excited some mirth, and in no way satisfied the Conservative backbencher who had unearthed this latest ministerial indiscretion, Rupert Gwynne—'Silver Market Gwynne' or 'Rupee Gwynne', as he was soon being called.[7]

The issue was fully debated on 13 February 1913, when Gwynne moved that a Select Committee be set up to 'inquire into the administration of Indian Finance and Currency by the Secretary of State for India and the Council of India, and the responsibility and powers vested in the Finance Committee, in special relation to the recent purchases of silver and the distribution of cash balances'.[8] In a letter to Venetia Stanley, Asquith commented that 'Bluetooth' [i.e. Baker] and he had 'championed the far-away Assyrian (Montagu), who was left without a stain on his character'.[9] It was, indeed, noticeable that Montagu was handled very gently by most MPs, even those on the Opposition benches. Thus, Bonar Law saw no reason to censure the Under-Secretary, but chose rather to commiserate with him for having been so badly treated by his insensitive relatives.[10] However, in an impressive speech later in the debate Lord Hugh Cecil, while agreeing with his Leader that Montagu was innocent, dissented from Bonar Law's view that British politicians could be relied upon to subordinate all considerations of money for the sake of a higher ambition; there was nothing inevitable, said Cecil, about British standards of honesty in public life, and the Government had behaved in a way that was 'very grossly indelicate', and though not in itself corrupt, its behaviour 'might easily be made a precedent for a transaction which was really corrupt'[11]—exactly the same charge that his brother, Robert, was to make later in the year in connection with Marconi. Earlier Strachey had written an article, 'The Appearance of Evil', which made rather similar points; what, he asked, would people have said if Cromer after having been sent out to Egypt had continued to do business with the house of Baring?[12]

Other aspects of the case worried the Opposition MPs who spoke in February 1913. For example, the India Office had initially reacted unhelpfully, even obstructively, to Gwynne's attempt to secure publication of its communications with Samuel Montagu & Co. It was

---

[6] *Parl. Deb.*, 5th ser. (Lords), xii. 971 (14 Nov. 1912). In a conversation with Strachey in Dec. 1919, Montagu asserted that his relationships with his brothers were not especially friendly and that he saw his elder brother at most three times a year, sometimes only once (HLRO, Strachey papers, S/10/13/1, Strachey's memo., 15 Dec. 1919).

[7] *Punch*, cxliv (1913), 145; Balcarres's diary, 22 Nov. 1912, in Vincent (ed.), *The Crawford Papers*, p. 286.

[8] *Parl. Deb.*, 5th ser., xlviii. 1224 (13 Feb. 1913).

[9] Asquith to Venetia Stanley, 18 Feb. 1913, in Brock (eds.), *Letters to Venetia Stanley*, p. 28.   [10] *Parl. Deb.*, 5th ser., xlviii. 1262.

[11] Ibid. 1330-1.   [12] *Spectator*, 30 Nov. 1912, pp. 887-8.

only at the fourth time of asking that the Government printed the full text of the really crucial letter: one which Montagu's brother-in-law, Ernest Louis Franklin, had written to the Chairman of the Finance Committee on 8 January 1912. This remarkable letter made it clear that Samuel Montagu had first approached the India Office, rather than vice versa: 'We particularly do not care about approaching Edwin Montagu on this matter for reasons that must be obvious to you', Franklin had said. 'We do not see, however, that our close relationship to this gentleman should militate against the Indian Council's doing business with us if they conscientiously think that it is to their advantage to do so.'[13]

There was also unease about the role of the Chairman of the Financial Committee of the India Office, Sir Felix Schuster, who was not a career civil servant, but served on a part-time basis (his salary being £1,200 p.a.), while his main work was as Governor of the Union of London & Smith's Bank—which happened to be the bank employed by Samuel Montagu. This in turn raised the issue of the huge Indian balances that had been allowed to accumulate in London amounting in 1912 to some £18 million; £3½ million from this fund had been lent out to the Union of London & Smith's Bank. Schuster was in any case disliked by Unionist politicians because he was a Liberal who had stood unsuccessfully for the City of London in the 1906 election. All of this suggested that, under a lax Radical administration, official policy, private business, and party activity were becoming dangerously intertwined.

In a way the criticisms of the Indian surpluses and of the uses to which they were being put helped save Montagu and the Government from being sucked into another controversy of Marconi-like proportions, since they raised highly technical issues which somewhat distracted attention from the political charges. From the start Asquith had been determined to resist Gwynne's call for a Select Committee, but after sounding out the mood of the House, he felt it would be prudent to offer as an alternative a Royal Commission which could examine at leisure the abstruse financial issues dear to the hearts of the small but enthusiastic band of Indian currency reformers.

From the remoteness of India Montagu lamented that 'a Commission has been promised as a direct result of the most unscrupulous of Parliamentary agitations' and declared it 'to be a bad precedent in Indian affairs'.[14] But Asquith's judgment was vindicated when the Royal Commission, chaired by Austen Chamberlain, produced a sober and authoritative Report in 1914, which included a sophisticated defence of the practice of including private bankers as members of the Finance Committee (though the Committee had actually been wound

[13] Special Report on Vacation of Seat, Appendix, p. xxiii.
[14] Montagu to Crewe, 16 Feb. 1913 (Montagu papers, AS-II-5, fo. 69).

up in late 1913). The way in which the deposits were distributed also met with its approval.[15] Moreover, J. M. Keynes, the Commission's Secretary, had already defended the Liberal Government in his suavest style in his book, *Indian Currency and Finance* (1913), which mocked the inability of most politicians to master the intricacies of this technical subject.[16] Consequently, those like Moreton Frewen who had hoped for dramatic 'exposures' of the manipulations of the silver market suffered a disappointment. 'Austen Chamberlain the best of men had a mind crammed with other matters,' Frewen ruefully observed, 'and thus his Commission will have made the elucidation of all this crookedness so much the more difficult.'[17]

But there was another more important reason why Edwin Montagu escaped relatively lightly from the 'Silver Scandal'. As he was informed by his colleague and friend, Walter Runciman, in a cable of early November 1912, the public attacks had started to switch to his cousin, Sir Stuart Samuel.[18] The offence of the latter was that, unlike Edwin Montagu, he was an active partner in the firm of Samuel Montagu, a position he combined with representing Whitechapel as a Radical MP. And this, as another tormentor of the Government, the Conservative MP, Sir Frederick Banbury, had pointed out as early as 7 November 1912, seemed to be a violation of the Contractors Act of 1782.[19]

On the other hand, there were grounds for supposing that this statute applied only to the British Government, not to the Government of India—which, of course, had not existed when the legislation was enacted. In short, the precise legal situation was obscure, and as Asquith admitted when he was challenged in the Commons by Banbury on 7 November and again on 11 November, the legal officers

[15] Final Report of Royal Commission on Indian Finance and Currency, 1914, Cd. 7236, esp. paras. 212, 202.

[16] *The Collected Writings of John Maynard Keynes*, i. *Indian Currency and Finance* (London, 1971), pp. 101–2. But his biographer notes that Keynes 'may have also wanted to help clear the name of Edwin Montagu, who had given him his first paper speech at the Cambridge Union. . .' (Skidelsky, R., *John Maynard Keynes: Hopes Betrayed 1883–1920* (London, 1983), p. 273.

[17] Frewen to Bonar Law, 17 Feb. 1914 (HLRO, Bonar Law papers, 31/3/31). But Moreton Frewen, who was Winston Churchill's uncle by marriage, had himself attempted to make his fortune by bringing off a corner in silver in 1899 (Andrews, A., *The Splendid Pauper* (London, 1968), pp. 136–40). Like many other prominent bimetallists, Frewen made a speciality of exposing financial scandals, but was himself something of a rogue. This in 1894 he had tried to blackmail Rhodes and was later shown to have made £16,000 profit out of the Deccan Mining Company promotion, a scheme in which he played a highly dubious role (ibid. 175–7, 127–33). For Frewen as sportsman, conversationalist, traveller, and English eccentric, see his obituary in *The Times*, 4 Sept. 1924.

[18] Runciman to Montagu, cable received 8 Nov. 1912 (Montagu papers, AS-II-5, fo. 22).

[19] *Parl. Deb.*, 4th ser., cxxix. 74–5 (2 Feb. 1904) and 194–9 (3 Feb. 1904). The Attorney-General, Sir Rufus Isaacs, thought the case of the Gibbs brothers might be a precedent. See his letter to Asquith, 11 Nov. 1912 (Bodleian, Asquith papers, vol. 24, fo. 220). See also Ch. 2, p. 44.

had been unable to give him a clear lead.[20] Ignoring the advice of Bonar Law and of some Liberal newspapers,[21] the Government then referred the issue to a Select Committee of the Commons, which met on eleven occasions under the Prime Minister's chairmanship but was also unable to reach a decision; it subsequently issued a very slender report which conveys little information, but very probably the Committee had split on straight party lines.[22] The problem was next referred to a Judicial Committee of the Privy Council, presided over by Haldane, the Lord Chancellor, its other members being Lords Halsbury, Loreburn, and Dunedin. Haldane complacently informed his mother that 'the judicial temper was perfect, although we were two Conservatives and two Liberals sitting to hear what had been a political question'.[23] In April 1913 the Committee delivered its ruling. While 'no suggestion [had] been made of any improper motive', it said, Sir Stuart Samuel had unwittingly infringed the 1782 statute and would have to resign his seat.[24] Herbert Samuel, Sir Stuart's brother, privately fumed that this was 'the grossest injustice'.[25] And clearly neither Sir Stuart nor his party welcomed the prospect of a by-election in what was a highly marginal East End constituency.

The Whitechapel by-election, where polling took place on 30 April, was a colourful affair. Sir Stuart had represented the constituency since 1900 and was popular with the Jewish community which comprised some 50 per cent of the voters. He went before his constituents protesting his innocence and protraying himself as a martyr to anti-Semitic prejudice. The Conservative candidate, Captain E. M. Browne, an ex-soldier and an 'all-round sportsman', tried to neutralize Samuel's campaign by rushing from synagogue to synagogue, and he also tried to work up an intense concern for the local costers and street traders, who felt threatened by the Government's Shops Act.[26] Browne also irritated

[20] *Parl. Deb.*, 5th ser., xliii. 1434–5 (7 Nov. 1912). Isaacs thought it wise to have the views of an expert Select Committee (Isaacs to Asquith, 11 Nov. 1912, Asquith papers, vol. 24, fo. 220), and Sir John Simon, the Solicitor-General, said that the case raised issues 'of great difficulty and considerable doubt since it depends in the main upon whether such a transaction on behalf of the Government of India is a contract "for or on account of the public service" within the meaning of the statute of Parliament of Great Britain in the year 1782' (Simon's opinion, Asquith papers, vol. 24, fo. 221).

[21] *Parl. Deb.*, 5th ser., lii. 62–3 (21 Apr. 1913); *Manchester Guardian*, 23 Nov. 1912; *Nation*, 28 Dec. 1912.

[22] Special Report on Vacation of Seat.

[23] Haldane to Mrs Haldane, 14 Mar. 1913 (National Library of Scotland, Haldane papers, vol. 5989, fo. 96). According to the Clerk of the Council there was at first some risk of the Court being divided, but the incipient division did not follow party lines, since Loreburn and Halsbury initially favoured 'the avoidance' and Haldane and Dunedin inclined to the other view (See Almeric Fitzroy's diary, 18 Mar. 1913, in Fitzroy, A., *Memoirs*, ii (London, n.d.), 508).

[24] *The Times*, 12 Apr. 1913.

[25] Herbert Samuel to mother, 21 Feb. 1913 (HLRO, Samuel papers, A156, fos. 1070–1). In this letter Samuel says that his brother had expected the decision to go in his favour.

[26] *The Times*, 12 Apr., 30 Apr., 1 May 1913.

the Unionist leaders by pestering them for assurances that the Party sympathized with the plight of British citizens of Jewish faith trying to enter Russia.[27]

Samuel held his seat. Although the majority was cut from 540 to 166 in an enlarged electorate, the Liberals could be pleased in the circumstances with having won the by-election at all. Interestingly, *The Times*'s correspondent thought that Browne would have come closer to victory 'if it had not been for the prevailing fear of anti-Semitism among the Jews of the East-end of London. Captain Browne did all he could to reassure the electors on this point, but matters pertaining to the Marconi Inquiry and the purchase of silver for the Indian Government by Sir Stuart Samuel's firm have taken deeper root among English Jews than is commonly supposed.' Browne agreed with this analysis: 'the bogey of anti-Semitism was the party cry of the Radical from first to last', he said, after the result had been declared.[28]

The Whitechapel by-election still left open the question of Sir Stuart Samuel's fine. Zealous supporter that he was of the Liberal Government, the unfortunate man had voted on 93 occasions since his firm had obtained its contract, making him liable to a fine of £46,500.[29] Nor was there any chance that this penalty would be waived; on 11 November two 'common informers', one of them serving a prison sentence, issued a writ for the recovery of the outstanding sum, thereby forestalling the *New Witness*, which wanted to have the 'honour' of striking the first blow.[30]

The Government's initial response was to bring in an Indemnity Bill. This met with the approval of 'old guard' Conservatives, like Lord Halsbury, but the *New Witness* had from the start been adamant that Samuel 'must be made to pay to the uttermost farthing, just as if he were a poor Englishman who told the truth about the rich',[31] and when the Indemnity Bill appeared in May 1913 it denounced this as 'another flagrant violation of the Constitution'.[32] Many Opposition papers protested at what they saw as a piece of blatant government favouritism to one of its supporters, and the protest was effective, in that Unionist MPs came forward in sufficient numbers to prevent the Indemnity Bill going through both Houses of Parliament within a single day. Among the speakers was Lord Hugh Cecil, who argued that Samuel should only be made to pay a moderate fine, but said that he disliked the idea of total indemnity. And Bonar Law would only agree to the Bill if Samuel Montagu threw open its books to inspection,

[27] Steel-Maitland to Bonar Law, 25 Apr. 1913, and enclosures (Bonar Law papers, 29/3/28).

[28] *The Times*, 1 May 1913.   [29] Ibid., 12 Apr. 1913.

[30] *New Witness*, 28 Nov. 1912, p. 97.

[31] Hobhouse's diary, 16 Apr. 1913, in David, E. (ed.), *Inside Asquith's Cabinet: From the Diaries of Charles Hobhouse* (London, 1977), p. 134.

[32] *New Witness*, 8 May 1913, p. 6.

which it resolutely refused to do.[33] No doubt many Unionist MPs were also taking advantage of the affair so as to waste government time and so obstruct Irish Home Rule and Welsh Disestablishment.

There was another twist to the story when on 23 May 1913 the India Office belatedly told the Attorney-General that Franklin had acted as a buyer as well as a broker in the silver market, a piece of information which had not been given to the Select Committee. The Government used this disclosure to force the firm of Samuel Montagu to beat a retreat. 'As far as the Indemnity Bill is concerned,' wrote the partners to the Patronage Secretary, 'Sir Stuart Samuel must leave himself in the hands of the House. If, however, there is to be official opposition, we have his authority for saying that, while thanking the Government for their intentions, he would prefer that the Bill should be withdrawn.'[34] But the firm continued to protest its innocence, and Sir Stuart lodged an appeal against his fine. Eventually a messy compromise was reached. In March 1914 the courts awarded the informer, Dr Bird, £13,000 costs against Sir Samuel—to the hearty approval of the *New Witness*, which admitted, however, that the Clean Government League and itself 'could have done very well with £13,000, and there would have been something delightful about financing them out of Samuel's pocket!'[35] Other appeals were dismissed on legal technicalities, but this still left Sir Stuart saddled with legal expenses that must have been enormous.[36]

Even harsh critics of the Government often tempered their amusement at the discomfiture of this very rich member of the Samuel–Montagu family with some sympathy for his plight. After all, if Franklin is to be believed, the India Office order had been handled in so confidential a manner that Sir Stuart was not even informed about the transaction. But the verdict of *The Times* was characteristic; it conceded that Samuel was 'morally innocent', but went on to argue that the purity of public life must be maintained: 'We need not fear the craft of placemen or pensioners. But influences, not less poisonous because subtle and indirect, exist. The moralist has not far to search to discover temptations new and dangerous.'[37]

The statute of 1782, however, could hardly be presented as an effective instrument for safeguarding the purity of public life in the early twentieth century, if only because its antiquity meant that it had nothing to say about the more recent phenomenon of the joint stock

[33] Goldsmid, 'Little Marconi Case', p. 285.

[34] Samuel Montagu & Co to Illingworth (copy), 7 Aug. 1913 (Bonar Law papers, 30/1/15).

[35] *New Witness*, 19 Feb. 1914, p. 491.

[36] Goldsmid, 'Little Marconi Case', p. 286. Goldsmid notes that 'Sir Stuart had been represented by a bevy of counsel both before the Select Committee and the Privy Council.'

[37] *The Times*, 12 Apr. 1913.

company. It was only the fact that Samuel Montagu was a private firm which exposed Sir Stuart Samuel to the rigours of the law; had the company been incorporated, his position would have been legally beyond reproach. What annoyed many Radicals and friends of the Government was the spectacle of Frederick Banbury, a director of the Great Northern Railway Company, which had made many public contracts, setting himself up as Samuel's judge.[38] The absurdity of this situation prompted Swift MacNeill, with his acute memory for the indiscretions of former Unionist Ministries, to introduce a Private Member's Bill in April 1913, aimed at barring directors of incorporated trading companies in contractual relationship with government departments from being elected to Parliament or sitting as Members.[39] (The Bill did not make significant progress.) Even the Marxist paper, *Justice*, a vitriolic critic of Liberal 'corruption', agreed that the existing rules bred hypocrisy.[40] This was obviously the line also pursued by the loyal Liberal press. The *Westminster Gazette* went further and actually claimed that Samuel had only incurred his fine 'because his firm came to the rescue of the Government of India in a difficulty, and saved that country something like half a million of money'.[41] For, if Samuel Montagu & Co. were to be believed, it had earned a trifling commission of £7,513 and had made no profit worth talking about out of its embarrassing assignment.[42]

But the extreme Unionist journals were not interested in justifications of this sort and exploited the Indian Silver Affair quite unscrupulously. The *Pall Mall Gazette*, for example, thundered in its editorial of 31 October 1912; 'It is quite evident now that the scandals of Indian finance are going to be brought into the light of day. Only an Edmund Burke could do full justice to their magnitude.'[43] It is also interesting to compare the relatively restrained language used by Rupert Gwynne when he moved his motion in the Commons in February 1913 with his article in *Our Flag* in that same month, which contained a genealogical table, delineating the family relationships of the Montagus and Samuels.[44] This was anti-Semitism by innuendo. More blatant was the approach of another Conservative backbencher, who used the Indian Silver Affair to 'demonstrate' to his constituents that Jews were in control of the Liberal Party.[45]

Equally ready to sound an anti-Semitic note was Maxse in the *National Review*. True, Maxse denied that he had a prejudice against

---

[38] *Parl. Deb.*, 5th ser., lii. 388 (23 Apr. 1913).   [39] Ibid. 387–90.
[40] *Justice*, 16 Nov. 1912.   [41] *Westminster Gazette*, 17 Feb. 1914.
[42] Colin Holmes comments: 'contrary to what was claimed in some quarters at the time, the India silver scandal might be considered as an attempt by Jews to prove their patriotism rather than an attempt to engage in a Jewish plot for Jewish interests.' (Holmes, *Anti-Semitism*, p. 84.)
[43] *Pall Mall Gazette*, 31 Oct. 1912.
[44] *Our Flag*, Feb. 1913, p. 26.   [45] Holmes, *Anti-Semitism*, p. 78.

Jews as such; a distinction had to be drawn, he said, between 'the best Jews, who make admirable citizens' and 'that type of Jews who regards the whole duty of man as consisting in scoring some material advantage'.[46] But clearly the *National Review* regarded the Samuels and Montagus as 'cosmopolitan financiers' of the latter type. Indeed, the founder of the firm of Samuel Montagu, Lord Swaythling, who had died in 1911, embodied nearly all the characteristics which supposedly defined the 'Radical Plutocrat'. He was a rich Jewish banker who had supported the Liberal Party, both financially and as an MP. In recognition of these services he had received a peerage in 1907. To commemorate this event, Swaythling commissioned a huge picture, which now hangs on the staircase separating the Lords from the main House of Commons lobby, depicting 'the Commons Petitioning Queen Elizabeth to Marry', in which the painter, Solomon J. Solomon, prominently displayed the donor—a blatant piece of self-advertisement which cannot have done much for Swaythling's popularity.[47] In addition to that, he had died leaving a will which attempted to bind his children to the strict observance of Jewish rites, so putting obstacles in the way of their marrying Gentiles—a will which Maxse interpreted as meaning that 'he regarded the people of the country in which the Montagus have taken up their abode as aliens unfit for family relationship.'[48]

Meanwhile, throughout 1912 and 1913 the *New Witness* poured endless abuse at 'the amazing Samuels', among whom, of course, the Montagus were included, since the first Baron Swaythling had been born a Samuel, before changing his name by deed-poll. Indeed, the original Samuel Montagu, disparagingly called 'old Samuel', was presented as a 'free-handed' man, who 'in his later years kept a stud of politicians as Joel keeps a stud of race-horses' and whose uncles and cousins were now swarming all over Whitehall and Westminster. 'For our part, little as we like corruption', sneered this bigoted journal, 'we would willingly pension off the whole Samuel family handsomely at the public expense and give them perquisites into the bargain, if, so only, could we persuade them to keep their hands off the Government of England.'[49]

There followed specific charges against the partners of the banking house which were clearly libellous. Edwin Montagu, enfuriated by this abuse, strongly urged his elder brother, the second Baron Swaythling, to get the family to bring an action against the *New Witness*, with a view to stopping the libels and possibly killing the paper by getting

---

[46] *National Review*, lx (1912), 553*.
[47] Goldsmid, 'Little Marconi Case', p. 284. See also Montagu, L. H., *Samuel Montagu, First Baron Swaythling* (London, 1913?).
[48] *National Review*, lx (1912), 557*.
[49] *New Witness*, 7 Nov., 14 Nov. 1912, pp. 8, 41.

heavy damages.[50] But Swaythling cabled back, 'Family think *New Witness* of no importance and would only advertise rag unnecessarily by criminally prosecuting. Action for damages not to be considered.'[51] In the privacy of his journal, however, Edwin wrote the following revealing note: 'a fine wave of Anti-Semitism results and Jews in the Liberal Party will be at a discount. Poor me, with Samuel and Isaacs ahead of me.'[52]

Back in London Herbert Samuel was writing to his cousin, Gerald Montagu, another partner in the house, commiserating with him over having been 'made the subject of some of the attacks in the *New Witness* to which I have long been accustomed, but which are new to you'. He added, 'fortunately the circulation of the new paper is almost nil' and its scurrilous articles were not likely to 'affect the opinion of anyone whose opinion [was] worth having'.[53] This was precisely the line of reasoning which convinced Herbert Samuel, Isaacs, and Asquith that it would be foolish to proceed against the *New Witness* for its libellous allegations over Marconi, and in both cases the contemptuous forbearance shown by ministers was possibly a major error of judgement.

This leads on to the question of what links, if any, there were between Marconi and the Silver 'Scandal'. Hilaire Belloc, of course, believed that the two had revealed different aspects of the same corrupt system; both were 'essentially cosmopolitan transactions in character', he told the Marconi Select Committee, and, together, they had had the effect of shaking what he called 'the old apathy' towards the Jewish Question.[54] In many ways the Indian Silver Affair could the more easily be fitted into an anti-Semitic frame of reference. True, the Conservative leadership continued in public to deprecate anything that bordered on Jew baiting, but, significantly, we find the Unionist Whip, Balcarres, confiding to his journal: 'A little knot of Radical Jews has secured the manipulation of millions of Indian money, and the case against this hateful jobbery is developing with a rapidity which causes deep alarm among ministerialists.'[55]

There was also an overlapping cast of characters in the two 'scandals'. Stuart Samuel, the laughing-stock of the Indian Silver

---

[50] Montagu to Lucas, 5 Jan. 1913 (Montagu papers, AS-II-5, fo. 50).
[51] Swaythling to Montagu, received 8 Jan. 1913 (ibid., fo. 51).
[52] Waley, *Edwin Montagu*, p. 56.
[53] Herbert Samuel to Gerald Montagu (copy), 17 Dec. 1912 (Samuel papers, A/38, fo. 52).
[54] Belloc's evidence, 24 Apr. 1913 (Select Committee on Marconi Wireless Telegraph Company, Limited, Agreement, 1913, vii. q. 8223).
[55] Balcarres's diary, 22 Nov. 1912, in Vincent (ed.), *Crawford Papers*, p. 286. Incidentally, Lloyd George himself was recounting with amusement the following *bon mot* about the Indian silver scandal: 'This is not the first occasion on which a Jew has got into trouble regarding a transaction in silver' (Riddell's diary, 23 Nov. 1912, in Riddell, *More Pages From My Diary*, p. 102).

Affair, was the elder brother of Herbert Samuel, who, as Postmaster-General, was in the thick of the Marconi controversy. Moreover, critics of the Government could not help noting that the minister who introduced the Indemnity Bill in April 1913 was none other than Rufus Isaacs. Conversely, the Opposition attack proceeded along similar lines. Lord Hugh Cecil was the moralizer in the one affair, his brother, Lord Robert, in the other.

There was another more tangible, though it later transpired unimportant, connection between Indian Silver and Marconi. When Herbert Samuel gave evidence to the Marconi Select Committee on 31 March, he was asked about a statement which had recently appeared in the *Financial News* to the effect that his cousin, Gerald Montagu, a partner in Samuel Montagu & Co., had acquired some 2,000 English Marconi shares on behalf of an Amsterdam client, Messrs. Wertheim & Gompertz.[56] This disclosure had very much excited certain organs of the press; the *New Witness* hailed Gerald Montagu as '"the missing link" between the Marconi and Indian scandals'.[57] Hyndman had also been intrigued by the information, which he assumed must reflect dishonour on the Liberal Ministry: 'altogether it is as unseemly a bit of scandal as has occurred in our time. Watch it carefully.'[58] Unfortunately for the scandalmongers, the *Financial News* disclosure proved to be a mare's nest. One historian has called it 'an outstanding example of how rumours and snippets of information could be fitted together to create a scandal'.[59] Gerald Montagu, privately interrogated by Herbert Samuel, was able to assure him that he had never held any Marconi shares himself, nor had the firm ever recommended any of its clients to buy or sell shares in any of the Marconi enterprises. Samuel duly passed on this information to the Select Committee, adding that he, too, could honestly say that he had never revealed any information of any sort nor had he so much as *mentioned* the pending Marconi Contract to any of his relatives.[60] Cynics were left to comment with mock admiration on the self-effacing silence of the Samuels and Montagus, who, it seemed, never discussed among themselves the work upon which each was severally engaged.

The Mexican Eagle Oil Co.

By the summer of 1913, with Marconi once more dominating the newspaper headlines, the Indian Silver Affair was beginning to slip out

[56] Select Committee on Marconi Agreement, qs. 1876–8.
[57] *New Witness*, 28 Nov. 1912, p. 98.
[58] *Justice*, 29 Mar. 1913.
[59] Holmes, *Anti-Semitism*, p. 74.
[60] Gerald Montagu to Samuel, 5 Dec. 1912; Samuel to Marconi Select Committee, 9 Dec. 1912; Samuel to Gerald Montagu (copy), 17 Dec. 1912 (Samuel papers, A/38, fos. 48–52).

of the politicians' consciousness. But at approximately the same time insinuations of a different kind were capturing attention and even securing a mention in newspapers and parliamentary debates. On 16 June 1913 the *Daily Mail* commented: 'The strong—and, we hope, baseless—rumours regarding oil contracts for the navy are exercising the public mind scarcely less than Ministers' dealings in Marconi shares.' And on 22 June the disgruntled former Lord Chancellor, Lord Loreburn, had a long conversation with Charles Hobhouse, in which he blamed the Prime Minister for not having grasped from the outset the seriousness of Marconi, before observing that 'every kind of evil rumour *had* been in circulation about Marconi, and *was* being said as to oil.'[61]

The new 'scandal' broke in the wake of the Admiralty's decision to convert its battlefleet from coal to oil. In April 1912 the Board of Admiralty had put into the Estimates provision for five oil-fired super-dreadnoughts; shortly afterwards, the First Lord, Winston Churchill, set up a Royal Commission on Fuel Oil, in an attempt to find out how the oil could best be procured, stored, and utilized. Then on 17 July 1913 Churchill made his historic statement to Parliament: oil-fired ships would gradually take the place of coal-fired vessels.[62] Unfortunately, whereas Britain had plentiful supplies of coal, it had no easy access to oil. It was this difficulty which brought about the negotiations that culminated in August 1914 in the British Government's acquisition of a controlling interest in the Anglo-Persian Oil Company. Of far less long-term significance, but possibly of greater interest to contemporaries, was the Admiralty's recommendation that the Government should sign a contract with the Mexican Eagle Oil Company to supply the Navy with part of its oil supplies.[63] Well-informed observers had been anticipating this announcement for some weeks past.

On one level, the proposed deal was very sensible, and Churchill was able to present it as highly advantageous both to the British Navy and to the general public. For Mexican Eagle was easily the largest British-controlled oil corporation in the world. And its position would be strengthened by this deal, so reducing the risk of the Admiralty falling dependent on the two giant foreign petroleum combines, Standard Oil (American) and the Royal Dutch Shell Group.[64]

But the announcement, coming in July 1913, was another source of embarrassment to the Government. For the company in question was one whose members were 'very closely related in a political sense with

---

[61] Hobhouse's diary, 22 June 1913, in David, *Inside Asquith's Cabinet*, p. 140.
[62] Marder, A. J., *From the Dreadnought to Scapa Flow, i. The Road to War 1904–1914* (Oxford, 1961), pp. 269–71.
[63] *Parl. Deb.*, 5th ser., lv. 1477 (17 July 1913).
[64] In fact, however, Standard Oil was broken up in 1911.

members of the Government', as the *Morning Post* put it.[65] Its director was the great contractor, Lord Cowdray, who as Weetman Pearson had sat as Liberal MP for Colchester between 1895 and 1910, before receiving a peerage, which his generosity to party funds had undoubtedly helped him to secure. With his wealth, business power, and political affiliations, Cowdray figured prominently on every Unionist list of 'Radical Plutocrats'.

Moreover, as we have seen, in late 1912 Cowdray had taken the former Patronage Secretary, the Master of Elibank, now Lord Murray, into his service, on a salary of £6,000. In addition, as political insiders were well aware, Lloyd George's son, Dick, had recently joined Murray in South America, where he had been put to work negotiating contracts with the Costa Rica Government, under Murray's avuncular supervision.[66] Also on Cowdray's staff was Churchill's brother-in-law. Since neither was wealthy or had special qualifications for his work,[67] the suspicion arose that the two men had been recruited by Cowdray in an attempt to 'dictate to the British Government'.[68] In January 1914, faced with a story which had appeared in the *Daily Mail*, Murray informed Lloyd George that he had 'thought it well in all our interests to state that Dick was a hard working engineer in the service of the Firm and in no way responsible for conducting negotiations with Foreign Governments'.[69] This was a blatant lie.

But most of the rumours concerned, not Lloyd George's relatives, but rather alleged ministerial investments in Mexican Eagle. As early as September 1912 the *Investors Chronicle* was carrying a paragraph claiming that Liberal Party funds had been put into the shares of Mexican Eagle in the name of Lord Murray.[70] Rumours gathered apace. On 4 April 1913 Strachey wrote an article for the *Spectator*, which, so he informed Lord Hugh Cecil, was intended 'to queer the pitch for politicians and naval men who are now tempted to dabble in oil and then say afterwards that it never occurred to them that there could be anything wrong in it or anything unbecoming their position. . . '.[71] Interestingly enough, Cecil was not impressed by this argument and had already warned Strachey that he might be falling into a Government trap: 'It is possible that some transaction has taken place which is really perfectly defensible and it occurred to some ingenious

---

[65] *Morning Post*, 17 June 1913.

[66] Murray to Lloyd George, 20 Aug. 1913 (HLRO, Lloyd George papers, C/6/5/6).

[67] Dick Lloyd George graduated from Christ's College, Cambridge, in 1910 and got his qualifications as a civil engineer two years later, working with the Cowdray organization. He then went to Spain, to acquire a fluency in Spanish, before leaving for South America early in 1913 (Grigg, *Lloyd George: From Peace to War*, p. 74).

[68] *New Witness*, 20 Nov. 1913, p. 70.

[69] Murray to Lloyd George, 26 Jan. 1914 (Lloyd George papers, C/6/5/9).

[70] See Archer-Shee's speech, *Parl. Deb.*, 5th ser., lv. 1562 (17 July 1913).

[71] 'A Journalist's Duty', *Spectator*, 5 Apr. 1913, pp. 562–3. Strachey to Hugh Cecil (copy), 27 May 1913 (Strachey papers, S/4/3/23).

member or supporter of the Government that, by starting a scandal which could be triumphantly disproved, good might be done in respect to Marconi by creating a general impression that the Unionist Party and press are foolish gossipers and slanderers. . .'.[72] Undeterred by this warning, Strachey went on to write another minatory article for the *Spectator*.[73]

On the same day, 14 June, the *Morning Post* published a similar piece, which repeated the rumour that Murray had invested as much as £20,000 in Mexican oil, some of it possibly party money.[74] Two days later the issue was raised in Parliament by the Conservative back-bencher, Archer-Shee, who pressed the Prime Minister to investigate the truth of the story which had first appeared in the *Investors Chronicle*; Asquith returned a predictably bland refusal.[75]

All these rumours and innuendos, however, were having an unsettling effect on both the Government and on Lord Fisher, the Chairman of the Fuel Oil Commission. From the moment that he agreed to take on this post, Fisher had sold all his many shares in Shell and other oil companies, at a considerable financial loss; this did not save him from libellous attack, fomented, in part, by his old enemy, Lord Charles Beresford,[76] and it needed Churchill himself to rescue the reputation of the old sea-dog.[77] Angry over these unjust aspersions, Fisher was also at one point so shaken by a paragraph in *The Times* hinting at scandals with regard to the Mexican Eagle contract that he even contemplated doing without Mexican oil altogether, momentarily forgetting that this would create an oil deficit which nobody knew how to bridge.[78]

Thus when Churchill addressed the Commons on 17 July, he felt himself obliged to make a strenuous vindication of the Government's good faith. MPs were assured by the First Lord that the Chief Whip had given him his word 'that no funds of the Liberal party have ever been invested in the shares of this company (laughter)'. He went on:

And I have been told, on high authority, that Lord Murray himself has bought no shares in it (laughter). But even if there were twenty Lord Murrays and if every one of them had 20,000 shares, and if all the funds of the Liberal party, past, present and prospective, were exclusively invested in this company (laughter), we cannot see in what way these facts would be relevant to the

[72] Hugh Cecil to Strachey, 22 May 1913 (ibid).
[73] *Spectator*, 17 June 1913, p. 998.
[74] *Morning Post*, 14 June 1913.
[75] *Parl. Deb.*, 5th ser., liv. 35 (16 June 1913).
[76] Fisher to Churchill, 20 Apr. 1913, in Churchill, *Winston S. Churchill*, ii. Companion Vol., Part III, pp. 1938–9; Morris, A. J. A., *The Scaremongers: The Advocacy of War and Rearmament 1896–1914* (London, 1984), p. 319.
[77] *Parl. Deb.*, 5th ser., lv. 1583 (17 July 1913).
[78] Hopwood to Churchill, 29 May 1913, Churchill, *Churchill*, ii. Companion Vol., p. 1943.

decision that the Admiralty have to take, or how they can be held to debar us from doing what is profitable to the public and necessary for the Navy (Cheers).

After referring to evil or unfounded suspicions spread abroad by malevolently minded persons, Churchill pompously announced that the Board of Admiralty had expressly desired to associate itself with the First Lord in the following statement:

We have not, and we have never had, any personal interest, direct or indirect, in the supply of oil fuel to the navy (Laughter). We do not hold, and we have never held during our tenure of office, any oil shares of any sort (Laughter). We occupy a position of complete disinterestedness and impartiality in regard to all oil enterprises, oil companies, oil magnates, and oil combinations (Loud cheers and laughter).[79]

Arthur Lee for the Opposition scoffed at this extraordinary declaration,[80] and Maxse in the *National Review* expressed amazement at the simplicity of sailors in allowing themselves to be used as 'the stalking-horse of mountebanks'.[81] In any case, the Government's critics thought it ominous that when a Conservative backbencher asked, apropos of Churchill's statement, 'Is that signed by the Government?', Churchill declined to reply.[82] This fell some way short of the categorical assurances being called for even by papers quite well disposed towards the Liberal Ministry. As for that inveterate critic, W. R. Lawson, unabashed by his recent humiliation at the hands of the Marconi Select Committee, he predicted that Churchill, by dragging the Mexican Eagle Company before the Commons, had given 'a fresh impulse to a controversy which [was] proving [the Liberals'] moral ruin'.[83]

Maxse gave the story a further twist when he expressed curiosity about a possible working arrangement between Mexican Eagle and the Standard Oil Company of the United States.[84] This was a shrewd trust. For in December 1913 Standard Oil had actually made an offer for Mexican Eagle. Cowdray told Lloyd George in a confidential letter that he wanted to resist this bid, but that, if he were going 'specifically to dedicate' his firm to the primary purpose of supplying the Admiralty with oil, he might be obliged to ask the British Government for £5 million; in return for this sum he would 'undertake not to sell its interests and to give the Government such security for the money as would be a full *quid pro quo* for their assistance and would be

---

[79] *Parl. Deb.*, 5th ser., lv. 1478–80 (17 July 1913); *The Times*, 18 July 1913.

[80] *Parl. Deb.*, 5th ser., lv. 1489–90. But Lee spoke of 'phantom slanders' and said: 'I, and so far as I know, speaking for my Friends behind me, . . . see no objection whatever to the Admiralty making contracts with any oil company in any portion of the world, if thereby the oil fuel reserves and supplies of the Navy will be more effectually guaranteed.'

[81] *National Review*, lxi (1913), 1018.   [82] *Parl. Deb.*, 5th ser., lv. 1480.

[83] *Outlook*, 26 July 1913, p. 124.   [84] *National Review*, lxi (1913), 1016–17.

satisfactory to the House of Commons'.[85] The matter was further discussed between Cowdray and Ministers—an easy matter to arrange, since Murray's brother, Arthur, was PPS to the Foreign Secretary, Edward Grey.[86] But of course, the British Government did not, in the event, act on Cowdray's suggestion. With Opposition newspapers baying at their heels, it would have been politically suicidal for them to have done so. (Control of Mexican Eagle later passed to the Royal Dutch group at the end of the Great War.)

The oil issue is nevertheless an interesting one, since, as G. Gareth Jones has shown, the relationship between the Government and the oil companies in this period saw an assault on *laissez-faire* from within private industry itself. All the oil companies, big and small, were anxious to involve governments in their affairs, because they realized that they needed diplomatic protection, or financial aid, or a secure outlet for their products, as well as the transport and marketing facilities, which only the state could provide.[87] But the Liberal Government had to step every carefully indeed through this minefield since, in the aftermath of Marconi and the Indian Silver Affair, all its moves were being closely scrutinized by critics and opponents predisposed to believe that Ministers were involved in every conceivable kind of chicanery and corruption. Such suspicions were being simultaneously reinforced by a series of patronage 'scandals'.

[85] Cited in Spender, J. A., *Weetman Pearson, First Viscount Cowdray* (London, 1930), p. 203. Cowdray had earlier asked to see Churchill, seemingly with the aim of setting up a similar kind of deal (Cowdray to Churchill, 14 June 1912, in Churchill, *Churchill, ii. Companion Vol.*, p. 1930).

[86] Arthur Murray's diary, 7 Jan., 8 Jan. 1914 (National Library of Scotland, Elibank papers, vol. 8814, fo. 117).

[87] Gareth Jones, G., 'The British Government and the Oil Companies, 1912–14: the Search for an Oil Policy', *Historical Journal*, xx (1977), 647–50. See also Kent, M., *Oil and Empire* (London, 1976), pp. 42 ff.

10
Patronage

Introduction

WHEN Lord Selborne addressed the Yorkshire Liberal Unionist Federation at Wakefield in October 1911, he prefaced his strictures on the Liberal Government for trading in honours with observations about another 'very dangerous tendency', namely, the practice of ministers nominating to vacant posts in the civil service. This should only happen occasionally, he said, since ministers were only human and would be tempted to use power for party purposes: 'this, they had been told again and again, had actually happened in America, and it had been our pride hitherto that we have avoided this snare of democracy.'[1]

Selborne's restrained phraseology was in contrast with the crude outbursts of many journalists, both on the extreme left and right. The Asquith Government was indulging in shameless jobbery, alleged one Conservative monthly:

With promises in their mouths, and hypocrisy in their hearts, [Liberal Ministers] prate loudly of the 'purity' of administration; while on every possible occasion, they utilise the spoils of the Civil Service to reward partisans, to the prejudice of men tried to the top, not only in examinations but in long and painstaking service. On a par with all their dealings—specious in words and promises, callous and partisan in act and deed, this last act of flagrant jobbery should at last open the eyes of the British public to the canting humbug of Mr Lloyd George and his parasites.[2]

Violent abuse from relatively obscure magazines could be dismissed. It was quite otherwise when the Leader of the Opposition repeated the substance of these accusations, as Bonar Law did in his speech at the Albert Hall in January 1912, in which the Liberal Government was accused of creating a vast spoils system on the American model.[3] Many Opposition MPs and peers sincerely believed in the existence of such malpractices. For example, the Duke of Somerset, in a private letter to Bonar Law, declared that Liberal Ministers were 'using the revenues as a huge fund for bribing their supporters by giving them posts'.[4]

A cynic might be tempted to observe that nothing new had happened under the years of Liberal rule. It might be argued that all governments were rightly concerned to exploit their considerable powers of

---

[1] *The Times*, 21 Oct. 1911. [2] *Throne*, 14 Feb. 1912.
[3] *The Times*, 27 Jan. 1912.
[4] Somerset to Bonar Law, 26 Mar. 1912 (HLRO, Bonar Law papers, 26/1/59).

patronage, and as a cursory examination of the correspondence of Victorian and Edwardian politicians shows, the ministers of those days were obliged to devote a significant portion of their time to dealing with importunate supporters, eager for public office for themselves, their relatives, or their friends. For instance:

I really hope the Government will be able to get me something, as I am *very hard up*, through no fault of mine. I suppose that my family have spent in all, in the last 70 years, some £30,000 or more in elections. I have spent £6,000 myself and you know my work in the Home Counties.

This letter was addressed to Lewis Harcourt in August 1907 and came from a Liberal anxious that his son be given a Civil Service Commissionership.[5] The Salisbury and Balfour Governments had been flooded with similar requests.

In one respect, however, the pre-war Liberal Administration was in a different position. Having been effectively twenty years in the wilderness, the claims of its supporters on the patronage at the disposal of the Government were correspondingly shrill. Moreover, the sheer scale of the Liberal electoral victory in 1906 apparently gave the Party the necessary popular mandate for effecting a decisive shift in the party distribution of public offices.

The Magistracy

Nowhere was this bid for greater recognition more vigorously pursued than in the Liberals' attempts to break up their opponents' near monopoly of places on the magistrates' benches in rural England. A sense of grievance at the party imbalance among JPs had been building up for over twenty years,[6] and by 1906 the issue was one that aroused very strong feelings. On the Shropshire Bench, complained the Patronage Secretary, Tories outnumbered Liberals by 214 to 10,[7] and, according to one Liberal backbencher, in one county division the only Liberal magistrates were the *ex-officio* incumbents.[8] Newly elected Radical MPs, flushed with triumph, understandably gave high priority to rectifying this anomaly. More was at stake than simply local prestige, since the magistrates wielded considerable political influence,

[5] Leveson-Gower to Harcourt, 14 Aug. 1907 (Bodleian, Lewis Harcourt papers, vol. 439, fo. 174).

Since this chapter was written, I have read Dr J. M. Bourne's excellent *Patronage and Society in Nineteenth-Century England* (London, 1986). Dr Bourne is concerned to destroy the notion that there is an inherent connection between patronage and corruption. I accept this proposition, but am simply showing that in the early 20th century patronage was in fact frequently condemned as corrupt.

[6] See Ch. 4, pp. 81–2.

[7] Whiteley to Loreburn, 11 Dec. 1906, cited in Heuston, R. F. V., *Lives of the Lord Chancellors 1885–1940* (Oxford, 1964), p. 156.

[8] *Parl. Deb.*, 4th ser., clxxii. 1005 (17 Apr. 1907).

for example, in interpreting and enforcing the controversial licensing acts.

Lord Loreburn, Halsbury's successor, was initially as keen as anyone in his party to promote speedy change; he regarded the party imbalance on the magistrates' benches as a great evil, because it impaired public confidence in the impartiality of the judicial process. He was also anxious to secure a fairer spread of social classes; and so in 1906 the Liberals abolished the £100 property qualification for county magistrates. But Loreburn did not believe that the Lords-Lieutenant were guilty of *conscious* partisanship and he felt it better to work through existing machinery, using discreet pressure to get the composition of the magistracy broadened.[9] As early as 1907 he was toying with the idea of setting up local committees, with representatives from all the political parties, which could advise on the suitability of candidates; but this proposal was not implemented until the Royal Commission of Inquiry endorsed it in 1911.[10] In the meantime Loreburn was not prepared to adopt a policy of 'positive discrimination' or to swamp the county benches with the nominees of local MPs, unless he was first convinced that the men were equipped to discharge their judicial functions and unless there were genuine vacancies to be filled.[11]

It was this refusal to manufacture Liberal JPs wholesale which gave rise to the determined campaign of a group of Liberal MPs, of whom Charles Solomon Henry, the Member for Wellington, was the most persistent. They began by inundating the Lords-Lieutenant with applications, accompanied by peremptory demands that their names be forwarded to the Lord Chancellor. When these demands were resisted, they pressed for a new procedure which would bypass the Lords-Lieutenant entirely. They then turned their criticisms on to the Lord Chancellor's Office. In December 1906 eighty-eight Liberal and Labour MPs signed a memorial, stating their grievances and requesting an interview with the Lord Chancellor. This was a mistake. Incensed by the tone of this document and convinced that the wirepullers in his party were subjecting him to improper pressure, Loreburn rejected the idea of a meeting and denounced the importunate MPs in a letter which was sent to *The Times*.[12]

The quarrel threatened to inflict serious damage on the morale of the Liberal Party. Members who impressed on the Lord Chancellor the unwisdom of his actions were liable to have the door slammed in their

---

[9] *Parl. Deb.*, 4th ser., clxxii. 1354–60 (22 Apr. 1907).

[10] Lee, J. M., 'Parliament and the Appointment of Magistrates: The Origin of Advisory Committees', *Parliamentary Affairs*, xiii (1959), 91–2; Report of Royal Commission on the Selection of Justices of the Peace, 1910, Cd. 5250.

[11] Heuston, *Lives of Lord Chancellors*, pp. 154–5.

[12] Minutes of Evidence taken by the Royal Commission on Selection of Justices of the Peace, 1910, Cd. 5358: Appendix 2, pp. 237–8.

face.[13] On 3 December 1906 the desperate Chief Whip, George Whiteley, wrote to the Prime Minister, complaining that Loreburn was 'upsetting and most seriously damaging our party. . . . We have honestly tried to keep our people quiet. But they are indignant beyond restraint, and I do not wonder at it.'[14] The County Members, he warned, were preparing to vote for a reduction in the Lord Chancellor's salary.[15] That same day Whiteley wrote to Loreburn personally, saying that his task was being made 'hopeless and heart-breaking' by his defiance of backbench opinion. 'Today I hear that Mr Neish [of the Lord Chancellor's Office] has told a defeated Liberal candidate that he has no right to make any recommendations. They must *all come* from the *sitting Tory Member*. I cannot believe this is true.'[16]

Loreburn again exploded: 'if', he wrote, 'the Liberal Party in the House of Commons wants to see done what the complaining Members privately ask me to do (viz, to job the judicial bench), I do not wish any longer to belong to that Party.' Whiteley's intervention he described as 'an attempt to force upon me what I regard as a prostitution of my office', and he added that he would 'resign the Great Seal sooner than do it'.[17] Whiteley patiently explained that it was the Conservatives who had jobbed the bench; all the Liberals were requesting was a redressing of the grave imbalance.[18]

It was not to be. Over the next year Loreburn appointed to the bench JPs who were Liberals in about three cases out of four, or so the Government claimed (exact figures were not, of course, compiled), but given Loreburn's determination not to increase the size of the county benches, this could do very little indeed to create a more equitable party distribution of offices, and the grievance lingered on.[19] In February 1908 a Party member complained to Bryce that 'the feebleness of the Lord Chancellor in pleading high principles for passing over Liberals and appointing Tories, has made him the joke of the clubs. . .'.[20] Looking at the problem from a very different perspective, Munro Ferguson informed Rosebery in December 1907 that Loreburn had 'led the life of a dog with the wirepullers all this summer. He could hardly talk of anything else. It even rumpled his

[13] Rowlatt to Ponsonby, 20 June 1907 (Bodleian, Ponsonby papers, vol. 654, fos. 110–11).
[14] Whiteley to Campbell-Bannerman, 3 Dec. 1906, cited in Heuston, *Lives of Lord Chancellors*, p. 155.
[15] Ibid.
[16] Whiteley to Loreburn, 3 Dec. 1906 (Bodleian, Asquith papers, vol. 127, fo. 129).
[17] Loreburn to Whiteley, 10 Dec. 1906 (ibid., fos. 130–1).
[18] Whiteley to Loreburn, 11 Dec. 1906, cited in Heuston, *Lives of Lord Chancellors*, p. 156.
[19] *Parl. Deb.*, 4th ser., clxxix. 152 (25 July 1907). But a question in the Commons in Nov. 1909 revealed that Loreburn had appointed 7,000 magistrates, of whom only 3,197 were known to be Liberals (Heuston, *Lives of Lord Chancellors*, p. 154).
[20] J. Andrew Strahan to Bryce, 24 Feb. 1908 (Bodleian, Bryce papers, UB 17).

relations with C-B.[21] Finally the setting up of a Royal Commission of Inquiry in 1910 stopped the agitation. Loreburn's career, however, never really recovered from the controversy, and he resigned office in 1911, an embittered and disappointed man.

The episode is relevant to the theme of this chapter in two respects. First, it illustrates the pressure from below which operated on Liberal Ministers through backbenchers eager to secure official posts for their supporters and dependents—unpaid ones, in this case. Secondly, the controversy played a significant part in bringing into the open the whole issue of jobbery and patronage. For, in publicly denouncing Liberal MPs for attempting to pack the benches with incompetent partisans, Loreburn created an embarrassing situation in which admiring Conservatives rushed to his defence. Thus in April 1907 the Marquess of Bath—himself a Lord-Lieutenant—drew the Lords' attention to the recent memorial and to the reply that it had elicited; the Marquess implied that he had no quarrel with the Lord Chancellor but that he wanted to help him in his brave resistance against those who were busily manipulating 'the rumblings and grumblings of disappointed politicians' in their localities.[22] When Loreburn then reiterated his views, Lansdowne, on behalf of the Opposition, greeted his words with relief.[23]

Yet notwithstanding Loreburn's assurances, the Unionist peers continued to believe—or so they professed—that grave dangers threatened the country. As the Marquess of Bath put it: 'to Americanise our system of administering justice by treating appointments to the magistracy as the legitimate spoil of political victors would be the last and worst form of *dementia Americana*. It would open the door to methods of retaliation to which we are at present happily strangers.'[24]

The Civil Service

The Government's announcement of the Royal Commission quietened this worry, but the spectre of Radicals presiding over a cynical spoils system continued to haunt many Conservatives. Underlying these fears were the innovations of the Government in the fields of taxation and social welfare. To administer these contentious pieces of legislation Whitehall dramatically expanded. By the spring of 1914 the established civil service numbered over 167,000, and on the eve of the Great War it was estimated that 5,387 established posts and 10,510 temporary posts

---

[21] Munro-Ferguson to Rosebery, 21 Dec. 1907 (National Library of Scotland, Rosebery papers, vol. 10,020, fo. 27).

[22] *Parl. Deb.*, 4th ser., clxxii. 1345–52 (22 Apr. 1907).

[23] Ibid. 1362.

[24] Ibid. 1352.

had been created in consequence of legislation passed by the Liberals.[25] The various bodies concerned with the administration of Health Insurance alone employed over 2,000 persons, and the Board of Trade had gone up to nearly 2,500.[26] The land valuation made necessary by the People's Budget was also very costly in terms of staffing, though much of the work was done by temporary officials drawn from the professions of surveying and auctioneering. To quote Avner Offer, 'Hundreds of qualified valuation staff had to be recruited in a hurry, and the opposition of property professions gave way to boundary disputes in competition for well-paid employment in a period of market depression.'[27]

Conservatives who disliked social welfare on principle would have been less than human if they had not drawn attention to the civil service expansion which it had necessitated. Thus, with further instalments of bureaucracy being promised by Lloyd George when he launched his Land Campaign, *Our Flag* commented: 'We may expect, of course, another Minister at £100 a week (think of it, ye agricultural labourers!), a band of Commissioners each with £1,000 or so a year, a regiment of assistants at salaries of something like £500 a year each, and a little army of minor officials at lower salaries, all of whom will be more or less engaged in pettifogging interference in local affairs.'[28] Nor was it just the expansion of the civil service and the resultant cost to the taxpayer of which complaint was made. It was also alleged that the creation of new posts was being used by Liberal Ministers to buy support and reward their followers. The same article in *Our Flag* grumbled that 'the Small Holdings Act, the National Insurance Act, and the Budget Land Taxes, were all recruiting grounds for "fat" appointments for faithful Radicals, and a new Ministry of Land [would] enormously widen the area.'[29]

What gave some substance to these accusations was that many of the new officials administering these social welfare services had not been selected by open competitive examination.[30] For this there were, it is true, perfectly respectable reasons. For example, William Beveridge, in building up his Labour Exchange organization, wanted to recruit people with practical experience of industrial life from a wide variety of backgrounds; the career civil servants who had entered the public service on the basis of an examination taken immediately after

---

[25] Numbers of Persons in Civil Service, Accounts and Papers, 1914, lvi. 538–9; Numbers of Additional Posts, Established and Temporary, Created in Consequence of Legislation Passed Since 1906 and Still in Existence, ibid. 550–3.

[26] Ibid. 539, 551.

[27] Offer, A., *Property and Politics 1870–1914. Landownership, Law, Ideology and Urban Development in England* (Cambridge, 1981), p. 366.

[28] *Our Flag*, Nov. 1913, p. 184. [29] Ibid.

[30] Though it is only fair to add that in the early 20th century open competition was still only being used for about one third of all civil service posts (Moses, R., *The Civil Service of Great Britain* (New York, 1914), p. 190).

graduation were not likely to meet this criterion. So the Board of Trade adopted a recruitment procedure whereby a special appointments committee invited applications for vacant Labour Exchange posts, sifted through the applications forms which they received, and then, after taking up references, drew up a short list of candidates who were summoned for an interview; those who passed the interview had finally to sit a qualifying examination before being placed on the establishment. Beveridge was not entirely satisfied with the results of his experiment, but it certainly produced an unusual and interesting collection of divisional officers. On the other hand, these seventeen men had in effect been appointed through the patronage of the President of the Board of Trade, and this bypassing of the standard selection procedure was bound to lead to unfavourable comment.[31]

Something similar occurred with the recruitment of certain officials connected with the National Insurance Act. Mr Leishman, the Chairman of the Scottish National Health Insurance Commission, defended his practice of relying on selection rather than examination for procuring certain categories of official:

We, of course, have been dealing with a rather special and a rather new department. In that department a good deal of special technical knowledge has been necessary, and I do not know that these qualities—for example, knowledge of Scots law and actuarial work—are found even in university men, except [when] they have been specially trained for that particular piece of work.[32]

The Chairman of the newly constituted Road Board, formerly a director of the North East Railway Company, similarly preferred to appoint to his office people whom he already knew from outside the public service.[33]

Though each of these procedures could be defended on its own merits, the cumulative result was a little worrying. By the autumn of 1914 there existed, to enforce the Liberal-inspired measures, 2,133 established and 9,887 temporary civil servants who had not had to sit an open competitive examination.[34] From late 1911 onwards backbench Conservative MPs and newspapers began to devote more and more time to probing these developments in search of irregularities that

[31] See Beveridge's evidence to Royal Commission (Third Report of Civil Service Commission, 1913, Cd. 6740, pp. 37–53); also, Harris, J., *Unemployment and Politics: A Study in English Social Policy 1886–1914* (Oxford, 1972), pp. 293–4. José Harris points out that the Treasury later insisted that, where possible, all new candidates should be examined by the Civil Service Commission or recruited from existing civil servants, and that this marked the end of Beveridge's bid to select men on the basis of their shop-floor experience and practical involvement in industrial life (Harris, J., *William Beveridge* (Oxford, 1977), pp. 185–6).

[32] Fourth Report of Civil Service Commission, Minutes, 1914, Cd. 7340, q. 24,383.

[33] Ibid., q. 32,457.

[34] Accounts and Papers, Vol. 56. Return Compiled as Answer to Question of Mitchel-Thomson, 7 Aug. 1914.

could be used to discredit the Liberal Government in general and Lloyd George in particular. In October 1912 Bonar Law, whose suspicions of the way in which government patronage was being distributed had already been voiced in his Albert Hall speech of January 1912, called for a return setting out the name, age, date of appointment, salary, and occupation for the five years preceding appointment of all persons who had been admitted to the civil service in any capacity since the Liberals' advent to power.[35] In an attempt to neutralize this piece of party propaganda, MacCallum Scott, a Liberal backbencher, promptly called for a similar list covering appointments made by the Unionists between 1895 and 1905.[36] As the *Saturday Review* pointed out, this was not an altogether wise move, since the Radical list turned out to be almost 100 pages longer than the Unionist one, which meant that 'on a rough estimate the Radical surplus [was] 2,500'; 'a lot can be done with 2,500 places judiciously distributed', it observed.[37] Since in fact the Liberal Government had presented the Commons with the requested information in a form that makes it virtually impossible to assess or analyse, one can neither prove nor disprove Opposition charges that jobbery had been perpetrated on a massive scale since the Liberals had assumed office.

Certain aspects of recent administrative developments, however, clearly invited comment. One was the large number of private secretaries to Ministers who had received permanent posts without open competition. The *Saturday Review*, in an article of 26 October 1912, cited a long list of cases where this had happened, commenting that its most serious consequence was that outsiders were promoted over the heads of the rank and file of civil servants, which in turn led to jealousy, wirepulling, and toadyism.[38] There was, for example, the case of Vaughan Nash, a journalist by profession, who had served as private secretary to first Campbell-Bannerman and then to Asquith, before being promoted in 1912 to the office of Vice-Chairman of the Development Commission. This was denounced as a flagrant piece of jobbery.[39] An outcry also greeted the news that a secretaryship in the Civil Service Commission, bearing a salary of £800 a year, had gone to the Liberal journalist and historian, J. L. Hammond, whose former position as leader writer on the *Daily News* had been terminated, in part because of ill health; critics alleged, and with some reason, that an invalid had been given a comfortable berth at the public expense.[40]

[35] But Bonar Law privately told Hugh Cecil that he was basically only concerned with 'improper appointments' like that of Soares, and even here felt that 'it would be very difficult to bring them home' (Bonar Law to H. Cecil, 15 Feb. 1912, Hatfield, Quickswood papers, 15/24).
[36] Accounts and Papers, lvi (1912–13), paras. 43,559, 47,845.
[37] *Saturday Review*, 8 Feb. 1913, p. 167.   [38] Ibid., 26 Oct. 1912, pp. 509–10.
[39] e.g. 'The Book of Jobs', *Throne*, 14 Feb. 1912.
[40] See Clarke, P., *Liberals and Social Democrats* (Cambridge, 1978) p. 105.

A number of Liberal MPs, some of whom had lost their seat at one of the 1910 general elections, were also provided for. Herbert Paul, MP for Northampton, retired from Parliament in January 1910 when his health broke down, and he was rumoured to have spent six out of the twelve months preceding his appointment as Second Commissioner in the Civil Service in a nursing home. Then there was Sir Ernest Soares, Liberal MP for Barnstaple, and a junior whip, who was made an Assistant-Comptroller in the National Debt Office in 1911. Conservatives also complained when they learned that T. W. Dobson, Liberal MP for Plymouth between 1906 and 1910, had been given a lecturing post by the Government; what need was there for government lecturers at all, they asked.[41]

The controversy even affected close relatives of Liberal Ministers. Questions were asked, for example, about what Lloyd George's son had done to warrant his post with the Port of London Authority.[42] And the *Norwich Unionist* cast aspersions on Augustine Birrell, one of whose stepsons had, it alleged, recently been appointed an Inspector to the Local Government Board of Ireland, while another had been taken into the Colonial Office, where he was drawing a salary of £750 p.a. We know and like Birrell, said this journal, 'but we don't like this kind of thing, and have never subscribed to the doctrine that the duty of a democratic Government is to find jobs for the dependents of Cabinet Ministers.'[43]

Also worrying was the Liberal Government's heavy reliance on part-time officials. The *Saturday Review* noted with dismay that the Official Return of 1913 contained over fifty pages of persons appointed to carry out land valuation under the terms of the 1909 Budget, and that many of these were temporary appointees:

This is the very essence of the American spoils system. Why does the American party nominee vote always for his party? Because his security of tenure depends on the maintenance of his party in power. . . . We do not pretend to have ascertained the political views of these temporary nominees. But they are human beings. They know that the return of the Unionists to power will put an end to the extravagance which means their livelihood, and we say that this is a list of potential Radical voters, maybe of potential Radical canvassers.[44]

When these insinuations were echoed by Opposition politicians, the Liberal Party reacted with fury. Its Publications Department issued a pamphlet, 'Unionist Lies About Government Appointments', in which

[41] For details of these cases, see *Gleanings and Memoranda*, xl (1913), 351–2, 166–7; Conservative leaflet, 'Jobs! Jobs!! Jobs!!!', 1914.

[42] *Throne*, 31 Jan. 1912; *Eye-Witness*, 25 Jan. 1912, p. 165.

[43] *Norwich Unionist*, May 1914. I am grateful for this reference, and others taken from the *Norwich Unionist*, to Barry Doyle.

[44] *Saturday Review*, 8 Feb. 1913, pp. 167–8.

their assailants were accused of misrepresenting official returns. Every care had been taken, said this pamphleteer, to ensure that the best men were appointed to public office, without any interference by ministers; in the case of Inland Revenue posts, it claimed, the vast majority of successful applicants were actually Unionist in politics. Moreover, the Liberals sought to reverse the accusations brought against them:

Unionists ask you to beware Liberal Bribery and Corruption and plead for 'Honesty in Politics'.
  Certainly if you want 'Honesty in Politics' you will not get it from these
                    LYING UNIONIST LEAFLETS.
  Show that you like fair criticism based on the truth by
                    Supporting the Liberal Party.[45]

But in 1914 the Conservative Party returned to the fray. Two pamphlets were issued in that year. The first, entitled 'The Very "Liberal" Radical Government', alleged that the Radicals had 'revived the bad old practice of giving civil service appointments by *nomination* which means THROUGH INFLUENCE, INSTEAD OF BY COMPETITIVE EXAMINATION, where all may have a fair chance and the best man gets the post'.[46] These charges were repeated at greater length in a later pamphlet, which bore the succinct legend, 'Jobs! Jobs!! Jobs!!!' The Government's methods were described as 'a system of unfair exclusion' that was leading to 'favouritism' and which, 'as worked by the Radical Government', was 'nothing less than downright jobbery!' Part of the pamphlet was concerned to whip up indignation against the Government's extravagance: '*Voters, this is the way your money goes.* Are the Radicals worth it?' But the main charge was that Ministers had 'filled Civil Service posts with their friends and supporters, in many cases creating the place to fit the man'.[47]

The critics were on stronger ground when they claimed that the Liberals were trying to buy the support of Labour MPs and Socialists friendly to the Progressive Alliance by giving them paid posts in the public service. One article in the *New Witness* alleged that the ILP had recently landed 374 public appointments, mainly at the Board of Trade, in National Insurance, at the Home Office, and so on, at a total cost of between £70,000 and £108,000. 'Is it any wonder', sneered the paper, 'that Mr Philip Snowden, MP, exalts Parliamentary action as preferable to Trade Union action? See what it has done for his friends!'[48] These charges formed an important part of the *New Witness*'s theory about the corrupt conspiracy which the Liberals were supposed to be conducting against the British people. But similar accusations appeared

---

[45] 'Unionist Lies About Government Appointments', 1912.
[46] 'The Very "Liberal" Radical Government', 1914.
[47] 'Jobs! Jobs!! Jobs!!!', 1914.   [48] *New Witness*, 16 Oct. 1913, p. 748.

in Maxse's *National Review*, where it was pointed out that the Labour leaders were a thoroughly middle-class set of men who had sold themselves to the Liberal Ministry.[49] Some Socialists were only too ready to repeat the taunt.[50]

How much evidence is there for the claim that the Government was trying to shackle organized labour by distributing favours to prominent working-class activists? Perhaps the earliest attempt to probe this claim was made by Elie Halévy in his *History of the English People in the Nineteenth Century*, first published in 1932.[51] The main piece of solid evidence Halévy employs is a statistical table compiled by *The Times* in July 1913, which was 'prepared from Government returns supplemented by private information setting out the number of active workers in the Labour and Socialist movement who have in the last six years been appointed to Government posts' (reproduced in Table 2). *The Times* adds the explanation that this table 'takes no account of trade union and other Labour officials appointed to minor posts, nor does it include a large number of Labour workers who, though given posts, cannot be said to have occupied permanent places in the Labour or Socialist movement. Included in the total are two former Labour members of Parliament and 17 Parliamentary candidates who proved unsuccessful at the polls.'[52]

TABLE 2: Number of Activists in Labour and Socialist Movements holding Government Office

Department	No. of Appointments	Annual Salaries (£)	
		Minimum	Maximum
Board of Trade	117	16,800	26,000
National Insurance	124	23,400	33,700
Home Office	48	8,200	13,640
Other Departments	85	22,730	34,680
TOTALS	374	71,130	108,320

Counting up names tells us little, of course, about the Liberal Government's motives, which do not necessarily bear the sinister interpretation placed upon them by their opponents. After all, Radical Ministers might well have felt it desirable to broaden the social composition and to extend the experience of the public service by bestowing patronage on able men and women from working-class backgrounds. But Churchill, for one, seems from an early stage to have

---

[49] This was a constant refrain of Maxse's.
[50] See material recorded in *Gleanings and Memoranda*, xli (1913), 501.
[51] Halévy, E., *History of the English People in the Nineteenth Century. The Rule of Democracy 1905–1914* (1932; English paperback, edn., 1961), pp. 446–7.
[52] *The Times*, 24 July 1913.

grasped the importance of using new posts, like those of divisional superintendants of Labour Exchanges, to reward trade union 'moderates' and to bind the Labour Party closely to Liberalism. At the Home Office, too, Churchill was quick to create 'two new posts of Labour Advisers, one of which he gave to an old official of the Textile Workers' Union, Shackleton, the other to the Welsh miner, T. Richards, and thirty posts of sub-inspectors of mines and quarries, to be reserved for miners and quarrymen'.[53] Again, however, such action could be defended as a shrewd and far-sighted way of managing labour and stabilizing the social order at a time when it was coming under increasing pressure.

But it was less easy to justify the practice whereby a government showered largesse on its *own* members and supporters, and Lloyd George was extremely sensitive to sneers about the Asquith Ministry being 'liberal' in more than one sense of that word. The Government, in its defence, could very reasonably point out that the much-abused Elibank, when Patronage Secretary, had at a stroke *destroyed* many of his Office's remaining rights in the matter of the appointment of porters, typists, messengers, and functionaries in government depart- ments. As the historian of the Treasury aptly comments: 'it was the end of an era, although one would be naive to suppose that it was the end of official patronage.'[54]

In fact, as we have seen, as old forms of patronage were abolished, new ones came into being. And by the end of 1911 MPs on all sides of the House were becoming.distinctly alarmed about what this new development might signify. In November 1911 over 400 MPs pressed for the establishment of a Royal Commission of Inquiry into the Civil Service which could give careful attention to the question of recruit- ment methods, as well as to other outstanding issues. One of the MPs most active in organizing this petition was Snowden, who had started life as an excise official and who deeply distrusted any innovation which bypassed the normal channels of appointment.[55]

In February 1912, with Bonar Law's Albert Hall speech still resounding through Westminster, Asquith was approaching suitable people to sit on the Commission. His initial hope was that Austen Chamberlain might serve as Chairman, but, pleading lack of time, Chamberlain refused. An equally strong reason for Chamberlain's

[53] Halévy, *Rule of Democracy*, p. 446. See also Churchill to Pease, 22 Aug. 1909 (Nuffield College, Gainford papers, vol. 86).

[54] Roseveare, H., *The Treasury* (London, 1969), p. 228. See also Hanham, H. J., 'Political Patronage at the Treasury, 1870–1912', *Historical Journal*, iii (1960), 83.

[55] Cross, C., *Philip Snowden* (London, 1966), p. 125. Snowden may have been influenced by the views of the Association of Second Division Clerks, who submitted a memorial to the MacDonnell Commission, in which, *inter alia*, they impugned the impartiality of the Civil Service Commission and accused the committee selecting labour exchange staff of 'notorious cases of jobbery' (Moses, *Civil Service*, p. 215).

refusal was his private belief that Bonar Law had been 'on very weak ground' in his accusation of corruption. He realized that the Commission would be expected to examine the charge that the Government had abused its patronage, and he wanted to avoid the embarrassing situation in which he had either to support or to throw over his Leader's strictures. 'The Government have done some bad jobs', Chamberlain confided to his stepmother, 'but it is not easy to bring home proof of them; whilst in regard to the great majority of appointments in connection with Valuation, Labour Exchanges and Insurance, I do not believe that any charge of extensive political partisanship can be sustained.'[56]

Under the chairmanship of Sir Antony MacDonnell, the Commission set to work and issued a series of Reports between 1912 and 1916. The leisureliness of its deliberations annoyed those Conservative MPs who were in a hurry to 'expose' the Government for corruption and could not understand why the proceedings of the Commission were 'most protracted'.[57] In general, the Reports exonerated the Liberals from the fiercer charges made against them by their opponents. True, the Commissioners expressed some criticism of the method of appointing Labour Exchange managers, many of whom, they thought, could have been transferred from existing departments.[58] While prepared grudgingly to defend what the Board of Trade had done as an 'emergency measure', they urged that in future appointments should be made in the standard way through open competitive examinations and a considered system of transfers. The MacDonnell Commission also wanted new offices, like the Road Board and the Development Commission, which employed many of their officials on a temporary basis, to reduce part-time staff to a minimum, and it censured the way in which the Road Board had exercised its patronage. Wherever possible, it insisted, the principle established by the Northcote–Trevelyan Report, that of selecting public officials through the impersonal mechanism of open competitive examinations, should form the basis of departmental practice.[59]

But the evidence brought before the Commission suggested that, especially in the case of the National Health Insurance Commission, preference had in fact been given in the majority of cases to career civil servants, and rigorous steps had been taken to prevent applicants from attempting to use political influence in securing a public post. J. Leishman of the Scottish National Health Insurance Commission,

[56] Chamberlain to Mrs Chamberlain, 6 Mar. 1912 (Chamberlain, A., *Politics From Inside* (London, 1936), p. 441).

[57] Herbert Nield to Bonar Law, 7 Aug. 1913 (Bonar Law papers, 30/1/14).

[58] Snowden, in particular, gave Beveridge a fierce grilling. See Third Report of Civil Service Commission, 1913, Cd. 6740, qs. 15,890–16,152.

[59] Fourth Report of Civil Service Commission, 1914, Cd. 7338, Ch. IX, paras. 57–9, 62, 66; Ch. IV, paras. 4–5.

which had received more than its fair share of criticism in the press, was particularly insistent, when giving his evidence, that Lloyd George had personally urged him 'to take the best man without any other consideration whatsoever' and had also directed his attention to a pledge that, with certain exceptions where special experience was required, civil servants should be employed. This advice, said Leishman, he had followed in the spirit and the letter.[60] Broadly speaking, the Royal Commission accepted this defence of the way in which Health Insurance was being administered, while adding: 'It makes a new departure in recruitment for the Civil Service, which calls for the most careful examination.'[61]

A minority of Commissioners, however, felt that a more whole-hearted exoneration of the Asquith Ministry was called for. In their dissenting note, they wrote:

We believe that, amongst the motives leading to the appointment of our Commission, one of the most prominent was a suspicion that, in the formation of new departments rendered necessary by recent legislation (such, for instance, as the Labour Department under the Board of Trade, and those of the National Health Insurance Commissioners), there has been a tendency to dispense with Competitive Examinations in favour of an extension of the system of Patronage. We are glad to be able to say that the evidence taken by us affords no support to this suspicion, and suggests that it arose from a misapprehension of the actual facts.[62]

But this, surely, was to go too far in the opposite direction. Perhaps Austen Chamberlain had summed up the situation as judiciously as possible in his private reflections of early 1912. Though a few flagrant jobs *were* perpetrated, a study of civil service expansion as a whole does not suggest that any systematic favouritism was shown to Liberal Party members or supporters. The departures from Northcote–Trevelyan principles which were made in these years carried risks with them, but this, arguably, was the price which the country had to pay for the benefits derived from the State's expansion of its responsibilities into the field of social welfare and industrial organization. If the Government was indeed using its powers of patronage to 'buy' the loyalty of its backbench followers, this was being achieved mainly by the distribution of honours. When in 1913 the jaundiced journalists of the *New Witness* tried to demonstrate that more than half of the Parliamentary Liberal Party had been 'rewarded' for the support they had given to the Ministry, they could find only ten MPs who had received appointments of profit (if one excludes the forty-six who had become Ministers); the

[60] Ibid., Minutes, Cd. 7340, q. 24,235.   [61] Ibid., Cd. 7338, Ch. I, para. 52.
[62] Ibid., Minority Report signed by H. W. Primrose, W. Guy Granet, and A. A. Booth, p. 146. Cecil Beck also wrote a reservation to Chs. 4 and 6 of the Report, in which he argued in favour of bringing certain categories of outsiders into the Civil Service and hoped that this would not stop 'because of allegations of Patronage'.

other 'bought' MPs had received nothing more than peerages and honours.[63]

The Development Commission and the Wick Burghs By-Election

But there were other ways in which the Asquith Ministry might conceivably have been deriving party advantage from the expansion of State activities. For example, Ministers could possibly have been allocating grants for economic development in such a way as to influence the behaviour of potential voters. This, as we have seen, had been the staple Liberal argument against Tariff Reform ever since Joseph Chamberlain had launched his great campaign. Similar warnings of the risk of corruption were now brought against the Liberal Government's economic policies. The fiercest controversy centred on the work of the Development Commission. This body originated in a relatively neglected innovation contained within the People's Budget. Exchequer money, Lloyd George announced in his budget speech, would in future be earmarked for a fund from which grants could be made to a Development Commission, whose task it would be to give financial aid to forestry, agriculture, rural industry and transport, harbours, canals, and fisheries. Later, in September 1909 the Commons duly passed the Development Act, which created the machinery for administering this new fund.[64]

Only six backbench MPs bothered to divide the House by voting against the establishment of the Development Commission, but from the start most Opposition spokesmen were suspicious of it. Some alleged that it would 'lead to a great waste of public money'; others predicted that it would result in 'a new swarm of officials' running over the country.[65] But the most serious accusation, which was made by Robert Cecil, Bonar Law, and Lord Winterton, was that, in Bonar Law's words, the Bill meant political corruption, because it would be used, as general elections approached, as a means of purchasing votes. Significantly, the parliamentary debate of September 1909 was enlivened by an Opposition complaint that the Liberals had only secured Irish Nationalist support for the measure after Lloyd George had assured them that part of the new Development Fund would be spent in Ireland.[66] There was also a discussion of the comparative dangers of state-aided development and Tariff Reform. Cecil, who was a Free Food Unionist, observed that 'the power of corruption under any scheme of Tariff Reform that has ever been suggested by a responsible statesman is as nothing to the power of corruption in this.'[67] The Tariff

[63] *New Witness*, 16 Oct. 1913, p. 748.
[64] Harris, *Unemployment and Politics*, pp. 340–6.
[65] *Parl. Deb.*, 5th ser., x. 906–1042 (6 Sept. 1909).
[66] Ibid. 944–7.   [67] Ibid. 917.

Reformers obviously took a different line. One of their advocates, Winterton, expressed his general approval of the principle of state-aided economic development, but he attacked the compulsory clauses in the Government's Bill and voiced his alarm over the wording of Clause 1, which defined the scope of the Development Commissioners' work; the Bill spoke of 'any other purpose calculated to promote the economic development of the United Kingdom'. This clause, said Winterton,

may, according as the Government which is in power chooses to administer it, mean practically anything or absolutely nothing. It may be merely used to throw dust in the eyes of the people of the country, or as a gigantic bribe for certain classes whose votes the Government at the time desire to obtain. A General Election may be approaching, and I see nothing to prevent the Government spending an enormous sum of money in prizes for the best form of light traction engine for commercial purposes; more particularly if at that moment the chairman of the Budget League happened to be the chairman of a Commercial Motor Transport Company.[68]

There were also references to the 'graft' and 'boodling' which occurred in new countries in connection with the construction of roads, railways, and bridges.[69] Nor were the critics reassured by Lloyd George's claim that the Development Commission which would administer the money would be an impartial body. In exasperation, the Chancellor rounded on Cecil: he 'talks as if we are all divided on both sides in politics into a sort of rampant politicians simply anxious for loot, bribery, or blackmail. Not at all. Thank heaven there are plenty of thoroughly upright, straightforward men in this country who can be depended upon to do their duty without any thought of corruption on both sides.'[70]

As a device for developing the economic resources of the country and for combating unemployment, the Development Commission was not a success. Moreover, from the start it was dogged by controversy. As we have seen, the composition of the body and the methods by which it was recruited came in for criticism. On top of that an embarrassing incident occurred in late 1913, which seemed to bear out the very worst fears of the Commission's critics.

In December 1913 a by-election was held at Wick Burghs in the Orkney Islands.[71] The contest was caused by the elevation of its sitting Member, Robert Munro, to the office of Lord Advocate for Scotland. Munro's own behaviour during the by-election campaign was

---

[68] Ibid. 1018–19. [69] Ibid. 1018. [70] Ibid. 974.
[71] This account of the Wick Burghs Affair is largely based on Vol. GD/113/108/2 of the Steel-Maitland papers (Scottish Record Office). However, the Wick constituency had a tradition of this sort of corruption and the former Conservative MP had probably indulged in very similar practices (See Pelling, H., *Social Geography of British Elections 1885–1910* (London, 1967), p. 383).

unexceptionable. But the same could not be said of the Scottish Liberal Whip, John Gulland, who made a series of speeches in the constituency in which he hinted that, should Munro be returned, the Government would reward the electorate by releasing public money from the Development Commission for economic improvements in the area. The most contentious of these speeches was delivered at Wick on 21 November, when, according to local reporters, Gulland said: 'Mr Munro had more power of worrying the Government to get things for his constituency than any member in Scotland. . . . Whether it was putting a word for money for a harbour in Wick or a naval base for Cromarty, Mr Munro had the faculty of putting his case in such an unanswerable way that the Government found it extremely difficult to refuse anything he asked.'[72]

The hint was duly taken up by the local newspaper, the *Northern Ensign*, which urged the return of Munro, largely on the ground that this would guarantee a government grant for harbour improvements— which was the issue which had stirred the constituency more than any other for at least a decade. Significantly, Munro did not dissociate himself from these remarks in the later stages of the campaign. Polling took place on 8 December. Although the Government was doing badly in by-elections at this time, Munro succeeded in increasing his majority to 443—higher than the majorities achieved by the Liberals in 1906 and the two general elections of 1910. The defeated Conservative candidate complained bitterly to the *Morning Post*: 'The harbour bribe proved its power.'[73]

Concern over what had happened in Wick Burghs spread over the next few weeks. Maxse told the Party Chairman that 'there seems to be very little doubt that the Radical Party won the election by pure corruption', yet the Opposition seemed content to take this lying down.[74] But Steel-Maitland was able to assure Maxse that he was 'being allowed [his] way over this quarry' and that steps were already on foot to destroy Gulland.[75] In fact, shortly after the election result had been declared, the National Union's Principal Agent was sent to the Orkneys to collect evidence from local people, in the hope that this might provide the Opposition with a legal case against the Government.

The Agent's report which Maitland received showed that, although Gulland's initial response to criticism had been to claim that he had been misreported, the *Northern Ensign* had in fact given a perfectly accurate account of his speech; it also seemed certain that the reference to harbour extensions had won over a significant number of votes from the fishing community. This report also cast doubt on two letters appearing under a *nom de plume* in the *Northern Ensign* which

[72] *Northern Ensign*, 25 Nov. 1913.   [73] *Morning Post*, 15 Dec. 1913.
[74] Maxse to Steel-Maitland, 2 Jan. 1914 (Steel-Maitland papers, GD/113/108/2).
[75] Steel-Maitland to Maxse (copy), 4 Jan. 1914 (ibid.).

purported to come from traditional Conservative voters who announced that this time they intended to vote Liberal on the harbour issue; internal evidence suggested that these two letters had in fact been penned by Munro's election agent! There also seemed to be a sinister significance in the fact that five days before polling the Government Surveyor arrived in the burgh and held a well-publicized meeting with the Harbour Board.[76]

Armed with this evidence, Steel-Maitland had high hopes of inflicting a severe blow upon the Asquith Ministry. In late December he discussed the whole matter at length with his subordinate, Sir George Younger, the Scottish Unionist Whip, and the two men agreed that an attempt should be made to force Gulland's resignation. They decided to proceed by placing in the press an article written by some responsible person and by tabling a motion in Parliament. 'The article', declared Maitland, 'shall be a direct attack on him for corruption, written after consultation with our lawyers, published if possible on February 1. It should be followed by notices in our press saying that clearly Gulland must either bring an action or resign and by jeers at Munro when escorted by Gulland to take the oath.' The Party's solicitors saw the editor of *The Times*, who agreed to publish an accusatory letter, provided that the paper was indemnified in case of libel; Steel-Maitland then set to work composing his letter.[77]

However, in late January Maitland fell ill and was ordered by his doctors to go abroad, so he delegated the work to that scourge of Liberal corruption, Lord Robert Cecil.[78] On 9 February Steel-Maitland's letter appeared in *The Times*. It described the recent events in Wick Burghs as a scandal:

True, no Act of Parliament was infringed. But there is no moral difference between promising to electors that if one of the candidates is successful they shall each have a gift of money and hinting to them that in the same event harbour works costing anything up to £150,000 will be carried out in their burgh. I therefore, in spite of his attempted disclaimer, definitely charge Mr Gulland with corruption, and corruption of a kind from which it is our boast that British politics have been conspicuously free.[79]

This challenge was taken up by other Unionist newspapers. On 17 February the *Pall Mall Gazette* referred sarcastically to the recent 'Buy-Elections'. Moreover, because the Wick Affair coincided with the Lords' debate on Elibank's part in the Marconi transactions and with Selborne's ventilation of the honours scandal, Gulland's

[76] GD/113/108/2.
[77] Ibid.
[78] Cecil's only reservation was that Maitland's original draft letter was not 'put quite strongly enough' and he succeeded in having it beefed up (Cecil to Mrs Steel-Maitland, 20 Jan. 1914, ibid.).
[79] *The Times*, 9 Feb. 1914.

misdemeanours were widely viewed as simply one episode in a larger pattern of governmental corruption.

Unfortunately for Steel-Maitland, the Liberals comprehensively outmanœuvred the Opposition when the issue came before Parliament on 16 February. A Scottish Liberal backbencher, Cathcart Wason, asked that the House should have an opportunity to debate the allegations.[80] Asquith thereupon apologized on Gulland's behalf:

I regret, and my hon. Friend shares my regret to the full, that such language was used. But he assures me . . . that when he employed the words which have been criticized, he did not intend to convey and did not realise that what he said was capable of the construction which has just been put upon it. My hon. Friend committed an error of judgment, but I feel that the House, always generous to its Members, among whom I believe he is one of the most generally esteemed, will accept his disclaimer of any corrupt or improper intentions.[81]

The Prime Minister was followed by Gulland, who stood up in a white sheet and threw himself upon the mercy of the House. At this point Bonar Law expressed satisfaction with the apology and announced that he would not now ask for public time in which to discuss the issue.[82] Asquith was well satisfied with the outcome: 'I managed with some difficulty at question time to extricate the "corrupt" Gulland from the scrape into which he got at Wick', was his complacent comment to Venetia Stanley.[83]

On his return from abroad, a frustrated Steel-Maitland, aware that Bonar Law had ignored his advice,[84] could do nothing but bombard the English and Scottish newspapers with further letters, complaining that the Prime Minister's statement of 16 February had misled the House and in no way disposed of the serious charges that had been laid against one of his Ministers.[85] As late as June 1914 the Conservative Chairman was in correspondence with the Deputy Speaker, claiming that he had a right to criticize Gulland in the Committee of Supply and that his actions were not inspired by personal rancour but by concern over the dangerous precedent which the Liberals had set.[86]

But the events in Wick Burghs could hardly compete with the Irish Crisis for political attention, and in the autumn of 1914 they disappeared entirely from view with the outbreak of war. Meanwhile, Gulland serenely proceeded with his political career. In January 1915 he stepped into the vacancy created by Illingworth's unexpected death

[80] *Parl. Deb.*, 5th ser., lviii. 589 (16 Feb. 1914).
[81] Ibid.
[82] Ibid.
[83] Asquith to Venetia Stanley, 16 Feb. 1914, in Brock, (eds.) *Letters to Venetia Stanley* (Oxford, 1982), p. 49.
[84] Steel-Maitland to Bonar Law, 13 Feb. 1914 (GD/113/108/2).
[85] e.g. *Daily Telegraph*, 3 Mar. 1914.
[86] Steel-Maitland to Whitley, 27 June 1914 (copy) (GD/113/108/2).

and continued as Liberal Chief Whip until, like so many Asquithian Liberals, he went down to defeat in the Coupon Election of 1918.[87] But by then the issue of corruption, which had briefly threatened Gulland's career, was about to take on an even greater political significance.

---

[87] But when Gulland became Chief Whip, Balcarres commented that his 'escapade at the Wick election, followed by some pretty brave romance in the House of Commons, will be remembered by old-fashioned Liberals if any such survive'. (Balcarres's diary, 25 Jan. 1915, in Vincent (ed.), *The Crawford Papers*, p. 347).

THE LLOYD GEORGE ERA
WAR AND COALITION
1914–1922

11
Wartime Xenophobia and Corruption

Spy Fever

IT might have been supposed that the outbreak of the Great War would have buried the scandals and rumours of scandals which had dogged the pre-war Liberal Government in its final years. In fact, this did not occur. For not only did the War throw up many fresh juicy scandals of its own, it also revived memories of the scandals of the Edwardian period, although these were now given a new twist and significance.

The reason for this was the peculiar atmosphere of fear, suspicion, and xenophobia which the War engendered. When the Allied Armies did not, as expected, sweep to victory in the first few months of hostilities, angry patriots began seeking for scapegoats. The Anglo-German relationship was, in any case, fraught with complexities. Once War had been declared, national interests seemingly required a clean break with the German Reich, the internment or expulsion of all Germans found on British soil, and a cessation of all friendly intercourse with a people dubbed by the press as a 'criminal race'. However, so closely connected were the British and German nations, on an economic, social, and cultural level, that this did not prove possible—at least, not in the short run. To take but one example: as late as the summer of 1918 Government and Parliament were still pondering what steps to take to shut down the German banks that were still openly operating in British cities. As *The Times* observed in an editorial of 20 June 1918, the general public could be forgiven if they explained this sort of thing as the result of 'some potent emanation of enemy influence'.

The presence in Britain of thousands of citizens with German names and German origins or connections was also something which patriotic editors and 'political independents' could and did effectively exploit. At times when emotions were running high, as, for example, after the sinking of the *Lusitania*, little was needed to encourage mobs to sack German shops or attack casual passers-by thought to have some affiliation with the hated enemy. The tirades which Horatio Bottomley hurled at the 'germ-Huns' in his popular weekly, *John Bull*, simply expressed, in intemperate language, emotions and attitudes that could be found in most of the patriotic press.[1]

When the War began, there were some 30,000 Germans resident in Britain. To cope with these unwelcome visitors, the Commons rushed

---

[1] See Bunselmeyer, R. E., *The Cost of the War 1914–1919* (Hamden, Connecticut, 1975), Ch. 7, for an account of 'The Anti-German Temper'.

through an Aliens Restriction Act on 5 August; under its terms enemy aliens who were not of military age had until 10 August to leave the country; others had to register with the police and were subject to various restrictions. Shortly afterwards the police were given orders to arrest aliens who were thought to constitute a national danger; by mid-September 10,500 civilians had been interned. This did not satisfy the Unionist backbenchers or 'ginger' Liberals, like Henry Dalziel, who argued that since all Germans were spies or potential spies, there should be a policy of wholesale internment. On 13 May 1915, following serious riots in East London, the Government ordered the imprisonment of all enemy aliens of military age and the repatriation of their dependents. But not even this could still the unrest.[2]

The real worries centred on Germans who had taken out British nationality just before or just after the declaration of War. These 'disguised' Germans were widely thought to include many who were secretly working for the 'Fatherland', and evidence that such persons had altered their names by deed-poll was given a sinister significance.[3] There were calls for a radical reform of the naturalization laws. For example, in November 1916 Henry Page Croft, MP, addressed a meeting at the Baltic Exchange, in which he said: 'We should insist that the Government should intern every Hun, even if their names were Brown or Jones . . . We must eliminate the German influence in our midst.'[4] In August 1918 there was a big rally in Hyde Park, as a result of which one million people were said to have endorsed the cry, 'Intern Them All!' Belatedly, the Government passed a new British Nationality and Status of Aliens Act, which enabled the authorities to revoke certificates of naturalization in certain cases.[5] But for almost the entire duration of the War there was an atmosphere of suspicion surrounding concealed Germans in high places. Such persons stood accused of sabotaging the Allied war effort and doing the work of Berlin, and Germans or alleged Germans were frequently the objects of employer victimization, press attacks, and casual mob violence.

Gruban v. Booth

Understandably enough, particular hostility was directed against munitions manufacturers who had German ties and connections,[6] and one of these cases has an important bearing on the subject of this study. Towards the end of 1915 Maxse learned about a meeting which

[2] This paragraph is based on the excellent article by French, D., 'Spy Fever in Britain, 1900–1915', *Historical Journal*, xxi (1978), 355–70.

[3] See Davenport-Hines, *Dudley Docker*, p. 89.

[4] *Morning Post*, 3 Nov. 1916.

[5] On the Hyde Park rally, see *Daily Mail*, 24 Aug. 1918.

[6] Anon. to Maxse, 16 Oct. 1917 (West Sussex Record Office, Maxse papers, vol. 474, N248).

the Minister of Munitions, Lloyd George, had held with the machine tool makers branch of the Munitions Committee in November 1915. In a confidential address, Lloyd George had talked frankly about the course of the War and about the Allies' munitions requirements, after first ensuring that no reporters were present. However, it was noted that among those present at this meeting was a certain Mr Gruban, who, said the informant, had only been naturalized after the outbreak of the War. The Chairman of the Munitions Committee had his attention drawn to Gruban, but thought it better not to make an issue out of the affair.[7] However, news of what had occurred soon reached the ears of others beside Maxse. Hostile references to Gruban appeared in the *Daily Mail* and the *Globe*, and the machine tools manufacturer understandably took fright.

At this time of personal crisis Gruban was approached with an offer of help and friendship from a Liberal MP who claimed to have it in his power to stop the attacks. According to Gruban when he later gave evidence in court, this friendly MP 'also referred to Mr Lloyd George as "George" and as a very special friend of his who would do all that he could do for him as he was under a deep obligation to him for services rendered from time to time',[8] adding that he had no personal animus himself against Germans, since his wife came from Frankfurt. The identity of this MP was Handel Booth, who had so assiduously shielded Lloyd George at the time of the Marconi Scandal; and though the word 'Marconi' was probably never used, Gruban assumed, reasonably enough, that Handel Booth's 'influence' with the Government and the Ministry of Munitions stemmed from the fact that he had some kind of 'hold' over Lloyd George.

Out of gratitude to this powerful friend, Gruban made Booth a co-director of his firm. W. B. Haigh Gruban & Co., and in March 1916 Booth acquired the financial interests of the firm at no cost to himself by telling Gruban that he had it on the authority of the Minister of Munitions and other high officials in that Department that he would otherwise be interned and his property expropriated. Believing this to be true, Gruban handed over his firm to Booth, only to be interned a week later. Far from intervening on Gruban's behalf, Booth then actually spoke out to his detriment.

Unlike many Germans victimized in such ways, Gruban successfully fought back. He appealed against his internment, and, when brought before the Appeals Tribunal, described what had happened to him. He was released, and, on the suggestion of the Tribunal and of other MPs, sued Booth for damages. The trial was held in May 1917, when feeling

---

[7] Undated memo. (1915?) (ibid., vol. 471, fo. 482).
[8] *The Times*, 8 May 1917. For a report of the trial, see *The Times*, 8, 9, 10, 11, 12, 15 May 1917; and for the Court of Appeal proceedings, ibid., 23 Nov. 1917. See also Hyde, H. Montgomery, *Sir Patrick Hastings: His Life and Cases* (London, 1960), pp. 57–67.

against Germans ran high, and it boded ill for Gruban when the presiding judge chose to deliver himself of a stinging attack on the German race. But, with the young Patrick Hastings as his counsel, Gruban was able to expose the Liberal MP as a villain and a liar. The jury, it is true, acquitted Booth on the charge of maliciously procuring Gruban's internment, but they ruled that he had 'falsely and fraudulently' claimed powers to protect the plaintiff and had pressurized him into resigning his business interests. Booth later appealed against this judgement and there was a settlement out of court. But Handel Booth's career was in tatters. He failed to secure readoption in his Pontefract constituency and was relegated to third place when he contested Wentworth in the 1918 General Election.[9] As Strachey later observed, 'it was one of the most appalling and humiliating stories that I ever remember'.[10]

The Gruban versus Booth Trial is interesting as one of many examples of the Marconi Affair resurfacing during the First World War. But it was untypical in its denouement. The man found guilty of 'corruption' in this case was a politician attempting to persecute and take advantage of a recently naturalized German. Usually the roles were reversed, and it was the 'alien' who found himself, justly or unjustly, accused of impropriety.

Attacks on Cosmopolitan Financiers

No group of men were so vulnerable in this respect as the great cosmopolitan financiers and businessmen from German backgrounds. As we have seen, they had been widely disliked and feared even before 1914. The Great War now provided their critics with a heaven-sent opportunity for revenge. The *National Review*, for example, renewed its vendetta against Sir John Brunner, who stood high on the hate list of all xenophobes because of his leadership of the Little Navy faction within the pre-war Liberal Party and because of his earlier attempts to secure an Anglo-German reconciliation.[11] Stories circulated that Sir John was in fact a spy. This was simply ridiculous, but in January 1915 the *Globe* touched a raw nerve when it accused Brunner's firm of shamelessly reaping huge profits by providing munitions for an army and navy he had once done his best to weaken.[12] Brunner's friend and partner, Alfred Mond, the son of a German Jew, excited even greater suspicion; and he was eventually driven to take legal action against

[9] But Hyde is in error when he says that Booth never contested another election (Hyde, *Hastings*, p. 67).
[10] Strachey to J. W. Hamilton (copy), 9 Jan. 1919 (HLRO, Strachey papers, S/8/12/4).
[11] Koss, S. E., *Sir John Brunner: Radical Plutocrat 1842–1919* (Cambridge, 1970), Ch. 11.
[12] Ibid., p. 275.

those who charged him with having treacherously and corruptly allocated shares in Mond Nickel & Co. to German citizens.[13]

The problems of the wealthy German-Jews in fact began at an early stage in the War when the playwright, Arthur Pinero, wrote to *The Times* suggesting that these men must be experiencing a divided loyalty now that Britain and Germany were at war and that they should clear their names by publicly denouncing Germany. This was the origin of the so-called 'loyalty letters' which appeared in *The Times* in May and June 1915.[14] One such letter was written by Sir Ernest Cassel, who also tried to ingratiate himself with the British people by subscribing generously to the War Loans and putting his international financial contacts at the disposal of the Allies. But a man with his world-wide interests could not escape the suspicion of being involved in organizations that were still trading with the enemy. Cassel also had to endure the indignity of defending his Privy Councillorship when a Scottish baronet, Sir George Makgill, brought an action against him. Cassel bore his misfortunes with stoicism and dignity.[15] So did Sir Felix Schuster, who was attacked in the *New Witness* in an article which linked his German ancestry to the 'disgraceful' part he had allegedly played at the time of the Indian Silver Affair.[16] This linking of pro-Germanism to allegations of corruption in the recent past was to become common practice.

One of the Jewish financiers arraigned in this way was Sir Edgar Speyer. His initial response was to offer Asquith the resignation of his baronetcy and his Privy Councillorship, an offer which Asquith refused. But he declined to write a 'loyalty letter' and the public attacks on him mounted. There were wild rumours that Speyer's family was using its house at Overstrand, near Cromer, to signal to the German Fleet.[17] It was also alleged, with greater plausibility, that Sir Edgar was involved, through his brothers, in commercial contact with Germany. Members of the family also had to suffer constant harrassment and threats.[18]

Riled beyond endurance, Sir Edgar made little effort to disarm his critics by a display of patriotic commitment, as Cassel had done, and when he too faced an action by Makgill to deprive him of his Privy Councillorship, he to all intents and purposes 'told the King and the Privy Council to go hang', as Lord Reading put it, and adopted a 'studiously disrespectful' attitude.[19] Before even waiting to hear the Privy Council's verdict, Speyer and his family then sailed for the United States, where they lived for the rest of the War. There they took

---

[13] *New Witness*, 6 Dec. 1918, p. 108. See below, Ch. 14.
[14] See Holmes, *Anti-Semitism*, Ch. 8, esp. pp. 122–3, 270 n. 13.
[15] Ibid., p. 123.   [16] *New Witness*, 29 Oct. 1914.
[17] There is material on the hysteria surrounding Speyer in the Maxse papers.
[18] Brock (eds.), *Letters to Venetia Stanley*, pp. 292–3.
[19] Fitzroy, A. *Memoirs* (London, n.d.), ii. 613–14; Fitzroy's diary, 19 Dec. 1915.

part in a number of anti-British activities, with the result that in December 1921 Sir Edgar was stripped by the Government of his Privy Councillorship, while he, his wife, and his three daughters also had their naturalization revoked—a decision which, according to the Clerk of the Council, 'was hailed with satisfaction by everyone present'.[20]

But how could such a man have been protected and befriended by politicians in high places in the early stages of the War? Asquith, it was recalled, had once publicly dismissed demands for the withdrawal of Speyer's titles with the words, 'I have known you long and well enough to estimate at their true value these baseless and malignant imputations.'[21] Indeed, in October 1914, when some of Asquith's friends were ostentatiously pulling out all their investments in Speyer's companies, the Asquiths had invited the Speyers to dinner. Distorted stories concerning this social event were soon circulating. The Conservative MP, Willie Bridgeman, for example, believed that Speyer was 'perpetually' in Downing Street.[22]

Why had Asquith taken such risks with his reputation? Some will admire his stance as showing a loyalty to friends in their adversity and will applaud his refusal to give way to mob hysteria. Others may doubt the soundness of Asquith's judgement and see this episode as evidence of a supercilious contempt for public opinion which fatally undermined his wartime premiership.

But there was another possible explanation for Asquith's conduct, namely, that he was under a personal or a party obligation to the unpopular financier. Milner's friend, F. S. Oliver, in a typically spiteful letter to Maxse of February 1916, expressing the wish that 'Squiff' would join his friend Sir Edgar in America, posed the question, 'Why do all great men have financial major domos?'[23] Maxse did not pursue this line of thought. But the *National Review* and the *New Witness* did draw a connection between Asquith's defence of Speyer and the latter's pre-war contributions to Liberal Party funds. For it was taken for granted that Speyer had only received a baronetcy from the Liberals in 1906 and a Privy Councillorship three years later because of his conspicuous 'generosity'. Was Asquith in 1915 still conscious of being indebted to the wealthy financier?

Such reflections brought to life old worries about the funding of the major parties, while giving a new twist to the debate about the dangers of honours trafficking. If one assumed, as the Radical Right did without question, that German-born financiers cared little for British

---

[20] Fitzroy, *Memoirs*, ii. 770; Fitzroy's diary, 13 Dec. 1921.

[21] Cited in Brock, *Letters to Venetia Stanley*, p. 292.

[22] Bridgeman to Maxse, 21 Feb. 1915 (Maxse papers, vol. 470, fo. 91). For other expressions of hostility to Speyer, see Long to Gwynne, 16 May 1915 (Bodleian, Gwynne papers, vol. 20); Balcarres's diary, 13 Nov. 1914, in Vincent (ed.), *The Crawford Papers*, pp. 344–5.

[23] Oliver to Maxse, 11 Feb. 1916 (Maxse papers, vol. 472, fos. 572–3).

interests and were even, in some cases, actively helping the Fatherland, what appalling dangers the Empire faced as a result of the dependence of the two governing parties (but especially of the Liberal Party) upon financial support from such men!

No one did more to dramatize this issue than the Conservative backbencher, Sir Henry Page Croft. In speech after speech he hammered away at this theme. The *Morning Post* backed him up. The country, it declared in October 1916,

desires to see a reformation in the system by which party funds are secretly used for party purposes. There is a presumption, strong and terrible, that Germany tried to corrupt the Government of this country from the national interest. . . . The country must never again run this hideous danger of being sold by the Judases of a Caucus to the national enemy. We have escaped by a miracle; let us never run the danger again.[24]

The insinuation of Page Croft and his friends was clear. The 'pacifist' strain in British policy before 1914 was the result of the Liberal Government's financial ties with 'cosmopolitans' who had no love for the British Empire. The call for the abolition of the party system, or, at the least, for the opening of the party accounts to public inspection, now acquired a new significance. Such a step, it was argued, would ensure that British parties did not fall under foreign control. The earlier concern with 'corruption' did not disappear, of course, but it was now harmoniously blended with a fierce insistence on extirpating all alien influences from public life.

Such an attack on secret party funds played an important part in Page Croft's launching of a new organization, the National Party, in August 1917. Among the initial aims of the Party were 'the eradication of German influence' and 'honest administration, a pure political system and no sale of honours'.[25] These objectives were thought to be mutually reinforcing. One National Party candidate, fighting a by-election in October 1917, even went so far as to claim that the 'vices of the party system' had had a pervasive and demoralizing impact on British politics and helped to explain why the country had not yet won the War.[26] More temperate were the views expressed by Page Croft, when he told a reporter in an interview in late November 1917 that contributors to party funds should be revealed for all to see: 'we shall never arrive at a better state until the "unseen hand" in party politics is exposed.'[27]

---

[24] *Morning Post*, 17 Oct. 1916.
[25] See Lord Croft, *My Life of Strife* (London, n.d.), p. 131. This manifesto was first published in the *Morning Post*, 30 Aug. 1917.
[26] *The Times*, 17 Oct. 1917.
[27] *Morning Post*, 23 Nov. 1917.

The 'Unseen Hand'

Page Croft's conspiratorial view of politics was one that was widely shared in late 1917. His invocation of the 'unseen hand' is also interesting. This phrase and its close equivalent, the 'Hidden Hand', seem to have come into currency during the course of 1915, when one often encounters them in private letters and newspaper articles. By the end of the War, if not earlier, they had become something of a popular joke.[28] But the Radical Right took the idea with deadly seriousness. It is not easy to discover quite what it was meant to signify. In practice the catch-words probably meant slightly different things to different people. Those who invoked the 'Hidden Hand', however, all felt baffled and frustrated at Britain's inability to bring the War to a quick conclusion. As the British armed forces suffered one set-back after another, it was tempting to imagine that more than incompetence, bad luck, or the existence of insuperable odds was responsible. There seemed to be some sinister, almost occult, force at work that was operating in Berlin's interest. Less mystical was the belief in a tight-knit group of spies and German dupes and sympathizers who had somehow managed to penetrate the very heart of Britain's war machine.[29]

Arnold White developed this theme in his pamphlet, *The Hidden Hand*, published in 1917. White had been a violent Germanophobe since the start of the century; and the events of the Great War, while confirming him in the truth of his former prophetic warnings, also seem to have unhinged a mind never known for its good judgement and balance. But White was not alone in recognizing 'the whorles, curves and lines of the finger-prints of the Hidden Hand in almost all the departments of State'.[30] Maxse, Gwynne, and other journalists shared his obsessive curiosity about the national origins and connections of politicians' wives, friends, and servants, and joined him in his vendetta against Haldane and in his hunt for officials and army officers with suspicious-sounding German names.

But xenophobic patriots still had to explain how native-born Britons, without a spot of German blood in their veins, could possibly have got caught up in a German conspiracy. One possible answer, as we have

---

[28] Atkins to Strachey, 19 Dec. 1918 (Strachey papers, S/8/12/5).

[29] Holmes, *Anti-Semitism*, p. 139.

[30] White, A., *The Hidden Hand* (London, 1917), p. 16. By the 1920s the phrase 'Hidden Hand' had become almost synonymous with the notion of a world-wide Jewish conspiracy. The journal of the 'Britons', one of several anti-Semitic bodies that sprang up in the post-war years, at first bore the title, *Jewry Ueber Alles*, before changing its name to *The Hidden Hand* (Lebzelter, G., *Political Anti-Semitism in England 1918–1939* (London, 1978), p. 54). But while the War was in progress, it was naturally fear of Germany which predominated. Surprisingly, in view of his earlier writings, Arnold White makes no mention whatever of Jewish influence in his 1917 pamphlet, *The Hidden Hand*.

seen, was that cosmopolitan plutocrats had been able to influence the actions of the British parties by the donations they had made to the secret funds. But in addition to *bribery*, it was quite widely believed during the War that prominent politicians were being *blackmailed* into pursuing an 'anti-national' line. And it was in this connection that a renewed interest was taken in the pre-war scandals, and particularly in Marconi.

To explain why this should have been so means returning to the events of 1912 and 1913. It is often forgotten that the attacks that Liberal Ministers sustained in these years were not confined to condemnation of their ill-judged speculations in American Marconi shares—the issue which dominated both Majority and Minority Reports of the Select Committee. Running parallel with this issue were highly scurrilous rumours, never substantiated or denied, that certain Ministers had also been involved in large-scale transactions in *English* Marconi shares, something which, if proved to be true, would have constituted a scandal of the utmost seriousness.

The accusation was formulated by Ellis T. Powell, Harry Marks's successor as editor of the *Financial News*, which by then claimed to have the largest circulation of any financial newspaper in the world.[31] In April 1913 he appeared before the Marconi Select Committee and told a story which was nothing if not sensational. It was also bizarre, involved, and not easy to believe. In brief, Powell was claiming that while the Government was negotiating with the English Marconi Company in the spring of 1912, large-scale purchases had been made of English Marconi shares, and the likelihood was that these dealings had originated with a person or persons who were 'in the know'. Moreover, the speculators, who were rumoured to include Cabinet Ministers, had taken care to conceal their identities by operating through assumed names and intermediaries and by transferring shares from London to Hamburg in an attempt to throw suspicious investigators off the scent.

At the time Powell's 'disclosure' did not make much of an impact. In fact, his appearance as a witness before the Select Committee is now usually remembered, if at all, in connection with Churchill. For Powell had mentioned Churchill as one of the Ministers said to be implicated in the transactions he was describing, and the Select Committee had then called upon the First Lord of the Admiralty to answer the allegation, which he did with theatrical indignation and fury. So much amusement and interest was aroused by this intervention that when the cross-examination of Powell was resumed, the press took little account of what he was saying. Since proof of Powell's charges was

---

[31] *Financial News*, 12 Aug. 1918. The paper's origins are discussed by Porter, Dilwyn, 'Journalist, Financier, "Dishonest Rogue", "Scoundrel": The Life and Times of Harry Hananel Marks, M.P.', *Moirae*, viii (1984), 65–7. In fact, Powell did not formally take over the editorship of the *Financial News* from Marks until July 1915.

almost entirely non-existent, even the more suspicious Unionist members of the Committee seem quickly to have switched their attention elsewhere.[32]

Yet long after the Marconi Affair had died down, Powell continued to work obsessively to assemble the supporting evidence he needed, and the long-suffering readers of the *Financial News* were regularly informed about the progress of his researches. But after August 1914 a new emphasis began to enter into his articles. In December 1915, for example, Powell asked:

Has the Kaiser, or has the German Government, any information with regard to some highly-placed persons which gives them the same 'pull' as a blackmailer who can reveal a dark secret if his conditions are not complied with? Are there people, capable of influencing the policy of the Government, who have a hourly fear of an *exposé* from Potsdam? If not, what is the paralysing 'influence' that seems to spread like a miasma over our national policy making it inert when it ought to be vertebrate, and flabby when it ought to be resolute?[33]

Three days later an editorial in the *Financial News* on 'The Hidden Hand' concluded: 'DRAG THE SKELETON OUT'.[34]

By the summer of 1916 Powell's story was almost complete. He now felt able to reveal that a music master named Cameron, who had made considerable purchases of English Marconi shares in 1912, was acting as Godfrey Isaacs's agent. He also alleged that further Marconi transactions carried out in the name of 'Madame Perelli' had been initiated by Godfrey's wife. What is more, Powell then tried to show that Lord Reading himself (the former Rufus Isaacs) must have been conversant with all these events. But that was not all. Shortly before the outbreak of War, Powell had visited Germany in a bid to unravel the Hamburg end of the story. In the course of this visit he discovered that the financial house which had handled the English Marconi share purchases was Salomon & Co., whose senior partner was a naturalized Austrian called Breisnach. Powell was convinced that Brisnach had promptly told everything he knew to both the Austrian and German Governments. There was thus, he concluded, a secret dossier in Berlin which contained information which could be used, should the opportunity arise, to blackmail prominent British Ministers.[35]

---

[32] Report of Select Committee on Marconi Wireless Telegraph Company, Limited, Agreement, 1913, PP vii (1913), qs. 8353–8402, 8620–9011. Powell's evidence was given on 24 and 28 Apr. 1913.

[33] *Financial News*, 11 Dec. 1915.

[34] Ibid., 14 Dec. 1915. But next day Powell raised an 'alternative hypothesis': 'Its sponsors regard the "influence" as arising from the extreme intimacy of certain German, and naturalised German, politicians with highly placed members of the Ministry.'

[35] Ibid., 6 Oct. to 22 Nov. 1916. As Powell told Bonar Law in Nov. 1918: 'I have satisfied myself, by enquiries in Germany before the War, that the whole of the concealed Maroni transactions are in a German secret dossier, which is capable of being

What prompted Powell to come out with his full sensational story was the shock of Kitchener's death, when the *Hampshire* hit a mine in June 1916. Like other paranoid patriots, Powell found it hard to accept the official account of how the War Secretary had died. The *National Review*, for example, speculated about the existence of some infernal machine which the Germans might perhaps have used to kill Kitchener.[36] Powell's explanation was far more dramatic: 'If Lord Kitchener is dead, the Unseen Hand killed him.' Someone 'very high up' in the Government who knew everything about the Allied war plans, claimed the *Financial News*, was being blackmailed by the Germans. 'Racial self-respect compelled one to the hypothesis that the person or persons were involved in the Marconi transactions via Hamburg', it added. 'The German Government sees that a distinguished career lies in the hollow of its hand. By a single disclosure it can precipitate political and social disaster so catastrophic as to amount to utter extinction.' Powell went on to chronicle the sinister work which the 'Hidden Hand' had accomplished since the start of the War:

German companies have been protected, German spies have been kept out of internment. . . . Every possible obstacle has been placed in the way of efficient measures with regard to dangerous naturalised Germans. German intriguers and co-operators have got off with fines of 10s and £1, while honest but indiscreet citizens have been mulcted in £100 at a time. As for our military and naval operations, nobody can study their history without seeing tricks of betrayal clearly marked in events which, at the moment, we need not enumerate.[37]

'WANTED, THE NAME', shrieked Powell. 'Let us have the name of the Man in the Iron Mask.'[38] And to whom was this appeal addressed? Inevitably, its recipient was Lord Reading, the trusted confidant of both Asquith and Lloyd George. To remove any lingering doubt that here was the source of many of the Empire's misfortunes, Powell reminded his readers that Reading's parents-in-law were the Cohens of Berlin. Nor did it seem a pure coincidence that it was Reading, in his judicial capacity, who had made difficulties in the early stages of the War over the removal of Speyer's Privy Councillorship, and who had also chaired the tribunal which had allowed foreign companies to register as British companies and enjoy all the accompanying advantages.[39] The *Financial News*, of course, was engaged in an almost non-

used as a means of intimidating politicians and other "persons of influence" into compliance with German wishes and into assisting German plans.' (Powell to Bonar Law (copy), 5 Nov. 1918, Strachey papers, S/9/8/18.)

[36] *National Review*, lxvii (1916), 664. But Maxse, too, speaks of the possibility that Kitchener's movements were betrayed to the Germans by 'a German spy in London—possibly moving in the best political society'.

[37] *Financial News*, 7, 8, 9 June 1916.

[38] Ibid., 18 Oct. 1916.

[39] Ibid., 6 Oct. 1916.

stop attack on foreign businesses operating in Britain, especially those 'spy organizations', the German banks. But by October 1916 Powell was convinced that no good would be done by the mere act of closing down German banks and companies; not until the questions he had posed in his paper had been answered could the process of de-Germanizing the country make any headway.[40]

How did the political world react to Powell's extraordinary allegations? Many politicians were initially intrigued, but puzzled. Jack Sandars, Balfour's Private Secretary, wrote to Maxse on 27 October 1916: 'I have been talking to a man who is in the City today. He says the Marconi articles in the Financial News are written by the editor—Powell, I think his name was—a barrister, an excellent lawyer who has been for some years at his job, and would not write as he does, had he not evidence which was sufficient for his purpose. . . .'[41] Others were not so sure. *Justice* was one of the few newspapers to give Powell support from the start. In a front page article of the 29 June edition, entitled 'What Are Our Rulers Doing?', it called for a public enquiry into the serious allegations carried by the *Financial News*, saying that failure to do this would administer 'a great shock' to 'the national confidence in our rulers'.[42] Other journalists, perhaps fearing they would be sued for libel, held back. Aware that he had a credibility problem, Powell bombarded leading politicians with letters in which he denied that he was a 'hair-brained crank' and cited his various qualifications: a barrister, an experienced financial journalist, the possessor of a London University doctoral degree and a Fellowship of the Royal Historical Society.[43]

In November 1916 one MP at least was persuaded by the *Financial News* articles to table a question in the Commons. This was Colonel Gretton, the future Diehard leader. But Bonar Law dismissed the allegations as being without basis, adding, however, that he was keeping in touch with the Director of Public Prosecutions on the matter.[44] Powell was furious: 'We should have thought that candid disclosure was a policy infinitely preferable to the "watching" of this newspaper by the Public Prosecutor, to say nothing of the tapping of our telephones and the dogging of the Editor's footsteps, which has now been going on for months', he complained.[45]

There are only two other aspects of Powell's campaign against

[40] Ibid., 19 Oct. 1916.

[41] Sandars to Maxse, 27 Oct. 1916 (Maxse papers, vol. 473, fo. 828).

[42] *Justice*, 29 June 1916.

[43] e.g. Powell to Bonar Law (copy), 5 Nov. 1918 (Strachey papers, S/9/8/18). Powell's obituary in the *Financial News* (2 June 1922) says that he mastered six or seven different tongues, including Hebrew, Latin, and Greek. It may also be significant that 'for many years Dr Powell interested himself in the study of psychic affairs.'

[44] *Parl. Deb.*, 5th ser., lxxxvii. 398 (9 Nov. 1916).

[45] *Financial News*, 13 Nov. 1916. Earlier, Powell had complained that he had 'been warned that he had better "look out for himself" if he persist[ed] in publishing Marconi

Reading which need be mentioned in this chapter. First, there were political commentators, like Loe Strachey, by no means taken in by the Ellis Powell saga, who were disturbed when Reading adamantly refused to defend his honour in court, despite the fact that he was being libelled day in, day out. Secondly, Reading's quiet confidence in the face of this assault and his seeming immunity to all criticism convinced many members of the Radical Right, not least Powell himself, that Reading must 'have a hold' of some sort over Lloyd George. In other words, the Lord Chief Justice was a blackmailer himself, as well as being the victim of blackmail. If this were true, then the tentacles of the Hidden Hand must be ensnaring even the statesman who had emerged as Britain's great war leader. And this in turn could be used to explain why, when Asquith had been replaced by a more vigorous Prime Minister, victory over Germany still proved to be so bafflingly elusive. Once again 'corruption' seemed to be the reason for the failure of the Government to prosecute British interests in a whole-hearted and effective way.

The Leverton Harris Affair

It was not always a case of 'unpatriotic' behaviour being presented as though it were a *consequence* of corruption. Sometimes financial malpractice and disloyalty to King and Country were treated rather as common symptoms of some underlying weakness of character. A particularly vivid example of this was provided by the political destruction of the Under-Secretary for Blockade, Leverton Harris, a personal friend and associate of Austen Chamberlain.

This little drama began in June 1918 when a young army officer facing a court martial alleged that Harris's wife, Gertrude, had visited a German in Wakefield Internment Camp, unsupervised, taking in with her various articles of contraband. Realizing the seriousness of the charge, Mrs Leverton Harris at once rushed off letters of explanation to her husband's perturbed constituents and to the readers of *The Times*. She admitted that she had indeed visited a German internee, Baron Leopold Plessen, but said that she had known his family for years: 'his mother and her sisters (who by birth are half English and half Austrian) were friends of mine, and the boy, until the war broke out, was an undergraduate at Oxford.' She had promised Leopold's aunt to see him occasionally and had done so four times, but she insisted that an official was always present and denied that she had received any particular privileges.[46]

articles', and hints were dropped that the paper might be closed 'as a result of strong Anglo-German pressure' (ibid., 17 Oct. 1916).

[46] *Parl. Deb.*, 5th ser., cvii. 866–8 (25 June 1918); *The Times*, 20 June 1918; Mrs Leverton-Harris's letter to her husbands' constituents, ibid., 21 June 1918.

Now, as she later ruefully admitted, Mrs Leverton Harris had behaved foolishly, in so far as the wife of a Unionist MP and of a Minister was not supposed to enjoy such close relationships with an Austrian family.[47] In fact, once the War had broken out, xenophobes had been constantly fuming over the alleged pampering of German POWs by leaders of British Society (Margot Asquith's name, for example, had been mentioned in this connection),[48] at a time when they believed that atrocities were being inflicted on British prisoners in Germany. Mrs Leverton Harris's kindness to àn enemy internee was also reckless because it was bound to be likened to the supposed softness to German interests being shown by the Ministry of Blockade, where her husband was employed. For the entire Radical Right treated it as axiomatic that the War was being needlessly prolonged by the 'treacherous' refusal of highly placed officials inside the Ministry to enforce an effective blockade against the Central Powers.[49]

To make matters worse, the unfortunate Leverton Harris then found himself four days later accused of corruption. Was this merely coincidental? His accuser was the founder of the newly created National Party, Page Croft, to whom an anonymous donor had sent a copy of an official letter which Harris had written when serving on the Admiralty War Staff in 1916. On the face of it, this letter seemed to suggest that Harris had abused his official position by granting special cable facilities to his family firm, Harris & Dixon. The rights and wrongs of this case are considered in Chapter 12. It is arguable that Harris had been careless and unlucky, rather than venal. Unfortunately, he was hardly helped by the tactless way in which Lloyd George, Asquith, and Bonar Law promptly rushed to his defence. The result was that Page Croft secured a great deal of publicity for his new party, which was partly the point of the exercise.[50]

Page Croft did at least temper the severity of his indictment of Leverton Harris by scrupulously separating it from the current furore caused by the Minister's indiscreet wife.[51] But few xenophobes showed a similar restraint. For example, the *New Witness*, in an article written by Percival Smith, the tormentor of Mond, linked the Minister's conduct with the behaviour of his Hun-loving wife.[52] *John Bull* also featured the luckless couple in a double-page spread, in which further doubt was cast on Harris's business probity; the article carried the stark message, 'Leverton Harris must go!'[53] Meanwhile, *Justice* was

[47] Gertrude Harris to Bonar Law, 24 Jan. 1919 (HLRO, Bonar Law papers, 96/9/20).

[48] Asquith, M., *The Autobiography of Margot Asquith*, ii. (London, 1922), 221; Davenport-Hines, *Docker*, p. 96.

[49] *Justice*, too, took this line, referring to what it called 'the pro-German blockade' (18 Oct. 1917).

[50] Croft, *My Life of Strife*, pp. 133–8. See also Ch. 12, pp. 276–8.

[51] *Parl. Deb.*, 5th ser., cvii. 758–9 (24 June 1918).

[52] *New Witness*, 27 Sept. 1918, pp. 427–8.　　　　　　　　[53] *John Bull*, 6 July 1918.

reminded (inevitably) of the Marconi Case by the way in which Asquith and Lloyd George had combined to rush to the support of a peccant minister, and it also dwelt on the misdemeanours of Gertrude, whose 'close intimacy with a German prisoner' it called 'contrary to law and military usage'; moreover, 'the officer who attempted to stop her carrying on in this way was arrested and court-martialled', it claimed.[54] *Justice* could easily be brushed aside, but it was a different matter when the *Daily Mail* joined in the hue and cry.[55]

At the end of his tether, Leverton Harris offered his resignation, which Bonar Law initially seemed inclined to accept. This aroused the fury of Harris's political chief, Lord Robert Cecil, the Minister of Blockade, who had himself had to endure the malicious hostility of the Radical Right press and who, despite his pre-war campaign for 'purity' in public life, was disgusted by the kind of muck-raking in which the jingo press was now engaging. Cecil curtly informed Bonar Law that if Leverton Harris resigned, he would resign too. Law replied that he thought Harris had behaved wisely in tendering his resignation, but felt sure that the Prime Minister would reject it; this answer, for the time being, mollified Cecil.[56]

But Leverton Harris's career never recovered from the onslaught made against himself and his wife in the summer of 1918. Despite loyal support from Austen Chamberlain, he decided to withdraw as a candidate from his safe Birmingham seat in the 1918 Election, rather than cause further embarrassment to his local Unionist Association.[57] Then soon after retiring into private life, Harris suffered a bad breakdown and had to go into a nursing home, too ill to work. The Government refused Cecil's request that they give Harris a peerage, and it was only when he died in 1926 that he received public recognition for his important war work. Cecil sent *The Times* his own tribute to his former colleague: 'it is, indeed, much to be regretted that his sensitiveness to unjust attack cut short a career of great public usefulness.'[58] But Harris's career had really been destroyed not by his own temperament, but by the kind of political agitation created by four years of bloody and frustrating warfare, in which scapegoats were sought for the British people's sufferings.

Pemberton Billing

When in August 1918 Cecil chivalrously linked his own ministerial career to that of his unpopular Under-Secretary, he gave Bonar Law this

[54] *Justice*, 27 June 1918.
[55] *Daily Mail*, 10 June 1918. On 8 July the *Mail* wished that the Prime Minister 'had dealt more energetically with the Leverton Harris embarrassment and had not earned the support of Mr Asquith'.
[56] Blake, *Bonar Law*, pp. 379–80.
[57] See his obituary in *The Times*, 16 Nov. 1926.   [58] Ibid., 17 Nov. 1926.

reason for taking so strong a line: 'I had rather sweep a crossing than be a member of a Ministry at the mercy of Pemberton Billing and his crew.'[59] For among Leverton Harris's assailants had been the most conspicuous and dangerous of all the wartime jingo demagogues.[60] We must now examine the career of Pemberton Billing in some detail, because it illustrates to perfection the way in which xenophobia and scandalmongering came together in the mind of the paranoid patriot.

Pemberton Billing had first attained prominence as a political 'Independent': as the self-styled 'Air Candidate' who in a barn-storming campaign nearly won the Mile End by-election in January 1916, before being triumphantly returned for Hertford three months later. Initially Billing concentrated almost exclusively on the question of Britain's air defences. At Mile End he toured the constituency accompanied by an aeroplane packed in a lorry, promising voters that, should his plan for a strengthened Air Force be adopted, Zeppelin raids would cease and the irritating black-out of London could be lifted.[61] He was joined in his campaign by his ally, Horatio Bottomley, who commended Billing as the inventor of a flying machine before which the Zeppelin would turn back.[62] The two men also spoke in favour of a relaxation of the licensing restrictions—a calculated and successful bid for the support of the Victuallers' Protection Association. The demagogic nature of Billing's appeal was further attested by the presence on his platform of Ben Tillett, the 'jingo Labour' leader, and of the ubiquitous Arnold White.[63] At Hertford Billing ran a similar campaign and afterwards attributed his victory to his concentration on one single issue: the imperative need to achieve air superiority.

In Parliament Billing showed the same single-mindedness, and was at first treated by many MPs and journalists with some respect as an acknowledged expert on his subject, to whom the Government would do well to listen; in some quarters he was even referred to as a possible candidate for office—a Minister of the Air, perhaps.[64] Consequently, there was a widespread willingness to tolerate Billing's marked eccentricities of speech and manner. And when shortly after his election he accused Ministers of 'murdering' British pilots by making

[59] Blake, *Bonar Law*, p. 379.

[60] See his obituary in *The Times*, 13 Nov. 1948.

[61] Ibid., 13, 14, 17, 18, 19 Jan. 1916.

[62] Symons, J., *Horatio Bottomley* (London, 1955), p. 187.

[63] *The Times*, 20 Jan. 1916. Interestingly, when he later won the Hertford by-election, Billing received the public congratulations of Dalziel and Handel Booth (ibid., 11 Mar. 1916).

[64] Spender, H., 'Coalition OR ——?', *Contemporary Review*, cix (1916), 562; Auditor Tantum, 'The Coalition and Its Critics', *Fortnightly Review*, xcix (1916), 794–5. On 20 Mar. 1916 Churchill wrote to his wife: 'Billing is not bad. His speeches are genuine products—& the facts are uncontrovertible.' (Gilbert, Martin, *Winston S. Churchill, iii. Companion Vol.* (London, 1972), Part II, p. 1474).

them fly defective machines, even this could be passed off as no more than an excess of patriotic zeal.[65]

But by the end of 1916 the 'Member for the Air' gradually started to launch out in new directions and to widen his appeal. Significantly for the future, it was Billing who first tried to raise the issue of Ellis Powell's Marconi articles in the Commons, and when the Speaker disallowed his question, only to permit Gretton to ask an almost identical question fourteen days later, the Member for Hertford could scarcely contain his indignation.[66] During the course of 1917 Billing's repertoire continued to grow. He persistently drew the attention of the House to the sinister presence of Germans, in most cases recently naturalized Germans, in public office, and he called on the Home Secretary to draw up a list of all such persons and their British guarantors, so that watchful patriots could see that vital national interests were not being jeopardized. Similarly, the award of a government contract to a person with a foreign-sounding name was unlikely to take place without the matter engaging the attention of this noisy, self-appointed 'people's tribune'.[67]

Predictably enough, Billing also developed an obsessive interest in the derivation and expenditure of the party funds. He shared Page Croft's fears that 'foreigners' were trying to control the activities of the British Government through political donations. In November 1917 the two men called on Bonar Law, in vain, to enforce the annual publication of the names of all party subscribers and to give the House an assurance 'that at least German money should not go into party funds'.[68] Moreover, a few months later Billing was excitedly proclaiming that many people believed that a significant proportion of the Liberal Party funds had been *invested* in Germany before 1914—something, he said, that must never be allowed to happen again.[69] Of course, Billing also waxed indignant over evidence that the Coalition Government was continuing the nefarious practice of honours trafficking.[70]

This professed concern with the purity of public life led Billing and his associates into populist denunciations of the rich and powerful. For example, Billing wanted the Prime Minister to prevent Ministers 'either personally or through the medium of a nominee investing any money in any company, either British or foreign, which may be either directly or indirectly affected by the progress of the War day by day'. This was a senseless demand, since, as Law pointed out, it was difficult

[65] *The Times*, 28 Mar. 1916.
[66] *Parl. Deb.*, 5th ser., lxxxvii. 398, 418–19 (9 Nov. 1916).
[67] e.g. ibid. xcviii. 1622 (1 Nov. 1917); cvii. 1373–4 (1 July 1918).
[68] Ibid. xcix. 30–1 (12 Nov. 1917). The accusation that the Free Trade Union was being funded, in part, by 'aliens' had first been made by the Tariff Reform League during the Edwardian period.
[69] *Parl. Deb.*, 5th ser., ciii. 1827–8 (5 Mar. 1918).
[70] e.g. ibid. 914 (21 Feb. 1918).

to imagine any business which was not so affected.[71] A similar concern to prevent unpatriotic citizens benefiting financially from their country's misfortunes lay behind Billing's hostility to the 'profiteer'. In November 1917 he suggested that a reward be offered to persons giving information leading to convictions for 'hoarding foodstuffs essential for the poor'. When the Government demurred, saying that this would 'merely increase the number of groundless complaints', Billing angrily asked whether Ministers were aware 'that the wealthier classes have laid in stores of tea, sugar and other food commodities, thereby decreasing the amount of food essentials available for poorer people'.[72] There was thus a distinctly populist strain in the agitation which Billing led. For example, in late 1918 one of his cronies was calling for 'a fairer distribution of profits among the workers, and improved homes and working conditions', as well as 'the purification of political life and the exposure of the sources of German influence'.[73] In the latter stages of the War, then, Billing and his friends were becoming more than a minor nuisance because they were stirring up a whole range of popular discontents by playing on the working man's xenophobia, his sense of economic deprivation, and on popular resentment against officialdom.

To channel these discontents, Billing in October 1917 founded a society called the 'Vigilantes'. It was a small, cranky body, whose members were mostly Billing's active supporters in his Hertford constituency, but its programme had a much wider appeal. This much became evident when Billing started to run his own candidates at by-elections, all of whom made a solemn pledge that they would accept neither office nor honour should they be elected. The first such intervention occurred in October 1917, when a vacancy was being filled at East Leyton. It was a bewildering contest for the electors, who found that as well as the official Coalition candidate, they had a choice between a National Party and a 'Vigilante' man, both campaigning on a similar programme.[74] It was the 'Vigilante' candidate who showed the greater vehemence and who made the greater impact; he came a respectable second, with over 32 per cent of the vote, while the National Party trailed a bad third.

There then occurred a series of events in France which gave an additional boost to the British Radical Right in general and to the 'Vigilantes' in particular. For in late 1917 Clemenceau unearthed evidence of various treasonable conspiracies against the French Government. No less a figure than Caillaux was arrested in January 1918 on the charge of having been in communication with the enemy. This was the start of a series of treason trials which brought to public

---

[71] Ibid. 1827 (5 Mar. 1918).   [72] Ibid. xcviii. 1779–80 (5 Nov. 1917).
[73] Captain Spencer's by-election address, printed in *Vigilante*, 13 July 1918.
[74] *The Times*, 19 Oct. 1917.

attention a charming and accomplished swindler, bearing the improbable name of Bolo Pasha. Paul Marie Bolo was the son of a Marseille café owner. He had dabbled in hairdressing, dentistry, and restaurant management, but his money had mainly been made through embezzlement and through contracting bigamous marriages with a number of wealthy women.[75]

After a futile attempt to control the emerald markets of the world and an ill-judged incursion into banking, Bolo was in desperate need of money. This he received when the Khedive of Egypt, who had earlier been so impressed by his financial genius that he had made him a pasha, was deposed by the British in December 1914. The ex-Khedive then became a German agent, whose job it was to channel funds into France with the aim of buying up 'patriotic' journals, so that, at an appropriate moment, they could be converted to a 'defeatist' line. Bolo undertook to carry out this work and received in all more than two million francs, nearly all of which stuck to his own fingers. But although he had successfully swindled his German employers, Bolo Pasha nevertheless persuaded them in 1916 to do business with him once more. On a visit to the United States he met the emissaries of Count Bernsdorff, German Ambassador at Washington, who gave him further sums of money for the capturing of a French paper, the *Journal*. However, these activities were being followed by both the British and American Secret Services, who passed on their information to Paris, where Clemenceau was now Premier.[76] Bolo was found guilty by a court martial, and in April 1918, elegantly clad in a new suit and white gloves, the amiable confidence trickster went out to face the firing squad at Vincennes.[77]

This dramatic news story was naturally followed with great interest on the other side of the Channel, not least by the Radical Right, who believed that there were 'Bolo Pashas' at work in Britain seeking to undermine national morale. Pemberton Billing was especially excited. His own pet theory was that Cecil Spring-Rice, the former British Ambassador at Washington, who had died suddenly and unexpectedly in February, had been murdered because he had had a part in the events leading to the arrest of Bolo and Caillaux, and, what is more, because he knew more than was good for him about many similar figures at large in British society. The Government's contemptuous dismissal of

[75] Watt, R. M., *Dare Call It Treason* (London, 1964), p. 121.

[76] The messages which Bolo had sent to Bernsdorff had been intercepted and decoded by the naval intelligence centre, Room 40. Its director, Admiral Hall, did not wish to pass on the messages directly to the French Government for fear of compromising the secrets of his organization, so instead they were transmitted to an official in the State Department at Washington, whence they were sent to Paris (Beesly, P., *Room 40: British Naval Intelligence 1914–18* (London, 1982), pp. 242–3).

[77] On the Treason Trials, see Watt, *Dare Call It Treason*; Adam, G., *Treason and Tragedy: French War Trials* (London, 1929). There is also some intriguing material in Fraser, P., *Lord Esher* (London, 1973), p. 458 n. 46).

this theory simply confirmed Billing in his belief that there was a sinister official plot to conceal the truth.[78]

Others too shared Billing's suspicion that 'enemy influences' might be operating in Fleet Street. After all, Lloyd George himself had urged his fellow countrymen to 'Beware of Boloism'. Ellis Powell and Gwynne, for example, were soon frightening themselves with the thought that some mysterious person, offended by the fearless patriotism of their respective papers, was out to silence them.[79] Rather illogically, perhaps, these fears became entangled with anxieties, quite widespread in early 1918, about the over-close relationship between the Prime Minister and the Press Lords, Beaverbrook and Northcliffe. Thus, in a rambling speech in Parliament on 12 February 1918, Billing denounced what he called the Government's attempt to run the country in alliance with Fleet Street, and asked some pointed questions about Beaverbrook's wartime meetings in Switzerland with representatives of the Deutsche Bank and other German banking concerns.[80] Was Billing insinuating that Beaverbrook was the 'British Bolo'?[81] Perhaps he was. But even more startling was his claim: 'There are many in this country in high positions being blackmailed by the German secret service. One of these days I propose to bring proof in this House to bear on that question.'[82]

As is generally known, Billing's startling revelations were made, not in Parliament, but in the law courts.[83] The famous Pemberton Billing Trial has often been described, but usually out of context. It must be remembered that this trial, which opened in late May 1918, took place at a time when the French treason trials were still fresh in most people's minds and when xenophobes were eagerly searching, though in a mood of some perplexity, for a Bolo to identify, denounce, and shoot.[84]

In the Pemberton Billing Trial rabid patriotism, Germanophobia, and scandalmongering combined to produce a highly potent brew. These were the standard ingredients of all Radical Right effusions at this time. But Billing supplied an extra ingredient, which the National Party, for example, would not have touched—sexual innuendo. To be

---

[78] *Parl. Deb.*, 5th ser., ciii. 622–3, 888–9 (19, 21 Feb. 1918).

[79] For Powell's fears, see letters from Powell to Gwynne in Gwynne papers (box 1).

[80] *Parl. Deb.*, 5th ser., ciii. 75–81 (12 Feb. 1918). Billing also asked some hostile questions about why Reading had been sent to the United States (ibid. 79–81).

[81] In April 1918 Maxse was complaining that the Prime Minister 'cannot bear an honest man, preferring Bolobrooks and such like crooks' (Maxse to Northcliffe, 15 Apr. 1918, Maxse papers, vol. 475, T256).   [82] *Parl. Deb.*, 5th ser., ciii. 79 (12 Feb. 1918).

[83] For an account of the trial, See Dean, J., *Hatred, Ridicule or Contempt: A Book of Libel Cases* (London, 1953), Ch. 1; Hyde, H. M., *Their Good Names: Twelve Cases of Libel and Slander with Some Introductory Reflections on the Law* (London, 1970), Ch. 7.

[84] *Vigilante's* notorious article, sparking off the libel case, was immediately followed by an item entitled 'Margot and The Snipers', in which it was claimed that Mrs Asquith 'aspires to the same position in English public life as Madame Caillaux holds in France' (16 Feb. 1918).

precise, it was not Billing himself, but his close associate, Captain Spencer, an army officer probably suffering from some kind of mental derangement, who penned the original indictment. According to Spencer, German agents had been engaged for years in promoting 'unnatural vice' in British society, and they had also compiled a 'Black Book' in which were listed the names of 47,000 English perverts, men and women, all of whom were consequently vulnerable to German blackmail.[85] Spencer's article was so absurd that it might well have been ignored, but for the fact that the dancer, Maud Allan, who had recently taken part in a private performance of *Salomé*, filed a libel suit against Billing over a short follow-up paragraph ('The Cult of the Clitoris') which clearly implied that she was a Lesbian.[86]

When the Trial was held in May and June 1918 Billing conducted his own defence. He did so by calling carefully selected witnesses, who proceeded to testify to the corrupting influence of *Salomé* and also to cast aspersions on various prominent figures in British public life. Mr Justice Darling, whose weak handling of the case was widely criticized, eventually ruled that the whole issue of the 'Black Book' was irrelevant, but not before Billing's witnesses had made outrageous attacks, at some length, on Mr and Mrs Asquith, Haldane, Rennell Rodd (Britain's Ambassador at Rome), and Mr Justice Darling himself; it was alleged that all these celebrities figured in the pages of the mysterious document. None of those libelled had an opportunity of answering back.

The Trial itself can logically be divided into three sections: the first concerns Miss Allan and *Salomé*, the second the role of Grein, the impressario responsible for the theatrical production, and the third revolves around the 'Black Book' and the supposed 'weaknesses' of prominent politicians. The first issue can be disposed of quickly. Billing soon withdrew any suggestion that he thought Miss Allan to be a Lesbian, but he continued to argue that *Salomé* was an indecent play 'calculated to deprave and debauch and to do more harm to all who saw it than even the German Army itself'.[87] Indeed, there were moments when it seemed as though the Oscar Wilde Trial was being re-run, especially when Lord Alfred Douglas entered the witness box to vilify Wilde's life and work. Other witnesses speculated on the effect which *Salomé* might have on performers and audiences. Among them was a person with whom we are already familiar, the Jesuit priest, Father Bernard Vaughan, who combined condemnation of the play (which he had never read or seen) with dark comments about the prevalence of sexual perversion amongst 'the highest classes', which it was his life's mission to try to stop.[88]

[85] *Imperialist*, 26 Jan. 1918.   [86] *Vigilante*, 16 Feb. 1918.
[87] *The Times*, 4 June 1918.
[88] Ibid., 3 June 1918. For Father Vaughan, see above, p. 23.

There is a sense, then, in which the Pemberton Billing Trial afforded an opportunity to exact revenge retrospectively on the Edwardian 'bad smart set' and on its hedonistic plutocrats. This might explain such otherwise bizarre aspects of the case as the denunciation of Mrs Keppel, Edward VII's former mistress, who was portrayed as a German spy. Nor was the introduction of the Asquiths' name into the affair simply a sign of disapproval of their attitude to the War. Early in his premiership, in June 1908, Asquith had displeased the staider kind of Liberal by inviting Miss Allan to one of his garden parties. Such episodes were recalled by an anonymous letter writer, who said that Maud Allan's 'intimacy with the then Prime Minister was talked of with scorn that a man at the head of our Government should associate with such people'.[89] It was also well known that the Asquiths had been on friendly terms with the homosexual, 'Robbie' Ross, Oscar Wilde's literary executor.[90]

What Billing was doing in the spring of 1918 was to play upon all these resentments and prejudices. *The Times* recognized this aspect of the case. In its leader comment it suggested that the jury's verdict of 'not guilty' probably signified 'an honest British repugnance for the whole *Salomé* business'. But, said the paper, it was also an expression of disapproval of the past carryings-on of fashionable Society. 'There has unquestionably been far too much excuse in the past for the suggestions of a lax moral outlook in high places', warned *The Times*, and it called upon all public men and women to remember 'that their responsibilities are not ended with their public functions'.[91]

The second issue, Grein's involvement in the affair, also aroused disquiet. J. T. Grein was the drama critic of the *Sunday Times*, but his main living was earned as the manager of a Batavian mercantile house which had originally been founded by two Germans. Grein was a Dutch Jew, but his brother had been expelled from France because he was thought to be pro-German. Indeed, J. T. Grein himself had been

---

[89] Anon. ('A.N.D.') to Beaverbrook, n.d. (HLRO, Beaverbrook papers, E/3/12). This informant insisted that Miss Allan was 'a female spy well versed in Lesbos'. He also had much to say about the prevalence of homosexuality within the acting profession, of which he was a member.

[90] Ross was given the post of Assessor of Pictorial Valuations to the Board of Trade. Douglas's charge that Ross was a 'bugger and blackmailer' and a corrupter of young boys led Ross to sue him for libel. The jury was unable to reach a decision when the case was tried in November 1914. Asquith was one of those who later signed a public testimonial to Ross. Thereupon Douglas started sending Asquith a series of abusive letters. Privately he talked of 'a pro-Sodomite Prime Minister' (Douglas to Arnold White, 27 Dec. 1915, National Maritime Museum, Arnold White papers, vol. 134).

Incidentally, Arnold White published an article in the *Daily Express* as early as 27 Dec. 1915 about the spread of homosexuality within the British army and navy: 'the vices of Berlin', he wrote, have been 'successfully exported and are now domiciled in the great cities of the British Empire.' Billing and his associates, therefore, were certainly not the first to make a connection between homosexuality and sinister German influences.

[91] *The Times*, 5 June 1918: editorial, 'A Scandalous Trial'.

under surveillance by both the City of London Police and MI5, and his firm had at one time been suspected of trading with the enemy, though this charge could not be substantiated.[92] Given his background, it is not surprising that Grein should have received rough treatment during the Trial.

Yet despite the strong reservations felt by the MI5 officers,[93] this seemingly suspicious character had been planning to take a theatrical company, including Miss Allan, to Holland, where *Salomé* and other plays were to be performed before the British POWs interned there. Moreover, there were grounds for believing that the tour was being sponsored by the Ministry of Information, whose chief, Beaverbrook, was already an object of deep suspicion to Pemberton Billing and his circle. In fact, the originator of the project was a part-time official, Robert Donald, and in his discussions with Grein no mention had actually been made of including *Salomé* in the repertory. Beaverbrook himself must have been entirely ignorant of the whole transaction. Unfortunately, despite being told by Donald that the prospective tour must not be publicly associated with the Ministry, Grein had rushed off and told the press that he had been appointed Director of Theatrical Propaganda in Neutral Countries! Moreover, he had then gone about London carrying an attaché case marked 'Ministry of Information'! When Basil Thomson, head of the Special Branch, interviewed him, he gave the lame explanation 'that if he lost the attaché case it would be more likely to be returned to him'.[94]

On learning of these developments, Beaverbrook quickly released a statement in which he denied that he had had any dealings with Grein, pointed out that Grein was not an employee of his Ministry, and categorically dissociated himself from the theatrical tour of Holland.[95] But Billing and others were not likely to be convinced by such disclaimers. And part of the Trial was given over to Billing's attempt to get Grein to admit that he had been officially chosen 'to represent British ideals in neutral countries'. Meanwhile, Beaverbrook was being subjected to some totally undeserved abuse for his alleged responsibility for the activities of Grein and Miss Allan. 'Are you a fool or a knave?', asked an anonymous actor who wrote to him at this time.

Why can't you find an English man for Propaganda work and not this Grein. Has he some power over you by heaven but these questions will have to be answered one day and soon. The thanks of the nation are due to Billing for exposing this infamy. . . . Believe me some of you will have to account for *our* money spent on these people.[96]

[92] Beaverbrook papers, E/3/12.
[93] H. G. Spencer to John Baird, 8 Mar. 1918 (ibid.).
[94] Thomson to Major Montague, 11 Apr. 1918 (ibid.).
[95] *The Times*, 18 Apr. 1918.
[96] Anon. to Beaverbrook, n.d. (Beaverbrook papers, E/3/12).

On the third issue, that of British public notables and the 'Black Book', Billing again seems to have touched a sensitive nerve. Of course, the two key witnesses who claimed to have seen this incriminating document, Captain Spencer and Mrs Villiers-Stuart, could have deceived no one of any intelligence or judgement. But what is interesting are the incidental accusations and comments which they chose to throw out. A. J. P. Taylor has commented on the significance of the fact that whereas the names of the Asquiths and of Haldane were said to be in the 'Black Book', Lloyd George's was not.[97] In fact, Spencer explicitly said that German 'influence' in government circles had now largely ceased, and, asked when this had happened, he replied: 'When Mr Lloyd George came into office. Previously, the party funds were filled from German pockets.' Spencer added that the Prime Minister was 'doing his best' to end this state of affairs, 'but he has a hard job.' By contrast, 'the appointments made by the old Liberal party machine were those of persons who are not very rigorous in the prosecution of the war.'[98] He also claimed that there had been 'a clique trying to restore Asquith and to make a German peace last September'.[99] It was presumably such insinuations as these that led a furious Margot Asquith to the erroneous conclusion that behind Pemberton Billing stood the figures of Lloyd George and Beaverbrook.[100] Billing, of course, denied the charge: 'What was behind him was the clean heart of the British people', he remarked.[101]

Another interesting feature of the Trial which is often missed is that the 47,000 names in the 'Black Book' were not *all* those of sexual perverts, but, as Justice Darling put it, also included people suffering from such moral failings as 'weaknesses for drink, for decoration or for social distinction'.[102] Under which category the Asquiths and Haldane were supposed to come was left for the public to decide, but clearly Billing and his associates wanted to broaden their attacks so as to bring in social climbers and 'title cadgers'—a common preoccupation of the Radical Right. Another theme was that while most politicians, Lloyd George perhaps excepted, were corrupt, Billing and his friends had a near-monopoly of honesty and patriotism. Thus Spencer at one point referred to Arnold White as a gentleman who had been fighting German influence in England for many years. 'In what capacity?', he was asked. 'As a public-spirited Englishman. One of the few', Spencer

[97] Taylor, A. J. P., *English History 1914–1945* (Oxford 1965), p. 103.
[98] *The Times*, 1 June 1918.   [99] Ibid., 31 May 1918.
[100] See Koss, S., *Asquith* (London, 1976), p. 234. According to her stepdaughter, Cynthia, 'Margot . . . attributes the whole thing to a political anti-Asquith plot—to make it impossible for him ever to return to office' (Asquith, Cynthia, *Diaries, 1915–1918* (London, 1968), p. 445: diary entry, 2 June 1918).
[101] *The Times*, 17 June 1918. Billing also observed: 'the names of Mr Bottomley, Lord Northcliffe, and Mr Lloyd George had been mentioned. They had nothing whatever to do with it. . .'.
[102] Ibid., 4 June 1918. This was Darling's reading of the article.

replied. 'He does not hold any official position?' 'No, that is why.'[103]

All these themes came together in Billing's final address to the court, in which he proudly announced himself as a libeller. 'I have libelled public men for the last two and a half years in the public Press, on public platforms, and in the House of Commons', he said. Amongst these libels had been his persistent call to the Lord Chief Justice to 'answer in the criminal dock to the Marconi scandal'. Billing linked these allegations to the operation of the 'Hidden Hand'—'the mysterious influence which seemed to have dogged our steps through the whole conduct of the war, which, after three and a half years of war, kept German banks open in England, which left Germans still uninterned in that Court at that moment, which had paralysed the Air Service of this country and had prevented our raiding Germany'.[104] Here is almost the entire catalogue of xenophobic complaints about corruption and treachery in high places.

Yet Billing, through his demagoguery and buffoonery, had introduced a new element into the politics of scandalmongering. For he had stepped entirely outside the bounds of conventional politics. Ellis Powell's articles can only have reached a small audience, but Billing had libelled the famous and the great in such a way as to secure the rapt attention of the entire nation. It could, perhaps, be argued that inadvertently the Member for Hertford had raised national morale at a difficult point in the War by his wild and often very funny antics. But the political 'Establishment' had some cause for wondering where such irresponsible attacks might lead. There had always been a subversive potential in the quest for greater purity in public life. That potential was now being realized.

This may be why Billing did not get a better press in those political quarters where one might have expected him to have found sympathizers. Perhaps it was not altogether surprising that the *Spectator* should have deplored 'the orgy of slander' which Billing had let loose.[105] But even the *New Witness* showed a certain circumspection; it rejoiced that 'the conspiracy of silence' surrounding the possibility of corruption on the Front Benches had been broken, but it declined to comment on Billing's specific accusations.[106] As for Maxse, he uttered a solemn warning:

We cannot help regretting that this question of German espionage should be perverted into cheap sensationalism, and that the public should be encouraged to believe what is not true—namely, that the State of Denmark is universally rotten. Things are sufficiently bad, but it is grotesque to treat Mr Asquith, e.g.,

[103] Ibid., 1 June 1918. White, whom Billing promised to produce as a witness but who in the event did not materialize, is alleged to have said that the names in the 'Black Book' had now gone up from 47,000 to 53,000!
[104] *The Times*, 4 June 1918.
[105] *Spectator*, 8 June 1918.   [106] *New Witness*, 7 June 1918.

and some of his colleagues as they were dealt with by the defendant and his witnesses. Patriots should be on their guard against playing the game of Defeatists and Pacifists by barking up the wrong tree.[107]

If independent critics of the Government felt in this way, little wonder if the two sets of political leaders should have made serious plans to silence Billing before he caused more mischief. Particularly worrying was the imminence of two by-elections, where the 'Vigilantes' had put up two of the witnesses who had recently appeared in the Trial: the Society's Treasurer, H. H. Beamish, the future libeller of Mond, who was contesting Clapham on 21 June, and Captain Spencer, no less, who was standing for Finsbury, where polling was due in mid-July. Buoyed up by the popular acclaim which had followed his acquittal, Pemberton Billing was also becoming more and more outrageous. On 11 July he was expelled from the Commons when the Speaker refused him leave to move the adjournment of the House on the subject of enemy aliens. Called to order, he yelled, 'I'm not going to sit down when there are a lot of damned Germans running about this country', and had to be forcibly ejected.[108] Billing's accusations against prominent politicians also became more reckless.

What happened during the Finsbury By-Election aroused widespread unease. Faced with a rival jingo candidate, an associate of the Seamen's leader, Havelock Wilson, the 'Vigilantes' embarked on strong-arm tactics. On the eve of polling Billing and a thousand of his supporters broke up their rival's meeting and severely damaged his car and the hall in which he was trying to speak. Then, inflamed by the oration which Billing had delivered from his famous torpedo-shaped motor car, the mob began to beat up anybody they could find who looked as though he might be foreign or of military age. The police were temporarily overwhelmed until outside reinforcements arrived.[109] The 'Vigilantes' were coming to pose a very real threat to public order.

A counter-attack was launched. Particularly subtle was the action of the Liberal newspaper, the *Daily Chronicle*, which published a series of short articles, starting in July, which alleged that Billing's own wife was a German! Mrs Pemberton Billing angrily replied that her father was Swiss and her mother Irish, and offered to go willingly into internment if it could be shown that she had a drop of German blood in her veins. The *Daily Chronicle* took up the offer and invited her to start packing her bags, since her father's birth certificate clearly showed him to be a Prussian, and he had never subsequently taken out naturalization papers.[110] The file which the *Chronicle* had built up on Billing was handed over to Gulland, the Asquithian Whip, and in June

[107] *National Review*, lxxi (1918), 560.
[108] *The Times*, 2 July 1918.
[109] Ibid., 16 July 1918.
[110] *Daily Chronicle*, 8–18 July 1918.

and July 1918 Asquith and his circle kept a close watch on the 'Vigilantes'—an ironic reversal of roles.[111]

On 4 June Inspector Basil Thomson noted in his diary:

The Pemberton Billing trial ended today in an acquittal amid acclamations both inside and outside the Court. In fact, every one concerned appeared to have been either insane or to have behaved as if he were. One might treat the case with contempt were it not for its pernicious influence throughout this and neutral countries. The German wireless has already been commenting upon it in the tone one would expect.[112]

Those with a suspicious mind must almost have been tempted to wonder whether Billing himself might not be the British Bolo and the whole trial some sinister manifestation of the 'Hidden Hand'. Thomson, who was in touch with Gulland, among others, certainly seems to have decided that Billing would have to be destroyed.[113] Towards the end of June he wrote to the Prime Minister's Private Secretary, 'Bronco Bill' Sutherland, giving the interesting information that Billing, 'the author of a "purity campaign", was living during the recent trial in illicit relations with one of his chief witnesses [i.e. Mrs Villiers-Stuart], who, by the way, has been·charged with bigamy'.[114]

A few weeks later the assiduous detective forwarded to Bonar Law a statement which he had persuaded Mrs Villiers-Stuart to sign. In it she claimed that Billing had used the impending bigamy case to blackmail her into giving false evidence at the recent trial, and that Captain Spencer had also been put under pressure to perjure himself. When she had threatened Billing with exposure, he had allegedly replied, 'If you do I shall stop at nothing you know.' Mrs Villiers-Stuart also claimed to have written to the Prime Minister, shortly before the Finsbury By-Election, informing him that Billing had compiled a list of factory workmen who had signed an undertaking to come out on strike if Billing asked them to do so.[115] Thomson hoped that Mrs Villiers-Stuart would repeat these remarks when she came to enter the dock in her bigamy trial,[116] but in the event she did not do so.[117]

Meanwhile even the Cabinet was getting drawn into the affair. On 6 June, Lord Curzon

---

[111] See material in Asquith papers (Bodleian, vol. 148, fos. 65–70).

[112] Thomson's diary, 24 June 1918, in Thomson, B., *The Scene Changes* (London, 1939), pp. 373–4.

[113] Gulland had earlier asked Thomson for help in getting information about Billing (Gulland to Thomson, 29 June 1918, Asquith papers, vol. 148, fo. 67).

[114] Hankey's diary, 22 June 1918, in Roskill, Stephen, *Hankey: Man of Secrets*, i. *1877–1918* (London, 1970), p. 566.

[115] Statement by Mrs Villiers-Stuart of 15 July, forwarded by Basil Thomson, with covering note, 16 July 1918 (Bonar Law papers, 85/C/28).   [116] Ibid.

[117] *The Times*, 17 Sept. 1918. Mrs Villiers-Stuart 'was originally employed by Maud Allan as a detective to find out what Billing knew and he had won her over as a weapon on his side' (Cynthia Asquith's diary, 6 June 1918, in Asquith, C., *Diaries, 1915–1918*, p. 448).

drew the attention of the War Cabinet to the publication in the press of the evidence taken in the Pemberton Billing libel action and stated that, in his opinion, such publication was doing more harm than anything that had appeared in this connection for many years. Opportunity was being taken to attack every section of society, and the social effect must inevitably be bad. Insinuations and accusations were being made against public men without a shred of foundation.

But the Lord Chancellor pointed out that Curzon's call for censorship could not be enforced. Lord Justice Darling, he believed, had asked the press not to publish some of the evidence—clearly to no avail. The only alternative would have been to hold the case *in camera*; but as Lord Cave observed, 'the suspicion and talk which would have arisen outside the Court, relative to what had been suppressed, would have been endless.'[118] A week later Bonar Law reported back to the Cabinet the Law Officers' view that there was nothing the Government could do, short of setting up a Commission of Enquiry, which no sensible person would contemplate doing. The Cabinet did, it is true, ask Bonar Law to pursue the idea of prosecuting some of the witnesses for perjury, but the Attorney-General, F. E. Smith, must have sent a discouraging reply, since nothing of the kind was attempted.[119]

By late 1918 public interest in Pemberton Billing declined. The *Vigilante* complained of a press boycott,[120] and in February 1919 Billing wound up his paper, saying that he felt unable to go on incurring such heavy financial liabilities.[121] It is true that the 'people's tribune' was still a Member of Parliament, since his Hertford constituents had returned him as an 'Independent' in the 1918 General Election, the Coalition leaders having 'honoured' him by declining to run a couponed candidate of their own.[122] But it needed another world war to bring Billing back into the national prominence he had briefly enjoyed in the summer of 1918.

Northcliffe's Suspicions

Yet belief in the existence of the 'Hidden Hand' was still strong in late 1918. So much is evident from the conduct of Lord Northcliffe. The Pemberton Billing Trial had been viewed with mixed feelings by the great press lord. Soon after it had started, he wrote to Marlowe, editor of the *Daily Mail*, expressing the view that public interest in this

[118] War Cabinet minute, 4 June 1918 (Cab. 23/6, item 17).

[119] Ibid., 10 June 1918 (Cab. 23/6, item 17). In early June Bonar Law gave a colleague to understand that the question of setting up a commission of judges to enquire into the 'Black Book' charges was being considered (Ramsden (ed.), *Real Old Tory Politics*, p. 106).

[120] *Vigilant*, 27 June 1918.   [121] Ibid., 8 Feb. 1919.

[122] An 'honour' he shared with Asquith! The result was: Billing (Ind.) 9628; E. B. Barnard (Nat. Party) 7158; C. Harding (Lab.) 1679.

'horrible business' was intense both in London and the country.[123] Two days later Northcliffe told Dawson that he wanted to discuss with him over the telephone what line *The Times* should take on the matter: 'if the Jury reflect the public opinion of the few people whom I have seen here in Gloucestershire', he wrote, 'they will not convict him, and the man, who is a fanatic, will continue his publications.'[124]

Yet though distrusting Billing, Northcliffe took very seriously the political position which Billing represented, and so he was furious with Dawson for writing a leader which laughed at Spencer's performance in the Finsbury By-Election: 'The facts are that a rowdy, who was opposed by both political associations and had no means of tracing removals, gets half as many votes as the man who wins, and only when the man has had to eat his words. . . . If you will enquire in Downing Street, you will discover how they regard the Election.'[125]

Such disagreements played a part in the growing estrangement between Northcliffe and Dawson which was to lead to the latter's resignation as editor in February 1919. Essentially, Northcliffe feared that Dawson was turning *The Times* into a government organ, just when he himself was on bad terms with Lloyd George and wanted to adopt a critical view of his Ministry.

Northcliffe's hostility to the Coalition took the form of pursuing some of Billing's lines of argument, albeit in a more 'respectable' way. Thus in late July he prompted the *Daily Mail* to attack the proviso that the Aliens Advisory Committee should work behind closed doors by offering them the following editorial:

The heart of every uninterned Hun must have leapt for joy when he read the fatal dictum that the work of these odious people was to be investigated in secret. . . . Rightly or wrongly, our people believe that the lives of our soldiers and sailors are now being sold. The Lord Chancellor, whose knowledge of modern Germany is particularly slight, went out of his way to say that he did not believe in the Hidden Hand. Ninety per cent of the people disagree with Lord Finlay in this remark. There are so many mysterious happenings—all favourable to the enemy—which have taken place in the last four years: there are so many Germans in high places in this country, that the coincidence of the presence of the Germans and the mysterious happenings is one that is obvious to any person of average intelligence.

Northcliffe posed a series of questions: 'Who warns the Hun submarine commander of the departure of certain ships? Who keeps Berlin informed by means of easily camouflaged telegrams from Holland and Sweden, or across the Atlantic? Who spreads amazing rumours of disasters? How many uninterned Huns are there really in this

[123] Northcliffe to Marlowe or Beattie (copy), 2 June 1918 (BL, Northcliffe papers, Add. MS 62,199). See also Pound and Harmsworth, p. 642.
[124] Northcliffe to Dawson (copy), 4 June 1918 (Northcliffe papers, Add. MS 62,245).
[125] Northcliffe to Dawson (copy), 17 July 1918 (ibid.).

country?' Lloyd George, he threatened, would 'find himself heavily handicapped in the forthcoming General Election' unless he quickly changed his views.[126]

Moreover, in ways with which we are now familiar, Northcliffe was able to convince himself that there was à sinister explanation for the Prime Minister's unbelievable softness towards the enemy in the country's midst:

Accountants state that the Deutsche Bank in London holds cheques paid to prominent English people on account of profitable sales of German securities up to the time of the War. Other accountants who are endeavouring to wind up German companies have told me that they have come to an impasse—that somebody stops or delays the proceedings.[127]

These suspicions were reinforced in November 1918 when the Prime Minister seemed to be reluctant to follow the French lead in making swingeing reparations demands on the Germans. Northcliffe privately hazarded the view that Lloyd George

is acting . . . at the instance of friends of people like Schröder, who are acting for the letting loose of interned Germans and who, like every other German financier [sic], is trying to prevent Germany having to pay for the war. I do not believe that Lloyd George is a free agent in this matter and I am determined to bring pressure to bear. . . . If we could get at the secrets of the Coalition cash box, we could get a good insight into the activities of the Germans.[128]

This outburst from Northcliffe shows clearly enough that the mere defeat of the Central Powers was not going to end the xenophobia and the hysterical scandalmongering which had brought Pemberton Billing his fleeting moment of glory. But before examining the feverish politics of the 1919–22 period, we must first turn our attention to other aspects of the wartime quest for corruption in high places. We have seen that the Radical Right was obsessed with the existence of 'notabilities' who had been bribed or blackmailed into treasonable behaviour. But they also believed that there were others who had been led by their own *greed* into playing Germany's game. And this takes us on to the theme of wartime profiteering.

---

[126] Enclosure in letter to Marlowe, 28 July 1918 (ibid, Add. MS 62,199). A slightly altered version of this outburst appeared as a leader in the *Daily Mail* on 29 July 1918.
[127] Northcliffe to Dawson (copy), 5 July 1918 (Northcliffe papers, Add. MS 62,245).
[128] Northcliffe to Dawson (copy), 30 Nov. 1918 (ibid.).

12
Profiteering

Trading with the enemy

ALTHOUGH it is convenient to discuss profiteering in a separate chapter from the one which concentrates on the hunt for corruption and treachery in high places, the distinction is not easy to draw and it would have made little sense to contemporary scandalmongers like Page Croft and Pemberton Billing, who moved effortlessly from one subject to the other. For who were profiteers if not antisocial people who had put their own financial advantage before the good of the community, and how in times of war could this not be of assistance to the enemy?

There was one area of activity in particular where greed and treachery were inextricably intertwined, and that was trading with the Central Powers. Royal Proclamations had been issued on 5 August and 9 September 1914 which made commercial contact with the enemy a criminal offence.[1] It was part of the 'patriotic' case against Sir Edgar Speyer that he had only reluctantly complied with these Proclamations by resigning his partnership in the American branch of the family firm, run by his brother James, which continued to trade with Frankfurt.[2] Even Cassel, anxious to display his patriotism, came under suspicion of having a stake in Swedish iron ore companies which were supplying the Germans with war materials.[3] In 1916 the Government tightened up its controls over Anglo-German commercial relations by passing the 'Trading With The Enemy Act', but it needed a special committee to advise the Board of Trade about the large number of 'hard cases' and ambiguous situations revealed by attempts to enforce this legislation.[4]

How easily a businessman through carelessness could find himself facing the risk of prosecution was revealed in the early stages of the War by the so-called Jacks Case, which has some importance, if only because it indirectly affected Bonar Law. In August 1914 the firm of William Jacks & Co., in which Bonar Law had once been an active partner and on whose Board his brother, John Law, still served, authorized the delivery of some 7,500 tons of iron ore to certain

---

[1] The Government gave statutory backing to these Proclamations with the Trading With The Enemy Acts of Sept. and Nov. 1914.

[2] Brock (eds.), *Letters to Venetia Stanley*, p. 293.

[3] See e.g. Leverton Harris's attempts to persuade Maxse that his suspicions of Cassel were groundless (West Sussex Record Office, Maxse papers, vol. 471, fos. 307–8: Harris to Maxse, 2 Sept. 1915).

[4] Report to President of the Board of Trade by Committee Appointed by Board of Trade on Matters arising under the Trading with the Enemy Act 1916, 1918, Cd. 9059.

German firms, one of them Krupps. The Censor intercepted the telegrams recording these transactions and in the summer of 1915 the Lord Advocate's Department decided to prosecute the firm. Two of the patners were found guilty, although they seem to have acted as they did in the mistaken belief that a business deal concluded before the Proclamation of 5 August was exempt from its provisions. In the end John Law himself was not prosecuted. But the whole affair greatly upset Bonar Law, who knew the gaoled businessmen well; he even tried at one stage to have the prosecution stopped—something which would undoubtedly have caused a storm of criticism if news of it had leaked.

Even as things stood, the connection between the Conservative Leader and a business company discovered to be trading with the enemy gave rise to scurrilous rumours. On 6 May 1915 *Justice* carried a letter from Hyndman maliciously implying that Bonar Law was as implicated in the affair as his brother. In fact, the Conservative Leader's involvement was confined to an arrangement whereby William Jacks & Co. acted as his banker, paying him a fixed rate of interest on the surplus cash which he deposited with them. Nevertheless, so shaken was Bonar Law by the attack on him that he actually prepared a statement for the Commons in which he promised to retire from public life should anything be proved that reflected on his brother's honour. In the event, Bonar Law thought better of making this reckless statement, and the only further public attack that he had to endure was a hostile question in the House from an Irish MP, Laurence Ginnell. But as others have observed, it seems unlikely that Bonar Law would have been treated so indulgently had he happened to be a Radical–Liberal politician.[5]

What about other aspects of profiteering? In December 1914 Walter Long was worried about 'the risk of scoundrels imposing upon the War Office and making wholly illegitimate profits out of war supplies . . .'.[6] Like other patriots, Long was appalled at the thought that, while some were making the supreme sacrifice in France and Flanders, others were living safe lives at home and acquiring fortunes at their country's expense. Similar feelings of indignation found expression in working-class communities. After the labour disturbances of May 1917 the Government set up a Commission of Enquiry. The regional commissioner for Scotland noted in his report that the chief cause of unrest was 'what the worker calls "profiteering", by which he means the amassing, by a few people, of abnormal wealth, out of the necessities of the country. The actual increase of the cost of living does not appear to be so important a factor in the workers' mind as the belief that

[5] Blake, *Bonar Law*, pp. 257–60; *Justice*, 1 July 1915: 'Mr Bonar Law and "Limited Liability"'; *Parl. Deb.*, 5th ser., lxxii. 1332–3 (24 June 1915).
[6] Long to Gwynne, 2 Dec. 1914 (Bodleian, Gwynne papers, Vol. 20).

"profiteering" exists.[7] The other seven regional commissioners made very similar comments.

'Profiteering' was easy to denounce, but it was more difficult to define. In practice it tended to involve two somewhat different, though related, issues: the involvement of businessmen in the running of the Departments of State, and the level of profit earned by the contractors who supplied the Government with munitions of war and other essential goods and services.

Businessmen in Government

Initially the Asquith Administration had attempted to keep a distance from the business community in the belief that market forces should be allowed full rein. This 'Business as Usual' attitude was maintained until political pressures and an angry public opinion forced modifications of policy. In retrospect, it is easy to argue that, from the very outset, the Government should have adopted a more interventionist role. But the fact remains that, to quote E. M. H. Lloyd, 'the economic system could not be transformed by a stroke of the pen' and 'elaborate preparation on the ground was necessary and various novel expedients in centralization and co-ordination had to be put into force' before the Government could assume effective control. Apart from anything else, the small pre-war Civil Service lacked the requisite experience and technical knowledge necessary for the implementation of 'war socialism'.[8]

In fact, it was this very deficiency which drove certain patriotic businessmen into volunteering their services to the Government. For example, George Macaulay Booth, from the famous Liverpool shipping line, had an interview with Asquith in late 1914, in which he offered to help the War Office get some of the supplies it urgently needed by putting prominent businessmen of his acquaintance in contact with the Director of Army Contracts. To his consternation Asquith replied that 'he didn't like the idea of introducing industrialists to such a position' and that 'his Government could not afford another Marconi scandal.' Booth said 'that the people he had mentioned, including himself, were not so fortunate as the Government—in their walk of life they could not afford even one scandal.'[9] Asquith apologized for his seeming discourtesy, but clearly he was not won over by Booth's appeal.

Asquith's premonition that it might prove difficult to establish a

[7] Cd. 8669, para. 4.
[8] Lloyd, E. M. H., *Experiments in State Control: At the War Office and Ministry of Food* (Oxford, 1924), p. 323.
[9] Crow, D., *A Man of Push and Go: The Life of George Macaulay Booth* (London, 1965), p. 69.

trouble-free arrangement between the Whitehall Departments and businessmen drafted in to government service was to be vindicated only a few weeks later with the outbreak of the so-called Meyer Scandal. In late 1914 the War Office faced the urgent task of building large numbers of huts that could accommodate the new recruits during the coming winter. It turned for help to the Office of Works, which promptly appointed a certain Montague Meyer as the Government's sole timber-purchasing agent, offering him a commission of 2½ per cent on the net value of the timber bought. The Timber Trade Federation later passed a resolution protesting at this appointment of a businessman who, they alleged, had had little prior experience of this kind of trade. They became even more indignant when the Government justified the virtual bypassing of the Federation's membership with the argument that it wanted to circumvent the operation of a 'timber ring'.

Perhaps, however, there would never have been much discussion of the affair in Parliament, had not the press seized upon Meyer's foreign-sounding name. On 11 February 1915 Dalziel asked why no British firms had been given the work.[10] Ministers eventually persuaded the most suspicious of MPs that Meyer was in no sense of the word an alien and that his family had been English for two or three generations, though some anti-Semitic sniping against Meyer continued.[11] But Dalziel and other MPs continued to criticize a contract which they thought to be a scandalously generous one. J. H. Thomas, the Labour politician, spoke of the resentment felt by manual workers over anyone making large profits out of the nation's terrible sacrifices,[12] and Handel Booth, a prime mover in the agitation, said that he had talked to trade unionists who could not 'get it out of their heads that there has been some corruption'.[13] The affair, it was claimed, was provoking labour unrest: 'How can you expect men, when prices of food are going up, to be content when they hear that Mr Montague Meyer is making thousands upon thousands of pounds by the mere purchase of timber?'[14]

Two full debates on the subject were held in the Commons. Some MPs, Bonar Law included, wondered out loud whether so much time should have been devoted, at a crucial stage of the War, to discussion of the allocation of a single contract.[15] But the issues ventilated in these debates were difficult and important ones. Should businessmen be allowed to combine government work with their own affairs? Was it wise to accept the services of businessmen who offered to help the Government gratis? Did the Meyer Affair illustrate a want of 'business

---

[10] *Parl. Deb.*, 5th ser., lxix. 718.
[11] *Parl. Deb.*, 5th ser., lxxi. 139 (15 Apr. 1915).
[12] Ibid. lxx. 1054 (4 Mar. 1915).
[13] Ibid. 509 (25 Feb. 1915). Booth said this was also the view of the Conservatives and Liberals he had met.
[14] Ibid. 510.   [15] Ibid. 1065–8 (4 Mar. 1915).

methods' on the part of the Government, in which case the remedy would presumably be a closer relationship between Whitehall and the business community? Or should the two sides keep one another at arm's length? Moreover, was the Meyer contract that exceptional? The *Daily Chronicle*, which harried the Office of Works relentlessly over this affair, suspected that it was not: 'What everybody sees is, that though Mr Meyer's spoils amount intrinsically to the merest drop in the ocean of war expenditure, his is just the single case which has happened to come out.'[16] And when Handel Booth announced his interesting discovery that one of Meyer's partners was an official in the Office of Works, the Government's critics, mainly jingo Liberal backbenchers, were convinced that they had unearthed a major scandal.[17]

A prudent politician might have deduced from this controversy that governments should revert to their traditional practice of reducing contacts with businessmen to a bare minimum. This, however, was not the strategy pursued by Lloyd George when he became Minister of Munitions in May 1915. In this newly created Department the dividing line between government officials and businessmen was deliberately blurred. As Lloyd George later observed, 'the Ministry of Munitions was from first to last a business-man organisation', which aimed at liberating the munitions industry from military direction and the restrictions of established official routine and in which a key role was played by prominent businessmen familiar with industrial problems.[18] Large firms lent over ninety directors and managers to the Ministry, many of whom were kept on their company's payroll. Gun production, for example, came under the control of representatives of firms like Armstrongs, Vickers, and John Brown, acting in the name of the Ministry.[19] Christopher Wrigley has shown that this gave rise to the problem of divided loyalties. Vincent Caillard of Vickers was worried about the position achieved within the Ministry by the rival firm of Armstrongs. And there was a small scandal when Christopher Addison, the Parliamentary Under-Secretary, discovered Colonel Wright, the Controller of Iron and Steel Production, trying to get better terms from the Ministry for the company from which he had been seconded, Port Talbot Steel Company Ltd. Lloyd George also had to prevent some businessmen turned civil servants from sending out business circulars from their ministry offices.[20] Those who had warned during the Meyer

---

[16] *Daily Chronicle*, 5 Mar. 1915.

[17] *Parl. Deb.*, 5th ser., lxxi. 92 (15 Apr. 1915).

[18] Lloyd George, D., *War Memoirs* (London, 1938 edn.), i. 147.

[19] Hinton, J., *The First Shop Stewards' Movement* (London, 1973), pp. 29–30.

[20] Wrigley, C., 'The Ministry of Munitions: An Innovatory Department', in Burk, K. (ed.), *War and the State: The Transformation of British Government, 1914–1919* (London, 1982), p. 42.

Affair of the dangers of receiving gratuitous help from businessmen[21] were, to a large extent, vindicated by what happened in the Ministry of Munitions, where unpaid officals proved to be much more difficult for the Treasury to control.

Nor were the businessmen brought into Whitehall confined to executive and administrative roles, since, especially after Lloyd George became Prime Minister in December 1916, conspicuously successful entrepreneurs were sometimes promoted to *ministerial* rank. The dizzy ascent of Eric Geddes from a managerial post in a railway company to the office of First Lord of the Admiralty is only the most dramatic example of this development.[22] Joseph Maclay, a prominent Glaswegian shipowner, was made Director of Shipping; Lord Rhondda, formerly D. A. Thomas, the South Wales coal magnate, served as President of the Local Government Board before taking over the Ministry of Food; and Albert Stanley brought his extensive experience of transport undertakings into the Board of Trade, of which he became President.

It may be significant that most of these businessmen-cum-ministers were supporters of Lloyd George. So too were Lord Rothermere, Air Secretary from November 1917 to April 1918, and his predecessor in that office, the one-time 'Radical Plutocrat', Lord Cowdray—though Cowdray resigned in a mood of deep anger against Lloyd George and subsequently put his great wealth at the disposal of the Asquithian Liberals.[23] The high visibility of these powerful businessmen lent substance to the Socialists' belief in a sinister union between private capital and state power, and also contributed to trade union discontent and to suspicions among manual workers that profiteering was rife.

The ambivalent position of the businessman in government was starkly revealed in the Leverton Harris Affair, which has already been touched upon in Chapter 11. Leverton Harris was not strictly speaking a businessman imported directly into ministerial office, since he had been a Unionist MP since 1900, but the various tasks which he performed for the wartime governments all required him to use the knowledge and experience he had gained through work for his family shipping firm, Harris & Dixon. Aware of a possible conflict of interest, Harris had, in fact, written to Bonar Law in December 1916 asking for guidance on what he should do now that he was about to become Under-Secretary at the Ministry of Blockade. He announced that he had already resigned his directorship in the firm and intended giving up his right to become its managing director, but he was worried about

---

[21] *Parl. Deb.*, 5th ser., lxxi. 107–8 (John Simon, 15 Apr. 1915).

[22] Cline, P. K., 'Eric Geddes and the "Experiment" with Businessmen in Government, 1915–1922', in Brown, K. D. (ed.), *Essays in Anti-Labour History* (London, 1974), pp. 74–104.

[23] See Wilson, T., *The Downfall of the Liberal Party 1914–1935* (London, 1966), p. 117.

the retention of his other directorships.[24] Bonar Law, who took a very relaxed view of such matters, curtly replied: 'I do not . . . see any reason why you should give up the Directorships which you speak of.'[25] That still left open the question of Harris's major shareholding in his family business. Later, when his conduct was attacked, he pointed out that a few weeks after joining the Government he had taken steps to dispose of his shares, though the death of a partner had held up the transaction so that the sale was not effected until early in 1918. But Harris insisted that since joining the Ministry of Blockade he had 'taken no share of the profits beyond fixed interest at 5% on the preference share . . . and a nominal and fixed interim dividend at the rate of 10% per an. till September 1917 on the ordinary shares'.[26]

This was very creditable of Leverton Harris, but it did not meet the main criticisms which Page Croft levied against him in the Commons in June 1918. Croft's complaint was that while Harris was serving in the Trade Division of the Admiralty in *1916* (i.e. *before* joining the Ministry of Blockade) he had been instrumental in securing favourable facilities for his family firm, in which he was still the principal shareholder. What had happened was that when Harris & Dixon submitted a request to the Admiralty to be given cable facilities, Harris had assured the Chief Cable Censor, under whom he worked, that these cables were mainly on Government business and that their delay was detrimental to national interests.[27] It was quite untrue, Harris later claimed, that Harris & Dixon had been given any privileges denied to their competitors, and the advice he had given had been inspired by disinterested patriotism. But Croft could not be persuaded that Harris had not used his official position for personal pecuniary advantage. 'The Government must take action in this case', he insisted. 'If we in this House condone what may be small matters . . . there is no hope that you are going to keep the administration in this country on pure lines. . . . We have had a great many vague charges made in recent times, which have been in some cases altogether unwise [presumably a reference to the recent Pemberton Billing Trial]. The result is that when anything of this kind arises, we naturally desire not to discuss it, but we have a duty' to do so.[28]

Attempts by other Ministers to help Harris simply made his position worse. Lloyd George, for example, categorically denied that Harris's family firm was given any particular advantage, but this denial was

---

[24] Harris to Bonar Law, 30 Dec. 1916 (HLRO, Bonar Law papers, 81/1/71).

[25] Law to Harris (copy), 2 Jan. 1917 (ibid. 84/6/32).

[26] Harris to Maxse, 14 Aug. 1918 (Maxse papers, vol. 475, T 313). In this letter, and an earlier one of 3 Aug. (T 299), Harris implored Maxse, with whom he had once had an amicable political relationship, not to attack him so unfairly in the *National Review*, and offered to put all the relevant papers before him, so that he could prove his innocence.

[27] *Parl. Deb.*, 5th ser., cvii. 726–8, 758–87 (24 June 1918).   [28] Ibid. 764.

buried in the middle of one of his most unconvincing kind of
blustering, hectoring speeches, in which he sought sympathy for the
plight of the businessman in politics: 'It is a very difficult matter for
businessmen to give their time to the Government. They cannot
altogether see their business go to grief.'[29] The Prime Minister's line
was immediately endorsed by Asquith, who waxed indignant at the
'gross breach of confidence' shown by the official who had leaked the
information concerning Leverton Harris's affairs—Asquith hoped that
the offender could be brought to book.[30]

That is exactly what the Government then tried to do. The War
Office inserted an advertisement in *The Times*, offering £100 to the
person who could give any information as to the identity of the official
who had divulged the material.[31] Moreover, scarcely had Croft
finished delivering his Commons speech, when the military authorities
raided the premises of the National Party in a vain search for the
offending letter. This enabled Croft to ask whether it was not a
violation of the privilege of a Member of Parliament when an attempt
to expose a public scandal led to 'his offices, or the offices of his
associates, or his private dwelling-house [being] ransacked by soldiers
and other Government agents'.[32]

The Speaker refused to give Croft satisfaction, but his complaints
were echoed by the *National Review*, the *Morning Post*, the *Globe*, and
other papers. Ministers, it was noted, seemed to be quite excessively
concerned over a minor breach of official security, while being quite
indifferent to an act of corruption.[33] Nor did Bonar Law silence the
critics when he told the Commons that Harris had 'done nothing
which might not have been done by any member of the House
including myself'. The *Daily Mail* commented: 'If this can be done
honourably by anyone in the House of Commons, at least we know
where we are and what to expect.'[34] And the eccentric aristocrat, Lord
Cecil Manners, was not slow to draw a connection between the Jacks
Affair and the sense of honour which allowed Bonar Law to overlook
Leverton Harris's 'indelicacies'. Manners, in an offensive letter to the
Conservative Leader, also had some sarcastic things to say about Bonar
Law's mentor, Lord Beaverbrook, who, as we shall see in Chapter 13,
was a figure who aroused widespread distrust.[35]

Leverton Harris had at least made an effort to divest himself of

[29] *Parl. Deb.*, 5th ser., cvii. 776.   [30] Ibid. 776, 786–7.
[31] *The Times*, 5 July 1918.   [32] Croft, *My Life of Strife*, p. 135.
[33] Ibid. 135–8; Croft's autobiography provides quite a full account of the Leverton
Harris episode.
The *Spectator* accepted Harris's 'honesty and probity', but said he should have avoided
the appearance of Caesar's wife, and added that in the newly formed Departments 'there
is a great deal of amiable jobbery by officials in the interests of their friends' (29 June
1918).
[34] *Daily Mail*, 31 July 1918.   [35] Blake, *Bonar Law*, p. 380.

economic interests that might conflict with his public duty. But there were other Departments, in particular the newly created Ministry of Information, where ministers and officials openly pursued their former occupations. In February 1918 parliamentary criticism induced the Patronage Secretary, 'Freddie' Guest, to suggest to the Prime Minister a judicial non-party Commission to consider the problems created by 'Ministerial appointments during the War' and the introduction of businessmen into Whitehall.[36] Nothing was done, and the grumbling continued. Briefed by Robert Donald, whose undistinguished career as Director of Propaganda in Neutral Countries had ended nearly four months earlier,[37] the *Westminister Gazette* published on 30 July an all-out attack on the Ministry of Information, giving details about the businessmen, many of them unpaid, who held office in it, while still following their normal careers. 'Ships, railways, rubber, tobacco, high finance in all its branches are spread out before us', sneered the *Gazette*; 'how exactly they spread information is not yet understood.'[38] The ambiguous position of the pressman in politics was also an issue which refused to go away. In November 1918 the Liberal MP, John Bernard Whitehouse, pointed out that before the war it was an 'established principle, which was known to be binding upon every Government, that when any Member received an office in the Government, he severed his connection with all commercial or other undertakings in order that there might be no conflict between his private interests and his public duties'. Where had that convention now gone, Whitehouse wondered.[39]

The exigencies of war pushed businessmen, civil servants, and politicians into many other kinds of collaboration involving the possibility of corruption. One of the most celebrated of these was the so-called 'Dope Scandal' of 1918.[40] During the War the Government needed large supplies of cellulose acetate, colloquially known as 'dope', which was an essential component in aeroplane manufacture. However, this important chemical was not being manufactured on a commercial scale in 1914, so the Government had to look to overseas sources of supply, and this was how they came to depend on a factory at Basle run by Henri and Camille Dreyfus, two Swiss citizens of

---

[36] Guest's Memo., cited in Lord Beaverbrook, *Men and Power 1917–1918* (London, n.d.), p. 283.
[37] Sanders, M. and Taylor, P. M., *British Propaganda During the First World War 1914–1918* (London, 1982), pp. 94–5. See Masterman to Beaverbrook, 9 Aug. 1918 (HLRO, Beaverbrook papers, E/43).
[38] *Westminster Gazette*, 30 July 1918. The paper continued its vendetta against Beaverbrook and his Ministry in its number of 5 Aug.
[39] *Parl. Deb.*, 5th ser., cx. 2374–5 (7 Nov. 1918).
[40] Coleman, D. C., 'War Demand and Industrial Supply: The "Dope Scandal", 1915–19', in Winter, J. M. (ed.), *War and Economic Development* (Cambridge, 1975), pp. 205–27. This and the succeeding paragraph rely heavily on Professor Coleman's excellent essay.

French–Alsatian origin. But because of the proximity of Basle to the German frontier, the Ministry of Munitions was anxious to establish manufacturing plant in Britain.

News of this situation came to a Canadian financier, Grant Morden, who in 1915 joined others to form a private company, the Acetate Manufacturing Company, which aimed to produce large quantities of 'dope' from a factory near London. The venture was a complete failure. Morden's group then entered into a complex agreement with the Dreyfus brothers, under which the British Cellulose and Chemical Manufacturing Co. Ltd. was formed, as part of a wider international combine. But once more there was a failure to deliver the goods. Then in March 1918 Morden's company was once more reconstructed. The Ministry of Munitions had already made a £200,000 loan to Morden and his friends and promised them effective relief from Excess Profits Duty for a limited period. These tax concessions were now withdrawn, but to offset this, yet more money—amounting to nearly £1½ million by June 1919—was pumped into the Company and new contracts drawn up worth nearly £3 million. Moreover, the earlier British Cellulose and Chemical Manufacturing Co. Ltd. had been launched with a suspiciously small initial capitalization, with the nominal share capital of £4,000 being divided into the unusually low denominations of 6d. shares. From early 1917 onwards these shares began to rocket; by the spring of 1918 they had become worth about £10 and later they went as high as £14. 10s.

Inevitably, there was soon public criticism. It was fomented in part by the rival company of Courtauld's, who suspected—with good reason—that Morden's main concern was to build up an enterprise, with the help of public money, which could break into the artificial silk market once the War was over. Representatives of Courtauld's and other firms which appeared before the sub-committee of the Select Committee on National Expenditure were pointing out in late 1917 the malpractices that were taking place. Then in July 1918 the Select Committee's Fifth Report appeared, the chairman of the sub-committee having earlier sent copies of the document to the press, with the criticisms of the British Cellulose Company underlined in blue pencil. This abrasive document called on the Government to take over the Company and suggested that the Ministry of Munitions should at once consider the advisability of finding another source of supply.

The result was predictable. Pressmen and politicians queued up to express their outrage. In particular, the *Daily Chronicle*, briefed, it would seem, by the Company's disgruntled former secretary, started a series of articles exposing the 'Dope Scandal'. This episode undoubtedly encouraged Lloyd George and his friends in their desire to buy up the *Chronicle*, which they did a few weeks later. But other newspapers were also quick to join in the denunciations. For example, the

Westminster Gazette, which, as we have seen, was already campaigning against the businessmen chosen by Beaverbrook to run the Ministry of Information, expressed the view that 'on the story as told by the Committee we are in the face of the greatest financial scandal of the war'.[41] Moreover, Strachey's sensitive conscience was once again troubled, while the *Morning Post* weighed in with a scathing indictment of the Ministry of Munitions.[42] In Parliament a defence of the Company was attempted by the Conservative, Sir William Bull, but he turned out to be a friend of Grant Morden and had been involved in the earlier reconstruction of the Company.[43] On the other side, Frederick Banbury, the veteran Tory, talked about 'financial methods which had been practised in the old days by a well-known man in the City called Baron Grant, and afterwards by Whitaker Wright and Ernest Terah Hooley'; and the Liberal shipowner, R. D. Holt, claimed that he had 'seldom read an account of a more gross scandal than this question of the Cellulose Acetate Company'. The Government was forced to set up a tribunal of enquiry.[44]

Possibly the outcry would not have been so great if the participants in the venture had been native-born Englishmen. But the Dreyfus brothers were Swiss, who had had extensive dealings with German firms both before and during the War, and, what is more, they were Jewish—which ensured that the *New Witness* would give the scandal extensive coverage in its own peculiar way.[45] Moreover, Grant Morden too was a highly controversial figure. The *Daily Chronicle* sourly commented on his career as follows: 'It is only a few years ago that Colonel Grant Morden burst as a new meteor on the financial world of London, after having made a reputation—good or otherwise—as a promoter in Canada.' Then, some time later, he had 'blossomed out as a country gentleman, of Heatherden Hall, Ivor Heath, Bucks, and is now a candidate for Parliament.' The *Chronicle* also drew attention to the links with Morden's fellow-Canadian friend and rival, Beaverbrook, whose *Daily Express* had given Morden a 'puff' ('A Man of Empire'), comparing him to Disraeli and Randolph Churchill, on the very eve of his adoption meeting as a Conservative candidate for Brentford and Chiswick; the author of this article, suggested the *Chronicle*, should be hauled before the tribunal as a witness. It also noted that similar praise had been published in *John Bull*, in which Morden had acquired a financial stake.[46]

In short, Grant Morden seemed to be the archetypal war profiteer—greedy, unscrupulous, and a corrupting influence in British politics.

[41] Cited in Coleman, 'Dope Scandal', p. 219.   [42] *Morning Post*, 29 July 1918.
[43] Coleman, 'Dope Scandal', pp. 218, 226 n. 42.
[44] *Parl. Deb.*, 5th ser., cix. 746–51 (1 Aug. 1918).
[45] *New Witness*, 16 Aug. 1918, pp. 301–2.
[46] *Daily Chronicle*, 10 Aug. 1918.

Such attacks, however, did not prevent him from being selected by the Conservative Association and returned to Parliament in the 1918 General Election. Moreover, like Beaverbrook, he then went on to combine politics with press-ownership—he became chairman of Odhams Ltd.—before his extravagance and mania for speculation led to his bankruptcy and to an early death in 1932.[47]

The 'Dope Scandal' was also worrying because it revealed the close tie-up between Whitehall and the business world. Ironically, in view of his earlier concern over war profiteers, Walter Long had a son who worked in the London office of one of Morden's companies and had money invested in it—a fact which may not have been unconnected with Long's role in lobbying the Treasury on Morden's behalf in the course of 1916.[48] It also transpired that a fellow director of Grant's in the Prudential Trust Company of Canada, which was heavily involved in all these complicated financial transactions, was a certain C. G. Bryan, whom the *Westminster Gazette* had already attacked as one of the undesirable unpaid businessmen whom Beaverbrook had recruited at the Ministry of Information.[49] Northcliffe wrote Beaverbrook a friendly note on 6 August 1918 warning him of the dangers of continuing to employ Bryan:

I am told that one Bryan, who is said to be concerned in the Dope scandal, has been sent to New York by your Ministry to work with a F.O. representative there. . . . If true, you can imagine what the attitude of the F.O. towards the Ministry of Information will be. They are slow, they are Roman Catholic, they are inefficient; but they do not get into the news in the Financial Scandal Department.[50]

Here, indeed, was a scandal, but it was one which, given the circumstances of the War, it would have been difficult to avoid. Almost overnight demand for a relatively little-used chemical dramatically increased. The Ministry of Munitions, in its desperate anxiety to increase supplies from native manufacturers, was tempted to cut corners, and it gave its backing to a company flotation without adequately thinking through the consequences of its action. Speculators and entrepreneurs like Morden were able to take advantage of the situation, while a number of politicians and officials eventually found that they had been compromised.

In view of such scandals as these, it is little wonder that, once the War was over, voices were raised for a speedy dismantling of economic

---

[47] Coleman, 'Dope Scandal', p. 223. On Morden, see Minney, R. J., *Viscount Southwood* (London, 1954), pp. 163–4; Koss, *Rise and Fall*, ii. 407.

[48] Coleman, 'Dope Scandal', pp. 210, 226.

[49] He was described as 'a director of six companies, including the Canadian Steamship Lines, the British Maritime Trust, and the Canada Securities Corporation' (*Westminster Gazette*, 30 July 1918).

[50] Northcliffe to Beaverbrook (copy), 6 Aug. 1918 (BL, Northcliffe papers, Add. MS 62, 161).

controls. And the move to disengage the State from business life was then given additional impetus by the occurrence of another mini-scandal, the St Omer Dump Affair, in which Page Croft and the National Party once again took the lead.

The end of the War had left the Ministry of Munitions with the task of disposing of surplus stores, a task entrusted to a special Disposal Board. In the course of 1920 parliamentary critics came upon information which cast doubt on both the efficiency and honesty of the Board's behaviour. As Page Croft was able to tell the Commons, the sale of the St Omer Dump, along with over 900 lorries, had been conducted in a seemingly irregular way, since the Disposal Board had given Messrs. Leyland, the purchasers of the site, advantages which were denied their rivals, Messrs. Lever. Could this have come about because Colonel Spurrier from the Ministry, who arranged the deal, happened to be the brother of Leyland's chairman and to have yet another brother sitting on its board?[51]

In time-honoured fashion, Croft denied that he was accusing Spurrier of corruption, but he insisted that the most cherished tradition of British public life was to avoid a situation in which an official could be involved in a conflict of interest—a subject on which he quoted Lloyd George's now legendary observations of December 1900![52] Since the Disposal Board's deal could also be represented as involving a 'serious loss to the State', and, hence, a waste of taxpayer's money, Croft was able to fit the 'scandal' into the current Anti-Waste Campaign.[53] But his more fundamental objection was to the fact that the many businessmen drafted into the Ministry of Munitions seemed never to have been inculcated with 'the spirit of the British Civil Service'. The sooner the Disposal Board handed over its work to a permanent Government Department and the sooner the gentlemen who were employed there 'return[ed] once more to [their] private avocations', the better it would be for all concerned, said Croft.[54] He went on to advocate the system of sealed tenders to prevent a recurrence of such an incident, and ended up moving a reduction of the Vote of the Ministry of Munitions, attracting the support of seventy-five MPs. Included in this number were many Diehards, a few Independent Liberals, and one or two Labour Members: in other words, representatives from all those groups which had expressed anxiety

[51] *Parl. Deb.*, 5th ser., cxxxii. 2278–90 (3 Aug. 1920).
[52] Ibid. 2288. [53] *Parl. Deb.*, 5th ser., cxxxii. 2280.
[54] Ibid. 2290. For another scandal involving the officials of the Ministry of Munitions, see Doig, *Corruption and Misconduct*, p. 82. This scandal was the occasion for the passing of the Tribunal of Inquiry (Evidence) Act of 1921, which was later employed to deal with the Budget Leak of 1936 and to investigate the activities of Lynskey (See Robinton, M.R., 'The British Method of Dealing with Political Corruption', in Heidenheimer, Arnold J. (ed.), *Political Corruption: Readings in Comparative Analysis* (New Brunswick, 1970; 1978 edn.), pp. 249–58.)

about profiteering and the close relationship between government and business which the War had brought about.

Not, of course, that businessmen seconded into Whitehall were responsible for all the irregularities. Under the intense pressure of work, many Ministers were unable to control the behaviour of their own permanent officials. Thus in September 1916 a case came before the courts involving employees of the Royal Army Clothing Department at Pimlico who were found guilty of running a number of fiddles on supply contracts. The employees were sentenced to five years' penal servitude under the 1861 Larceny Act, because the judge thought that the penalties allowed by the 1906 Prevention of Corruption Act were too limited.[55] This prodded Parliament into passing a new Prevention of Corruption Act, which raised the maximum sentence which an offender could serve and forced defendants, for the first time, to prove their innocence if apprehended in suspicious circumstances.[56] This piece of legislation reached the statute book in December 1916. As it passed through the Commons, backbench MPs had an opportunity to voice their disquiet at the want of sound business method shown by many Ministries. The egregious Booth actually claimed that 'there was far more jobbery going on, about ten times as much, as during the Boer War under the Unionist Government'[57]—an allegation which he was vainly pressed to substantiate.[58]

Profit Levels

Those exercised about the evil of profiteering were also concerned with the apparently exorbitant profits which some businessmen were making out of the nation's difficulties, regardless of whether or not they actually held office. Though he later took action to reduce the public's anxieties on this score, Lloyd George himself unwittingly did much to create the setting in which such profiteering could flourish, when as Minister of Munitions he based his policy on the notion that the prime necessity was to expand production whatever the cost. The Ministry of Munitions, by offering generous inducements to its business contractors, did in time succesfully overcome the initial armaments shortages, but the social price that was paid for this achievement was a high one.[59]

Many businessmen stood to gain from other artificial shortages created by war conditions. It was probably the publication of several company balance sheets at the end of 1914 which first aroused public

---

[55] Ibid. 77–9.   [56] Ibid. 80.
[57] *Parl. Deb.*, 5th ser., lxxxvii. 475 (9 Nov. 1916).
[58] Ibid. 479–82 (F. E. Smith).
[59] See discussion in Wrigley, C. J., *David Lloyd George and the British Labour Movement* (Hassocks, 1976), pp. 84–5.

opinion on this subject and led to calls for the introduction of some sort of profit tax. The most discussed case was that of Spillers and Bakers, the millers, whose profits were shown to have increased from £89,352 in 1913 to £367,868 for 1914.[60] Snowden ironically observed that 'even Tory newspapers [were] now agitating with a great deal of enthusiasm' for a war profits tax and floating proposals that made him feel 'moderate and old fashioned'.[61] The 'injustice' of high profits was also a favourite theme in the speeches of 'ginger' Liberals, like Chiozza Money and the coalowner, Arthur Markham. The latter, under the shadow of death, pursued his campaign for the heavy taxation of the profiteer with intense zeal and in a highly personalized way: 'If only I can make old —— pay up all he's got I don't mind how much I pay', he would privately exclaim.[62]

But of all the political parties it was Labour which put the record profits registered by many companies to greatest use in its wartime propaganda. Labour argued that the sacrifices being made by the working class should be complemented by the 'conscription of wealth', and evidence that the business community was doing well out of the War was used to support this campaign. Thus in 1917 the Labour Party produced a pamphlet entitled 'Profiteers and their Plunder: A Call for Restitution'. 'CAPITALIST INTERESTS HAVE BEEN ENORMOUSLY ENRICHED BY THE WAR', declared this pamphlet, and it backed up this assertion with a wealth of telling detail.[63]

Shipping profits aroused particularly strong feelings. High freight charges, caused by a scarcity of tonnage, meant that shipowners fortunate enough not to have their vessels requisitioned were able to draw what Lord Salter later called 'immense and possibly unique profits'.[64] It has been calculated that in the first twenty-six months of the War, the shipping companies made total net profits of at least £262 million, while their property appreciated from £175 million to £500 million.[65] The Conservative MP, Robert Houston, who had extensive shipping interests, complained in the Commons:

The shipowner has been held up in the Press—and principally in that portion of the Press which has supported the Government—as being a rapacious profiteer, and in one paper in particular—a Sunday paper, which usually expresses the views of the Government—the most offensive cartoons have constantly appeared from week to week showing the shipowner to be a sort of bloated villain.[66]

During the Asquith Coalition Government's term of office the key

[60] Stamp, Josiah, *Taxation During the War* (Oxford, 1932), pp. 39–40.
[61] Ibid. 43. [62] Ibid. 63–4.
[63] Labour Party Pamphlets, 1917/19.
[64] Cited in Hurwitz, S. J., *State Intervention in Great Britain* (New York, 1949), p. 186.
[65] Ibid. [66] *Parl. Deb.*, 5th ser., xcv. 972 (3 July 1917).

Ministers, Runciman, the President of the Board of Trade, and McKenna, the Chancellor of the Exchequer, inclined to the view that the earnings of the shipping companies had been much exaggerated.[67] But Lloyd George, on coming to the premiership, gave a promise that 'during the war shipping would be nationalized in the real sense of the term', whatever that might mean.[68] And Bonar Law, the new Chancellor, bowed to the political pressure by discriminating against the shipping companies in his 1917 Budget when he cancelled their right to claim Excess Profits Duty refunds in certain circumstances.[69] The shipowners angrily protested that the Government had broken its agreement with them. To this Bonar Law replied by bringing before the Commons, during the committee stage of the Budget, detailed information about the returns he had recently received on his various shipping investments. He announced that he had put some £8,100 into fifteen shipping companies. Whereas in peacetime he would have expected to draw 5 per cent on his investment, that is to say, £405, he had, in fact, been lucky enough to receive £3,624 in 1915 and £3,847 in 1916. Amongst other examples cited by the Chancellor was this one:

There was another shipping company, in which I invested £350. The other day I received a letter from the managing owners of that company, saying that because the cost of building was so high and was likely to continue high, it was not probable they would wish to invest the money in ships for a long time to come; therefore, they were going to make a division out of the surplus capital. For that £350 capital, on this division, I received a cheque for £1,050. That is the trade we are ruining![70]

McKenna was amazed at what he considered the Chancellor's 'naïvety' in making this frank disclosure.[71] And, in fact, Bonar Law's statement about his personal finances was later to be used against him. In December 1918 one of his supporters asked Bonar Law for material with which he could refute Snowden, who had been putting about a statement describing the Chancellor's private affairs. Law could only say in reply: 'There is nothing to be done about Snowden's statement for the facts are true', though he added that they rested on figures which he had produced in 1917 'as a reason for cutting down shipowners' profits'—something for which he had been denounced at the time by many Liberals.[72]

How widespread, then, was profiteering? In an important, pioneering article, 'Patriots or Profiteers?', Jonathan Boswell and Bruce Johns

---

[67] Wrigley, *Lloyd George*, p. 260 n. 21; McKenna to Northcliffe, 9 Feb. 1916 (Northcliffe papers, Add. MS 62, 157).

[68] Hurwitz, *State Intervention*, p. 194.   [69] Stamp, *Taxation*, p. 194.

[70] *Parl. Deb.*, 5th ser., xcv. 985–6 (3 July 1917).

[71] Stamp, *Taxation*, p. 116.

[72] Law to John Rutherford (copy), 17 Dec. 1918 (Bonar Law papers, 84/7/121). This is a reply to Rutherford's letter of 16 Dec., with report of Snowden's election speech enclosed (ibid. 84/4/9).

argue that it was only a minority of businessmen who deliberately extorted money from the Government. These 'rogues', they suggest, were particularly to be found 'exploiting army supply shortages during the early months, food and clothing scarcities in later periods and anomalies in shipping controls whenever they existed'. Whitehall's anger was especially aroused by 'outside speculators' who moved into industries where they had not previously been employed—armaments, clothing, and shipping—in search of quick profits. But most profiteering, Boswell and Johns believe, was 'partial, involuntary or intermittent', and most businessmen displayed a mixture of public-spiritedness and acquisitiveness, the blend varying from person to person and from industry to industry.[73]

But, as Boswell and Johns also recognize, profiteering is an imprecise concept. It has, they say, four possible meanings: '(a) a substantial increase in profit over a pre-war "standard", (b) profit rates exceeding some general or industrial norm, (c) profits disproportionate to contributions of effort, organisation or risk, or (d) profits from excessive market power related to categories familiar from economic theory'.[74] But these were economic definitions, and as the authors of the article go on to show, neither Government nor press was discussing profiteering within a strictly economic frame of reference. When the Government took action against some alleged abuse, it did so because something was happening which 'offended public opinion or damaged civilian morale'.[75]

It was just such a concern for equality of sacrifice and fairness which shaped the debate about fiscal policy as it developed during and after the Great War. Hence, Excess Profits Duty—which embodied the first and second of the Boswell and Johns definitions—failed to satisfy the Labour Movement, which condemned it on the simple moral ground that it was too lenient.[76] According to the Labour representatives on the Ministry of Reconstruction Committee of Enquiry into Trusts, the system of free competition had irretrievably broken down under pressure of war, and EPD was an inadequate way of checking the profiteering which had resulted. They therefore called for monopolistic combines to be taken into public ownership, in addition to which they wanted Government Departments to 'cost' each stage in the production of a commodity and then impose a maximum price.[77]

This suggestion proved far too extreme for 'mainstream' political

[73] Boswell, J. S. and Johns, B. R., 'Patriots or Profiteers? British Businessmen and the First World War', *Journal of European Economic History*, xi (1982), 423–45.
[74] Ibid. 426.   [75] Ibid.
[76] Hicks, J. R. and U. K. and Rostas, L., *The Taxation of War Wealth* (Oxford, 1942), pp. 72–3. For Labour's dissatisfaction, see e.g. *Parl. Deb.*, 5th ser., lxxxvi. 463–4 (W. C. Anderson, 17 Oct. 1916).
[77] Report of Committee of Ministry of Reconstruction on Trusts, 1918, Cd. 9236, pp. 13–14.

opinion, but another possible course of action favoured by Labour, the Capital Levy, initially enjoyed much wider support. The reason for this was that it seemed as though a carefully devised scheme could be framed to catch the hated profiteer. Thus Masterman, in his pamphlet, *The New Liberalism* (October 1920), argued that the War had redistributed wealth in the most inequitable way: 'It has given to those who stayed at home with the defence of ill-health or the excuse of indispensible public service the opportunity of acquiring wealth which was denied to the actual combatants.' Since, in Masterman's view, the effect of the War had been to help the old at the expense of the young, and those who possessed wealth to the detriment of those trying to create it, the mission of Liberalism should be the paying off of the War Debt in such a way as to redress this imbalance and to remove this injustice. The Capital Levy, argued Masterman, served such a purpose much better than would raising income tax to punitive levels or imposing taxes on the poor which might provoke revolution.[78]

But despite the endorsement of the Capital Levy by the all-party Select Committe on War Wealth,[79] the Coalition Government eventually submitted to the wishes of its backbenchers, most of whom by 1920 were clearly against any kind of levy on wartime profits.[80] A year later Ministerialists and Independent Liberals alike had discarded their former radical notions in their anxious quest for Economy and Anti-Waste. 1921 also saw the expiry of the Profiteering Acts, first introduced in 1919 in an attempt to damp down industrial unrest.[81]

In fact, even in the middle of the War there were many whose doctrinaire belief in the working of the market and whose dislike of state interventionism made them wary of the concept of 'profiteering'. For example, the *Spectator*, ever on the look-out for evidence of individual corruption and of the decay of national morals, went on record in July 1917 with the claim that high prices were not, in general, caused by profiteering.[82] Its editor, Strachey, very much hoped that Rhondda's work at the Ministry of Food would 'prove that the suspicion of profiteering is exaggerated', but he feared 'his good endeavours will end in measures which, intended to prevent famine, are the exact method to bring it on.' As he put it in a letter to Garvin in June 1917:

You remember how Bacon says that suspicion clouds the mind. L. G.'s talk

---

[78] Masterman, C. F. G., *The New Liberalism* (London, 1920), pp. 75–9.

[79] Report of Select Committee on Increase of Wealth (War), vol. cii.

[80] Morgan, K. O., *Consensus and Disunity: The Lloyd George Coalition Government 1918–1922* (Oxford, 1979), pp. 240–1; Masterman, *New Liberalism*, pp. 87–8.

[81] The Profiteering Bill received its Second Commons Reading on 11 Aug. 1919. It was an experimental measure designed to lapse after six months. It was renewed in 1920, but allowed to expire in the following year.

[82] *Spectator*, 28 July 1917, p. 79. See also the article, 'The Dangers of Food Control', in the issue of 4 Aug. 1917 (p. 110).

about profiteering and all the talk in the D[aily] M[ail] is clearly clouding the mind of the democracy. What we ought to do is to lift the clouds. Meantime let the Press denounce the bad cases. I have heard of them in the abstract but curiously enough never come across any specific instances—surely a bad sign.[83]

This was essentially the position of another old-fashioned believer in *laissez-faire*, Tommy Lough, who disliked the implication that the Government should somehow or other stop profiteering by extending its controls; Lough believed on the contrary that the Government was already doing *too much*.[84] Such fears were articulated by J. H. Balfour-Browne in an article in the *Fortnightly Review*:

There has been a good deal of silly talk and fluid thinking about what is called 'profiteering', and it is quite certain that many persons, in denouncing what they regard as an economic abuse, may really, as vapid talk always does, be doing a disservice to the community. 'Profiteering' is, as I understand it, nothing more than the taking of profits, and although the taking of excessive profits is bad for the community, and is an extortion of the same kind as the money-lender's extortionate interest on money lent, or, for that matter, the demand for excessive wages, the abolition of profiteering or the taking of profits would be productive of an economic paralysis, which would surprise those glib persons who have been denouncing capitalists in much the same way that the Church, for a long time, denounced usury.[85]

It is not difficult to discern ulterior motives behind this kind of reasoning!

But a multitude of complex motives also animated those who were attacking profiteers and profiteering. These criticis, for convenience, can be divided into four main groups: Socialists, Tory aristocrats, intellectual Liberals, and the Radical Right.

Images of the Profiteer

The attitudes adopted by spokesmen for the Labour–Socialist movement are the easiest to analyse and explain. The profiteer played a central role in Labour's propaganda in the 1915–22 period, and the stereotype of the ruthless money-grubbing capitalist, who exploited the hardships of the working class and the sufferings of the fighting men, is a stock-in-trade of all socialist newspapers of this period. At election time the stereotype was especially in evidence. 'NO PROFITEERING! NO UNEMPLOYMENT! NO CONSCRIPTION!' was one of Labour's slogans in 1918.[86] And in the run-up to the 1922

---

[83] Strachey to Garvin (copy), 20 June 1917 (HLRO, Strachey papers, S/7/1/3).
[84] *Parl. Deb.*, 5th ser., lxxxvi. 473 (17 Oct. 1916). Lough was a Liberal backbencher of the old school.
[85] Balfour-Browne, J. H., 'Profiteering', *Fortnightly Review*, ciii (1918), 714.
[86] Labour Party pamphlets, 1918/53.

General Election a Labour leaflet repeated the question which Clynes had recently put to Lord Birkenhead: 'Why did the Government allow a few thousand persons to make thousands of millions during the war period while nearly a million men got only a soldier's grave for their service?'[87]

On occasions Labour politicians followed the line of the Radical Right and presented the profiteer as belonging to a kind of German 'fifth column'.[88] But usually they identified profiteering with 'capitalist interests'. And it was this which differentiated the Labour position from that of the other three groups. However useful the profiteer may have been as a stereotype and a slogan, the Labour Movement was not really interested in personalities and only incidentally interested in the wartime conditions in which profiteering was supposed to have flourished. Here there was a complete contrast to the stance of Lloyd George, who can be found publicly insisting in August 1919 that profiteering was 'not a normal problem—it is a problem which has arisen in consequence of the circumstances of the War, and the circumstances which have followed the War.'[89] Far from believing this to be true, Labour spokesmen followed the line taken by Bevin, Webb, and Hobson on the Reconstruction Committee on Trusts and presented profiteering as a form of exploitation which monopoly capitalism inevitably produced; the growth of cartels and combines, they thought, may have been speeded up by the War, but it was at the same time a necessary stage in economic development. The profiteer was, therefore, not a man of evil and antisocial disposition, nor was he the product of 'abnormal' conditions; he was simply a capitalist who had been found out. True, Labour used the censorious language customarily employed about individual wrongdoers ('robbery'), but it used this language about an entire class and as a way of indicting an entire social system.

Non-Socialists were obviously aware of the 'dangers' inherent in Labour's denunciation of the War Profiteer. However, many of them responded, initially at least, by stepping up their *own* attacks on profiteering in the hope of neutralizing Labour's appeal. 'The legitimate father of the Bolshevik is the Profiteer', wrote Masterman in 1920;[90] the epigram was neat, the sentiment it expressed something of a commonplace. 'There must be no profiteering in the shortages of the necessities of life', pontificated the *Pall Mall Gazette*. 'That way lies Bolshevism.'[91]

---

[87] Ibid. 1922/7. Predictably enough, *Justice*, too, took a strong line on profiteering (e.g. 30 Aug. 1917, 'Milliardaires and Their Milliards').

[88] 'Not even the food of the civilian population has been free from the activities of the exploiters. The submarine menace of the enemy outside the realm has only strengthened the grip of speculators posing as patriots inside' ('Profiteers and Their Plunder. A Call for Restitution', Labour Party pamphlets, 1917/19).

[89] *Parl. Deb.*, 5th ser., cxix. 658 (7 Aug. 1919).

[90] Masterman, *New Liberalism*, p. 202.   [91] *Pall Mall Gazette*, 5 July 1922.

But quite apart from their concern to stem the advance of the Labour Party and to stabilize society in the face of revolutionary Socialism, those Liberals and Conservatives who joined in the denunciation of the Profiteer did so because this was an effective way of propounding their own alternative view of society. Discussing the problem of profiteering was also apt to generate a mood of nostalgia for a vanished past and indignation over the corrupt present. And this mood was reflected in two of the most famous political manifestoes produced in these years, Lord Henry Bentinck's *Tory Democracy* (1918) and C. F. G. Masterman's *England After War* (1922).

Lord Henry Bentinck was an independent Conservative MP who had been sitting in the Commons, with a few interruptions, since 1886. He was a Conservative of the traditional type. His half-brother was the 6th Duke of Portland and his wife the daughter of an earl. As Lord-Lieutenant of Westmoreland he was obliged to fulfil the functions of a leader of 'County' Society, and a similar sense of duty drove him to serve in the army at Gallipoli, though he was then over 50 years old. In the immediate pre-war years he had been a member of the Tory Social Reform Group, and had held quite advanced views on a number of welfare issues; in hindsight, he saw the function of this Group as being to demonstrate that the Conservative Party was sincere in its commitment to social progress and was 'destined for higher things than to be the dumping ground for disgruntled Liberals, or a mere appendage to the Tariff Reform League, with its purely commercial and material ideals'.[92]

However, by the end of the War Bentinck had come to accept that his 'vision of the Commonwealth'—an organic society in which each social group worked for others in a spirit of disinterestedness—was further away from realization than ever before. 'While everything generous, self-sacrificing and noble is shedding blood on the fields of France and Flanders', complained Bentinck, 'Plutocracy is on the war-path at home.'[93] Bentinck assimilated the two stereotypes of 'Plutocrat' and 'Profiteer' in a famous and much quoted passage:

Plugson of Undershot, having conquered shells and cellulose, will capture our political life. . . . The Golden Calf will be set up; those who worship will be rewarded with the crumbs that fall from the rich man's table, while those who refuse will be denounced as Pacifists and Bolsheviks. The Tory Party will be thoroughly commercialized and vulgarized, and a liberal distribution of office and honours will promote contentment in its ranks.[94]

In the future, predicted Bentinck, the State and the political parties were likely to be more closely connected with national industry than ever before. In view of this, he reasoned, 'it is of all things most vital

---

[92] Bentinck, H., *Tory Democracy* (London, 1918), p. 78.
[93] Ibid. 2.   [94] Ibid.

that the connexion should be pure and clean; that neither the State itself nor any of its parties should be yoked to the horses of Croesus; that wealth should be made to serve the Commonwealth, and industry to produce not wealth for a few, but welfare, abundant welfare, for all.'[95]

The post-war Coalition merely confirmed Bentinck's worst forebodings. He saw this Government as the apotheosis of vulgarity and plutocracy. A capitalist class bent on personal enrichment was setting the tone of political life, and provoking amongst manual workers an understandable reaction and commitement to class warfare. During the Coal Strike of 1921 Bentinck led a Labour deputation to the Home Office protesting at the arrest of some miners who had clashed with the police, and later he presided over meetings in March and April 1922 at which Lord Robert Cecil preached his gospel of international conciliation and class harmony—to be achieved through the League of Nations abroad and schemes of profit-sharing at home.

As Maurice Cowling has written, 'Bentinck was not a figure of consequence, but he shared in an off-beat way the dislike felt by all three Cecils [i.e. Robert, Hugh, and Lord Salisbury] for the threat presented to their style of politics by the Tariff Reform League and by Lloyd George's employment of the plutocracy in high places.'[96] In Bentinck's own words, his was a protest against those who were 'all-powerful' in present-day politics; people who believed that 'a great Empire [could] be governed on the principles of the counter', and that the common man could be kept subservient by the propagation of 'synthetic truth or manufactured falsehood' pumped out by the capitalist press—a clear reference to Beaverbook.[97] To an aristocratic Conservative like Bentinck, trying to resurrect the 'best' traditions of the now largely superseded ruling class, the profiteer was a symbol of all that was corrupt and degraded in modern political life. 'The longer the war lasts,' he wrote despairingly in early 1918, 'the stricter will be the monopoly and the larger the spoils, the more will Plutocracy be ennobled, decorated, knighted and enriched. That way lies disruption and damnation.'[98]

It is an interesting commentary on the political changes effected by the War that there should be so much common ground between a book like *Tory Democracy* and Masterman's disillusioned survey of the post-war world, *England After War* (1922). Before 1914 Masterman had been an ardent land reformer, anxious 'to spread the "Virus" in every

---

[95] Ibid. 139.

[96] Cowling, M., *The Impact of Labour 1920–1924* (Cambridge, 1971), p. 67.

[97] Bentinck, *Tory Democracy*, pp. 68–9, 2. Bentinck clearly had Beaverbrook in mind: 'A Ministry of Information, strengthened and enlarged by Imperial financiers and lumber-men, will provide the right brand of synthetic truth and manufactured falsehood. The "pious Editor" will spread whatever trash will keep the people in blindness' (ibid. 2).

[98] Ibid. 3.

village, even the neighbourhood of Hatfield'.[99] Yet by 1922, with landed society on the point of total collapse, Masterman was describing that social order—to which Bentinck essentially belonged—in a mood of nostalgic affection. Indeed, some of the most telling pages in *England After War* are those in which Masterman sings his threnody over aristocratic England.

While other men were receiving 'increased wealth and emoluments by sharp contracts for munitions with a Government Department lax in cutting prices so long as the goods could be delivered speedily', writes Masterman, the old landed families had made the supreme sacrifice: their sons had gone off to be slaughtered; then, weighed down by death duties and high taxation, many families which had worked their estates and provided leadership for their localities for generations now found themselves obliged to sell out and see their land and home pass into the hands, perhaps of tenant farmers, perhaps of the local authorities, and often of a War profiteer 'climbing upwards towards gentility, a title, and a seat in the House of Lords'. What had happened to such dispossessed aristocrats, Masterman asked. In reply to his own question, he cited a case where 'the great house having been bought by a profiteer from Tooting, the ladies who once owned it [were] living in the lodge at the gate; being reluctant to cut themselves entirely apart from their old home'—an apocryphal story, this, maybe, but one which conveys Masterman's sense of the pitiable state to which many ancient families had been reduced.[100]

However, in Masterman's view, the political and social advancement of the despised profiteer had been achieved at the expense not only of landed society, but also of the average 'middle-class citizen', including Masterman's favourite social group: hard-working and socially responsible professional men, now suffering from high taxation and the effects of inflation:

[The] profiteer not only amasses his ill-gotten gains. He flaunts these in the open street, in full vision of the despairing Middle Class. He (or generally she) is swaggering in all the luxury shops . . . while the Middle Class is hurriedly endeavouring to pick up a remnant of cloth or a scrap of cheap nourishment. He is at gigantic motor shows competing ostentatiously for cars of a thousand or two thousand pounds apiece. The Middle Class reads of the splendour of such displays, as he contemplates ruefully the renewal of his third-class ticket at double the old rate. . . .[101]

Yet in Masterman's view, the middle class was the victim of a

---

[99] Masterman to Lloyd George, 1913, cited in Masterman, *C. F. G. Masterman*, p. 259. On the other hand, even during the Edwardian period Masterman was commenting on the poignancy of the supersession of landed aristocrats by wealthy parvenus. See Masterman, C. F. G., *In Peril of Change* (London, 1905), p. 311.

[100] Masterman, C. F. G., *England After War* (London, 1922), esp. pp. 35, 40, 46.

[101] Ibid. 73–4.

bourgeois kind of 'false consciousness', because, far from protesting at the injustice of its lot, it took things lying down. 'For the profiteer has only to mention "Bolshevik" and the Middle Class scurries off to its dilapidated home.' Yet it was Masterman's belief that in reality suburbia faced *two* oppressors: 'The Middle class, like Issacha of old, is crouching down between two burdens. The one is the demand of the proletariat. The other is the demand of the profiteer.'[102]

But that, indeed, could also be said to symbolize the plight of the Liberal Party itself—or at least of the kind of democratic Radical Party which Masterman had spent his life trying to construct. It is noticeable, in this connection, that by 1922 the spokesman for the 'New Liberalism' had abandoned all pretence of sympathy with Organized Labour. Consequently, unlike the Socialists, who portrayed the profiteer as the exploiter of the working class, Masterman is actually *coupling* proletariat and profiteer. Both represented, in his view, the forces of materialism and coercion—'collective power'—in contrast to Liberals who, Masterman thought, were articulating the convictions and energies of intelligent, independent-minded, and disinterested citizens. The profiteer plays such a large part in *England After War* precisely because he symbolizes for Masterman the triumph of the kind of class politics to which the Liberal Party found it difficult, perhaps impossible, to adapt.

It is also characteristic of the 'Liberal Mind' that Masterman should fail to provide an economic explanation of the 'profiteering phenomenon'. When in Chapter VI of *England After War* he attempts to categorize different types of profiteer, he does so on *moral* grounds, by differentiating between successful businessmen who displayed a sense of responsibility from those who did not. For the risk-taking entrepreneur he actually has a very considerable admiration.[103] Masterman reserves his contempt for those who deliberately squeezed the nation in its hour of need because of 'the love of money' and 'the desire for accumulation of great fortune for its own sake'. These lost souls, as Masterman views them, were unlikely ever to achieve true happiness; but meanwhile they were able to gratify their sense of being alive and rich, while more than half a million of their fellow-countrymen were neither, by ostentatious displays of wealth which merely drew attention to their own vulgarity. ' "You see great motors travelling the roads", said one observer to me, "which are finished to the last degree, and containing occupants who are not".'[104] This remark tells us little about the profiteering mentality but a great deal about Masterman.

This leads finally to Masterman's denunciation of modern politics and his assertion of the superior moral stature of the pre-war Liberal

---

[102] Ibid. 74, 76.   [103] Ibid. 141.   [104] Ibid. 142–3.

Party. Once again he makes his point vividly by use of the pointed anecdote, and two of these have become famous. On the consequences of the Coupon Election, Masterman quotes Keynes, who said he had asked a Conservative friend who had known previous Houses what he thought of the present one, to which he had received the reply: 'They are a lot of hard-faced men who look as if they had done very well out of the war.'[105] There is also Masterman's story of how Asquith had once responded to a colleague's report that a certain shipping speculator had made 400 or 500 per cent profit out of a single cargo of food or munitions: 'disgusting', observed Mr Asquith, 'with a characteristic shrug of the shoulders'.[106]

Bentinck, the aristocratic Tory, and Masterman, the Radical Liberal, were alike in celebrating a world they had lost. Profiteering, however, presented itself in a somewhat different guise to the Radical Right. Here *patriotism* was the driving force. Profiteering was therefore denounced, not as exploitation of the worker or as something inconsistent with the nobler traditions of public life, but rather as a kind of subversion or treachery, and profiteers as scoundrels who, intentionally or otherwise, were playing the game of the Hun.

We have seen the populism with which Pemberton Billing handled this theme in 1917 and 1918. Page Croft, and his National Party colleagues, seldom went to such extremes, but they too were prepared to denounce 'big capitalists' if the latter happened to be 'aliens', naturalized Britons, or doctrinaire free traders. Thus in a newspaper article of October 1916 Croft denounced the Free Trade Union and other Cobdenite societies for being 'composed largely of wealthy capitalists who have amassed huge fortunes as cosmopolitan traders and financiers, and have invariably put their own individual trading interests before the interests of the country'.[107] There is a sense in which much of this can be seen as a continuation of the attacks directed against the 'Radical Plutocrats' before 1914.

Yet Croft's devotion to the ideal of national unity could at times lead him to quite substantial criticisms of the existing economic dispensation. In September 1916, for example, he called for 'radical change in the relationship of employer and employed, based on the principle of mutual forebearance and consideration'.[108] By 1920 the National Party had converted this vague aspiration into what it called its 'Industrial Charter', which proposed the establishment in each industry of a joint council representing both employers and employees

[105] Ibid. 140.
[106] Ibid. 143.
[107] *Daily Graphic*, 14 Oct. 1916.
[108] *Hertfordshire Mercury*, 30 Sept. 1916.

for the regulation of working conditions and the establishment of what was called 'a standard comfort wage'.[109]

The fact is that the leaders of the National Party felt little affinity with Big Business and their convictions inclined them to favour any scheme that might have the effect of subordinating particularist economic interests to the good of society as a whole. Nor did they have any principled objection to the extension of the powers of the State; indeed, as ardent tariff reformers, they positively advocated such a development. This encouraged the National Party on occasions to recommend unorthodox measures for curbing profiteering. In the North Norfolk by-election campaign, its candidate, Captain Crewdson, spoke about the evils of inflation, and he singled out profiteering as one of its three main causes. 'In regard to profiteering', Crewdson held that 'the one way of stopping it was this: let us appoint Commissionaires to sit in public; let consumers be represented on it. Let Labour and manufacturers be represented on it, sitting together with financial experts. This Commission should deal with alleged cases of profiteering, and all proved cases should be treated as criminal offences.'[110]

However, this pioneering exercise in 'Corporatism' ran somewhat ahead of what the National Party was usually prepared to countenance.[111] Croft himself clearly had ambiguous feelings about profiteering. His anxiety to protect the agricultural interest led him, for example, to question the fixing of wheat prices.[112] The National Party also took a strong stand on the upholding of property rights, and viewed with dismay the Labour Party's campaign for the 'conscription of wealth'. This was not needed, explained Croft in January 1917, since 'people with property and capital were paying great chunks at the present moment'.[113]

Once the War had ended, the National Party tended to adopt an orthodox stance on economic issues. Thus in August 1919, against a background of feverish speculation and company promotion,[114] Croft told Parliament that the high cost of living and 'undue profits' were 'causing . . . a great unsettlement in the country'; but he ventured the opinion that the word 'profiteer' was 'a most unfortunate one', since it blurred the important distinction between 'legitimate profits essential

[109] Rubinstein, W. D., 'Henry Page Croft and the National Party 1917–22', *Journal of Contemporary History*, ix (1974), 141–2.
[110] *Eastern Daily Post*, 8 Dec. 1920.
[111] e.g. the National Party's two MPs, Croft and Cooper, abstained on the Second Reading of the 1919 Profiteering Bill.
[112] *Bournemouth Echo*, 5 Jan. 1917.
[113] Ibid. Instead, Croft favoured a 3% 'patriotic loan', plus the payment to public servants of part of their salaries in 3% bonds (letter to *The Times*, 29 Dec. 1917).
[114] Davenport-Hines, *Dudley Docker*, p. 165. 'The invasion of Lancashire by London financiers is creating a very uneasy feeling among all classes in this great centre of cotton manufacture', wrote the Manchester correspondent of the *Morning Post* on 25 Nov. 1919.

to an industry and excessive profits which are gained at the expense of the country', and he urged the Government to spend more time *explaining* economic facts to working-class audiences, so that the latter might be brought to see 'that what is generally and widely described as profiteering is very frequently due to natural causes'.[115] Moreover, as unemployment rose from 1920 onwards, the National Party joined in the hue and cry about 'waste' and took the fashionable line of deploring extravagant public expenditure.[116] It was an ironic end to the Party's once radical economic programme when its members could be found parroting the same slogans as Lord Rothermere's Anti-Waste candidates, and a greater irony still, when the National Party formed a loose working alliance inside Parliament with Horatio Bottomley and his friends.

So much for the National Party's claim to stand for the purification of public life! But this sort of 'apostasy' was not confined to Croft. In the closing period of the Coalition Government the *National Review*, too, was presenting 'Economy' as a universal panacea. In fact, the National Party itself had from the start shown a certain caution on the subject of profiteering. 'Where prices have risen it is sometimes due to "profiteering", sometimes not', ran the Party's manifesto of October 1917. 'Where it is due to this cause it must be stopped ruthlessly; where it is due to other causes they must be explained to the people clearly, which has never yet been done.' Some of the unrest, the Party added darkly, might be the product of 'something in our present social and political system' which was sowing suspicion and strife.[117] The profiteer might indeed be doing the work of the Germans. But those who denounced him too vigorously ran the risk of being charged with the self-same offence.

Thus on an economic plane, the attack on profiteering eventually proved to be a divisive one. To generalize somewhat broadly, the Labour Movement used it to assail the profit-making system, whereas others were only concerned with 'abuses' which had crept into that system under the pressure of war.

But at a social level, dislike of the profiteer could unite people who otherwise would have agreed on little else. It is noticeable, for example, that during the 1922 Honours Scandal, all the critics of the Coalition tended to assume that if a businessman who had done nothing special to distinguish himself was given an honour, this must be because he was a profiteer who had bought his title.

By 1922, in fact, Lloyd George was widely viewed as the political ally

---

[115] *Parl. Deb.*, 5th ser., cxix. 626–7 (7 Aug. 1919).

[116] See articles in the Party journal, *National Opinion*. But Croft could still win applause by claiming that 'German goods were turning our ex-Service men on the streets' (*Morning Post*, 24 Nov. 1920).

[117] *National Review*, lxx (1917), 247.

and protector of the 'profiteering classes'. But this had not always been his public image. On the contrary, as we have seen, in the middle of the War many professed to believe that the Welshman was a fearless patriot whose zeal for victory made him the profiteer's natural foe. The following chapters will describe how Lloyd George came to acquire this reputation—before later forfeiting it.

13
Lloyd George and the Politics of the Great War

Views of Lloyd George before December 1916

IT is a commonplace to say that the First World War brought about a reversal of the image and reputation of many politicians. For example, Asquith, the Liberal Imperialist of the early twentieth century, had become by the middle of the War a popular target for 'patriots' of every hue, whereas Lloyd George, the former 'Pro-Boer' and Radical economist, had emerged as the strong war leader. Similarly, the Welshman, once the darling of the Radical Left of his party, had broken with many of his one-time admirers, but had developed close ties with the Tories, including their ultra-patriotic right wing.

It is not often noted, however, that very much the same thing was happening in public perceptions of corruption. On the eve of the War Lloyd George was identified by nearly all his opponents—and by some of his colleagues—as a threat to the integrity of British politics, being intimately associated not only with the Marconi transactions but with allegations of jobbery and unscrupulous wire-pulling. Yet towards the end of 1916 many of his former detractors had not only pushed these events into the backs of their minds but were actually presenting Lloyd George as an agent of political purification. This remarkable transformation was, in turn, part of the wider re-evaluation of reputations which smoothed the path of Lloyd George to the premiership in December 1916.

Though it was circumstances, more than conscious planning, which brought about this 'role reversal', it owed something, initially at least, to the activities of the so-called 'Liberal Ginger Group' or Liberal War Committee. The Committee was not formally established until January 1916, but long before then its leading lights—Handel Booth, Henry Dalziel, Arthur Markham, 'Freddie' Guest—were pressing for a more vigorous prosecution of the War, a course of action which often brought them into conflict with the Asquithian leadership, but not, of course, with Lloyd George, of whom they were open admirers. Even in early 1915 these backbenchers, like other ardent patriots of that time, were combining their calls for an all-out assault on the enemy with an obsessive quest for spies and enemy aliens and with hunting down cases of mismanagement and corruption. There is a striking paradox here. Many of these Liberals were businessmen (Booth and Dalziel, for example), and some of them, like Markham, a colliery-owner, had frequently figured in pre-war days on their opponents' lists of 'Radical Plutocrats'. But these men, presented to the world in 1913 and 1914 as shady politicians on the make, were able, once the War had started, to go over from defence to attack, under cover of the party truce. Previously they had been cast as 'suspects'; now they assumed the more congenial roles of 'detectives' and 'prosecuting counsel'.

A good example of their methods is furnished by the Meyer Affair, described in the preceding chapter. Almost without exception, the MPs who harried the unfortunate timber merchant were Liberals known to have close associations with Lloyd George—a Minister who was, of course, completely uninvolved in the allocation of the timber contract. But the attacks on Meyer had a wider political significance than that, as is shown by what happened in the parliamentary debate of 25 February 1915. In the course of this debate Booth expressed furious disbelief at the lack of business method displayed by the Government and said that this had created the opening for corruption. 'There has been nothing since I have been a Member of this House', he said, 'which has staggered me like this transaction. . . . I have spoken to Conservatives, I have spoken to Liberals, I have spoken to leading trade unionists, and they cannot get it out of their heads . . . that there has been some corruption.' This led Booth to make a startling demand: 'If there is no other way to prevent these things I am going to advocate a Coalition Government.'[1] Trevor Wilson, in *The Downfall of the Liberal Party*, glancingly refers to this outburst as one of the earliest instances of a Liberal MP friendly to Lloyd George publicly commending a coalition government, but he does not explain the context.[2] What was actually happening in early 1915 was that a group of 'jingo' Liberals was linking an attack on alleged corruption with calls for a fundamental change in the running of the War—a change, moreover, which was intended to enhance the Chancellor's authority. The transformation of Lloyd George's reputation was already under way.[3]

Political opponents who had taken part in the mud-slinging against the pre-war Asquith Government could obviously not be expected to drop their prejudices overnight and to see things in Handel Booth's way. Lloyd George's apparent hesitation in August 1914, before the issuing of the ultimatum to Germany, had not exactly boosted his reputation in the eyes of the Diehard Tories, and in the early months of the War their distrust of his methods and viewpoint often spilled over

[1] *Parl. Deb.*, 5th ser., lxx. 507–10 (25 Feb. 1915).
[2] Wilson, Trevor, *The Downfall of the Liberal Party 1914–1935* (London, 1966), p. 53.
[3] But though the agitation had strong backing from the *Daily Chronicle*, many Conservative journals consciously distanced themselves from it. The *Saturday Review*, for example, said: 'We do not consider the Meyer contract agitation an honest agitation at all, and we will have nothing whatever to do with it. The company which is—on the surface—so eager about it is not at all to our liking' (1 May 1915).

into public and private expressions of hostility. Willoughby de Broke wrote bitterly in June 1915: Lloyd George 'seems rather proud of our being so badly prepared for war. He admits that we were worse prepared for war than any other nation. He then goes on to say he is not altogether sorry. Why should he be? His own friends are not being killed, while yours and mine are being picked off every day.'[4]

Maxse, the recipient of this letter, was also hearing complaints from his Tory and Radical Right associates about the Liberals' continuation of their partisan methods of distributing patronage, for which Lloyd George was given much of the blame.[5] More specifically, many Tories suspected that prominent Liberals were receiving more than their fair share of 'cushy' Staff appointments, while patriotic Conservative youths were left to get on with the bloody unglamorous side of the fighting.[6] Thus there were mutterings about the situation occupied by Lloyd George's sons, Dick and Gwilym, who, thanks to their father's influence, spent the first months of the War serving as ADCs to Generals. One must, in fairness, add that both men later took part in actual combat, facing danger with great bravery. But Lloyd George's earlier attempts to shield them, though understandable, were, as his biographer says, rather difficult to reconcile with his oratorical flights on the recruiting platform.[7] The Liberal Ministry, it seemed, was still up to its old tricks; and few Tories, as yet, suggested that Lloyd George was not as much involved in such petty jobbery as his colleagues.

Moreover, the shadow of Marconi still hung over Lloyd George's career in 1915. 'Did you see in the Daily Mail the photo of Lloyd George in Paris accompanied by Lord Murray?', wrote Lord Crawford to Maxse in February. 'I think it indecent how the latter and Lord Reading are rivetting their fetters round the Treasury.'[8] Comments of this kind continued to be made after Lloyd George became Minister of Munitions in May. This was not surprising, since Lloyd George made regular use of Murray's political services, believing him to be a good friend, though Frances Stevenson confided to her diary that she did not trust him at all.[9]

Meanwhile, Lord Reading, the Lord Chief Justice, was very much in Lloyd George's company and privy to many of his secrets.[10] The result was the reconstitution of the 'Marconi gang' in 1915–16—something which alarmed many political observers. Among the latter was Lord

[4] Willoughby de Broke to Maxse, 5 June 1915 (West Sussex Record Office, Maxse papers, vol. 470, fo. 225).

[5] e.g. Page Croft to Maxse, 14 Jan. 1915, with enclosure (ibid., fos. 14–21).

[6] Raymond Greene to Maxse, 5 Apr. 1915 (ibid., fos. 118–20).

[7] Grigg, *Lloyd George: From Peace to War*, pp. 171, 404.

[8] Crawford to Maxse, 10 Feb. 1915 (Maxse papers, vol. 470, fo. 77).

[9] Frances Stevenson's diary, 21 Jan. 1916, in Taylor, A. J. P. (ed.), *Lloyd George. A Diary by Frances Stevenson* (London, 1971), p. 88.

[10] For Lloyd George's use of Reading in the early stages of the War, see Grigg, *Lloyd George*, p. 152.

Esher, acting as an informal liaison officer at British Headquarters in France. When Lloyd George, now War Secretary, arrived there in September 1916, accompanied by the Marconi gang and a large press entourage, Esher was appalled.

Lloyd George made the *worst* impression and showed himself to be what he really is, a clever political adventurer seeking limelight. He came surrounded by satellites, Lord Reading who lowers the dignity, authority and status of the great office he holds by dabbling in finance and politics, Murray of Elibank whose reputation for honest dealing is more than doubtful and lesser lights of equally questionable character.[11]

It was probably on this occasion, or perhaps a little earlier, that, according to Esher's letter to Maxse of 29 September, Lloyd George showed his lack of breeding by asking the French Generals in private what they thought of Haig and of the British High Command. In addition, complained Esher, 'he allows Lord Reading and Lord Murray of Elibank to follow suit. All this trotting about, followed by the old Marconi Gang, including Godfrey Isaacs who turned up simultaneously in our hotel, gives one a very uncomfortable feeling.' Yet in this same letter Esher expressed his divided feelings about Lloyd George: he 'says things that are eminently right in themselves, and although he says them in a common way, they *are* so right, that one disregards his mannerisms.'[12] That Lloyd George, while undoubtedly a 'phenomenal little cad', was the one Minister with flair, drive, and a capacity to get things done was a fact which Esher clearly grasped. But why, he wondered, could the man not keep better company? When a few months later he stumbled upon further evidence of Murray's political and financial skulduggery, Esher once more subsided into a state of unhappy bewilderment.[13]

Some of the politicians and journalists active in the pre-war campaign against the Marconi gang never managed to revise their view of Lloyd George, despite the latter's growing reputation as an efficient and determined war minister. For example, although *Justice* adopted a stridently jingoistic line, of a kind that was commonly associated with support for Lloyd George, it would have required a more important event than the Great War to induce Hyndman to abandon his contempt for the Welsh politician, whose moral and political failings his readers were never allowed to forget.[14]

A patriot and crusader for 'political purity' of another hue was Loe Strachey, editor of the *Spectator*. Strachey, too, could never forgive the

---

[11] Esher's War Journal, 17 Sept. 1916, cited in Fraser, Peter, *Lord Esher: A Political Biography* (London, 1973), p. 331.

[12] Esher to Maxse, 29 Sept. 1916 (Maxse papers, vol. 473, fo. 801).

[13] See Fraser, *Esher*, pp. 349–50 and 451 nn. 95 and 96, for Elibank's relationship with the suspicious Baron Gunzburg.

[14] *Justice*, 6 May 1915: 'Lloyd George: A Danger to the Country'.

'guilty men' of the Marconi Scandal. Indeed, the *Spectator*'s hostility to Lloyd George actually intensified during 1916 when it became apparent that there was some sort of alliance between him and Northcliffe; for Strachey viewed with dismay the scurrilous attacks on Asquith and the official Unionist leaders being mounted by patriotic 'independents'. So strongly did Strachey feel about this that in April 1916 he wrote to Bonar Law, offering to stand as a Coalition Unionist candidate 'to give my indignation rein against the Kennedy Jones', the Pemberton Billings and the Gibson Bowles' '; he added, unnecessarily perhaps, that he would not be asking for help from the party funds![15] The offer was not taken up. Strachey never, at any stage in the War, fell under Lloyd George's spell; the kindest thing he could think to say of him was that he lacked 'weight of mind'.[16] Significantly for the future, Lord Salisbury was another sceptic. In June 1916 he wrote to his cousin, Balfour, urging Milner's claims to the vacant war secretaryship, comparing Milner favourably with Lloyd George, who eventually landed the job: 'Lloyd George has I admit enthusiasm, and patriotism too if you like. But for the rest he is a windbag and a liar, inspiring no confidence and useless as a man of business . . .'.[17] This remained Salisbury's view.

However, other former critics of Lloyd George were anxious to bury the hatchet. Notable among their number was Oliver Locker-Lampson, who had brought in the Traffic in Titles Bill on the eve of the War. Moreover, in his anxiety to stamp out what he saw as corruption, Locker-Lampson, together with a Conservative solicitor called Peter Wright, had in 1913 bought some English Marconi shares, so that the two men, in their capacity as shareholders, could bring an action for fraud against Godfrey Isaacs and his co-directors for the way they had handled the issue of the American Marconi shares—a course of action which had been suggested to them by the judge in the Cecil Chesterton Trial.[18]

The outbreak of the War delayed the hearing of this case. Then in late 1916 the solicitors representing Godfrey Isaacs and those representing the plaintiffs decided to reach a settlement out of court; the

---

[15] Strachey to Bonar Law (copy), 17 Apr. 1916 (HLRO, Strachey papers, S/9/8/16).

[16] Strachey to Garvin (copy), 20 June 1917 (ibid., S/7/1/3). In this letter Strachey conceded that Lloyd George might mean well, 'but I am genuinely alarmed as to what he is going to do next.'

[17] Salisbury to Balfour, 15 June 1916 (BL, Balfour papers, Add. MS 49,758, fo. 311).

[18] See Donaldson, *Marconi Scandal*, p. 235. From 1914 until the end of the War, Wright was in receipt of regular sums of £50, out of a fund which Locker-Lampson had set up to further 'our great enterprise'. Locker-Lampson realized that the War would interfere with their litigation, but he wrote in Nov. 1914: 'I do not intend to forego any chance of righting a wrong and the recent case only strengthens me in my belief that I am right.' (Norfolk Record Office, O. Locker-Lampson papers, vol. 2682, Wright to Locker-Lampson, 2 Mar. 1915; ibid., vol. 2238, Locker-Lampson to Charles Bright (copy), 23 Nov. 1914).

charge of fraud was dropped, but Isaacs admitted committing an irregularity and agreed to contribute to the legal costs of the case. The settlement was formally announced in October 1916.[19] A partial explanation for what had happened was then provided by Isaacs's counsel, Sir John Simon, in an interesting letter which he sent to Lloyd George on 23 October. 'The action if tried', he wrote, 'would necessarily have aroused the old Marconi storm in some degree and I am glad on public and national grounds it is ended. Oliver Locker-Lampson has behaved very well about it and I think there is no doubt he felt that in present circumstances the continuance of such an action was regrettable.' Simon went on: 'He feels distressed at the idea that he should be supposed to have wanted to persist in it for political reasons or by way of attacking *you* and he would very much appreciate the chance of telling you so.' It would be a nice gesture, Simon suggested, if Lloyd George could shake hands with Locker-Lampson before the latter returned to the Russian Front.[20] Whether this touching reconciliation occurred we do not know.

Moreover, it was a sign of Lloyd George's growing reputation that even those concerned to keep alive the memories of Marconi were now shifting their attack from Lloyd George to Reading. Ellis Powell of the *Financial News*, for example, had been a fierce critic of the Chancellor of the Exchequer in 1912 and 1913,[21] but under the pressure of war he was beginning to re-evaluate the whole episode. The sensational articles of late 1916 made no mention of Lloyd George at all, and Powell admitted that some of his readers had asked the reason for this omission. 'The answer is quite simple', he wrote on 22 November 1916. 'Mr Lloyd George was only interested to an infinitesimal extent. . . . He was "roped in" at the time of the Marconi boom, to protect other people.' Lloyd George had soon afterweards realized how he had been made a 'stalking-horse, or else a scapegoat'. Powell described Lloyd George as 'impulsive and confiding, like all true Celts'. But he brusquely dismissed the suggestion that such a man could ever have been subjected to the 'German "screw"'. 'His own admirable achievements would be the all-sufficient answer to anybody who should suspect *him*' of being animated by anything 'save his own passionate desire to do the best for his country within the scope of his special activities.'[22]

This new-found confidence in Lloyd George on the part of the Radical Right was accompanied by, and even in part the consequence

[19] There is much information on this in the Gwynne Papers (Bodleian, Box 1), which contains many of the letters which Wright sent to Gwynne.
[20] Simon to Lloyd George, 23 Oct. 1916 (HLRO, Lloyd George papers, E/3/8/1). Incidentally, Locker-Lampson backed Lloyd George in the Dec. 1916 crisis (Locker-Lampson to Bonar Law (copy), 5 Dec. 1916, Locker-Lampson papers, vol. 2141).
[21] See e.g. the comments on Marconi in the *Financial News*, 14 June, 20 June 1913.
[22] Ibid., 22 Nov. 1916.

of, its growing disillusionment with the official Conservative leadership. Up to a point, this was almost bound to happen. Throughout most of the Edwardian period, as we have seen, right-wing Tories, like Maxse, had voiced their suspicions of *both* Front Benches, believing them to be in 'collusion'. By leading the Unionist Party in an aggressive assault on the pre-war Asquith Administration, Bonar Law had momentarily removed such suspicions and captured the allegiance of his own Diehard backbenchers. But with the formation of the First Coalition Government in May 1915, the old anxieties quickly returned. In any case, members of the Radical Right only felt really happy in opposition. They had no patience with or tolerance of the compromises of office. So as Bonar Law became more and more implicated in the failures of the Asquith Coalition, in whose defence he soon found himself making a series of rather limp speeches, the discontent of the Diehards grew. 'We must get rid of Bonar, Chamberlain and Lansdowne', the Duke of Northumberland was writing in March 1916. 'It is quite as necessary to get rid of them as it is to get rid of "Squiff".'[23]

Moreover, the Unionists' entry into the Government had in no way destroyed the traditional party system. All that had happened was that there were now *two* sets of party managers and *two* groups of party loyalists pressing their claims to an honour. And after ten years in the wildnerness the Unionists had accumulated a very large number of debts, some of which were rather embarrassing. Scarcely had the first Coalition Government been formed than the Unionist Chairman, Steel-Maitland, and the Chief Whip, Lord Edmund Talbot, found it necessary, metaphorically speaking, to put up crush barriers outside Unionist Party headquarters to control the queues of supplicants who waved 'pledges' in their face, uttered threats, and, in some cases, betrayed their feelings in weeping and hysteria.[24]

When they actually came to draw up their honours lists, Maitland and Talbot gave due weight to these obligations, and their recommendations to Law frequently carried such phrases as 'promise of Hood' and 'has spent close on £10,000 for party purposes'.[25] The result was a further 'inflation' of honours which in turn led to public anger. The Birthday List of June 1916 was particularly unpopular, in part because, by an unfortunate coincidence, the long list of new party and official honours appeared in some newspapers on the same page as the news of the casualties incurred at the Battle of Jutland. As Jack Sandars bitterly complained, countless party loyalists and social climbers had been 'advanced in their strange ambitions', but the Navy, by contrast,

---

[23] Northumberland to Maxse, 16? Apr. 1916 (Maxse papers, vol. 472, fo. 657).
[24] See correspondence in the Bonar Law papers (HLRO), esp. vol. 52.
[25] See memo. in Bonar Law papers, Dec. 1915 (63/A/1).

had been 'practically ignored'—'yet it is the Navy that we are all thinking of to-day.'[26]

There was a further disturbing feature of the June 1916 Honours List, as far as Conservatives were concerned, which was that most of the 'indefensible' promotions, like the grant of a barony to Astor, clearly fell within the responsibility of the Unionist Party.[27] At a personal level, it is true, Bonar Law viewed the whole honours business with extreme distaste, but, like Asquith, he wearily accepted it as an inescapable part of the British party system, and, once in office, he showed not the smallest desire to stop, or even to make a fuss about, those 'abuses' in the system which both traditional Conservatives and the Radical Right found so offensive.[28]

One name on the 1916 Birthday Honours List was especially unpopular with many Conservatives: that of Max Aitken, who was made a baronet. *The Times* explained that the award was given for Aitken's wartime services to Canada, adding: 'Politically he is the close friend and adviser of Mr Bonar Law.'[29] A. J. P. Taylor has told the involved story of Aitken's baronetcy: how Asquith had succeeded in blocking this promotion a year earlier, how timid Bonar Law had proved to be in pressing the claims of his friend, how the devious behaviour of the Duke of Connaught, the Governor-General, left the understandable impression that the honour conferred on Aitken had ignored the advice of the Canadian Government, and how King George V had made difficulties over this use of his royal prerogative.[30]

Aitken's acquisition of a baronetcy, even without these complications, would probably have stirred up controversy. In his masterly biography of Beaverbrook, Taylor discounts the rumours according to which Aitken was supposed to have left Canada in a storm to escape the scandals which his unscrupulous money-making methods had aroused in his homeland.[31] But the vital point is that these rumours were widely believed. Indeed, in 1912 Aitken received a warning that the Liberals were assembling material about his business past with a

[26] Sandars to Maxse, 3 June 1916 (Maxse papers, vol. 472, fo. 685).

[27] Page Croft alleged in Dec. 1919 that Astor had bought his peerage and also that his daughter-in-law was adopted as a Conservative 'solely because the local Association desired to retain the advantage of the Astor wealth'. Croft suggested a modification of the Act of Settlement to restrict the right of foreigners to sit in Parliament. Astor's American origins clearly contributed to the unpopularity of his promotion (Page Croft to Salisbury, 1 Dec. 1919, Hatfield, 4th Marquess of Salisbury papers, 94/93–5).

[28] e.g. he referred in a letter to Mond (16 Dec. 1918) to 'the wretched honours list' (Bonar Law papers, 84/7/118), and he later suggested that a party supporter should be given the Order of Merit for not wanting a title! (Bonar Law to Younger (copy), 25 Apr. 1919, ibid., 101/3/53).

[29] Taylor, A. J. P., *Beaverbrook* (London, 1972), p. 99. Taylor wonders who inspired this sentence, which only *The Times* published.

[30] Ibid. 98–9.

[31] Ibid. 41.

view to discrediting him with his constituents.[32] Bonar Law was thus running a certain risk in keeping up this rather odd friendship. Certainly, during the succession struggle following Balfour's resignation as Leader, Conservative Central Office and the Whips were expressing anxiety about Aitken's influence over Bonar Law, while Jack Sandars commented: 'the way in which the *Daily Express* is promoting that candidature is American—and sinister.'[33]

What seems initially to have drawn the two men together, apart from their common Canadian links, was a passion for speculation. Aitken and Bonar Law had first done a business deal in 1908, two years before Aitken entered the Commons. Later the Canadian adventurer had persuaded Law to put down £100,000 and enter a syndicate with himself and others for the purpose of selling Price Brothers bonds.[34] Such activities linked the two men to one another for the rest of their lives. Taylor has calculated that nine-tenths of the voluminous Aitken–Law correspondence is given over to financial matters and that by the end of the War the Conservative Leader was possibly benefiting from the relationship to the tune of £10,000 a year, tax free.[35] To use F. S. Oliver's phrase, Aitken was, indeed, Bonar Law's 'financial major domo'.[36]

But if Aitken was the type of person with whom the Conservative Leader chose to associate, what claim did his Party have to moral superiority over Lloyd George and his highly controversial Radical friends? 'None whatsoever' was the answer which most of the Diehards would have given in the course of 1916. By contrast, Lloyd George seemed to have much more to offer the right wing of the Tory Party. For example, his commitment to the cause of conscription in late 1915 and his 'Knock Out Blow' interview in September 1916 delighted the patriotic Right, for the same reason that traditional Liberals were filled with indignation and dismay. Moreover, the growing alliance between Lloyd George and the Tory Right was not based simply on policy agreements. For Lloyd George was articulating—and far more effectively than Law and most official Unionist leaders were able to do—the *mood* which prevailed in Diehard circles.

The developing political views of Page Croft illustrate this point.

---

[32] See the correspondence between Steel-Maitland and Aitken in Aug., Sept., and Oct. 1912 in the Beaverbrook papers (HLRO, C/239).

[33] Balcarres's Diary, 10 Nov. 1911, in Vincent (ed.), *The Crawford Papers*, p. 246.

[34] Taylor, *Beaverbrook*, p. 45.   [35] Ibid.

[36] Oliver to Maxse, 11 Feb. 1916 (Maxse papers, vol. 472, fo. 573). Of the many letters about investments which passed between the two men, this one will suffice: 'As arranged on Sunday I enclose cheque for £1700 which I think is somewhere about the amount of my debt to you. After sending this I have still £8000 left as the return on an investment of £2200 so that the want of money is not one of my worries. I need not tell you how grateful I am to you for all your have done in this matter' (Bonar Law to Beaverbrook (copy), 20 Sept. 1917, Beaverbrook papers, C/203).

During his spell of service at the Front, Croft had reached the conclusion that the social relationships being formed in the trenches provided a model that civilian society ought to follow. As he told the *Daily Graphic* in November 1915: 'I could give many instances to prove how effective the New Socialism has become both between the men themselves and between officers and men as they enter the crucible in which Peer and Ploughboy are fused in one common fellowship.'[37] Page Croft contrasted this social solidarity with the perennial bickering of the House of Commons, where what divided people was always emphasized, not what united them. In place of the existing political system Croft called for a new National Party and a new kind of government that would stand fairly and squarely on the Union Jack and keep clear of the old, decaying party issues. Now this simple-minded appeal echoed what was being said on the public platform by Lloyd George, himself an embodiment of the will to victory which transcended party political strife.

Little wonder, then, that when Lloyd George became Prime Minister in December 1916 Croft was delighted. Addressing a public meeting at Queen's Hall, the brigadier expressed his satisfaction with the recently formed 'National Government', with the stream-lined War Cabinet, and, indeed, with the personality of the Premier. 'They had suddenly felt a great relief', he told his cheering audience. He explained that he himself 'had always been bitterly opposed to Mr Lloyd George in the past and it was an extraordinary thing that he should now find himself in this situation where his heart and his support went out to Mr Lloyd George. It was because the new Prime Minister meant business.'[38]

This was by no means an uncharacteristic Diehard reaction. The *Morning Post* took the same line,[39] and so, incredibly, did the *National Review*, which declared a clear preference for the Lloyd George Government, with all its faults, to the 'Old Gang' of the former Administration. 'While doing lip service to the War', quipped Maxse, the Asquith Ministry had 'somehow conveyed the impression that it regarded the War as an inconvenient interruption of the more serious business of life, ie Party strife—which Mr Asquith was for ever glorifying'.[40] There was no irony in the letters which stalwart readers of the *National Review* sent the editor in early 1917, congratulating him on the part he had played in helping Lloyd George to supreme power.[41] For, at least during the first half of 1917, these people could

[37] *Daily Graphic*, 23 Nov. 1915.
[38] *The Times*, 13 Dec. 1916.
[39] Gwynne's own changing views on Lloyd George during the first half of the War are recorded in his letters to Lady Bathurst. See Koss, *Rise and Fall*, ii. 285.
[40] *National Review*, lxix (1917), pp. 7–8.
[41] H. Norman Ballantyne to Maxse, 28 Jan. 1917 (Maxse papers, vol. 474, N. 12). But one Tory, Sir Thomas Edwards-Moss, cancelled his subscription to the monthly when Maxse took this line. As he later explained to Esher, he had first taken the *National*

convince themselves that the Welshman had seen the errors of his ways and now stood for all the goals which *they* had long been pursuing. For example, many Diehards made what in retrospect seems the extraordinary error of supposing that Lloyd George, compared with his predecessor, would be less likely to 'interfere' with the conduct of the War. Another odd idea gripped many Diehards in December 1916, and that was that Lloyd George might join them as an ally in their attempts to clean up the abuses of the party system.

Attempted Reform of the Honours System

There were probably two reasons for this latter belief. Having committed themselves to the view that the Empire, in its danger, needed Lloyd George's leadership, the Diehards seem to have been under a powerful psychological compulsion to believe, in the teeth of all the evidence, that the new Premier would act as an agent of political purification. This was, perhaps, simply the reverse side to the belief, explored in Chapter 11, that pro-German, anti-war, and defeatist figures in public life were also liable to be corrupt. But equally important was the conviction in these circles that corruption was an integral part of the unreformed party system. The formation of a 'National Government' headed by a vigorous and patriotic statesman who had reached the highest office in the land without any organized party to sustain him could therefore be seen as prefiguring a complete and radical change of political methods—especially in the vexed matter of honours.

Indeed, it did seem at first that, with Lloyd George as Prime Minister, the Government had turned over a new leaf. Thus, while giving credit to Gwynne and the *Morning Post* for the improvements, the *National Review* expressed pleasure with the new Premier's 1917 New Year's Honours List, which was compared favourably with 'the jobbery and snobbery' of his predecessor's recommendations; it contained, thought Maxse, 'no man whom the King had been advised to ennoble because of his cheque-book or for unspeakable Party services which no man dare specify'. The paper added that this 'was all the more to Mr Lloyd George's credit, because the old gang are understood to have captured the Party Funds'. The new Premier, it concluded, might open an entirely new chapter in public life by building up whatever war chest he needed by launching an open appeal, rather on the lines of the recent appeal for money to build the

because of its 'independent and strong line' at the time of Marconi. He later gave it up 'because it formerly denounced George as a dead wrong 'un, and now called upon us to support him as Premier. People who shift about like this are of no use to me . . . ' (Edwards-Moss to Esher, 5 Apr. 1918, Imperial War Museum, Henry Wilson papers, 34A).

'Eton memorial to the fallen', which had brought in £58,000.[42] One must add that Maxse seems not to have been joking! Even in private, there were similar expressions of optimism. Writing to Lord Salisbury in March 1917, the veteran Tory politician, Harry Chaplin (now Lord Chaplin) agreed that the 'pitch' to which the honours scandals had got was 'unbearable', and he admitted that there had been 'some glaring cases of late'. But he concluded: 'Lloyd George—I should think—would be very likely to take it up "con amore". He is very open minded and never wanting in pluck.'[43]

At that very moment Lord Salisbury, who had perhaps unwisely been left out of the new Coalition Government,[44] was in communication with some eminent peers and privy councillors who he knew shared his own anxieties about the operation of the honours system.[45] The result was an appeal to the Prime Minister signed by forty signatories. Salisbury assured Lloyd George that he did not want to raise the issue in Parliament during 'the present emergency', but he begged him to use his 'exceptional position' to ensure that British public life was 'pure and free from reproach'.[46] The signatories added that they 'had no thought of attacking the Government of which you are the head, or any other Government'. But they strongly urged three proposals upon Lloyd George: that in future a public statement should be made explaining why an honour or dignity had been conferred; that the Prime Minister should assure himself that 'no payment or expectations of payment [was] directly or indirectly associated with the grant or promise of an honour'; and that an audit of party funds should be instituted.[47]

Many of Salisbury's associates seem initially to have been confident that their appeal would be sympathetically received, though such confidence was somewhat dampened by 10 Downing Street's prolonged silence.[48] Then on 1 June there appeared the Birthday Honours list, one of the longest ever compiled, with twelve new peerages and no fewer than twenty-four baronetcies. Lord Rosebery, who had been reluctant to sign the appeal in the first place,[49] took a rueful pleasure in the

[42] National Review, lxix (1917), 42.

[43] Chaplin to Salisbury, 8 Mar. 1917 (Salisbury papers, S(4), 233, fo. 20).

[44] Salisbury had been offered the Leadership of the Lords, but had turned down the post when he learned that he would not be given a Department of State to run or a seat in the Cabinet (Rose, Later Cecils, p. 86).

[45] See material in Salisbury papers, S(4), 233.

[46] Memo. to the Prime Minister, 25 Mar. 1917, accompanied by Salisbury's letter to Lloyd George (copy), 25 Mar. 1917 (ibid., fos. 3–7).

[47] Ibid.

[48] Salisbury was encouraged by Stamfordham, who ended one of his letters: 'It is impossible to overrate the feelings of nausea with which the ever recurring consideration of honours fill yours very truly' (Stamfordham to Salisbury, 23 May 1917, ibid., fo. 29).

[49] Rosebery later explained to Salisbury that he had signed the Memorial 'agreeing heartily with the principle, though not with every clause. Both parties are tarred with the same brush in this matter. There ought of course to be a much stricter control vested in

event: 'Surely that swollen list of birthday honours was a sufficient answer to the memorial', he told Salisbury on 9 June, 'and indeed the only one that I expected.'[50] But more typical was the response of *The Times*, which published a censorious editorial on the subject, but also showed sympathy with 'Mr Lloyd George's difficulties' and hoped that the List would be the last of its kind; now that old-style party politics had disappeared, it observed, the 'accumulated funds in existence could perhaps be diverted by common consent to some national object'. In June 1917 it was still possible to talk with a straight face about the possibility of Lord Edmund Talbot and Captain 'Freddie' Guest handing over unwanted money to some deserving war charity.[51] In short, there was still a general disposition to give the new Prime Minister the benefit of the doubt.

Salisbury himself had all along taken a more realistic view of Lloyd George's character and intentions and did not feel so sanguine.[52] He had needed to nag the Prime Minister's Office even to get a considered reply to his appeal.[53] And though Lloyd George eventually met him on 20 June and expressed a readiness to arrange a friendly response to all three of the proposals if a parliamentary question were put down in the House of Lords, a subsequent meeting between Lord Selborne and Curzon, the Leader of the Upper House, strongly suggested that the Prime Minister was having second thoughts.[54] 'The Prime Minister has turned out exactly the humbug I expected in relation to the matter of your interview with him', Selborne reported to Salisbury.[55] The two campaigners then reassembled the forty original signatories at Salisbury's

the King. But the only practical remedy that I can see, and that only a partial one, is the laying of election expences on the constituencies and not on the candidates. But I rejoice that the protest has been made' (Rosebery to Salisbury, 20 June 1917, ibid., fo. 64).

[50] Rosebery to Salisbury, 9 June 1917 (ibid., fo. 36).

[51] *The Times*, 4 June 1917. Beresford declared, however, that the List made him feel sick. He ran down the names of the recipients: 'Devonport, a failure, to be made Viscount, Lord Astor, an American, who must have bought the Viscountcy, for what possible reason was he made a Peer and promoted? Lord Farquhar, whose services to the State are of such a transcendent character' (Beresford to Salisbury, 4 June 1917 (Salisbury papers, S(4), 233, fo. 30). Farquhar had become Lord Steward of the Household in 1915, and in 1917 was promoted to a viscountcy (Rose, Kenneth, *King George V* (London, 1983), p. 276). Many newspapers referred disapprovingly to Astor's receipt of a viscountcy coming, as it did, so quickly after his barony (e.g. *Daily News*, 8 Aug. 1917: editorial, 'The Fount of Honour').

[52] In May 1917 Salisbury created a 'ginger group' in the House of Lords, the Unionist War Committee, many of whose members were involved in the honours agitation.

[53] Salisbury to signatories of March Memo., 7 June 1917, and Salisbury to Lloyd George (copy), 7 June 1917 (Salisbury papers, S(4), 233, fos. 32, 34).

[54] J. T. Davis to Salisbury, 8 June 1917; Salisbury's Notes on a Conversation with Lloyd George, with accompanying letter to Lloyd George (copy), 20 June 1917; Salisbury to Selborne (copy), 26 June 1917 (ibid., fos. 35, 59–60, 66). 'The miraculous has happened', Salisbury told Selborne on 26 June. See also Selborne to Curzon (copy), 27 June 1917; Curzon to Selborne, 27 June 1917; Selborne to Salisbury, 4 July 1917 (ibid., fos. 79, 85–6).

[55] Selborne to Salisbury, 6 July 1917 (ibid., 80/6–7).

London house on 17 July, where it was decided that they should bring in their own Resolution in the Lords, with or without Government approval.[56]

This was duly done on 7 August, though, interestingly, Selborne, who opened the discussion, omitted all reference to the audit of party funds, which had been dropped as too 'radical'.[57] It was a poorly attended debate and also an inconsequential one. Crewe, for the Independent Liberals, poured cold water on Selborne's suggestions,[58] while Curzon orated about the difficulties of reform and questioned the whole notion that any real corruption was occurring. For this he earned a stinging rebuke from Salisbury, who insisted that of course corruption existed: 'My noble friend said that he knew nothing about it, and had never heard of it. *O sancta simplicitas!*'[59] Wrote Selborne to his wife: 'G[eorge] N[athaniel] C[urzon] took just the line on the honours debate which I anticipated, minimising the evil, exaggerating the difficulties of dealing with it, and professing pious sentiments—an adroit speech for its purpose. He has no ideals. Jem [Salisbury] trounced him in reply quite admirably.'[60]

But the Government's stalling tactics worked. Salisbury agreed to amend one of the resolutions to make it clear that only party contributions, not charitable donations, were to be disassociated from the award of honours, and the Lords agreed to defer further consideration of the matter until the autumn.[61] This time the Lords did pass Selborne's Resolution, with the Government agreeing to put its provisions into operation. Henceforward, the Prime Minister was committed to ensuring that the award of an honour was not simply the reward for contributions to the party funds, and, except in the case of public servants, he would have to issue a statement of why the honour had been conferred.[62] Whether the Government really accepted the *spirit* of these reforms was quite another matter.[63]

Salisbury and his friends were unable to make much further progress

---

[56] Selborne's Memo. of 17 July 1917 (ibid., fo. 90); Selborne to Salisbury and Midleton, 17 July 1917 (ibid., fos. 91–2); Salisbury's Notes on Meeting of 17 July 1917 (ibid., fo. 88).

[57] *Parl. Deb.*, 5th ser. (Lords), xxvi. 172–212 (7 Aug. 1917).

[58] Ibid. 182–4.   [59] Ibid. 172–212.

[60] Selborne to Wife, 7 Aug. 1917 (Bodleian, Selborne papers, vol. 103, fo. 27). Lord Montagu was also delighted by Salisbury's retort (Montagu to Salisbury, 10 Aug. 1917, Salisbury papers, S(4), 233, fo. 108). Salisbury had had a tense relationship with Curzon for many years. His wife, Alice, had been the recipient of Kitchener's complaints against Curzon when the latter was Indian Viceroy (Rose, *Later Cecils*, pp. 83–4).

[61] *Parl. Deb.*, 5th ser. (Lords), xxvi. 208–12 (7 Aug. 1917).

[62] Ibid. 835–86 (31 Oct. 1917).

[63] Thus it took another initiative from Selborne in March 1918 before Ministers could be persuaded to specify in the *Gazette* what services to their country the newly created peers and baronets were supposed to have performed. Before then Downing Street had simply given out a brief and erratic description of the background and career of new recipients of honours, which newspapers could either ignore or print, as they chose—so evading the purpose of the reform (ibid. xxix. 513–33 (20 Mar. 1918).

while the War was being waged. Indeed, they did their cause positive damage when, against their better judgement, they decided to release to *The Times* a letter, mainly drafted by Lord Loreburn, which protested, *inter alia*, at the wholesale distribution of minor honours, like the recently instituted Order of the British Empire.[64] This was a mistake. Granted that there might be something faintly absurd about a title allocated so generously that a recent OBE List had covered 600 printed pages, was it really sensible to annoy thousands of harmless, respectable citizens—especially in view of the fact that nobody seriously believed that the OBE was being *sold* to fill the party coffers? Those peers who had all along been unhappy at the content and phraseology of the Loreburn Letter[65] were vindicated by the response it elicited. *The Times*, for example, published the irate reflections of an anonymous correspondent calling himself 'ONLY AN MBE', who quoted the words of Dr Johnson, 'Madam, *I* never counted *your* cups of tea', and complained that 'this detraction of the British Empire Order [was] bitterly resented by many recipients of the Order, especially in the lower grades.'[66] Government Ministers quickly realized that Salisbury and his aristocratic friends were wide open to this sort of attack and employed it quite effectively when in November 1918 Selborne made yet another attempt to tackle the honours question—this time by resurrecting his own favourite nostrum, the scrutinizing committee of the Privy Council.[67] And there matters rested at the time of the Armistice.

The honours question was to give Lloyd George much trouble in the future. But this could not easily have been predicted in the summer of 1917, when even the Radical Right tended to believe that the new Prime Minister was secretly on their side and actually wanted to be rescued from the abuses of the political system he had inherited.

[64] Salisbury's Memo. of 5 July 1918; Loreburn to Salisbury, 9 July 1918; Salisbury to Loreburn (copy), 18 July 1918 (Salisbury papers, S(4), 233, fos. 128, 137, 150–2). Loreburn's letter was read out to the meeting. It painted a lurid picture of creeping corruption in British politics. 'I believe that the party machines in this country are in great danger of falling over the precipice,' declared Loreburn, 'and there are some signs that they have slipped down towards the brink already. For example, I believe that Ll. George was really free from any dishonesty in the Marconi affaire and was really what he said himself exceedingly foolish, but I also greatly fear that there was a deep-laid and most dangerous plot to corrupt our public life of which he was innocent and one cannot help fearing that the party machines or one of them, if not both, have helped to cover up the scandal.' Loreburn concluded by suggesting that a public letter should be sent to the press, preparatory to another discussion in Parliament. (Loreburn to Salisbury, 9 July 1918, ibid.)
[65] e.g. Plymouth to Salisbury, 14 July 1918; Donoughmore to Salisbury, 18 Aug. 1918 (ibid. fos. 145–6, 171). See also Midleton to Salisbury, 7 Aug. 1918 (ibid., fo. 167). But so touchy was Loreburn that the other peers hesitated to correct his draft.
[66] *The Times*, 3 Sept. 1918. See other letters on this subject published in *The Times* on 31 Aug. and 3 Sept. 1918.
[67] *Parl. Deb.*, 5th ser. (Lords), xxxii. 4–34 (13 Nov. 1918).

Renewed Anxieties about Lloyd George

So long as the War lasted, then, there was still widespread confidence in the Prime Minister. But doubts and criticisms were more and more frequently voiced in its closing stages. Perhaps the most important single reason for growing Diehard disillusionment was the realization that the new Government was more, not less, tempted to interfere in the determination of strategy than Asquith's had been. In April 1918 Maxse was reacting to this by urging a Robertson Dictatorship![68] But it was the Maurice Debate of May 1918 which brought the relationship between Lloyd George and the Diehards almost to breaking point. Gwynne, expecting the fall of the Government and Asquith's return to power, actually wrote to Asquith a letter full of unsolicited advice, as was his wont. He admitted that he had once favoured Asquith's supersession by Lloyd George (though he said he had 'had no hand in the vulgar intrigue' which brought this about). But now, wrote Gwynne, he could see that Lloyd George had failed—partly because he was still playing the party game, partly because he would not leave his generals and admirals alone, but also, more basically still, because he was such an 'intriguer' that 'even his political friends and supporters confessed that they could not believe a word he said.'[69]

This view of Lloyd George's premiership as being flawed by moral weakness took a number of forms. First, there was the widely-held belief that Lloyd George was not a free agent, in that his past misdemeanours during the Marconi Affair had exposed him to blackmail from his more unscrupulous colleagues and associates. Shortly before the fall of the Asquith Coalition, C. P. Scott, on a visit to London, picked up a rumour that 'Northcliffe has some information about [Marconi] which he holds over George *in terrorem.*'[70] This rumour, and variations on it, enjoyed a long lease of life. For example, Moreton Frewen wrote to Strachey in January 1919 saying that he had been told by Gilbert Parker in strict confidence the following story: 'There are two Marconi letters of the PM's in Northcliffe's hands and to a degree they are compromising. These letters are about to come out in a libel action now ripening'; but when Northcliffe had tried to use these documents to influence the composition of the Peace Delegation, Frewen added, the Prime Minister had 'told him to "go to Hell!" '[71] Oddly enough, on the very same day that this communication was penned, Walter Long, the First Lord of the Admiralty, took it upon himself to warn Lloyd George of the dangers he faced:

[68] Maxse to Northcliffe, 15 Apr. 1918 (Maxse papers, vol. 475, T 256).
[69] Gwynne to Asquith (copy), 8 May 1918 (Gwynne papers, vol. 14).
[70] Scott's journal, 20–2 Nov. 1916, in Wilson (ed.), *Political Diaries of C. P. Scott*, p. 236.
[71] Frewen to Strachey, 23 Jan. 1919 (Strachey papers, S/6/4/17).

The talk of the town is that Northcliffe is out to destroy you, and rumours are going about that he has some Marconi letters of yours. I knew nothing about these; perhaps you would care to instruct your solicitors to make inquiries. Of this I am perfectly certain, that if he attempts anything of the kind, public opinion will be unanimous in condemning him as a blackmailer and supporting you; and speaking for a moment for my own Party, I am absolutely certain that they will be behind you and outspoken in their condemnation of such cowardly and un-English tactics.[72]

But, even when presented as the more or less innocent victim of blackmail, Lloyd George was bound to suffer in reputation as a result of such rumours. In September 1917 L. S. Amery met Kipling, who told him that 'the British people profoundly distrust the present Government, mainly because of Marconi' and he referred to 'a man in the train' who 'had told him the other day that the only reason why Churchill had been brought back was that he knew too much about that business and so was able to blackmail the Prime Minister'.[73]

Yet another version of this story was being put about by Hyndman, who linked Ellis Powell's conspiracy theory to his own belief in the villainy of Ramsay MacDonald. Why had MacDonald some sort of 'hold' over the Prime Minister, asked Hyndman in a private letter in April 1918:

Political and personal blackmail pure and simple. Ramsay was *in every detail* of the peace intrigue with George, Harcourt, Beauchamps, Morley, Burns and Co at the beginning of the War. Much went on then that is not publicly, or even privately, known. Then he has been kept—I believe is now—thoroughly well posted as to all the dirty work that went on at Amsterdam, Hamburg and Berlin about 'Marconi'. This from Berlin.[74]

A few months later he elaborated on this story:

MacDonald knows from Berlin, and has long known, the details of the dealings in Marconi shares at Amsterdam and Hamburg. More than that, he is aware *why* certain well-known Jews, here and on the Continent, have power over George, apart from the Marconi transactions. And political blackmail in this connection is not confined to MacDonald. Why does the Government protect so many of its friends by refusal to investigage scandals? 'There are millions in it!' . . . [75]

The belief that Lloyd George was compromised by his Marconi past was 'proved' in the eyes of many people by the serene progress of Lord Reading's career. Further honours and marks of recognition continued to come the Lord Chief Justice's way. He was made a viscount in 1916

---

[72] Long to Lloyd George, 23 Jan. 1919 (Lloyd George papers, F/33/2/7).
[73] Amery's diary, 10 Sept. 1917, in Barnes and Nicholson (eds.), *Leo Amery Diaries*, p. 171.
[74] Hyndman to Maxse, 6 Apr. 1918 (Maxse papers, vol. 475, T 241).
[75] Hyndman to Maxse, 1 May 1919 (ibid., vol. 476, M 48).

and an earl in November 1917. Lloyd George employed him in a number of capacities, including that of financial adviser to the Cabinet. Then in January 1918 the British Government sent Reading to Washington to replace the failing Cecil Spring-Rice. This in turn led to some ugly rumours; Northcliffe, from London, warned Reading that it was being said that the new Ambassador had recently been seeing Sir Edgar Speyer.[76] It was also alleged that he had been sent to the USA to protect the German Metal Trust.[77] Moreover, Reading was being subjected to the harrassment of a pamphleteer called J. W. Hamilton, who had already written to the Prime Minister and to the Director of Public Prosecutions, urging them to investigate the charges contained in Ellis Powell's *Financial News* articles.[78] He then started to distribute scurrilous leaflets, such as 'The Wireless Ghost', in which Reading was libellously attacked for his part in the Marconi Affair.[79] Once again, however, the Lord Chief Justice took absolutely no notice of his tormentors.

Meanwhile, in January 1918 Powell had sent Lloyd George an outspoken letter, pleading with him to end his association with 'the chief foreign conspirator', as Powell dubbed Reading. The public had come to suspect, he said, that Lord Reading was blackmailing the Government into not prosecuting the War with sufficient vigour:

In fact . . . the rumour is persistently and mischievously spread that Lord Reading has a 'hold' upon you, and that he can make you dance to any tune he pleases. . . . Add the continual appearance of Lord Reading's name in combination with yours as if you were his secretary or his servant, and the reiterated (and of course carefully arranged) publication of his portrait showing you in his company, and finally his appointment to Washington, a position for which, in public opinion, (in spite of the applause of an obvious claque) he is the most unsuitable man who could possibly have been chosen, and you will understand why you . . . are suffering inestimable damage by the present public association with an individual who is more distrusted even than Lord Haldane.[80]

The anti-Reading agitation threatened to flare up in a big way in late 1918, when it was thought that the Lord Chief Justice had been selected as a member of the Versailles Peace Delegation. Even moderate critics of the Government felt a little uneasy over the Prime

[76] Northcliffe to Reading (copy), 8 Mar. 1918 (BL, Northcliffe papers, Add. MS 62,156, fo. 87).

[77] J. M. Clark to Mond, 17 July 1918, forwarded to Reading (India Office Library, Reading papers, F 118/58, fo. 4).

[78] See material in Gwynne papers, box 1. Hamilton was a civil engineer who sued the Marconi Company for damages for wrongful termination of an agreement under which he was to be the Company's sole representative in Australia.

[79] Hamilton to Strachey, 7 Dec. 1918, with enclosures (Strachey papers, S/8/12/4).

[80] Powell to Lloyd George, 24 Jan. 1918 (Lloyd George papers, F/94/3/1).

Minister's determination to stick by Reading through thick and thin, in the face of so much criticism.

In addition, there were numerous complaints, quite unconnected with Marconi, that Lloyd George was discrediting his reputation and his office by continually associating with the wrong type of person. Before December 1916 such complaints originated in the main with Radical Liberals and their friends. In January of that year, for example, John Dillon spoke regretfully to C. P. Scott about 'the degeneracy of Lloyd George'. 'On the principle of *Noscitur a sociis* he said it was lamentable to see the sort of man with whom he had now surrounded himself and with whom he was to be seen in frequent conference in the tea-room—Dalziel and Booth, Chiozza Money, an adventurer on the make, and Markham—a sort of lunatic.'[81]

Friendly critics of Lloyd George hoped that, once he had attained the premiership, he would choose a new set of political companions. As Donald Maclean observed: 'the PM had been surrounded too long by a poisonous crew, whom practically everyone at Westminster knew all about, but who were apparently admitted to his inner Councils.'[82] Handel Booth was indeed 'found out' in the course of 1917, but other cronies of Lloyd George from the former Liberal War Committee saw their political fortunes rise along with that of their hero. David Davies and Addison had a meeting with Thomas Jones, of the Cabinet Secretariat, in December 1916, at which they agreed to urge Lloyd George 'to drop Sir Hy Dalziel of "Reynolds" and rotters of his type'.[83] But Dalziel soon made himself indispensable to Lloyd George by acting as his unofficial press manager, and he continued to be a constant visitor to 10 Downing Street.

There were even more unpopular members of Lloyd George's entourage. Travelling to London in December 1916 Hankey found himself in the company of 'an odious fellow called Sutherland, some sort of political parasite of Ll.G.'s'.[84] This was the aptly named 'Bronco Bill' Sutherland, Lloyd George's Private Secretary, whose uncouth manners and cynical press manipulations were soon making an unfavourable impression on politicians of all persuasions. 'The really filthy William Sutherland', as Belloc dubbed him in one of his satirical verses,[85] could be counted upon to promote his master's interests with unscrupulous loyalty. But a mystery surrounded the position of Basil Zaharoff, the cosmopolitan arms salesman, whose easy entrée into 10

---

[81] Scott's Journal, 10–11 Jan. 1916, in Wilson (ed.), *Political Diaries of C. P. Scott*, p. 170.
[82] Jones's journal, 10 Jan. 1917, in Middlemas, K. (ed.), *Thomas Jones, Whitehall Diary*, i (Oxford, 1969), 20.
[83] Jones to his wife, 7 Dec. 1916 (ibid. 9).
[84] Hankey's diary, 10 Dec. 1916, in Roskill, *Hankey: Man of Secrets*, i. 329.
[85] See Koss, *Rise and Fall*, ii. 293.

Downing Street was soon generating a series of extraordinary rumours.[86]

The key members of the Prime Minister's 'Garden Suburb', Professor Adams, Philip Kerr, W. W. Astor, did not, admittedly, suffer the fate of having *their* personal characters impugned. But Mrs Astor was complaining in December 1917 that 'men of moral worth', like her husband and Philip Kerr, were being used by Lloyd George 'as virtuous windowdressers while in the background he works through Sutherland, Northcliffe and Co.'. Thomas Jones, the recipient of this complaint, could only observe that the Prime Minister could not be changed and that he was the one man possible.[87]

Beaverbrook

When such discussions as these were taking place about the Prime Minister's 'unsavoury' entourage, it is interesting to note that the name of Beaverbrook was frequently mentioned. Four changes had taken place in the circumstances of this remarkable Canadian since the early stages of the War. First, by acquiring control of the *Daily Express* in December 1916, he had for the first time joined the ranks of the great Press Lords, alongside Northcliffe and Rothermere. Second, his political affiliations had to some extent changed, in so far as he was now usually spoken of as a personal friend of the Prime Minister, rather than as the intimate of Bonar Law.[88] Third, a mere six months after receiving his controversial baronetcy, he had been made a peer of the realm, Baron Beaverbrook, once again to the distress of the King and of most traditional Conservatives.[89] Finally, in February 1918 he was given public office when he was put in charge of the Ministry of Information.

How Beaverbrook was viewed in the latter part of the War can be learned from this unflattering pen portrait which the Secretary of the Cabinet, Maurice Hankey, put down in his diary on 26 February 1918:

He is a Canadian, who made a fortune in a fortnight, came to England and by various obscure methods obtained first a baronetcy and then a peerage. He owns the Daily Express and there is intense feeling against his appointment in the Government, the House of Commons, and the country. I can only suppose

---

[86] See the account by McCormick, D., *The Mask of Merlin: A Critical Study of David Lloyd George* (London, 1963), pp. 201–8. A more sober presentation of Zaharoff is to be found in Trebilcock, C., *The Vickers Brothers. Armaments and Enterprise 1854–1914* (London, 1977).

[87] Jones's journal, 7 Dec. 1917, in Middlemas, *Whitehall Diary*, p. 40.

[88] On the other hand, Bonar Law's friends were still expressing anxiety over the possibility of Beaverbrook compromising his reputation. See e.g. Amery's diary, 10 Oct. 1917, in Barnes and Nicholson, *Leo Amery Diaries*, p. 173; James, Robert Rhodes (ed.), *Memoirs of a Conservative: J. C. C. Davidson's Memoirs and Papers 1910–37* (London, 1969), pp. 28–9.

[89] On the King's unhappiness at the way his hand had been forced on the Beaverbrook peerage, see Rose, *King George V*, p. 247.

that Ll.G. put him in the Government in order to induce him to finance the new party machine, which, as he tells me, he is about to found. A shady business![90]

But when Lloyd George was warned of how unpopular Beaverbrook was, he merely observed that the Canadian 'was extremely clever and though he was described as a "shady financier" he was not aware of any real foundations for the charge'.[91] In any case, Lloyd George was the last man in the world to be shocked by the company of a 'shady financier'. Nor would Beaverbrook's unconventional early career and lack of a traditional 'ruling class' education have been seen by the Prime Minister as any kind of disqualification from holding high office.

Nevertheless, most orthodox Liberals and Conservatives held Beaverbrook in intense dislike, probably because his career underlined the significance of two contemporary developments which were arousing widespread unease in 1917 and 1918: these were, first, the continuing abuses in the honours system, and, second, the growth in the political power of the newspaper proprietors.

As we have seen, Lord Salisbury and his friends had resumed their agitation over honours trafficking in March 1917. And Beaverbrook's ascent into the peerage provided them with an excellent example of what was wrong with the current system. Gwynne informed Lady Bathurst that he had refrained from public comment on 'Aitken's dirty peerage' because he 'did not want to foul the nest of the new Government', but he wondered whether he had done the right thing, for 'it was one of the worst jobs ever perpetrated and I am ashamed of it all!'[92] Moreover, indignation over the Beaverbrook peerage was kept alive by the former Governor-General of Canada, Lord Grey, whose objections to this particular honour soon became the common property of London clubland. The following letter, written to Salisbury in June 1917, makes clear the reasons for his disgruntlement:

I had never heard of Mr Max Aitken's existence before I saw his name at the head of the list of honours for which, in the opinion of the Canadian public, H.M.'s Canadian Ministers and I were jointly responsible. On making enquiries about him I was informed that he had recently been blackballed for the two principal clubs in Montreal! I regard the bestowal of this honour as a serious blow to Imperial interests.[93]

Grey believed, in other words, that Beaverbrook lacked the moral character and public reputation necessary for promotion to the House of Lords and he also considered that the proper constitutional procedures had been flagrantly ignored.

[90] Roskill, *Hankey*, pp. 502–3.
[91] Scott's journal, 4 Mar. 1918, in Wilson (ed.), *Political Diaries of C. P. Scott*, p. 336.
[92] Cited in Koss, *Rise and Fall*, ii. 307.
[93] Grey to Salisbury, 20 June 1917 (Salisbury papers, S(4), 233, fos. 47–52).

Why, then should such a man have been singled out for this high distinction? Esher thought it was in part a reward for Beaverbrook's role in detaching Bonar Law from Asquith during the December 1916 crisis, but that it was also not unconnected with his payment of £30,000 'to get F. E. Smith out of a scrape'.[94] Was there any substance in this rumour? Beaverbrook was certainly on friendly terms with Smith (who, incidentally, was an object of growing distrust to both the Diehards and Conservative traditionalists), and A. J. P. Taylor has shown that Beaverbrook was to play a decisive part in securing Smith his baronetcy in the 1918 New Year's Honours List.[95] Further than that it is impossible to go.

Beaverbrook's entry into the Government created even more resentment than his peerage. In a speech to the Lords on 12 February, Lord Charles Beresford expressed the doubts that were in many people's minds. 'Everybody wants the Prime Minister to remain where he is', said Beresford, 'but what I deplore about him is that he is weakening himself through the people he puts around him', and he singled out Beaverbrook's personal character for censure: 'If you want to know the qualifications of the last named for governing here, you had better go to Canada, where I was, and found them.'[96] As he later explained to Maxse, Beresford felt that his duty was to expel 'the crooked Beaverbrook' from office, come what may. 'If we get rid of Beaverbrook, we will stem the torrent of corruption that started in our public life with the Marconi incident.'[97] On the other hand, he observed, 'if we go on as we are doing, we shall have none but unscrupulous people in power.'[98]

Although Beresford's attempts to 'expose' Beaverbrook went off at half cock, the Government had to absorb much more effective criticism in the Commons on 19 February when Austen Chamberlain made some stinging comments on the appointment of so many newspaper proprietors to public office. For of course, in early 1918 Northcliffe was the Director of Propaganda in enemy countries, while Rothermere ('a very shady looking personage', thought Hankey[99]) still held the office of Air Secretary. Beaverbrook's personal reputation aside, the appointment of yet another newspaper proprietor to the newly created Ministry of Information was bound to confirm the suspicion that Lloyd George was trying to build up a power base of his

---

[94] Esher's war journal, 2 Jan. 1917, in Fraser, *Esher*, p. 464.
[95] Taylor, *Beaverbrook*, p. 131. In fact, Beaverbrook had also been handling F. E.'s investments for him, certainly from September 1913 onwards, and was plying him with presents. 'I think you are under no illusions', wrote Smith on 9 June 1917, 'as to the extent to which I would render you services if, which seems unlikely, circumstances should ever put it in my power' (Beaverbrook papers, C/39).
[96] *Parl. Deb.*, 5th ser. (Lords), xxix. 33–6 (12 Feb. 1918).
[97] Beresford to Maxse, 3 Mar., 10 Mar. 1918 (Maxse papers, vol. 475, T 203, T 207).
[98] Beresford to Maxse, 7 Mar. 1918 (ibid., T 206).
[99] Hankey's Diary, 26 Feb. 1918, in Roskill, *Hankey*, p. 503.

own by 'capturing' the syndicated press. Chamberlain thus caught the prevailing mood when he spoke of 'an atmosphere of suspicion and distrust' caused by the Government's actions.[100] This speech delighted Salisbury,[101] and, interestingly, a junior minister wrote Chamberlain the following congratulatory note: 'You have given expression to what every decent man has been preaching for months.'[102] That junior minister was Stanley Baldwin.

Of more immediate importance was the fact that on the same day as Chamberlain's speech, the Unionist War Committee, chaired by Salisbury, passed a resolution which called, *inter alia*, for a ban on newspaper proprietors joining the Government or holding responsible posts under it so long as they retained control of their journals. Esher had written to Haig on 14 February:

The feeling of the House of Commons is hostile to his [ie the PM's] surroundings and disgruntled with the Northcliffes, Beaverbrooks and Sutherlands . . . The hostility to Northcliffe & Co is widespread, but no one dares to openly attack except a few more or less insignificant MPs. The powers of the Amalgamated Press are greater than were those of the Inquisition. The King blasphemes but he does not resist.[103]

But Chamberlain's speech had broken any taboo there might once have been concerning criticism of Lloyd George's relationship with Fleet Street, and the Government, for a while, was seriously worried. Guest, who had originally suggested Beaverbrook's appointment as a Minister ('I want him anchored'),[104] now tried to put the blame on 'Bronco Bill' Sutherland's unseemly methods of press management.[105] Incidentally, there was some validity in Guest's argument, since, in private, Chamberlain was writing to Salisbury: 'the Press appointments to Government are only a part of the evil—the most conspicuous and therefore perhaps the least poisonous part of the evil. But the PM's direct and indirect inspiration of, and intrigue with, the Press is worse and more difficult to tackle . . .'.[106]

Nevertheless, in early March Lloyd George thought it necessary to

[100] *Parl. Deb.*, 5th ser., ciii. 657 (19 Feb. 1918).
[101] In a note on Beaverbrook, written at this time, Salisbury wrote: 'My informant is not aware that he has done anything crooked, but he is shady, a schemer, a man good business men would not care to be associated with . . .' (Fourth Marquess of Salisbury papers, 81/98).
[102] Baldwin to Chamberlain, 20 Feb. 1918 (Birmingham University Library, Austen Chamberlain papers, AC/15/7/3).
[103] Esher to Haig, 14 Feb. 1918, in Fraser, *Esher*, p. 382. Two months later, Esher mused: 'Democracy means government by cads like Northcliffe and Rothermere. But patriotism means that gentlemen obey the cads rather than set an example of disobedience' (Esher to Haig, 29 Apr. 1918, in Fraser, *Esher*, p. 393).
[104] Sanders, M. and Taylor, P. M., *British Propaganda During the First World War 1914–18* (London, 1982), pp. 77–8.
[105] Guest to Lloyd George, 26 Feb. 1918, in Lord Beaverbrook, *Men and Power 1917–1918* (London, n.d.), pp. 383–4.
[106] Chamberlain to Salisbury, 27 Feb. 1918 (Salisbury papers, 81/93).

meet the Unionist War Committee to defend his recruitment of the newspaper proprietors. His speech, Amery noted, 'was a masterpiece of adroitness; nothing could equal the neatness with which he suggested that Beaverbrook had been selected Director of Propaganda because he was an unscrupulous ruffian, or that Northcliffe would be ideal for sowing, in enemy countries, distrust of the Government and lack of confidence in the General Staff. Of ourse he blew away the whole ponderous attack.'[107] Balcarres, who had heard the Prime Minister utter similar sentiments at a meeting a week earlier, observed that Lloyd George's defence was hardly one that could be repeated in public; but he grudgingly admitted that it had a certain cogency: 'in these times we must not be squeamish. For dirty work give me the dirty man.'[108]

Yet in the wider political world, the grumbling against the Ministry of Information and the over-close links between 10 Downing Street and the Press Barons rumbled on. In March, Beresford was particularly agitated over rumours that Beaverbrook, through a Government Minister, was involved in an attempt to capture the *Daily Chronicle*.[109] When, towards the end of 1918, a syndicate, headed by Dalziel, at last took control of the *Chronicle* and promptly sacked its respected editor, Robert Donald, the affair was raised in the Commons.[110] Earlier, the *Westminster Gazette*, in an article probably inspired by Donald (who had himself once been briefly employed in the Ministry of Information), published a memorable attack on Beaverbrook:

He has many irons in the fire, financial and political; his friends say that he has boundless energy, and ambition to match. He is supposed to have played a more formidable part behind the scenes in the making and unmaking of Cabinets that even the rival potentate, Lord Northcliffe. Anyhow, he was given a peerage by a special creation before his services to the nation had become known or even been explained to the public, and during the subsequent fifteen months the noise of his approach to the seats of the mighty has become rapidly louder.'[111]

In November the Ministry of Information came under critical scrutiny, and MPs from all quarters of the House attacked the ambiguous position of the great Press Lords.[112] Ministers were 'selling their souls' and becoming 'the servants' of the newspaper proprietors, complained

[107] Amery's Diary, 5 Mar. 1918, in Barnes and Middlemas, *Leo Amery Diaries*, p. 208.
[108] Balcarres's Diary, 28 Feb. 1918, in Vincent (ed.), *The Crawford Papers*, p. 386.
[109] Beresford to Maxse, 7 Mar., 10 Mar. 1918 (Maxse papers, vol. 475, T 206, T 207). But Beresford thought it unwise to launch an attack lest Beaverbrook sought to defend himself.
[110] *Parl. Deb.*, 5th ser., cx. 78–94 (15 Oct. 1918).
[111] *Westminster Gazette*, 30 July 1918. Later, on 6 Aug., the paper cast doubt on Beaverbrook's qualifications to direct British propaganda, and it went on to sneer at his 'vulgarity' and at the music hall antics sponsored by the Ministry of Information.
[112] *Parl. Deb.*, 5th ser., cx. 2345–2408 (7 Nov. 1918).

Dillon.[113] Another MP accused Beaverbrook of using ministerial office to distribute publicity material in praise of himself.[114] And the Liberal backbencher, Hogge, claimed that the Ministry of Information was making a film—with the aid of a firm of persons with German names who had recently assumed 'good old John Bull names'—which aimed to present the Prime Minister to the public in a very heroic light.[115] Given the imminence of a general election, was this desirable?

Lloyd George and his Critics in 1918

By the end of 1918 the suspicion was growing that Lloyd George's predilection for the company of 'cads' was not a mere personal foible at all, but was the inevitable result of the kind of regime which had been set up in December 1916. Lacking an organization of his own to back him, Lloyd George needed to build up a personal fund as quickly as possible, while at the same time creating favourable publicity for himself by adroitly managing the press. And to help him in this work, political operators like Sutherland were clearly indispensable. As this insight slowly sank in, public attitudes to Lloyd George began to change.

Yet, so long as the War lasted, there was an understandable reluctance to stir up controversies which might weaken national morale. Gwynne, for example, refused to launch a major campaign against Godfrey Isaacs and Reading when pressed to do so in late 1917: 'The chief reason', he explained, 'is that at the present time when we are "up against it", as it were, I don't think we should have such a scandal, for it would be an appalling scandal.'[116] For similar reasons Salisbury was very anxious, as he assured the Prime Minister in March 1917, to eradicate abuses in the honours system quietly and discreetly and to avoid at all costs making attacks upon ministers during 'the present emergency'.[117]

Quite apart from such patriotic considerations, there was still a temptation in 1917–18 to believe that the Prime Minister should not be held personally accountable for the 'dirty' things that were done in his name. Perhaps, as Milner suggested to Maxse, in extenuation of the June 1917 Honours List, the Prime Minister was 'so absorbed in the War and so careless of what he considers—wrongly—a matter of small importance that he passes every rotten thing which the party managers put before him'.[118] It is also significant that in the letter in which

---

[113] Ibid. 2359.   [114] Ibid. 2368.

[115] Ibid. 2390. The *Westminster Gazette*, too, warned that Beaverbrook had his eye on home propaganda (30 July 1918).

[116] Gwynne to Powell, 3 Dec. 1917 (Gwynne papers, box 1).

[117] See Ch. 15, pp. oo–o.

[118] Milner to Maxse, 13 June 1917 (Maxse papers, vol. 474, N 120).

Beresford fumed against Beaverbrook, he included the following observation: 'I am alarmed for the future, L.G. ought to be kept where he is, but he is bound to come down by his associates.'[119] In other words, the tendency was still for criticism to focus on the Prime Minister's 'evil councillors' rather than on the Prime Minister himself.

Subjected as they were to these contradictory pressures and emotions, right-wing patriots were somewhat ambivalent in their attitude towards both the Coalition and Lloyd George himself in 1917 and 1918. Nothing illustrates this ambivalence better than the stance taken up by Page Croft's National Party, founded in August 1917. Unlike Salisbury and his friends, Croft did not shrink from declaring open war against the corruption he believed to be destroying the British State.[120] At Wallasey in January 1918, for example, he is reported as saying: 'The House of Commons, at the present moment, was a corrupt House. Out of the 680 Members, eliminating the Irish Members, they would find 225 men who had received reward, by way of title, place, job, or in some other way. Probably another 100 were on the waiting list for reward . . . '.[121]

But did that make the National Party an out-and-out opponent, or merely a friendly critic, of Lloyd George and his Coalition Government? At a sociological level the National Party can indeed be said to represent a protest at the kind of Ministry that Lloyd George was heading. Although seven right-wing Conservative MPs joined the new party when it was launched (only two stayed the course), most of its active supporters were peers.[122] The Morning Post, which together with the National Review did everything it could to build up the new party, claimed that large numbers of businessmen were coming forward to join.[123] But this should be taken with a pinch of salt. Only one of the National Party's prominent members, Richard Cooper, MP, was a businessman.[124] Nearly all the identifiable leaders were traditional aristocrats and elderly public servants, of whom most were drawn from the armed services, diplomacy, and the Imperial administration. Amongst the best known personalities were Beresford and Lord Ampthill, whose pursuit of corrupt politicians had begun way

[119] Beresford to Maxse, 3 Mar. 1918 (ibid., vol. 475, T 202).

[120] See the Party's opening manifesto, cited in Ch. 11, p. 247.

[121] Liverpool Daily Courier, 31 Jan. 1918.

[122] For an able account of the National Party, see Rubinstein, W. D., 'Henry Page Croft', pp. 129–47, esp. 134–5. See also Wrigley, C., ' "In the Excess of their Patriotism": the National Party and Threats of Subversion', in Wrigley, C. (ed.), Warfare, Diplomacy and Politics: Essays in Honour of A. J. P. Taylor (London, 1986), pp. 93–119.

[123] Morning Post, 14 Sept. 1917.

[124] Despite his strong line on corruption, Cooper was nearly arrested for sending a letter by hand to the United States, where he wanted to set up a subsidiary company in order to evade EPD. This evasion of the censorship regulations nearly led to his prosecution, although the Solicitor-General eventually decided against it (Bonar Law papers, 83/6/25).

back in February 1914 when he had led the parliamentary attack on Lord Murray. William Rubinstein has analysed the social backgrounds of the forty people about whom information is available who signed the Party's original manifesto or who subsequently served on its Provisional or on its Grand Council; and he finds that eight were industrialists, ten were professional army officers, eleven were peers or heirs to a peerage, and a disproportionately large number had some kind of connection with the Empire. As Rubinstein notes, the 'socio-economic profile resembled that of the die-hard group within the Unionist party in 1922.'[125]

Yet the National Party at the end of the War was playing a different political role from that which the Diehards were later to assume. Whereas by 1920 or 1921 the Diehards had come to see Lloyd George as the embodiment of all that was most corrupt in British public life, Page Croft and his friends had as yet by no means arrived at so clear-cut a conclusion. Their quarrel was with the party machines and with the men who financed and managed these machines, rather than with the Prime Minister, whose patriotic rhetoric and commitment to a new kind of 'national' government freed from the party catchcries of the past the members of the National Party enthusiastically shared. Even Lloyd George's personal motives did not meet with total hostility. Rather, suspicion and grudging admiration lay uneasily alongside one another. 'I have faith in Lloyd George, though I do not trust him', Beresford observed in October 1916,[126] and this continued to be the viewpoint of most National Party members. This ambivalence was to continue for the next two years. The National Party, like the 'Vigilantes', was not so much out to destroy Lloyd George, but to keep him up to the mark—to pressurize him into acting out his patriotic rhetoric.

Especially interesting is the attitude of Ampthill, who in September 1917 was still expressing relief at the thought that Lloyd George and not Asquith was the Premier. 'What a comfort it is to feel that the danger of political treachery had been removed and that the fighting men will now be allowed to finish the job thoroughly at any cost!' Writing from abroad, Ampthill took the view that 'he need not hurry back to the National Party until the war is over and the old parties resume their old game.'[127] It was because a number of prominent figures in the National Party took this view that Page Croft had difficulty in knowing whether he should be exposing the Prime Minister or bolstering up his authority against his detractors. As the General Election approached, this dilemma became more and more acute. For example, the decision to contest the Election as an

[125] Rubinstein, 'Henry Page Croft', p. 139.
[126] Beresford to Maxse, 10 Oct. 1916 (Maxse papers, vol. 473, fo. 815).
[127] Ampthill to Maxse, 29 Sept. 1917 (ibid., vol. 474, N 227).

independent organization provoked Lord Montagu of Beaulieu into resignation; Montagu explained that he admired Lloyd George and shared his general objectives.[128]

Moreover, Page Croft had some difficulty in identifying the precise areas of difference between himself and the Prime Minister in late 1918. He talked rather vaguely about the National Party's concern with 'Efficiency and Purity in Public Life', but there was little in the Party's election manifesto with which most Coalition supporters would not have agreed—except perhaps the attack on 'the secret party funds'.[129] This similarity of programme and outlook for a time worried Bonar Law and the Conservative Whips who feared that many of their own rank-and-file members might be tempted to join the new organization.[130] Yet it was also the case that Lloyd George, by appropriating the 'national' label for himself and his associates and by detaching himself from the political parties, had already succeeded in occupying the political ground on which Page Croft had designs. It was not really surprising, then, that the National Party made so little mark in the 1918 Election, with only two of its candidates, Croft and Cooper, being returned.

A similar dilemma confronted the Cecil brothers, who were trying in 1918 to put distance between themselves and the Coalition, without committing themselves to outright opposition. In March, Lord Robert, along with Curzon, had advised 'against touching [Lloyd George] on the ground that he is such a dirty little rogue'.[131] In the event he stayed on in the Government until November, when he resigned in protest against Welsh Disestablishment. Meanwhile, Lord Salisbury prepared for the election by campaigning on the slogan 'Trust the People'. Labour unrest, he proclaimed, could only be checked by telling the people 'the truth' and by the espousal of 'clean politics'.[132] But Salisbury's avowed concern was merely to maintain the Unionist Party as an independent organization, not to attack Lloyd George and the Coalitionists as such.

1917 and 1918, in short, were transitional years in British politics. Lloyd George had come to supreme power in December 1916 carrying with him the hope that a new era was about to be inaugurated in which the shoddy compromises and corrupt practices of the past, like honours trafficking, might disappear. So long as Lloyd George was

[128] *Daily Telegraph*, 27 Nov. 1918.

[129] *Morning Post*, 19 Nov. 1918. During the 1918 election campaign Croft said he was prepared to support the Coalition Government so long as it stood by its reconstruction programme (*Daily Telegraph*, 27 Nov. 1918).

[130] But some Conservatives viewed the National Party with derision. See Peter Sanders's Diary, 3 Oct. 1917, in Ramsden (ed.), *Real Old Tory Politics*, pp. 89–90.

[131] Peter Sanders's Diary, 3 Mar. 1918, in Ramsden, *Real Old Tory Politics*, pp. 101–2.

[132] See his letters to the *Morning Post*, 6 Nov., 27 Nov., 2 Dec. 1918. The 6 Nov. letter is entitled, 'Unrest and Distrust. Need for Clean Politics'.

perceived as a vigorous and successful war leader, these hopes
survived. But by the middle of 1917 there was disquiet over Lloyd
George's entourage and it was impossible to repress memories of
earlier controversial episodes in the Prime Minister's career. In
particular, the ripples from the Marconi Incident continued to disturb
the surface of political life. There was even the faintest premonition
discernible in 1918 that Lloyd George's break with the conventions of
the traditional party system might perhaps be doing more to *encourage*
corruption than to end it. Yet Diehards and aristocratic Conservatives
alike took a long time to think their way through to this conclusion.
Once they had done so, the foundations of Lloyd George's political
power were to be seriously shaken, but this did not occur until 1920 or
1921.

14

The Politics of Coalition, 1919–1922

Anti-Semitic Attacks

RUMOURS and scandals flourished in the atmosphere of acute anxiety and tension during the First World War. But the signing of the Armistice did not produce that tranquillity or 'normalcy' for which so many Britons yearned. For the post-war period, too, was one of almost constant turmoil. From many different quarters came threats to the social order and to British world interests. Ireland was in rebellion, India in upheaval. The problems of post-war reconstruction were complicated by the existence of Bolshevik Russia, whose menacing posture was complemented at home by a powerful and angrily assertive Labour Movement imbued with a vaguely revolutionary ethos. In this febrile political atmosphere the Lloyd George Coalition Government was stumbling from one crisis to another, or so its detractors believed.

Paradoxically, Lloyd George was on occasions not averse to dramatizing, even exaggerating, the difficulties by which his Ministry was beset, since he calculated that this might impress upon the moderate, constitutionally-minded, property-owning sections of the population his own indispensability and the continuing need for a broad-based Coalition such as the one he was heading. This tactic sometimes paid off.[1] On the other hand, the more the Radical Right was conscious of the revolutionary turmoil, the more tempted it was to explain the Government's predicament in conspiratorial terms. One can see the germs of one such conspiracy theory in Kipling's letter to Maxse of 20 January 1920:

What impresses me most is the . . . accurate *timing* of events to our disadvantage. A Montaguized India handed over to chaos at the *exact* moment that a Bolshevized Central Asia is getting ready to act; and (lest the match should be lacking to the petrol) Dyer's 'trial' stage-managed in time and effect to start everything up again. Then as soon as LlG has to go to Paris the strike threat breaks out behind him—exactly as they did before. I wish you'd publish a table of synchronization in the N[ational] R[eview] balancing strike and crisis and the needs of the enemy since 1915. You'd see how perfectly they nick[?] in.[2]

---

[1] Thus Selborne ruefully conceded that Lloyd George, by successfully confronting the miners in the autumn of 1920, had 'done himself more good' with the Conservatives than he had 'in all his other record since the armistice' (Selborne to Maude Selborne, 12 Oct. 1920, Bodleian, Selborne papers, vol. 103, fos. 144–5).
[2] Kipling to Maxse, 20 Jan. 1920 (West Sussex Record Office, Maxse papers, vol. 476).

Men like Maxse scarcely needed to be given such encouragement. The links between the events Kipling mentions were not accidental, they believed, but had been brought into existence by some mysterious deep-laid plot, with the 'Boche', Bolsheviks, Sinn Fein, International Jewry, and Labour militants in league with one another to destroy British interests. With only a little more exercise of the imagination they could then explain the inability of the Government to fend off this many-pronged challenge to its authority by supposing that Lloyd George and certain of his Ministers were *colluding* with sinister alien forces.

In this conspiratorial view of politics anti-Semitism played a prominent part, finding outlet in the small-circulation journals which proliferated in these years—for example, the Duke of Northumberland's *Patriot*; the scurrilous broadsheet, *Plain English*, which Lord Alfred Douglas edited until he was ousted by Captain Spencer, of Pemberton Billing fame; and *Plain Speech*, which Douglas founded after his 'displacement'.[3]

Moreover, these anti-Semitic journals continued to find much Marconi material to interest them, for the litigious nature of Godfrey Isaacs ensured that the word 'Marconi' was seldom out of the public gaze for any length of time. In any case, many individuals continued to hope that sooner or late they would destroy Godfrey Isaacs and his illustrious brother. No one was more persistent in these attempts than Captain Peter Wright, best known as the man who libelled Gladstone's memory in the 1920s.[4] This former associate of Oliver Locker-Lampson had not been pleased when his fellow-plaintiff had allowed their joint case against Godfrey Isaacs to be settled out of court in 1916. Momentarily he dropped his grievance on being appointed, at Amery's suggestion, to the staff of the Supreme War Council in Paris. However, the Secret Service felt that Wright was a security risk, and forced Hankey to have him dismissed.[5] He thereupon returned to England, and resumed his bombardment of Gwynne with endless letters rehearsing his Marconi allegations. Along with Ellis Powell, Wright was particularly exercised over some of the evidence which had emerged during the earlier Seager Case relating to the Isaacs brothers,[6] and, given a certain amount of publicity, the two men were confident that they could use this material to destroy Lord Reading's career.

In the closing stages of the War Gwynne was tempted to help them out in this respect. But before doing so he wrote to Carson asking for

[3] See Holmes, *Anti-Semitism*, Ch. 9.
[4] Hyde, H. M., *Norman Birkett* (London, 1964), Ch. 5; Hyde, H. M., *Their Good Names: Twelve Cases of Libel and Slander with Some Introductory Reflections on the Law* (London, 1970), Ch. 10.
[5] Roskill, *Hankey*, i. 491 n. 1.
[6] On the intriguing Seager Case, the *The Times*, 31 Oct. 1914, 3, 4, 5, 11, 12, 20, 21 Nov. 1914. The Appeal proceedings are reported in *The Times*, 17 Dec. 1915.

advice; he said that his information came from 'a man who knows the Marconi thing inside out' and was trying to prove that 'Lord Reading [was] nothing else but a common thief.'[7] But Carson, of course, had acted as Godfrey Isaacs's counsel in a number of legal actions— including the Seager Case itself—so, predictably, his response was to warn Gwynne of the dangers ahead, 'especially as Lord Reading occupies such an important public position at the present time'.[8] The *Morning Post*'s main leader writer, Ian Colvin, also urged restraint on Wright, agreeing with him 'as to the fishiness of the whole case as it affects the reputation of the Isaacs family', but adding that 'he was not sure if your points would be maintained if the matter came into court.'[9] Gwynne had already explained to Wright that driving Reading from public life presented 'enormous difficulties' and that he felt that he ought not to risk a libel suit unless he was sure of winning: 'This paper is a private property and not in the hands of a public company, and the costs, even of a successful libel action, are enormous.'[10]

Meanwhile, as we have seen, Reading, while serving as Ambassador in the United States, was the object of several vicious attacks, and in January 1918 Powell had written a vain appeal to the Prime Minister, urging him to distance himself from Reading.[11] In November Powell sent a similar effusion to Bonar Law, who curtly replied that he did not think he was 'called upon to express any opinion upon the statements which it contains'.[12] Powell wrote back that he had expected him to be 'indignant at the deception practised upon you, and through you, upon the public' and said that he now had little option but to publicise the whole affair, hinting at a campaign of meetings in the autumn.[13]

Powell was obviously hoping for the very thing that Gwynne feared—that Reading would be goaded into bringing a libel action. Reading's refusal to do so dismayed Strachey, who was not sure whether he believed in the current rumours or not, but thought the Lord Chief Justice's silence sinister: 'nothing in public affairs has made me so anxious or so miserable for a long time', he confided to Lord Cave.[14]

But Strachey had other things to worry about. For in November 1918 Fleet Street was alive with stories that Reading was about to be appointed to the Peace Delegation at Versailles. Indeed, the renewed protests which Wright made in November and December were intended to stop the Government from taking this step. Without

[7] Gwynne to Carson, 18 Oct. 1918 (Bodleian, Gwynne papers, box 1).

[8] Carson to Gwynne, 22 Oct. 1918 (ibid.).

[9] Colvin to Wright (copy), 6 Jan. 1919 (ibid.).

[10] Gwynne to Wright (copy), 2 Jan. 1919 (ibid.).   [11] See Ch. 13, p. 316.

[12] Powell to Bonar Law (copy), 5 Nov. 1918 (HLRO, Strachey papers, S/9/8/18); Bonar Law to Powell (copy), 7 Nov. 1918 (ibid.).

[13] Powell to Bonar Law (copy), 12 Nov. 1918 (ibid.).

[14] Strachey to Cave (copy), 25 Jan. 1919 (Strachey papers, S/8/12/7).

making specific charges, papers like the *Spectator* and the *Morning Post* did their best to warn Lloyd George of the dangers that such an appointment would entail. For example, the *Morning Post* declared that Reading's career was 'not clean'. 'He deceived the House of Commons in the Marconi affair, and the British people have never trusted him since.'[15] Strachey meanwhile was making a private appeal to Lord Robert Cecil, still a member of the Coalition. 'I am exceedingly loath', he wrote, 'to rake up the Marconi business, either as it affects Lord Reading or Lloyd George, at this moment, or, indeed, at any other moment; but I don't see how it is to be helped if the scandal of having our country represented by Lord Reading cannot be prevented by some other means.' The thought was 'unendurable', said Strachey, that two of the British Delegates at Versailles would be 'tarred with the Marconi brush'.[16]

But Cecil's perspectives had slightly changed since his Opposition days. He offered to discuss the matter confidentially with Strachey, but he deprecated the idea of a public controversy. Cecil assured the newspaperman that he knew of no plan for appointing Reading as one of the British representatives in Paris and he doubted whether Reading would accept the job if it were offered to him. 'At the same time,' wrote Cecil, 'I must in fairness say that I believe his influence in the Government is for good. What may be the secret history of the Marconi transactions I now know no more than I ever did. But if we were ever to know the truth I shall be very much surprised to find that Reading was the chief mover in the transactions . . . '.[17]

Cecil was right when he discounted the idea of the Lord Chief Justice taking part in the Paris negotiations. However, in January 1919 it was announced that he would head the British delegation at the Inter-Allied Council, whose concern was the supplying and victualling of allied, neutral, and enemy countries. Depressed by the *Morning Post*'s attacks, Reading had initially turned down the assignment, and Hankey had had to talk him round to accepting it.[18]

Meanwhile, Powell was active in trying to organize a protest meeting in the City of London. Particularly excited by this project was Lord Cecil Manners, the third son of the Duke of Rutland and a former Conservative MP. His niece, Lady Diana Cooper, remembers her

---

[15] *Morning Post*, 20 Nov., 21 Nov. 1918. On 29 Nov. the leader writer said that he had been sustained in his 'disagreeable duty' 'by the many letters on this subject which we receive from members of the public—letters convincing us that if Mr Lloyd George persists in the intention that is accredited to him he will have gone far to forfeit the confidence which his conduct of the war has earned'.

[16] Strachey to Robert Cecil (copy), 21 Nov. 1918 (Strachey papers, S/4/4/31).

[17] Robert Cecil to Strachey, 25 Nov. 1918 (ibid.). But he added that probably 'none of us can ever quite forget' Marconi.

[18] Hankey's diary, 24 Nov. 1918, in Roskill, *Hankey*, ii. 25–6; Judd, Dennis, *Lord Reading* (London, 1982), pp. 181–2, where G. K. Chesterton's famous letter on the subject is quoted.

'Uncle Cecil' as 'a big success with children, being always on all fours', and says that he quarrelled with his family, 'suffered from spy-fever and at the age of eighty . . . could no longer endure life itself so ended it beneath a train at Crowborough'.[19] Both the childishness and the spy-mania were strongly in evidence in 1918. Early in the year, as we have seen, he had sent Bonar Law an impudent letter about his part in the Jacks Case and his relationship with his 'mentor', Beaverbrook.[20] This was only one of a number of similarly eccentric missives which he posted that year.

Manners felt that he had a mission to purify British public life. Initially he tried to enlist the support of Lord Salisbury in this quest. However, he set about his task in a peculiarly inept way, since he peppered his letters to Salisbury with innuendoes against the latter's relative, Lord Selborne, whose offence, in Manners's eyes, was to have involved himself in Mond's business empire.[21] In fact, as early as 1913, when Selborne had accepted a place on the Board of Natal Ammonium Ltd., Conservative eyebrows had been raised; what, critics asked, was a prominent Unionist doing aligning himself in this way with the 'Liberal plutocracy' and 'Jewish finance'?[22] Later, in December 1914, Balcarres heard 'a good deal of acrid comment' about Selborne's joining another Mond company. This, perhaps, was the Mond Nickel Company, which later came under suspicion, as we shall see, of improperly allotting shares to German citizens in wartime.[23] But despite his disapproval of Selborne's conduct, Manners was still trying in early December 1918 to associate Salisbury with the proposed Reading protest meeting—an idea, incidentally, which Belloc had been the first to float.[24] But he must have received a dusty answer, since shortly afterwards he was dismissing Salisbury as 'really stupid—weak—and not very courageous—and much too closely connected by ties of relationship—marriage and other connections—with what Maxse calls the "Mandarinate" '.[25]

Who, then, was to chair the protest meeting? Strachey's deputy, Mr Atkins, agreed to meet Manners to discuss the problem, but came away unimpressed; Manners, he reported, seemed to have his head full of ' "unseen hands", secret wireless installations, Jewish international finance, secret party funds, the corruption of the Honours List and so on', between all of which he saw connections, and it was

---

[19] Cooper, D., *The Rainbow Comes and Goes* (London, 1958), p. 33. On the subject of Manners's suspiciousness, see also Lyon, L., *By The Waters of Babylon* (London, n. d.), pp. 185–6.

[20] See Ch. 12, p. 278.

[21] Manners to Salisbury, 6 Nov. 1918 (Hatfield, Fourth Marquess of Salisbury papers, 84/77–8).

[22] Vincent (ed.), *The Crawford Papers*, p. 348 n. 65.

[23] Balcarres's diary, 3 Dec. 1914 (ibid., p. 346).

[24] Manners to Salisbury, 11 Dec. 1918 (Salisbury papers, 84/125).

[25] Manners to Strachey, 15 Dec. 1918 (Strachey papers, S/8/12/5).

hard to ascertain exactly what crimes Reading was supposed to have committed.[26] Strachey himself showed more sympathy for what Manners was trying to achieve, but it was a sign of the latter's desperation that he could think of no one better to preside over his protest meeting than the Duke of Northumberland![27]

In any case, none of this discussion came to anything, since shortly afterwards Powell, the principal organizer behind the scenes, decided to abandon his meeting because of the refusal of weighty and responsible City figures to take part in it. Strachey wrote to Manners on 3 January 1919 to express his disgust at the timidity of those who feared to incur 'the ire of the Lord Chief Justice and his devoted friend, the Prime Minister'.[28] But one senses also a certain relief on Strachey's part at not having to commit the *Spectator* to what was likely to be a dubious cause. His line was that he would publicize Powell's charges, once they had been openly produced, but that he would not take the initiative in the matter.[29] Gwynne reacted in the same way, although he admitted in private that he distrusted Reading so much that he was afraid his appointment as Food Controller would be 'one in which corruption will very largely figure'.[30]

The vendetta against Reading then abated for a couple of years, until his promotion to the office of Indian Viceroy in January 1921 brought all the old rumours and allegations back into circulation again. Moreton Frewen, for example, told Strachey that this appointment had finally destroyed his confidence in Lloyd George as Premier. Reading, he declared, 'was a moral leper'. He had compiled a complete dossier on him, and sent it to Lloyd George—clearly without effect! Frewen's objections are interesting because they do not simply centre around Reading's part in the Marconi Affair but also deal with the opportunities which the new Viceroy would have of speculating in Indian securities. 'What we do know', wrote Frewen, 'is that he has a record as a Stock Exchange gambler, and THE autocrat of the silver market—on whose advice the India Office relies as to WHEN the Government buys silver to coin and what amount it buys—that man is the Viceroy. When he buys heavily the price of silver and of thousands of millions of silver securities . . . *just jump*; when on the other hand he keeps out of the silver market all the silver exchanges with all Asia fall.'[31]

In addition, the Government's Radical Right critics, almost to a man, were disturbed at the prospect of having a Jew in charge of the Indian Government as well as a Jew running the India Office. For the

[26] Atkins to Strachey, 19 Dec. 1918 (ibid.).
[27] Strachey to Manners (copy), 13 Dec. 1918 (ibid.); Manners to Strachey, 15 Dec, 1918 (ibid.).
[28] Strachey to Manners (copy), 3 Jan. 1919 (ibid.).
[29] Ibid.; Strachey to J. W. Hamilton (copy), 9 Jan. 1919 (ibid., S/8/12/4).
[30] Gwynne to Foster, 2 Jan. 1919 (Gwynne papers, box 1).
[31] Frewen to Strachey, 10 Jan. 1921 (Strachey papers, S/6/4/22).

Indian Secretary at this time was Edwin Montagu. And around Montagu, too, rumours of corruption continued to flourish. Leaving aside pure anti-Semitic prejudice, there were bound to be doubts about the wisdom of appointing as Indian Secretary a man so closely related to the bullion-broking and merchant-banking house of Samuel Montagu, especially when one recalls the embarrassing 'Silver Scandal' of 1912–13. For if, as Frewen was suggesting, Reading might be tempted to use his official position to enrich himself by playing the Indian silver market, how could Montagu—however disinterested he might try to be—escape similar imputations?

This issue was raised in the *Spectator* on 6 December 1919, where it was argued that Montagu should never have accepted this office because of the interest taken in India by his family's firm: 'When asked by a careless and possibly ignorant Prime Minister, he would at once have replied that the India Office was the one post which owing to family circumstances he ought not to hold, lest suspicion, almost as injurious as corruption itself, should be the result of his appointment.' At the very least, the *Spectator* asserted, Samuel Montagu & Co. should have followed the example of Baring's, which, as soon as Cromer became the Agent-General in Egypt, declared that they would take no part in loans to that country so long as a relative was in office. The author of this article insisted that such fastidiousness was now more necessary than ever, since a good example would have to be set to the working classes.

As even his critics readily acknowledged, Edwin Montagu had actually divested himself of all personal financial interest in the family firm, so the *Spectator's* strictures certainly erred on the side of severity. Indeed, the Indian Secretary himself was moved to write Strachey a pained letter, saying that he had read the recent article 'with great regret' and would be glad of an opportunity to talk the matter over. The two men then met for a long, agonized conversation on 14 December, in the course of which Montagu pointed out how tenuous was now the connection between the family firm and the India Office, and Strachey offered him the columns of the *Spectator* to publicize his case. This offer momentarily cheered up the neurotic Indian Secretary, who at one stage in the interview had hinted that he might feel compelled to leave office altogether.[32]

Edwin Montagu did not, of course, carry out this 'threat'. But press attacks on him continued. The *Morning Post*, for example, declared that it was 'intolerable for any Government servant to be placed in a position where his private interests and his duties to the State [might] possibly clash'. 'Mr MONTAGU's brother's firm', it went on, 'has

[32] Montagu to Strachey, 11 Dec. 1919; Memo. of Conversation with Montagu, dated 15 Dec. 1919 (ibid., S/10/13/1); Strachey to Robert Cecil (copy), 19 Dec. 1919 (ibid., S/4/4/34).

certain business relations with the Government of India, and we contend that in fairness to Mr MONTAGU he should not have been appointed Secretary for India.'[33]

Ignoring all the abuse, Montagu pressed on with his liberal reforms of the Indian machinery of government. But this only served to increase his unpopularity in the eyes of his critics, especially after his response to the Amritsar Massacre. Frewen had a sinister explanation for Montagu's apparent refusal or inability to rule India with a firm hand. In July 1918 he told Strachey that Indian finance was 'totally in the hands of a Jew oligarchy—Abrahams Montagu Schuster Meyer', who gambled heavily in silver securities. 'If Parliament only knew one sixth of what I know', wrote Frewen, 'there would be an anti-Semitic explosion about the India Office and Silver, but the whole thing is so cryptic that they can sin safely.' He concluded: 'My conviction is that the junta would welcome a prodigious explosion in India later such as would shake our rule to its foundations, in order that their work of the last few years might be covered up by the fire.'[34] Once again, a conspiratorial theory of corruption was being invoked to explain the Government's seeming lack of patriotism and Imperial resolve.

Anti-Semites, raging at the wickedness and folly of the 'Jew-alition Government',[35] had another inviting target to attack in their old bugbear, Sir Alfred Mond, who had been made First Commissioner of Works in 1919. Mond was already under heavy criticism even while the War was in progress. The most specific allegations against him were made by a South African journalist, Percival Smith, who wrote a series of articles for the *New Witness*, starting in September 1918. According to Smith, Mond had allocated 17,775 shares in Mond Nickel to German citizens. Mond, however, ignored these imputations of treachery and corruption.[36] Then, during the 1918 General Election campaign, Percival Smith went down to Mond's constituency, Cardiff, and held a mass meeting under the auspices of the New Witness League. Smith threw down a challenge to Mond: 'with all his millions', he sneered, the Liberal MP 'was afraid to attack an insignificant Englishman' by meeting him in court where their conflicting stories could be assessed by a British jury. Smith's resolution, protesting at the Board of Trade's condoning of Mond's share transactions, was seconded by a shareholder in the Mond Nickel Company and carried unanimously.[37]

H. H. Beamish, the 'Vigilante' candidate who had stood unsuccessfully at the Clapham By-Election in June 1918, also joined in the hunt.

---

[33] *Morning Post*, 11 June 1920.
[34] Frewen to Strachey, 25 July 1918 (Strachey papers, S/6/4/11).
[35] Holmes, *Anti-Semitism*, p. 145. This gibe was occasioned by the choice of Herbert Samuel as High Commissioner for Palestine in July 1920.
[36] Ibid. 144, 276 n. 21.   [37] *New Witness*, 6 Dec. 1918, p. 108.

In early 1919, together with a Lt.-Commander Harry M. Fraser, founder of an ex-serviceman's organization, he displayed a poster bearing the legend, 'Sir Alfred Mond is a traitor, he allotted shares to the Huns during the war.' For this Mond successfully sued the two men for libel and was awarded £5,000 damages, although Beamish speedily made off for his former home in South Africa to avoid paying the fine.[38]

Far harsher was the fate suffered by Lord Alfred Douglas, like Beamish a recent witness in the Pemberton Billing Trial. Oscar Wilde's old friend, now displaying acute symptoms of persecution mania and an obsessive desire to vindicate himself in the courts, became convinced that Winston Churchill had written a misleading statement on the Admiralty's behalf about the Battle of Jutland, with the aim of helping a syndicate of rich Jews, including Cassel, which was alleged to have bought government stock cheaply when the first gloomy news of Jutland was released to the public and then to have sold at a high profit after the later and more reassuring statement had been released. The syndicate was supposed to have made £18 million out of transactions in British stock and £36 million from German stock. Douglas also treated as truth rumours which had been current since 1916 concerning the 'murder' of Kitchener, whom 'traitors' were alleged to have sent to his watery grave. All these 'amazing' revelations duly appeared in the pages of Douglas's small-circulation magazine, *Plain English*.[39]

Strangely enough, the first response to this piece of provocation came from the *Morning Post*, which on 26 April 1922 printed a paragraph accusing Douglas of inventing 'vile insults against the Jews' from pecuniary motives. Douglas thereupon sued the *Morning Post*, and in the course of the trial sought to convince the world that Churchill, 'short of money and eager for power, was trapped by the Jews', who were also responsible for Kitchener's death. Balfour, the First Lord of the Admiralty at the time of Jutland, and Churchill were both called in to refute Douglas's charges, and the business secretary of the late Sir Ernest Cassel also appeared as a witness to deny that his former employer had either bought or sold stocks in the period before and after the Battle. The jury eventually found in Douglas's favour, though they only awarded him a farthing's damages—a verdict which they reached, not because they thought Douglas's story was true, but because they did not agree with the *Morning Post* that it was a deliberately fabricated lie.[40]

Unfortunately, Lord Alfred was encouraged by the outcome to pursue his personal crusade. His friends set up a body called the 'Lord

---

[38] Lebzelter, G. C., *Political Anti-Semitism in England 1918–1939* (London, 1978), pp. 50–1.
[39] Croft-Cooke, R., *Bosie; The Story of Lord Alfred Douglas: His Friends and Enemies* (London, 1963), pp. 302–4, 306.
[40] Hyde, *Their Good Names*, Ch. 8.

Kitchener and Jutland Publicity Committee', which held a public meeting in the Memorial Hall on 3 August 1923, where Douglas made a speech, later published in pamphlet form. In November he was arrested and charged with having libelled Churchill. At this well-reported Old Bailey Trial it transpired that one of Douglas's main informants was none other than Captain Spencer, who, since the summer of 1918, had briefly held the editorship of *Plain Speech* as well as serving a six-month prison sentence for libel. By the time of the Churchill Trial he was clearly insane. The court proceedings did, at least, provide the world with some tantalizing glimpses of Churchill's relationship with his old friend, Cassel, whose image once again took a cruel buffeting, this time at the hands of Douglas's lawyer, who mocked Cassel's German accent and his well-known difficulties in riding a horse. However, much to the relief of Churchill and Balfour, Douglas was duly sentenced to six months imprisonment and bound over for a further six months with a surety of £100 to keep the peace and not to persist in his libels.[41]

Lloyd George and Birkenhead

Meanwhile, Lloyd George himself was largely spared this kind of treatment, though, of course, there were many insinuations that he, too, showed a disturbing preference for Jewish company.[42] Indeed, in January 1922 Sir Henry Wilson actually went so far as to complain, in private, that the Prime Minister had 'so enmeshed [himself] with Zaharoff and the Jews' that he had been 'forced to back the Greeks against the Turks which will result in the loss of India and Egypt'.[43]

Two months later the question of Lloyd George's liking for 'plutocratic' Jews was raised by Douglas's journalistic colleague, T. W. Crosland, who had dealt with it in a book which Beaverbrook wanted to serialize in the *Daily Express*, thinking it to be 'good journalism'.[44] But the Prime Minister, who had been sent a copy, was not amused, and urged Beaverbrook not to publish the extracts from the book: 'It is gratuitously offensive and libellous. It is grossly unfair to the Jews, and I resent very strongly his attack upon the Welsh people.' Lloyd George attributed Crosland's malevolence to disappointment at not having

---

[41] Ibid.; Croft-Cooke, *Bosie*, pp. 305–10.

[42] See D. R. Daniel's MS biography of Lloyd George, cited in Kinnear, M., *The Fall of Lloyd George: The Political Crisis of 1922* (London, 1973), pp. 186–7.

[43] Wilson to General Rawlinson, 26 Jan. 1922 (Imperial War Museum, Henry Wilson papers). Beamish, not surprisingly, believed that Lloyd George was 'controlled by this Jew gang' (Beamish to J. H. Clarke, in Lebzelter, G. C., 'Henry Hamilton Beamish and the Britons: Champions of Anti-Semitism', in Lunn, K. and Thurlow, R. C. (eds.), *British Fascism* (London, 1980), p. 43).

[44] Beaverbrook to Lloyd George, 30 Mar. 1922 (HLRO, Lloyd George papers, F/4/6/11). On Crosland, see Brown, W. Sorley, *The Life and Genius of T. W. Crosland* (London, 1928). The Prime Minister would also have disliked one of Crosland's earlier books, *Taffy Was A Welshman*.

received the grant from the Civil List Fund for which he had asked: 'This is his way of paying me out.'[45]

The overt anti-Semites of the post-war years sometimes played deliberately on memories of Marconi. In a letter of abuse directed at 'that accursed little Welsh Bolshevik thief', one of Maxse's correspondents observed: 'The *Hidden Hand* the Jew saved him at the Marconi time. He has been in the hands of the Jews ever since.'[46] More commonly, as we have seen, it was assumed that the Prime Minister was being blackmailed because compromising information about Marconi had come into the hands of his enemies. This charge could be raised in the most unlikely of contexts. For example, when Horatio Bottomley was finally gaoled for fraud in June 1922, many wondered why he had been allowed to act with impunity for so long. The explanation offered by the *New Witness* was that 'Mr Bottomley knew a great deal about Mr Lloyd George, Lord Birkenhead, and other members of the Coalition . . . He kept silent during the Marconi scandal, though he was very obviously in the know as to the contract and the consequent manipulations of the market by the Brothers Isaacs.'[47]

Strachey, too, continued to be obsessed by Marconi, though, unlike the Radical Right, which tended to link the Affair to charges of treachery, conspiracy, and blackmail, the editor of the *Spectator* was more concerned with the ways in which it might have set a *bad precedent*. In July 1921 he received a letter from a friend complaining of the ill-treatment he thought he had received at the hands of a business associate. In his sympathetic reply, Strachey observed: 'I hope you won't think me a man of one idea when I say that I believe in these matters we took a wholly wrong turn at the time of the Marconi business and that we have never got back to the right road either in politics or in commerce.' In Strachey's view, the real threat to public morality came, not so much from the wrongdoer, but from otherwise honourable men who, out of misplaced loyalty, *acquiesced* in wrongdoing. At present, he argued, the country was being damaged by the 'way in which men like Curzon and Austen Chamberlain and other men who ought to and do know so much better, and are personally high-minded men, let themselves be ordered about and forced to endure mean actions' because they could not bring themselves to abandon Lloyd George.[48] And here, too, the fateful precedent had been set when Asquith chose to protect Lloyd George in 1913. That

[45] Sylvester to Beaverbrook, 31 Mar. 1922 (Lloyd George papers, F/4/6/12). Sylvester, one of Lloyd George's secretaries, was here transmitting his employer's words.

[46] R. Carew to Maxse, 9 Apr. 1922 (Maxse papers, vol. 478, K17–18).

[47] *New Witness*, 2 June 1922. The paper suggested that, with the loss of his press, Bottomley had 'ceased to count, in the Ministerial mind, as an asset'.

[48] Bledisloe to Strachey, 26 July 1921 (Strachey papers, S/2/12/1); Strachey to Bledisloe (copy), 30 July 1921 (ibid., S/2/12/2). Bledisloe was an idealistic young Tory

was why Strachey was so annoyed when Margot Asquith wrote to him in 1921 deploring the immorality of the Coalition Government. 'I am amused that you should write as if I was responsible for L.G.', he replied. 'You Liberals nursed him and brought him to power and place. In order to save him you condoned Marconi, and now you throw him at my head!'[49] The two of them were still wrangling about the rights and wrongs of Marconi after the Coalition had collapsed: 'I should have thought that you would have seen after all that has happened that LG sinned against the light in the Marconi business and that your husband made a great mistake in shielding him out of loyalty and kind-heartedness to a colleague', he told Margot Asquith for the umpteenth time on 21 December 1922.[50]

This almost insane preoccupation with the Marconi Affair, ten years after the 'scandal' had first broken, testifies to a widespread belief, by no means confined to Strachey and Margot Asquith, that the whole *tone* of public life had been lowered by the Coalition experiment and by Lloyd George's Premiership. One did not have to be anti-Semitic in any way to take this view, nor was it necessarily bound up with the kind of conspiratorial theories favoured by 'extremists', like Northumberland, or 'cranks', like Manners, Douglas, and Captain Spencer.

As far as the more traditional Diehards were concerned, the profession of concern about the spread of corruption was often, in part, an expression of simple snobbery. For it must be remembered that in the wartime and post-war Coalition Governments there were politicians, most of them Liberals, some Conservatives, whose social backgrounds were different from those enjoyed by the majority of Ministers who had served in the pre-war administrations—and were to serve in the Conservative Ministries of the mid-1920s. Thus, of the twenty-one Ministers who comprised Lloyd George's Cabinet in 1919, as many as nine were Scotsmen, one was Welsh, and one Jewish; only eight had attended one of the big public schools and only eight had graduated from Oxford or Cambridge University. 'Gentlemen' from traditional ruling-class families accounted for barely one-third of the Cabinet. In addition, the huge influx of 'business' MPs, like Grant Morden, into the Commons following the 1918 Election dismayed many aristocratic Members, who feared that their chamber was becoming indistinguishable from the Stock Exchange.[51] J. C. C. Davidson later alleged that

peer. For his later protest at the readmission of Birkenhead to the Conservative Front Bench, see Ch. 16, p. 395.

[49] Strachey to Margot Asquith (copy), 14 May 1921 (ibid., S/11/7/70).
[50] Strachey to Margot Asquith (copy), 21 Dec. 1922 (ibid., S/11/7/71).
[51] As Kinnear has shown, the Diehard critics of the Coalition came, in general, from more aristocratic backgrounds than did the loyal Government supporters, 43% of whom were businessmen (Kinnear, *Fall of Lloyd George*, p. 77). On the other hand, there were many links between some aristocratic Diehards and the businessman, Dudley Docker (see Davenport-Hines, *Dudley Docker*, pp. 96, 125, 245 n. 2).

some disreputable Tories who would otherwise never have secured adoption as Conservative candidates had actually been *sold* coupons by Lloyd George.[52]

No evidence exists to corroborate this claim. But it remains true that the social composition of both Cabinet and Parliament was changing, and that the Diehards tended to equate the arrival of 'parvenus' with a lowering of standards in public life. There is thus a sense in which 'independent Conservatism' can be seen, as Kenneth Morgan argues, as an aristocratic reaction against 'the passing of ancient patterns of deference, control, and stability' and as a protest at vulgar *arrivistes* like Lloyd George, Birkenhead, and Horne.[53]

In fact, as was the case before 1914, such politicians were quite unable to disarm their critics. If they advertised their relative poverty—for example, by supplementing their ministerial salaries by writing for newspapers—this was attacked as improper. If, on the other hand, they displayed signs of affluence, they were denounced as vulgar plutocrats. In 1921 and 1922 Maxse was pillorying Lloyd George, using much the same rhetoric that he had once turned on the 'Radical Plutocrats' of the Edwardian period—suggesting, for example, that the slogan, 'One Man One House' might be a suitable one for a 'democratic' Premier!

But Maxse was not alone in seeing Lloyd George as the 'Welsh Walpole', nor in mocking F. E. Smith (now Lord Birkenhead) as a 'cad' and a drunkard. The very qualities of intelligence and resourcefulness which had brought these two men to high office were now widely viewed with suspicion, the argument being that 'character' mattered more than 'cleverness'. 'It is strange how our beloved P.M. inspires all who come near him with complete mistrust of his having any fixed principles', wrote Neville to Austen Chamberlain in November 1921[54]—and several Cabinet Ministers would have endorsed this judgement. To Stanley Baldwin the Lloyd George Government was a 'thieves' kitchen'.[55] In January 1922 he wrote to his wife complaining of the atmosphere of intrigue and wishing he were at work in a cleaner environment.[56]

But if, as Baldwin believed, Lloyd George was personally responsible for creating the prevailing mood of swaggering cynicism, who was there to replace him? In the late summer of 1921 Salisbury was briefly

[52] James (ed.), *Memoirs of a Conservative*, p. 265. However, I have come across no evidence that this did actually occur.

[53] Morgan, K. O., *Consensus and Disunity*, p. 160.

[54] Neville Chamberlain to Austen Chamberlain, 23 Nov. 1921 (Birmingham University, Austen Chamberlain papers, AC 26/4/43).

[55] Thomas Jones's diary, 26 Apr. 1926, in Middlemas, K. (ed.), *Thomas Jones, Whitehall Diary, ii. 1926–1930* (Oxford, 1969), p. 23.

[56] Baldwin to Mrs Davidson, 16 Jan. 1922, in James (ed.), *Memoirs of a Conservative*, p. 112.

driven to contemplate the creation of a Birkenhead Administration, but, as Lord Robert Cecil observed, that 'would be a pale edition of Lloyd Georgism without his genius'.[57] Indeed, to the 'moral' critics of the post-war Coalition Government, 'F.E.' symbolized all that was degenerate in contemporary political life. Undoubtedly, such strictures were a little unfair. For example, many thought that Birkenhead was animated by a mere desire to make money; yet by accepting the Woolsack, he was in fact deliberately sacrificing wealth for power.[58] Moreover, Birkenhead brought wisdom, intelligence, and sound judgement both to his legal work and to the deliberations of the Cabinet. But, as Lloyd George later remarked, 'F.E.' had a dual personality; he was arguably the greatest Lord Chancellor of modern times, but 'the public only saw him at the Embassy Club with a lot of girls, when he was probably drunk, a most foolish thing to have done in his high office.'[59] Birkenhead also had a streak of dare-devil recklessness which attracted him to 'scoundrels' and 'lovable rogues'. Thus he always had something of a soft spot for Bottomley, in whom he may have discerned certain of his own qualities. Then there was his association with dubious characters like Warden Chilcott, 'Buns' Cartwright (his personal secretary, who may have been blackmailing him),[60] and Maundy Gregory, the honours tout—from all of whom he was happy to receive gifts and hospitality, indifferent to the thought that he might thereby be incurring obligations. The seamy side of Coalition politics was particularly visible in the character of James White, a ruthless and cynical company promoter, who eventually died by swallowing prussic acid and chloroform, after his swindles had caught up with him.[61] White, however, was used by Lloyd George's managers to help out in their newspaper purchases.[62] And on his desk, prominently displayed, there rested a book on international law, with an inscription from 'his sincere friend, Lord Birkenhead'.[63]

The Coalition System

But the moralists were not content with attacking the prominent personalities in the Lloyd George Coalition. They also expressed anxiety about the political system within which these individuals were operating. If there was an abuse of power, this, they argued, was

[57] Robert Cecil to Wife, 26 Aug. 1921 (Hatfield, Chelwood papers, CHE 6/124).
[58] Campbell, *F. E. Smith*, p. 458.
[59] A. J. Sylvester's diary, 22 Apr. 1933, in Cross, C. (ed.), *Life With Lloyd George: The Diary of A. J. Sylvester* (London, 1975), p. 95.
[60] Campbell, *F. E. Smith*, pp. 288, 472.
[61] Johnston, T., *The Financiers and the Nation* (London, 1934), pp. 94–6.
[62] See also Memo, 'The Prime Minister's Attempt To Control The Press' (Gwynne papers, vol. 8).
[63] Lyon, *By The Waters of Babylon*, pp. 211–12.

because Lloyd George and his little clique of favourites had effectively created a personal dictatorship.[64] When Edwin Montagu was dismissed from the Government in March 1922, he reinforced this line of criticism by calling the Prime Minister 'a great genius' but also 'a dictator' who had bypassed the Cabinet in favour of Conferences from which Ministers not in his good books were systematically excluded.[65] There was also grumbling from all sides of the political compass about Lloyd George's Personal Secretariat—the so-called 'Garden Suburb'. Some of its members enjoyed considerable influence, but they worked solely for the Prime Minister, having no responsibility to the Ministers on whose terrain they encroached, and they could not be cross-examined in Parliament. In June 1922 there was a debate in the Commons on the constitutional propriety of the Personal Secretariat and also about the role of the Cabinet Secretariat, and Hankey, the latter's Secretary, had good reason for fearing that the Conservatives might abolish his office altogether when they came into power.[66]

These fears of a 'Lloyd George Dictatorship' were also kept alive by disquiet over the power of the press barons who enjoyed prime ministerial favour. Lloyd George was unlike his predecessors in cultivating the company of pressmen and Fleet Street proprietors. Moreover, in his search for political support, he was assiduous in his attempts to acquire papers through which he could transmit his own point of view to a wider public. We have already heard that in late 1918 a group of Lloyd George's friends headed by Dalziel brought off a dramatic coup by seizing control of the *Daily Chronicle*; they sacked Robert Donald, its editor, and turned it into an organ sycophantically loyal to the Prime Minister.[67] The close ties between Lloyd George and the *Chronicle* were then emphasized when Philip Kerr left the Prime Minister's Secretariat in May 1921 and took over as the paper's manager. It is also well known that attempts were made after Northcliffe's death in August 1922 to purchase *The Times*; it was even seriously mooted that Lloyd George might exchange 10 Downing Street for the editor's office at Printing House Square, or even combine the two posts![68] Though this grandiose project foundered, Lloyd

---

[64] *National Review*, lxxviii (1922), 759.

[65] *The Times*, 13 Mar. 1922.

[66] Roskill, *Hankey* vol. ii, Ch. 11. One of Hankey's assailants in the press was Peter Wright, probably bent on revenge (ibid., p. 309).

[67] See the Memo., 'The Prime Minister's Attempt To Control The Press', probably drawn up by the Asquithian Liberals, Vivian Phillipps and Lord Buckmaster (Gwynne papers, vol. 8); Koss, *Rise and Fall*, ii. 333–7.

[68] Campbell, *F. E. Smith*, p. 604, where it is shown that the venture was being jointly organized by Lloyd George and Birkenhead, with Warden Chilcott handling the delicate negotiations. Koss also suggests that Rothermere, had he obtained control of *The Times*, would have installed Lloyd George as editor (Koss, *Rise and Fall*, pp. 401–3). See also Cregier, D. M., *Chiefs Without Indians* (Washington, 1982), pp. 123–8.

George's friends did succeed in taking over and 'muzzling' a string of provincial papers and a few metropolitan ones.

Lloyd George's opponents became obsessed also by the ways in which the Government, through the Whips' Office and through 'agents' like Riddell and Dalziel, sought to 'manage' the press by showering honours on newspaper proprietors and editors. What upset them were episodes like the one in which the Lancashire millionaire, John Leigh, was persuaded to buy up the *Pall Mall Gazette* and turn it into a pro-Coalition paper by a veiled promise of a peerage (which, in fact, was never delivered) and the prospect of becoming a famous figure in the House of Commons, to which Leigh got elected as a Conservative MP in May 1922.[69] Ugly rumours also surrounded the Government's wooing of the Berry brothers, who were building up their huge press empire in these years. It was alleged that the three men should have entered the Army when the Military Service Act extended the age of liability, but that they had extricated themselves by invoking the Prime Minister's patronage and opening a munitions factory as an alternative.[70]

Lloyd George's reputation as a skilful manipulator of press opinion was obviously exaggerated. Northcliffe, as we have seen, had quarrelled with the Prime Minister in 1918, and then developed into an implacable enemy. Beaverbrook, it is true, helped organize the press in the Coalition's favour when he brought Rothermere and Hulton to dine with the Prime Minister just prior to the Coupon Election: Hulton was promised a barony (though in the event the King would not go beyond a baronetcy) and Rothermere a viscountcy, and both of them agreed to throw their newspapers behind the Coalition.[71] But Lloyd George and his associates could never quite bring themselves to trust 'Max', and shortly after the Election Beaverbrook successfully asserted his right to play the 'independent critic' through the columns of the *Daily Express* whenever he chose to do so.[72]

Lord Rothermere also proved to be a difficult customer.[73] He soon forsook his promise to help Lloyd George. Instead he sent him a hectoring letter, complaining of ill-treatment, trying to make his support for the Government conditional upon its acceptance of the policies he thought necessary to save the country from 'Bolshevism', and expressing gloom at the prospect of an increased number of

---

[69] Memoranda in Gwynne papers, Vol. 8.

[70] Ibid. Sutherland was particularly anxious to cultivate William and Gomer Berry and to 'keep them substantially in hand' (Sutherland, Memo., 14 Dec. 1919, Lloyd George papers, F/93/2/18).

[71] Taylor, *Beaverbrook*, p. 160.   [72] Ibid.

[73] Amery's diary, 8 Nov. 1918, in Barnes and Nicholson (eds.), *Leo Amery Diaries*, i. 242. Peter Sanders made a similar observations in his diary: 'Rothermere struck me as rather more of a bounder than I imagined' (Sanders's diary, 10 Nov. 1918, in Ramsden (ed), *Real Old Tory Politics*, p. 112).

Conservatives being returned to Parliament.[74] Although in May 1919 he did receive the viscountcy he had been promised, despite the furious objections of the King, by late 1920 Rothermere had broken with the Coalition, and in January 1921 he founded the Anti-Waste League, a pressure group which ran independent candidates, three of whom were elected.[75] Despite, or perhaps because of, all this, Rothermere wrote to the Prime Minister's Office in 1922, asking for a baronetcy for his brother, Hildebrand, an honour which he claimed Lloyd George had promised to include in the next Honours List.[76] Hildebrand, an undistinguished backbench Liberal MP, was indeed made a baronet, to the amusement of his family who thought him a worthless idler, but when Rothermere then asked for a Privy Councillorship for another of his brothers, Cecil, the party managers turned a deaf ear.[77]

These squabbles notwithstanding, the critics of the Coalition could not be shaken out of their conviction that a corrupt alliance existed between the Government and the great press barons, and that there was enough evidence to support this conviction. For example, some Cabinet Ministers, notably Birkenhead, regularly supplemented their salaries by writing newspaper articles for inflated fees.[78] Then there were 'the "nobble" breakfasts in Downing Street, at which, over a muffin and a poached egg, ingenuous Pressmen were primed in the way they should go', as Maxse put it.[79] Moreover, honours were showered on newspapermen, while the Prime Minister, as well as being on terms of intimacy with Riddell and Dalziel, also encouraged Beaverbrook and Rothermere to imagine that they had a right to bargain with Cabinet Ministers on equal terms. Even if Lloyd George's exercises in 'squaring and squashing'[80] often failed, the fact is that the exercises had been seriously attempted.

Lord Robert Cecil and his Friends

Yet what was to be done to arrest these disturbing new developments and to restore the traditional 'decencies' of public life? There were among the Coalition's critics those who contended that national interests would continue to be neglected until such time as 'English gentlemen' recovered their rightful inheritance. Page Croft put this point of view with his customary directness in a speech at Manchester in September 1919: 'This country would never recover', he said, 'so

[74] Taylor, *Beaverbrook*, pp. 161–2.

[75] See Cowling, M., *The Impact of Labour 1920–1924* (Cambridge, 1971), pp. 47–52.

[76] Rothermere to Lloyd George, 7 May 1922 (Lloyd George papers, F/44/5/15).

[77] Rothermere to Lloyd George, 5 July 1922 (ibid., F/44/5/16); King, Cecil H., *Strictly Personal* (London, 1969), pp. 78, 84–6.

[78] e.g. he was paid £100 a piece of his three short articles in the *Weekly Dispatch* on the lessons of the Spen Valley by-election (Koss, *Rise and Fall*, p. 366).

[79] *National Review*, lxxix (1922), 189.   [80] See Koss, *Rise and Fall*, Ch. 9.

long as the "Welsh Wizard" promised the moon, surrendered to blackmail, and broke his pledges.' Since the Salisbury era, he observed, Britain had had as its Prime Minister a succession of lawyers, Scots, and a Welshman. He concluded: 'we now need a straight, honest Englishman who will give us deeds instead of frothy rhetoric, whom the people will trust to go straight, and who in turn will trust our long-suffering, splendid people!'[81] The implicaton here was that Scotsmen and Welshmen, particularly if they also happened to be lawyers, tended to be dishonest. Gwynne, a Welshman himself, was prepared to go along with this prejudice and actually put his 'disadvantage' to good use by claiming that this gave him an especially acute insight into Lloyd George's character: 'I know the type'![82] In private such sentiments were expressed more freely than in public. Selborne, for example, told his wife that there were doubts about whether Lord Edmund Talbot was 'clever enough' for the Irish Viceroyalty which he had just accepted; but, Selborne commented, he personally had a 'great belief in the administrative power of an absolutely straight English gentleman'.[83] Once again, the connection was being established between honesty, Englishness, and the social position of a gentleman.

Now, the elder statesman who best fitted this description in 1921 and 1922 was Edward Grey. Strachey thought that Grey was 'in politics like a good bank reserve is in commerce. If anything goes wrong we have always got him in the background to serve and save the state.'[84] Grey's appeal was one which crossed party lines. Hence his central role in the so-called 'Grey Conspiracy' of 1921, instigated by Lord Robert Cecil, who had resigned from the Coalition over the Welsh Church question in December 1918 and returned to his pre-war role as a bitter critic of Lloyd George's character and policies. Cecil believed in particular that a return to principle was necessary to restore the good name of the British Government abroad and to reduce social tension at home. In words which almost echo Page Croft's, Cecil lamented the fact that 'a Welsh Wizard' was controlling the affairs of the country: 'I am beginning to believe that there is nothing so dangerous as cleverness in an administrator. Give me a stupid old country gentleman.'[85]

Cecil was buoyed up in 1921 and 1922 by a strong sense of mission. In a revealing letter to his wife of June 1921 he described how deeply he had been moved by listening to his brother, Lord William ('Fish') preaching on the subject of 'England and responsibility', 'the immense

[81] *Manchester Guardian*, 23 Sept. 1919.
[82] Gwynne to Austen Chamberlain (copy), 18 May 1921 (Gwynne Papers, vol. 17).
[83] Selborne to Maude Selborne, 4 Apr. 1921 (Selborne papers, vol. 104, fo. 47).
[84] Cited by Bentley, M., 'Liberal Politics and the Grey Conspiracy of 1921', *Historical Journal*, xx (1977), 476.
[85] Cecil to Gertrude Bell, 11 Apr. 1921, cited in Morgan, *Consensus and Disunity*, p. 207.

opportunity for moral leadership open to us English and the certainty
of destruction if we neglected it', and the need for 'statesmen who were
not opportunists'. Lord Robert, though aware of the dangers of
hypocrisy and self-deception, felt that this message spoke directly to
him, and that he had 'been "called" to preach the League spirit in
public affairs' along lines laid down in the Bible. If Grey refused to
respond, he mused, he would have to strike out by himself, 'asking the
people to follow me'.[86] It was this strong sense of mission, plus his
saintly persona, and not just his abhorrence of Lloyd George ('a
spiritual vampire'[87]) which presumably explains the enormous appeal
Lord Robert made to many dissident Conservatives, to Liberals like
Massingham,[88] and even to some Labour men—Harold Laski, for
example, momentarily fell under Cecil's spell, emerging from an
interview 'feeling cleaner by contact with him'.[89]

Nevertheless, Lord Robert persisted for several months in his
attempts to exercise his moral influence through the instrumentality
of Grey. This was a sensible strategy, since the programme of the
movement which Cecil envisaged was based on co-partnership,
'economy', and support for the League of Nations—all quintessentially
Liberal concepts. Whether Grey entirely understood what others
expected of him is not entirely clear. But in a well-publicized speech at
Berwick in October 1921 he struck exactly the right note, denouncing
the Coalition as a dangerous compound of 'great ability and extreme
instability' and calling up in opposition to it the spirit of 'class co-
operation'.[90] Even more pertinently, in a speech in January 1922, the
Liberal elder statesman announced that he had returned to politics
because 'since the last election, there has been a House of Commons
which has allowed any apparent scandal, however great, to remain
unexposed, which has allowed any policy, however extravagant, to go
on unchecked, which has allowed any inconsistency, however flagrant,
to take place.' In its place he advocated 'wholesome, straightforward
politics in this country'.[91] This was precisely Cecil's language. Could
the two men combine, as Cecil himself hoped, to create a new kind of
Centre Party, which, with the ageing Asquith pushed into the
background, might then go on and successfully appeal to the conscience
and better moral instincts of the nation?

Michael Bentley has ably analysed the reasons for the ultimate
failure of the 'Grey Conspiracy'.[92] In retrospect the scheme seems to

[86] Cecil to Wife, 12 June 1921 (Hatfield, Chelwood papers, CHE 6/105).
[87] Cecil to Wife, 29 Mar. 1922 (ibid., CHE 6/148).
[88] Havighurst, A. F., *Radical Journalist: H. W. Massingham 1860–1924* (Cambridge, 1974), pp. 291–2.
[89] Laski to Holmes, 15 May 1922, in Howe, M. (ed.), *The Holmes–Laski Letters* (Oxford, 1953), pp. 427–8.
[90] Liberal Party pamphlets, 1921/2.
[91] Ibid., 1922/3.   [92] Bentley, 'Grey Conspiracy', 461–78.

have been foredoomed. The Liberal 'organization men' like Herbert Gladstone and Donald MacLean and the chief financial backer of the Independent Liberals, Lord Cowdray (himself an unlikely protagonist of a new 'moralized' politics!) saw advantages in Cecil joining their Party and had no scruples about demoting Asquith, whom they rightly judged to be an increasing electoral liability. But Cecil did not wish to join the Liberal Party and Asquith shrewdly blocked all attempts to demote him, while Grey's aloofness and fragile health still further reduced the feasibility of the enterprise. By April 1922 Cecil was again ploughing his lonely furrow, but his personal manifesto, a document full of admirable sentiments, made little political impact when it was released to the press.[93] What Kenneth Morgan has rightly called an anachronistic attempt to revive Bentinck's Young England Movement ended in anticlimax, and 'the revolt of the high-minded' simply petered out.[94]

In a sense the 'Grey Conspiracy' may have got under way too late in the day. Cecil's ambition was to create a new kind of Centre Party, under leaders of high moral stature, and to displace the unscrupulous, power-seeking centrism of Lloyd George and his Coalition supporters. But by late 1921 disillusionment with the Coalition was producing a mood of nostalgic longing for the old party system. The 'corruption', levity, and cynicism of the Lloyd George entourage could not, it seemed, be explained merely as personal defects accentuated by social and educational disadvantage. Instead, they were perhaps the inevitable consequence of coalition government itself, which encouraged politicians to combine in the pursuit of power without giving thought to the policy differences that might divide them. In short, there was something 'dishonest' about coalitionism as a *phenomenon*, and from that flowed all the other unsavoury aspects of contemporary politics which were so widely deplored.

Both Independent Liberals and many Conservatives can be found deploying this line of argument. For example, the Asquithian journalist, Harold Storey, in his September 1920 pamphlet, *The Case Against the Lloyd George Coalition*, writes: 'The truth is that government under Mr Lloyd George's Coalition is neither honest Conservatism nor honest Liberalism.' In 1918 the country had been invited to elect a caucus and that was what it had now got: 'a party without a principle, a combination of persons with no common policy, with nothing to recommend it except the legend that it had won the War'.[95] And Grey in his January 1922 Edinburgh speech called for a return to pre-war conditions and expressed the hope that in the election shortly to be

[93] Cecil's letter to Col. Heaton-Ellis, chairman of the Hitchin Unionist Association (*The Times*, 22 Apr. 1922).
[94] Morgan, *Consensus and Disunity*, pp. 207, 210.
[95] Storey, H., *The Case Against the Lloyd George Coalition* (London, 1920), p. 36.

held the country would 'have a straight contest between parties who are agreed in principle, opposing parties holding different principles, with the object of having again, as we have had before, a homogeneous Government which can be trusted not to swing this way and that, but to adhere to principles and policy which are know to the country'.[96] That was indeed the stance which the Independent Liberal Party adopted in the 1922 General Election. In its leaflet, 'What the Liberal Party Stands For', there was a section on 'Honest Government' in which 'the present method of Government by make-belief' was denounced and the call made for a 'return to the system under which Statesmen say what they mean and do what they say'.[97]

But the Diehards were expressing almost identical sentiments. In fact, by a supreme irony men like Page Croft, who for years had been identifying party politics with corruption, were now discovering that the disciplines of party rivalry might assist in restoring morality to public life. Faced by Labour militancy and 'direct action', they were also abandoning their former contempt for parliamentary institutions. Ampthill actually claimed that 'you cannot choose between Parliamentary government and party government . . . they go together'; and he went on to call for a re-establishment of the two 'historical parties . . . on the foundations of their ancient and purest principles'.[98] This revival of confidence in the two-party system played a part in the decision to wind up the National Party in April 1921, leaving Page Croft and his friends free to return to the Conservative fold.

The Diehards' abhorrence of coalition as a political system also found expression in April 1922, when Joynson-Hicks moved the following motion: 'That in the opinion of this House, the lack of definite and coherent principle in the policy of the present Coalition Government can only be remedied by the establishment of a Ministry composed of men united in political principle.' The Government saw off this challenge to its authority easily enough—by 288 votes to 95— but Austen Chamberlain may have been unwise to boast of his crushing victory.[99] For there was some cogency in the critics' argument that conservatism and liberalism simply did not mix. In Lord Hugh Cecil's view, the impression was being given that Ministers, lacking clear convictions, were solely concerned with hanging on to office, even if this accorded 'very little with their dignity and still less with their honour'. Such an administration, Cecil warned, 'imperils

---

[96] Liberal Party pamphlets, 1922/3.

[97] Ibid., 1922/18. Montagu made the same point in his Cambridge speech: 'Believe me, you make the principle of Coalition ridiculous if you try to apply it by standing first on one leg and then on the other: by making up for . . . every Liberal measure by doing something for the Conservatives the next day' (*The Times*, 13 Mar. 1922).

[98] *Daily Telegraph*, 6 Apr. 1922.

[99] Austen Chamberlain to George V (copy), 6 Apr. 1922 (Austen Chamberlain papers, AC 33/3/65).

our public life as it imperils the national good'.[100] This, in short, was the heart of the critics' case: that coalition government bred dishonesty, so that the country was 'dishonoured'.

This theme was taken up again two months later in the Diehard Manifesto of 2 June 1922 which appeared in the newspapers over the signatures of eleven peers (including Salisbury, Selborne, and Ampthill) and thirty MPs. 'Our purpose', they declared, 'is not to break up the Conservative and Unionist Party, but to rally and revive the true Conservative and Unionist principles.'[101]

Particularly significant in this anti-Coalition demonstration was the part played by Salisbury. Unlike his brother, Lord Robert, Salisbury had never relished the prospect of associating with Liberals, Edward Grey alone excepted,[102] but had always preferred the strategy of undermining Lloyd George through a re-establishment of 'independent Unionism'—a concept which, according to Selborne and himself, entailed 'clean and straightforward politics' and the repudiation of 'unavowable methods of securing office'.[103] By the summer of 1922 Salisbury felt that the moment was ripe for making a public stand. And in so doing he supplied the Diehards with something they had hitherto lacked: respected and credible leadership. As Maurice Cowling has argued, Salisbury's importance lay in the fact that he was able to appeal simultaneously to the various Diehard polit: ans, Gretton, Northumberland, Page Croft, Ampthill, and so on, and also to such independent Conservatives as his brother, Lord Robert Cecil, and to unite all these dissidents in a movement which presented 'a modest, humane, decent, uncorrupt, patriotic *Conservative* face to the people'.[104]

The attempt to 'cleanse' British life of corruption and simultaneously to destroy Lloyd George's Coalition Government had begun in earnest. Predictably enough, the movement was soon focusing on abuses in the honours system—the issue which had been engrossing Salisbury's attention for several years past.

[100] *Parl. Deb.*, 5th ser., clii. 2382 (5 Apr. 1922).
[101] *Morning Post*, 2 June 1922.
[102] Robert Cecil to Wife, 27 Aug. 1921 (Chelwood papers, CHE 6/125).
[103] Cited in Morgan, *Consensus and Disunity*, p. 241.
[104] Cowling, *Impact of Labour*, p. 90.

15
The 1922 Honours Scandal

Prelude

DISCONTENT with the honours system, which had been simmering away for over a decade, flared up quite suddenly in the summer of 1922, with the announcement that the unpopular South African financier and mineowner, J. B. Robinson, was about to receive a peerage. This really 'put the fat in the fire', as one observer put it.[1] In both Commons and Lords the award was denounced as an insult to the nation and a humiliation to the Crown. Robinson was obliged to decline the honour. The incident seems to have broken the existing taboo about naming names and giving concrete examples of honours trafficking. The Duke of Northumberland in the House of Lords and Ronald McNeill in the Commons denounced other recent creations. The press, sensing that here was a very juicy news story, began unearthing scandals and publishing documents which showed how the 'honours touts' plied their peculiar trade. A mood of angry righteousness gripped MPs, 279 of whom eventually signed a motion calling for a Select Committee of Enquiry. Lloyd George and his inner Cabinet initially underestimated the significance of the protests and tried to fend off the demand, until, in the parliamentary debate of 17 July, Lloyd George was forced to concede the appointment of a Royal Commission of investigation in a half-apologetic, half-defiant speech which inspired general derision. 'The PM was lamentable,' confided Churchill to his wife, 'and is universally pronounced to have made the worst speech of his career.'[2] The 17 July debate dramatized the decline in Lloyd George's fortunes and the eagerness of large sections of the Conservative Party to break free from the Coalition. Few observers of the political scene were that surprised when, three months later, the Chanak Crisis sparked off the rebellion which put Lloyd George out of office.

It would be fruitless to attempt to estimate the precise contribution made by the Honours Scandal to the fall of the Coalition. Historians, of late, have tended to play down its significance. But a high percentage of the Tory rebels spoke of their unwillingness to continue following Lloyd George, and it is clear that their objections to what Austen

---

[1] Peter Sanders's diary, 2 July 1922, in Ramsden (ed.), *Real Old Tory Politics*, p. 177.
[2] Churchill to Clementine Churchill, 18 July 1922. Mrs Churchill replied: 'The Honours Debate made me blush—our public life is not really squalid but the whole ways these last two years have been managed politically makes one doubt.' See also Churchill to Clementine Churchill, 16 July (Gilbert, Martin, *Winston S. Churchill*, iv. *1917–22* (London, 1975), p. 787; ibid., *Companion Vol.* (London, 1977), Part III, pp. 1932–3).

Chamberlain called 'the defects of Lloyd George's character' had been powerfully reinforced by the recent revelations of Government complicity in honours trafficking.[3] Talking with Salvidge in April 1923, Birkenhead even ventured the opinion that nothing had damaged the Coalition more than the 'prodigal' way in which the Prime Minister had distributed peerages.[4] Certainly, the debate of 17 July created an atmosphere highly favourable to those Conservatives who had for long been anxious to extricate their party from the Coalition. It is not enough to write dismissively of 'the political trivialities of the honours scandal'.[5]

In a sense it was the belief that only unworldly moralists and cranks took the honours issue seriously that encouraged leading Coalition Ministers to ignore the serious anger that was being aroused until it was too late. One can understand this point of view. Since the mid-1890s there had been intermittent attempts to bring about radical changes in the system of party funding and the award of honours. A brief period of excitement had always been followed in the past by apathy and indifference.

At the end of the War the issue certainly did not look like creating great public interest. Admittedly, the theatre-going public was being regaled in the summer of 1918 with Arnold Bennett's satirical comedy, *The Title*, which received 285 performances in London and was a great success there—though it failed in the provinces.[6] But, as we have seen, Lords Selborne and Salisbury had made only modest headway when they tried to interest Parliament in honours trafficking in 1917 and 1918.[7]

This left the field open, for the time being, to Page Croft and his friends, who had founded the National Party in August 1917 partly out of disgust at the spectacle of war profiteers buying their way into the peerage.[8] In May 1919 Croft had his big chance to persuade Parliament to share this concern. With the War still fresh in everyone's memory, he brought a motion about honours trafficking before the Commons. Characteristically, he emphasized the dangers of foreign infiltration: aliens with guttural accents, he complained, were being foisted on the the constituencies, and later their wives were gaining entry into the nobility, something which could only have happened because they were generous contributors to the party funds. In the recent Honours List, said Croft, were the names of people 'whom no decent man would

---

[3] On the views of the Tory rebels, see Kinnear, *Fall of Lloyd George*, pp. 87–8. On Chamberlain's remark, see Petrie, Sir C., *Life and Letters of the Right Hon. Sir Austen Chamberlain* (London, 1940), ii. 204.

[4] Salvidge, S., *Salvidge of Liverpool* (London, 1934), p. 252.

[5] Morgan, *Consensus and Disunity*, p. 375.

[6] Pound, R., *Arnold Bennett* (London, 1952), p. 279. One consequence was that when Bennett was offered a knighthood later that year, he felt obliged to refuse!

[7] See Ch. 13, pp. 310–13.   [8] Croft, *My Life of Strife*, pp. 129–30.

allow to enter his house'. He deprecated the fact that relatively few awards had gone to the fighting services, while honours were heaped on pressmen; the hackneyed phrase, 'The pen is mightier than the sword', had now acquired a new meaning! The National Party, whose accounts were audited annually by a chartered accountant, was held out as a model, and Croft also suggested, rather casually, the idea of a vetting committee.[9]

Seconding Croft's motion was the recently re-elected Bottomley, who noisily congratulated himself on having escaped promotion to the House of Lords and voiced his contempt for 'the old party shibboleths'.[10] No wonder that Lord Hugh Cecil, speaking later in support of the motion, said that it was important to rescue it from previous speakers who did not command much confidence, since exaggeration and the suspicion of crankery were to be avoided at all costs.[11] From the Government benches the only contributor was Bonar Law, who dismissed the audit of party funds as impractical, but said that he was agreeable to a motion which would disallow the exchange of honours for party donations; however, he then weakened the force of this apparent concession by adding that the Whips had assured him that there never had been, and never would be, such bargains![12] In a subsequent letter to Lloyd George, who was absent in Paris, Freddie Guest, the Coalition Liberal Chief Whip, called Bonar Law's contribution an 'absolutely first-rate speech'![13]

Inevitably, the Government easily beat off this feeble threat to its position. According to the *Morning Post*, which enthusiastically backed Page Croft, five Coalition Whips 'were stretched across the entrance to the division lobby to persuade Members to go the official way'. It hinted, moreover, that Croft had made a tactical mistake in pressing his motion to a vote and ignoring Bonar Law's somewhat ambiguous 'offer'.[14] Be that as it may, the division gave victory to the Government by 112 votes to 50. The minority, if one adds in the two tellers, comprised twenty Labour MPs, most of whom wanted the total abolition of all hereditary honours, seventeen Unionists, six Asquithian Liberals, the two National Party Members, two Independents, and, more surprisingly, two Members of the generally pro-Coalition

[9] *Parl. Deb.*, 5th ser., cxvi. 1334–44 (28 May 1919).   [10] Ibid. 1344–7.
[11] Ibid. 1353. Page Croft was not thought well of by the Salisbury family. In December 1919 Croft wrote to the Marquess, saying he had 'often wished to have a talk with you about this question of political corruption in which I am so glad to realize that you are interested. . . . I should very much like to have a talk with you before the "little Welsh scoundrel" has destroyed every tradition of British statesmanship' (Croft to Salisbury, 1 Dec. 1919, Salisbury papers, 94/93–5). But the rivalry between the National Party and Salisbury's Independent Conservatives made any kind of co-operation difficult at this stage.
[12] *Parl. Deb.*, 5th ser., cxvi. 1367.
[13] Guest to Lloyd George, 30 May 1919 (HLRO, Lloyd George papers, F/21/3/24).
[14] *Morning Post*, 29 May 1919.

National Democratic Party and three Coalition Liberals. It is also surprising to note that four MPs who were firm Diehards by 1922 *supported* the Government, one of them being Ronald McNeill.[15]

Probably few Members who took part in the May 1919 debate apart from the self-important National Party MPs, whom one Coalition Unionist dismissed as 'the most stupid set of men that ever walked',[16] took the occasion too seriously. On the other hand, it did make the party leaders proceed more cautiously over the following weeks. Guest, in his letter to the absent Premier, wrote:

There is no doubt . . . that there is still considerable restlessness in the public mind on this subject, more particularly on the grounds that soldiers and sailors have, so far, failed to achieve recognition. . . . I have consulted Bonar Law, Younger, Talbot and 'F.E.' separately, and we are all of opinion that the ordinary political list should be deferred until Peace is declared and the soldiers and sailors recognised.

Agitators, he warned, were looking for something 'to seize [?] upon and exploit'.[17] A day later Bonar Law wrote to Lloyd George in the same sense: 'I am thankful that you have agreed not to have a political honours list just now. I was frightened of it after my speech the other night.'[18] The special List announced in the autumn largely consisted of 'war heroes': Beatty, Haig, Plumer, Rawlinson, Allenby, and so on, and the critics were momentarily silenced.

But in 1920 and 1921 there was another avalanche of honours, many of which aroused controversy. True, only seven new peers were created in 1920, but there were twenty in 1921, as well as the forty-two and forty-three baronetcies awarded in these two years. This is to omit all mention of new knights, over 1,500 of whom had come into existence between December 1916 and July 1922—an 'inflation of honours' by comparison with which Asquith's creations seemed timidly modest. Moreover, Lloyd George was bound to ruffle the feathers of his aristocratic critics by bestowing so many awards on men and women from 'unconventional' backgrounds, particularly pressmen and business-men with no strong record of public service; according to Laski, the latter accounted for 30 per cent of Lloyd George's peers (as against 13 per cent of Asquith's), 55 per cent of his baronetcies (as against 50 per cent), and 30.5 per cent of his knights (as against 18 per cent).[19] There would have been unease over this development, even had all the new

---

[15] *Parl. Deb.*, 5th ser., cxvi. 1379–82. See list of 1922 Diehards in Kinnear, *Fall of Lloyd George*, pp. 222–42.

[16] *Parl. Deb.*, 5th ser., cxvi. 1349 (Lane-Mitchell).

[17] Guest to Lloyd George, 30 May 1919 (Lloyd George papers, F/21/3/24). Guest had sent the Prime Minister a similar letter of warning earlier in the year (Sutherland to Lloyd George, early 1919, with enclosed letter from Guest, 16 Feb. 1919, Lloyd George papers, F/93/2/13).

[18] Bonar Law to Lloyd George (copy), 31 May 1919 (Bonar Law papers, 101/3/92).

[19] Laski, H., 'The Prime Minister's Honours Lists', *Nation*, 15 July 1922.

creations possessed irreproachable records and characters, which was far from being the case.

Before the row over the Robinson Peerage, the person whose honour gave the Government most trouble was Sir Rowland Hodge, who was made a baronet in the New Year List of January 1921. That Hodge had for some time been anxious for recognition is plain from the letter which Churchill's Secretary, Eddy Marsh, sent to Lloyd George's Secretary in November 1918:

Mr Churchill thinks he ought to let you know that he was approached on Saturday, to his great surprise, by an acquaintance, who should have known better, with a suggestion that he should procure a baronetcy for a certain Hodge, a Newcastle shipowner, and receive £5000 on delivery of the goods. Naturally the intermediary received short shrift—and Mr Churchill thinks you may wish to make a note, to be borne in mind if the idea of any honour for Mr Hodge is mooted again.'[20]

Rebuffed in this direction, Hodge and his friends then approached Conservative Central Office, and, as Younger, the Party Chairman, later explained to Bonar Law, 'made offers so brutally frank that I made up my mind to have nothing to do with him, and showed him the cold shoulder'. Younger's supposition was that Hodge must then have 'gone to Freddie and captured him'.[21] For Hodge's name had somehow or other appeared on the list of new baronetcies released in January 1921.

This was indeed a scandalous promotion, since Hodge had been convicted of food-hoarding during the War and fined £450. Nor, as Lloyd George initially tried to claim when the issue was raised in public, was Hodge's offence merely a technical one.[22] In fact, if Page Croft, who quickly carried out his own investigations, was to be believed, the Newcastle businessman had gone to the length of erecting a special partition in his house behind which the goods could be concealed. After his conviction, Hodge had been driven out of Newcastle by the hostility of his neighbours, and settled in Rochester, where his disreputable past was unknown. But Conservatives in the North-East did not forget the episode, and of course the Hodge Affair soon became a political talking point.[23]

Challenged by Croft in the Commons, the Prime Minister at first made light of the offence and spoke of Hodge's public services to the country during the War.[24] Anxious to cut short all further discussion, Lloyd George then sent an urgent message to Page Croft to meet him before Question Time; at this meeting the Prime Minister confessed

[20] Marsh to J. T. Davies, 9 Dec. 1918 (Lloyd George papers, F/8/2/44).
[21] Younger to Bonar Law, 7 Jan. 1921 (Bonar Law papers, 100/1/2).
[22] *Parl. Deb.*, 5th ser., cxxxviii. 1417 (28 Feb. 1921).
[23] Croft to Lloyd George (copy), 1 Mar. 1921 (Bodleian, Gwynne papers, vol. 8).
[24] *Parl. Deb.*, 5th ser., cxxxviii. 1417.

that he was 'much worried about the Hodge Case' and volunteered the information that the title had in fact been pressed by the Admiralty to mark its appreciation of Hodge's services to shipbuilding during the War. Croft was not convinced of the truth of this and informed the Premier that he could not let the matter drop: 'on this occasion I have got the sympathy of the House', he told Gwynne. 'If we can get this title annulled, a great blow will be struck for public honesty.'[25] The wrangle continued in the Commons. Croft was by now convinced that the Northumberland Shipbuilding Company had received 'very substantial profits' on its barges.[26] So Hodge, who had been its managing director, stood condemned, not just as a petty criminal, but also as a 'war profiteer'.

Another interesting aspect of the Hodge Affair was the active involvement of the King, who was already disgusted at the inflation of honours and at the cavalier way in which Ministers were making use of the Royal Prerogative. Clive Wigram, one of George V's Secretaries, had received a letter from an informant in the North-East describing Hodge's food-hoarding. The King had a good memory and this letter reminded him that he had once been introduced to Hodge during a wartime tour of the Newcastle shipyards. As Stamfordham wrote to 10 Downing Street: 'His appearance, dress and manner left an indelible mark on His Majesty's mind. Such appointments react upon the Sovereign, and the King has expressed to me his feelings of annoyance and indeed disgust that this man should have received any honour, let alone a baronetcy.'[27] But the Government stuck to its guns, refused to annul Hodge's title, and eventually the controversy died down.

Origins of the 1922 Scandal

Why, then, did the 'Honours Scandal' erupt in the summer of 1922, although discontent had been building up for almost a decade? One obvious answer is that the Coalition had already become discredited by then, and honours abuses just happened to offer a convenient target. A sense that the Government's life was drawing to its end may also have played its part in precipitating the crisis by pushing the Coalition Liberals and 'honours cadgers' into a series of quick deals, while there was still time. According to one of the gentlemen who had been approached by an honours tout, the tout had said: 'the Government would not last very long, and . . . when Mr Lloyd George went to the country he wanted funds for contesting certain seats, etc.'[28] Such considerations as this may have led the Whips and their unofficial

[25] Croft's Memo. of 1 Mar. 1921 (Gwynne papers, vol. 8).
[26] *Parl. Deb.*, 5th ser., cxxxix. 1024 (14 Mar. 1921).
[27] Stamfordham to Lloyd George, 19 Jan. 1921 (Lloyd George papers, F/29/4/34).
[28] The correspondence was published in the *Morning Post*, 28 Aug. 1922.

agents to ignore the warning signs of public anger and to take risks which in other circumstances they would have avoided.

But there were other reasons why the Honours Scandal should have broken when it did. By an odd coincidence the 1922 Birthday Honours List appeared just a day after the appearance of the Diehard Manifesto of 2 June, when the Diehards, with Salisbury as their acknowledged leader, were better organized than they had ever been in the past for an attack on the Lloyd George regime.[29] Moreover, Salisbury and his friends were currently engaged in one of their periodic efforts at getting 'Second Chamber Reform' brought into the forefront of politics. Salisbury and Selborne hoped that the Conservative Peers, aided by the National Union and by press sympathizers, might succeed in impressing upon the Coalition leaders that Conservative support was conditional upon progress in this field. But Selborne had reached the conclusion by May that 'we are being simply sold';[30] not only was Lloyd George obviously dragging his feet on Second Chamber Reform, he was seemingly intent on weakening the House of Lords still further by stuffing it with discreditable creations. In Maxse's words, the Prime Minister had 'always despised the Upper House, and was killing at least two birds with one stone every time Coalition-Liberalism secured a cheque through some unattractive peerage'.[31] Interestingly, the House of Lords was debating its own future at the very time the honours crisis exploded.

Meanwhile, the Labour Movement, which usually put honours trafficking rather low down its agenda, also had reasons for emphasizing the issue in the summer of 1922. A private member's bill, heavily supported by the Coalition Parties, had recently been brought in: the Trade Union Act (Amendment) Bill, which aimed at replacing contracting out by contracting in. Its introduction had generated the usual flood of rhetoric about the 'tyranny' of the political levy and the superiority of a system of voluntary contributions. Labour men could not resist the opportunity of pointing out that, in practice, 'voluntary contributions' were not all that they appeared. 'The rich man's political levy' was how one socialist newspaper described the purchase of honours.[32]

Another factor influencing Labour attitudes was the Party Conference held in Edinburgh in late June, where 'democratic' feeling ran high and more than usual enthusiasm was aroused by calls for the abolition of all hereditary honours. The Labour Leaders even had to ward off attempts from the floor to prevent members of the Party from becoming privy councillors. Arthur Henderson's line was to claim that

---

[29] Ibid., 2 June 1922.
[30] Selborne to Wife, 3 May 1922 (Selborne papers, vol. 104, fo. 77).
[31] *National Review*, lxxx (1922), 36.
[32] See also the cartoon in *Labour Leader*, 13 July 1922, reproduced in Figure 8.

8. A Socialist View of the 1922 Honours Scandal

(*Labour Leader*, 13 July 1922)

a privy councillorship 'was the only honour that was pure in the whole of the honours given in the country' and thus the only one that a Labour man could ever, with a clear conscience, accept.[33]

Oddly enough, then, the summer of 1922 saw an unconscious convergence between Left and Right, the one wanting the abolition of the Upper Chamber, the other its restoration to effective power, but both feeling that a further 'adulteration of the peerage' was an insult to the ideals they held dear. It was at this moment that the Birthday Honours List was published on 3 June. Some newspapers that one would have expected to react angrily took a little time to appreciate its significance. In its initial comment, the *Morning Post*, for example, opined that there were 'fewer ostensibly political honours than usual', and although it had some sharp observations to make about 'the Lloyd Georgian model [of] making up in quantity what it lacks in quality', there was as yet no sense of an 'enormity' having been perpetrated.[34]

But the appearance on the List of the name of Sir J. B. Robinson was bound to create controversy. The Liberals' bestowal of a baronetcy on the South African mineowner in 1908 had been unpopular enough. But Robinson had also been recently fined £500,000 for fraudulent practices in South Africa, and the Privy Council had refused him permission to appeal against this judgement as late as November 1921. Though he was a South African citizen, it was immediately apparent that the recommendation did not come from the South African Government, and one did not have to be unduly cynical to suspect that a large cheque had recently been paid into the coffers of the Coalition Liberal Party. Since virtually no one cared about wounding Robinson's feelings, critics of the Coalition queued up to denounce this flagrant misuse of the Royal Prerogative. They were actively encouraged by Buckingham Palace. On 15 June Stamfordham wrote to Salisbury assuring him that the King had had nothing to do with Robinson's peerage and knew nothing about the man except what he had read in the newspapers since the *Gazette* was published. 'The whole question of honours grows more and more disagreeable and distasteful to the King', wrote Stamfordham, 'whose one object is to reduce the numbers that are submitted to him twice a year, and naturally to secure their being conferred upon reputable people; but you will naturally be inclined to reply that His Majesty's efforts are not very successful!'[35]

In the event, the man who first denounced the Robinson creation in Parliament was not Salisbury but Lord Harris, whose concern was not solely with the health of British public life, since he had personal grievances against the South African mineowner which went right

[33] *Labour Party Annual Conference Report* (Edinburgh, 1922), p. 214.
[34] *Morning Post*, 3 June 1922.
[35] Stamfordham to Salisbury, 15 June 1922 (Salisbury papers, S(4), 232, fos. 31–2).

back to the 1890s.[36] But that did not weaken the impact of the statement which he made in the House of Lords on 22 June. Harris was followed by Selborne, who burst out angrily about 'a public scandal of the first magnitude'.[37] The sequel is well known. Robinson was prevailed upon with some difficulty to decline his peerage in a letter which Lord Birkenhead read out in the Lords on 29 June.[38]

Development of the Scandal

The agitation now developed along two fronts, in the press and in Parliament, with journalists and politicians often co-operating with one another. No newspaper played a more important role than the *Morning Post*. Dismayed by the 1922 Birthday Honours List, Gwynne concluded that only the Diehards stood between the country and 'National Dishonour'. Yet it was his belief that Lloyd George's 'vast political machine, fed by the sale of honours' was impeding these 'honest men' in their attempts to win support in the constituencies. Accordingly, on 13 June the paper launched an appeal for funds, under the banner headline: 'AN APPEAL TO THE NATIONAL HONOUR. THE RESTORATION OF CLEAN GOVERNMENT. SUPPORT THE DIEHARDS'. The condemned practice of honours trafficking was explicitly linked to the existence of a Coalition, and the remedy for both was said to be a movement of national repentance and moral renewal:

If righteousness exalteth a nation, how shall unrighteousness not debase it? Political corruption is one cause of the decay. It began with the Marconi scandal which went unpunished. It continued in a system of mendacity and illicit influence unparalleled since the Reform Act. The sale of honours has become so notorious that names and prices are openly quoted, and the profits amount to a handsome fortune. The existence of that secret hoard, available for every device of the unscrupulous politician, is a public danger.[39]

The *Morning Post*'s solution was to raise by clean and open methods a rival fund, so that the forces of good could combat the forces of evil on more or less equal terms. 'Are you interested in cleaning British politics of the Coalition stains?', readers were asked on 15 June. If so, they were invited to contribute to the Appeal. All England, it was claimed, had been 'moved' by it. 'Our appeal does not reach the wealthy war profiteers', said the paper. 'Their great cheques go to old party political funds for "value received". It is the people who are

---

[36] Harris was Chairman of Gold Fields, Rhodes's former company, and a business rival of Robinson (see Emden, P. H., *Randlords* (London, 1935), p. 121).
[37] *Parl. Deb.*, 5th ser. (Lords), l. 1126–40 (22 June 1922).
[38] On the Robinson scandal, see Cullen, T., *Maundy Gregory, Purveyor of Honours* (London, 1974), Ch. 8.
[39] *Morning Post*, 13 June 1922.

almost crushed under the burden of taxation who respond; and the sacrifice they make in responding is manifest.'[40]

Day by day the *Morning Post* described the building up of its Fund, which it saw as a sign 'of an awakening of the national conscience' and of a renewed commitment 'to the old ideals and the traditional justice and seemliness of British public life'.[41] True to its belief in publicizing the names of donors and the amounts donated, the paper solemnly recorded every contribution, however small, along with extracts from the considerable mail which the Appeal was generating. 'POOR LOVER OF ENGLAND. Thank you, Sir! God and St George prosper you and all honest Englishmen', ran one not untypical message.[42] The newspaper staff, too, burst out into prayer: 'How long, oh Lord, how long?', was the title of one of the editorials.[43] The assassination of Field Marshal Sir Henry Wilson on 22 June intensified this mood and probably helped the *Morning Post* Appeal; a number of subscribers sent money 'in memory' of the great man.[44] It is also interesting that Gwynne should claim that support was by no means confined to Diehards but had touched the hearts of thousands of 'decent-minded citizens', including former Liberals who disliked the paper's Conservative principles but respected the fact that it *had* principles, and who could at least share the commitment to 'clean government'.[45]

The *Morning Post* Appeal clearly did better than Gwynne had expected. By the time it was closed in August 1922, it had brought in nearly £22,000.[46] Great pains were taken to ensure that this Fund would be administered efficiently and honestly. Gwynne persuaded Salisbury to assume over-all responsibility for the disbursement of the money, in conjunction with two Trustees, Sir Reginald ('Blinker') Hall and the Duke of Bedford, while Gretton acted as business manager. Salisbury and Gwynne had a few private differences of opinion, but they were in total agreement over financial arrangements. The Fund, they insisted, must be audited by a respected firm of London accountants, and the world should be informed of this fact. As Salisbury put it: 'we are up against the misuse of Party funds, both in the way they are obtained and the way they are spent, and it would be a point in our favour that we do not hesitate to have *our* funds audited.'[47]

However, somewhat to the embarrassment of all concerned, the Coalition collapsed in October and did so before the Fund could be used in the ways which its creators had intended. This led in time to

[40] Ibid., 15 June 1922. [41] Ibid., 17 June 1922. [42] Ibid., 20 June 1922.
[43] Ibid., 23 June 1922. [44] Ibid. [45] Ibid., 21 June 1922.
[46] Ibid., 2 Aug. 1922.
[47] Salisbury to Gretton, 15 Aug. 1922 (Gwynne papers, vol. 8, which contains much other information about the Fund).

some public bickering and internal dissension about what to do with the unspent balances.[48] Nevertheless, the exercise had been worth attempting, if only in order to dramatize the fact that there were alternative methods of fund-raising to those practised by the major parties. Yet was that really true? As the *Scotsman* rather unkindly pointed out, the cardinal fact was that 'this sustained appeal' had failed to raise as much money as was customarily given for one single knighthood, if the Duke of Northumberland was to be believed.[49] Thus, if politics were ever to be cleansed in the way the *Morning Post* desired, honours trafficking would have to be stopped *first*. And this in turn meant that more concrete evidence of abuses would have to be furnished than had ever been produced in the past.

On this matter Gwynne had in fact already taken the lead. On 24 June the *Morning Post* asked all 'decent-minded Englishmen who [had] been approached and insulted' by a tout to 'communicate with us privately and recount their experiences and the names of the unfortunates who are compelled in this fashion to earn a living'. No information given in confidence, it said, would be made public except with the assent of the donor, but it was hoped that some of it could later be transmitted to MPs and peers anxious to erase this blot from public life.[50] This straightforward appeal, coming as it did in the wake of the 'Robinson Scandal', was timed to perfection. Interesting revelations were soon coming in, some to Gwynne, some to the Diehard peer, the Duke of Northumberland, and the two men were soon discussing how best to use this material. Especially important was the information supplied by a certain Mr Charles Sales. 'I always strive to avoid publicity,' Sales said, 'but, in view of the national importance of the subject, would be prepared in case of need to sacrifice my feelings and to give evidence before any fair or impartial tribunal which might be appointed to make a complete investigation.'[51]

The *Morning Post* Appeal did not, surprisingly perhaps, lead to the unmasking of Maundy Gregory, who is said to have been the brains behind the sale of honours racket,[52] but it did lead to the naming

---

[48] Gretton, for example, was arguing in 1924 that the money should be returned to support the Irish Loyalists in Ulster and in Southern Ireland. Northumberland in 1925 asked for financial support for his extremist paper, the *Patriot*. Finally, in 1933 the unspent money, amounting now to about £14,000, was devoted to the 'defence of India', i.e. to oppose the National Government's Indian policy (ibid.).

[49] *Scotsman*, 7 July 1922.

[50] *Morning Post*, 24 June 1922.

[51] Sales to Northumberland, 6 July 1922 (Gwynne papers, vol. 8). But Gwynne got into hot water with one of the informants, who was furious when material sent in confidence to Northumberland was published without his permission in the *Morning Post* (ibid.).

[52] Cullen, *Maundy Gregory, passim*. Cullen, whose account is largely based on interviews with survivors who claim to have known Gregory well, believes that Gregory had been introduced to his trade by Elibank, when the latter was Liberal Chief Whip, and that in December 1918 Elibank (now Lord Murray) brought him into contact with Guest, who was delighted at the prospect of being able to raise the money he needed without

of three honours touts, some or all of whom may have been Gregory's agents: Captain Wells, Douglas Moffat, a former prospective Conservative Party candidate, and Henry Shaw.[53] It was the Duke of Northumberland who made this information public when he read out a number of the juicy letters which had come into his hands in the big House of Lords honours debate of 17 July.[54] And this, in turn, led to still further revelations; for example, an intrepid reporter from the *Morning Post* actually tracked Henry Shaw down to his London apartment and 'forcibly' interviewed him in August.[55] For the first time incontrovertible evidence of a circumstantial kind existed to show that a systematic traffic in titles was taking place. No longer could Ministers sweep the issue under the carpet.[56]

Meanwhile, a parallel agitation was afoot in the House of Commons. On 21 June Godfrey Locker-Lampson, a Conservative MP and former associate of Lord Robert Cecil at the time of the 'Grey Conspiracy',[57] asked that a Joint Committee of both Houses should be set up to review the procedure for awarding honours. Austen Chamberlain, on behalf of the Government, refused, saying that dissatisfaction and objections had been expressed for a long time, but most of the complaints were quite unfounded.[58] The following day Lloyd George fended off the same request by invoking the Royal Prerogative—a ploy which received some support a week later from the Speaker.[59] Still hoping to 'tough it out', the Prime Minister bluntly told the Commons on 27 June that no time existed for debating the honours issue. 'A great

having to soil his hands by personal dealings with the actual touts (pp. 92–5). It is, however, puzzling that so little reference is made to Gregory's role in honours trafficking prior to the collapse of the Coalition Government.

[53] On Moffat, see Ch. 7, p. 154, Northumberland suspected that he was a mere imposter. Midleton, however, thought that he was acting as Shaw's partner and said he had received information from a City friend that Moffat had been offering a knighthood for £25,000 in a deal which also involved the Prime Minister's Private Secretary (presumably Sutherland) and Sir Alfred Mond, who wanted the money for a building project he was interested in (Northumberland to Gwynne, 3 Sept. 1922, Gwynne papers, vol. 8). This sounds like idle gossip. What is certain is that by the early 1930s Moffat was Gregory's agent (Cullen, *Maundy Gregory*, pp. 46–50) and he may also have been acting in that capacity during the Coalition period. Cullen thinks that Shaw, too, was part of Gregory's organization (ibid., pp. 95–7). Lord Derby knew 'something about him from a racing point of view' and dubbed him 'an out-and-out scoundrel' (Derby to Austen Chamberlain, 11 Sept. 1922, Birmingham University Library, Austen Chamberlain papers, AC 33/2/15).

[54] *Parl. Deb.*, 5th ser. (Lords), li. 507–10 (17 July 1922). Northumberland gave a 'trailer' to this speech when he addressed the Lords on 29 June (ibid., 128–9).

[55] *Morning Post*, 29 Aug. 1922.

[56] However, both Lloyd George and the Conservative Whip, Leslie Wilson, publicly denied any knowledge of Shaw (ibid.).

[57] Robert Cecil to Wife, 2 May 1921 (Hatfield, Chelwood papers, CHE 6/92); Cowling, *Impact of Labour*, p. 68. Godfrey Locker-Lampson was actually the brother of Oliver Locker-Lampson.

[58] *Parl. Deb.*, 5th ser., clv. 1298 (21 June 1922).

[59] Ibid. 1497 (22 June 1922); ibid. 1843–4 (27 June 1922).

scandal! They are afraid of an inquiry', exclaimed Locker-Lampson.[60] Meanwhile, day by day the number of MPs signing the motion that called for an enquiry grew, so that when eventually the long-awaited Commons debate was held on 17 July, it had attracted the support of 279 MPs, a clear majority of Members not holding office.[61] The party breakdown is worth noting: fifty-eight Labour MPs (out of seventy-five) backed the motion, as did 134 Coalition Unionists, well over half the parliamentary party, and nearly all the Independent Liberals, twenty-nine in all. The Coalition Liberals, however, showed greater 'loyalty' to the Government, since only twenty of them signed the motion. But this may simply reflect the fact that Coalition Liberals were better represented in the Ministry, in proportion to their numbers, than were the Conservatives. The remaining signatories were eleven Ulster Loyalists and twenty-seven representatives of the minor parties.[62]

In the House of Lords a similar agitation was being organized by Selborne, whose satisfaction at the prospect of finally ending the abuse of honours trafficking was somewhat tempered by sadness as he contemplated the depths to which public life had sunk. 'Up to the Elibank regime and including it', he confided to his wife, 'I do not believe that any of the party managers ever "touched" for themselves, all the loot went into the party treasury. I no longer feel sure of this. The kind of man who is now doing it will be taking commissions or percentages for themselves [sic].'[63]

The parliamentary critics were egged on by Buckingham Palace, disappointed, perhaps, that George V's private appeal to Lloyd George in January 1922 had been ignored.[64] Samuel Hoare, the Conservative who was to second Locker-Lampson's motion, was in regular communication with Clive Wigram, the King's Assistant Private Secretary. On 1 July Wigram wrote to Hoare to say how angry the King was to learn that Taft had expressed the belief that the monarch himself had 'made something out of the sale of Honours'![65] And three days later, with the Commons debate drawing near, he wrote Hoare another encouraging note in which the hope was expressed that 'this scandal will be quashed for all time'.[66]

The King even tried in person to shame Lloyd George into a reformation of his ways. 'For some time', he wrote on 3 July, 'there have been evident signs of growing public dissatisfaction on account of

[60] Ibid. 1844–5, 1848 (27 June 1922).
[61] Ibid. clvi. 1745 (17 July 1922). [62] Ibid.
[63] Selborne to Maude Selborne, 8 June 1922 (Selborne papers, vol. 104, fo. 82).
[64] Stamfordham to Lloyd George (copy), 2 Jan. 1922, and Stamfordham to Austen Chamberlain, 3 May 1922 (Austen Chamberlain papers, AC 23/5/13–14).
[65] Wigram to Hoare, 1 July 1922 (Cambridge University Library, Templewood papers, I.ii).
[66] Wigram to Hoare, 4 July 1922 (ibid.).

the excessive number of honours conferred; the personality of some of the recipients; and the questionable circumstances under which the honours in certain instances have been granted.' The case of Robinson, he went on, 'must be regarded as little less than an insult to the Crown and to the House of Lords'. He appealed to the Prime Minister to establish some mechanism 'to protect the Crown and the Government from the possibility of similar painful if not humiliating incidents' in the future.[67] Lloyd George's reply was coolly insolent. He said that he was discussing with his colleagues 'what further safeguards [could] be taken', but he actually defended Robinson's peerage at some length and offered the view that of recent years there had been few cases which had elicited just criticism or complaint! 'I doubt if any change of system would result in fewer accidents and errors than have marked the Honours Lists of the last seven years', he cheekily claimed.[68] This missive cannot have been much appreciated by HRH, and it is not surprising that, after the Lords had again debated the honours question, Stamfordham should have written Salisbury an encouraging note: 'Far from the King being dissatisfied with what was said . . . His Majesty is only glad that the truth should be known "better late than never".'[69]

Buoyed up by royal encouragement and general press support, the parliamentary critics were in no mood to back down, and the Government was soon desperately looking for a compromise. Before the 17 July Commons debate, it seems that attempts were made to square the rebels. According to a memorandum in the Salisbury papers, Hoare 'was caught by a Whip and carried into the Prime Minister's room'—quite when is not specified. Lloyd George declared his readiness to accept a Select Committee, if Hoare and his friends would give an honourable undertaking not to use the enquiry 'for digging up the past'. Hoare replied that he personally was agreeable to this, and so, he believed, were the peers with whom he was in contact. However, on an earlier occasion the Conservative Whip, Leslie Wilson, had buttonholed Locker-Lampson, who took a tougher line; he said 'he had no authority to speak for the peers but that his impression was that they were in favour of the unrestricted reference'.[70] This was worrying for the Government, as was Salisbury's threat that the Upper House would hold up all legislation until their grievance was remedied.[71] Though perhaps they did not know it at the time, Bonar Law, refreshed by eighteen months away from office, was also moving round to the

---

[67] Nicolson, H., *King George the Fifth* (London, 1952), pp. 512–13.

[68] Lloyd George to George V (copy), 4 July 1922 (Lloyd George papers, F/29/4/104).

[69] Stamfordham to Salisbury, 26 June 1922 (Salisbury papers, S(4), 233, fo. 33). The King told Chamberlain that he was 'not surprised' at the feeling shown by the Commons (Stamfordham to Austen Chamberlain, 22 June 1922, Austen Chamberlain papers, AC 23/5/22).

[70] Salisbury Memorandum, n.d. (Salisbury papers, S(4), 232).

[71] Peter Sanders's diary, 2 July 1922, in Ramsden (ed.), *Real Old Tory Politics*, p. 177.

view that changes in the system were necessary to 'restore public confidence'.[72]

In fact, Ministers were in something of a quandary in July 1922. On the one hand, the hard-headed operators inside Conservative Central Office and among the Conservative Whips were perfectly familiar with the time-honoured bargaining in which contributions to party funds were linked to the offer of a title. But the fund-raising methods employed by their Coalition Liberal counterparts were filling them with mounting exasperation. In a letter to Beaverbrook of May 1919 Younger neatly summed up his grievance: 'I am getting rather sick of being held responsible for the sins of no. 10, but it seems quite impossible to restrain them. Everything is fish which comes near their net and poaching is the order of the day.'[73]

The complaint was threefold. First, the Conservative managers saw their Liberal allies as 'interlopers' who were interposing themselves between the Conservative Party and its wealthy business supporters. This was obviously resented because it meant that money was being diverted away from their own war chest. In a much quoted letter to Bonar Law, dated 7 January 1921, Younger angrily pointed out that the Liberals had placed many more of their nominees on to the recent Honours List than the Conservative Whips had been able to do. *'There must be a stop to Freddie poaching our men'*, he cried. But, secondly, Younger was cross because some of the men recommended by Guest were supporters of the Conservative Party whose characters and records made them, in his opinion, unsuitable for recognition. The consequence of this, as Younger pointed out, was that the Conservatives were 'blamed for giving honours which it never would have occurred to us to bestow'.[74] Thirdly, the Coalition Liberals' cynical and reckless manipulation of their powers of patronage was bringing the entire system into disrepute. More than once the Conservative Whips warned their Coalition Liberal counterparts that there might be an explosion unless they showed greater restraint. Similar anxieties had been expressed by Curzon[75] and by other senior Conservatives. In particular, Austen Chamberlain, the Leader since March 1921, privately shared the King's view that 'the swollen lists of the war and post-war period

[72] Bonar Law's paper to the Royal Commission later in the year said: 'the amount of suspicion had become an evil and whether this was well founded or not it would be an advantage to the P.M. to have some intermediate body, not to go into merits but to be a kind of guarantee to the public that the persons recommended were not in character unworthy of an Honour' (Templewood papers, I.ii).

[73] Younger to Beaverbrook, 12 May 1919 (HLRO, Beaverbrook papers, C/334).

[74] Younger to Bonar Law, 7 Jan. 1921 (Bonar Law papers, 100/1/2).

[75] In December 1918 Curzon had written the Prime Minister a reproachful letter after having encountered an honours tout, Mrs Parrish, whom he assumed must have some connection with the Coalition Liberals. Curzon had warned that unless the touts were disowned and stopped, they could 'very well bring us to the ground' (Curzon to Lloyd George, 5 Dec. 1918, Lloyd George papers, F/11/9/25).

should now be reduced to reasonable proportions', though he also insisted on 'parity' between the two Coalition parties.[76] Moreover, Chamberlain had made his organization men aware that he could not personally countenance anything resembling an exchange of money for the reward of an honour.[77]

But of course, the Conservative Leader also knew that his own party was to some extent implicated in the scandals that were under attack in the summer of 1922.[78] Not all the 'dubious' peerages in the recent List, for example, had been created on the recommendation of the Coalition Liberals; William Vestey, who stood accused of moving his business to Argentina during the War to escape taxation, had actually been sponsored by Younger, not, as was widely assumed, by Lloyd George's friends.[79] No wonder, then, that the Conservative organizers forgot their earlier anger with Sutherland and Guest and rallied round the Government in the summer of 1922.

In their anxiety to protect their familiar little world from invasion, Younger and the Conservative Whips expressed fierce hostility to any notion of a fundamental change in the honours system.[80] They would have been reinforced in their fears, had they realized the nature of the relationship between the Conservative Treasurer, Farquhar, and Lloyd George—though this embarrassing disclosure was not made until later in the year.[81] Finally, there is evidence that the notorious honours touts had not been working solely with the Coalition Liberals. For example, Shaw, in his interview with the *Morning Post*, made the ominous observation that he had 'friends' in *both* of the Coalition parties.[82] And there are some intriguing passages in the letters sent to Gwynne by friendly informants, warning that it might be imprudent to pursue certain lines of investigation too far, lest the Conservatives themselves suffer discredit.[83]

So what the Honours Crisis of 1922 in fact did was temporarily to

[76] Chamberlain to Athelstane Baines (copy), 19 May 1922 (Austen Chamberlain papers, AC 26/4/60); Chamberlain to Stamfordham (copy), 3 May 1922 (ibid., AC 23/5/12).

[77] See Chamberlain to Balcarres (copy), 25 Nov. 1921 (ibid., AC 26/4/39); Chamberlain to G. Locker-Lampson (copy), 16 Jan. 1922 (ibid., AC 26/4/52).

[78] Informed by Balcarres about an attempt to buy a peerage by an act of public benevolence and a contribution to Conservative Funds, Chamberlain coyly observed: 'The less I know about offers of that kind the better. They should be made only to the Whips!' (Chamberlain to Balcarres (copy), 25 Nov. 1921, ibid., AC 26/4/39).

[79] See Younger to Austen Chamberlain, 27 June 1922 (Lloyd George papers, F/252). Interestingly, Vestey had received a baronetcy from the Asquith Government in 1913.

[80] Balcarres to J. T. Davies, 5 July 1922 (ibid.). In this letter Balcarres urged the Prime Minister to confine the membership of any scrutinizing committee that might be set up to Secretaries of State and Ministers and to exclude all outsiders.

[81] See Ch. 16, pp. 388–9. [82] *Morning Post*, 29 Aug. 1922.

[83] e.g. Northumberland to Gwynne, 30 Aug. 1922; and note on Sir Alfred Stevens, who is said to have paid £25,000 to Conservative funds for his knighthood, a deal clinched by the Party's South Wales agent (Gwynne papers, vol. 8).

strengthen the unity of the Coalition at leadership level, while dividing the leaders from their respective followers. True, five junior Ministers, including Willie Bridgeman, threatened to vote against the Government in the summer of 1922 unless an enquiry was set up.[84] But when the Cabinet met to discuss the matter on 11 July it did so in cautious and hesitant mood. The two Coalition Whips, McCurdy and Wilson, attended the meeting, where they warned that 'a point-blank refusal of any enquiry would result in a very bad Division in the House of Commons.' But there was also a very strong desire that any enquiry 'should be confined to the future', as the instigators of the agitation themselves were alleged to want. The Cabinet then divided fairly evenly between those who grudgingly accepted the idea of a Select Committee and those who demurred. The deadlock was finally broken by Balfour, who argued that it would be best to wait on events and leave the Prime Minister full discretion to take whatever line in the 17 July debate that he thought appropriate.[85]

Two days after this Cabinet meeting Lloyd George had worked out his strategy. The Commons was told that the Government intended to treat Locker-Lampson's motion as a vote of no confidence. But newspapers were also soon carrying the story that the Prime Minister was about to announce the establishment of a Royal Commission. The Government's line was that this was the only constitutional way of examining an issue that touched the Royal Prerogative; but probably it was preferred to a Select Committee mainly because this gave the Government greater control over the composition and terms of reference of the enquiring body.

And there matters stood when the fateful debate took place on 17 July. It is important to note that the mover and seconder of the motion, Godfrey Locker-Lampson and Hoare, were neither of them Diehards. They had abstained or remained away from the House during the debate of May 1919, and, unlike Page Croft and his friends, they had not previously identified themselves with the honours question. This made their opposition all the more dangerous to the Government. Moreover, in keeping with their political reputations, both men took up a moderate stance on 17 July. Locker-Lampson, for example, dissociated himself from any wish to rake over the scandals of the past, and Hoare, while earnestly calling for changes to 'restore confidence', emphasized that he was making 'no charge of general corruption'.[86] But he did delicately discuss some of the more controversial recipients of recent honours, a theme, of course, later developed by Page Croft.[87]

---

[84] Bridgeman's unpublished diary, cited in Cross, J. A., *Sir Samuel Hoare: A Political Biography* (London, 1977), p. 68.
[85] War Cabinet (39) Minute, 11 July 1922 (Cab. 23/30, item 5).
[86] *Parl. Deb.*, 5th ser., clvi. 1746–8, 1749–52 (17 July 1922).
[87] Ibid. 1750, 1784–5.

However, it was left to the Diehard Ronald McNeill to make the really dramatic disclosures. In a fiery speech McNeill denounced not only Robinson, but also two other new peers: Lord Waring, who, he pointed out, was the managing director of a business which had gone bankrupt in 1910 and who had subsequently made a personal fortune out of aeroplane contracts; and Sir Archibald Williamson, now Lord Forres, the merchant and former Liberal MP, whose firm, according to McNeill, had traded with the enemy during the War. This outburst probably did the critics of the Government more harm than good. Four days later McNeill publicly withdrew his charges against Forres.[88] Meanwhile, others had expressed unease about the propriety of attacking public men in this way, without warning and under cover of parliamentary privilege.[89]

If McNeill's outburst is ignored, however, the Government fared badly in the 17 July debate. Only one Conservative backbencher, Walter Elliott, spoke up on its behalf. Others, including Robert Cecil, censured it with greater or lesser severity.[90] From the other side of the House, Clynes pointed out the superiority of the Labour Party's methods of fund-raising—though, somewhat illogically, he also pleaded for more honours to be bestowed on members of the Co-operative Movement![91]

The Independent Liberals were characteristically unable to agree on a common line. Asquith had a particularly difficult task to perform. He chose to praise his own record as Prime Minister, claiming that though some of his Lists were criticized for their 'mediocrity', he could not 'remember a single occasion during the whole of [his premiership] when the name of any person recommended for distinction by the Crown was adversely commented upon on the ground of unworthiness or of a bad record on the part of the recipient'—a bold claim which Page Croft surprisingly endorsed. Asquith said he was willing for the enquiry to go back as far as anyone liked. Looking to the future, he insisted that any Prime Minister must assume responsibility for his nominations, but perhaps outside assistance and advice would improve the system.[92]

This measured response was in contrast to a violent speech from Donald Maclean, who combined a bitter denunciation of Lloyd George with sneers at the self-professed probity of the Diehards. MacLean even managed to fall foul of the Deputy Speaker after delivering an intemperate attack on the war profiteers, who, he claimed, had thrown in their lot with the Prime Minister.[93] Shortly afterwards, Wedgwood

---

[88] *Parl. Deb.*, 5th ser., clvi. 1802–7; ibid. 2413–16 (21 July 1922). But both the Foreign Office and the City had grave doubts about Forres (Rose, *King George V*, p. 251; Ramsden (ed.), *Real Old Tory Politics*, p. 179).

[89] *Parl. Deb.*, 5th ser., clvi. 1810 (17 July, 1922, Donald Maclean).

[90] Ibid. 1821–3, 1791–6.

[91] Ibid. 1774–82.   [92] Ibid. 1770–4.   [93] Ibid. 1814–15.

Benn tried unsuccessfully to move an amendment for the aboliton of all titles—a remedy more favoured by Labour than by his fellow Liberals.[94] But at least the Government's attempts to 'square' the Independent Liberals over the honours question had failed[95]—to the relief of the *Westminster Gazette* which had half feared that Asquith might be bullied into silence by the veiled threats of the Coalitionists.[96]

It was, therefore, in an overwhelmingly hostile Chamber that Lloyd George and Austen Chamberlain had to make their defence. The Prime Minister had gone to considerable lengths in the preparation of his case, using his large personal secretariat to assemble evidence that would support his claim that his own Ministry had distributed patronage in just the same way as all recent Ministries.[97] But though the Government-inspired press had gleefully anticipated a stunning performance in which the Prime Minister would rout his critics, this triumph did not materialize. Lloyd George's speech was long and rambling, and when at one point he seemed to be attributing Germany's collapse in 1918 to the absence of a party system sustained by secret funds, the response was derisive.[98] Churchill was not alone in thinking this to be the worst speech that Lloyd George had ever made. Austen Chamberlain fared little better.

At the end of the debate, however, the Government had one lucky break. Lloyd George had announced the Government's intention of setting up a Royal Commission. Yet the House had before it a motion supporting a Joint Select Committee—a device which the Cabinet was determined to resist. Clearly, many of the MPs who had signed the Locker-Lampson motion were prepared to accept Lloyd George's alternative solution, but others undoubtedly wanted to press the motion to a vote. But no vote was ever taken, because at the crucial moment Lord Hugh Cecil, of all people, rose to his feet and prolonged the debate until it was talked out.[99] Was this a planned move or did it happen by accident? Cecil later confessed that he had acted deliberately because 'it would have been the sort of rotten division that would have been no good to anyone.'[100] Chamberlain declared himself disappointed

---

[94] Ibid. 1831.

[95] Robert Cecil to Wife, 12 July 1922 (Chelwood papers, CHE 6/160).

[96] *Westminster Gazette*, 18 July 1922. But there were barely concealed divisions within the Liberal press on the honours question. The *Westminister Gazette* seemed to have no objection to the existing system, but believed that there needed to be a change of government before public confidence could be restored (24 June, 18 July 1922). By contrast, the *Nation*, while accepting Selborne's idea of a scrutinizing committee, would have preferred the publication of party contributions (1 July 1922).

[97] One of Lloyd George's secretaries engaged in this task, Geoffrey Shakespeare, was quite sure that the Prime Minister was innocent of all corruption, but had been badly let down by his subordinates! (Shakespeare, G., *Let Candles Be Brought In* (London, 1949), p. 108.)

[98] *Parl. Deb.*, 5th ser., clvi. 1755–70 (17 July 1922).   [99] Ibid. 1862.

[100] Peter Sanders's diary, 19 July 1922, in Ramsden (ed.), *Real Old Tory Politics*, p. 179.

by the outcome.[101] But perhaps in the end both the Cabinet and its implacable critics were pleased to have avoided a division which neither side was likely to have won comfortably.

Battered by their enemies in both Houses of Parliament, Lloyd George and his Coalition colleagues were also receiving a very bad press. A few journals, it is true, gallantly rushed to the Prime Minister's defence. Among these was Lloyd George's 'tame' newspaper, the *Daily Chronicle*, which commented on the 17 July debate in an editorial entitled, 'Much Cry and Little Wool'. There were no skeletons in the cupboard for the Royal Commission to discover, declared the *Chronicle*, and British public life was conspicuously free from corruption precisely because 'the system of conferring Honours [enabled] Governments and parties to live without selling the public interest'—a claim which reduced the *Daily Herald* to hysterical mirth.[102] Berry's *Sunday Times* and the *Pall Mall Gazette* both came to the aid of the Government,[103] while, interestingly in view of what was to come, the *Daily Mail* played down the issue.[104]

But although Lloyd George's critics were fond of accusing him of attempting to 'muzzle' the press, the events of 1922 do not suggest that this attempt had been particularly successful. On the honours question, the Government was assailed from all quarters: from Labour journals, from Independent Liberal and most Conservative papers, and from *The Times*, which employed its most magisterial language of censure.[105] Naturally, the *Morning Post*, *National Review*, *Spectator*, and *New Witness* expressed satisfaction that their long campaign was at last coming to fruition, while Page Croft's *National Opinion* portrayed the establishment of the Honours Commission as a justification for the founding of the National Party five years earlier in the face of the 'contempt' shown towards its proposals by the Mandarins.[106]

The Royal Commission

But *had* the Diehards won so decisive a victory over the party organization men? The critics had wanted the widest possible investigation into honours abuses and were disappointed when the

[101] Chamberlain to George V (copy), 18 July 1922 (Austen Chamberlain papers, AC 33/3/106).

[102] *Daily Chronicle*, 18 July 1922; *Daily Herald*, 19 July 1922.

[103] *Sunday Times*, 9 July 1922; *Pall Mall Gazette*, 18 July 1922. See also the cartoon in *Punch*, 12 July 1922, reproduced in Figure 9.

[104] Its main contribution to the Robinson drama, apart from factual parliamentary reports, was a 'human interest' interview with 'Old J.B.', who was made to sound a very jolly fellow (*Daily Mail*, 30 June 1922).

[105] *The Times*, 18 July 1922; *Daily Express*, 30 June 1922; *Daily Telegraph*, 19 July 1922; *Manchester Guardian*, 18, 19 July 1922; *Labour Leader*, 20 July 1922.

[106] *National Opinion*, Aug. 1922.

9. *Punch's* view of the 1922 Honours Scandal
(*Punch*, 12 July 1922)

Government set up a Royal Commission rather than a Select Committee. The *National Review* denounced this expedient as 'eyewash' and pointed out that the Commission's terms of reference were restricted to that of advising on what procedure should be adopted *in future* to 'assist the Prime Minister in making recommendations to His Majesty of the names of persons deserving of special honour'.[107] Moreover, with the exception of the Duke of Devonshire, the members of the Commission did not give Maxse much confidence. He would have liked to see it staffed with men like Gretton, Rupert Gwynne, McNeill, Page Croft, Selborne, Northumberland, and Ampthill—the seasoned scandalmongers, in fact—since all these men 'meant business'; whereas instead a selection had been made from the ranks of the professional politicians, most of whom had a prior commitment to the existing system.[108]

Was the work of the Royal Commission in practice the anti-climax which the Diehards anticipated? The body first met in October 1922 and by the end of the year had submitted its report. It recommended the setting up of an advisory committee of not more than three privy councillors to scrutinize the names of everyone receiving a political honour, along with the reasons for the recommendation. This, essentially, was the solution which Selborne had been pressing for over ten years. Support was also given to the idea of making it a criminal offence to offer money for a title or to act as an intermediary in such a transaction.[109]

However, these recommendations did not go far enough for one of the Commissioners, the Labour MP, Arthur Henderson. He would have preferred the abolition of all political honours, at least those which carried a title. In his note of dissent Henderson also expressed regret that neither the touts, nor the persons who had been approached by touts, had been called to give evidence. The cynics were confirmed by this in their premonition that the Commission was mainly concerned to stamp out the worst abuses, while leaving the existing system largely intact.[110] They also took note of the fact that the report was a discreetly worded and slender document (only nine pages in length), which was published without the usual minutes of evidence and with only a brief description of the methods of investigation that had been adopted.

Fortunately, the papers of Samuel Hoare (Lord Templewood), one of the Commissioners, enable us to go behind the bland report and reconstruct what actually occurred behind closed doors. At the opening meeting the autocratic Chairman, Lord Dunedin, had emphasized the importance of keeping within the Commission's narrow terms of reference and had suggested that it would be enough to hear

---

[107] *National Review*, lxxix (1922), 821–2.   [108] Ibid. lxxx (1922), 37.
[109] Report of Royal Commission on Honours, 1922, Cmd. 1789.   [110] Ibid.

the evidence of those who had filled the office of Prime Minister and Patronage Secretary. Devonshire agreed with this conservative line. But Henderson then argued that 'such an enquiry would not go far enough' and urged that Shaw and other honours brokers should be summoned. Lord Denman, one of the Liberals on the Commission, backed Henderson up, adding that Northumberland, too, should be approached. Hoare then pressed the idea of summoning party officials like Younger in the hope of getting to the roots of the scandal. Eventually a compromise was clearly reached between Dunedin, who continued to hanker after a restricted enquiry, and Henderson, who wanted to stray far and wide over the whole honours question, with the decisive voice being that of 'liberal' Conservatives like Hoare who held an intermediate position.[111]

In the event all living Prime Ministers were quizzed, except Rosebery, who declined the invitation on the ground that he was too old and his premiership too distant for him to be of much use. Of the Whips and ex-Whips who were still alive, all appeared before the Commission, bar Murray, who once again contrived to be unavailable at the crucial moment! Younger, Selborne, and Northumberland made up the remaining witnesses. However, Northumberland's offer to bring some of the touts before the Commission was not taken up. It was, of course, accepted that touts did exist (by October 1922 this could no longer be denied), but the majority of Commissioners thought it better to look to the future, and obviously did not want to make disclosures that might deeply embarrass prominent political figures.

The testimony of the party leaders and of some of the Whips does throw light on the fund-raising methods employed by the two major parties over the previous twenty years. But, in general, the party organizers showed considerable reticence whenever the contentious side of their work came up for discussion, and they did what they could to discourage all bold innovations. Younger, for example, submitted a memorandum which argued that the compilation of the Honours Lists should be treated as a strictly party matter. The former Conservative Whip, Lord Edmund Talbot (now Lord Fitzalan) was even more negative, denying the need for any changes at all and deprecating any interference with the confidential relationship between Prime Minister and Sovereign: 'The public uneasiness would soon subside', he claimed, once the Lists had been reduced to more moderate dimensions. Nor did Guest or McCurdy show any great reforming zeal!

In any case, one gets a strong sense from the material in the Templewood papers that the cross-examination of the witnesses was not that important. Most Commissioners seem to have decided, at a fairly early stage, that they were going to recommend a scrutinizing

---

[111] Hoare to Godfrey (Locker-Lampson?), 10 Oct. 1922 (Templewood papers, I.ii).

committee of the Privy Council. The formal proceedings then became an opportunity, not for probing into some of the murkier areas of political life, but rather for trying to convert the witnesses to an acceptance of the reform that they were about to propose. In this venture, interestingly enough, the Commissioners clearly enjoyed more success with the Prime Ministers than they did with the Whips and Party Chairmen.

Yet the Commissioners shied away from all really radical ideas. Thus, when Selborne suggested that Honours Lists should in future be drawn up on non-party lines, he was listened to politely, but ignored. And when he spoke of the steady drift into a state of affairs where party chicanery was only narrowly separated from personal corruption, he was not invited to explain what he meant. The Commissioners showed no interest, either, in the views of Northumberland, and they certainly had no intention of establishing Lloyd George's relative 'guilt' or 'innocence', compared with his predecessors. Thus what had, only a few months earlier, been a topic capable of generating considerable political excitement was in the process of being taken out of party politics altogether.

The Honours Commission Report enjoyed, by and large, a friendly press, and there was no serious opposition to any of its principal recommendations, Northumberland being one of the few critics.[112] At an official level, too, the Report was welcomed. By now Lloyd George had fallen from power, and Bonar Law, his successor, had swung round to an acceptance of the need for change.[113] The new Government promised to bring in the necessary legislation as soon as possible. And that, for the time being, effectively killed the honours question as an important political issue. The only interesting question still open in early 1923 was the membership of the new scrutinizing committee; would Selborne be prepared to serve, for example, or even perhaps Edward Grey?[114]

Conclusion

Nevertheless, the Honours Scandal, so long as it lasted, was not a trivial matter. Quite apart from the contribution it made to the

---

[112] See Northumberland's article, 'Whitewash', in *National Review*, lxxx (1923), 837–44. The very least that was needed, he said, was a scrutinizing committee appointed directly by the Crown. The new committee, by contrast, would be appointed by the Prime Minister and consist of party men: 'that is all the safeguard we shall have against corruption!' (ibid. 843). On this score Northumberland was in agreement with the Socialist, Fenner Brockway (Brockway, A. F., *Lloyd George and the Traffic in Honours* (London, 1922), pp. 15–16.

[113] Bonar Law had sympathized with the proposed scrutinizing committee when he appeared as a witness before the Royal Commission (Templewood papers).

[114] Devonshire to Salisbury, 2 Jan. 1923 (Salisbury papers, S(4), 232, fo. 46).

estrangement between Lloyd George and the Conservative Party, the spotlight that had so cruelly played on some of the Coalition Government's controversial creations had powerfully reinforced the existing suspicion that corruption was rife in public life. Almost all the 'social types' which had excited the disapproval of political moralists were shown to figure on the post-war Honours Lists. There were bankrupts (Waring), food-hoarders (Hodge) and tax-avoiders (Vestey). One new peer (Forres) and one new baronet (Drughorn) stood accused of trading with the enemy. There was even the sinister, foreign-born Zaharoff, who had somehow or other succeeded in securing the Grand Cross of the Bath.[115]

In particular, the Honours Lists were thought to contain the names of numerous war profiteers who had 'bribed' Lloyd George into protecting them and helping them realize their social ambitions. This allegation became something of a cliché in the post-Armistice period.[116] The critics of the Government also compiled lists of pressmen granted honours by the Coalition Government to illustrate their contention that the Prime Minister was seriously abusing his powers of patronage to boost his public image.[117] The fact that some of these men had disreputable business or matrimonial pasts further compounded the offence.[118]

Finally, the honours scandals were treated seriously because they seemed to symbolize the restlessness and cynicism which marked the Coalition Ministry in general and its leader in particular. In the past the *New Statesman* had taken little interest in the campaign against corruption in public life, but after Lloyd George's fall from power in October 1922, it made this revealing comment:

When the Marconi scandal was exposed, we refused in these columns to treat it very seriously. There was nothing that could really be called corruption on the part of Mr Lloyd George, and but for his rather silly attempt to conceal the truth about his Stock Exchange transactions, there need have been little scandal. But the incident has a profound importance, out of all proportion to the actual turpitude of the deal. It was a portent—a revelation of moral slackness to which, no doubt, more heed should have been given; for it is precisely that side of Mr Lloyd George's character which has led to the disasters of the last four years.

Like many Liberals and Conservatives, the *New Statesman* ended up

[115] According to Maxse, Zaharoff was 'the Mystery Man of our day', a cosmopolitan financier who had the ear of Lloyd George and bore a responsibility for the British Government's recklessly pro-Greek foreign policy ('Who Tempted Greece?', *National Review*, lxxvii (1921), 308).

[116] e.g. Page Croft's article, 'Corrupt Sale of Honours', in *John Bull*, 20 May 1922; editorial in *Labour Leader*, 20 July 1922.

[117] e.g. *National Review*, lxxviii (1922), 598–600.

[118] Rose, *King George V*, pp. 249–50, for the King's dislike of Riddell's peerage, on account of the latter being a 'guilty party' in a divorce case.

by viewing the ugly quarrel between the Premier and public opinion over the honours question as symptomatic of a loss of confidence in the integrity and reliability of the British Government, which had contributed to its foreign policy failures, culminating in the Chanak fiasco.[119]

[119] *New Statesman*, 21 Oct. 1922, p. 65.

AFTERMATH

16
Removing the 'Coalition Stain', 1922–1931

The Lloyd George Fund and its Critics

It is only in retrospect that the collapse of the Lloyd George Coalition seems to mark a watershed in British politics. When he left Downing Street in October 1922, Lloyd George was in high spirits and his many admirers thought that it would not be long before Britain's 'greatest living statesman' was Premier again. Moreover, he possessed a political fund, amounting perhaps to about £1,500,000, which both ensured the continuance of his career and also gave him maximum room for political manœuvre. With these impressive resources behind him, Lloyd George could apparently choose between a number of options: he could re-unite with his former Liberal colleagues on his own terms, or put together another coalition government, or even, perhaps, reach some sort of concordat with Labour. A. G. Gardiner publicly called the Fund 'a source of personal influence which can be directed to any occult end, an *imperium in imperio*, as sinister and disruptive in its possibilities as it is . . . unprecedented in the whole history of British political life'.[1] Lloyd George undoubtedly believed that wealth meant power and influence, and critics like Lord Irwin agreed: 'any man with so much money, however tainted, to his hand is bound to be a political force', wrote Irwin in September 1927.[2]

But this was a faulty assessment. In fact, the Lloyd George Fund soon came to constitute a considerable liability for its owner. For the continuing scandals surrounding this Fund played a significant part in finally discrediting Lloyd George, in destroying the Liberal Party, and in neutralizing those politicians, both Liberal and Conservative, who had linked their names too closely to his. From these developments the greatest benefits accrued to Stanley Baldwin, and the Conservative Party that established its dominance in the 1920s was partly shaped by the widespread revulsion against Lloyd George's methods and personality.

The main significance of the Lloyd George Fund after October 1922 was that it kept alive memories of the Honours Scandal of that year, which might otherwise have been quickly forgotten. Every time the Fund came up for discussion, Lloyd George's enemies had an opportunity of reminding the general public of the unsavoury methods

---

[1] *Manchester Guardian*, 12 June 1926, cited in Cregier, *Chiefs Without Indians* (Washington, 1982), p. 135.

[2] Irwin to Davidson, 24 Sept. 1927 (HLRO, Davidson papers). But Irwin also thought that Davidson need not 'greatly fear S[tanley] B[aldwin] being killed in order to open the succession to Lloyd George . . . '.

by which it had been accumulated. Moreover, with the collapse of the Coalition, Lloyd George was on much weaker ground when he claimed, as he always did,[3] that his Fund differed in no way from that of the other parties. For the party funds were administered by treasurers and whips who acted as trustees for the organization as a whole. But especially after the National Liberal Party had been formally wound up, the sole purpose of the Lloyd George Fund seemed to be the promotion of a single individual's career.

The situation naturally gave rise to scandalous gossip. The bitterly anti-Lloyd-George Liberal, Vivian Phillipps, was firmly of the opinion that 'after the General Election of 1922 there was a considerable "share-out" and that, among others, J. T. Davies—now Sir J. T. Davies—received a considerable sum with which he was reputed to have purchased a big house in Hampstead!'[4] This accusation—probably false—was not one that could be made publicly. But Lloyd George's critics often subtly conveyed the notion that the Welshman had in some way or another 'trousered' the money and was spending it on himself.[5]

Such insinuations were somewhat unfair. By the time he was Prime Minister, Lloyd George was in comfortable financial circumstances. Andrew Carnegie had settled £2,000 a year for life upon him, and this income he supplemented after 1922 by writing articles for newspapers, including the Hearst chain in America. Charles Mallett calculated that in the four years since leaving office, Lloyd George must have been earning about £20,000 a year.[6] The writing of the War Memoirs also brought him a lucrative contract.[7] The money thus earned more than covered Lloyd George's personal expenditure, which was not especially extravagant. Moreover, before 1927 much of the Fund was locked up in newspaper investments. So there seems no reason for doubting Lloyd George's indignant denial that he had ever touched a penny of the money in his private capacity.[8] Instead, the Fund was used to subsidize legitimate political activities, among them the staffing of a large secretariat and running the ambitious investigation of the land question and of Britain's industrial problems.[9] But was this what was intended by the donors who had given the National Liberals the money in the first place?

[3] See Owen, F., *Tempestuous Journey: Lloyd George His Life and Times* (London, 1954) for two of Lloyd George's public statements on the issue.

[4] Phillipps to Gwynne, 3 Aug. 1927 (Bodleian, Gwynne papers, vol. 21).

[5] e.g. the insinuations in the *Morning Post*, 14 Nov. 1927.

[6] Owen, *Tempestuous Journey*, p. 662; Mallet, C., *Mr Lloyd George: A Study* (London, 1930), pp. 282–3. The sum mentioned by Mallett refers to Lloyd George's income from his syndicated American column.

[7] Owen, *Tempestuous Journey*, pp. 699–701.

[8] Ibid. 688, quoting Lloyd George's statement of 3 Dec. 1927. But for evidence to the contrary, see Cregier, *Chiefs Without Indians*, p. 245 n. 127.

[9] Campbell, John, *Lloyd George: The Goat in the Wilderness* (London, 1977), pp. 176–7.

Lloyd George could perhaps have silenced his critics had he given a convincing and unambiguous account of the Fund's status and of the way in which it was being administered. But it suited his purposes to leave this issue blurred. Depending upon circumstances, the Fund was described as a party war chest, as a trust fund, or—on occasions—as personal property.[10] Such tactics reinforced the public's image of Lloyd George as evasive and untrustworthy—if not actually dishonest. Moreover, even if the Fund really was under the control of trustees, what effective independence did these men have?[11] These issues were not resolved until 1938 when the courts ruled that the Fund was Lloyd George's, to dispose of as he pleased.[12]

The capriciousness and irresponsibility shown by Lloyd George when challenged to explain the status of his Fund enraged and disgusted his enemies. But they too had mixed motives, of which a concern with the purification of British public life was only one. This is manifestly true of the Asquithian Liberals. Initially, these men wanted to distance themselves from the Fund. Thus Herbert Gladstone, writing to Beauchamps in January 1923, gave as one reason for not uniting with the National Liberals the risk of entanglement 'in the whole Georgian machinery . . . [with] its ill-gotten funds, its bought press, its Sutherlands and McCurdys and all that made the Lloyd George regime so detestable in the country'.[13] Six months later he was still striking a moralistic note: 'What is to become of this fund? . . . It is the proceeds of corruption and we have protested against corruption', he told C. P. Scott.[14]

But in that same conversation Gladstone acknowledged the power which the Fund gave Lloyd George when he discussed the 'defection' of J. M. Hogge, the former Independent Liberal Whip, who had recently gone over to Lloyd George's service, where he was receiving a salary of £1,000—£400 more than the Asquithians were prepared to pay him.[15] In any case, the moral posturing had to stop after Baldwin's declaration in favour of Protection at Plymouth in October 1923, when the Asquithians found themselves obliged to co-operate with the 'traitors'

[10] Owen, *Tempestuous Journey*, pp. 688–93; Cregier, *Chiefs Without Indians*, pp. 113–47.

[11] See Memo. on Lloyd George Fund, 2 Aug. 1927 (Gwynne papers, vol. 21).

[12] Cregier, *Chiefs Without Indians*, p. 145.

[13] Gladstone to Beauchamps (copy), 15 Jan. 1923 (Bodleian, Maclean papers, vol. 467, fos. 4–5). A month later Asquith wrote in a private letter that many of the 'faithful' disliked the idea of co-operating with the Coalition Liberals: 'They think we ought not to handle the unclean thing, and I have a good deal of sneaking sympathy with them' (Asquith to Friend, 15 Feb. 1923, in MacCarthy, D. (ed.), *H.H.A.: Letters of the Earl of Oxford to a Friend: Second Series 1922–1927* (London, 1934), p. 44).

[14] Scott's diary, 1 July 1923, in Wilson (ed.), *Political Diaries of C. P. Scott*, p. 441.

[15] Ibid. Hogge's departure, however, was something of a relief to the Asquithians, since during the recent election Hogge had run off to Scotland with the waitress who looked after his table in the Commons restaurant—a young lady known to MPs as 'The Fairy'—and they feared exposure and a scandal.

whom they had been ostracizing. The logical consequence of Liberal reunion was a 'pooling' of resources. And although Gladstone felt moral scruples about handling 'tainted money', the Liberal Party organizers were now very eager to get access to the Lloyd George Fund. For the Party had been largely living on its capital since the War. An appeal for contributions prior to the 1922 General Election had been answered by only a handful of the wealthy faithful; all but £7,000 of the £45,523 raised came from twelve subscribers, headed by the indispensable Cowdray (£12,000) and Walter Runciman (£10,000).[16] The threat to Free Trade in 1923 boosted the Liberals' income, as it had done in 1906, almost £75,000 coming in to party headquarters. But a year later subscriptions had fallen again—to about £40,000.[17] Thus the Asquithians needed Lloyd George's money if they were to present themselves as credible contenders for office. In addition, some of them seem to have thought that Lloyd George, by transferring his Fund into their hands, would expiate the various 'sins' he had committed since 1916.

Faced by Liberals animated by such emotions as these, it is hardly surprising that Lloyd George, after giving the Party £90,000 for the 1923 Election campaign, should have been reluctant to continue subsidizing it thereafter. Perhaps, as Trevor Wilson suggests, Lloyd George should be seen as 'a typical Welsh peasant, who had got hold of some cash and did not want to part with it'.[18] But tactical considerations also came into play. By teasing and prevaricating and keeping hold of his Fund, Lloyd George preserved his freedom of action and ensured that, if there was to be a genuine Liberal reunion, he would be in a position to influence Liberal policy and strategy, even though Asquith and his nominees formally controlled the party machine.

The farcical story of how Lloyd George and his Liberal opponents manœuvred for control of the notorious Fund between 1924 and 1926 has already been clearly and ably told.[19] In the background lurked the mysterious figure of Guest, now slowly gravitating towards the Conservative Party, but believed by Gladstone and Hudson to be Lloyd George's 'evil genius'[20]—an impression fostered by Lloyd George himself, who darkly muttered that 'Guest knew too much' and was 'the dangerous man'.[21] Whether Lloyd George really went in terror of exposure from his former Whip we will never know.

---

[16] Pinto-Duschinsky, *British Political Finance*, p. 84 n. 2. Based on material in Asquith papers (Bodleian), vol. 141, fo. 45.   [17] Ibid.

[18] Wilson, T., *The Downfall of the Liberal Party 1914–1935* (London, 1966), p. 297. This view seems to be supported by Lloyd George's amused account of a conversation he had had with the Labour politician, 'Jimmy' Thomas (Lloyd George to Frances Stevenson, 11 Aug. 1925, in Taylor, A. J. P. (ed.), *My Darling Pussy* (London, 1975), p. 84).

[19] The best account is that of Cregier, *Chiefs Without Indians*, pp. 113–47.

[20] Ibid. 131.

[21] Phillipps to Gwynne, 3 Aug. 1922 (Gwynne papers, vol. 21); Gladstone to Maclean, 23 Jan. 1924, cited in Cowling, *Impact of Labour*, p. 344.

The long-drawn-out negotations between Lloyd George and the Asquithians finally broke down in late 1925, when Vivian Phillipps, Chairman of the Party's Organization Committee, exasperated by the Welshman's deviousness, delivered a speech in Hull, in which he gave vent to his feelings and proclaimed that the Party was not up for sale. Asquith himself had no forewarning that Phillipps was about to make this speech, but loyally backed him up.[22] By this time the relationship between the two Liberal leaders was close to breaking point. Six months later the final rupture occurred with the disagreement over the General Strike. Asquith was forced into resigning his leadership, whereupon Gladstone took advantage of the quarrel to publish an attack on Lloyd George for the way in which he had treated his fellow Liberals over the Fund.[23]

Nothing did more than these events to demoralize the Liberal Party in the 1920s. Michael Bentley has captured very well the 'flavour of distilled bitterness' which characterized the utterances of the Asquithians as they contemplated the misfortunes of their Party, and the language of 'regret and recrimination which [was] such a feature of the Liberal Mind after 1914.'[24] In their revulsion against Lloyd George's methods—from his part in the 'Palace Revolution' to his haggling over the Fund—the 'Holy Family' surrounding the aged and ineffectual Liberal Leader (Gladstone, Vivian Phillipps, Donald Maclean) sought to define their own tradition of Liberalism in severely moral terms. What Asquith himself made of this display of chilly self-righteousness, so different from the atmosphere which had permeated 10 Downing Street when he was Prime Minister, is less certain. But his wife willingly subscribed to the Manichean view of politics now fashionable amongst the official Liberals, according to which virtuous Asquithians were locked in conflict with unprincipled Lloyd Georgians and 'gentlemen' struggled with 'cads' for the soul of the British people. 'You'll smile at me', wrote Margot Asquith to Keynes (of all people!), 'but in the end character is better than intelligence—especially intelligence without *intellect'*.[25] Meanwhile the Liberal Leader was being written up by his friends and relatives as a much-wronged saint.[26]

So strongly did the Asquithians denounce Lloyd George's financial chicanery that they felt obliged to attempt a clean break with the fund-raising methods which they, as well as Lloyd George, had always pursued in the past. As the *Liberal Magazine* explained in February

[22] Wilson, *Downfall of Liberal Party*, pp. 324–5; Cregier, *Chiefs Without Indians*, p. 133.
[23] Wilson, *Downfall of Liberal Party*, p. 331.
[24] Bentley, M., *The Liberal Mind 1914–1929* (Cambridge, 1977), pp. 95, 213.
[25] Quoted in Bentley, *Liberal Mind*, p. 162.
[26] Even Amery now described him privately as 'a man of high character' (Amery to Baldwin, 1 Nov. 1924, Cambridge University Library, Baldwin papers, vol. 159, fo. 179).

1925, the Trustees of their newly launched Million Fund intended to publish each year the audited accounts of its income and expenditure.[27] In the event, this promise was dishonoured.[28] But the Asquithians continued to present themselves as the political group which was offering the British people the values of 'decency' and 'honesty'. What else, the cynic might ask, could they claim to stand for after 1924?

This emphasis became even more pronounced once Lloyd George had taken control of the Liberal Party in 1926. In self-defence his enemies formed the Liberal Council, whose President, appropriately enough, was Grey, who saw its purpose as being not only to attack Lloyd George's 'corrupt' finance,[29] but also to 'save the soul of the Liberal Party' by a root-and-branch denunciation of all that Lloyd George represented. One of the Liberal MPs who attached himself to the Council was Richard Holt, who believed that Liberal politics had for too long been controlled by 'clever men of bad character'; he blamed the degeneration on to the activities of Coalition Ministers whose lack of common principle had allowed the 'villainy', 'roguery and the dirty ways of the Welshmen' to have free play.[30] This was also the view of Charles Mallet, who concluded his hostile biography of Lloyd George, published in 1930, by asking:

Is sincerity, or is it not, a part of statesmanship? Is it necessary, in following a political leader, to be able to trust the individual who leads? That is the plain issue between those who share the views expressed in this essay, and those who are content to accept Mr Lloyd George's domination on the ground that in modern politics money matters more than principle and forcefulness pays better than good faith.[31]

'Clean hands', unfortunately, was all that Lord Grey and his friends could offer Liberalism in the late 1920s. It was not enough.[32]

Moreover, the Asquithians' lofty principles did not inhibit them from entering into some fairly unscrupulous intrigues in the hope of discrediting the hated Lloyd George. Even before the fall of the Coalition, some prominent Liberals, Phillipps and Lord Buckmaster among them, had been assembling confidential information about the financial circumstances and methods of Lloyd George and his circle, which they then passed on to the receptive editor of the *Morning*

[27] *Liberal Magazine*, Feb. 1925, p. 66: 'The day of secret funds, so far, at all events, as the Liberal Party is concerned—is over. The accounts will be audited, and a full summary of disbursements will be published every year.'
[28] Pinto-Duschinsky, *British Political Finance*, p. 90 n. 18. The Fund was also a miserable failure from the fund-raising point of view (Cregier, *Chiefs Without Indians*, pp. 132–3).
[29] For Grey's anxieties about the Fund and Reading's tactful attempts to mediate between him and Lloyd George, see Reading papers, EUR F 118/27 (India Office Library).
[30] Cited of Waller, P. J., *Democracy and Sectarianism. A Political and Social History of Liverpool 1868–1939* (Liverpool, 1981), p. 278.
[31] Mallet, *Lloyd George*, p. 312.
[32] Bentley, *Liberal Mind*, p. 110.

Post.[33] In August 1927 Phillipps again plied Gwynne with a mass of material giving highly detailed accounts of the Party's internal affairs and including writings and memoranda which gave the frank opinions of, for example, Pringle, Mond, Buckmaster, and Margot Asquith.[34] Some of this information had already been published and would have been familiar to Gwynne, but much of it must have been a revelation to him; and without revealing its sources, the *Morning Post* made good use of the material in a series of articles published in November 1927 and later reissued as a pamphlet, entitled *Lloyd George and His Millions*.[35]

In taking this line Phillipps was well aware of the possible consequences of his actions. 'My own view', he told Gwynne on 12 August, 'is that there is no hope for the Liberal Party, so long as it acquiesces in this scandal and disgrace to our public life. It had far better perish in a struggle for cleaner and more upright standards than survive under the present dishonouring conditions.'[36] Pringle, who met Gwynne on 11 August, apparently took the same view: 'He looked upon the Lloyd George Fund as a great national danger', according to the notes Gwynne made of this conversation, 'and realises that in smashing Lloyd George the Liberal Party may also be smashed. But he is quite prepared for that, and thinks it a small price to pay for Lloyd George's disappearance from public life.'[37] When the *Morning Post* editorials and articles started appearing, Phillipps cheered the paper on from the sidelines; today's leader, he told Gwynne in an undated note (probably August 1927) 'was the subject of much approving comment at the Reform Club'.[38] Nothing could better illustrate the extent of the demoralization and the feuding amongst the Liberals than the readiness of men like Phillipps to risk the destruction of their party by entering into an informal alliance with a Diehard editor.

It might be thought that only a common hatred of Lloyd George could have maintained this incongruous alliance. Over Ireland, India, and fiscal policy, for example, Independent Liberals and Diehards were poles apart. Yet, despite their differences, the two sides could sometimes come together on the basis that they both subscribed to certain standards of 'decency'. 'I have said it 1000 times you are the *most* honest man I have ever known except my husband', gushed

---

[33] See the Memoranda in Gwynne papers (vol. 8): 'The Prime Minister's Attempt to Control the Press' and 'Mr Lloyd George's Personal Affairs'.

[34] 'Memorandum on Lloyd George Fund', 2 Aug. 1927 (ibid., vol. 21).

[35] *Morning Post*, 7, 8, 9, 11, 12, 14 Nov. 1927. In addition, a number of editorials in the autumn and winter of 1927 were devoted to the subject.

[36] Phillipps to Gwynne, 12 Aug. 1927 (Gwynne papers, vol. 21).

[37] Notes on Conversation with Pringle, 11 Aug. 1927 (ibid.).

[38] Phillipps to Gwynne, n.d. (ibid.).

Margot Asquith, in a letter to Gwynne.[39] And Gwynne, for his part, was only too willing to listen to Margot Asquith's almost demented denunciations of Lloyd George, which he wished she would repeat publicly:

I share so cordially your views about Lloyd George and the dangers of his possible return to power [he wrote in March 1928] that I become more persistent in asking you to think over the idea I placed before you in my last letter. Looking round our public men to-day, I can see nobody who is able or willing to stop Lloyd George's career. To my mind the man is a crook. The money with which he has bribed a portion of the Liberal Party is not his, and, at any rate, was obtained by corrupt methods. You, and you alone, it seems to me, could, by telling the truth about him, bring home to the British public the fact that he is a crook.[40]

Yet Gwynne's purpose in trying to destroy Lloyd George differed from that of the 'Holy Family' in one important respect. The Asquithians wanted initially to prevent and, later, to end Lloyd George's control of their party. The Diehards were less worried about this than about the prospect of Lloyd George using his wealth to re-create, at some propitious moment, a variant on the old Coalition Government. They also took a slightly different view of the Fund itself. The Asquithians wanted Lloyd George to hand over his ill-gotten gains to them, so regularizing an anomalous situation. Gwynne's point of view was, rather, that Lloyd George was behaving with rank dishonesty in treating as his personal property money which donors thought would be used for specific political purposes. Totally abandoning the view of the Coalition which he had entertained when it was still in existence, Gwynne now declared that the Coalition had been 'predominantly Conservative'; was it not natural to suppose that many of the donors intended their contributions to be used 'in the interests of the country' on Conservative lines, he asked.[41] Yet in 1924 Liberal MPs, some of whom had been returned to Westminster with support from the Fund, had actually put Labour in office. Surely this was a betrayal of trust. With bitter memories of Freddie's Guest's 'poaching', Page Croft joined in the hue and cry, asking in the columns of the *Morning Post* 'whether any proportion of these funds was collected from and titles bestowed upon gentlemen who have never claimed to belong to any party other than that of the Conservatives?'[42] The 'tainted money' of the Lloyd George Fund, it almost seemed, could only be cleansed if it were first returned to where it rightly belonged: the Conservative Party war chest!

---

[39] Margot Asquith to Gwynne, n.d. (Gwynne papers, vol. 14).
[40] Gwynne to Margot Asquith (copy), 6 Mar. 1928 (ibid.).
[41] *Morning Post*, 26 July 1927.
[42] Ibid., 27 July 1927.

The Role of Baldwin

But what, meanwhile, was the view of the official Conservative leadership towards the Fund? To answer this question we must first go back to the fall of the Lloyd George Coalition in October 1922. Lloyd George's resignation had led to the formation of a purely Conservative Administration under Bonar Law. But many leading Conservatives, including Austen Chamberlain, Balfour, and Birkenhead, deeply resented the decision made at the Carlton Club and went into the 1922 Election as a semi-autonomous group, complete with a fund of their own. The young man appointed to administer this fund was John Reith, soon to become the first Director-General of the BBC, acting under instructions from Sir William Bull (already encountered in the 'Dope Scandal' of 1918) to distribute money to those Conservative candidates which his group favoured. Reith later claimed to have paid out £15,000, incurring Bull's displeasure by making a meticulous record of all his transactions![43] The provenance of the money is unclear. But Birkenhead subsequently spoke of Lloyd George providing £50,000 to cover the election expenses of 'the members of the Coalition Government'.[44]

However, during the course of 1924 nearly all the leading 'Conservative Coalitionists' at last reconciled themselves to the notion that the Coalition was dead and made their peace with the new Conservative Party Establishment. And this meant working with a group of men who had declared from the outset their determination to make a clean break with the political methods that had prevailed during the Coalition era.

Significantly, on the first evening of his premiership Bonar Law ordered his Private Secretary, J. C. C. Davidson, 'to clean up Downing Street'.[45] The 'Garden Suburb', which was being ferociously attacked in the popular press, was promptly swept away, and even the Cabinet Secretariat came under threat. Eventually Hankey was able to secure the future of his office, but its staff was cut down from 129 to 37[46]—a gesture which not only signalled Law's determination to effect economies in public spending, but also his desire to distance himself from the kind of 'prime ministerial government' which had led the critics of the late Coalition to fear that a 'dictatorship' was in the process of being established. The message went out from 10 Downing Street that the new administration intended to govern through the Cabinet and the Departments and that Lloyd George's extensive

[43] Reith, J. C. W., *Into The Wind* (London, 1949), p. 82.
[44] Neville Chamberlain's diary, 4 Dec. 1927. See Dilks, D., *Neville Chamberlain, Vol. 1 1869–1929* (Cambridge, 1984), p. 538.
[45] James (ed.), *Memoirs of a Conservative*, p. 139.
[46] Ibid. On background to this, see Roskill, *Hankey*, vol. ii, Ch. 11.

system of press management would be discontinued. The *National Review* expressed its delight: 'Mr Bonar Law has made a salutary start towards restoring clean and sound Government by his announcement that "the Dope Department" of Downing Street has been closed, and that no Ministerial influence will be brought to bear on the Press . . . '.[47]

The new Administration also wanted to put an end to the convention according to which the great press barons had automatic access to government offices. Rothermere discovered this to his cost when he called upon Bonar Law soon after the fall of the Coalition and demanded as the price of his newspaper support a Cabinet position for his son, Esmond, and an earldom for himself. The Prime Minister pretended not to have heard the request, but immediately Rothermere had left the room dictated an account of what had happened in case he needed it later for his own protection. In fact, the Rothermere Press proved to be friendly enough to the new Administration in the 1922 Election. However, different rumours of what had occurred in the Bonar Law—Rothermere interview were soon circulating through London clubland, and in March 1923 the Duke of Somerset and the aged Willoughby de Broke considered raising the issue in the Lords, before Lord Salisbury, himself a fierce critic of press influence, managed to persuade them that this would be an unwise step.[48] 'The scoundrel ought to be exposed—and smashed in the process', commented Balcarres, who suspected that Rothermere 'must be approaching the lunacy which overtook Northcliffe'.[49]

If the great press proprietors were no longer to be treated as the confidants of Ministers, neither, it was thought, should members of the Conservative Cabinet seek to supplement their incomes by doubling up as freelance journalists, as had happened during Lloyd George's premiership. And so in January 1923 the Government formally resolved 'to refrain from the practice . . . of writing signed articles on current topics in the Press during their tenure of office'.[50]

The re-establishment of the traditional proprieties of public life also necessitated an overhaul of the Conservative Party's fund-raising methods. Bonar Law soon discovered, in fact, that the party finances were in a state of confusion. The Treasurer was still the aged banker-cum-politician, Lord Farquhar, to whom Lloyd George had awarded an earldom in his Resignation Honours List. In January 1923 the Conservative leadership learned with horror that Farquhar was refusing to sign a £20,000 cheque to meet expenses incurred by the Party during the recent General Election, justifying this with the

---

[47] *National Review*, lxxx (1922), 505.

[48] Blake, *Bonar Law*, pp. 472–3. But Koss claims that 'The *Daily Mail*, the *Evening News*, the *Daily Mirror*, and the *Sunday Pictorial* all fell into line after Bonar Law threatened to expose Rothermere's attempted extortion' (Koss, *Rise and Fall*, ii. 417).

[49] Balcarres's diary, 14 Mar. 1923, in Vincent (ed.), *The Crawford Papers*, p. 477.

[50] Cabinet Conclusion of 26 Jan. 1923, (Baldwin papers, vol. 56).

argument that the money in his Fund had been collected to sustain the Coalition. But as an angry Younger pointed out, the Conservatives and the Coalition Liberals had always had their separate Funds, and, now that the Coalition had collapsed, Farquhar's behaviour was simply incomprehensible. Bonar Law then met his Treasurer and grimly noted that 'poor old Farquhar' had gone ' "gaga" '. It also transpired that, out of a donation of £200,000, which the late Lord Astor had entrusted to Farquhar, some £40,000 had been given to charities approved of by the King, while of the residue, £80,000 had been handed over to the Coalition Liberals; the remaining £80,000 had simply disappeared. Farquhar was dismissed and died later in the year, leaving lavish bequests to various members of the Royal Family; but when the executors came to divide the estate, they found that Farquhar was almost penniless.[51] In all probability, to quote Beaverbrook's coarse words, 'Horace had spent the lot.'[52] Moreover, further financial irregularities of Farquhar's later came to light.[53]

At least this débâcle gave the new Conservative Administration an incentive to put its financial affairs on to a completely different footing and to disentangle itself from the methods of the Lloyd George era. Whether or not this really happened will be considered in due course. Meanwhile, Bonar Law put on a show of virtue by declining to confer any new peerages until the Royal Commission on Honours had submitted its Report, and as soon as it had done so the Government declared its willingness to implement its recommendations. The scrutinizing committee of the Privy Council was set up without delay, but parliamentary congestion meant that legislation making honours trafficking a criminal offence did not reach the statute book until the late summer of 1925—over two years after Bonar Law's death.

Perhaps Law's actions mattered less than his style. In the oft-quoted words of Philip Guedalla, the country was looking in late 1922 for a political leader totally unlike Lloyd George, and Bonar Law's great strength was that he was 'more indubitably not Mr Lloyd George than the other competitors'.[54] This was possibly true. On the other hand, the new Prime Minister had been a central figure in the Lloyd George Coalition prior to his retirement through ill-health in March 1921, and he had often had the unheroic task, as Leader of the Commons, of defending some of the Government's more controversial activities—as Curzon had had to do in the Lords. Bonar Law was also known to be a

[51] Blake, *Bonar Law*, pp. 496–8; Lord Beaverbrook, *The Decline and Fall of Lloyd George* (London, 1963), pp. 203–4, 298–300.

[52] Ibid., p. 204. But, contrary to the accepted version, Stamfordham later told Balcarres that he *had* received a legacy—one of 100 guineas (Balcarres's diary, 2 Feb. 1926, in Vincent (ed.), *The Crawford Papers*, p. 510).

[53] See Rose, *King George V*, pp. 279–80.

[54] Cited in James, R. R., *Churchill: A Study in Failure, 1900–1939* (London, 1970), p. 148.

close personal friend of Beaverbrook—another black mark against his name.[55]

It can therefore be argued that the decisive break with the ethos of the Lloyd George Government did not occur until May 1923, when renewed ill-health drove Bonar Law into final retirement and the King chose as his successor the as yet little-known Stanley Baldwin. In later years Baldwin was fond of describing how uncomfortable he had felt as a relatively junior Minister in the post-war Coalition, cooped up 'in a thieves' kitchen'.[56] The fact that Baldwin seems quite successfully to have concealed his distaste at the time does not mean that later utterances of this kind should be dismissed as humbug. Baldwin clearly loathed Lloyd George, viewed him as a dangerous and corrupt influence in public life, and was motivated by more than self-interest when he consistently worked after 1922 to exclude the Welshman from office.

In fact, though he may not have realized it at the time, Baldwin was really the main beneficiary from the vote at the Carlton Club in October 1922. His tenure of the post of President of the Board of Trade had given him the experience and status which eased his path, first to the Treasury, and then to the Premiership. But such had been his inconspicuousness and 'insignificance' that once the Coalition had collapsed, no one seriously contended that Baldwin should be held accountable for its 'misdeeds'.

In short, though Baldwin's accession to the Premiership is sometimes treated as a fortuitous event, there is clearly a sense in which Baldwin was ideally fitted by temperament and background for the role of 'cleanser' of British public life and restorer of its time-hallowed traditions—a role which Lloyd George's critics had been trying to fill for the last couple of years. Having a strong party base, he was much more effectual than Lord Robert Cecil or Grey. Yet, despite his loyalty to party—which was actually an asset after 1922—Baldwin was never thought of as being partisan and his appeal was one which stretched out to the uncommitted and even to some of his party opponents. Moreover, by 1922 Baldwin had gone far to distancing himself from his industrial upbringing and was self-consciously projecting himself as the embodiment of the underlying traditions of English rural life. Yet, in contrast to the aristocratic Salisbury, he seemed a 'modern' politician endowed with the common touch necessary for popularity with the new mass electorate. He was also able, as Salisbury and the Diehards were not, to discuss social problems in a sympathetic way,

---

[55] 'It is alleged (though not by Stanley B.) that the sinister influences of Beaverbrook over BL had been pretty strong. If Lloyd George was surrounded by bad advisers, BL's trusted councillor is far more dangerous—not the common scheming parasites who clung to Ll.G. but a much more efficient and cunning intriguer . . .' (Balcarres's diary, 14 Mar. 1923, in Vincent (ed.), *The Crawford Papers*, p. 477).

[56] Thomas Jones's diary, 26 Apr. 1926, in Middlemas (ed.), *Whitehall Diary*, ii. 23.

and this appealed to the young progressives in the Party, who thought it imperative that Labour should not be seen as having a monopoly of 'idealism'. For, while resolutely defending the interests of capitalism, Baldwin had a happy knack of conveying a belief in the overriding importance of spiritual values. Of course, he did not define these values in a narrowly Anglican way, as the Cecil brothers did, but he shared with Lord Robert Cecil and Grey a rhetorical commitment to the League of Nations abroad and class harmony at home.

Finally, Baldwin deliberately cultivated the image of a man who was 'honest to the point of simplicity', and subtly suggested that to be clever was somehow not quite English. For Baldwin, above all else, presented himself as the quintessential Englishman. Moreover, no hint of scandal had ever touched his public or private life. In short, more perfectly than Grey or Robert Cecil or Selborne, Baldwin made a homely appeal to those who equated 'Englishness' with decency, decorum, and honesty.

That, at least, was how Baldwin was seen by his many admirers. In a pamphlet published in July 1924, for example, the Conservative Leader was described as 'a plain, blunt, simple-hearted countryman', lacking, perhaps, in 'the commercial cleverness of the professional politician', but 'a man of the most impressive and beautiful selflessness'. The writer also emphasized Baldwin's 'sincerity' and natural goodness—'his heart is clean.' And, in fulsome language, the pamphlet described how this saintly man had put the country for ever in his debt.:

The corruption of our public life had reached a festering height which threatened the health of the whole nation. There was an air of Tammany in Westminster, a touch of Bottomley in the party organisations. All that was morally bad in politics had gathered a courage and intensified an insolence which were carrying every successive barrier of decency and virtue before them. Men who could never have personally addressed the second secretaries of Salisbury and Gladstone were the close intimates, the gossips, and the go-betweens of the greatest ministers of state. There was no limit to the demands of these insurgents. They were not content with securing honours for themselves and their parasites, not even content with dominating the organisation of their parties and degrading the once noble profession of journalism; they were determined, these gross and ignorant men, to govern the British Empire. From this disgraceful state of things Mr Baldwin delivered the reconstructed Conservative Party. He has restored the old standards. He has repaired the ancient barriers . . . [57]

Baldwin was well aware of the usefulness of this image, and he took care to surround himself with men of a similar stamp. A particularly close confidant was Bonar Law's one-time private secretary, J. C. C. Davidson, whom Baldwin made Conservative Party Chairman in 1926—a promotion which Davidson himself attributed to his familiarity

[57] 'A Gentleman With a Duster' (Harold Begbie), *The Conservative Mind* (1924), p. 19.

with Lloyd George's political methods and personality.[58] Protecting Baldwin's reputation for wholesomeness and decency was clearly seen by Davidson as an important part of his work.[59]

While Baldwin and Davidson set out to clean up the 'thieves' kitchen' they had inherited, other Conservative Ministers strove to purify the national life in their own particular ways. At the Home Office, for example, Joynson-Hicks, a zealous Evangelical, waged war on London's night clubs and kept a sharp watch for obscene publications—a role which earned him the title of 'God's Policeman'.[60] Up-and-coming Ministers who benefited from Baldwin's patronage, like Douglas Hogg and Lord Irwin, also took a sternly moralistic view of politics. So, in a somewhat different way, did Lord Robert Cecil, whom Baldwin brought back into office in May 1923,[61] and Lord Salisbury, who served in all the Conservative Administrations of the 1920s.

Baldwin's reputation for 'honesty' may have been grossly inflated, but there is little doubt that the Conservative Leader was able to generate emotions of trust and even love in people from different parties and with different convictions from his own. Most Diehards, in particular, had confidence in Baldwin at this stage of his career. Gwynne, for example, finally severed his relationship with Lord Derby when the latter took part in the anti-Baldwin intrigue of January 1924. 'We have at last thrown up a man of such conspicuous ability, statesmanship and honesty of purpose', wrote Gwynne reprovingly, 'that he is bound in the long run to win the suffrages of his fellow-countrymen.'[62] Baldwin's 'honesty of purpose' seemed, for the time at least, to outweigh those qualities of mildness, caution, and moderation that were eventually to estrange the militant Diehards from the Conservative Leader. In April 1929 Gwynne's admiration for Baldwin was still strong: 'The greatest thing you have done for England', he told him, 'is to begin the job of making politics clean. Given another five years of office I believe you will succeed in making honest men of politicians. L.G. has debauched politics, you are making them clean again.'[63]

The attitude of the Asquithians to Baldwin was much more

---

[58] James (ed.), *Memoirs of a Conservative*, p. 262. But, though he approved of Baldwin's refusal to see the press lords or to bargain with them, Neville Chamberlain agreed with Hoare that Davidson was 'the wrong man' to act as the intermediary between the Prime Minister and the press (Birmingham University, Neville Chamberlain's diary, 18 Dec. 1923).

[59] See Davidson's letter to Vansittart, 19 Feb. 1929 (Davidson papers).

[60] Taylor, H. A., *Jix Viscount Brentford* (London, 1933), pp. 242–5.

[61] But Cecil soon lost his respect for Baldwin, and in Oct. 1927 he resigned from the Cabinet.

[62] Gwynne to Derby (copy), Jan. 1924 (Gwynne papers, vol. 22).

[63] Cited in Campbell, *Goat In Wilderness*, p. 243.

ambiguous.[64] Yet, as contemporaries noted, Baldwin and Asquith had one important thing in common: they both hated Lloyd George, and for much the same reasons. One is tempted to dismiss as 'gush' Margot Asquith's frequent protestations that she 'loved' Baldwin, in whom she affected to see many of her husband's qualities.[65] But it is significant that almost all members of the Asquith family wrote to Baldwin saying that his parliamentary oration on the death of the Liberal Leader was the one which had given them particular satisfaction.[66] In this speech Baldwin had chosen to emphasize Asquith's serenity, personal integrity, and loyalty, and had spoken of a 'character' that was proof against all temptation and all disappointment.[67] These, in fact, were just the qualities for which Baldwin himself was often praised.

Indeed, many Liberals professed themselves to be rather proud of Baldwin. For example, the former Liberal MP, Gerald France, congratulated him in February 1923 on his success as Chancellor of the Exchequer: 'I am more glad than I can say that character as a foundation for ability with an added grace of humour' could still bring political success. 'I can now almost forgive you for the "Safeguarding" Act', he joked.[68] Margot Asquith made a similar point four years later. Protection, she told Baldwin, 'is your only flaw—your belief in a Policy that spells Corruption'.[69] Otherwise, the values which Baldwin represented could be seen as a homespun provincial variant on all that was best in the great Liberal tradition, which was why Baldwin seemed to be so perfect a foil to Lloyd George. The extraordinary affinity between some of the Asquithians and the Conservative Leader is most memorably captured in the famous exchange of letters between Baldwin and Grey in early 1929. Grey gently turned down the Prime Minister's suggestion that perhaps he might be offered the Foreign Office if the Conservatives won the forthcoming General Election, but he went on to express his appreciation of the wonderful gifts which Baldwin had brought to the Premiership:

Personality is more than any special qualifications, more than all special qualifications put together. As long as you are at the head of a Government, it will stand for what is honourable. The iron entered into my soul, when Ll.G.'s Govt. after the war let down and corrupted public life at home and destroyed our credit abroad. Ever since, it has been a relief to have public honour re-established and you will always stand for that . . . [70]

---

[64] See Cowling, *Impact of Labour*, p. 401.

[65] 'A man that we love personally and the country trusts' (Margot Asquith to Gwynne, 30 Jan. 1925 (Gwynne papers, vol. 14)); Margot Asquith to Baldwin, 3 Aug. 1928 (Baldwin papers, vol. 163, fo. 221).

[66] See letters in Baldwin papers, vol. 163.

[67] Baldwin, S., *Our Inheritance: Speeches and Addresses* (London, 1928), pp. 229–32.

[68] France to Baldwin, 17 Feb. 1923 (Baldwin papers, vol. 159, fos. 57–8).

[69] Margot Asquith to Baldwin, 3 Aug. 1928 (ibid., vol. 163, fo. 222).

[70] Grey to Baldwin, 5 Jan. 1929, in Middlemas (ed.), *Whitehall Diary*, ii. 165–6.

Baldwin's Enemies

Baldwin's image was one which came naturally to him, but it was also a matter of deliberate contrivance. And when it occasionally conflicted with the other side of his nature, that of the shrewd party manager, his admirers, both colleagues and followers, were bewildered. One such conflict occurred in late 1923, and again in early 1924, when the Conservative Leader, confident that reunion could be achieved on his own terms, moved to invite the principal Carlton Club rebels back on to the Front Bench. Few of Baldwin's friends took serious exception to the readmission of Austen Chamberlain, but real anger and dismay broke out when it was realized that reconciliation with Chamberlain entailed co-operation with Lord Birkenhead.

For the former Lord Chancellor, unpopular with most backbench MPs for many years past, had continued to behave as if the Coalition were only momentarily in abeyance and as if the 'second eleven', as he insolently dubbed the members of the Conservative Administration, would very shortly be displaced by the 'first class brains', including himself.[71] In the 1922 Election he had publicly referred to Lloyd George as Britain's 'greatest living statesman', and in early 1923 was spending much time in Rothermere's company, before the two men quarrelled in April.[72] For Baldwin, Birkenhead had a scarcely veiled contempt, and, following the Conservative Party's electoral set-back in the 1923 Election, he had been the centre of an intrigue against his leadership.[73]

Quite apart from these unfriendly acts, Birkenhead's reputation violently jarred against the public's perception of Baldwin and his circle. In particular, his 'morals' (i.e. his heavy drinking) and his swaggering cynicism were said to be anathema to the woman voters. According to Amery, it was this consideration which induced Baldwin to withdraw his offer of a government place to Birkenhead in November 1923. 'The women of England', he observed, 'want either political or moral respectability (if they can't get both!) and F.E. was too much all round for them.'[74]

A few weeks previously Birkenhead had confirmed all the prejudices of his detractors when he delivered his notorious Glasgow Rectorial Address, in which he proclaimed the necessity and desirability of strife in social and international life, mocked the League of Nations, praised self-interest, and informed his youthful audience that 'the world continue[d] to offer glittering prizes to those who have stout hearts and

---

[71] Campbell, *F. E. Smith*, Chs. 20–1.

[72] On the quarrel, see Neville Chamberlain's diary, 26 Apr. 1923.

[73] Cowling, *Impact of Labour*, Ch. 17.

[74] Amery's diary, 10 Nov. 1923, in Barnes and Nicholson (eds.), *Leo Amery Diaries*, i. 355–6; Cowling, *Impact of Labour*, p. 323.

sharp swords'.[75] Lord Robert Cecil, already angry over Baldwin's public conversion to Protection, could not understand how an invitation could have been extended to Birkenhead after such an effusion.[76]

In January 1924, with Labour now in office, the Conservative politician, Ormsby-Gore,[77] wrote to Baldwin saying that any association with Birkenhead would 'spell disaster for the Unionist party at the next election'. 'The chief reason we admire you so much and want to keep you as leader', he went on, 'is that you broke from Mr Austen Chamberlain and Lord Birkenhead in October 1922, and definitely and we hope finally severed yourself from Lloyd George and all he stands for.' Ormsby-Gore added: 'The two men in British public life ... whom I dislike and distrust most' are Lloyd George and Birkenhead; 'I would far rather have a Labour Government than support a party dominated by either of those two powerful personalities.'[78]

This was far from being an isolated or eccentric protest. Lord Bledisloe, an emotional young Tory peer, who, significantly, had been closely associated recently with Lord Robert Cecil, informed Baldwin on 31 January that he was about to leave the Conservative Party, mainly because he so disliked 'the Gospel of sordid self-assertion, greed (and contempt for the under-dog) furnished by Birkenhead—now the chief apostle of modern Conservatism'. Birkenhead's cynical materialism, he said, was 'the very negation of the lessons' which he had learned at his mother's knee. This aristocratic Tory professed a preference for Labour: 'Their idealism at least is stimulating.'[79]

Baldwin may have smiled at Bledisloe's excitable outburst, but he must have taken more seriously a letter which he had received from Salisbury five days earlier. Reconciliation with Chamberlain, said the Marquess, he could reluctantly accept, but F. E. was simply 'disreputable'. Salisbury continued:

I do not imagine he has got many political principles and most of what he has got are wrong. Poor devil, he will probably drink himself to death. What, however, we have to consider is what effect the quasi-public reception of him may have on the leaders of thought in the democracy. *They are panting after ideals which they are afraid may be slipping from them. They have no*

[75] Campbell, *Smith*, p. 640. But Campbell points out that this passage—then as now—was often taken out of context (ibid. 640–2).

[76] Cecil to Baldwin (copy), 1 Feb. 1924 (BL, Cecil of Chelwood papers, Add. MS 51,080, fos. 116–17).

[77] Ormsby-Gore, son of the Third Lord Harlech, had been concerned about 'corruption' in public life for many years. He had taken part in the pre-war Radical Plutocrats Enquiry, he had been a follower of Lord Robert Cecil at the time of the 'Conspiracy', and his 'political moralism' was doubtless reinforced by the influence of his father-in-law, Lord Salisbury.

[78] Ormsby-Gore to Baldwin, 29 Jan. 1924 (Baldwin papers, vol. 42, fos. 182–7).

[79] Bledisloe to Baldwin, 31 Jan. 1924 (ibid., vol. 159, fos. 183–4). On Bledisloe, see Cowling, *Impact of Labour*, pp. 88–9. Despite Bledisloe's high-minded outburst, he did not leave the Conservative Party; indeed, he became a junior minister in Baldwin's next Administration, in which Birkenhead served as Indian Secretary!

sympathy with the hard-shelled defence of the Haves against the Have Nots. I think F.E.—without ideals and with his crude attachment to the interests of wealth—would lose us more than Austen would gain us.

Salisbury concluded on a threatening note, saying that he would take no responsibility for the consequences for the Party and country which would follow Birkenhead's rehabilitation.[80]

Ignoring both the plea and the threat, Baldwin went ahead and invited Birkenhead, along with other senior Chamberlainites, to the Shadow Cabinet meeting of 19 February 1924. But the relationship between the Party Leader and the former Lord Chancellor was still uneasy. Baldwin resented it when Birkenhead continued to write articles for Beaverbrook's *Sunday Express*, a paper in which his own leadership was constantly held up to ridicule.[81] And an embarrassing incident occurred on 18 May when the *People* published some off-the-cuff comments which Baldwin had made, in which the press lords were scathingly dismissed and the opinion ventured that 'Lord Birkenhead, if his health does not give way, will be a liability to the Party'. The publication of these indiscreet remarks was possibly a piece of malice on the part of the paper's proprietor, Grant Morden (the 'villain' of the 'Dope Scandal'), who was hostile to Baldwin and had ordered his staff to print anything favourable to Birkenhead.[82]

Despite all this, Baldwin's political instincts told him that it was better to control his political enemies by having them inside his Government than to force them into the role of external critics. Consequently, when Baldwin returned to office in November 1924, he appointed Churchill Chancellor of the Exchequer, Austen Chamberlain Foreign Secretary, and Birkenhead Indian Secretary. This arrangement caused never-ending anxiety to staunch Baldwinites like J. C. C. Davidson, who feared that the ex-Coalitionists were still engaged in an intrigue to destroy the Prime Minister's authority, with the aim of re-creating a coalition government including Lloyd George.[83]

Such suspicions were quite unfounded, so far as Birkenhead was concerned. For, whatever the rumours to the contrary,[84] once he had become Indian Secretary, he showed a general loyalty to Baldwin, committed himself completely to the Conservative Party, and abandoned

---

[80] Salisbury to Baldwin, 26 Jan. 1924 (Baldwin papers, vol. 159, fos. 258–61).

[81] Cowling, *Impact of Labour*, p. 400.

[82] Ibid. 401; Middlemas, K. and Barnes, J., *Baldwin* (London, 1969), pp. 213, 267. But R. J. Minney attributes the article to the editor, Swaffer, and claims that when it appeared, Morden was furious (Minney, R. J., *Viscount Southwood* (London, 1954), p. 181).

[83] e.g. James (ed.), *Memoirs of a Conservative*, p. 213.

[84] e.g. Blumenfeld was told that at the St James' Club Birkenhead 'began abusing Mr Baldwin and giving away Cabinet secrets and then said, "If Baldwin does not make me the next Viceroy of India I will torpedo his Government"' (C. Stuart Menzies to Blumenfeld, 11 Apr. 1925, HLRO, Blumenfeld papers).

his earlier concern for the establishment of a Centre grouping as a barrier against Socialism. Moreover, his sympathy for his old Liberal friends evaporated once they had placed Labour in office in 1924, while his former political friendship with Lloyd George virtually ended when Lloyd George adopted a sympathetic attitude towards the trade union movement during the General Strike. Birkenhead also drifted away from Beaverbrook and Rothermere, whose attacks on the Baldwin Administration he strongly resented.[85]

However, though no longer a threat, Birkenhead still constituted something of an embarrassment to Baldwin. Not only did his drink problem grow worse after 1924; he also did unwitting damage to the image of the Conservative Government through the political company he kept. For example, there was the continuing association with the Conservative Party manager in Liverpool, Alderman Salvidge, who Davidson thought was little better than a corrupt Tammany Boss.[86] More damaging still was F.E.'s reckless friendship with the Conservative MP who had inherited his former Liverpool seat, the sybaritic Commander Warden Chilcott.[87] The two men seem to have been intimates of Maundy Gregory and frequenters of the infamous Ambassador's Club, and Chilcott's activities were soon the subject of much political gossip.[88]

The critics would have been strengthened in their views had it been generally known how Chilcott maintained his luxurious lifestyle. For in 1926 Hankey discovered with dismay that the Conservative MP was engaged upon an audacious swindle of certain rich Indian princes. Under cover of leading a parliamentary delegation to India to promote agricultural development, Chilcott had persuaded a number of princes to set up a fund, which totalled £100,000, the proceeds of which were supposedly to be used to safeguard their interests in London. One of the most disquieting features of the affair was that, as Hankey put it, 'Chilcott was given to bragging about his influence with Lord [B]irkenhead, and seems to have boasted that he managed Lord B's financial affairs.' This story was confirmed by the former editor of *The Times of India*, who told Hankey that the Indian princes 'universally believed that Lord B. was in Chilcott's pocket for financial reasons, and that consequently Chilcott could do what he liked with Lord B.' Hankey did not 'for one moment suspect B. of any corruption', but he felt that, by publicly associating himself with Chilcott, the Indian Secretary was laying himself open to serious misunderstanding. Hankey eventually decided that it would be too embarrassing to bring

[85] Campbell, *Smith*, pp. 789–90, 819.
[86] James (ed.), *Memoirs of a Conservative*, p. 117. Davidson said that he once accused Salvidge of taking party funds, and the latter admitted it and broke down.
[87] See the sketch in Waller, *Democracy and Sectarianism*, p. 307.
[88] Amery's diary, 20 Mar. 1928, in Barnes and Nicholson (eds.), *Leo Amery Diaries*, p. 539; Cullen, *Maundy Gregory*, pp. 132–7.

the matter before the Prime Minister. Belatedly Birkenhead seems to have realized what use was being made of his name by his so-called friend, whom he now referred to as 'that sewer rat'.[89]

The Chilcott Affair, and Birkenhead's innocent involvement in it, remained more or less a secret. But a blaze of publicity surrounded Birkenhead's continued attempts to solve his largely self-created financial problems by writing for the press. Pointed questions were asked in Parliament,[90] and Baldwin was obliged to remind his Indian Secretary of the Cabinet ruling of January 1923. As his son explains, 'Birkenhead yielded with an ill grace and nourished an abiding grievance.'[91] The matter came before the Cabinet in the course of 1925, when it was decided that, in order to retain the Indian Secretary's 'great legal knowledge and long Parliamentary experience', Birkenhead should be paid a special pension out of party funds, as a compensation for his loss of earnings at the Bar. In 1926 two cheques, one for £3,500 and one for £6,500, were paid by Conservative Central Office into Birkenhead's bank account.[92]

But in April 1927 the Indian Secretary, still hampered by financial difficulties, was tempted by an outside offer to earn £15,000 a year 'in gilt edged surroundings'. Contemporaries suspected that this had something to do with the Berry brothers, with whom Birkenhead was friendly and for whose papers he had earlier written.[93] The temptation was resisted. However, eventually in October 1928, to the relief of most of his colleagues, Birkenhead resigned and promptly joined his City friends from whom he received a number of lucrative company directorships; for example, he was put on the board of ICI and of Tate & Lyle and became chairman of the Greater London & Counties Trust.[94] Within two years he was dead.

The departure of Birkenhead, however, did not solve the main problem confronting Baldwin in the late 1920s: how to cope with the press barons, Beaverbrook and Rothermere. As we have seen, neither of these two powerful men had been unequivocal supporters of Lloyd George during the Coalition period. But the Baldwin coterie suspected them—with good reason—of working secretly for the destruction of Baldwin's leadership and for Lloyd George's return to power as one of the leaders of a new Centre Party. These anxieties were bound up with

[89] Roskill, *Hankey*, ii. 420–4; Cullen, *Maundy Gregory*, p. 132. Chilcott seems also to have made an effort to 'nobble' Reading, the Indian Viceroy (Chilcott to Reading, 5 Nov. 1924, Reading papers, EUR F 118/10, fo. 40).
[90] *Parl. Deb.*, 5th ser., clxxxiv. 1735–7 (9 June 1925); ibid. clxxxix. 34 (7 Dec. 1925).
[91] Second Earl of Birkenhead, *F. E., The Life of F. E. Smith First Earl of Birkenhead* (London, 1960), p. 544. On Birkenhead's writing for the press, see Koss, *Rise and Fall*, ii. 451.
[92] Campbell, *Smith*, pp. 719–20.
[93] Ibid. 810–11; Birkenhead to Baldwin, 13 Apr. 1927 (Baldwin papers, vol. 162, fos. 31–4).
[94] Campbell, *Smith*, p. 811.

a fear of the presumed political influence of the syndicated press. In a private conversation of October 1928 Baldwin expressed the view that it was 'disgraceful that L.G. writes for such a scoundrel' as Hearst—a view shared, of course, by many Liberals, who thought it 'unpatriotic' of a leading British politician to criticize his own government in a foreign newspaper. But Baldwin also bracketed Hearst with his British counterparts; the syndicated press, he said, was 'the most obvious peril to democracy today', and he hoped 'to see the day when Rothermere, Hearst, and Co. will be sent to the gallows for spreading lies'.[95]

Apologists for Baldwin often indulged in similar outbursts. In late December 1923 Massingham wrote an article for the *Spectator* in which, much to the delight of Strachey's readers, the Rothermere Press was declared to be 'a *masked* power . . . a *monopoly* power . . . a *non-moral* power'.[96] And an anonymous pamphleteer asked how the country proposed 'to guard itself against this domination at the hands of two or three men who have turned to journalism, not as a man turns to schoolmastering or to preaching, but for the sake of money or for their own personal aggrandisement?'[97]

Of the two great press lords, most Conservatives had a slight preference for Beaverbrook. Davidson, for example, distrusted the Canadian, yet could not help liking him, while he recognized that the latter had had a genuine affection for his former 'Chief', Bonar Law.[98] Then, too, Beaverbrook had played an important role in the destruction of the Coalition, which was another sign of grace. Nevertheless, as Maurice Cowling says, 'in the Conservative party [Beaverbrook] was as unpopular as Birkenhead.'[99] Typically, it was at Beaverbrook's house, Cherkeley, that the 'old Coalition gang', Lloyd George, Churchill, Austen Chamberlain, and Birkenhead, had assembled on 12 November 1923. Here it was decided, half jokingly perhaps, that the two Liberals present should pretend to defend Free Trade, while the two Conservatives promoted Protection; they could then link up again on an Empire Free Trade platform after Baldwin had lost the Election.[100] In the event Birkenhead committed himself so enthusiastically to the Conservative campaign that the cynical Beaverbrook soon concluded that money had passed into F. E.'s hands from Conservative Central Office.[101] Beaverbrook, by contrast, was anxious not to separate himself so cleanly from Lloyd George; so was Rothermere. Later, with

[95] Jones to Wife, 23 Oct. 1928, Middlemas (ed.), *Whitehall Diary*, ii. 153.

[96] Havighurst, A. F., *Radical Journalist: H. W. Massingham 1860–1924* (Cambridge, 1974), p. 305.

[97] 'Gentleman With a Duster', *Conservative Mind*, p. 112.

[98] James (ed.), *Memoirs of a Conservative*, p. 28.

[99] Cowling, *Impact of Labour*, p. 319.

[100] Ibid. 320; Taylor, *Beaverbrook*, p. 218.

[101] Lloyd George to Frances Stevenson, 23 Nov. 1923, in Taylor (ed.), *My Darling Pussy*, p. 73.

Labour in office, the hostility between Baldwin and the press lords grew in intensity. In the unfortunate *People* interview Baldwin allegedly remarked that Beaverbrook and Rothermere were 'both men I would not have in my house'.[102]

After 1924 the two newspaper proprietors continued what Strachey indignantly called their 'private vendetta' against the Conservative Leader.[103] Moreover, in 1925 Beaverbrook was also spending much of his time in Lloyd George's company, which loyal Conservatives found ominous and which moved Margot Asquith to denounce the press baron as 'that scoundrel'.[104] In fact, a freelance journalist who wrote for both the *Daily* and *Sunday Express* came forward in November 1924 and offered to keep the Conservative leadership 'well posted concerning the machinations of Lord Beaverbrook and his political associates provided the source of [the] information [was] not divulged'. Beaverbrook, said the informant, was using the *Daily Express* attacks on Baldwin as a way of promoting his own oil interests in the Middle East.[105]

By 1927 Davidson was becoming positively paranoid about the plotting of the press lords. His suspicions were fuelled by the former editor of the *Daily Mail*, Marlowe, who told him in September that Rothermere was being blackmailed by Beaverbrook (who knew embarrassing things about the circumstances in which Rothermere had been ennobled) into espousing Lloyd George's cause: 'The game is for R. and Max to give half-hearted support to the Conservative Party before and during the [forthcoming] Election, and at the critical moment to stab Baldwin in the back and run in Ll.G.' Marlowe believed that Beaverbrook was the master mind in this dirty business.[106]

But it was Rothermere who aroused the fiercer antipathy in the circles surrounding Baldwin. In December 1923 the mere rumour that Baldwin had invited Rothermere round to 10 Downing Street forced the Prime Minister's Secretary to put out an embarrassed apology cum denial.[107] In fact, Rothermere's crude attempt to impose terms on the Conservative Leader just prior to the 1923 Election had led to a complete breach in the relationship between the two men. Amery recorded in his diary that Rothermere had 'repeated with Baldwin what he had done with Bonar, asking as the price of his support for a place in the Cabinet for himself and an under-secretaryship for Esmond'.

[102] *People*, 18 May 1924.

[103] Strachey to Baldwin, 7 May 1924 (Baldwin papers, vol. 159, fo. 264). Strachey described their behaviour as a 'scandal'.

[104] Margot Asquith to Gwynne, 30 Jan. 1925 (Gwynne papers, vol. 14).

[105] Memo. by E. J. Moyle of Unionist Central Office, 12 Nov. 1924 (Baldwin papers, vol. 159, fos. 192–3).

[106] Davidson's note of 24 Sept. 1927 (Davidson papers).

[107] Boyd-Carpenter to Baldwin, 27 Dec. 1923 and the reply thereto (Baldwin papers, vol. 159, fos. 9–11).

Baldwin enquired whether he wanted anything else and Rothermere had requested a further step in the peerage, only to be told that he could have none of these things![108]

Rothermere took the rebuff badly. In February 1924 Derby found him consumed with hatred of Baldwin and threatening to oppose him, even to the extent of supporting Arthur Henderson in the Burnley by-election.[109] However, Rothermere's intense fear of Socialism in all its forms caused him to throw the *Daily Mail* behind the Conservatives in their assault on MacDonald's Minority Administration in the 'Red Scare' election of 1924. But far from expressing gratitude, Baldwin had subsequently put out a statement denying that his electoral triumph owed anything to 'the Stunt Press', and, this, as F. E. later noted, was taken by the press proprietor as a 'gratuitous insult' which had never been forgiven.[110] In 1928 Churchill, who wanted the quarrel buried, held a meeting with Esmond Harmsworth and told him that he had recently spoken in that sense to Baldwin; but, he went on, Baldwin had said in reply, 'I am not clever. I can't speak, yet here I am Prime Minister. It is chiefly because I am regarded as an honest man that I can't go and have any truck with these people [i.e. Rothermere and Beaverbrook].'[111]

Held at arm's length as he was by Baldwin, Rothermere swallowed his dislike of Lloyd George's Land Campaign and renewed commitment to radical domestic reform and offered his support to the Liberal Leader, whom he now hailed as 'the Man of Emergency'.[112] How seriously Lloyd George took such protestations of friendship it is difficult to say, but he was prepared on occasions to humour the press baron—possibly to his own long-term detriment, since, as John Campbell observes, 'Rothermere recalled the Lloyd George of the Coalition, the anti-Socialist national saviour, while the enforced conservatism of his last spell in office was exactly what Lloyd George was trying to get the public to forget.'[113]

The Honours Scandal Revived, 1927

Rothermere's chosen method of demonstrating his loyalty to Lloyd George took the form of an intervention in the public dispute which had once again broken out on the issue of Lloyd George's by now

[108] Amery's diary, 17 July 1923, in Barnes and Nicholson (eds.), *Leo Amery Diaries*, p. 334. Note Amery's probably mistaken belief that Rothermere had asked for Cabinet office for *himself*.
[109] Derby's diary, 7 Feb. 1924, in Churchill, R. S., *Lord Derby, 'King of Lancashire'* (London, 1959), p. 565.
[110] James (ed.), *Memoirs of a Conservative*, p. 201; Koss, *Rise and Fall*, ii. 443.
[111] Note by Victor Cazalet, cited in James, R. R., *Victor Cazalet. A Portrait* (London, 1976), p. 125.
[112] Rothermere to Lloyd George, 11 Aug. 1925 (HLRO, Lloyd George papers, G/17/1/9).
[113] Campbell, *Goat in Wilderness*, p. 181.

famous Fund. In January 1927 a deal had been struck which, as his critics bitterly complained, made Lloyd George 'for the time the paymaster of the Liberal Party'.[114] It was this which prompted Lord Rosebery, a self-confessed 'embarrassed old fogey', to write a 'naïve' letter to *The Times*, asking for detailed information about the provenance and nature of the Lloyd George Fund.[115] Lloyd George had 'a fair conjecture as to who persuaded him to rush into a controversy, from which a mere perusal of his own Honours List would have induced him to refrain'.[116] Augustine Birrell then joined in the hue and cry, publicly deriding Lloyd George's 'Coalition swag, or booty, or loot' and alleging that one half of the money raised by honours trafficking during the Coalition period had gone into the coffers of the Conservative Party.[117] This forced Conservative Central Office into issuing a formal denial: 'Lord Younger . . . states that he has no knowledge of Mr Lloyd George's Fund or the purpose for which it was subscribed, and at no time has he had any financial interest in it.'[118] This statement was literally true, but, of course, as Younger virtually conceded in a private letter to Baldwin, Conservative fund-raising had not been radically different from Lloyd George's.[119]

For this reason alone Baldwin probably hoped that the subject of the Lloyd George Fund would quickly disappear. But this was to overlook the blundering zeal of Gwynne, who could not resist the temptation of once more denouncing the 'corrupt' Welshman. Puzzled by the fact that Conservative Ministers and officials were not giving him more support,[120] Gwynne mounted another press campaign, starting with an article in the *Morning Post* on 26 July, which challenged Lloyd George to give a proper reply to the political crimes of which he stood accused. The challenge was then taken up, not initially by Lloyd George himself, but by Rothermere, whose *Daily Mail* contemptuously castigated the *Post*'s behaviour as 'un-English'. The attacks on Lloyd George, it said, had 'about them an unpleasant flavour of hypocrisy'; 'it

[114] Mallet, *Lloyd George*, p. 288.

[115] *The Times*, 16 Feb. 1927.

[116] Lloyd George to Perks, 29 Mar. 1927, cited in Cregier, *Chiefs Without Indians*, p. 243 n. 110.

[117] Cited in Ramsden, J., *The Age of Balfour and Baldwin 1902–1940* (London, 1978), p. 222.

[118] Ibid.

[119] Ibid. Younger writes: 'The charge against LG is not that he raised such subscriptions but that he used his position as P.M. to fill his own *political* coffers, while ours were placed in trust and solely used for the necessities of the Party to which the donor belonged.'

[120] See Gwynne to Davidson (copy?), 7 Nov. 1927 (Gwynne papers, vol. 18). It must also be remembered that the *Morning Post*, with a small and declining circulation, was held in derision even by many Conservatives. A contemporary quip was 'that no cause could be regarded as completely lost until the *Morning Post* took it up' (Seymour-Ure, C., 'The Press and the Party System Between the Wars', in Peele, G. and Cook, C., (eds.) *The Politics of Reappraisal, 1918–1939* (London, 1975), p. 239.

is sheer affectation', argued the *Daily Mail*, 'to pretend that any Government has abstained from this method of raising the supplies of money which it requires for party purposes.'[121]

Vivian Phillipps was delighted at the outcome: 'I have not seen the "Daily Mail" ', he told Gwynne on 12 August, 'but it is all to the good that it has taken the field in defence of Lloyd George and your two articles will certainly worry him. There is nothing that he is more sensitive about than the Fund question and I doubt whether he will bless Rothermere for rushing to his aid.'[122] From the standpoint of an 'Independent' Liberal, this was fair comment. However, Conservatives cannot have been too happy at the resulting slanging match between the two newspapers.[123] For the *Daily Mail* continued to disparage the *Post*'s attacks as hypocritical because, it alleged, the Conservatives themselves did not have 'clean hands'. Why, asked the *Mail*, did the Conservative Party not publish its own financial accounts, so allowing members of the public to judge for themselves 'what equivalent in knighthoods, baronetcies, and peerages was given in return for these sums?'[124] On a more threatening note, the *Daily Mail* editorial of 15 August 1927 alleged that the late Lord Farquhar had 'often in his indiscreet old age . . . recounted to his friends the names of individuals for whom he procured titles, with the exact sums they paid'. In thus launching a counter-attack Rothermere may have been encouraged by Beaverbrook, who claimed to have telephoned him to offer congratulations on one of the *Mail*'s leaders: 'I told him that honours had been sold through Baldwin's administration and named to him certain recipients who had probably contributed to the Conservative fund. I hope he will make something of it.'[125]

Meanwhile, Conservatives close to Baldwin were viewing the whole wrangle with dismay. This is reflected in the letter which Davidson wrote to Irwin on 17 August:

During the last few weeks it has become clear that Rothermere is definitely backing Lloyd George. The reason of course is perfectly obvious. He wants troubled and somewhat muddy water to fish in, and the smooth and crystal stream of the Baldwin Government, in spite of a certain proportion of muddy water at the fringes where some of the old gang in and outside the Government operate, is no possible good to Rothermere, Lloyd George and Co. It would be most amusing to know whether Lloyd George has agreed to the same terms

---

[121] *Daily Mail*, 8 Aug. 1927.

[122] Phillipps to Gwynne, 12 Aug. 1927 (Gwynne papers, vol. 21).

[123] See the *Morning Post*'s ragging of the *Daily Mail* (11, 13 Aug. 1927).

[124] *Daily Mail*, 12 Aug. 1927.

[125] Beaverbrook to Lloyd George, 10 Aug. 1927 (Lloyd George papers, G/3/6/16). But Lloyd George suspected that Beaverbrook was somehow in league with the *Morning Post* and there was temporary ill-feeling between the two men (Frances Stevenson's diary, 18 Aug. 1927, in Taylor, A. J. P. (ed.), *Lloyd George: A Diary by Frances Stevenson* (London, 1971), p. 251.

Aftermath

Bonar rejected in '23 in return for Rothermere's support in his newspaper. Nearer the election it may be necessary to tell the truth but not yet . . . [126]

What loyal Conservatives *could* do was to attempt to show Rothermere up as a mere client of Lloyd George. The *Morning Post* itself followed this ploy when on 13 August it referred dismissively to the *Mail* as 'a Lloyd Georgian organ, just as effectively as the "Daily Chronicle" itself'.[127] Marlowe also favoured this line of attack, telling Davidson in September that the Prime Minister should publicly challenge Rothermere and ask him 'where he stands and declare who is his master, Beaverbrook or Ll.G. . . . R[othermere] will no doubt fall for it, and then the P.M. can say, "oh no, I don't believe the man who bartered his papers for an earldom etc, can be pure of heart, etc." R. is a coward and won't sue for libel.'[128] Without going quite that far, Baldwin did indeed act in the general spirit of this advice, after his leadership had once more been brutally assailed in the *Daily Mail*. Addressing the Cardiff meeting of the National Union in October, he asked Rothermere to say where his party allegiances lay. In reply the press lord described himself as an 'independent'; 'after years of experience', he disingenuously remarked, 'I am convinced that the less politicians see of newspaper people and the less newspaper people see of politicians the better.'[129]

Well pleased with the furore it had provoked, the *Morning Post* went on in November to publish a series of articles on the Lloyd George Fund, which was later issued as a pamphlet entitled *Lloyd George and His Millions*. The issue also came up for debate in Parliament. On 10 November the Labour backbencher, Ernest Thurtle, asked the Prime Minister whether he had read the allegations in the *Daily Mail* that honours were still being sold by his own Administration, and whether he intended to instigate an enquiry.[130] When Baldwin brushed aside the request, Thurtle raised the issue again in a debate on the Adjournment of the House on 14 November. Several members of the Labour Party, smarting from the recent enactment of the Trade Union Act, which had substituted 'contracting in' for 'contracting out', took this opportunity of sneering at Conservative fund-raising methods.[131] The Government, of course, insisted that the *Mail*'s story was 'completely false from beginning to end'.[132]

The debate petered out without a division. But the *Morning Post* articles and Rothermere's reply to them had probably done something

[126] Davidson to Irwin, 17 Aug. 1927 (Davidson papers).
[127] *Morning Post*, 13 Aug. 1927.
[128] Davidson's Note of 24 Sept. 1927 (Davidson papers).
[129] See newspaper cuttings in Baldwin papers, vol. 56.
[130] *Parl. Deb.*, 5th ser., ccx. 355–6 (10 Nov. 1927).
[131] Ibid. 785–94 (14 Nov. 1927).
[132] Ibid. 788 (Col. Gibbs, Treasurer of the Household, speaking on behalf of the Government).

to unsettle certain sections of the Conservative Party. One MP, for example, complained in this debate that he and his friends were being faced with critical questions from their constituents on the subject of honours trafficking and were thus 'being made the scapegoats for the actions of the right hon. Gentleman the member for Carnarvon Boroughs'.[133] There is a certain humour in the situation when one realizes that the Conservative making this point was Lord Apsley, the heir to the Bathurst peerage and a director of the *Morning Post*, which his mother had once owned!

If ordinary voters were indeed confused about the difference between Conservative finances and the Lloyd George Fund, their confusion could only have increased after Lloyd George had released a statement to the press on 3 December. In this statement he categorically reaffirmed that his Fund had been assembled in the same way as other party funds and that during the Coalition years he had drawn up the Honours Lists in conjunction with the Conservative Leader, that is to say, firstly with Bonar Law and then with Austen Chamberlain. This claim stung Chamberlain into writing a private letter to Lloyd George, in which he strongly objected to the use that had been made of his name and gave 'a friendly warning not to force me to take a part in a controversy from which I should wish to continue to hold aloof'.[134] Lloyd George immediately went on to the counter-attack. He resented, Chamberlain was told, being made responsible for some of the honours that had actually been conferred at the instigation of Leslie Wilson, the Conservative Whip. Two of Wilson's nominees, he claimed, had filled him at the time with 'grave misgivings'. 'Subsequently it came to my knowledge that substantial cheques passed in respect of both these cases to the managers of your party fund.' The *Morning Post*, Lloyd George continued, could be ignored.

[But] it is another matter when Ministers take a hand in circulating this slander. That is why I have come to the conclusion that if Joynson-Hicks, Douglas Hogg, J. C. Davidson and others persist in their charges I shall be driven in self-defence to mention these and other cases publicly. . . . Since you have sent me a 'friendly warning' perhaps you will accept this warning in the same spirit. I have just had enough of it. . . . [135]

In the face of this explosion, Austen Chamberlain, it is interesting to note, wrote a somewhat ingratiating letter to the Liberal Leader which exhibited a clear anxiety to drop the whole Honours issue; he expressed particular regret that the phrase 'friendly warning' should have been construed as a threat.[136]

Lloyd George also employed more blatant methods of intimidation.

---

[133] Ibid. 794.
[134] Austen Chamberlain to Lloyd George, 3 Dec. 1927 (Lloyd George papers, G/4/3/4).
[135] Lloyd George to Austen Chamberlain (draft?), 5 Dec. 1927 (ibid., G/4/3/5).
[136] Austen Chamberlain to Lloyd George, 15 Dec. 1927 (ibid. G/4/3/7).

Using first Birkenhead and then Guest as intermediaries, he threatened to go to the House and read the names of Conservatives to whom he had sold honours and the amounts paid and then to announce what honours had been sold by the present Government. Birkenhead favoured a deal, but an angry Churchill 'marched up and down the room . . . very excited and saying "The Little Devil! I know enough about him to hang him!"' Baldwin shared Churchill's view that Lloyd George was bluffing and ignored the approach.[137]

The Second Baldwin Administration: Image and Reality

Was there, then, no truth in Lloyd George's charge—one which the *Daily Mail* had earlier raised—that the Baldwin Government was continuing the practice of honours trafficking? Davidson later denied all such accusations, devoting many pages of his Memoirs to a description of how he had destroyed Maundy Gregory by infiltrating a 'spy' into his organization and then ensuring that none of Gregory's clients ever found their way on to Baldwin's Honours Lists.[138] There is indeed, corroborative evidence that the Conservative Ministry wished to distance itself from the Lloyd George regime. Thus, when George Lloyd, the Governor of Bombay, pressed for a peerage, the Indian Secretary explained that the prevailing view in the Cabinet was that 'honours have been cheapened by too lavish a distribution in the past', and that the number of awards was being deliberately restricted.[139] In fact, during the course of his second Administration Baldwin created only forty-two new peeers (which averages out at nine a year, compared with Lloyd George's sixteen), and none of these creations stirred any serious controversy. Moreover, the conventionally-minded would have been reassured by the fact that, by comparison with what happened during the Coalition years, few men were elevated to the peerage who did not possess the 'appropriate' educational qualifications and career backgrounds.

Perhaps the existence of the Honours Scrutinizing Committee made a small contribution to this state of affairs. On the other hand, among a number of genuinely self-made men granted peerages by the Conservatives, it is interesting to observe the name of William Berry, who became Lord Camrose in 1929. Berry had by this time abandoned his former hostility to Baldwin and was now one of his most enthusiastic admirers.[140] Davidson, for his part, trusted Berry, helped him in his

---

[137] Neville Chamberlain's diary, 4 Dec. 1927.

[138] James (ed.), *Memoirs of a Conservative*, p. 280.

[139] Peel to Reading, 3 Oct. 1923; also Peel to Reading, 26 Sept. 1923 (Reading papers, EUR E238/6 fos. 144, 152). I am grateful to my colleague, Dr John Charmley, for drawing my attention to these letters.

[140] Compare the editorial comment on Baldwin in the *Sunday Times* in 1924 and in 1927: 'A conspicuously honest man, he would probably be the first to agree that, as the

commercial rivalry with Rothermere, and almost certainly interceded with the Prime Minister to secure him the barony he coveted.[141] Thus, for all its professions of concern about the political influence of the syndicated press, the Conservative leadership clearly appreciated the importance of securing the goodwill of powerful proprietors like the Berrys, with their weekly circulation of 34,000,000, and, when this could be achieved with safety and advantage to themselves, they were prepared to reward assistance from such men in the customary way.

Moreover, as several historians have argued, it seems unlikely that fund-raising methods changed that abruptly after 1922.[142] Interestingly, Ramsay MacDonald wrote to Salisbury in July 1925 expressing disquiet 'about the way that public honours are being given, and my brief experience in office led me to the conclusion that the old methods have not been abandoned'.[143] It may also be significant that Maundy Gregory was able to maintain his expensive establishment throughout the decade. Of course, as Gregory's biographer points out, the Honours (Prevention of Abuses) Act of 1925 may actually have helped swindlers like Gregory, since the tout could now, if he chose, pocket the entire sum he received from a client virtually safe from exposure by the would-be honours purchaser.[144] Gregory, it seems, was also doing a lucrative trade in the sale of foreign titles, while he probably supplemented his earnings by the proceeds of blackmail.[145]

But there is in any case clear evidence that honours touts, who may or may not have been Gregory's agents, were still plying their customary trade in the late 1920s. For example, in April 1925 (admittedly, a few months before the enactment of the Honours (Prevention of Abuses) Act), Gwynne heard from an old friend who had recently been approached by a man called Carew offering to procure him an honour. 'Under the present regime such a thing was impossible', Gwynne replied. The incriminating correspondence was then forwarded to Baldwin's Secretary, Captain Waterhouse, with whom the tout, on his own initiative, shortly afterwards arranged an interview. Waterhouse had by now come across other attempts at honours broking.[146] Was all this information duly passed on to Conservative Central Office?

Leader of the Unionist Party and as Prime Minister, he found himself in a position too big for him' (27 Jan. 1924); but on 14 Aug. 1927 he was being depicted as an English batsman who could be relied upon to keep a straight bat and hit the ball squarely with the middle of it.

[141] James (ed.), *Memoirs of a Conservative*, pp. 294–7.
[142] Ramsden, *Age of Balfour and Baldwin*, pp. 223–4; Pinto-Duschinsky, *British Political Finance*, pp. 110–11.
[143] MacDonald to Salisbury, 28 July 1925 (Hatfield, Fourth Marquess of Salisbury papers, S(4) 232, fo. 56).
[144] Cullen, *Maundy Gregory*, p. 126.   [145] Ibid. 136, 156.
[146] Gwynne to Waterhouse, 30 Apr. 1925; Waterhouse to Gwynne, 29 Apr. 1925 (Gwynne papers, vol. 18).

When Davidson became Party Chairman in 1926, he quickly proved his prowess as a fund-raiser, attracting, by his own admission, over a million pounds in three years.[147] However, the way in which he achieved this was probably not quite so open and above-board as he wanted the readers of his Memoirs to believe. After all, Davidson's stratagem for putting Gregory out of business necessarily involved him in co-operating to some extent with the man he was working to destroy, at least in the short run. Moreover, when Gregory was eventually apprehended and prosecuted under the 1925 legislation for trying to sell an honour to a naval officer, Conservative Central Office persuaded Gregory to plead guilty and say as little as possible in court. Then, after serving a short prison sentence, Gregory was paid out of a 'hush fund' to go into exile in France and to stay there.[148] According to Ramsay MacDonald's diary, Baldwin feared that the presence of Maundy Gregory in the country might lead to unsavoury revelations that would poison public life. He also informed the dismayed MacDonald that some leading Labour politicians—the names of Clynes and Henderson were mentioned—may have been compromised by Gregory and his organization.[149]

Nor was Davidson himself averse to trading honours for contributions to party funds and for other party services. The Davidson Papers make it quite clear, for example, that the wealthy Indian merchant, A. J. David, purchased his baronetcy for £30,000 after propositioning the Party Chairman in the most blatant way.[150] Further honours were given to wealthy businessmen who had put up money for the Conservative College at Ashridge.[151] These incidents have led John Ramsden to the conclusion that 'apart from tidying up the worst excesses of the Lloyd George era, Davidson did not materially alter his party's attitude to honours.'[152]

But, then, it must be remembered that even vociferous Conservative critics of 'Coalition corruption' were not (the *Morning Post* excepted) proposing *fundamental* changes in the methods by which their party was funded. When the 1925 Bill came up for debate in the Commons, for example, the Attorney-General, Douglas Hogg, a self-professed crusader for 'purity' in public life, wrote anxiously to Salisbury about the possibility that certain Liberal and Labour MPs might press for the publication of the names of those who had subscribed to party funds; he also feared that Labour might denounce the Honours System

---

[147] Ramsden, *Age of Balfour and Baldwin*, p. 219.
[148] Cullen, *Gregory*, Chs. 2–3; Pinto-Duschinsky, *British Political Finance*, pp. 106–7 and 107 n. 59.
[149] MacDonald's diary, 13 Dec. 1933, in Marquand, D., *Ramsay MacDonald* (London, 1977), p. 746.
[150] Material in Davidson papers. David's sponsor was Oliver Locker-Lampson!
[151] Ramsden, *Age of Balfour and Baldwin*, p. 224.
[152] Ibid.

itself.[153] Fortunately for the Baldwin Government, Labour did not exploit its opportunity. Was MacDonald still suffering from embarrassment over his part in the ludicrous McVitie & Price affair?[154] As for the backbenchers, they too failed to rise to the occasion. Loud-mouthed ranting against all hereditary honours such as came from the Labour MP, J. Jones, could easily be shrugged to one side by the leaders of the traditional parties.[155] What worried the Conservative Cabinet and Central Office was the possibility of a campaign being launched for the audit of all party accounts. And this, in the event, never materialized.

In short, though the Conservative Ministries of the 1920s prudently avoided the 'excesses' which had brought such opprobrium on the post-war Coalition, one should view with some scepticism the claim that Baldwin and his colleagues were living on a much higher plane than their predecessors. If, as indeed happened, anxieties about corruption abated somewhat during the Baldwin Era, this was because wider changes were taking place in public life which made the scandalmongering and political moralizing described in this book seem increasingly unimportant and peripheral.

Epilogue

The 1929 Election did not provide Lloyd George with the electoral breakthrough for which he had so determinedly worked. Nevertheless, it left the Liberal Party under his leadership holding the balance of seats in the Commons and so with the power, theoretically at least, to make and unmake Ministries. With Baldwin's stock at a very low ebb, many Conservative officials and loyalists were understandably nervous that the Welshman might exploit the situation so as to create another 'centre' grouping. Hence, when Lloyd George, Churchill, Birkenhead and the Press Lords, as well as the Diehards, attacked the Irwin Declaration on the future of India, which Baldwin broadly endorsed, Davidson jumped to the conclusion that this was some sort of plot to destroy Baldwin's Leadership.[156] In fact, it was nothing of the kind. Nor was there now any great likelihood of Lloyd George featuring as the leader of a new anti-Socialist Coalition.[157]

But Conservative loyalists really did have legitimate cause for

[153] Hogg to Salisbury, 27 July 1925 (Salisbury papers, S(4) 232, fo. 54).
[154] See Appendix II.
[155] *Parl. Deb.*, 5th ser., clxxxvii. 1317–19 (4 Aug. 1925). Typical of Jones's oratory is the following: 'There is only one kind of blood worth having—clean blood, blood of the common people, the people who have made all the Governments and done all the work.' The only serious objections to the Honours (Prevention of Abuses) Bill were that the penalties (a maximum of two years' imprisonment or a fine of £500 or both) were too light, and that the Bill was unenforceable (ibid. clxxxvi. 2618–19; 24 July 1925).
[156] Davidson to Irwin, 9 Nov. 1929 (Davidson papers).
[157] Campbell, *Smith*, pp. 822–3; Campbell, *Goat In Wilderness*, p. 255.

anxiety when Rothermere, whose papers were fiercely opposed to Irwin's Indian policy, linked up informally with Beaverbrook, who in October 1929 had flamboyantly launched a 'Crusade' for Empire Free Trade. This strong 'Imperial' line won the Press Lords support in sections of the Conservative Party which had previously viewed them with distaste. For example, Salisbury joined in the attack on Baldwin over India, while many of the Diehards, swallowing their dislike of the syndicated press, now aligned themselves with Beaverbrook and Rothermere.

Baldwin's response was subtle. Instead of attempting to separate the more amenable Beaverbrook, with whom a deal was clearly feasible, from the totally irreconcilable Rothermere, he spurned Beaverbrook's advances and publicly presented the two newspaper proprietors as intimate friends and allies.[158] Then, in the famous St George's By-Election of March 1931, both Baldwin and the official Conservative candidate, Duff Cooper, ignored the issues which their opponents had raised, centering the contest instead on whether the syndicated press had the right to 'dictate' terms to a political party. This was a constitutional issue not unlike the late General Strike, or so Baldwin affected to believe.[159] Here Rothermere had played into his hands by sending the Conservative Leader a letter in 1930 in which he made his support conditional upon receiving 'complete guarantees' about the policy which the Party would pursue when in office and upon his being 'acquainted with the names of at least eight, or ten, of [Baldwin's] most prominent colleagues in the next Ministry'.[160] Baldwin read this letter out to a Party meeting in June 1930 so as to dramatize what he saw as a sinister attempt by the press 'to impose Ministers on the Crown'. 'A more preposterous and insolent demand was never made on the Leader of any political party', he said.[161] This proved to be a dress-rehearsal for Baldwin's later eve of poll speech at St George's when he lashed out at Rothermere—but also, by implication, at Beaverbrook—for seeking 'power without responsibility—the prerogative of the harlot throughout the ages'.[162]

Baldwin's identification of his personal cause with that of 'decency' and constitutional rectitude probably paid electoral dividends. One Labour MP resident in the St George's constituency publicly announced his intention of voting for Duff Cooper: 'the return of your opponent would be a calamity from the point of view of clean fighting in

---

[158] See Gwynne's comment on this in his letter to Beaverbrook, 22 Feb. 1930, cited in Koss, *Rise and Fall*, ii. 500.

[159] Peele, G., 'St George's and the Empire Crusade', in Cook, C., and Ramsden, J. (eds.), *By-Elections in British Politics* (London, 1973), p. 95. 'I accept the challenge as I accepted the challenge of the TUC. . . . When I fight I go on to the end, as I did in 1926' (*The Times*, 25 June 1930).

[160] Middlemas and Barnes, *Baldwin*, pp. 573–4.

[161] *The Times*, 25 June 1930.   [162] Middlemas and Barnes, *Baldwin*, p. 600.

politics', he said.[163] And when news came through that Petter, the Press Lords' candidate, had been defeated, Duff Cooper was inundated with congratulations. 'I am delighted that you have triumphed over those two unclean newspaper men', wrote H. A. L. Fisher.[164] Earlier, in his speech of June 1930, Baldwin, who privately suspected that Lloyd George must somehow be involved in the Press Lords' campaign,[165] had also slyly conveyed the impression that there was actually some affinity between the two 'insolent plutocrats', as he dubbed them, and the Liberal Leader and his tainted Fund: 'We are told that unless we make peace with these noblemen', he told his audience, 'candidates are to be run all over the country. The Lloyd George candidates at the last election smelt; these will stink.'[166] The link between Lloyd George's followers and the United Empire Party, in Baldwin's mind, was that both were engaged in a corrupt attempt to convert wealth into political authority.

Of course, in practice the relationship between politicians and the press was far more complex than a reading of Baldwin's moralistic speeches would suggest. Still less was the St George's By-Election a clear-cut fight between 'decency' and 'indecency'. Petter, ironically, had earlier stood as a candidate for Page Croft's National Party, with its strong commitment to political purity, while Duff Cooper was somewhat miscast as the knight in shining armour.[167] Nevertheless, Baldwin's intervention in the by-election gave it a symbolic significance it might otherwise have lacked, and the outcome had an important influence on the future of British Conservatism.[168]

In other respects, however, the events in St George's were an irrelevance. In August 1931 the mounting economic crisis brought down the minority Labour Government and forced a startled Baldwin into participating in a new kind of National Government designed to stave off a total collapse of the capitalist order. In this crisis-laden atmosphere the brand of political moralism which Baldwin had so effectively deployed in his own defence in 1930 and 1931 could only have a subordinate place.

[163] Peele, 'St George's and the Empire Crusade', p. 101.

[164] H. A. L. Fisher to Duff Cooper, 21 Mar. 1931 (Duff Cooper papers, currently in the hands of his biographer, Dr John Charmley. Reproduced by kind permission of Sir Rupert Hart-Davis). Fisher's comment is perhaps surprising, coming from a Coalition Liberal whose pride in his association with Lloyd George's post-war Government reminded Lionel Robbins of 'a good man who had unwittingly entered a brothel—*and rather enjoyed it*' (Morgan, *Consensus and Disunity*, p. 2). See also Charmley, J., *Duff Cooper: The Authorized Biography* (London, 1986), Ch. 9.

[165] See Baldwin's letter to John Buchan, cited in Middlemas and Barnes, *Baldwin*, p. 558.

[166] Ibid. 573.

[167] Charmley, *Duff Cooper*, Ch. 9; Taylor, *Beaverbrook*, p. 304. Taylor notes that Duff Cooper himself had actually congratulated Beaverbrook over the South Paddington By-Election. See also Peel, 'St George's and the Empire Crusade', p. 96.

[168] Ibid. 107. See also Ramsden, *Age of Balfour and Baldwin*, p. 314.

Conclusion

THIS study ends as it began, with a City scandal involving a crooked company promoter. In September 1929 the companies controlled by the financier, Clarence Hatry, suddenly collapsed; subsequent investigations revealed that Hatry had issued forged scrip certificates, and he and several of his associates received heavy prison sentences.[1] 'There have been rogues in finance before', thundered *The Times*, 'but downright fraud and treason like this in the very citadel have not been known. . . . A signalman has deliberately tampered with the signals. A rogue has traded upon the common expectation of integrity in finance.'[2] There are certain parellels between these events and the Hooley Affair of thirty years earlier: for example, the involvement of aristocrats like the luckless Marquess of Winchester, the chairman of the Hatry group of companies.[3] But here the parallel ends. For the Hatry collapse, followed a month later by the far more serious New York Stock Exchange Crash, seemed to be part and parcel of a wider crisis of international capitalism which climaxed in Britain with the flight of sterling from London and the establishment of the National Government in August 1931. With the electoral triumph of the Conservatives in the 1931 General Election, and the slow but gradual recovery of the economy, this sense of crisis lifted. But what remained was a class-based political system polarized between a radicalized Labour Movement and a Conservative Party which represented the interests of capitalism more directly than it had ever done before. And this had consequences for the politics of scandalmongering.

The challenge of Labour was particularly important in this respect. Socialists and trade unionists, as we have seen, had never been very interested in attacks on 'corruption'.[4] It had taken a threat to the political levy, for example, to goad the Parliamentary Labour Party into mounting an assault on honours trafficking in the summer of 1922. Nor were Socialists and politically conscious working men much concerned with the peccadilloes of individuals, be they businessmen or politicians, preferring to attack what they saw as a 'rotten' economic

---

[1] Fanning, D., 'Charles Clarence Hatry', *DBB*, iii (1985), 110–11. Fanning argues that Hatry made an inaccurate confession to the DPP when he took responsibility for the issue of the forged scrip. For an amusing story of Hatry's attempts during the Coalition years to acquire a baronetcy, see Lyon, L., *By the Waters of Babylon*, pp. 209–11.

[2] *The Times*, 25 Jan. 1930.

[3] See Marquess of Winchester, *Statesmen, Financiers and Felons* (London, n.d.), Ch. 12.

[4] In Feb. 1914 an angry Lord Robert Cecil burst out: 'Nothing is more discreditable . . . to the Labour party than the fact that during the whole of their existence they have not, so far as I can recollect, taken a single action in order to promote purity in public life' (*Parl. Deb.*, 5th ser., lviii. 1269 [19 Feb. 1914]). Cecil was mainly thinking here of Labour's refusal to back him over Marconi.

and political system: hence their concentration on 'profiteering' during the First World War. Earlier, while the politicians from the established parties had argued over the rights and wrongs of Marconi, the ILP, as we have seen, had instead set out to expose the interests which sustained the 'Armaments Ring', which Socialists believed to be busily fomenting a European war. To Socialists 'corruption' was an endemic part of capitalism.[5] But, conversely, to many businessmen 'corruption' was integral to socialistic experiments, like 'Poplarism'.[6] And as politics settled down into a class mould in the 1920s, the debate about corruption increasingly came to be seen in these class terms.

The change of perspective is evident from the events of July 1926. In that month the PLP called for an enquiry into the position of Ministers of the Crown associated with companies in contractual relationship with the Government of which they were members.[7] The Minister being attacked here was Neville Chamberlain, who had retained his directorship of Hoskins when he entered the Cabinet. True, Hoskins was a private, not a public, company, which exempted it from the ministerial ban on company directorships laid down by Campbell-Bannerman in 1906. Chamberlain had also cleared his position with the various Prime Ministers under whom he had served, including the current Premier, Baldwin. On the other hand, both Hoskins and Elliott's, a public company in which Chamberlain was a major shareholder, had been allotted Admiralty contracts in 1925 and 1926. Although, as the Attorney-General said in reply to the Labour Party critics, only 2.08 per cent of Hoskins's contracts were accounted for in this way,[8] Chamberlain's position certainly laid him open to criticism. On one level, then, the parliamentary debate of 12 July 1926 afforded an opportunity for raising a whole series of interesting issues concerning where best to draw the dividing line between private interests and public duty. Thus Sir John Simon, in a thoughtful speech, pointed out that private companies had only been given legal recognition in the Companies Act of 1907, over a year *after* Campbell-Bannerman had delivered his historic ruling, and firms like Hoskins were not small partnerships of the kind that the former Liberal Leader presumably had in mind when discussing permissible 'exemptions'.[9] Indeed, as several Labour MPs argued, the situation of the private company was 'illogical and anomalous' and badly needed clearing up.[10]

[5] A similar view was taken by early 20th-century French Socialists. See Vèrdes-Leroux, J., *Scandale financier et antisémitisme catholique: Le Krach de l'Union Générale* (Paris, 1969), pp. 205–6.
[6] See Ryan, P. A., ' "Poplarism" 1894–1930', in Thane, P., (ed.), *The Origins of British Social Policy* (London, 1978), pp. 56–83.
[7] *Parl. Deb.*, 5th ser., cxcvii. 2258–80, 2277–81 (8 July 1926); ibid. cxcviii. 85–159 (12 July 1926).
[8] Ibid. 148–9. [9] Ibid. 128.
[10] Tom Johnston, for example, argued that the prohibition on ministerial directorships should logically apply to private, rather than public companies, since directors in private

But of course, the 1926 debate was not really 'about' such issues as these. Conducted against the backcloth of the recently concluded General Strike, Labour's attack on Neville Chamberlain originated in the latter's move against Labour-controlled Boards of Guardians who were giving generous help to the families of miners currently on strike. Shortly before the July debate Chamberlain had moved to put a stop to this 'abuse', as he saw it, by introducing the Board of Guardians (Default) Bill, and in the course of justifying this measure he had spoken of 'open and unabashed corruption'.[11] Furious at this 'class attack', the Labour MP, Tom Johnston, retaliated by raising the question of Chamberlain's relationship with Hoskins.[12] Meanwhile, *Lansbury's Labour Weekly* was keeping up a barrage of abuse against both Chamberlain and Baldwin, whose family firm, it alleged, was about to profit from the Government's recently introduced bill to increase the miners' maximum working week—a 'murder bill', Lansbury dubbed it.[13] The Conservative backbencher, Cadogan, was therefore surely right when he described the motion before the House as being inspired by 'the undying ambition to break down the capitalist system'.[14] And though there were obvious parallels with the famous Boer War contracting 'scandals' of 1900, to which many of the speakers referred, the political context had significantly changed. The July 1926 debate was, in essence, a minor skirmish in the class war. This is reflected in the Division Lists. The motion calling for an enquiry, which Arthur Henderson introduced, attracted no support outside Labour's ranks. Lloyd George, Joe Chamberlain's tormentor in December 1900, prudently absented himself, and the only Liberal MP who joined the debate, Simon, welcomed an enquiry to be carried out at some later date, but would not associate himself with what he saw as a discreditable attack on an individual.[15] As for Lord Hugh Cecil, the one-time custodian of 'delicacy' in public life, he it was who successfully moved the amendment castigating Labour's 'organised campaign of calumny and insinuation which ha[d] no justification in fact'.[16]

The politics of scandalmongering, as they had developed from the 1890s onwards, were thus rapidly becoming obsolete. In retrospect, such activities can be seen as belonging to that phase in the country's

companies were better placed to influence policy and contracts (ibid. 100). Thurtle made the same point (ibid. 114). See also Platt, 'Commercial and Industrial Interests', pp. 286–7. Eventually in 1939 Neville Chamberlain, now Prime Minister, was forced by parliamentary opinion to modify the 1906 ruling by agreeing that in future 'private companies' would apply only to 'concerns dealing wholly or mainly with family affairs or interests and not primarily engaged in trading' (ibid. 187–8).

[11] Feiling, K., *Life of Neville Chamberlain* (London, 1946), pp. 139–40.
[12] *Parl. Deb.*, 5th ser., cxcvii. 2258 (8 July 1926).
[13] Ibid. cxcviii. 126 (Lansbury); ibid. 146–7 (Hogg) (12 July 1926).
[14] Ibid. 135.
[15] Ibid. 130–1.
[16] Cecil's amendment was carried by 341 votes to 98.

life when politics were in the process of democratization but had not yet developed a class base.[17] In this environment Liberals and Conservatives were tempted to bid against one another for the support of an enlarged electorate by employing various demagogic weapons, including attacks on the integrity of their opponents both collectively and as individuals. But the growth of Labour eventually caused Liberals and Conservatives to close ranks in defence of the established order, and once this started to happen, as it did in the 1920s, the now 'traditional' methods of political invective lost their relevance.[18]

Even before the emergence of Labour, political mud-slinging had presented dangers, since abuse of opponents could easily rebound on its instigators, something which Front Bench politicians were quicker to appreciate than backbench MPs and political journalists. For attempts to probe into such 'scandals' as honours trafficking invited counter-exposure, which in turn threatened to bring into discredit the entire party system of government to which nearly all Liberals and Conservatives felt a strong commitment.

Potentially damaging though the politics of scandalmongering were to *both* the party political machines, it was the Liberal Party which undoubtedly suffered the greater damage. In part, this was an 'accidental' by-product of Lloyd George's domination of Liberal politics throughout the period under examination. One is not denying Lloyd George's immense achievements as a social reformer and as a war leader when one draws attention to the more sinister side of this complex and baffling personality, which included a cynical attitude towards matters of money—a trait which led, for example, to episodes like the 'disappearance' of the £20,000 which the American industrialist, Solomon Guggenheim, had intended Lloyd George to donate to a British charity during the Great War.[19] Contemporaries were sensitive to the moral atmosphere in which Lloyd George and his retinue did their wheeling and dealing, even if they seldom had the detailed evidence to substantiate their suspicions, and Liberalism undoubtedly suffered damage in the process.

But one can easily exaggerate Lloyd George's personal responsibility for this state of affairs. Equally important was the high-minded, even priggish, tone of voice in which many Liberal activists, notably the

---

[17] This period closely coincides with what Pinto-Duschinsky has called 'the Plutocratic Era' (Pinto-Duschinsky, *British Political Finance*, Ch. 2).

[18] I am not, of course, arguing that corruption was peculiarly a feature of the early 20th century, nor even that issues that agitated public opinion during these years, like honours trafficking, have not surfaced, in slightly different ways, in more recent years (see e.g. De-La-Noy, M., *The Honours System* (London, 1985), Walker, J., *The Queen Has Been Pleased* (London, 1986)).

[19] See John Grigg's article in the *Sunday Telegraph*, 31 May 1981, entitled 'Lloyd George and the Missing £20,000'.

Nonconformists, conducted political debate. The Liberal Party gave off an atmosphere of moral earnestness and devotion to principle which its parliamentary leaders found difficult to match in their day-to-day activities. Little wonder if opponents chose to draw attention to the gap between the profession and the practice of Liberalism.

But there was another, more fundamental, reason why, almost to the end, scandal dogged the Liberal Party. Paradoxically, despite its early links with manufacturing industry and finance, Liberal politicians were slow to adapt to changes in the structure of the capitalist economy. By the late 1920s, for example, the Conservative Party Chairman, J. C. C. Davidson, had grasped the importance of building up a mass party of small subscribers on the one hand, and of appealing to the institutional interests of the big financial and industrial corporations on the other. Prior to the 1929 Election Baldwin was persuaded to attend carefully planned fund-raising meetings in the City, where his warnings of the dangers of Socialism brought in some sizeable corporate donations. The central election fund of that year contained contributions from many of the biggest business institutions in the country, among them General Electric Co., Watney's Brewery, and Vickers, as well as from employers' associations, like the West Yorkshire Coal-Owners.[20]

The Liberals, by contrast, never seem to have made a serious bid for corporate donations; instead both Asquithians and Lloyd George continued to rely on the support of very wealthy *individuals* sympathetic to their cause. It is obviously arguable—and many Socialists were making precisely this point—that there was enormous potentiality for corruption in the growing links between Conservatism and big business. But the highly *personalized* links between the Liberal leaders and their financial backers were more likely to spark off an eye-catching scandal: partly because of the direct association between politicians and businessmen which this style of politics involved, and also because many of the businessmen who gave the Liberals money had personal ambitions to promote as well as ideological and institutional interests to defend.

Finally, how does scandalmongering in British politics compare with similar events in other contemporary societies? As we observed in the Preface, the countries against which Britain was usually measured were the United States and France. Journalists like Maxse and Strachey were certainly well aware of the writings of the American 'muckrakers', by whom they may have been slightly influenced, and many Americans took an interest in British political developments. But whereas to Britons the United States represented a warning of

[20] Pinto-Duschinsky, *British Political Finance*, pp. 112–13; Ramsden, *Age of Balfour and Baldwin*, pp. 219–21.

what to avoid, to many American 'reformers' the United Kingdom offered a model to be copied. Thus the civil service reform movement in the United States between 1865 and the mid-1880s was in large part an attempt to replace the native 'spoils system' with selection procedures based on open competitive examinations, British-style.[21] Many Americans also admired British urban government, which they saw as being both efficient and 'pure'—hence the high-powered delegation which the National Civic Federation sent to the United Kingdom in 1906–7.[22]

But the American civil service reformers achieved only limited success; to this day patronage methods form the cement of party and lie at the very centre of political life at all levels.[23] Efforts to 'purify' American municipal life have also proved particularly difficult. Indeed, at the start of the century the condition of many American cities, dramatized by 'muckrakers' like Ida Tarbell and Lincoln Steffens, aroused horror and dismay on both sides of the Atlantic.[24]

However, the very scale of the malpractices revealed by the 'muckrakers' stimulated more thoughtful Americans into attempts at *explaining* the role of political corruption in their country. Very important in this respect was Henry Jones Ford's 1904 review of Steffens's *The Shame of the Cities*. In it he advanced three suggestions as to why 'corruption' was seemingly so prevalent in the United States. First, he argued, it was a pragmatic way of concerting the activities of legally independent branches of government through an exchange of favours; in other words, Tammany and similar machines had come into existence in response to the separation of powers enshrined in the American Constitution. Second, much so-called corruption served as a way of assimilating parvenu groups into American society and politics—groups which, given the rigidity of the existing order, might otherwise have been dangerously alienated. As Ford put it, America's 'party feudalism' 'perform[ed] a valuable office by the way it establish[ed] connections of interest among the masses of the people'. And he went on to compare 'the disintegration of government through strife of classes and nationalities' in Europe with 'the strong tendency shown in this country towards national integration of all elements of the population'. Third, Ford questioned whether corruption was the unmitigated evil which most moralists supposed. 'Slackness and decay

---

[21] Both the Report of the Grant Commission into the Civil Service (1871) and Pendleton's Bill of 1880 took specific account of British administrative procedures (Hoogenboom, A., *Outlawing the Spoils: A History of the Civil Service Reform Movement 1865–1883* (Urbana, 1968), pp. 94, 200).

[22] Kellett, J. R., 'Municipal Socialism, Enterprise and Trading', *Urban History Yearbook*, 1978, p. 36.

[23] See Tolchin, M. and S., *To The Victor: Political Patronage From the Clubhouse to the White House* (New York, 1971).

[24] See Filler, L., *The Muckrakers* (Pennsylvania, new edn., 1976).

are more dangerous to a nation than corruption', he provocatively wrote.[25] All these ideas were to be refined and systematized by later generations of American sociologists and political scientists, whose theories have a considerable relevance to an understanding of British politics, as I will shortly show.

With France, 'the classic land of political scandal', as one historian has called it,[26] it is much easier to draw direct parallels. Indeed, many British scandals have the appearance of being somewhat feeble replays of earlier French ones. Thus the 1922 Honours Scandal in Britain bore a considerable resemblance to the 'Wilson Affair' of 1887, which saw the exposure of Daniel Wilson, President Grévy's son-in-law, who had been selling the Legion of Honour and committing other abuses from his room in the Élysée Palace.[27] One also catches faint echoes of the Panama Scandal[28] in the events surrounding the disgrace of Hooley and Whitaker Wright. Anglo-French comparisons are most readily applicable to the time of the Great War, when in both countries a search for scapegoats found outlet in an obsessions with traitors, who were assumed to be also engaged in corruption.

But the contrasts are as obvious as the superficial similarities. For a start, most of the French scandals took place earlier than their British counterparts. Was this because France had acquired universal manhood suffrage so much earlier than Britain, scandals needing a moralized mass electorate to achieve their full impact? There was also a difference in scale. It is arguable that Britain could do no more than produce small-scale scandals, while one of France's most notable contributions to Western Civilization was the '*Affaire*', a much more imposing phenomenon. The French '*Affaire*' was (and indeed, is) an elaborate national ritual, whose rhythms, conventions, and traditional symbolism have been subjected to analysis and aesthetic appraisal.[29]

In particular, French scandals have tended to be considerably more intense than British ones. In both the Wilson and Panama Affairs journalists, politicians, and businessmen hurled acrimonious accusations against one another. Although some of the customary restraints were breaking down, British political culture seems, by contrast, to be based on reticence and concealment. Compare, for example, the extremely reserved, nine-page document produced by the 1922 Honours Com-

---

[25] Ford, H. J., 'Municipal Corruption: A Comment on Lincoln Steffens', republished in Heidenheimer (ed.), *Political Corruption*, pp. 284–97.

[26] Williams, P. M., *Wars, Plots and Scandals in Post-War France* (Cambridge, 1970), p. 3.

[27] Dansette, A., *L'Affaire Wilson et la chute du Président Grévy* (Paris, 1936).

[28] The literature on the Panama Scandal is voluminous. But I have found particularly helpful Jean Bouvier's *Les Deux Scandales de Panama* (Paris?, 1964). See also Watson, D. R., *Georges Clemenceau: A Political Biography* (London, 1974), pp. 123–30.

[29] Williams, *Wars, Plots and Scandals . . .*, Ch. 1; Vèrdes-Leroux, *Scandale financier*, esp. pp. 194–200; Blocq-Mascart, M., *Du Scandale* (Paris, 1960).

mission with 'la boîte à ordures', as it was aptly named, which came
out of the Parliamentary Enquiry into the Wilson Affair, to say nothing
of the exposure of individuals in a series of court cases. Moreover, how
striking it is that whereas the French public were regaled with the
minutiae of the activities of French honours touts and their agents,
like 'la Limouzin' and 'la Ratazzi',[30] Maundy Gregory and his
associates were *not even summoned* before the 1922 Royal Commission,
and when Gregory, by a mishap, later landed up in court he was
prepared—albeit for a consideration—to seal his lips and after serving a
short prison sentence go into a discreet foreign exile. Note, too, how
differently the two affairs ended. Wilson and many of his associates and
agents were put on trial and sentenced to imprisonment (though most
had their sentences quashed or reduced on appeal),[31] whereas in Britain
the 'guilty parties' escaped scot-free, such was the anxiety to avoid a
public scandal.

What underlay these differences? France had much weaker libel laws
than Britain, which encouraged an often venal press to indulge
in a brand of vituperative and defamatory journalism; for example,
Drumont's anti-Semitic *La Libre Parole* played a crucial part in
unleashing the Panama Scandal. Interestingly, a number of the British
scandalmongers had a close knowledge of French political journalism,
by whose style and mannerisms they may have been affected. Maxse,
for one, enjoyed a close relationship over several decades with
Clemenceau and, along with other members of his family, paid regular
visits to Paris. As for Hilaire Belloc, he had a French father, fulfilled his
year of service in the French Army, and, most significantly of all, was
an admirer of his one-time neighbour and family friend, Paul
Déroulède, the demagogue who had taken a leading role in the Panama
exposures.[32] Perhaps one reason why the *Eye-Witness* never acquired
the authority in British political circles to which its writers aspired
was precisely because it too much resembled a school of French
journalism with which most Englishmen felt uncomfortable.

Another difference between the two countries was that in France the
scandalmongers had to hand a mass of discontent and disillusionment
with the entire system of government that did not exist in Britain. The
'integrity' of nearly all the institutions of the State was in question
during the period of the Third Republic. Court procedures were lax and

[30] Dansette, *L'Affaire Wilson*, esp. pp. 92–103.
[31] The touts and Wilson himself were not prosecuted for trafficking in the Cross of
the Legion of Honour, the pretence being that this could not happen, but for swindling!
Later, in July 1889 a law was passed punishing under article 177 of the penal code 'toute
personne investie d'un mandat électif qui aura agrée des offres ou promesses, reçu des
dons ou présents pour faire obtenir ou tenter de fair obtenir des décorations, médailles,
distinctions, etc.' (ibid. 262). This measure, it will be observed, was much more
restricted than Britain's later Honours (Prevention of Abuses) Act.
[32] McCarthy, J. P., *Hilaire Belloc: Edwardian Radical* (Indianapolis, 1978), pp. 40–1.

the level of competence among judges extremely variable. It was suspected, with good reason, that both the legal system and the police could be deflected from the course of impartial justice by political interference, as happened, blatantly, during the protracted Stavisky Affair of the inter-war period.[33] No such widespread suspicion existed in Britain during the years under study. Thus the British scandals never seriously threatened to subvert the existing regime.

Political life in the Third Republic was conducted in an atmosphere of intense partisanship. Neither the Wilson nor the Panama Affair can be properly understood outside the context of the politics of parliamentary manœuvre at a time when 'boulangisme' constituted a real threat.[34] But though the French Chamber was organized around 'blocs', it lacked an organized party system on the British model. According to the Francophile J. E. C. Bodley, writing in 1898, this went far to explaining 'the indifference of an honest people to the political dishonesty of its representatives chosen by universal suffrage'. For it was the party system, Bodley argued, which supplied 'the great motive power to keep wavering members on the path of parliamentary integrity'.[35]

Of course, this claim is highly contentious; indeed, as we have seen, the British party system bred its own brand of corruption. Perhaps it would be more accurate to say that organized parties put a break on *scandalmongering*. The British Opposition Front Bench, willing and ready to assume office at short notice, did not usually take kindly to the activities of zealous supporters who threatened to stir up the kind of trouble that might weaken popular confidence in the existing dispensation. That is why exposures of corruption often came from mavericks like Belloc and Arnold White, on whom party loyalties sat lightly.

When Bodley emphasized the importance of a party system as an agency for purifying public life, his especial concern was to scotch the notion that there was something politically dangerous about republican institutions themselves. 'Laxity of morals, whether public or private, displayed by persons in authority' could be found, he said, in all regimes, though the impact on public opinion might be greatest under a Republic.[36] Accepting this as true, one might nevertheless wish to argue that in one important respect the institutions of the Third Republic did lead to political instability. In France the head of State was more directly involved in political controversy. In fact, as the Wilson Affair gathered momentum, it became obvious that many

[33] See the discussion in Martin, B. F., *The Hypocrisy of Justice in the Belle Epoque* (Baton Rouge, 1984), pp. 225–32.
[34] Dansette, *L'Affaire Wilson, passim*; Bouvier, *Deux Scandales de Panama*, pp. 140–1; Watson, *Clemenceau*, p. 125.
[35] Bodley, J. E. C., *France* (London, 1898; revised edn. 1899), pp. 510, 515.
[36] Ibid. 494–7.

deputies were out to destroy not only Wilson but also his father-in-law, President Grévy—which by the end of 1887 they had succeeded in doing. In Britain, by contrast, those who attacked trafficking in titles were able to pose, sincerely enough in most cases, as protectors of the Monarchy; far from being weakened, George V, if anything, emerged from the 1922 Honours Scandal with increased popular sympathy and respect. In short, the British Royal Family stood outside the arena of party strife, and this helped minimize the impact of political scandal. (Such a situation, though, required royalty to behave in an exemplary way—hence the anxiety caused for a time by the behaviour of the Prince of Wales and his entourage.)

Here we come to the heart of the difference between the British and French political systems. As Philip Williams has argued, in France the extreme Right had never accepted popular government and Republican institutions. But neither had it ever won sufficient electoral support for its views. Hence, 'in their search for weapons by which they [could] protect the political bastions they control[led] and undermine those of their opponents', the Far Right alternated (as they had done ever since the great Revolution) 'between the exploitation of scandal and the organisation of conspiracy'. 'Denounced by the Left for treason against a régime they regarded as illegitimate', the Right sought retaliation 'by accusing their enemies of treason to the nation itself'. Moreover, in France—and also, to some extent, in America—political power tra- ditionally flowed from the countryside, with its inherent distrust of a big city life seen as 'remote, cosmopolitan and suspect'. These anxieties were then systematically made use of by certain right-wing journalists and lawyers, 'nihilists rather than Conservatives by temperament', who specialized in mendacity and scandalmongering as a method of discrediting the Republic and its adherents.

This style of political combat, thinks Williams, grew more bitter and intense during the 1890s, when the French Right, 'violently nationalist, bitterly anti-parliamentary', came to terms with urbanization and popular government, and started to link itself 'with the new plebeian forms of revanchist Catholicism'.[37] In this new alignment anti- Semitism clearly acted as a unifying force. Significantly, Jews were often singled out for harassment during the classic French scandals— not just Dreyfus, but also, for example, the Panama Canal Company's banker, Jacques de Reinach, and his sinister agent, Cornelius Herz.

Inextricably linked with such agitations was what one historian has called 'nationalism as a hidden agenda'.[38] The humiliation of 1870–1, the loss of Alsace-Lorraine and the invasion of the 'patrie' in 1914 created an atmosphere of aggrieved nationalism, which readily encour- aged a search for 'traitors within'. The association in people's minds

[37] Williams, *Wars, Plots and Scandals . . .* , Ch. 1.
[38] Martin, *Hypocrisy of Justice*, p. 229.

between corruption and treason, which we have observed in British politics, was even more prominent in France. The paper which first broke the Wilson story by implicating an army officer employed in the War Ministry (General Caffarel) revealingly commented: 'qui trafique des décorations peut aussi bien trafiquer des secrets de la défence nationale'.[39] Apropos of Panama, Drumont castigated Reinach as 'voleur, agent allemand, et corrupteur d'hommes politiques'.[40] It seemed significant that Herz himself had been born in Germany, while his political ally, Clemenceau, momentarily discredited, found himself branded an English agent ('aoh yes!', opponents shouted at his meetings). A similar mixture of accusations faced Joseph Caillaux in 1914; the journalist Calmette accused him of 'treason' during the Agadir Crisis but also of having officially intervened in 1911 to protect a convicted swindler.[41] And in the depths of the Great War French patriots set out to expose the 'defeatists', like Bolo, as corrupt individuals who were acting, consciously or unconsciously, in Germany's interests.[42]

Some of this is familiar to us from our study of British politics in the same period. But in Britain political paranoia assumed a much milder form. This was undoubtedly because in France the very concept of patriotism was problematical, with the Right promoting a brand of nationalism which brought it into conflict with the existing institutions of the State. The nearest parallel to this in modern British history is the situation during the years 1909 to 1914; this was a period when different versions of what was 'constitutional' came into violent collision with one another and when, significantly, the air was also alive with rumours and suspicions.

But (if Ireland be left out of account) Britain during the last century has been a relatively integrated Nation-State, with a near-universal commitment to parliamentary institutions which even the extremists of the Radical Right have seldom challenged head-on. Moreover, whereas in France (and, in a different way, America, as in the case of the 'muckrakers') scandalmongering largely originated *outside* the political system, in Britain the situation was very different. Despite the doubts of many of the 'party Mandarins', accusations of corruption, impropriety, and 'indelicacy' were usually channelled through the political party machines. Indeed, those who posed as the custodians of political purity often came from families with a long tradition of service to the State, like the Cecils.

---

[39] Dansette, *L'Affaire Wilson*, p. 56.
[40] Bouvier, *Deux Scandales de Panama*, p. 142.
[41] Martin, *Hypocrisy of Justice*, p. 169.
[42] Slater C., *Defeatists and Their Enemies, Political Invective in France 1914–1918* (Oxford, 1981), esp. pp. 89–98.

Can one, despite these national differences, generalize about the nature and significance of political scandal? Engels was for a time much excited about the Panama Affair, and in a number of private letters expressed the hope that the discrediting of so many deputies heralded the collapse of the 'bourgeois Republic' itself. 'It is clear that this business brings the moment considerably nearer when our people will become the only possible leaders of the state in France', he told Sorge in December 1892.[43] But Engels's confidence soon evaporated, and few of his followers and disciples believed in the scandal as an instrument of historical change. Whether we are Marxists or not, we must surely sympathize with the French historian who has insisted: 'Les régimes et les systèmes économiques et politiques ne meurent jamais de leurs scandales. Ils meurent de leurs contradictions. C'est tout autre chose.'[44]

Indeed, in the case of France it can easily be demonstrated that scandal was a favourite device of political reaction; its practitioners invariably sought to establish a connection between demoralization and corruption on the one hand, and parliamentarism and democracy on the other, as well as whipping up demagogic anti-Semitism.[45]

Etymologically, too, the connotations of scandal are broadly conservative. The word literally means a 'snare', and originally it was used to denote an offence to spiritual life, an incitement to sin; only in the course of the eighteenth century did the word come to mean not just an occasion for sin, but the evil deed itself, particularly an evil deed exciting popular disapprobation and rumour. Arguably, some of the earlier connotations of the word have been carried forward into the modern language of scandalmongering. In particular, there is the assumption that highly placed individuals have a duty to maintain the dominant moral and political code, and if they are seen by the public not to be doing so, their conduct becomes 'a cause of offence' and a potential threat to the existing order.[46] Perhaps that explains the common linkage between the concepts of political corruption and treachery; both tend to be seen as instances of *subversion*.

The assault on corruption has often been conservative in yet another sense. For example, in the United States the early civil service reformers mainly came from socially prestigious East Coast backgrounds

---

[43] Engels to Sorge, 31 Dec. 1892, in Karl Marx and Friedrich Engels, *Correspondence 1846–1895* (London, 1934), pp. 501–4. Engels's correspondence on this same subject with Paul and Laura Lafargue is discussed in Vèrdes-Leroux, *Scandale financier*, pp. 184–8. Engels had been initially influenced by Marx's emphasis on the role of scandal in the destruction of the July Monarchy in his *The Class Struggles in France 1848–1850*.

[44] Bouvier, *Deux Scandales de Panama*, p. 204.

[45] Vèrdes-Leroux, *Scandale financier*, esp. pp. 10–13.

[46] In the following discussion I have been influenced by the reflections of Jeannine Vèrdes-Leroux (ibid. 178–94).

and many of their leaders only took up the attack on the spoils system when they realized that it was working to the benefit of 'parvenus'.[47] The same configuration of forces could be found in municipal politics. That is why some American academics have recently tended to focus their criticisms not on corrupt city bosses, but rather on the 'reformers', who are portrayed as 'aristocratic, condescending, rigid, and cold, in contrast to the warm, friendly machine'.[48]

In Britain a more complicated situation can be discerned. In this country there was a political tradition, going back to Bolingbroke, which linked the notion of 'patriotism' to the defence of 'Constitutional Liberty'. Politicians holding a wide variety of beliefs defined themselves as 'patriots' in this sense, including, as Hugh Cunningham has shown, many late eighteenth- and early nineteenth-century Radicals, including the Chartists. Here the characteristic stance was the defence of the traditional rights of freeborn Englishmen against usurpers and tyrants, who, it was claimed, were undermining the Constitution by their 'corruption'.

However, as Cunningham also shows, 'the vocabulary of patriotism' began to shift away from Radicalism in the middle years of the nineteenth century, and by the late 1870s it had become indelibly associated with the political Right.[49] But the same thing was perhaps occurring with the vocabulary of corruption-mongering. In the early twentieth century it was not the spiritual descendants of the Chartists but men like Sir Henry Page Croft who were raising the alarm about 'corruption' and the 'threat to the Constitution'! Moreover, though scandalmongering had by now come to involve a great deal of party 'tit-for-tat', those who most passionately and most consistently denounced the abuses of the age were men who tended to look back, in a mood of gentle nostalgia, to an earlier era. This is evidently true of the Cecil brothers and Loe Strachey, and it is true, to a lesser degree, of the Radical Right, whose attitudes, however, were more ambiguous.

Possibly, too, the very notion of corruption, like scandal, carries with it many conservative implications. Of course, those accused of corruption seldom recognize, still less admit, the validity of the charge. But what are the assumptions of those making the accusation? The *OED* gives eight different meanings of the word 'corruption', only one

---

[47] This is argued forcibly by Ari Hoogenboom in 'Spoilsmen and Reformers: Civil Service Reform and Public Morality', in Heidenheimer (ed.), *Political Corruption*, pp. 276–83.

[48] See Hoogenboom, *Outlawing the Spoils*, p. 73. Also, Abraham Eisenstadt's essay in Eisenstadt, A. S., Hoogenboom, A., and Trefousse, H. L. (eds.), *Before Watergate: Problems of Corruption in American Society* (New York, 1978), where the 'reformers' are superciliously dubbed 'the gentility'.

[49] Cunningham, H., 'The Language of Patriotism, 1750–1914', *History Workshop*, xii (1981).

of which is directly applicable to the political realm: 'perversion or destruction of integrity in the discharge of political duties by bribery or favour'. But there are two other definitions which seem relevant to the attitudes of the scandalmongers: 'the perversion of an institution, custom, etc. from its primitive purity', and, more generally, 'the perversion of anything from an original state of purity'. These latter meanings were clearly very much in the minds of late Victorian and Edwardian moralists anxious about the delinquencies of their day.

I am not suggesting that Maxse, Strachey, the Cecil brothers, and others believed in the existence of a 'golden age' when the British Constitution had existed in a state of pristine virtue (though that was precisely what 'radical patriots' of an earlier generation *had* believed). The fact that Maxse could dub Lloyd George 'the Welsh Walpole' is proof that he, for one, was no uncritical admirer of eighteenth-century parliamentary politics! But they all assumed that standards of political morality had been higher in the fairly recent past. The historical location of this era of purity tended, of course, to shift as the years passed by. In the 1890s nostalgic glances were cast back to the hey-day of Gladstone and Disraeli; yet after the Armistice the period around the turn of the century had taken on a rosy, retrospective glow. In any case, we are really concerned here, not with a precise historical epoch, but with a mental world. And it was by the standards of this imaginary world that Lloyd George, Beaverbrook, 'F. E.', and Rothermere were measured and found wanting.

There were small variations of interpretation. When Conservatives (with a capital 'c') thought about a purer past, they tended to conjure up an image of enlightened aristocratic rule—of a period when landed society had been purged of the contamination of 'Old Corruption' but had yet to face the dangers of association with the 'new plutocracy'. Liberals were more inclined to look back longingly to an era of 'political rationality', when responsible, moral citizens had calmly reached their verdict on public affairs undistracted by the vulgar clamour of the 'Yellow Press'. But nearly all the 'purity crusaders' were 'conservative', not in any party political sense, but because they had a deep-rooted prejudice against new social forces which threatened their familiar world.

But arguably the converse of this argument is that much of the behaviour that stood arraigned for corruption was innovative, even 'progressive'. That, indeed, is the claim of some American political scientists. We have already encountered Henry Jones Ford's three 'explanations' of corruption. The first, which has to do with the separation of powers under the American Constitution, is not applicable to the British case. But the other two are, especially in the form in which they have recently been developed. Samuel P. Huntington, for example, has claimed that 'corruption may . . . be functional to the maintenance of a political system in the same way that reform is.'[50] By that he and others mean that corruption can sometimes serve as an 'irregular' device for the assimilation into the political system of 'new' groups (American immigrants, for example).[51] This is a most interesting concept. Viewed from that perspective 'honours trafficking' might be understood as a beneficial mechanism for integrating emergent élites, like the 'Park Lane Millionaires', into the established ruling class, so stabilizing British society, at least in the long run. Whether such putative benefits outweighed the political and moral costs of the enterprise is quite another matter.

A more profitable line of enquiry is suggested by Huntington's hypothesis that 'corruption may be one way of surmounting traditional laws or bureaucratic regulations which hamper economic expansion.' The growth of the American economy in the 1870s and 1880s, according to this interpretation, was on balance *assisted* by the corrupt condition of the state legislatures and city councils of that period.[52] Now it is obviously beyond the scope of this book to test the validity of this claim. But even to mention it draws attention to a very significant issue. For it is hard to envisage any British person, in the early twentieth Century or subsequently, talking in this way. Even Lloyd George, in a frank, private justification of the sale of honours, only went so far as to present his conduct as a *pis aller*, a preferable alternative to the American situation, where parties were controlled by the big business interests—something which he professed to deplore.[53] Sociological theories of corruption, like the cheery defence by an early twentieth-century American machine politician of 'honest graft', jar on the sensibilities of most Britons.[54]

Underlying these differences is a sharp conflict of national values. Bryce and other foreign observers, confronted by American 'corruption', often lamented that the 'best men' in the United States did not enter politics. But of course, talent and energy in America usually made their way into business. This in turn had implications for the political system. As one American scholar has argued, 'American politics was part of the domain of American entrepreneurship'. Yet 'where social

[50] Huntington, Samuel P., *Political Order in Changing Societies* (New Haven, 1968), p. 64.
[51] This and other recent sociological theories of corruption are usefully summarized and discussed in Benson, G. C. S., *Political Corruption in America* (Lexington, Mass., 1978).
[52] Huntington, *Political Order*, pp. 68–9.
[53] See James (ed.), *Memoirs of a Conservative*, p. 279.
[54] 'Honest graft' was the famous phrase employed in 1905 by George Washington Plunkitt of Tammany Hall (cited in Hofstadter, R. (ed.), *Great Issues in American History From Reconstruction to the Present Day, 1864–1969* (New York, 1969 edn.), pp. 253–6). But a reaction against this approach has also occurred in America itself, George Benson protesting that social scientists have over-emphasized the psychological and sociological benefits of corruption while ignoring its administrative consequences (Benson, *Political Corruption in America, passim*).

purpose was largely identified with individual acquisition, who could say at what point political morality ended and political corruption began?'[55] In Britain, by contrast, the promotion of a dynamic economy has never enjoyed a very high priority, indeed has often been ignored altogether. The 'moralists' featured in this book exemplify this point. These men were not exactly 'anti-capitalist', but they tended to value business enterprise only to the extent that it fostered vital national and imperial interests (which was how most Tariff Reformers saw their creed), or else they relegated 'money-making' to a lower plane of activity from that occupied by politics.

Another difference between the two countries is that the American spoils system may, as Ernest Griffith has argued, have encouraged the belief that office-holding was a reward or even a right, not a privilege. Such a belief would have destroyed the 'aura' surrounding public office which was so marked a feature of British political culture.[56] Certainly, the British scandalmongers had a very highly developed sense of the State and a lofty conception of public duty, which, perhaps, left them little sympathy to spare for the 'entrepreneurial virtues'. That is probably why 'profiteering', for example, excited such widespread revulsion, and not just on the Left. It must also be significant that the figures in British public life who automatically came under suspicion were men like Lloyd George, Birkenhead, Beaverbrook, and Rothermere, who possessed the entrepreneurial qualities in abundance.

Meanwhile, the role of custodian of 'decency' devolved upon Baldwin, a man who seemed intent on putting as much distance as possible between his political career and his business background. Note his frequent public expressions of distaste for go-getting materialism and for the modern industrial system. The fact that Baldwin managed to dissipate much of the business fortune he had inherited could even be held to his credit, as something which proved his 'honesty'. It is possible to argue, then, that the preoccupation with 'standards of probity' in public life and the extreme sensivity to charges of 'corruption', characteristic of political controversy in the late nineteenth and early twentieth centuries were, at least in part, symptoms of what is sometimes called 'the British disease', by which is meant an ingrained national hostility to the very notion of an 'enterprise culture'.[57] In short, the quest for purity in British public life may well have had its admirable features; but, some might wonder, was it an entirely healthy phenomenon?

[55] Abraham Eisenstadt, in Eisenstadt, Hoogenboom, and Trefousse (eds.), *Before Watergate*, pp. 204, 210–11.
[56] Cited in Benson, *Political Corruption in America*, p. 218.
[57] This argument has been forcefully, if one-sidedly, argued in Wiener, M. J., *English Culture and the Decline of the Industrial Spirit 1850–1980* (Cambridge, 1981).

Appendix I: The 'Armaments Trust'

IN 1913, inspired by Karl Liebknecht's revelations in the Reichstag about the operation of the German armaments interests, a group of British anti-war Radicals and Socialists, with the ILP very much to the fore, began an agitation against the so-called 'merchants of death'. Their contention was that the process of 'trustification' had produced a vast international Armaments 'Ring', which held all the major European States in thrall. 'The Armaments Trust is the most terrible of all Capitalism's evils', said the ILP paper, *Labour Leader*; the British Government, it alleged, was 'far more under the control of the Armaments ring than under the control of the National Liberal Federation'.[1] 'It has friends at Court, its directors in the Press and Commons, supported by scores of shareholders', wrote Walton Newbold; 'its voice is heard in the Press, and its apostles in the pulpits of cathedrals and tabernacles.'[2]

Two influential books were spawned by the agitation: George Herbert Perris's *The War Traders: An Exposure* (1913) and J. T. Walton Newbold's *The War Trust Exposed (1916)*. Both set out to demonstrate that not only bishops and aristocrats but also prominent MPs and peers, some of them Liberals, had large shareholdings in the seven large armaments firms. They went on to offer this as a major explanation for why the Asquith Government had embarked upon an expensive and dangerous arms race with Germany.

This anti-war campaign reached its climax at just the time when the 'Liberal scandals' were breaking. But the two developments were largely separate. True, Snowden, who had some caustic things to say about Marconi, as we have seen, spearheaded the attack on the 'merchants of death' in the Commons. But in general the anti-war crusaders took little interest in such incidents. Perris, for example, said he wanted to draw his readers' interest to the fact that the armaments interests were 'part and parcel of the British governing system', saying that episodes like Netheravon and Marconi 'were small in comparison with the normal and accepted conditions of the trade in arms'.[3] Perris did, however, express the hope that Marconi might have 'set up new currents of political thought' which would possible result 'in a generally higher standard of public duty'; should this occur, the sinister influence of the merchants of death could the more easily be countered.[4] Newbold, on the other hand, bluntly rejected this approach and insisted on a straightforward socialist solution: 'only by nationalisation can we strike at the heart of the octupus.'[5]

In short, the 'exposure' of the Armaments Trust in 1913–14 had very little in common with the other 'scandals' of the period, and that is why I have omitted it from my book. Also, the subject has already been very competently described and analysed. See, in particular, Clive Trebilcock's sceptical assessment of the anti-war campaign in 'Radicalism and the Armaments Trust', in Morris, A. J. A. (ed.), *Edwardian Radicalism 1900–1914* (London,

[1] Cited in Morris, A. J. A., *Radicalism Against War*, p. 335; Morris, A. J. A. (ed.), *Edwardian Radicalism*, p. 187.
[2] Newbold, J. T. Walton, *The War Trust Exposed*, p. 13.
[3] Perris, G. H., *The War Traders*, pp. 20–1.
[4] Ibid. 11.
[5] Newbold, J. T. Walton, *The War Trust Exposed*, p. 18.

1974), pp. 180–201, and his article, 'Legends of the British Armaments Industry, 1890–1914: A Revision', *Journal of Contemporary History*, v (1970). See also Morris, A. J. A., *Radicalism Against War 1906–1914* (London, 1972), esp. pp. 325–39. On the background to this subject, see Marder, A. J., *The Anatomy of British Sea Power* (Hamden, Connecticut, 1940), Ch. 3. On the links between certain retired civil servants and the armaments firms in this period, see Doig, A., *Corruption and Misconduct in Contemporary British Politics* (London, 1984), pp. 84–5.

Appendix II: Ramsay MacDonald's Daimler

ON 11 September 1924 the *Daily Mail* carried a story by its City Editor which began: 'At a time when many investors are uncertain about the industrial outlook in this country, it is useful to have the guiding example of no less an authority than the Prime Minister himself. A comparatively recent £30,000 investment in his name appears on the files of the Registry of the Joint Stock Companies at Edinburgh', revealing him to be the owner of 30,000 Preference Shares in the biscuit firm of McVitie & Price Ltd. The significance of the *Daily Mail* story, although the City Editor did not himself mention the fact, was that the owner of McVitie's, Sir Alexander Grant, had received a baronetcy in the recent Birthday Honours List.

Two days later a flustered MacDonald, from his home in Lossiemouth, put out a statement to the correspondent of the Central News agency. In it he admitted that Sir Alexander Grant had given him a Daimler car and £30,000 of shares with which to endow it. It was an offer, said the Prime Minister, that he had initially been reluctant to accept: 'I did not fancy myself as the owner of a motor-car. It was against the simplicity of my habits.' He referred to his friendship with Sir Alexander, which went back to their boyhood days. 'I am sick at heart to have to talk of this', he went on, 'but I must protect my dear old friend in the enjoyment of the honour which the King so worthily bestowed upon him, and with which this act of personal kindness to myself had as much to do as the man in the moon.'[1]

As his biographer has argued, it was almost unbelievably foolish of MacDonald to have landed himself in this embarrassing situation a mere two years after the Lloyd George honours scandal.[2] But was his behaviour in any way corrupt? The Prime Minister's papers make clear that the transaction with Grant was broached in February 1924 and finalized in March, a month before the Prime Minister recommended him for a baronetcy.[3] Yet clearly MacDonald saw no connection between the two events; had he done so, he would have acted on his solicitor's advice and arranged matters so that the money from the shares was paid to him by trustees.[4] Moreover, the initiative in this affair almost certainly did not lie with MacDonald himself. His Private Secretary, Ronald Waterhouse, an official 'inherited' from Baldwin, later claimed that it was he, anxious about the dangers to his Chief's health and morale, who had first put the idea of equipping a motor car into Sir Alexander's head.[5] In any case, the latter was eminently worthy of his baronetcy, having regularly disbursed some £200,000 a year, perhaps more, to a number of public causes; particularly striking was his donation to the National Library of Scotland of the Advocates' Library.[6] Even Snowden, no lover of MacDonald, has written that it was within his personal knowledge that Grant's name had been on the waiting list for a baronetcy *before* Labour's advent to power.[7]

---

[1] *The Times*, 13 Sept. 1924.
[2] Marquand, D., *Ramsay MacDonald* (London, 1977), p. 359.
[3] Ibid. 357–9.   [4] Ibid. 361.
[5] Waterhouse, N., *Private and Official* (London, 1942), pp. 298–9.
[6] Ibid. 300.
[7] Snowden, Viscount Philip, *An Autobiography* (London, 1934), ii. 688. Writing in the

While generally exonerating MacDonald, his biographer, David Marquand, has nevertheless criticized him for a want of frankness, arguing that the preference shares would have brought in an income far greater than what was necessary to cover the running costs of a car, and the Prime Minister should have admitted this from the outset. Moreover, Marquand points out that MacDonald's statement to the Central News correspondent was inaccurate; the shares he had been given were worth £40,000, not £30,000.[8] This last charge is a little harsh. As we have seen, the sum of £30,000 was first mentioned by the *Daily Mail* journalist who broke the story, and MacDonald then repeated this figure, perhaps because he had confused the *number* of shares with their *monetary value*. The whole episode suggests unworldliness rather than dishonesty. MacDonald, be it recalled, had a well-deserved reputation for scrupulosity in financial matters.[9] He was also genuinely shocked by the 'fearful morass' into which the conferring of honours had fallen and was determined to 'clean up' the system.[10]

Yet it was precisely the strain of Scottish sanctimoniousness and puritanism in the Prime Minister's character which encouraged many of his political opponents to pursue the issue.[11] Masterman went further than most when he dubbed the transaction 'deplorable' and told a public meeting that 'this case appeared to afford a precedent for unlimited corruption in the future', since a subsequent Prime Minister 'might receive a gift from a man to whom he gave a peerage, and plead that he was only doing what Mr MacDonald did'.[12] But it was undoubtedly Labour MPs and candidates who were most cross with the Prime Minister's behaviour. According to A. G. Gardiner, their 'peace of mind' had 'been profoundly disturbed by the affair'.[13] An embarrassed *Daily Herald* said that it did not think 'that any useful purpose would be served by publishing' readers' letters on so personal a matter.[14] Communist papers openly jeered.[15]

On the painfully sensitive MacDonald the impact was severe, even though we should take with a pinch of salt Philip Snowden's claim that the Prime Minister was so shaken by the ordeal that his nerve deserted him when faced by the Campbell Case shortly afterwards.[16] Once Parliament had been dissolved, the campaign of calumny gathered momentum. Hecklers at public meetings took advantage of the Prime Minister's fear of ridicule by shouting 'Biscuits' at him. Nor were his colleagues pleased at being forced back on to the defensive over this affair.[17] For though nobody thought that MacDonald had

---

Nation (20 Sept. 1924, p. 742), A. G. Gardiner, too, expressed the view that Grant had been expected to receive an honour from the last Government.

[8] Marquand, *MacDonald*, p. 360. [9] Ibid. 360.

[10] See MacDonald's letter, published in Waterhouse, *Private and Official*, p. 300.

[11] Thus, a Conservative 1924 election pamphlet mischievously quoted MacDonald's remarks in a speech of Feb. 1921 in which he said: 'I detest the idea that a man cannot serve his country in its highest offices without an income of several thousand pounds a year.' Why could not former ministers, MacDonald had asked, 'go back to the simple life with its porridge and plainness' (Conservative pamphlet, 1924/60).

[12] *The Times*, 23 Sept. 1924.

[13] *Nation*, 27 Sept. 1924, p. 771. [14] *Daily Herald*, 17 Sept. 1924.

[15] *Workers' Weekly*, 19 Sept. 1924, cited in *Gleanings and Memoranda*, lx (1924), 464.

[16] Snowden, *Autobiography*, ii. 689–90.

[17] Marquand, *MacDonald*, p. 360; Dalton, H., *Memoirs: Call Back Yesterday* (London, 1953), p. 151.

behaved corruptly, many Socialists agreed with their opponents that there was something incongruous about the Labour Party Leader riding around the country in a luxury motor-car, *however acquired.*[18] It was thus a great relief to them when MacDonald returned both car and shares at the end of the year.

Perhaps the most balanced reaction was that of Baldwin, who linked MacDonald's Daimler with Margot Asquith's lecture tour of the United States and Lloyd George's writing for the Hearst Press. The moral of all three episodes, he thought, was that Prime Ministers should be provided with a pension.[19]

[18] As Neville Chamberlain, one of the few Conservative Frontbenchers to raise the issue, put it, there seemed something inconsistent in a man whose moral sense was revolted by capitalism accepting from a capitalist provision in the shape of an income on £30,000 in order that he might ride in a lordly motor-car for the rest of his days (*Birmingham Post*, 18 Sept. 1924).

[19] Thomas Jones's diary, 8 Nov. 1924, in Middlemas, (ed.), *Whitehall Diary*, i. 304–5. Characteristically, Baldwin added that if he were to introduce a bill to this effect he would of course exclude himself from its provisions.

BIBLIOGRAPHY

A. MANUSCRIPT COLLECTIONS

1. Asquith Papers (Bodleian Library, Oxford).
2. Baldwin Papers (Cambridge University Library).
3. Balfour Papers (British Library).
4. Beaverbrook Papers (House of Lords Records Office).
5. Blumenfeld Papers (House of Lords Records Office).
6. Bonar Law Papers (House of Lords Records Office).
7. Bryce Papers (Bodleian Library, Oxford).
8. Campbell-Bannerman Papers (British Library).
9. Cecil of Chelwood Papers (British Library).
10. Chelwood Papers (Hatfield House).
11. Austen Chamberlain Papers (Birmingham University Library).
12. Joseph Chamberlain Papers (Birmingham University Library).
13. Neville Chamberlain Papers (Birmingham University Library).
14. Crewe Papers (Cambridge University Library).
15. Page Croft Papers (Churchill College, Cambridge).
16. Davidson Papers (House of Lords Records Office).
17. Elibank Papers (National Library of Scotland, Edinburgh).
18. Gainford Papers (Nuffield College, Oxford).
19. Haldane Papers (National Library of Scotland, Edinburgh).
20. Herbert Gladstone Papers (British Library).
21. Gwynne Papers (Bodleian Library, Oxford).
22. Lewis Harcourt Papers (Bodleian Library, Oxford).
23. Lloyd George Papers (House of Lords Records Office).
24. Oliver Locker-Lampson Papers (Norfolk and Norwich Records Office).
25. Maclean Papers (Bodleian Library, Oxford).
26. Maxse Papers (West Sussex Records Office, Chichester).
27. Montagu Papers (Trinity College, Cambridge).
28. Northcliffe Papers (British Library).
29. Ponsonby Papers (Bodleian Library, Oxford).
30. Quickswood Papers (Hatfield House).
31. Reading Papers (India Office Library, London).
32. Rosebery Papers (National Library of Scotland, Edinburgh).
33. Third Marquess of Salisbury Papers (Hatfield House).
34. Fourth Marquess of Salisbury Papers (Hatfield House).
35. Samuel Papers (House of Lords Records Office).
36. Sandars Papers (Bodleian Library, Oxford).
37. C. P. Scott Papers (British Library).
38. Selborne Papers (Bodleian Library, Oxford).
39. Spender Papers (British Library).
40. Steel-Maitland Papers (Scottish Public Records Office, Edinburgh).
41. Strachey Papers (House of Lords Records Office).
42. Templewood Papers (Cambridge University Library).
43. Wargrave Papers (House of Lords Records Office).
44. Henry Wilson Papers (Imperial War Museum).

45. Arnold White Papers (National Maritime Museum).
46. Willoughby de Broke Papers (House of Lords Records Office).

B. OFFICIAL PAPERS

Cab./23 (Cabinet Minutes, 1917–22).
Hansard, *Parliamentary Debates*, Fourth and Fifth Series.
Select Committee on Members of Parliament (Personal Interest), PP (1896), xi.
Select Committee on War Office Contracts, PP (1900), ix.
Committee Appointed by Army Council to Consider the question of Sales and Refunds to Contractors in South Africa (1905), Cd. 2435.
Royal Commission on War Stores in South Africa (1906), Cd. 3127.
Royal Commission on Selection of Justices of the Peace (1910), Cd. 5250; Minutes of Evidence (1910), Cd. 5358.
Select Committee on Vacation of Seat (Members Holding Contract), PP (1912–13), ix.
Select Committee on Marconi Wireless Telegraph Company, Limited, Agreement, PP (1913), vii.
Select Committee of House of Lords on the Charges Against Lord Murray of Elibank, PP (1914), lxvi.
Number of Persons in Civil Service, Accounts and Papers (1914), lvi.
Royal Commission on Indian Finance and Currency (1914), Cd. 7236.
Royal Commission on the Civil Service: Third Report (1913), Cd. 6739; Minutes of Evidence (1913), Cd. 6740.
Royal Commission on the Civil Service: Fourth Report (1914), Cd. 7338; Minutes of Evidence (1914), Cd. 7340.
Commission of Enquiry into Industrial Unrest (1917), Cd. 8662–8.
Committee Appointed to Advise the Board of Trade on Matters Arising under the Trading with the Enemy Act, 1916 (1918), Cd. 9059.
Ministry of Reconstruction Committee on Trusts (1918), Cd. 9236.
Select Committee on Increase of Wealth (War), PP (1920), cii.
Royal Commission on Honours (1922), Cmd. 1789.

C. PARTY POLITICAL LITERATURE

I have consulted the following pamphlets and leaflets: collected pamphlets and leaflets of Liberal, Conservative, and Labour Parties; National Liberal Federation Reports; Reports of Annual Conferences of the National Union; Labour Annual Conference Reports; Annual Conference Reports of the Independent Labour Party.

D. NEWSPAPERS AND PERIODICALS

Annual Register	*Daily Mail*	*Globe*
Blackwood's Magazine	*Daily News*	*Imperialist*
Clarion	*Daily Telegraph*	*Independent Review*
Contemporary Review	*The Economist*	*John Bull*
Critic	*Eye-Witness*	*Justice*
Daily Chronicle	*Financial News*	*Labour Leader*
Daily Express	*Fortnightly Review*	*Liberal Magazine*
Daily Herald	*Gleanings and Memoranda*	*Manchester Guardian*

Morning Leader
Morning Post
Nation
National Opinion
National Review
New Age
New Statesman
New Witness
Nineteenth Century
Norwich Unionist

Observer
Our Flag
Outlook
Pall Mall Gazette
Punch
Quarterly Review
Referee
Saturday Review
Speaker
Spectator

Star
Sunday Sun
Sunday Times
Throne
The Times
Truth
Vigilante
Westminster Gazette
Westminster Review

SELECT BIBLIOGRAPHY OF PRINTED WORKS

(place of publication London, unless otherwise stated)

Biographies, Autobiographies, Diaries, and Memoirs

BARNES, J., and NICHOLSON, D. (eds.), *The Leo Amery Diaries*, i. *1896–1929* (1980).

BROCK, M. and E. (eds.), *H. H. Asquith: Letters to Venetia Stanley* (Oxford, 1982).

RAMSDEN, John (ed.), *Real Old Tory Politics: The Political Diaries of Robert Sanders Lord Bayford 1910–1935* (1984).

TAYLOR, A. J. P., *Beaverbrook* (1972).

CAMPBELL, John, *F. E. Smith: First Earl of Birkenhead* (1983).

BLAKE, Robert, *The Unknown Prime Minister: The Life and Times of Andrew Bonar Law 1858–1923* (1955).

ROSE, Kenneth, *The Later Cecils* (1975).

CHURCHILL, Randolph S., *Winston S. Churchill*, ii. *Young Statesman, 1901– 1914* (1967).

——, *Winston S. Churchill*, ii. Companion Volumes (1969).

GILBERT, Martin, *Winston S. Churchill*, iii. Companion Volumes (1972).

——, *Winston S. Churchill*, iv. *1917–1922* (1975).

——, *Winston S. Churchill*, iv. Companion Volumes (1977).

VINCENT, John (ed.), *The Crawford Papers. The Journals of David Lindsay, twenty-seventh Earl of Crawford and tenth Earl of Balcarres 1871–1940 during the years 1892 to 1940* (Manchester, 1984).

Lord CROFT, *My Life of Strife* (n.d.).

JAMES, Robert Rhodes (ed.), *Memoirs of a Conservative: J. C. C. Davidson's Memoirs and Papers 1910–37* (1969).

DAVENPORT-HINES, R. P. T., *Dudley Docker. The Life and Times of a Trade Warrior* (Cambridge, 1984).

FRASER, Peter, *Lord Esher: A Political Biography* (1973).

ROSE, Kenneth, *King George V* (1983).

CULLEN, Tom, *Maundy Gregory, Purveyor of Honours* (1974).

ROSKILL, Stephen, *Hankey: Man of Secrets*, i. *1877–1918* (1970).

ROSKILL, Stephen, *Hankey: Man of Secrets*, ii. *1919–1931* (1972).

DAVID, Edward (ed.), *Inside Asquith's Cabinet: From the Diaries of Charles Hobhouse* (1977).

MIDDLEMAS, K. (ed.), *Thomas Jones, Whitehall Diary*, i. *1916–1925* (Oxford, 1969).

——, (ed.), *Thomas Jones, Whitehall Diary*, ii. *1926–1930*, (Oxford, 1969).

CAMPBELL, John, *Lloyd George: The Goat in the Wilderness* (1977).

GRIGG, John, *The Young Lloyd George* (1973).

——, *Lloyd George: The People's Champion 1902–1911* (1978).

——, *Lloyd George: From Peace to War 1912–1916* (1985).

MARQUAND, David, *Ramsay MacDonald* (1977).

MASTERMAN, Lucy, *C. F. G. Masterman* (1939).

WALEY, S. D., *Edwin Montagu* (1964).

POUND, R., and HARMSWORTH, G., *Northcliffe* (1959).

HYDE, H. Montgomery, *Lord Reading* (1967).
JUDD, Dennis, *Lord Reading* (1982).
RIDDELL, Lord, *More Pages From My Diary 1908–1914* (1934).
WILSON, Trevor (ed.), *The Political Diaries of C. P. Scott, 1911–1928* (1970).
MACKENZIE, Norman and Jeanne (eds.), *The Diary of Beatrice Webb*, vols. ii and iii (1983, 1984).

Other Books

BENTLEY, Michael, *The Liberal Mind 1914–1929* (Cambridge, 1977).
CAMPLIN, Jamie, *The Rise of the Plutocrats: Wealth and Power in Edwardian England* (1978).
COWLING, Maurice, *The Impact of Labour 1920–1924* (Cambridge, 1971).
CREGIER, D. M., *Chiefs Without Indians* (Washington, 1982).
DANSETTE, A., *L'Affaire Wilson et la chute du Président Grévy* (Paris, 1936).
DAVIDOFF, Leonora, *The Best Circles: Society, Etiquette and the Season* (1973).
DOIG, Alan, *Corruption and Misconduct in Contemporary British Politics* (1984).
DONALDSON, Frances, *The Marconi Scandal* (1962).
HEIDENHEIMER, Arnold, J. (ed.), *Political Corruption: Readings in Comparative Analysis* (New Brunswick, 1970; 2nd edn., 1978).
HEUSTON, R. F. V., *Lives of the Lord Chancellors 1885–1940* (Oxford, 1964).
HOLMES, Colin, *Anti-Semitism in British Society 1876–1939* (1979).
KINNEAR, M., *The Fall of Lloyd George: The Political Crisis of 1922* (1973).
KOSS, Stephen, *The Rise and Fall of the Political Press in Britain*, i. *The Nineteenth Century* (1981), and ii. *The Twentieth Century* (1984).
LEE, A. J., *The Origins of the Popular Press, 1855–1914* (1976).
MIDDLEMAS, Keith, *The Pursuit of Pleasure: High Society in the 1900s* (1977).
MORGAN, K. O., *Consensus and Disunity: The Lloyd George Coalition Government 1918–1922* (Oxford, 1979).
PINTO-DUSCHINSKY, M., *British Political Finance 1830–1980* (Washington, 1981).
RAMSDEN, John, *The Age of Balfour and Baldwin 1902–1940* (1978).
THOMPSON, F. M. L., *English Landed Society in the Nineteenth Century* (1963).
WILLIAMS, P. M., *Wars, Plots and Scandals in Post-War France* (Cambridge, 1970).
WILSON, Trevor, *The Downfall of the Liberal Party 1914–1935* (1966).

Articles and Essays

BOSWELL, J. S. and JOHNS, B. R., 'Patriots or Profiteers? British Businessmen and the First World War', *Journal of European Economic History*, xi (1982).
COLEMAN, D. C., 'The "Dope Scandal", 1915–19', in Winter, J. M. (ed.), *War and Economic Development* (Cambridge, 1975).
D'AVIGDOR-GOLDSMID, H., 'The Little Marconi Case', *History Today*, xiv (1964).
HANHAM, H. J., 'The Sale of Honours in Late Victorian England', *Victorian Studies*, iii (1960).
LEE, J. M., 'Parliament and the Appointment of Magistrates: The Origins of Advisory Committees', *Parliamentary Affairs*, xiii (1959).

LLOYD, T. O., 'The Whip as Paymaster: Herbert Gladstone and party organization', *English Historical Review*, lxxxix (1974).

LUNN, K., 'Political Anti-Semitism Before 1914: Fascism's Heritage?', in Lunn, K. and Thurlow, R. C. (eds.), *British Fascism: Essays on the Radical Right in Inter-War Britain* (1980).

PLATT, D. C. M., 'The Commercial and Industrial Interests of Ministers of the Crown', *Political Studies*, ix (1961).

PORTER, Dilwyn, 'Journalist, Financier, "Dishonest Rogue", "Scoundrel": The Life and Times of Harry Hananel Marks, M.P.', *Moirae*, viii (1984).

RUBINSTEIN, W. D., 'Henry Page Croft and the National Party 1917–22', *Journal of Contemporary History*, ix (1974).

WRIGLEY, Christopher, 'The Ministry of Munitions: An Innovatory Department', in Burk, K. (ed.), *War and the State: The Transformation of British Government, 1914–1919* (1982).

INDEX

Abbott, Speaker 42
Acetate Manufacturing Company *see* 'Dope Scandal'
Acland-Hood, Sir Alexander 91–4, 146, 162, 305
Addison, Christopher 275, 317
Agricultural Land Rating Act (1896) 80–1
Aitken, Max *see* Beaverbrook
Akers-Douglas, Aretas 89, 91
Albermarle, Lord 10, 12
Albu, Sir George 133
Aliens Act (1905) 119
Aliens during First World War 241–2, 257, 269–70
Allan, Maud 124, 261–2, 263
American Marconi Company *see* Marconi Scandal
Americanization 27, 71, 94–5, 218, 222, 307
Americans 26–7
Amery, L. S. 125 n., 173, 178, 180, 187, 189, 315, 322, 394, 400–1
Ampthill, Lord 164, 189, 190, 324–5, 348, 349, 372
Anderson, W. C. 29
Anglo-Persian Oil Company 213
anti-Imperialism 65–72, 76, 96
  see also Imperialism
anti-Semitism 2–3, 25–6, 68–9, 119–20, 206–7, 209–11, 244–6, 248, 274, 281, 329, 332–3, 421, 423
  see also Jews
anti-waste 283, 288, 297, 344
Apsley, Lord 405
Archer-Shee, Maj. 139, 215
arms ring 78, 197, 413, 428–9
Arnold-Forster, H. O. 76
Ashton, Lord *see* Williamson, J.
Asquith, Henry Herbert 47, 123 n., 137, 213, 215, 229, 236, 253, 305, 308, 325
  and Boer War contracting scandals 58, 62
  social life of 124, 135
  and honours system 147, 148, 149, 152–3, 156, 159, 163–4
  and Marconi 175–6, 180, 183, 211, 338–9
  and Indian Silver Scandal 203, 204, 205–6
  and Edgar Speyer 245–6
  and Leverton Harris affair 254, 255 n., 278
  and Pemberton Billing 261, 264, 265, 267
  and war-time economy 273, 295

and 'Grey Conspiracy' 347
and 1922 Honours Scandal 353, 368
attitude to Lloyd George Fund 381 n., 383
and Baldwin 393
Asquith, Margot 21, 124, 125, 149, 254, 260 n., 261, 262, 264 and n., 339, 383, 385–6, 393, 400, 432
Asquith, Raymond 124
Asquithians 347–8, 352, 381–6, 392–3
Astor, William Waldorf (First Viscount Astor) 13, 16, 306 and n., 311 n., 389
Atkins, Mr 332–3

Baker, Harold ('Bluetooth') 202, 203
Balcarres, Lord (Earl of Crawford) 106, 124, 126, 145, 211, 237 n., 301, 322, 332, 366 nn., 388
Baldwin, Stanley 321, 340, 379, 381, 390–401, 402, 403–4, 406, 407–11, 413, 416, 427, 432
Balfour, Arthur James 50–1, 52, 61, 79, 81, 82–3, 113, 114, 127, 157, 367, 387
  and company directorships 44–5, 47
  and London & Globe 48, 192–3
  and honours system 84, 91–4, 145, 162, 164
  and Marconi 189, 193–4
  libelled by Lord Alfred Douglas 336–7
Balfour, Gerald 48, 104 n.
Balfour-Browne, J. H. 289
Banbury, Sir Frederick 139, 205, 209, 281
Banister, Joseph 26
Bath, Marquess of 222
Bathurst, Lady 319, 405
Beamish, H. H. 266, 335–6, 337 n.
Beauchamps, Earl 140, 315, 381
Beaverbrook, Lord (Max Aitken) 194, 260, 278, 281, 324, 332, 337, 343, 344, 389, 390 n., 404, 425, 427
  and Pemberton Billing trial 263
  as Minister of Information 282, 292 n., 320–3
  receives baronetcy 306–7
  receives peerage 318–20
  vendetta against Baldwin 394, 399–400, 403 and n., 410–11
  see also *Daily Express*; Press
Bedford, Duke of 80, 360
Beit, Alfred 13, 67
Belloc, Hilaire 3, 26, 68–9, 99, 119, 149, 158–60, 169, 211, 317, 332, 419
Benn, Wedgwood 368–9
Bennett, Arnold 351 and n.
Bentinck, Lord Henry 291–2, 295